Exceptional Children

Exceptional Children

Introduction to Special Education

Fifth Edition

DANIEL P. HALLAHAN

JAMES M. KAUFFMAN

University of Virginia

ALLYN AND BACON
Boston London Sydney Toronto Tokyo Singapore

Library of Congress Cataloging-in-Publication Data

HALLAHAN, DANIEL P.
    Exceptional children: introduction to special education/Daniel
P. Hallahan, James M. Kauffman.—5th ed.
        p. cm.

    Includes bibliographical references (p.) and indexes.
    ISBN 0–13–293333–0
    1. Special education—United States.   I. Kauffman, James M.
II. Title.
LC3981.H34 1991   90–45579
371.9′0973—dc20   CIP

CHAPTER OPENING QUOTES: (1) and (3) Richard H. Hungerford, "On Locusts," *American Journal of Mental Deficiency*, 1950, 54, 415–418. (2) "The Times They Are A-Changin' " (Bob Dylan). 1963 Warner Bros. Inc. (Renewed). All rights reserved. Used by permission. (4) Neil Diamond, "Brooklyn Roads." Copyright © 1968 Stonebridge Music. All rights reserved. Used by permission. International copyright secured. (5) Neil Diamond, "Shilo." Copyright © 1967 Tallyrand Music, Inc. All rights reserved. Used by permission. International copyright secured. (6) D. Shields, *Dead Languages*. New York: Alfred A. Knopf, Inc. (7) Helen Keller, *The Story of My Life*. New York: Doubleday, 1954. (8) Leonard Gershe, "Butterflies Are Free." Copyright © 1969 by Leonard Gershe. (9) Words by Chuck Mangione. Copyright © 1971 Gates Music, Inc. All rights reserved. (10) Excerpt from *The Autobiography of Mark Twain*, edited by Charles Neider. Copyright 1927, 1940, 1958, 1959 by the Mark Twain Company, copyright 1924, 1945, 1952 by Clara Clemens Somossoud, copyright 1959 by Charles Neider. Reprinted by permission of HarperCollins Publishers Inc. (11) Christopher Nolan (1987). *Under the Eye of the Clock: The Life Story of Christopher Nolan*. New York: St. Martin's Press, pp. 37–38.

Printed in the United States of America
10 9 8 7 6 5 4 3 2   95 94 93 92 91

ISBN 0-13-293366-7 (AIE)
ISBN 0-13-203333-0 (Student)

Contents

CHAPTER *3* *Mental Retardation* 77

CHAPTER *4* *Learning Disabilities*   *121*

CHAPTER 7 *Hearing Impairment*   263

CHAPTER *8* *Visual Impairment*   *301*

CHAPTER *9* *Physical Disabilities*   *343*

Preface

This book is a general introduction to the characteristics of exceptional individuals and their education. Although we have placed major emphasis on classroom practices, we have also covered the psychological, medical, and sociological aspects of disabilities. We begin with an introductory chapter in which we present an overview of exceptionality and special education, including definitions, basic legal requirements, and the history and development of the field. The second chapter contains a discussion of major current issues and trends—normalization, integration, and cultural diversity. Following that are eight chapters covering the major categories of exceptionality—mental retardation, learning disabilities, emotional/behavioral disorders, communication disorders, hearing impairment, visual impairment, physical disabilities, and giftedness. The last chapter pertains to parents and families of persons with disabilities.

MAJOR CHANGES FOR THIS EDITION

More Emphasis on Mainstreaming

A predominant theme of this edition is the recognition of the significant role that the general educator plays in dealing with students with a variety of learning and behavioral problems. Indeed, most of the changes we made for this edition were in response to the rapidly growing numbers of general education students who are now taking an introductory course in special education. We believe this emphasis on the student with disabilities in the mainstream also enhances the relevance of the text for preservice and inservice special education teachers. We have added two new features to each of the eight categorical chapters that are designed to help teachers teach exceptional children in general education settings. They are:

- **Suggestions for Teaching Students in General Education Classrooms** Written by Dr. E. Jane Nowacek, an experienced resource teacher and teacher educator, this section at the end of each of the categorical chapters provides the teacher with a variety of teaching ideas and strategies. In addition to many practical, how-to-do-it suggestions, Dr. Nowacek provides lists of additional resources, books, and software. They are not meant to equip the teacher with everything needed to teach children with disabilities. However, we think these sections serve as an excellent starting place for general education teachers faced with their first mainstreamed student.

- **Collaboration: A Key to Success**   For each categorical chapter we asked two expert teachers, one from general education and one from special education, to write about how they collaborate to provide effective integration of exceptional students into the mainstream. We believe these sections serve as models of best practices for mainstreaming.

Important Trends: Parents and Families, Cultural Diversity, Transition

- **Parents and Families**   Recent legislation and research make it imperative that today's educator be able to work with parents and families of students with disabilities. In recognition of this, we have added a new chapter (11) on this topic.
- **Cultural Diversity**   Demographic changes in the United States compel educators to understand the role that cultural diversity plays in education. We have expanded our coverage of this topic with a new section in Chapter 2.
- **Transition**   Practitioners, researchers, legislators, and persons with disabilities alike recognize the need for more and better programming for individuals with disabilities as they leave secondary schools and enter the work force or college life. We have expanded our coverage of this topic in Chapter 1 as well as in each of the eight categorical chapters.

Organization

In response to instructors' and students' suggestions, we have moved the content relating to normalization, mainstreaming, and attitudes toward persons with disabilities from the last chapter into Chapter 2 on Issues and Trends. Given the current emphasis on mainstreaming, we believe this makes for a more logical progression.

Readability

Although we have prided ourselves on the readability of previous editions, we have taken special care with this edition to write clearly and concisely. With the reformation of teacher education, we are aware that preservice and inservice teachers are being asked to do and know more than ever before. They don't have the luxury of knowing everything there is to understand about persons with disabilities and their education. Without compromising depth of coverage, we believe we have streamlined the coverage in this book so that the reader will come away knowing the essentials.

MAJOR FEATURES RETAINED FOR THIS EDITION

Based on responses from users, students and instructors alike, this edition preserves some of the popular features from previous editions:

Boxed Material on Misconceptions

We start each chapter with a box of myths and facts. These serve as an excellent advance organizer for the material covered in the chapter.

Boxed Material on Special Topics

Sprinkled throughout the text are a liberal number of boxes. These boxes are primarily of three types: first, some highlight research findings and their applicability to educational practice; second, some discuss issues facing educators in the field; and third, some present the human side of being exceptional. In the last case, they stress the inherent paradox of being exceptional—that the exceptional individual is, at once, both different from and the same as the rest of humanity.

Glossary

We include a glossary for readers' convenience. Words appearing in boldface within the text are listed in the glossary at the end of the book.

SUPPLEMENTS

The Annotated Instructor's Edition contains all the material in the student's edition of the text plus special annotations in the margins describing new class activities, points to emphasize in lecture, additional examples, other research citations, and cross-references to teaching ideas in the instructor's manual, transparency masters, and study guide.

The Instructor's Manual is referenced by the marginal annotations in the AIE and includes chapter outlines, objectives, terminology, class activities, discussion questions, and a list of audio, video, and print resources.

The separate test item file has been substantially revised and is based on class testing. These items are also available on computer (IBM, Apple, and MacIntosh) and through the Prentice Hall telephone testing service. The telephone testing service will provide typed or dittoed test masters of the items you specify. For more information, contact your locate Prentice Hall representative.

The Student Study Guide has been redesigned to help the student move from rote memorization of material to understanding and applying the concepts to new situations. It also includes projects that students can do outside of class to help their understanding and application of concepts. The Student Guide is also available for IBM and IBM-compatible computers.

ABC News/PH Video Library is comprised of professionally produced videos designed to coordinate and enhance *Exceptional Children 5E* and your course. These videos explore a variety of issues in special education today that correspond to topics found in *Exceptional Children 5E*. Based on ABC News award-winning programs—Nightline, 20/20, This Week with David Brinkley, World News Tonight and Health Show—ABC and PH have combined to select the most current videos which will provide especially good support for your class. The Instructor's Manual contains information about how to integrate this video with the book and the content of your course.

PH Datamanager is a state-of-the-art computerized class management package that will help the professor give and record tests and help students learn. It consists of a test construction program which uses questions from the test item file and allows the professor to alter or add questions, a gradebook, and a computerized study guide using questions from the Student Study Guide. Available for IBM only.

To add even more emphasis to key points, we are now offering electronic transparencies using Storyboard^R program by IBM. With two or three very basic key punches on an IBM computer, transparencies come alive with color and movement. To see a demonstration of this very simple yet exciting supplement, please call your local Prentice Hall representative.

Special Ed On A Disk is a student-oriented computer program that helps students learn and apply concepts from the text in an interactive way.

The Handout and Transparency Masters Booklet will provide you with ready-made, professional visuals to give emphasis to key points in your lectures. In addition to key points in the text, there are also transparency masters for classroom activities that are listed in the Annotated Instructor's Edition or the Instructor's Manual.

ACKNOWLEDGMENTS

By way of appreciation, we are thankful to reviewers of our previous edition and drafts of some of our revised chapters: Rebecca Dailey Kneedler, University of Virginia; Donald Moores, Gallaudet University; Ann Turnbull, University of Kansas; June H. Elliott, Lyndon State College; Carol Jo Yanek, Howard Community College; Charlene Lingo, Pittsburg State University; Linda C. Knicker, College of DuPage; Louise Pitt, Florida Southern College; Jerome J. Schultz, Lesley College: Antoinette Heppler, Nova University; B. C. Moore, Arizona State University; Linda Reese, Northeastern State University; Deborah Gartland, Towson State University; Ann C. Candler, Texas Tech University; T. Hisama, Southern Illinois University; Rhoda Cummings, University of Nevada; Kay Butler, Syracuse University; Mara Sapon-Shevin, University of North Dakota; Jeanne E. Legan, Joliet Junior College; Joseph S. Renzulli, University of Connecticut; Agnes Rainwater, Eastern Michigan University; Patricia Mulhearn Blasco, University of North Carolina; Donald F. Moores, Gallaudet University– Research Institute; Carolyn Callahan, University of Virginia; Rebecca R. Fewell, Tulane University; Ruth Buehler, Millersville University; Bruce L. Mallory, University of New Hampshire; Richard M. Gargiulo, University of Alabama at Birmingham; and Steward Ehly, University of Iowa.

We want to thank Tim Landrum for his assistance on various phases of the project. At Prentice Hall, we are grateful to Carol Wada and Mary Anne Shahidi for their help during the project.

We also want to thank those instructors and students who have given us feedback on our previous editions. Your comments are always welcome.

DANIEL P. HALLAHAN
JAMES M. KAUFFMAN

THE NEW YORK TIMES and PRENTICE HALL are sponsoring A CONTEMPORARY VIEW: a program designed to enhance student access to current information of relevance in the classroom.

Through this program, the core subject matter provided in the text is supplemented by a collection of time-sensitive articles from one of the world's most distinguished newspapers, THE NEW YORK TIMES. These articles demonstrate the vital, ongoing connection between what is learned in the classroom and what is happening in the world around us.

To enjoy the wealth of information of THE NEW YORK TIMES daily, a reduced subscription rate is available. For information, call toll-free: 1-800-631-1222.

PRENTICE HALL and THE NEW YORK TIMES are proud to co-sponsor A CONTEMPORARY VIEW. We hope it will make the reading of both textbooks and newspapers a more dynamic, involving process.

About the Artists . . .

The cover art is a hooked rug created by Erma Eleanor Hackett. Ms. Hackett is an artist with mental disabilities, as well as vision, hearing, and speech problems. She was born in Boise, Idaho, into a family of eight siblings and now lives in Oakland, California. She has been attending the Creative Growth Art Center since 1985 where her drawing, painting, and rug/tapestry design skills have been developed.

Much of Ms. Hackett's artwork reflects her bucolic remembrance of life on a farm in Idaho. Her favorite subjects are rural scenes with barns and animals, gardens, flowers, and especially roses. She creates her work using layers of impressionistic color with objects defined by overlapping feather-like scratchy lines. She defines most pieces with a border design which she equates with a border in a garden. Her work has been featured in *Northern California Home and Garden*.

The art work that opens each chapter of the book was done by people associated with Very Special Arts or the Creative Growth Art Center. We are extremely proud of these talented people.

Chapter 1: Louis Estape, Creative Growth Art Center
Chapter 2: Helen Yoon, Creative Growth Art Center
Chapter 3: Camille Holvoet, Creative Growth Art Center
Chapter 4: Eleanor Hackett, Creative Growth Art Center
Chapter 5: Robert Lauricella, Creative Growth Art Center
Chapter 6: William Tyler, Creative Growth Art Center
Chapter 7: America Sites, Courtesy Very Special Arts
Chapter 8: William Tyler, Creative Growth Art Center
Chapter 9: Micky Doolittle, Courtesy Very Special Arts
Chapter 10: Udith A. Morton, Courtesy Very Special Arts
Chapter 11: Camille Holvoet, Creative Growth Art Center

SKY DANCER
Louis Estape, Creative Growth Art Center

Exceptionality and Special Education

Only the brave dare look upon the gray—
upon the things which cannot be explained easily,
upon the things which often engender mistakes,
upon the things whose cause cannot be understood,
upon the things we must accept and live with.
And therefore only the brave dare look upon difference
without flinching.

(*Richard H. Hungerford, "On Locusts"*)

*T*he study of exceptional children is the study of *differences*. The exceptional child is different in some way from the "average" child. In very simple terms, such a child may have problems or special talents in thinking, seeing, hearing, speaking, socializing, or moving. More often than not, such a child has a combination of special abilities or disabilities. Today over 4 million such "different" children have been identified in public schools throughout the United States. About one out of every ten children in U.S. schools is considered exceptional. The fact that even many so-called normal children also have school-related problems makes the study of exceptionality very demanding.

The study of exceptional children is also the study of *similarities*. Exceptional children are not different from the "average" in every way. In fact, most exceptional children are average in more ways than they are different. Until recently, professionals, and laypeople as well, tended to focus on the differences between exceptional and nonexceptional children, almost to the exclusion of the ways in which all children are alike. Today we give more attention to what exceptional and nonexceptional children have in common—to similarities in their characteristics, needs, and ways of learning. As a result, the study of exceptional children has become more complex, and many so-called facts about handicapped and gifted children have been challenged.

Students of one of the hard sciences may boast of the difficulty of the subject matter because of the many facts they must remember and piece together. The plight of students of special education is quite different. To be sure, they study facts, but the facts are relatively few compared to the unanswered questions. Any study of human beings must take into account inherent ambiguities, inconsistencies, and unknowns. In the case of the child who deviates from the norm, we must multiply all the mysteries of normal human behavior and development by those pertaining to the child's exceptionalities. Because there is no single accepted theory of normal child development, it is not at all surprising that relatively few definite statements can be made about exceptional children.

There are, however, patches of sunshine in the bleak gray painted by Hungerford (see page 1). It is true that in the vast majority of cases we are unable to identify the exact reason why a child is exceptional, but progress is being made in determining the causes of some disabilities. In a later chapter, for example, we discuss the rather recent detection of causal factors in Down syndrome—a condition resulting in the largest number of children classified as moderately retarded. Likewise, retrolental fibroplasia—at one time a leading cause of blindness—has been greatly reduced since the discovery of its cause. The cause of mental retardation associated with a metabolic disorder—PKU (phenylketonuria)—has been discovered. Soon after birth, infants are now routinely tested for PKU so that any mental retardation can be prevented if they should have the disorder. Besides these and other medical breakthroughs, research is bringing us a more complete understanding of the ways in which the child's psychological, social, and educational environments are related to learning. For example, special educators, psychologists, and pediatricians are increasingly able to identify environmental conditions that increase the likelihood that a child will have learning or behavior problems (Werner, 1986).

Educational methodology has also made strides. In fact, in comparison to what is known about causes, we know a lot about how exceptional children can be taught and managed effectively in the classroom. Although special educators constantly lament that all the questions are not answered, we do know considerably more today about how to educate exceptional children than we did ten or fifteen years ago.

Before moving to the specific subject matter of exceptional children, we must

MISCONCEPTIONS
ABOUT EXCEPTIONAL CHILDREN

Myth	*Fact*
Public schools may choose not to provide education for some children.	Federal legislation specifies that to receive federal funds, every school system must provide a free, appropriate education for every child regardless of any disabling condition.
By law, the handicapped child must be placed in the least restrictive environment (LRE). The LRE is always the regular classroom.	The law does require the handicapped child to be placed in the LRE. However, the LRE is *not* always the regular classroom. What the LRE does mean is that the handicapped child shall be segregated as little as possible from home, family, community, and the regular class setting while appropriate education is provided. In many, but not all, instances this will mean placement in the regular classroom.
The causes of most disabilities are known, but little is known about how to help children overcome or compensate for their disabilities.	In most cases, the causes of children's disabilities are not known, although progress is being made in pinpointing why many disabilities occur. More is known about the treatment of most disabilities than about their causes.
People with disabilities are just like everyone else.	First, no two people are exactly alike. People with disabilities, just like everyone else, are unique individuals. Most of their abilities are much like those of the "average" person who is not considered to have a disability. Nevertheless, a disability is a characteristic not shared by most people. It is important that disabilities be recognized for what they are, but individuals with disabilities must be seen as having many abilities—other characteristics that they share with the majority of people.
A disability is a handicap.	A disability is an inability to do something, the lack of a specific capacity. A handicap, on the other hand, is a disadvantage that is imposed on an individual. A disability may or may not be a handicap, depending on the circumstances. For example, inability to walk is not a handicap in learning to read, but it can be a handicap in getting into the stands at a ball game. Sometimes handicaps are needlessly imposed on persons with disabilities. For example, a student who cannot write with a pen but can use a typewriter or word processor would be needlessly handicapped without such equipment.

point out that we vehemently disagree with Hungerford on an important point: We must certainly learn to "live with" disabling exceptionalities, but we must never "accept" them. We prefer to think there is hope for the eventual eradication of many of the disabling forms of exceptionality. In addition, we believe it is of paramount importance to realize that even children whose exceptionalities are extreme can be helped to lead a fuller life.

Some exceptional individuals learn to live with their disabilities or special abilities

Jim Abbott was born with a disability, but he's about to realize a lifelong dream

IT IS THREE-quarters of a mile from Room 111, Rumsey Hall at the University of Michigan, to the baseball field at Ray Fisher Stadium, and as Jim Abbott walks across the sprawling campus, he has plenty of time to think and fret, as any freshman pitcher would. He thinks freshman thoughts. He has freshman doubts. He wonders if a high school fastball is good enough for college hitters.

"I feel the pressure," he says. "After all that's happened to me in my life, I don't want to get lost in the shuffle now. I don't want to be just another high school pitcher who got lost in college."

Jim Abbott, 18, is not just another lefthanded high school phenom, no matter what happens when the varsity baseball season begins for real this month in Ann Arbor. Jim Abbott was born without a right hand.

As he heads across campus each day, he smiles nervously as he readies himself for practice. He has come too far to fail. He smiles because he is eager.

"I'm battling against the odds again," Abbott says. "I've got to prove myself all over again, because I'm different. I'm back at the bottom, working my way up. But I'm going to make it."

In the 10 years of my job as a newspaper columnist, I have never been as touched by an athlete as I have by Jim Abbott, the one-handed kid from Flint, Mich., who has been different, at least so far in his young life, because he has been better, not because he is crippled.

"I'm just at another crossroads," he says, "with people staring at me."

His right arm ends at a narrow stub—a wrist that quit—with one small finger protruding. The right arm is about 10 inches shorter than the left. On the mound, Abbott starts with the stub stuck in the pocket of his glove, which has the pocket turned around, facing home plate. At the end of his follow-through, as a fastball already is being Federal Expressed to the plate, the good hand slides into the glove as easily as a knife going into soft butter.

When he must catch the ball, he takes it in the glove. Then, with deftness and economy, the glove is being turned around as it is tucked under his right arm, the ball comes out, and Abbott has it in his left hand, ready to throw again.

Ted Mahan, Abbott's Connie Mack League coach in Flint, says, "He used to drop the glove once in a while. I can't remember the last time he did *that*."

If Abbott could not make the switch, he could not pitch. He was outfitted with a hooklike prosthesis when he was 4. He threw out the hook when he was 5. He would play the hand he was dealt.

"I *hated* that [artificial] hand," Jim Abbott says now. "That's why I gave it up before I got to the second grade. It limited the things I could do. It didn't *help* me do anything. It was ugly, it drew attention to me, and I threw it out."

I say to him: "But you had to know having one hand was going to draw attention to you your whole life."

He says: "I planned to be different because I was a great baseball pitcher."

His boyhood seems artificial because it is out of some improbable storybook. Jim Abbott knew hurts. There were, briefly, nicknames like "Stub."

"He heard all the predictable mean things that 5- and 6-year-olds say," says his father, Mike Abbott. But the jokes and nicknames did not last long. Jim Abbott became the best in the

Freshman Jim Abbott holds baseball in University of Michigan locker room. He's battling the odds again, but it's an old familiar battle, and the outcome is always the same.

The Kid Who Wins One-Handed

BY MIKE LUPICA

SOURCE: *Parade Magazine*, March 2, 1986, pp. 4–5. Reprinted by permission of International Creative Management.

in ways that surprise most of us. Their differences from most people do not keep them from leading full and normal lives as children or as adults. Sometimes special education plays no role in their lives because their abilities, motivation, and support from their families and communities are sufficient to allow them to overcome obstacles without special assistance. A case in point is Jim Abbott, a former student at the University of Michigan (see the box above). After college, Abbott was neighborhood, in all the games. But mostly baseball. "He was going to show everybody," his father says.

The father, a 37-year-old account executive for Anheuser-Busch, watched the son over hundreds of boyhood hours throwing a ball against a brick wall. He would throw. Switch the glove. Catch. Put the glove under the arm. Take the ball out. Throw again. And again.

Jim started in a Flint Midget League when he was 12. There was a story about him in *The Flint Journal*. The road to deciding between a University of Michigan baseball scholarship and a Toronto Blue Jays bonus contract as a high school senior had begun.

"The only thing that would have been a handicap for me," Jim Abbott said one day last summer, sitting on his stoop, pounding his fist into a new Rawlings glove, "is if anyone had ever been negative around me. If anyone at any point had said, 'You can't do this' or, 'How do you expect to do *that* with one hand?' I probably wouldn't be playing ball of any kind right now. But my mom and dad and my coaches and my teammates have always said, 'Just go do it.' So I've played. I love playing basketball. I love football. I'm going to miss playing football now that I'm out of high school. But I just kept getting better and better at baseball. And I've been successful at every level I've pitched."

"We told him a long time ago," says his mom, Kathy Abbott, 37, a Flint attorney, "that if he wanted to play, he had to be able to do what the other kids do."

"I'm not going to tell you there weren't nights when he came home crying," says Mike Abbott. "But there really weren't a lot. He has been blessed with a great heart."

Jim Abbott is 6 feet 4 and 200 pounds. With his shock of sandy hair and open, ingenuous face, he looks like he ought to be starring in one of those summer movies for teens. He shot up to his present size between his sophomore and junior years at Flint Central High. No more brick walls by then, of any kind. Most times when the ball came back to him, it came from his catcher, because the batters were swinging and missing so often. Abbott was throwing baseballs past high school teams in the spring. Connie Mack teams in the summer. The scouts, college and pro, began to hear about this one-handed kid ("Huh? One-handed pitcher? *Come on!*") who was lighting up the radar guns with a 90 mph fastball. The scouts came to watch. When they saw the left arm, they forgot about the missing right hand.

In his senior year at Flint Central, Abbott had a 10-3 record with a 0.76 earned run average. He struck out 148 batters in 73 innings. He gave up just 16 hits. That works out to two strikeouts an inning, a hit every four or five innings. When batting, he stuck the stub at the end of the bat, near the handle, and closed his big left hand around it.

Using this system, Jim Abbott only managed to hit .427 for Flint Central, with seven homers. He also played quarterback on the football team. Flint Central went 10-2. Against Midlands High, Abbott threw four touchdown passes in the first half. There isn't a rule anywhere that says The Natural has to have two hands.

Jim Abbott, bottom, at age 4 with prosthesis he later discarded; right, warming up for college photo session (note glove cradled on right hand); and in football uniform.

Asked if there's anything he can't do, he replies: "I can't button the darn buttons on my left cuff."

When I first heard about Jim Abbott, one-handed pitcher, I remembered Monty Stratton, the one-legged pitcher for the White Sox, and how hard it was for him to field bunts. I asked Jim about bunts, first thing.

Jim: "One game when I was pitching in the ninth grade, they bunted on me eight times in a row. I threw out the last seven. That was enough of that."

Mike and Kathy Abbott married young. They were each 18 when their first son was born without a right hand. Like him, they have learned as they've gone. They have helped him turn the abnormal into the normal, a potential negative into an inspiring and uplifting positive. Jim Abbott would be a more complete baseball player with two hands. I find it impossible to believe he could be a more complete person.

"We think," says Mike Abbott, "that if the baseball thing went up in smoke tomorrow, Jimmy would be adjusted enough to go live his life without baseball."

Once, quite seriously, I asked Jim Abbott what he *can't* do.

Quite seriously, he replied: "I can't button the darn buttons on my left cuff."

"Who does it?"

"My mom, usually. My roommate in college."

"After watching him pitch, I didn't think of the right hand at all—*at all*," says Don Welke, one of the scouts who has helped make the Toronto Blue Jays' farm system into one of the best in baseball. "For me, he was just another outstanding prospect."

The Blue Jays felt that Abbott's impairment might discourage other teams, so they waited until the 36th round of last year's amateur draft before taking him. Some saw it as a publicity stunt—as a backhanded compliment, if you will. The Blue Jays were, and are, serious about Jim Abbott's future.

"His drafting wasn't for publicity," says Don Welke, who urged the team to take Abbott. "We look down the road and see him as a major leaguer. He has a major league arm, a major league heart."

Jim Abbott, however, had that major league heart set on Michigan.

"A couple of years ago," he says, "to play college ball at any level was a dream I never thought could come true. I remember on my first visit to Ann Arbor, I looked at the campus and thought how pretty things were and how neat it would be for someone to go there. Then I stopped short and said to myself. '*You* can have this. It's you they want. You can play college baseball here.' I think I can have both my dreams. I can play college ball and have pro ball still waiting for me down the road."

A week before he left for college, I asked Jim if he was afraid about the future. "I am," he said. "But I really think they're just normal fears for a guy going off to college. You're talking about my hand, right? I had to stop being afraid a long time ago. What fear there's been, I've used to get better."

We were sitting in front of the Abbott house. He was showing me his new glove. "You know," he said, "I hear a lot about how inspirational I am. But I don't see myself as being inspirational. Whether you're rich or poor or one-handed or whatever, your own childhood just seems natural, because it's the only one you know. I've met kids with one hand lately, or one arm—8-year-olds, in that range—and they tell me I've helped them by example, and I do feel great about that. But I don't think *I'm* that great. If I can inspire kids in any way, I'd just hope they could get the same enjoyment out of sports I've had."

And now, on this afternoon, it was time for a game of catch. Jim Abbott walked about 30 yards away and began tossing the ball to me. It began to make bigger and bigger popping noises in my glove as the kid got loose. After about five minutes, I promise I did not notice the shortened right arm, or the glove switch, any of it. I just made sure to watch the ball. I wanted to be sure I was quick enough with *my* glove so that a baseball thrown by Jim Abbott did not hit me between the eyes.

I thought: I'm like the hitters. I feel overmatched. But I wanted to remember this game of catch, because I began to feel strongly that it would be important someday that I knew Jim Abbott when.

I have used the word hero a lot in writing about sports, carried away by the moment. Jim Abbott is a hero. He is like most true heroes. He doesn't make a big deal out of what he does. He just gets on with things. He plays the hand dealt him, at the University of Michigan now. Without bitterness and without complaint, he has become a champion, no matter what happens in Ann Arbor this spring.

drafted by the California Angels—"for his ability, not his disability" (Anderson, 1989, p. 27)—and began a successful career in professional baseball. One of his teammates thought that he might have to help Abbott with everyday tasks but found that "You don't have to ask [Jim] what he can't do . . . just sit back and watch what he *can* do" (p. 27).

Jim Abbott is exceptional in two ways. First, he is an extraordinarily good baseball player. Second, he is a person with one hand. Perhaps the media have given more attention to him than to many other players because we do not expect a one-handed person to be able to play baseball, much less to excel. His achievements in a high-profile profession make a forceful point—that we must not let people's disabilities keep us from recognizing their abilities. Many children and youths with disabilities have abilities that go unrecognized because their disabilities become the focus of our concern and we do not give enough attention to what they *can* do. We must study the disabilities of exceptional children and youths if we are to learn how to help them make maximum use of their abilities, and some students with disabilities less obvious than Jim Abbott's need special programs of education and related services to help them live full, happy, productive lives. However, we must not lose sight of the fact that *the most important characteristics of exceptional children are their abilities.*

DEFINITION OF EXCEPTIONAL CHILDREN

For purposes of their education, *exceptional children are those who require special education and related services if they are to realize their full human potential.* They require special education because they are markedly different from most children in one or more of the following ways: They may have mental retardation, learning disabilities, emotional disturbances, physical disabilities, disordered speech or language, impaired hearing, impaired sight, or special gifts or talents. In the chapters that follow we define as exactly as possible what it means to be a member of a group of exceptional individuals.

Most exceptional individuals have a disability, and they are often referred to as "handicapped" in laws, regulations, and everyday conversations. In this book we sometimes use the colloquial term *handicapped* to refer to individuals with disabilities, but we make an important distinction between disability and handicap. A disability is an inability to do something, a diminished capacity to perform in a specific way. A handicap, on the other hand, is a disadvantage imposed on an individual. A disability may or may not be a handicap, depending on the circumstances. Likewise, a handicap may or may not be caused by a disability. For example, blindness is a disability that can be anything but a handicap in the dark. In fact, in the dark the person who has sight is the one who is handicapped. Being in a wheelchair may be a handicap in certain social circumstances, but the disadvantage may be a result of other people's reactions, not the inability to walk. Other people can handicap a person who is different from themselves (in color, size, appearance, language, and so on) by stereotyping them or not giving them an opportunity to do the things they are able to do. When working and living with exceptional individuals who have disabilities, we must constantly strive to separate the disability from the handicap. That is, our goal should be to confine their handicap to those characteristics that cannot be changed and to make sure that we impose no further handicap by our attitudes or our unwillingness to accommodate their disability.

PREVALENCE OF EXCEPTIONAL CHILDREN

Prevalence refers to the percentage of a population or number of individuals having a particular exceptionality. The prevalence of mental retardation, for example, might be estimated at 2.3 percent, which means that 2.3 percent of the population, or twenty-three people in every thousand, are assumed to be mentally retarded. If the prevalence of giftedness is assumed to be between 3 percent and 5 percent, we would expect somewhere between thirty and fifty people in a sample of a thousand to have special gifts of some kind. Obviously, accurate estimates of prevalence depend on our ability to count the number of people in a given population who have a certain exceptionality.

At first thought, the task of determining the number of children and youths who have exceptionalities seems simple enough, yet the prevalence of most exceptionalities is uncertain and a matter of considerable controversy. Several factors make it hard to say with great accuracy and confidence just how many exceptional individuals there are. Some of the most important factors are vagueness in definitions, frequent changes in definitions, and the role of schools in determining exceptionality.

An accurate count of the number of individuals who are exceptional and in need of special education depends on having a clear, unambiguous definition of exceptionality. Ultimately, this means that accurate estimates of prevalence depend on definitions of the various categories of exceptionality. However, as we discuss in following chapters, most exceptionalities do not have unambiguous definitions. There may be honest disagreement among professionals regarding whether a child has a certain condition. Tests and other means of evaluating individuals' abilities and characteristics are not so accurate that we can always trust them. To complicate matters further, a given individual may have more than one pertinent set of characteristics. For example, he or she may have both mental retardation and blindness or cerebral palsy, blindness, and a gift for writing. Furthermore, a diagnosis that fits an individual today may be inappropriate in the following year, or even in a month. Children and youths with some exceptionalities may change so much over a period of a year or two that they are no longer considered exceptional.

Definitions of exceptionality, because they are arbitrary distinctions, are subject to change. A case in point is the definition of mental retardation, which includes but is not based solely on the intelligence quotient (IQ). Several decades ago, mental retardation was defined to include individuals scoring below about 85 on an individually administered intelligence test. Today, the criterion is a score below about 70. What the change means is simply this: A lot of people who used to be considered mentally retarded are not considered retarded by today's standard. Today, some educators are suggesting that most of the students now considered mildly handicapped have only relatively minor problems and should not be classified as exceptional for special education purposes. We could, of course, dramatically lower the prevalence of exceptionalities simply by setting different criteria for the definitions of mental retardation, learning disability, emotional disturbance, and other conditions.

Still another factor that makes it difficult to determine the prevalence of exceptional individuals is the role of the schools. That is, some exceptionalities are defined primarily by the student's response to the demands of school. Failure to achieve at school plays the major role in defining learning disabilities and mild mental retardation; children who perform as expected in school almost never receive one of these labels. The point is this: When we base our definitions on how students do in school, we have no accurate way of estimating the prevalence of that exceptionality in preschoolers or individuals beyond school age. Furthermore, a student who is considered exceptional in one school might not be considered exceptional in another.

Government figures show that about 10 students out of every 100 have been identified as handicapped for special education purposes (U.S. Department of Education, 1989). The total number of students served by special education is over 4 million. Most of these children and youths are between the ages of six and seventeen.

Although preschoolers and youths eighteen to twenty-one are being identified as handicapped with increasing frequency, school-age children and youths in their early teens make up the bulk of the identified population. In subsequent chapters we discuss the prevalence of specific categories of exceptionality.

DEFINITION OF SPECIAL EDUCATION

Special education means specially designed instruction that meets the unusual needs of an exceptional child. Special materials, teaching techniques, or equipment and/or facilities may be required. For example, children with visual impairment may require reading materials in large print or Braille; students with hearing impairment may require hearing aids and/or instruction in sign language; those with physical disabilities may need special equipment; those with emotional disturbances may need smaller and more highly structured classes; and children with special gifts or talents may require access to working professionals. Related services—special transportation, psychological assessment, physical and occupational therapy, medical treatment, and counseling—may be necessary if special education is to be effective. The single most important goal of special education is finding and capitalizing on exceptional children's *abilities*.

Where and by Whom Special Education Is Provided

Several administrative plans are available for the education of exceptional children and youths, from a few special provisions made by the student's regular teacher to twenty-four-hour residential care in a special facility. Who educates exceptional students and where they receive their education depends on two factors: (1) how and how much the child or youth differs from average students and (2) the resources of the school and community. We describe various administrative plans for education according to the degree of physical integration—the extent to which exceptional and nonexceptional students are taught in the same place by the same teachers.

Beginning with the most integrated intervention, the *regular classroom teacher* who is aware of the individual needs of children and skilled at meeting them may be able to acquire materials, equipment, and/or instructional methods that are appropriate. At this level the direct services of specialists may not be required—the expertise of the regular teacher may meet the child's needs.

At the next level the regular classroom teacher may need consultation with a *special educator* or other professional (e.g., school psychologist) in addition to the special materials, equipment, or methods. The special educator may instruct the regular teacher; refer the teacher to other resources; or demonstrate the use of materials, equipment, or methods.

Going a step further, a special educator may provide *itinerant services* to the exceptional child and/or the regular classroom teacher. The itinerant teacher establishes a consistent schedule, moving from school to school and visiting the classroom to instruct exceptional children individually or in small groups, to provide materials and teaching suggestions for the regular teacher to carry out, and to consult with the regular teacher about special problems.

At the next level, a *resource teacher* provides services for the children and teachers in only one school. The children being served are enrolled in the regular classroom and are seen by the specially trained teacher for a length of time and at a frequency determined by the nature and severity of their particular problems. The resource teacher continually assesses the needs of the children and their teachers

The emphasis today is on providing special education services that are tailored to individual students' unique needs. Here one student who has difficulty controlling a pencil for written work is using a manual typewriter in the conventional way, and another who hasn't the use of his arms and fingers is learning to use a headstick to type his written work. Meanwhile, other students in the class are completing their assignments with paper and pencil. (Ann Chwatsky/Leo de

and usually teaches children individually or in small groups in a special classroom, where special materials and equipment are available. Typically, the resource teacher serves as a consultant to the regular classroom teacher, advising on the instruction and management of the child in the classroom and perhaps demonstrating instructional techniques. The flexibility of the plan and the fact that the child remains with peers most of the time make this a particularly attractive and popular alternative.

Diagnostic-prescriptive centers go beyond the level of intervention represented by resource rooms. In this plan children are placed for a short period of time in a special class in a school or other facility so their needs can be assessed and a plan of action can be determined on the basis of diagnostic findings. After an educational prescription is written for the child, the recommendations for placement may include anything from institutional care to placement in a regular classroom with a particularly competent teacher who can carry out the plan.

Hospital and homebound instruction is most often required by children who have physical disabilities, although it is sometimes employed for emotionally disturbed or other handicapped children when no alternative is readily available. Typically, the child is confined to the hospital or the home for a relatively short period of time, and the hospital or homebound teacher maintains contact with the child's regular teacher.

One of the most visible—and in recent years, controversial—service alternatives is the *special self-contained class*. Such a class typically enrolls fifteen or fewer exceptional children with a particular diagnostic label (e.g., mental retardation). The teacher ordinarily has been trained as a special educator and provides all or most of the children's instruction. Those assigned to such classes usually spend the whole school day segregated from their normal peers, although sometimes they are integrated with nonhandicapped children during part of the day (perhaps for physical education, music, or some other activity in which they can participate well).

Special day schools provide an all-day, segregated experience for exceptional children. The day school is usually organized for a specific category of exceptional children and may contain special equipment necessary for their care and education. These children return to their homes during nonschool hours.

The final level of intervention is the *residential school*. Here exceptional children receive twenty-four-hour care away from home, often at a distance from their communities. These children may make periodic visits home or return each weekend, but during the week they are residents of the institution, where they receive academic instruction in addition to management of their daily living environment.

The major features of each type of placement or service alternative, examples

TABLE 1.1   Examples of Service Alternatives for Special Education

Most Integrated ←———————————————————————————————

Type of Placement	Regular Class Only	Regular Class with Consultation	Itinerant Teacher	Resource Teacher
Major features of placement alternative	Regular teacher meets all needs of student; student may not be officially identified or labeled; student totally integrated	Regular teacher meets all needs of student with only occasional help from consultant(s); student may not be officially identified or labeled; student totally integrated	Regular teacher provides most or all instruction; special teacher provides intermittent instruction of student and/or consultation with regular teacher; student integrated except for brief instructional sessions	Regular teacher provides most instruction; special teacher provides instruction part of school day and advises regular teacher; student integrated most of school day
Types of students typically served	Student with mild learning disability, emotional/behavioral disorder, or mild mental retardation	Student with mild learning disability, emotional/behavioral disorder, or mild mental retardation	Student with visual impairment or physical disability; student with communication disorder	Student with mild to moderate emotional/behavioral, learning, or communication disorder
Primary role of special education teacher	None	To offer demonstration and instruction and to assist regular class teacher as requested	To visit classroom regularly and see that appropriate instruction, materials and other services are provided; to offer consultation, demonstration, and referral for regular teacher and assessment and instruction of student as needed; to work toward total integration of student	To assess student's needs for instruction and management; to provide individual or small-group instruction on set schedule in regular class or resource room; to offer advice and demonstration for regular teacher; to handle referral to other agencies for additional services; to work toward total integration of student

of the types of students most likely to be served in each, and the primary roles of the special educators who work there are shown in Table 1.1. Note that although these are the major administrative plans for delivery of special education, variations are possible. Many school systems, in the process of trying to find more effective and economical ways of serving exceptional students, combine or alter these alternatives and the roles special educators and other professionals play in service delivery. Furthermore, the types of students listed under each service alternative are *examples only*; there are wide variations among school systems in the kinds of placements made for particular kinds of students. Note also that what any special education teacher may be expected to do includes a variety of items not specified in Table 1.1. We discuss these expectations for teachers in the following section.

Special education law requires placement of the child in the **least restrictive environment (LRE).** What is usually meant is that the child should be segregated

Least Integrated →

Diagnostic Prescriptive Center	Hospital or Homebound Instruction	Self-Contained Class	Special Day School	Residential School
Special teacher provides most or all instruction for several days or weeks and develops plan or prescription for receiving teacher; student totally segregated while in center but may be partially or totally integrated following diagnosis and prescription	Special teacher provides all instruction in hospital or home until student is able to return to usual school classes (regular or special) from which he or she has been temporarily withdrawn; student totally segregated for short period	Special teacher provides most or all instruction in special class of students with given categorical label; regular teacher may provide instruction in regular class for part of school day; student mostly or totally segregated	Special teacher provides instruction in separate school; also may work with teachers in regular or special classes of regular school; student totally or mostly segregated	Same as special day school; special teacher also works with other staff to provide a total therapeutic environment or milieu; student totally or mostly segregated
Student with mild disability who has been receiving no services or inadequate services	Student with physical disability; student undergoing treatment or medical tests	Student with moderate to severe mental retardation or emotional/behavioral order	Student with severe or profound physical or mental disability	Student with severe or profound mental retardation or emotional/behavioral disorder
To make comprehensive assessment of student's educational strengths and weaknesses; to develop written prescription for instruction and behavior management for receiving teacher; to interpret prescription for receiving teacher and assess and revise prescription as needed	To obtain records from student's school of attendance; to maintain contact with teachers (regular or special) and offer instruction consistent with student's school program; to prepare student for return to school (special or regular)	To manage and teach special class; to offer instruction in most areas of curriculum; to work toward integration of students in regular classes	To manage and teach individuals and/or small groups of handicapped students; to work toward integration of students in regular school	Same as special day school; also to work with residential staff to make certain school program is integrated appropriately with non-school activities

from normal classmates and separated from home, family, and community as little as possible. That is, his or her life should be as "normal" as possible, and the intervention should be consistent with individual needs and not interfere with individual freedom any more than is absolutely necessary. For example, children should not be placed in a special class if they can be served adequately by a resource teacher, and they should not be placed in an institution if a special class will serve their needs just as well. Although this movement toward placement of exceptional children in the least restrictive environment is laudable, the definition of *least restrictive* is not as simple as it seems. Cruickshank (1977) has pointed out that greater restriction of the physical environment does not necessarily mean greater restriction of the child's psychological freedom or human potential. In fact, it is conceivable that some children could be more restricted in the long run in a regular class where they are rejected by others and fail to learn necessary skills than in a special class or day school where they learn happily and well. It is important to keep the ultimate goals for the child in mind and to avoid letting "least restrictive" become a hollow slogan that results in shortchanging children in terms of their education. As Morse has noted, "The goal should be to find the most productive setting to provide the maximum assistance for the child" (1984, p. 120).

Although considerable variation in the placement of handicapped students is found from state to state and among school systems within a given state, most exceptional children are educated in regular classes. Nationwide, over two-thirds of handicapped children and youths are served primarily in regular classes. Most of these students receive special instruction for part of the school day from special education resource teachers. About one-fourth of all handicapped children and youths in the United States are placed in separate special classes, and only about 7 percent are segregated in separate schools or other environments (e.g., institutions, hospital schools, and homebound instruction).

Children under the age of six less often receive education in regular classes and more often attend separate schools than do children who have reached the usual school age. Special classes, separate schools, and other environments such as homebound instruction are used more often for older teenagers and young adults than for students of elementary and high school age. We can explain these differences by two facts. First, preschoolers and young adults who are identified for special education tend to have more severe disabilities than children of school age. Second, some school systems do not have regular classes for preschoolers and young adults, and thus placements in other than regular classes are typically more available and more appropriate.

The environment that is least restrictive depends in part on the child's exceptionality. Figure 1.1 illustrates the differences in educational placement of children with different disabilities. There is almost never a need to segregate in a separate class or separate school a child whose primary disability is a speech or language impairment. Most children with learning disabilities can be appropriately educated primarily in regular classes. On the other hand, the resources needed to teach deaf and blind children require that most of them attend separate schools or classes.

WHAT TEACHERS ARE EXPECTED TO DO

We have noted that most students in public schools who have been identified as exceptional are placed in regular classrooms for at least part of the school day. Furthermore, there is good reason to believe that a large number of public school

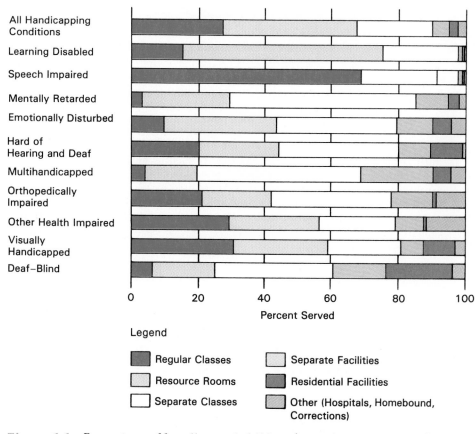

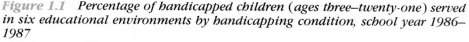

Figure 1.1 *Percentage of handicapped children (ages three–twenty-one) served in six educational environments by handicapping condition, school year 1986–1987*

SOURCE: *Eleventh Annual Report to Congress on the Implementation of the Education of the Handicapped Act.* (Washington, DC: U.S. Department of Education, 1989.)

students not identified as disabled or gifted share many of the characteristics of exceptional children. Thus all teachers must obviously be prepared to deal with exceptional children.

The roles of general and special education teachers are not always clear in a given case. Sometimes uncertainty about the division of responsibility can be extremely stressful; for example, teachers may feel very uneasy because it is not clear whose job it is to make special adaptations for a child or just what they are expected to do in cooperating with other teachers.

Relationship Between General and Special Education

During the 1980s, the relationship between general and special education became a matter of great concern to policymakers, researchers, and advocates for exceptional children. Proposals for changing the relationship between general and special education, including radical calls to restructure or merge the two, came to be known as the *regular education initiative* (REI). Moderate proponents of REI suggested that general educators take more responsibility for many students with mild or moderate disabilities, special educators serving more as consultants or resources

What Should I Do Before I Make a Referral?

Probably the most important thing you should do is to contact the student's parents if you are thinking about referring him or her. If you cannot reach them by phone, try a home visit or ask the visiting teacher (or school social worker, psychologist, or other support personnel) to help you set up a conference. It is very important that you discuss the student's problems with the parents *before* you refer. Parents should never be surprised to find that their child has been referred; they should know well in advance that their child's teachers have noticed problems. One of the most important things you can do to prevent conflict with parents is to establish and maintain communication with them regarding their child's progress.

Before making a referral, check *all* the student's school records. Look for information that could help you understand the student's behavioral or academic problems.

Has the student ever:
- had a psychological evaluation?
- qualified for special services?
- been included in other special programs (e.g., programs for disadvantaged children or speech or language therapy)?
- scored far below average on standardized tests?
- been retained?

Do the records indicate:
- good progress in some areas, poor progress in others?
- any physical or medical problem?
- that the student is taking medication?

Talk to the student's other teachers and professional support personnel about your concern for the student.

Have other teachers:
- also had difficulty with the student?
- found ways of dealing successfully with the student?

The analysis of information obtained in these ways may help you teach and manage the student successfully, or help you justify to the parents why you believe their child may need special education.

Before making a referral, you will be expected to document the strategies that you have used in your class to meet the student's educational needs. Regardless of whether the student is later found to have a handicapping condition, your documentation will be useful in the following ways: (1) you will have evidence that will be helpful to or required by the committee of professionals who will evaluate the student; (2) you will be better able to help the student's parents understand that methods used for other students in the class are not adequate for their child; and (3) you will have records of successful and/or unsuccessful methods of working with the student that will be useful to you and any other teacher who works with the student in the future.

Your documentation of what you have done may appear to require a lot of paper work, but careful record keeping will pay off. If the student is causing you serious concern, then you will be wise to demonstrate your concern by keeping written records. Your notes should include items such as the following:

- exactly what you are concerned about
- why you are concerned about it
- dates, places, and times you have observed the problem

- precisely what you have done to try to resolve the problem
- who, if anyone, helped you devise the plans or strategies you have used
- evidence that the strategies have been successful or unsuccessful

In summary, make certain that you have accomplished the following before you make a referral:

1. Held at least one conference to discuss your concerns with the parents (or made extensive and documented efforts to communicate with the parents).
2. Checked all available school records and interviewed other professionals involved with the child.
3. Documented the academic and behavioral management strategies that you have tried.

Remember that you should refer a student only if you can make a convincing case that the student may have a handicapping condition and probably cannot be served appropriately without special education. Referral for special education begins a time-consuming, costly, and stressful process that is potentially damaging to the student and has many legal ramifications.

SOURCE: Patricia L. Pullen and James M. Kauffman, *What Should I Know About Special Education? Answers for Classroom Teachers* (Austin, TX: Pro-Ed, 1987). © 1987 by P. L. Pullen and J. M. Kauffman.

to regular classroom teachers and less as special teachers of children. More radical REI proponents recommended that special education be eliminated as a separate, identifiable part of education. They called for a single, unified educational system in which all children are viewed as unique, special, and entitled to the same quality of education. Although many of the suggested reforms have great appeal and some could produce benefits for exceptional children, the basis for REI and its ultimate consequences have been questioned.

We discuss REI and its implications further in Chapter 2. Regardless of how one views REI, the controversy about the relationship between special and general education has made teachers more aware of the problems of deciding just which students should be taught with specific curricula, which students should receive special attention or services, and where and by whom these should be provided. There are no pat answers to the questions about how special and general education should work together to see that every child receives an appropriate education. Yet it is clear that the relationship between them must be one of cooperation and collaboration. They must not become independent or mutually exclusive educational tracks. Neither can we deny that general and special educators have somewhat different roles to play. With this in mind, we summarize some of the major expectations for all teachers as well as for special education teachers in particular.

Expectations for All Educators

Whether specifically trained in special education or not, a teacher may be expected to participate in educating exceptional students in any one of the following ways:

1. *Make maximum effort to accommodate individual students' needs.* Teaching in public schools requires dealing with diverse students in every class. All teachers must make an effort to meet the needs of individuals who may

differ in some way from the average or typical student in their classroom. Flexibility, adaptation, accommodation, and special attention are to be expected of every teacher. Special education should be considered necessary only when a teacher's best efforts to meet a student's individual needs are not successful.

2. *Evaluate academic abilities and disabilities.* Although psychologists or other special school personnel may give a student formal standardized tests in academic areas, adequate evaluation requires the teacher's assessment of the student's performance in the classroom. Teachers must be able to report specifically and precisely how the student can and cannot perform in all academic areas for which they are responsible.

3. *Refer for evaluation.* By law, all public school systems must make extensive efforts to screen and identify all handicapped children and youths of school age. Teachers must observe students' behavior and refer those they suspect of having disabilities for evaluation by a multidisciplinary team. *We stress here that a student should not be referred for special education unless extensive and unsuccessful efforts have been made to accommodate his or her needs in regular classes. Before referral, school personnel must document the strategies that have been used to teach and manage the student in general education. Only if these strategies have failed is referral justified* (see the box on pp. 14–15).

4. *Participate in eligibility conferences.* Before students are provided special education, their eligibility must be determined by an interdisciplinary team. Therefore teachers must be ready to work with other teachers and with professionals from other disciplines (psychology, medicine, or social work, for example) in determining a student's eligibility for special education.

5. *Participate in writing individualized education programs.* A written individualized program for his or her education must be on file in the records of every disabled student. Teachers must be ready to participate in a conference (possibly including the student and/or parents, as well as other professionals) in which the program is formulated.

6. *Communicate with parents or guardians.* Parents (sometimes surrogate parents) or guardians must be consulted during the evaluation of their child's eligibility for special education, formulation of the individualized education program, and reassessment of any special program that may be designed for their child. Teachers must contribute to the school's communication with parents about their child's problems, placement, and progress.

7. *Participate in due process hearings and negotiations.* When parents, guardians, or disabled students themselves are dissatisfied with the school's response to the child's needs, they may request a "due process" hearing or negotiations regarding appropriate services. Teachers may be called on to offer observations, opinions, or suggestions in such hearings or negotiations.

8. *Collaborate with other professionals in identifying and making maximum use of exceptional students' abilities.* Finding and implementing solutions to the challenges of educating exceptional children are not the exclusive responsibility of any one professional group. General and special education teachers are expected to share responsibility for educating students with special needs. In addition, teachers may need to collaborate with other professionals, depending on the student's exceptionality. Psychologists, counselors, physicians, physical therapists, and a variety of other specialists may need the teacher's perspective on the student's abilities and disabilities, and they may rely on the teacher to implement critical aspects of evaluation or treatment.

A high level of professional competence and ethical judgment is required to conform to these expectations. Teaching demands a thorough knowledge of child development and expertise in instruction. Furthermore, teachers are sometimes faced with serious professional and ethical dilemmas in trying to serve the needs of students and their parents, on the one hand, and in attempting to conform to legal or administrative pressures, on the other. For example, when there are indications that the child may have a disability, should a teacher refer that child for evaluation and possible placement in special education, knowing that only inadequate or inappropriate services will be provided? Should a teacher who believes strongly that teenage students with mild retardation need sex education refrain from giving students any information because sex education is not part of the prescribed curriculum and is frowned on by the school board?

Expectations for Special Educators

In addition to being competent enough to meet the preceding expectations, special education teachers must attain special expertise in the following areas:

1. *Academic instruction of children with learning problems.* The majority of students with disabilities have more difficulty learning academic skills than do the nondisabled. This is true for all categories of handicapping conditions because sensory impairments, physical disabilities, and mental or emotional disabilities all tend to make academic learning more difficult. Often the difficulty is slight; sometimes it is extreme. Special education teachers must have more than patience and hope, though they do need these qualities; they must have the technical skill to present academic tasks so that students with disabilities will understand and respond appropriately.

2. *Management of serious behavior problems.* Many students with disabilities have behavior problems in addition to their other exceptionalities. Some, in fact, require special education primarily because of their inappropriate or disruptive behavior. Special education teachers must have the ability to deal effectively with more than the usual troublesome behavior of students. Besides understanding and empathy, they must possess the mastery of techniques that will allow them to draw out particularly withdrawn students, control those who are hyperaggressive and persistently disruptive, and teach critical social skills.

3. *Use of technological advances.* Technology is increasingly being applied to the problems of teaching exceptional students and improving their daily lives. New devices and methods are rapidly being developed, particularly for students with sensory and physical disabilities. Special education teachers need more than mere awareness of the technology that is available; they must also be able to evaluate its advantages and disadvantages for teaching the exceptional children with whom they work.

4. *Knowledge of special education law.* For good or ill, special education today involves many details of law. Disabled students' rights are spelled out in considerable detail in federal and state legislation. The laws, and the rules and regulations that accompany them, are constantly being interpreted by new court decisions, some of which have widespread implications for the practice of special education. Special education teachers do not need to be lawyers, but they do need to be aware of the law's requirements and prohibitions if they are to be adequate advocates for students with disabilities.

We caution here that the specific day-to-day expectations for special education teachers vary from school system to school system and from state to state. What are listed here are the general expectations and areas of competence with which every special educator will necessarily be concerned.

HOW AND WHERE
SPECIAL EDUCATION BEGAN

There have always been exceptional children, but there have not always been special educational services to address their needs. During the closing years of the eighteenth century, following the American and French revolutions, effective procedures were devised for teaching children with sensory impairments—those who were blind or deaf (Winzer, 1986). Early in the nineteenth century the first systematic attempts were made to educate "idiotic" and "insane" children—those who today are said to be mentally retarded and emotionally disturbed. In the prerevolutionary era the most society had offered exceptional children was protection—asylum from a cruel world into which they did not fit and in which they could not survive with dignity, if they could survive at all. But as the ideas of democracy, individual freedom, and egalitarianism swept America and France, there was a change in attitude. Political reformers and leaders in medicine and education began to champion the cause of handicapped children and adults, urging that these "imperfect" or "incomplete" individuals be taught skills that would allow them to become independent, productive citizens. These humanitarian sentiments went beyond a desire to protect and defend handicapped people. The early leaders sought to normalize exceptional children to the greatest extent possible and confer on them the human dignity they lacked.

The historical roots of special education are found primarily in the early 1800s. Contemporary educational methods for exceptional children can be traced directly to techniques pioneered during that era. And many (perhaps most) of today's vital, controversial issues have been issues ever since the dawn of special education. In our discussion of some of the major historical events and trends since 1800, we comment briefly on the history of people and ideas, professional and parent organizations, and legislation and litigation.

People and Ideas

Most of the originators of special education were European physicians. They were primarily young, ambitious people who challenged the wisdom of the established authorities, including their own friends and mentors (Kanner, 1964).

Jean Marc Gaspard Itard (1775–1838), a French physician who was an authority on diseases of the ear and on the education of deaf students, is the person to whom most historians trace the beginning of special education as we know it today. In the early years of the nineteenth century, this young doctor began to educate a boy of about twelve who had been found roaming naked and wild in the forests of France. Itard's mentor, Philippe Pinel (1745–1826), a prominent French physician who was an early advocate of humane treatment of insane persons, advised him that his efforts would be unsuccessful because the boy, Victor, was a "hopeless idiot." But Itard persevered. He did not make Victor nonhandicapped, but he did dramatically improve the wild child's behavior through patient, systematic educative procedures (Itard, 1962).

Itard's student, Edouard Seguin (1812–1880), emigrated to the United States in

1848. Before that, Seguin had become famous as an educator of retarded children, even though most thinkers of the day were convinced that such children could not be taught anything of significance. His book *Idiocy and Its Treatment by the Physiological Method* (published in the United States in 1866) described in detail his interpretation and elaboration of Itard's methods. It also provided much of the foundation for the work of Maria Montessori (1870–1952). Montessori became known not only as an educator of mentally retarded children but also as an advocate of early education for children.

The ideas of the first special educators were truly revolutionary for their times. These are a few of the revolutionary ideas of Itard, Seguin, and their successors that form the foundation for present-day special education:

- *Individualized instruction*, in which the child's characteristics rather than prescribed academic content provide the basis for teaching techniques.
- *A carefully sequenced series of educational tasks*, beginning with tasks the child can perform and gradually leading to more complex learning.
- *Emphasis on stimulation* and awakening of the child's senses, the aim being to make the child more aware of and responsive to educational stimuli.
- *Meticulous arrangement of the child's environment*, so that the structure of the environment and the child's experience of it lead naturally to learning.
- *Immediate reward for correct performance*, providing reinforcement for desirable behavior.
- *Tutoring in functional skills*, the desire being to make the child as self-sufficient and productive as possible in everyday life.
- *Belief that every child should be educated to the greatest extent possible*, the assumption being that every child can improve to some degree.

So far we have mentioned only European physicians who figured prominently in the rise of special education. Although it is true that much of the initial work took place in Europe, many U.S. researchers contributed greatly during those early years. They stayed informed of European developments as best they could, some of them traveling to Europe for the specific purpose of obtaining first-hand information about the education of handicapped children.

Among the young U.S. thinkers concerned with the education of handicapped students was Samuel Gridley Howe (1801–1876), an 1824 graduate of Harvard Medical School. Besides being a physician and an educator, Howe was a political and social reformer, a champion of humanitarian causes and emancipation. He was instrumental in the founding of the Perkins School for the Blind in Watertown, Massachusetts, and was also a teacher of deaf and blind students. His success in teaching Laura Bridgman, who was deaf and blind, greatly influenced the education of Helen Keller. Howe was also a force behind the organization of an experimental school for retarded children in Massachusetts in the 1840s and was personally acquainted with Seguin.

Thomas Hopkins Gallaudet (1787–1851) was a minister who had met and tried to teach a deaf girl when he was a student at Andover Theological Seminary. He traveled to Europe to learn about the education of deaf students, and on his return to the United States in 1817 established the first American residential school for deaf students in Hartford, Connecticut (now known as the American School of the Deaf). Gallaudet University in Washington, D.C., the only liberal arts college for deaf students in the world, was named in his honor.

The early years of special education were vibrant with the pulse of new ideas. It is not possible to read the words of Itard, Seguin, Howe, and their contemporaries without being captivated by the romance, idealism, and excitement of their exploits. The results they achieved were truly remarkable for their era. Today, special education remains a vibrant field in which innovations, excitement, idealism, and controversies are the norm. Teachers of exceptional children—and that includes, as discussed earlier, *all* teachers—must understand how and why special education emerged as a discipline.

Growth of the Discipline

Special education did not suddenly spring up as a new discipline, nor did it develop in isolation from other disciplines. The emergence of psychology and sociology, and especially the beginning of the widespread use of mental tests in the early years of the twentieth century, had enormous implications for the growth of special education. Psychologists' study of learning and their prediction of school failure or success by means of tests helped focus attention on children with special needs. Sociologists, social workers, and anthropologists drew attention to the ways in which exceptional children's families and communities responded to them and affected their learning and adjustment. As the education profession itself matured and as compulsory school attendance laws became a reality, there was a growing realization among teachers and school administrators that a large number of children must be given something beyond the ordinary classroom experience. Thus contemporary special education is a professional field with roots in several academic disciplines—especially medicine, psychology, sociology, and social work—in addition to professional education. It is a discipline sufficiently different from the mainstream of professional education to require special training programs but sufficiently like the mainstream to maintain a primary concern for schools and teaching.

Contemporary special education draws heavily on all disciplines concerned with child development. Special educators must know not only the developmental characteristics of exceptional children but also how these characteristics differ from those of nonhandicapped children. In addition to an understanding of normal and delayed development, special educators must have a foundation of technical knowledge in the disciplines that involve a given exceptionality. For example, to be an adequate teacher of deaf children, one must have some knowledge of audiology (the science of hearing) and otology (the medical specialty of the ear and its diseases), as well as of communication and teaching techniques. We are not suggesting that an educator of deaf children must also be a developmental psychologist, an audiologist, and an otologist. But unless the educator of children with impaired hearing has the ability to communicate intelligently with professionals from these other disciplines, he or she will not be an effective teacher.

Becoming a special educator means preparing to *teach* exceptional children. It means preparing to spend one's time helping children change their behavior— grasp new concepts and perform new responses. Usually, but not always, it means working in public schools and classrooms. Always, it means working with other professionals and contributing to an interdisciplinary effort to help the child and the people the child lives with.

Professional and Parents' Organizations

Individuals and ideas have played crucial roles in the history of special education, but it is accurate to say that much of the progress made over the years has been achieved primarily by the collective efforts of professionals and parents. Professional groups were organized first, beginning in the nineteenth century. Effective national parents' organizations have existed in the United States only since 1950.

The earliest professional organizations having some bearing on the education of handicapped children were medical associations founded in the 1800s. Organization of a professional association devoted to special education did not occur until 1922, when the Council for Exceptional Children (CEC) was founded. CEC and its divisions have become the primary professional organizations of special educators, although other professional groups, such as the American Orthopsychiatric Association and the American Association on Mental Retardation, welcome special educators as members and work toward many of the same goals as CEC. Today CEC has a national membership of over 50,000, including about 10,000 students. There are state CEC organizations and hundreds of local chapters. The divisions of CEC (see Table 1.2) have been organized to meet the interests and needs of CEC members who specialize in a particular area.

TABLE 1.2   The Divisions of CEC

CASE	Council of Administrators of Special Education. Members are administrators, supervisors, or coordinators of special education programs and college faculty in special education administration. Designed to deal with administrative and supervisory problems (organized 1952).
DVH	Division for the Visually Handicapped: Partially Seeing and Blind. Concerned with the education of children with blindness or partial sight (organized 1952).
TED	Teacher Education Division. Designed to assist professionals who are involved in the education and training of teachers, such as the instructors of college courses and the supervisors of field experiences or student teaching, in all areas of special education (organized 1953).
DPH	Division for the Physically Handicapped. Concerned with the education of children with physical disabilities and health impairments (organized 1957).
TAG	The Association for the Gifted. Devoted to the education of gifted and talented children (organized 1958).
CEC–MR	Division on Mental Retardation. The division for educators of children with mental retardation (organized 1963).
CCBD	Council for Children with Behavioral Disorders. Deals with the problems of teaching children and youths with emotional/behavioral disorders (organized 1964).
DCCD	Division for Children with Communication Disorders. Focuses on children with disorders of speech and language (organized 1968).
DLD	Division for Learning Disabilities. Designed to deal with the problems of teaching children who have learning disabilities (organized 1968).
DEC	Division for Early Childhood. Deals with the special concerns of those who are involved in the education of young handicapped children (organized 1973).
CEDS	Council for Educational Diagnostic Services. Concerned with problems and issues in testing and diagnosing exceptional children (organized 1974).
DCD	Division on Career Development. Founded to serve teachers who are involved in vocational training and job placement for exceptional children and youths (organized 1976).
TAM	Technology and Media Division. Organized to keep interested professionals informed of new technological developments related to the education of exceptional children (founded in 1984).
CEC–DR	Division for Research. Founded to promote research relating to the education of exceptional individuals (organized in 1987).
CEC–PIO	Pioneers Division. For retired, life, and long-time members of CEC (organized in 1989).

Although the parents' organizations offer membership to individuals who do not have handicapped or gifted children of their own, they are made up primarily of parents who do have such children and concentrate on issues of special concern to them. Parents' organizations have typically served three essential functions: (1) providing an informal group for parents who understand one another's problems and needs and help one another deal with anxieties and frustrations, (2) providing information regarding services and potential resources, and (3) providing the structure for obtaining needed services for their children. Some of the organizations that came about primarily as the result of parents' efforts include the Association for Retarded Citizens, the National Association for Gifted Children, the Association for Children and Adults with Learning Disabilities, and the National Society for Children and Adults with Autism.

Legislation and Litigation

Private schools and tutors have played a part in the education of children with disabilities since the beginning of special education. Services supported by public funds began early in the nineteenth century. But as Martin (1976) points out, a national commitment to the right to a free public education for *every* individual, including every person with a disability, represented a new level of maturity for the United States.

In the earliest years of special education, government funds were first appropriated to support "experimental" schools to see whether children with disabilities could actually be educated. Over time, legislation gradually began to provide a more permanent foundation for special education as an integral part of the public education system.

Legislation providing for special education may be of two types: permissive or mandatory. *Permissive* legislation states that schools *may* provide special education; *mandatory* legislation says they *must.* At the federal level, legislation was permissive until 1975. The assumption was that control over the education dollar is a state's right. Funds were provided as incentives for the states to develop their own special education services, with little federal control.

Federal law became mandatory in 1975 with the enactment of a legislative landmark **PL 94-142,*** the Education for All Handicapped Children Act. This law contains a *mandatory* provision, stating,

> in order to receive funds under the Act every school system in the nation must make provision for a free, appropriate public education for every child between the ages of 3 and 21 (unless state law does not provide free public education to children 3 to 5 or 18 to 21 years of age) regardless of how, or how seriously, he may be handicapped.

In 1986, PL 99-457 extended the requirements of PL 94-142 to children aged three to five, even in states that do not provide free public education to children that young. To continue receiving federal special education funds, every state education agency *must* now provide free and appropriate education and related services to all handicapped children three to five years of age. PL 99-457 also includes

---

* Legislation is typically designated PL (for public law), followed by a hyphenated numeral, the first set of digits representing the number of the Congress that passed the bill and the second set of numerals representing the number of that bill. Thus PL 94-142 is the 142nd public law passed by the 94th Congress.

incentives for states to develop early intervention programs for handicapped infants and infants at risk, from birth to age thirty-six months.

Responsibility for implementing the provisions of PL 94-142 and other federal laws is shared by local, state, and federal governments. Although PL 94-142 spells out what must be provided in the way of special education and related services, another law passed by the 93rd Congress (Section 504 of PL 93-112, the Rehabilitation Act of 1973) prohibits discrimination against handicapped people. Section 504 and PL 94-142 both require every handicapped child to be provided a free and appropriate education (Bateman & Herr, 1981).

PL 94-142, passed and signed into law in 1975, is the most significant bill in a long chain of federal enactments affecting the education of students with disabilities. We do not try to lead you through the thicket of that legislation here. Neither do we try to give you a review of current litigation related to federal and state education laws. We do, however, discuss general trends in legislation and litigation and the relationship between the two.

TRENDS IN LEGISLATION AND LITIGATION

Trends in Legislation

Legislation has historically been increasingly specific and mandatory. In the 1980s, however, the renewed emphasis on states' rights and local autonomy, plus a political

Handicapped people have increasingly been motivated to become skilled in working through government agencies at all levels to ensure their rights and obtain equal opportunities.
(© Bob Daemmrich/Uniphoto)

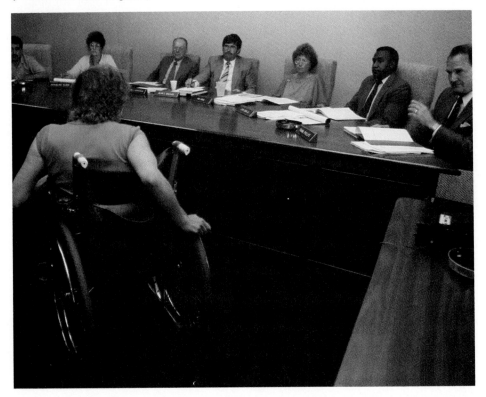

strategy of federal deregulation, led to attempts to repeal some of the provisions of PL 94-142 and loosen federal rules and regulations. Federal disinvestment in education and deregulation of education programs were hallmarks of the Reagan administration (Clark & Astuto, 1988; Verstegen & Clark, 1988), so it is not surprising that federal mandates for special education have come under fire. Dissatisfaction with federal mandates is due in part to the fact that the federal government contributes relatively little to the funding of special education. Although the demands of PL 94-142 are detailed, state and local governments must pay most of the cost of special education programs.

Relationship of Litigation to Legislation

Legislation requires or gives permission to provide special education, but it does not necessarily result in what legislators intended. Whether the laws are administered properly is a legal question for the courts. That is, laws may have little or no effect on the lives of exceptional children until courts interpret the meaning of those laws—exactly what the laws require in practice. Within the past few years, there has been a flurry of litigation involving the special education programs offered by states and local school districts. Exceptional children, primarily through the action of parents' and professional organizations, have been getting their day in court more frequently since PL 94-142 and related federal and state laws were passed (Bateman & Herr, 1981). Thus we must examine trends in litigation to complete the picture of how our legal system may safeguard or undermine appropriate education for exceptional children.

Trends in Litigation

Zelder (1953) noted that in the early days of public education school attendance was seen as a *privilege* that could be awarded or withheld from an individual child at the discretion of local school officials. The courts typically found, during the late nineteenth and early twentieth centuries, that disruptive or mentally retarded children could be excluded from school for the sake of preserving order, protecting the teacher's time from excessive demands, and sparing children the "pain" of seeing others who are disabled. In the first half of the twentieth century the courts tended to defend the majority of school children from a disabled minority. But now the old excuses for excluding students with disabilities from school are no longer thought to be valid. Today, the courts must interpret laws that define school attendance as the *right* of every child, regardless of his or her disability. Litigation is now focused on ensuring that every child receives an education *appropriate for his or her individual needs.*

Litigation may involve legal suits filed for either of two reasons: because special education services are not being provided for children whose parents want them, or because children are being assigned to special education when their parents believe they should not be. Suits filed *for a child's special education* have been brought primarily by parents whose children are unquestionably disabled and are being denied any education at all or being given very meager special services. The parents who file these suits believe that the advantages of their child's identification for special education services clearly outweigh the disadvantages. Suits *against a child's special education* have been brought primarily by parents of children who have mild or questionable disabilities and who are already attending school. These parents believe that their children are being stigmatized and discriminated against rather than helped by special education. Thus the courts today are asked to make decisions in which the individual child's characteristics are weighed against a specific educational program.

Major Provisions of PL 94–142

Each state and locality must have a plan to ensure

Child identification	Extensive efforts must be made to screen and identify all handicapped children.
Full service, at no cost	Every handicapped child must be assured an appropriate public education at no cost to the parents or guardians.
Due process	The child's and parents' rights to information and informed consent must be assured before the child is evaluated, labeled, or placed, and they have a right to an impartial due process hearing if they disagree with the school's decisions.
Parent/guardian surrogate consultation	The child's parents or guardian must be consulted about the child's evaluation and placement and the educational plan; if the parents or guardian are unknown or unavailable, a surrogate parent to act for the child must be found.
LRE	The child must be educated in the least restrictive environment that is consistent with his or her educational needs and, insofar as possible, with nonhandicapped children.
IEP	A written individualized education program must be prepared for each handicapped child. The program must state present levels of functioning, long- and short-term goals, services to be provided, and plans for initiating and evaluating the services.
Nondiscriminatory evaluation	The child must be evaluated in all areas of suspected disability and in a way that is not biased by the child's language or cultural characteristics or handicaps. Evaluation must be by a multidisciplinary team, and no single evaluation procedure may be used as the sole criterion for placement or planning.
Confidentiality	The results of evaluation and placement must be kept confidential, though the child's parents or guardian may have access to the records.
Personnel development, in-service	Training must be provided for teachers and other professional personnel, including in-service training for regular teachers in meeting the needs of handicapped students.

Detailed federal rules and regulations govern the implementation of each of these major provisions. The definitions of some of these provisions—LRE and nondiscriminatory evaluation, for example—are still being clarified by federal officials and court decisions.

Parents want their disabled children to have a free public education that meets their needs but does not stigmatize them unnecessarily and that permits them to be taught in the regular school and classroom as much as possible. The laws governing education recognize parents' and children's rights to such an education. In the courts today, the burden of proof is ultimately on local and state education specialists, who must show in every instance that the child's abilities and disabilities have

Section 504

Section 504 of the Rehabilitation Act of 1973 states,

No otherwise qualified handicapped individual . . . shall, solely by reason of his/her handicap, be excluded from participation in, be denied the benefits of, or be subject to discrimination under any program or activity receiving federal financial assistance.

This means that if free public education is provided for nonhandicapped children, it must also be provided for handicapped children. If free public education is denied to a handicapped child when it is available to others, there is discrimination, and federal funds to the program may be cut off. Section 504 is more general than PL 94-142 in its prohibition of discrimination. States must comply with Section 504 if they receive any form of federal financial assistance. They must meet the requirements of PL 94-142 only if they wish to receive funds specific to that act.

been completely and accurately assessed and that appropriate educational procedures are being employed.

One court case of the 1980s deserves particular consideration. In 1982 the U.S. Supreme Court made its first interpretation of PL 94-142 in *Hudson* v. *Rowley*, a case involving a deaf child, Amy Rowley. The Court's decision was that "appropriate" education for a child with a disability does not necessarily mean education that will produce the maximum possible achievement. Amy's parents had contended that she might be able to learn more in school if she were provided with a sign language interpreter. But the Court decided that because the school had designed an individualized program of special services for Amy and she was achieving at or above the level of her nondisabled classmates, the school system had met its obligation under the law to provide an "appropriate" education. Court cases in the 1990s will undoubtedly help to clarify what the law means by "appropriate" education and "least restrictive" environment (Yanok, 1986).

The Intent of Legislation: An Individualized Education Program

The primary intent of the special education laws passed during the past two decades has been to require educators to focus on the needs of individual students with disabilities. The individualized education program (IEP) is the most important aspect of this focus; it spells out just what teachers plan to do to meet an exceptional student's needs, and the plan must be approved by the student's parent or guardian. IEPs vary greatly in format and detail and from one school district to another. Some school districts use computerized IEP systems to help teachers determine goals and instructional objectives and to save time and effort in writing the documents. Many school systems, however, still rely on the teachers' knowledge of students and curriculum to complete handwritten IEPs on the district's forms. Federal and state regulations do not specify exactly how much detail must be included in an IEP, only that it must be a *written* statement developed in a meeting of a representative of the local school district; the teacher; the parents or guardian; and, whenever appropriate, the child, and that it must include certain elements (see the box on p. 30). Figure 1.3 shows excerpts from IEPs written by teachers in school districts that do not use computer-generated goals, objectives, or forms.

Figure 1.2

SE 10

Confidential Information

INDIVIDUALIZED EDUCATION PROGRAM

School Year _89-90_

Name _Kevin Doe_ DOB _1-9-84_ School _Curry Elementary_ Grade _1 (primary EMR)_

Handicapping condition _mild mental retardation/speech-language delay_ Date of IEP meeting _4-11-90_ M-D-Y Notification to parent _4-6-90_ M-D-Y

Initiation and anticipated duration of services _4-90_ M-Y to _6-92_ M-Y Eligibility/Triennial _4-1-93_ M-D-Y Plan to be reviewed no later than _9-90_ M-Y

Educational/Vocational Program

Special Education Services	Regular Education Services
Self-contained EMR class	_first grade homeroom_
	art, music, lunch, field trips with first grade

Total Amount Times/Wk _5_ Hrs./Day _3_ Total Amount Times/Wk _5_ Hrs./Day _2_

Related Services

Type	Amount
Speech-language therapy 2 30 min./wk	

Physical Education

Adapted Class Amount _none_

Regular Class Amount _as scheduled for homeroom_

Transportation

Special _____ Regular _✓_

Current Level of Performance _Orally spells his name but cannot write it without help (often gets letters in wrong sequence). Names sounds m, a, ē, r, s, f, d inconsistently. "Counts" to 14, but not always sequentially ("1, 2, 5, 8..."). Names numerals, but not consistently. Has one-to-one correspondence to 10. Knows only colors red and green. Difficulty with plurals. Does not consistently answer who, what, where, when questions. Impulsive in group. Imitates misbehavior and doesn't stop when asked. Usually falls asleep by 11:00 am._

Participants in Plan Development

Name	Title
Corine Doe	_mother_
Jessica Via	_first grade teacher_
Pat Hassie	_teacher (EMR)_
Dan Ruffner	_principal_

For High School Students ONLY (to be initially completed at 9th grade IEP meeting and reviewed annually).

This student is a candidate for: High School Diploma _____; Special Ed. Certificate _____; GED Equivalency Diploma _____.

Is the Minimum Competency Test to be administered this school year? Yes _____ No _____ If yes, attach addendum.

White: Confidential Folder Yellow: Parent Copy

SE 10a

INDIVIDUALIZED EDUCATION PROGRAM

School Year _89-90_

ANNUAL GOAL: The student _Kevin Doe_ will _increase reading/language skills commensurate with ability_

PROGRESS REPORTS

SHORT TERM OBJECTIVES	Grading Periods	COMMENTS
Objective: _will name following sounds with 100% accuracy when presented randomly (2 trials): m, a, d, ē, f, r, s, i, t_ Beginning Skill Level: _inconsistent on above_ Date Initiated _4-16-90_	1. 2. 3. 4.	
Objective: _will name color of object when presented with object and asked what color for red, blue, yellow, green, orange, black, brown (100% accuracy, 2 trials)_ Beginning Skill Level: _Knows only green and red_ Date Initiated _4-16-90_	1. 2. 3. 4.	
Objective: _will identify and name letters a-9 with 100% accuracy on 2 trials._ Beginning Skill Level: _inconsistent on above_ Date Initiated _4-16-90_	1. 2. 3. 4.	
Objective: _will blend consonant-vowel-consonant words using sounds m, a, d, ē, f, r, s, i, t with 100% accuracy on 2 trials._ Beginning Skill Level: _no current skills_ Date Initiated _4-16-90_	1. 2. 3. 4.	

Evaluation Procedures: Annual goals will be evaluated during the annual review. Short term objectives will be monitored at each nine week marking period. Beginning skill level indicates the student's performance prior to instruction.

Progress Key: No mark—Objective not initiated P—Progressing on the Objective D—Having difficulty with the objective (comment to describe difficulty)
M—Objective mastered M/R—Objective mastered, but needs review to maintain mastery

White: Confidential Folder Yellow: Parent Progress Report Pink: Teacher Working Copy Goldenrod: Parent Original

SPECIAL EDUCATION
INDIVIDUALIZED EDUCATION PROGRAM

Section A

School __Howe__

I. Student __Jimmy Joh__   Date of Birth __12-7-80__ Age __9__   Date of Eligibility __3/24/90__

Parent/Guardian __Carolyn Green__   Date of IEP Meeting __5/6/90__

Address __1464 Minor Hill__   Phone __555-1212__   Handicapping Condition _____

__Mountainwood, VA__   __Learning Disability__

Expiration Date of IEP __5/6/91__

II. Present Level of Performance (Summary Data).

Language Arts: Jimmy is reading on a 2.9 grade level as measured by the Woodcock Reading Mastery Test. When he works slowly and carefully, he has good word attack skills. When he rushes, however, he will guess at words based on their initial consonants. His sight word skills are on a mid-third grade level and are improving quickly. He has excellent comprehension and remembers what he has read quite well. Jimmy's interest in reading is increasing rapidly. He is very motivated to read books on certain topics like hunting, fishing, sports, and popular books. English: Jimmy writes neatly, in full sentences, and applies basic rules of punctuation and capitalization. He is beginning to work on word endings and should continue working on the parts of a sentence.
Content Areas: Jimmy has a wide range of general knowledge. His knowledge of science is particularly impressive. He is very enthusiastic about science, social studies, and health. He contributes a lot to class discussions, learns material very thoroughly and does creative projects.

Behavior: Jimmy is a pleasant, sociable young man. He gets along well with peers and adults. He becomes very frustrated at times. He becomes stubborn and may refuse to work. Occasionally, he will try to avoid work in a playful, kidding manner. A firm statement of what is expected and the consequences for continuing the off-task behavior will usually remedy the situation.

CONFIDENTIAL: The information on this page must be maintained in the student's confidential file.

Student: __Jimmy Joh__   Date of Birth: __12/7/80__

ANNUAL GOAL: Jimmy will display language arts skills on a late third grade level by May, 1991.

SHORT TERM OBJECTIVES	EVALUATION PROCEDURES/ SCHEDULES	ANTICIPATED BEGIN DATE	ANTICIPATED COMPLETED DATE	CONTINUATION AND/OR MODIFICATION DATE
① Complete one book report each nine weeks.	① 80% or better on written book report each nine weeks.	① 9/90	① 6/1/91	
② Write creative stories, at least 1 per week.	② 80% or better on weekly creative writing assignments.	② 9/90	② 6/1/91	
③ Complete assignments and tests involving regular and irregular spelling words on his reading level.	③ Teacher-made tests, given weekly, to be completed at 80% or better.	③ 9/90	③ 6/1/91	
④ Write a descriptive paragraph of at least 6 sentences at least 1 per week.	④ 80% or better on weekly descriptive writing assignments, as homework or in class.	④ 9/90	④ 6/1/91	
⑤ To edit and rewrite all work to include correct spelling, capitalization and punctuation.	⑤ Monitoring of all written assignments by special education teacher to insure that they are edited.	⑤ 9/90	⑤ 6/1/91	

(One page for each Annual Goal)

NOTE: Information on this page may be maintained in the student's cumulative file and/or teacher file.

III.

Special Education and Related Services	Frequency and Duration (Per Wk)	Date to Begin	Anticipated Completion Date	Location/Provider
LD Resource	11¾ hours/week	9/90	6/91	Howe/Ms. Pullen

Transportation: General ✓ Special _____

IV. Extent of participation with non-handicapped students:

ACTIVITIES	AMOUNT OF TIME PER WEEK
Academic	
Math	5 hours
Social Studies	} 12 hours, 15 minutes
Science	
Health	
Non-Academic	
Music	½ hour
P.E.	2½ hours
Lunch	2½ hours
Extra-Curricular	
Homeroom	

*Note: The Individualized Education Plan does not include the summer vacation.

CONFIDENTIAL: Information on this page <u>must</u> be maintained in the student's confidential file.

Participant--Individualized Education Program

DATE	SIGNATURE OF PERSONS PRESENT	RELATIONSHIP TO STUDENT
5/6/90	James Goh	father
5/6/90	Carolyn Green	mother
5-6-90	Ellen Pullen	LD Teacher
5/6/90	David Washko	Admin. Designee

I GIVE PERMISSION FOR MY CHILD, ___Jimmy Goh___, to be enrolled in the special program described in the Individualized Education Plan. I understand that I have the right to review his/her records and to request a change in his/her Individualized Education Program at any time. I understand that I have the right to refuse this permission and to have my child continue in his/her present placement pending further action.

I did participate in the development of the Individualized Education Program. YES ____ NO ____

I did not participate in the development of the Individualized Education Program, but I do approve of the plan.

YES ✓ NO ____

DATE: ___May 6, 1990___ SIGNATURE: ___Carolyn Green___
(PARENT OR GUARDIAN)

CONFIDENTIAL: The information on this page <u>must</u> be maintained in the student's confidential file.

Individualized Education Program (IEP)

WHAT IS AN IEP?

An IEP is a written agreement between the parents and the school about what the child needs and what will be done to address those needs. It is, in effect, a contract about services to be provided for the student. By law an IEP must include the following: (1) the student's present levels of academic performance; (2) annual goals for the student; (3) short-term instructional objectives related to the annual goals; (4) the special education and related services that will be provided and the extent to which the child will participate in regular education programs; (5) plans for starting the services and the anticipated duration of the services; and (6) appropriate plans for evaluating, at least annually, whether the goals and objectives are being achieved.

ARE TEACHERS LEGALLY LIABLE FOR REACHING IEP GOALS?

No. Federal law does not require that the stated goals be met. However, teachers and other school personnel are responsible for seeing that the IEP is written to include the six components listed above, that the parents have an opportunity to review and participate in developing the IEP, that the IEP is approved by the parents before placement, and that the services called for in the IEP are actually provided. Teachers and other school personnel are responsible for making a good-faith effort to achieve the goals and objectives of the IEP.

SOURCE: Patricia L. Pullen and James M. Kauffman, *What Should I Know About Special Education? Answers for Classroom Teachers* (Austin, TX: Pro-Ed, 1987). © 1987 by P. L. Pullen and J. M. Kauffman.

We believe these IEPs are about average in detail and specificity for the areas of the curriculum they address.

The process of writing an IEP and the document itself are perhaps the most important features of compliance with the spirit and letter of the law. When the IEP is prepared as intended by the law, it means that

- The student's needs have been carefully assessed.
- A team of professionals and the parents have worked together to design a program of education to best meet the student's needs.
- Goals and objectives are clearly stated so that progress in reaching them can be evaluated.

Legislation and litigation were initially used to include exceptional children in public education with relatively little regard for quality. In the 1980s they have been used to try to ensure individualized education, cooperation and collaboration among professionals, parental participation, and accountability of educators for providing high-quality, effective programs.

ISSUES AND TRENDS IN SPECIAL EDUCATION

Some issues in special education have remained remarkably constant over the past 100 years. How to define specific exceptionalities, how to train teachers of children with particular exceptionalities, and how to provide public funding for special education programs are examples of issues with which previous generations and our own have struggled. In fact, nearly every current issue in special education has been a matter of controversy since its beginning. Still, some issues are key concerns of special educators of the 1990s. Among the most important present-day issues and trends in special education today are the following:

1. *Normalization*—making the education and everyday living environment of every student with a disability as "normal" as possible
2. *Integration*—educating exceptional and nonexceptional students together so that students are not separated into ability groups or removed from their "normal" peer group
3. *Cultural diversity*—recognizing and valuing cultural differences and diversity in the classroom so that "normal" differences associated with a particular culture are not mistaken for exceptionality
4. *Early intervention*—identifying exceptionalities as early in the child's life as possible and providing effective programs of education or other services designed to maximize the child's potential and minimize any disability
5. *Transition*—preparing exceptional students for the world of work and adult living, including continued education and career opportunities, so that they are able to achieve their maximum level of independence and productivity following their high school years

There is extensive discussion of normalization, integration, and cultural differences in Chapter 2 because these issues cut across all age levels. Early intervention and transition are included in special sections of each chapter on a specific exceptionality because they are issues related to specific developmental levels. Educators and other professionals now recognize the critical importance of what happens to exceptional children in their preschool years and in adulthood. That is, how exceptional individuals are treated before and after the usual school years, as well as how they are educated in kindergarten through high school, may help us achieve the goals of normalization, integration, and acceptance of cultural diversity.

Early Intervention

Many educators and social scientists believe that the earlier in life an exceptionality is recognized and a program of education or treatment is started the better the outcome for the child. Bricker (1986) states three basic arguments for early intervention: First, a child's early learning provides the foundation for later learning, so the sooner a special program of intervention is begun the further the child is likely to go in learning more complex skills. Second, early intervention is likely to provide support for the child and family that will help prevent the child from developing additional problems or disabilities. Third, early intervention can help families adjust to having an exceptional child; give parents the skills they need to handle the child effectively at home; and help families find the additional support services they may need, such as counseling, medical assistance, or financial aid.

As mentioned previously, PL 99-457 now extends the right to special education and related services to children as young as three years and encourages development of programs for infants. PL 99-457 also calls for education of young children with disabilities in the least restrictive environment, meaning with nonhandicapped peers to the greatest extent possible (Jenkins, Odom, & Speltz, 1989). Thus infants and preschoolers with disabilities are increasingly likely to be seen in the usual or typical public setting or preschool for nonhandicapped young children.

Children whose disabilities are diagnosed at a very young age tend to be those with a specific syndrome (Down syndrome, for example) or an obvious physical disability. Many have severe and multiple disabilities. Typically, these young children's needs cannot be met by a single agency or intervention, so many professionals must work together closely if the child is to be served effectively. If the child's exceptionalities are recognized at an early age and intervention by all necessary professionals is well coordinated, the child's learning and development can often be greatly enhanced. The development of effective early intervention programs leads us to hope that we shall soon see dramatic decreases in the degree of disability that results from being born with a specific condition or acquiring a disability in early childhood. For example, we see the possibility of greatly reducing the handicaps—and enhancing the development—of children with Down syndrome, autism, cerebral palsy, and many other disabilities acquired through diseases or accidents.

We caution, however, not to assume that early intervention alone will mean fewer children with disabilities. Although we are devising more effective programs of early intervention, the number of children with disabilities is increasing. The reasons for this increase are many and complex and are related to changes in economic and social conditions in the United States during the 1980s. Today, compared to a decade or two ago,

- More young children and their mothers are living in poverty, have poor nutrition, and are exposed to environmental conditions likely to cause disease and disability.
- More babies are born to teenage mothers.
- More babies are born to mothers who receive inadequate prenatal care, have poor nutrition during pregnancy, and abuse substances that can harm the fetus.
- More babies are born with a low birth weight.
- Environmental hazards, both chemical and social, are increasing.
- More children are subjected to abuse and an environment in which violence and substance abuse are pervasive.
- Cuts in social programs have widened the gap between needs and the availability of social services.

These facts prompted the President's Committee on Mental Retardation and the National Coalition on Prevention of Mental Retardation to speak of a new morbidity— a new set of disabilities (Baumeister, Kupstas, & Klindworth, 1990). The new morbidity includes a variety of behavioral, health, and school problems that affect a growing number of U.S. children and are caused by many of the preceding factors. Implementing and expanding the services provided under PL 99-457 and training the early childhood specialists necessary to provide effective early intervention are major challenges of the 1990s.

Transition

Preparing students for continued education, adult responsibilities, independence, and employment have always been goals of public secondary education. Most students complete high school and find jobs, enter a vocational training program, or go to college without experiencing major difficulties of adjustment. We know that dropout and unemployment rates are far too high for all youths, especially in economically depressed communities, but the outlook for students with disabilities may be even worse (Hendrick, MacMillan, & Balow, 1989; Wolman, Bruininks, & Thurlow, 1989). Published figures on dropout rates must be viewed with caution because there are many different ways of defining *dropout* and computing the statistics. Studies of what happens to students with disabilities during and after

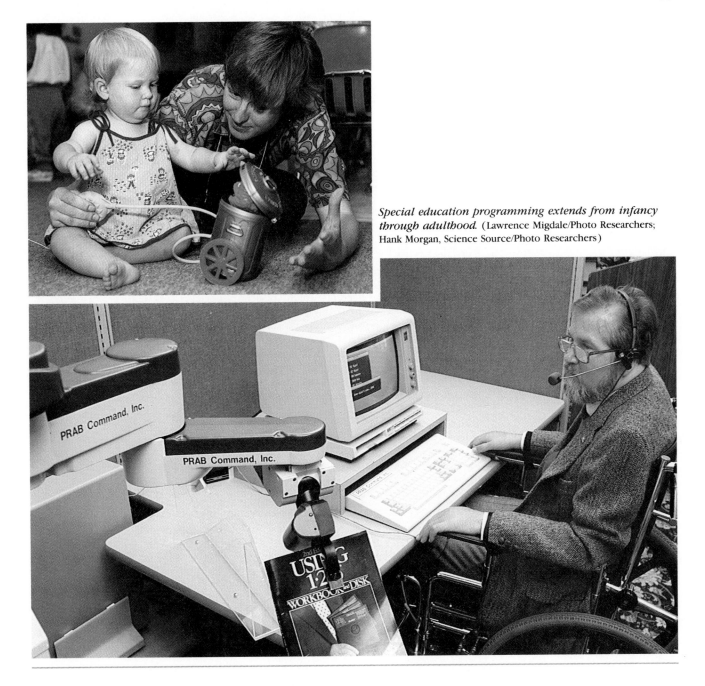

Special education programming extends from infancy through adulthood. (Lawrence Migdale/Photo Researchers; Hank Morgan, Science Source/Photo Researchers)

their high school years strongly suggest, however, that a higher percentage of them, compared to students without disabilities, have difficulty in making the transition from adolescence to adulthood and from school to work. Many drop out of school, experience great difficulty in finding and holding a job, do not find work suited to their capabilities, do not receive further training or education, or become dependent on their families or public assistance programs (Edgar, 1987; Neel, Meadows, Levine, & Edgar, 1988).

Today, transition to adulthood is a special concern for most adolescents with disabilities. The concern is not necessarily greater for individuals who have more

Case Study: Tom

Tom is average in height and slightly immature physically. He is relatively low functioning with an attained IQ of 70, second-grade reading skills, and third-grade math skills. His behavior is noticeably inappropriate at times; he is very excitable and difficult to get along with. His speech tends to be disjointed and he often uses clichés (which he generally misstates) to appear more knowledgeable and on top of things. He has only one friend, a slightly higher functioning special education peer, whom he tries to dominate during social interactions. He drives and has his own car. He lives at home with his family and has no plans to move out.

He was adopted at birth; his parents were unaware of his disability until he was referred for testing in kindergarten. As he was growing up, they made every effort to provide a supportive and protective environment for him although Tom thought they babied him too much.

Throughout high school, Tom saw himself as competent and intelligent. He never admitted to having a learning disability and dismissed any conversation suggesting such an idea. He felt he had been incorrectly placed in special classes that were below his ability and was anxious to graduate. He thought a lot about what he should do after graduation, and on one self-description survey indicated "need advice on what to do after high school." He talked about becoming an electrician, a contractor, a welder, and a forest ranger, but mostly he aspired to be a contractor (he had worked part time for a contractor, a family friend since ninth grade). Tom finally decided to enroll in a training program at the junior college to prepare him for a contractor's license. The summer after graduation, he began attending classes but again felt they were below his ability and he had been incorrectly placed (a college counselor had enrolled him in an Independent Living Skills class for disabled students). Tom dropped the course and took a leave of absence from school for a year so he could work full time with the contractor. Shortly afterward, the contractor's company went out of business and Tom lost his job. Tom's family arranged for him to work with an uncle who was also a contractor and welder (two of his cousins worked for Tom's uncle as well). After a few months, Tom lost that job, too.

At this point, no school, no job, Tom confided in the field researcher (whom he had known for over a year) of his fear that he might not have a "normal" future (he had confided in few people before about his learning problem). He acknowledged the extent of his learning disability and his concern about its impact on his future plans for contractor's work. He seemed hopeless and his self-confidence had dropped markedly. He felt tremendous pressure "to decide about something" and asked the field researcher for help. Tom had one last hope, that perhaps he could enroll in a vocationally oriented junior college (i.e., trade technical college), and that maybe his uncle (the contractor) and the field researcher could help him check out the school. Tom seemed to be identifying with his uncle—Tom described him as "also learning disabled"—as though his uncle more than anyone could understand Tom's problem. It also seemed to reassure Tom to know he was not alone in the world with his learning disability.

Tom pursued admission to the contractor's program at the trade tech junior college and began attending classes during the spring semester. Within a few weeks of his starting the program, Tom's self-confidence and hopes for the future were restored. He boasted that going to trade tech is the best thing he has ever done.

SOURCE: A. G. Zetlin and A. Hosseini, "Six Postschool Case Studies of Mildly Learning Handicapped Young Adults," *Exceptional Children*, 55(5) (1989), 405–411. Copyright 1989 by the Council for Exceptional Children.

severe disabilities. The more obvious a student's disability, in fact, the easier it is to recognize the need for special support services that continue into adulthood. Services that help severely disabled adolescents make the transition are likely to be available. But adolescents with mild disabilities, many of whom have received special education during most of their school years, may find themselves suddenly without help in coping with societal expectations. The result may be serious difficulties in adjusting to the expectations for young adults in our society (see the box on p. 34). As Zetlin and Hosseini (1989) have noted in their case studies of young adults with mild learning handicaps,

> Once the child comes of age and departs from school, families experience an abrupt cutoff of this long-term resource and support (Johnson, Bruininks, and Thurlow, 1987). The mildly handicapped individual is set loose in the community to test the waters of young adulthood without further mandated guidance or support services (p. 405).

> The case histories indicate that these six learning handicapped young adults are anxious and frustrated by the uncertainty of their future. They have no clear course that they are following; rather, they move around from part-time job to part-time job, from class to class, from school to school (p. 411).

A smooth and successful transition to adult life is difficult for any adolescent. Individuals find many different routes to adulthood, and we would be foolish to prescribe a single pattern of transition. Our goal must be to provide the special assistance needed by adolescents and young adults with disabilities that will help them achieve the most rewarding, productive, independent, and integrated adult life possible. This goal cannot be achieved by assuming that all adolescents and young adults with disabilities, or even all individuals falling into a given special education category, will need special transition services or that all will achieve the same level of independence and productivity. One of education's great challenges of the 1990s is to devise an effective array of programs that will meet the individual needs of students on their paths to adulthood.

SUMMARY

The study of exceptional children is the study of similarities and differences among individuals. Exceptional children differ from most other children in a specific way, but they are also similar to most others in most respects. Children's exceptionalities—their differences—must not be allowed to blind us to the ways in which they are like other children. We distinguish between an exceptionality that is a disability and one that is a handicap. A disability is an inability to do something. A handicap is a disadvantage that may be imposed on an individual. A disability may or may not be a handicap.

For purposes of education, *exceptional children* are defined as those who require special education and related services if they are to realize their full human potential. Special education strives to make certain that students' handicaps are confined to those characteristics that cannot be changed.

Determining the number of exceptional children with accuracy is difficult. Definitions of exceptionality are sometimes vague, and they are subject to change. Children may have multiple exceptionalities. Furthermore, some exceptionalities are defined by school performance, making it difficult to assess the prevalence of these exceptionalities in preschoolers and those older than the usual school age. Current government figures show that approximately one student in ten is identified as exceptional and receiving special education services. Most children and youths identified as exceptional are between the ages of six and seventeen, although identification of infants and young adults with disabilities is increasing.

Special education refers to specially designed instruction that meets the unusual needs of exceptional children. The single most important goal of special education is finding and capitalizing on exceptional children's abilities. Special education may be provided under a variety of administrative plans. Some exceptional children are served in regular classrooms by their regular classroom teacher, in some cases, in consultation with other professionals, such as psychologists or teachers with more experience or training. Some children are served by an itinerant teacher who moves from school to school or by a resource teacher. Itinerant and resource teachers may teach children individually or in small groups for certain periods of the school day and provide assistance to regular classroom teachers. Sometimes children are placed in a diagnostic-prescriptive center so their special needs can be determined. The special self-contained class is used for a small group of children, who are usually taught in the special class all or most of the day. Special day schools are sometimes provided for students whose disabilities necessitate special equipment and methods for care and education. Hospital and homebound instruction is provided when the student is unable to go to regular classes. Finally, the residential school provides educational services and management of the daily living environment for disabled students who must receive full-time care.

Present law requires that every exceptional child be placed in the least restrictive environment so that educational intervention will be consistent with individual needs and not interfere with individual freedom and the development of potential. Today, therefore, most students with exceptionalities are educated primarily in regular classes.

All teachers need to be prepared to some extent to deal with exceptional students because many of these students are placed for part of the day in regular classrooms. Furthermore, many students not identified as exceptional share some of the characteristics of disability or giftedness. Although the relationship between general and special education must be one of collaboration and shared responsibility for exceptional students, the roles of special and general educators are not always clear. Both may be involved in educating exceptional children by making maximum efforts to accommodate individual students' needs, evaluating academic abilities and disabilities, referring students for further evaluation, participating in eligibility conferences, writing individualized education programs, communicating with parents, participating in due process hearings, and collaborating with other professionals. In addition, special educators must have particular expertise in instructing children with learning problems, managing serious behavioral problems, using technological aids, and interpreting special education law.

Systematic attempts to educate children with disabilities, especially mentally retarded ("idiotic") and emotionally disturbed ("insane") children, began in the early 1800s. European physicians like Itard, Pinel, Seguin, and Montessori pioneered in these educational efforts. Their revolutionary ideas included individualized instruction, carefully sequenced series of educational tasks, emphasis on stimulation and the awakening of the child's senses, meticulous arrangement of the child's environment, immediate reward for correct performance, tutoring in functional skills, and the belief that every child should be educated to the greatest extent possible. Howe and Gallaudet brought special education techniques and ideas to the United States.

Many other disciplines, especially psychology and sociology, were involved in the emergence of special education as a profession. Much of the progress in special education has resulted from the efforts of professional and parents' organizations. The Council for Exceptional Children (CEC) is an influential group with many divisions devoted to such things as the study of specific exceptionalities; the administration, supervision, and implementation of special programs; teacher training and placement; and research. Organizations such as the Association for Retarded Citizens (ARC) provide parents, schools, and the public with information about exceptionalities and the structure for obtaining needed services.

The legal basis of special education has evolved over the years from permissive legislation, allowing public funding of special programs for exceptional children, to mandatory legislation, requiring such expenditures. The contemporary commitment to the principle that every individual has the right to as normal a life and education as possible has prompted much legislation and litigation in the 1970s and 1980s. The Education for All Handicapped Children Act, PL 94-142, mandates that in order to receive funds under the act *every school system in the country must make provision for a free, appropriate education for every handicapped child*. PL 99-457 mandates free appropriate public education for three- to five-year-olds with disabilities.

Special education legislation has historically been increasingly specific and mandatory. The 1980s, however, saw movement toward deregulation and curtailment of the federal role in education. Reform proposals suggested that special education, as well as general education, should be governed by fewer federal rules and regulations, leaving more decisions to state and local authorities. Laws and regulations may have little effect until their meanings are interpreted by the courts through litigation. Litigation today focuses on ensuring that every exceptional child receives an education that is appropriate for his or her individual needs. Suits filed *for* special education have tended to be filed on behalf of children who are unquestionably disabled but are receiving no education at all or only meager services. Suits filed *against* special education have tended to be filed on behalf of children whose disability is mild or questionable and for whom special education is thought to be more stigmatizing and discriminatory than helpful. Future court cases will undoubtedly result in clarification of the term *appropriate* with reference to education for exceptional children. The primary intent of special education legislation has been to require educators to focus on the needs of individual students. Thus, a central feature of PL 94-142 is the requirement that every student receiving special education under the law must have an individualized education program (IEP). An IEP is a written plan, which must be approved by the child's parent or guardian, that specifies the following: (1) the child's current level of performance, (2) annual goals, (3) instructional objectives, (4) special services to be provided and the extent to which the child will participate in regular education, (5) plans for starting services and their expected duration, and (6) plans for evaluation.

Although many issues in special education have remained for over 100 years, some are particularly important today: normalization, integration, cultural diversity, early intervention, and transition. Early intervention may improve the functioning of children with disabilities and provide support for the family. Although early intervention programs may minimize a young child's disabilities, they do not necessarily mean that there will be fewer disabled young children. Many complex social and environmental causes are producing a variety of new disabilities, including behavioral, health, and school problems for a growing number of children. Transition programs are designed to help students make a successful change from adolescence and secondary education to adulthood and work. Transition is a concern of most adolescents regardless of the severity of their disabilities, but special programs to assist those with mild disabilities have recently been recognized as a particular need.

VILLAGE LIFE
Helen Yoon, Creative Growth Art Center

2

Issues and Trends: Normalization, Integration, and Cultural Diversity

Come writers and critics
Who prophesies with your pen
And keep your eyes wide
The chance won't come again.
And don't speak too soon
For the wheel's still in spin
And there's no tellin' who
That it's namin'
For the loser now
Will be later to win
For the times they are a-changin'.

(*Bob Dylan, from "The Times They Are A-Changin'"*)

The lyrics of Bob Dylan's song "The Times They Are A-Changin'" (excerpts on previous page), could have been written for the field of special education. The 1980s have seen especially dramatic changes in the education of exceptional individuals, and current thinking of special educators, as reflected in the professional literature, indicates that the field is poised for still more changes.

In this chapter we explore recent major changes and issues in the field. The chapter is divided into three main sections: Normalization, Integration, and Cultural Diversity. Although we believe in the logic of this division, it should also become evident that many of the issues are interrelated. For example, much of what we discuss in this chapter is derived from the topic to which we now turn—normalization.

NORMALIZATION

Normalization, first espoused in Scandinavia and later popularized in the United States by Wolfensberger (1972), is the philosophical belief that every person with a disability should have an education and living environment as close to normal as possible. No matter what the type or level of the individual's disability, normalization dictates that he or she should be integrated as much as possible into the larger society. PL 94-142's insistence on the *least restrictive environment* was a direct result of lobbying by advocates for people with disabilities to get the principle of normalization legally mandated.

In this section, we explore some of the major themes in special education that grow out of the normalization principle: the antilabeling movement, the disability rights movement, society's attitudes toward disabled newborns, technology and the goal of normalization, and the media's treatment of disabilities.

The Antilabeling Movement

Some people fear that a "special education" label can cause a child to feel unworthy or to be viewed by the rest of socety as a deviant, and hence grow to feel unworthy. This fear is not entirely unfounded. Most of the labels used to designate students for special education carry negative connotations. *Retarded, disturbed*, and other labels that designate disabilities associated with special education are not kind words. Being so described may lower a person's self-esteem or cause others to behave differently toward the labeled individual. Consequently, advocates for people with disabilities have suggested using different labels or, to the extent possible, avoiding the use of labels altogether.

The antilabeling movement is based in part on the theory that disabilities are a matter of social perceptions and values, not inherent characteristics. Therefore, labels can reflect biases or prejudices that are damaging to the labeled person. Labeling can also change the way a person is perceived—changing what is noticed about them and what is expected of them. Furthermore, damaging labels may be applied more frequently to members of certain ethnic groups, compounding society's discrimination against them. Chinn and Hughes (1987) note that overrepresentation of ethnic minorities in special education has been a pressing and volatile issue during the 1970s and 1980s.

Bogdan (1986) suggests that disability is a socially created construct. Its existence depends on social interaction (see the cartoon on p. 42). Only in a very narrow sense, according to Bogdan, does a person *have* a disability. For example, the fact that a person cannot see only sets the stage for his or her being labeled blind.

MISCONCEPTIONS
ABOUT EXCEPTIONAL INDIVIDUALS

Myth	*Fact*
Labeling a child *retarded*, *disturbed*, or *blind* is totally inappropriate.	Although there are dangers in using labels, there are advantages as well. Labels are an efficient way of describing a general set of characteristics and are useful in making appeals for services for specific groups of exceptional children. Labels of some kind are necessary for efficient communication about any group of children.
Mainstreaming has been embraced wholeheartedly by general educators.	General educators are often reluctant to accept exceptional children into their classrooms. A good deal of pre- and in-service training is required to prepare regular educators to work with exceptional students.
Physicians are always in a position to advise parents about what kind of "quality of life" their newborn child will have.	In many cases no one is able to predict the future development of infants with disabilities, and some have questioned whether it is possible to define "quality of life."
Deinstitutionalization is easily achieved.	Communities need to be educated before group homes can be established without resistance.
Group homes can be established only in marginal neighborhoods; if set up in other kinds of neighborhoods, property values will decline.	If handled appropriately, group homes can be set up in almost any kind of neighborhood without causing declines in property values.
Research has established beyond a doubt that special classes are ineffective and that mainstreaming is effective.	Research comparing special versus mainstream placement has been inconclusive. In fact, many are now saying that these "efficacy studies" are not very helpful in deciding the issue of what the best placement is for exceptional children. Instead, researchers are focusing on finding ways of making mainstreaming work more effectively.
A given disability always has predictable effects on a child's life and calls for specific accommodations in school, family, and community.	How any disability will affect a child's life depends a lot on the culture of the child's school, family, and community. Different cultures may value specific personal characteristics, including abilities and disabilities, very differently. Consequently, a child who has a specific disability may not be handicapped or stigmatized in one culture but be highly stigmatized and suffer many social penalties in a different culture.

Once we call a person blind, there are a variety of undesirable consequences. Our interactions with the blind person are different because of the label. That is, we view the person primarily in terms of the blindness. We tend to interpret everything the blind person can or cannot do in terms of the blindness, and the label takes precedence over other things we may know about the individual. This labeling opens the door for viewing the blind person in a stereotypical and prejudicial manner because, once labeled, we tend to think of all blind people as being similar to one another but different from the rest of society.

Cutter John Cuts through Prejudicial Barriers

Most special education professionals and people with disabilities would agree that there are many ways to break down attitudinal barriers toward those who have disabilities. Humor may be one of the most effective weapons against such prejudices. If that is the case, the well-aimed salvos of Cutter John, the creation of Pulitzer Prize-winner Berke Breathed, may be doing their fair share of winning the war against stereotypical and negative attitudes toward people with disabilities.

Appearing in the comic strip "Bloom County," syndicated by the *Washington Post,* Cutter John takes a no-nonsense approach to his disability. He has his tenderhearted moments with his girlfriend, Bobbi, and he loves to joyride with his penguin companion, Opus, whose friendship he won when Opus realized they were "birds of a feather" because they both had "a couple of useless limbs." He is at his best, however, when he directly, but gently and humorously, forces others to confront their own feelings about his disability. The following strip demonstrates in the blink of an eye what theorists often take several paragraphs to explain when positing that disability is a socially created construct whose existence depends on social interaction.

© 1983 Washington Post Writers Group. Reprinted with permission.

Research on the effects of labeling has been inconclusive (Brantlinger & Guskin, 1987). On the one hand, studies indicate that most people tend to view a labeled person differently from a nonlabeled one (Foster, Ysseldyke, & Reese, 1975). People are more likely both to expect deviant behavior from labeled individuals and to see abnormality in nondisabled individuals if told (incorrectly) that the nondisabled individuals are deviant. On the other hand, labels may also make nondisabled people more tolerant of those with disabilities. That is, labels may provide explanations or justifications for differences in appearance or behavior for which the disabled person otherwise might be blamed or stigmatized even more (Fiedler & Simpson, 1987; Gottlieb & Leyser, 1981). The effects of the label seem to depend on the other information that is available about the labeled person (Brantlinger & Guskin, 1987).

Given the logical likelihood that labeling *might* result in negative consequences, are there any reasons for doing it? Five reasons are usually given for the continued use of labeling:

1. Federal and local funding of special education programs is based on labeling. This says nothing regarding the value of labeling in and of itself. Because funding guidelines use particular labels does not mean that the labels are appropriate.

2. Labeling a population helps professionals communicate with one another. For example, in assessing a research study it is helpful to know that the investigation was carried out with visually impaired, hearing-impaired, or mentally retarded students. Unfortunately such labels are not always clear; they do not always result in accurate communication.

3. With the abolition of the present labels a new set of labels and/or descriptive phrases would evolve to take their place. In other words, individuals with special problems will probably always be perceived as being different. People do not necessarily need a given label to recognize individual differences. Nevertheless, we cannot talk about differences without using labels of some sort—words that describe differences.

4. Whether right or wrong, labeling helps spotlight the problem for the general public. Gallagher notes, "Like it or not, it is a fine mixture of compassion, guilt, and social conscience that has been established over these many years as a conditioned response to the label 'mental retardation' that brings forth . . . resources [monies for specialized services]" (1972, p. 531). The taxpayer is more likely to react sympathetically to something that can be labeled. Gallagher maintains that the crux of the labeling problem is that it does not always guarantee appropriate services.

5. Labeling may, to a certain extent, actually make the nondisabled majority

We must be careful not to let labels for handicapping conditions lead to inappropriate restrictions on children's exploration of their environment and participation in activities. (Glyn Cloyd/Taurus Photos)

more tolerant of the disabled minority (Fiedler & Simpson, 1987). Gottlieb and Leyser (1981) speculate that the label may influence people to view people with disabilities more favorably by justifying some of the latter's inappropriate behavior. For example, it is probably fairly common for the nondisabled adult to tolerate the socially immature behavior of the mentally retarded child while finding the same behavior unacceptable in his or her own child.

The Disability Rights Movement

In their quest for normalization, more and more handicapped people have become disability activists. They are a part of a disability rights movement that in the late 1970s began to confront various societal institutions that proponents believe discriminate against handicapped people.

In many ways, the seeds of the movement were sown in the civil rights movement of the 1960s. Disability activists claimed that they, like blacks and other ethnic groups, were an oppressed minority. They even coined the term *handicapism*, a parallel of *racism* (Bogdan & Biklen, 1977). **Handicapism** is "a set of assumptions and practices that promote the differential and unequal treatment of people because of apparent or assumed physical, mental, or behavioral differences" (p. 14).

Although more and more disabled people—and professionals too—are supporting the disability rights movement, there are several impediments to its achieving the same degree of impact as the civil rights movement. Some believe that the political climate in the United States has not been conducive to fostering yet another rights movement. Whereas the civil rights movement of the 1960s was spawned in an era of liberal ideology, the disability rights movement has coincided with a more conservative climate (Gartner & Joe, 1986). Activists themselves have been unable to agree on the best ways to meet the movement's general goals. For example, some believe that disabled individuals should receive special treatment in such things as tax exemptions or reduced public transportation fares. Others maintain that such preferential treatment fosters the image of handicapped people being dependent on the nonhandicapped for charity (Gartner & Joe, 1986).

As we have pointed out repeatedly, disabled people are an incredibly heterogeneous population. Although general goals can be the same for all handicapped people, specific needs vary greatly, depending to a large extent on the particular type and severity of handicap the person has. The *particular* problems a blind, severely retarded adolescent faces are considerably different from those of a Vietnam veteran who has lost the use of his or her legs. Although activists admit it would not be good for the public to believe that all handicapped people are alike any more than they already do (Gartner & Joe, 1986), the heterogeneity does make it more difficult for disabled people to join forces on specific issues.

But perhaps what has been most missing and what is hardest to achieve is a sense of pride. The civil rights movement for blacks and the women's movement fostered a sense of pride. For example, there has been no equivalent of the "Black is beautiful" slogan within the disability rights movement, although the movement is attempting to develop a sense of identity and community. One of the vehicles for accomplishing this is a publication, *The Disability Rag*, which highlights disability as a civil rights issue (see the box on pp. 45–46).

Society's Attitudes toward Newborns with Disabilities

The recent revolution in neonatal technology has made it possible to keep alive many newborn children who previously would have died because of various anomalies or illnesses. Unfortunately, many of these infants who now survive are seriously

Puncturing The Pathos for The Disabled

INSTEAD, THE GADFLY 'RAG' SEEKS THE REMOVAL OF BARRIERS

The advertisement by the National Society to Prevent Blindness seems inoffensive. Designed to produce a catch in the throat and induce a little checkbook action, it no doubt does both.

"Save the Stars," reads the text, which is illustrated by a photo of the night sky. "When you lose your vision, you lose the stars. You lose the sunsets. The rainbows. The snowflakes and moonlight. This year, 50,000 Americans will lose all that and more. Forever. Yet in many cases, blindness can be prevented . . . Help us save the stars. Give to Prevent Blindness."

Simple, touching and effective, no? Not according to readers of The Disability Rag, a spirited magazine out of Louisville, Ky. Their reactions were a tad harsher.

"They're worrying about me seeing stars," said one. "I wish they'd worry about why we never see paychecks." Another commented: "It reinforces the myth that blind people's lives are unbearably sad, and that's simply not true."

The advertisement may be well-meaning, but it "goes for the negative, and plays on the fears of everyone who can see," says Rag editor Mary Johnson. "A sighted person reads that and says, 'How awful it must be to be blind!' Of all the ways they could have got people to contribute money, they chose the one that made blindness look tragic and pathetic."

The 4,200-circulation Rag, which claims to be the only periodical that covers disability as a civil rights issue, takes aim at anyone or anything that, in the magazine's opinion, patronizes, stereotypes or takes advantage of the disabled. As with the Prevent Blindness ad, which ran in the magazine's "We wish we wouldn't see . . ." section, it's not reluctant to tackle groups devoted to improving conditions for the disabled. Some other recent targets:

- Telethons for the handicapped. ("Why isn't the space program—or Star Wars defense research—paid for by a national telethon? . . . [Why is it that] vital services for disabled people—and research for cure, research this country pays such lip service to—must await the nickel-and-dime generosity of people who give money out of 'thankfulness' that they're not like the poor unfortunates they believe their money is going to 'save.'")
- The National Handicapped Sports and Recreation Association slogan "If I can do this, I can do anything." ("What do the people who are learning to live by that slogan do when they come up against an attitude in society they can't conquer? Or a real barrier like a flight of stairs?")
- And then there's exercise guru Richard Simmons, whose *Reach for Fitness: A Special Book of Exercises for the Physically Challenged* has provoked special ire.

"His whole approach tends to sanctify the concept that disabled people have to 'overcome' and they're very 'special,'" says Johnson. "It's really sappy, and also misguided and superficial. He's gotten on this bandwagon—help the gimps and be trendy at the same time."

It reminds her, she adds, of the "dress for success" philosophy that asserted that the solution to a woman's pay inequities was to buy a nice navy blue suit. "It's trivializing the very real problems that are caused by society . . . All this junk about 'challenging,' where you become good by exercising and making your body perfect—I never can figure out what those people are supposed to do when they need to ride a city bus and they can't get on it."

The Rag doesn't spend all its time firing broadsides. Features in the November-December issue include a book review, an article on the abuse of the handicapped by attendants and family, and several personal testimonies. Yet every piece displays an underlying conviction that the problems of the disabled aren't just medical, but can arise out of prejudice, denial of access and discrimination.

"We wanted disabled people to realize that getting about is not totally up to them," said Cass Irvin, the Rag's publisher and a contributing editor. "Society needs to take some responsibility for people getting around easier. That's why we have roads and mass transit, and that's why we should have accessible buses." Buses are a frequent topic in the Rag: The editors estimate that fewer than 10 cities in the country have satisfactory public transport systems.

Some of those who work with the disabled have mixed views of the Rag, seeing it as well-intentioned but abrasive. Says John Kemp, general counsel for the National Easter Seal Society and the director of its telethon:

"They cover a perspective that no one else does, and they provide a valuable service by rounding out readers' perspectives." He adds, however, that "I resent the strident, shoot-from-the-hip approach. Much of what the Rag offers is good, but the accusatory tone they use can diminish the impact of their message."

As for their criticism of telethons, "It would be wonderful if we could get the federal government to accept its responsibility to provide all disabled people with minimal but essential services. But until then, money will have to come from elsewhere, like telethons."

Bob Ruffner, the director of public affairs for the President's Committee on Employment of the Handicapped, also sees the Rag as a "strong voice for those who may not be associated with a lot of well-organized groups. It's very forceful in arguing that disabled people should get their heads out of the clouds and confront society with their needs."

The Rag, some critics feel, often places more importance on being disabled and staying that way than on taking risks with technology that might remove the barriers.

"There can be dignity in disability, but this is a world of hearing, sight and ambulation, and if you could accomplish these things, life would certainly be easier," says Kemp. "I'm a quadruple amputee, and if I could miraculously grow arms and legs, I would take them in a second."

The Disability Rag, P.O. Box 145, Louisville, Ky. 40201, is available in regular type, large print or cassette. Subscription is $9 a year ($6 if you're on a tight budget, $12 if you're generous, $15 if you want it sent first class).

David Streitfeld, *Washington Post*, November 6, 1986, p. D5. © *The Washington Post*. Reprinted by permission.

disabled, sometimes so severely that some physicians and parents have serious reservations about whether these newborns should be kept alive. And, in fact, medical treatment has often been withheld from such children, resulting in their death, even though it was impossible to predict with complete accuracy how severe the disabilities would eventually have been. Hentoff (1985), for example, provides the following illustrations of how difficult it is to predict the future physical and mental status of some newborns:

Some physicians' prophecies about imperfect babies are shown to be startlingly wrong when the child has a chance to live long enough to confound the prediction. A particularly vivid illustration of auguries turned upside down appeared as part of *Death in the Nursery*, a 1983 series on the Boston television station WNEV-TV. The segment focused on two classmates in a West Haven, Connecticut, elementary school, Jimmy Arria and Kimberly Mekdeci. The boy, born prematurely, had weighed only four and a half pounds at birth, contracted pneumonia a day later, and suffered seizures. The girl was born with spina bifida.

A pediatrician suggested to the parents of both infants that they choose death as the preferred management option. Kimberly Mekdeci's father remembers that doctor saying that his daughter would probably grow up to be a vegetable. The quality of Jimmy Arria's life, the doctor predicted, would be very poor.

Jimmy Arria is [now] a good student. Kim is also bright. (p. 58)

Nevertheless, the practice of withholding treatment from handicapped newborns has been relatively common. Duff and Campbell (1973) report, for example, that in one special-care nursery forty-three infants died in a two and one-half year period because treatment was withheld.

Today, however, some denounce withholding treatment from any handicapped newborn, and this denouncement has been seen as indicating a more positive attitude toward exceptional individuals. Some make the case that an index of a society's attitudes toward disabled people is how that society resolves the moral dilemma of caring for disabled infants. They believe a society that allows doctors and parents to decide not to treat disabled infants is one that does not place much value on the lives of individuals with disabilities.

Conversely, some maintain that physicians and parents together should be able to make a judgment regarding the quality of life the child is likely to experience and then decide whether to withhold treatment. Quality of life is sometimes very hard to judge or predict, however (Zaner, 1986). But from the perspective of some physicians a society that does not allow anyone to make quality-of-life judgments under any circumstances ignores other moral and ethical problems, especially the problem of perpetuating pain and suffering (Kopelman, Irons, & Kopelman, 1988).

The survival of handicapped newborns is a complex issue. Whether considered from the perspective of a professional or a parent, resolution of the problem is no easy matter. No matter where one stands on the issue, one should agree that open discussion is a healthy sign for special education as a profession and for disabled people themselves. Whereas in the past decisions regarding the treatment of newborns with severe disabilities were sometimes made on the almost automatic assumption that defective babies were destined to lead meaningless lives, the difference that special educators and other professionals can make in the lives of many of these infants is now being recognized.

Some may argue that "quality of life" is not quantifiable, but most of us can recognize happiness when we see it. (David H. Grossman/Photo Researchers, Inc.)

Technology and the Goal of Normalization

Technology is rapidly changing the way special educators and other professionals work with exceptional individuals. In addition, it is changing how disabled people themselves participate in various aspects of society, from leisure to job activities. Personal computers (PCs) are perhaps the technology affecting the lives of disabled people most obviously (Brody, 1989). Throughout this book we provide numerous examples of how technology has bettered the lives of people with disabilities. In particular, some technologies have helped disabled individuals lead more independent lives. By allowing for greater independence, technology is making it possible for more and more people with disabilities to take part in activities that previously were inaccessible to them. Thus technology serves in many instances as a means for achieving normalization. Recent government action has supported this goal (see the box below).

A View from Capitol Hill

I know a young girl, 11 years old, who is severely impaired by cerebral palsy and mental retardation. Hers was an isolated childhood. She could not play as other children do. And she was unable to communicate at all until the University Affiliated Program at the University of Iowa offered her a childhood through the use of customized devices. Today she communicates by using a head-mounted light pointer the university program developed for her; she points the light at pictures on a board. With the help of another device the university developed using microswitches that require minimal hand movement, she also plays with battery-operated toys.

Astrophysicist Stephen Hawking suffers from Lou Gehrig's disease (ALS) and cannot talk or write. Assistive technology has allowed him to write a best-selling book and to lecture internationally. But most importantly to the world, it allows him to continue his work and contribute to scientific knowledge.

Just as it did for the girl in Iowa and for Hawking, adaptive technology can make a tremendous difference in the lives of all of us. Disabilities confront everyone in varying degrees. As we age, more and more of us may find ourselves or someone we know facing a disability. It is estimated that nearly two-thirds of America's population will one day suffer partial or total hearing loss. Glaucoma and cataracts threaten our vision as we grow older. Stroke victims may find themselves unable to communicate and function independently; others are rendered immobile by falls and accidents.

Optacon, VersaBraille, speech synthesizers, voice communication boards, and the emerging brain/computer interface are just a few products on the growing list of devices that are breaking down barriers for the disabled.

Last year, as chairman of the Senate Subcommittee on the Handicapped, I introduced a bill called the Technology-Related Assistance for Individuals with Disabilities Act of 1988. Following two days of testimony on how technology has already helped the disabled to lead productive lives, it became clear that America needs a comprehensive, responsive, and coordinated system to stimulate new developments and make them accessible and affordable to disabled people.

The act, which was approved by both houses and signed by President Reagan in just two months, was designed to do just what its name suggests. It established a federal program through which states receive money to conduct research in assistive technologies, disseminate information on those technologies, and offer assistance to the disabled to obtain them.

Rarely had a bill received the kind of support from both sides of the aisle and from consumer and professional groups that this one did. Obviously, many people believe in the promise that technology brings to the lives of people with disabilities. And they welcome the help of the federal government in turning that promise into reality.

Support for that vision continued into this year when the Bush administration recommended more than doubling funds to implement the bill. The appropriation, which will increase from $5,000,000 to nearly $11,000,000, is the largest percentage increase in a domestic program. But while we have made real progress in the past several years, far more needs to be done.

Today, the federal government funds hundreds of millions of dollars in unemployment disability payments to persons who could be employed if they had access to assistive technology. Investments in technology to keep people working can save taxpayers and employers much of the cost of long-term disability payments.

As a nation dedicated to freedom, independence, and the dignity of all human beings, it is the responsibility of all of us to look at disabled people and see what they can do, not what they can't. Assistive technology gives us a very powerful means to support the "can dos."   *Tom Harkin*

Tom Harkin (D-Iowa), whose brother is deaf, is the only United States senator proficient in sign language. He is chairman of the Senate Subcommittee on the Handicapped and of the Subcommittee on Appropriations for Labor, Health and Human Services, and Education.

SOURCE: Herb Brody, "The Great Equalizer: PCs Empower the Disabled," *PC Computing*, 2(7) (July 1989), 91. Copyright © 1989, Ziff Communications Company.

Yet some people have expressed the opinion that technology can, in some cases, actually work against the goal of normalization. First, there is the danger that some disabled individuals might be too quick to rely on technology for assistance instead of working to improve their own abilities. Reliance on artificial means of interacting with the environment when more natural means are possible could jeopardize a person's quest for normalization. A controversy reported in the March 1984 issue of *The Braille Monitor* highlights how sensitive some disabled individuals are to the issue of technology and independence. The National Federation of the Blind of New Mexico was upset about an electronic guidance system for blind people being used at the University of New Mexico. In this system wires under the floor transmit a signal to an electronic cane used by the blind person. The cane acts as a receiver, beeping whenever it is near a wire. Fred Schroeder, president of the federation, wrote a letter to the developer of the electronic system in which he listed his complaints:

The guidance system which you have installed . . . poses a limitation to independent travel rather than an opening of new freedom of movement for the blind.

The fundamental problem with an electronic guidance system is the philosophical premise upon which it is based. The underlying attitude behind its creation stems from an image of the hopeless, helpless blind groping their way timidly through the world fraught with danger and uncertainty.

By installing an electronic guidance system the public is reinforced in its belief that the blind are unable to travel without elaborate accommodation. . . . Our success in improving social and economic conditions for the blind has come from our ability to adapt ourselves to the world rather than relying on the benevolence of the world to adapt to us.

Second, some professionals fear that an emphasis on technology may be dehumanizing (McMurray, 1986). They argue there is a danger that a heavy stress on technology leads to viewing disabled people as "broken persons," like broken machines whose parts need fixing (Cavalier & Mineo, 1986). An indication of this dehumanization, they claim, is the tendency for technologists to concentrate on trying to fit people with disabilities into existing technology rather than developing technology to fit the needs of disabled individuals.

Although most technology does not usurp the independence of exceptional individuals and technology need not lead to dehumanization, a couple of points are worth keeping in mind. First, those who develop technology for disabled people need to consult with them at every stage of research and development. The consumer needs to be considered.

As technology becomes ever more sophisticated, the issue of independence will become ever more important. One general guideline might be that if the technology allows disabled people to do something they could not do without it, then the technology is in their best interest. If, however, it allows them to do something new or better but at the same time imposes new limitations, then one might need to weigh the technology's benefits.

The Media's Treatment of Disabilities

In the mid-1980s, disability activists began claiming that the media have been often guilty of representing people with disabilities in stereotypic and inaccurate ways.

Klobas (1985) and Longmore (1985) criticize television and movies for stereotyping disabled individuals. They argue that the electronic media use five common disability images: A person with a disability is portrayed as criminal, monster, suicidal, maladjusted, or sexually deviant. Longmore maintains that these characterizations reinforce common prejudices and stereotypes; for instance, images of disabled people as criminals (Dr. Strangelove is used as an example) foster three common prejudices.

1. Disabled individuals have been punished for doing evil.
2. They are embittered by their fate.
3. They resent nondisabled people and seek to destroy them.

These prejudices offer the viewer absolution for any difficulties faced by people with disabilities and allow nondisabled people to "blame the victims" for their own problems. Rarely do movie themes acknowledge society's role in creating attitudinal barriers for people with disabilities.

Just how difficult it is to portray disability and society's response to it in a way that is judged by all to be appropriate was illustrated by the motion picture *Rain Man*. In this film, Dustin Hoffman played the role of Raymond, a man with **autism.** Raymond spent most of his life in an institution, where he was found by his younger (nondisabled) brother, played by Tom Cruise. Aside from the artistic merits of the film, was autism and society's response to it portrayed appropriately or inappropriately? Some advocates for disabled people praised the film highly for what they saw as a sensitive portrayal of autism and of the relationship that evolved between a disabled man and his nondisabled brother. Others, however, had harsh words for a film that ended with a disabled man's return to an institution. *Rain Man* did not show how a man who had inherited considerable wealth and had just demonstrated great progress outside the institution could be helped to live in the community.

When television attempts to portray disabled people in a positive light, it often

Dustin Hoffman's portrayal of a man with autism in "Rain Man" raised issues regarding the appropriate depiction of people with disabilities in the media. (AP/Wide World Photos)

ends up highlighting phenomenal accomplishments—a one-legged skier, a wheelchair marathoner, and so forth. This superhero image, according to some disability activists, is a mixed blessing. It does promote the notion that being disabled does not automatically stop achievement. Activists claim, however, that such human interest stories

> suggest that disabled people can best prove their social acceptability, their worthiness of social integration, by displaying some physical capability. Finally, these features also reiterate, with the active complicity of the disabled participants themselves, the view that disability is a problem of individual emotional coping and physical overcoming, rather than an issue of social discrimination against a stigmatized minority. (Longmore, 1985, p. 35).

Although disability activists, for the most part, have been extremely displeased with television's handling of disabilities, they have been more complimentary of TV advertising that uses disabled characters (Longmore, 1985). Beginning in the mid-1980s, a few TV commercials have used people with disabilities. One example is a Levi jeans commercial showing a group of young people going down the street in time to music. One of the characters is in a wheelchair. Ads such as this one, and others using disabled actors, have been applauded by activists because they present disabled people in a casual or "normalized" manner. They promote what activists call "disability cool," an approach that neither denies nor overdoes the disability (see the box on pp. 52–53 for an example involving TV acting).

Besides the electronic media, journalism and literature often reinforce negative stereotypes about disabled people (Biklen, 1986; Kent, 1986; Kriegel, 1986). Considering physical disabilities, for example, Kriegel states that Melville's Ahab is an example of a physically disabled person being portrayed as evil. Even more important, he is depicted as demonic *because* of his disability. His obsession over the loss of his leg drives him to seek revenge on the great white whale. Kriegel notes that another literary image is that of the charity case, like Dickens's Tiny Tim.

Kent's (1986) analysis focused on twenty-four twentieth-century novels and plays, which contained a total of twenty-seven disabled women characters. She

This commercial for Levi Strauss 501 Jeans has been applauded by disabled people and special education professionals. It shows a disabled person in a natural and nonstereotypical way. (Levi Strauss)

states that the predominant characterization of these women is one of passivity, helplessness, and victimization. Almost one-third of them, in fact, owe their disability to an act of violence or an accident, often caused by someone else's carelessness. According to Kent, relationships with men are rarely normal. The man is either perversely attracted to the woman because of her disability or repulsed by it. In either case, the man's feelings toward the woman center on the disability: The disability defines the relationship.

Those who criticize the media's treatment of issues relating to disability have made a strong case by pointing to the many instances in which disabled individuals were portrayed in an inappropriate manner. More systematic research on this topic, however, might help to document even more convincingly the failure of the media to educate rather than merely entertain (Crowley, 1986). For example, how much of the media's depiction of disabled people is a reflection of society's views toward disabilities, and how much does it actually shape society's attitudes? Another important question is whether different characterizations have different effects on attitudes. For instance, does the superhero result in better or worse public perceptions than the maladjusted characterization? Are any of these portrayals better than no exposure at all? Finally, an important issue is how much disabled people, in general, agree with activists' harsh criticism of the media. It would be interesting to know which portrayals draw the strongest criticisms from disabled people themselves, and why.

Summary

Normalization has as its goal making the lives of people with disabilities as much like the lives of nondisabled people as possible. Movement toward normalization has included dropping most or all of the labels used to describe disability, emphasizing the civil rights of disabled people, fostering treatment of newborns with severe disabilities, developing technology that enhances the independent functioning of people with disabilities, and encouraging the nonstereotyped portrayal of people

Handicapped Actress Wants To Make A Difference

LOS ANGELES—Actress Madlyn Rhue: "I'm always on time, I'm in makeup on time, I know my lines, I'm funny on the set and I bring a professionalism to the show I'm on.

"I think I've made a difference for handicapped people," added Miss Rhue, who is confined to a wheel chair because of multiple sclerosis.

This season she stars in an episode of CBS' "Murder, She Wrote" and has a recurring role as the judge in the new syndicated series "Trial by Jury," which stars Raymond Burr. She's also in discussions for another series role.

"The part on 'Murder, She Wrote' was written for a woman in a wheelchair," she said. "I'm so happy thay cast an acress in a wheelchair for the role.

"On 'Trial by Jury' I'm on the bench so no one will know that I'm in a wheelchair. I won't be making a statement. Yet it does make a statement because a handicapped actress is doing the part. I love to do parts for people not in a wheelchair. Just get them because I read better than anyone else."

In addition, Miss Rhue has made a television public-service announcement for the Multiple Sclerosis Society. The campaign, called "Profiles in Courage," encourages all people to lead fuller lives whether they are disabled or not.

"When I was first in the wheelchair, I had to stay on the set when I was working," she said. "Now I have a driver. He gets me everywhere on time. I don't cost the show anything. He also takes me to therapy three times a week."

Multiple sclerosis is a progressive neurological disease, she explained. "The three worst things are heat, fatigue and stress. What you should do is exercise in water so you stay cool.

"I first knew I had MS in 1973 or '74. I didn't tell anyone because all I had was a little dropped foot. Then I had to walk with a cane. Then I had to walk with two canes. I've been in the wheelchair since 1981, but I wasn't wheelchair-bound at first. I could get up, drive, dress myself. I've been confined to the wheelchair for two years."

While she was interviewed in her Beverly Hills apartment, a huge flower arrangement from the producers of "Trial by Jury" was delivered. The apartment walls were decorated with several of her oil paintings and sketches. She is a talented artist whose works have been exhibited in galleries around the country and are in the private collections of many celebrities.

Miss Rhue has been an actress since the 1950s, appearing in more than 15 feature and television movies. She's also done numerous guest roles on television and been a regular in "Bracken's World," "Executive Suite," and "Houston Knights." She had recurring roles in "Fame" and "Days of Our Lives."

The actress was in "Mad, Mad, Mad, Mad World" and was one of the nurses aboard the pink submarine in "Operation Petticoat" with Cary Grant and Tony Curtis.

Her professional name comes from the title of a movie. "I was looking for a name and remembered a James Cagney movie called '13 Rue Madeleine.' That's an address in Paris and I had grown up thinking my father was French," said Miss Rhue, who was born Madeline Roche in Washington, D.C.

"I tried Madeline Rue. My mother said it needed something. We played around with it and settled on Madlyn Rhue."

SOURCE: Jerry Buck, The Associated Press, *Daily Progress*, September 12, 1989, p. A12.

with disabilities in the mass media. All of these facets of normalization are intended to enhance the integration of children and adults with disabilities into the mainstream of society, the topic to which we now turn.

INTEGRATION

Integration is the normalization of where and with whom people with disabilities live, work, go to school, and play. Like other aspects of normalization, integration as a broadly supported social issue began in the 1960s. Integration involves the movement of people with disabilities from institutions to community living, from special schools to regular public schools, and from special classes to regular classes. Ultimately, in the opinion of the most radical advocates of integration, it entails the dissolution of special education. Special education and general education should, according to some, merge into a single educational system in which all students are perceived as special. Proponents of less radical views of integration suggest that we should integrate exceptional individuals into communities and into general education as much as possible but that we should maintain special education— including the full range of placement options from special schools and classes to full-time placement in regular classes with help from a special teacher. Two aspects of integration that have been especially important issues since the late 1960s are deinstitutionalization and mainstreaming.

Deinstitutionalization

The first part of the twentieth century witnessed a growth in the numbers of large residential facilities. Starting in the late 1960s, however, the trend has been to place individuals with disabilities in closer contact with the community. More and more exceptional children are being raised by their families. In addition, smaller facilities, constructed within local neighborhoods, are now common. Halfway houses are being used as a placement for disturbed individuals who no longer need the more isolated environment of a large institution. For people with mental retardation, group homes are being used to house small numbers of individuals whose retardation may range from mild to severe.

One of the reasons large residential institutions are less popular today is that both the general public and the special education profession have become aware of the grossly inadequate care provided by many of them. Blatt and Kaplan's now-classic *Christmas in Purgatory* (1966), a pictorial essay on the squalid conditions of institutional life, did much to raise sentiment against institutions. This book and others like it have shown how bad residential living for exceptional individuals *can* be. But a caution is in order here. Not all institutions are dehumanizing and grossly mismanaged. Actually, there is a great variety in the quality of institutional programs (Zigler, 1988).

Research on the results of institutionalization has shown that the effects may be quite varied, depending on the individual's characteristics and the way institutional life is managed. The following conclusions are based on reviews of research by Balla (1976), Butterfield (1967), Landesman and Butterfield (1987), and Zigler (1973, 1988).

1. Institutionalization can result in a lowering of cognitive abilities. The most likely areas to be affected are those involving verbal and abstract abilities.
2. Whether cognitive deficiencies are due to decreased intelligence per se or are the result of motivational changes is a debatable issue. There is evidence showing that institutionalization can deprive retarded individuals of social reinforcement.
3. Not all retarded individuals are affected in the same way by institutionalization. For example, those who have come from a socially deprived home environment to an institution are less likely to be harmed.
4. Most important, not all institutions are alike. Those that make an effort to provide a noninstitutional atmosphere are more likely to produce positive behavioral changes in the residents. In other words, a restrictive regimen can be harmful; a program offering residents an opportunity to live as normally as possible can be beneficial. Wolfensberger's concept of "normalization" is important here (see Soeffing, 1974; Wolfensberger, 1972). He believes that every attempt should be made to make retarded individuals' living, working, and playing arrangements like those of the rest of society.

As the negative aspects of institutionalization became more and more apparent during the 1960s, advocates for people with disabilities began developing alternative living arrangements in more normalized community settings. These were typically referred to as group homes or community residential facilities (CRFs). Because the trend to place individuals in CRFs only started in the 1970s, not as much research has been conducted on the effects of such placement. Most authorities agree, however, that at the very least the potential for better treatment is higher in smaller CRFs than in larger residential facilities. Researchers have demonstrated that the fewer the number of residents served in a residential setting, the more likely it is that the treatment environment will be characterized as positive and homelike (Rotegard, Hill, & Bruininks, 1983). In addition, the limited research done thus far suggests that residents of CRFs achieve better adjustment than do residents of larger facilities. We can draw the following conclusions from studies of CRFs:

1. Movement from larger facilities to CRFs results in better adaptive behavior (Conroy, Efthimiou, & Lemanowicz, 1982; Kleinberg & Galligan, 1983).
2. CRFs provide more social and occupational opportunities for their residents than do larger institutions (Jacobson & Schwartz, 1983).
3. Successful adjustment of CRF residents is related to personal variables such as good vocational skills and mild behavior problems, as well as to environmental factors such as appropriate social supports and clinical services (Jacobson & Schwartz, 1983). With regard to the latter, it is important that residents in the CRF be given genuine access to the various community service agencies.
4. Evidence suggests that better resident care is generally associated with staff job satsifaction, and studies indicate that there is better job satisfaction in CRFs with decentralized, community-oriented service delivery systems (Jacobson & Schwartz, 1983).

Deinstitutionalization has been one of the hallmarks of the normalization movement. It has the potential to improve the quality of life for most people who in previous generations would have been lifelong residents of institutions. Yet it is doomed to fail unless careful steps are taken to ensure its success. Turning disabled people out of institutions onto the streets places them in even greater jeopardy. Placement in CRFs will not automatically make life more normal for disabled people, although for many it has meant a greatly enhanced quality of life (see the box below). Landesman and Butterfield (1987) note the difference between controversy and facts regarding deinstitutionalization. "As goals, normalization and deinstitutionalization are not terribly controversial; as *means* to achieving these goals, many of the current *practices* related to deinstitutionalization and normalization are" (p. 809). Research on the effects of deinstitutionalization does not clearly confirm all the hopes of the proponents of normalization (Landesman & Butterfield, 1987), but some see further research on normalization as unnecessary. Greenspan and Cerreto (1989), for example, suggest that normalization, which implies deinstitutionalization, represents a value system that does not need to be subjected to empirical testing. In their view, "Deinstitutionalization is a highly desirable policy whose time has come. Researchers should focus on how to implement it most successfully instead of trying to demonstrate that it may not work" (1989, p. 448). No doubt the controversy regarding the rightness and effects of deinstitutionalization will continue into the next century.

Is Life in a CRF Really Normal?

The reason for moving individuals out of large institutions and into smaller community residential facilities is to give them a more normal existence. It is fair to ask, then, how close these small group living arrangements come to achieving the goal of normalization, especially with severely and profoundly handicapped persons. In other words, do individual residents actually participate in the small-group living experience? The answer to this question undeniably varies according to which group home one visits, but Rothman and Rothman, in their investigation of group homes in New York, were able to find CRFs in which residents participated actively and meaningfully in the group life of the home.

The first impression of group-home life at the Lincoln Apartments may be of an elaborate puppet show. Normalization seems a script for the staff-puppeteers to follow as they manipulated the resident-puppets. One puppet is very bright, another very funny, another very affectionate, but all these characteristics appear to be imposed by the staff on residents who are too handicapped physically and mentally to be capable of scripting their own parts. So when one resident wears a Mets cap and has a schedule of the team's games on his wall, the staff is assigning him an interest that he does not possess. Similarly, when the residents sit in front of the TV set with their legs up, the staff is arranging a scene. When two boys of the same age are said to have exchanged gifts, once again there is the suspicion that the staff has set the stage and written the lines. The group home takes on the quality of a performance—an amiable one, to be sure. The atmosphere is relaxed and the residents well cared for; there is no bad puppet. The staff relates to everyone without making anyone into a scapegoat. So even if group homes were nothing more than elaborate puppet shows, that would justify them.

Sustained observation of the daily routine alters this initial impression. Perhaps the enterprise had begun as a puppet show, but in *Pinocchio* fashion, life had been breathed into the puppets. The residents, too, were involved in making some of the decisions. They were not simply plopped in front of the TV, but often "asked" for programs by giving the staff signals that a casual observer might miss. Albert and Ted, both nonverbal, had word boards (one with thirty words, the other with eighty). When they wanted to watch television, they would move a spastic arm until it more or less hit the character for TV. The staff would respond by positioning them in front of the set. There is no way of knowing how much they understood of the program. But they made the request, and that required effort and forethought.

Rothman and Rothman also address the question of whether group homes are ever really integrated into the social fabric of the community. According to the Rothmans, it is really a matter of what you mean by integration:

It may also be time to bury the question of whether group homes are or are not in the community. If critics go on at length about the difficulty of getting normals to be friends with the retarded—as though community living is the equivalent of intimate ties—supporters get rhapsodic about the visit to the museum or the zoo—as if living in a community involves a checklist of events attended. Are group homes in the community? No, if one means choosing acquaintances by preference (not by the accident of a shared residence), or attending different functions with different social circles (basketball games with one, weddings with another). Yes, if by community one is talking about visibility (so that residents are better protected from abuse) or convenient location (so that staff would prefer to work there). And finally, yes, if one means the opportunity to exercise some degree of choice and enjoy a variety of life's ordinary experiences.

SOURCE: David J. Rothman and Sheila M. Rothman, *The Willowbrook Wars*, (New York: Harper & Row, 1984), pp. 228–229 and 252–253. Copyright © 1984 by David J. Rothman and Sheila M. Rothman. Reprinted by permission of Harper & Row, Publishers, Inc.

Mainstreaming

Many professionals have viewed **mainstreaming**—the integration of handicapped students into general education classes—as the primary method by which schools can help exceptional children achieve normalization. Even though the concept of mainstreaming has been around for many years, special educators have changed their approach to the topic. From about 1950 to 1980, they emphasized research on the effectiveness of special classes (efficacy studies) for students with mild disabilities. During the 1980s, however, they have argued for mainstreaming on ethical grounds and have tried to devise ways of making it more apt to work.

One of the problems with the efficacy studies was that they focused on physical placement and did not address what kind of instruction goes on in those settings. (Jeff Lowenthal/Woodfin Camp & Associates)

Studies of the efficacy of special classes typically produced mixed results, showing social but not academic benefits. That is, the efficacy studies typically found that students with mild disabilities learned as much or more academically in regular classes compared to special classes but that regular class placement tended to result in lower acceptance of these students by their nondisabled peers. Much of the efficacy research was poorly done, and therefore the results are questionable. Even the well-designed studies are inconclusive. Efficacy researchers have tended to focus on the physical placement of students to the exclusion of what goes on in the class—how the teacher manages and instructs and what actually happens in the peer group. Consequently, researchers have tended to overestimate the extent to which the setting per se affects students' learning and social development (Bickel & Bickel, 1986; Hallahan, Keller, McKinney, Lloyd, & Bryan, 1988).

In spite of the serious flaws in many efficacy studies and the inconclusive findings of the research, many now view these studies as an indictment of special classes. Special classes—even those that students may attend for only part of the school day—segregate exceptional children from their peers. Because segregation is unethical unless its benefits are clearly demonstrated and because, some argue, no benefits of special classes have been demonstrated, the case is closed: Special classes are indefensible (Wang, Reynolds, & Walberg, 1989). Others are more cautious, pointing out that we have not resolved all the problems in making special education classes effective (Vergason & Anderegg, 1989).

Since about 1980, those advocating mainstreaming have used two general arguments:

1. Some, who have written on the topic from the perspective of advocates, have emphasized ethical issues: Mainstreaming is the *right* thing to do because, unlike special class and resource class programming, it does not require segregating handicapped students from their peers.
2. Some, in general agreement with the arguments concerning overemphasis on physical setting in most efficacy studies, have begun to look at the educational process with the goal of finding ways of facilitating the principle of

mainstreaming. They have investigated different ways of structuring what goes on in the classroom, as well as different ways in which educational personnel can be used to enhance the chances of successful mainstreaming.

Implementing the Principle of Mainstreaming

A variety of recommendations have been made about how to better the chances that mainstreaming will work. We briefly discuss six of the most common strategies.

1. To encourage general education teachers to use teaching practices with exceptional students that have been found to be effective with nonexceptional students
2. To use special educators as consultants to help general education teachers cope with the special problems presented by exceptional children
3. To establish prereferral teams to ensure that only those who truly need special education services are identified for them
4. To structure classroom activities to encourage cooperative learning among students of different ability levels
5. To structure classroom activities so that nonexceptional students act as tutors for their exceptional peers
6. To use commercially available curriculum materials designed to change nonexceptional students' attitudes toward their exceptional peers

ENCOURAGING GENERAL EDUCATION TEACHERS TO USE EFFECTIVE TEACHING PRACTICES. In the late 1970s, educational researchers began experimentally to address the question of which teaching behaviors in general education classrooms lead to students' achievement. This body of literature has been referred to as the **effective teaching research.** Those conducting effective teaching studies have arrived at a relatively consistent set of findings (Rosenshine, 1983; Walberg, 1984). Although very few of these investigators have included disabled students in their samples, they have often included low-achieving pupils. A review of experiments that included students who were younger, slower, and/or had little prior knowledge concluded that teachers were most effective with these students when they

structure the learning; proceed in small steps at a brisk pace; give detailed and redundant instructions and explanations; provide many examples; ask a large number of questions and corrections, particularly in the initial stages of learning new material; have a student success rate of 80% or higher in initial learning; divide seatwork assignments into smaller assignments; and provide for continued student practice so that students have a success rate of 90%–100% and become rapid, confident, and firm. (Rosenshine, 1983, pp. 336–337)

In one of the few studies to include disabled mainstreamed students, a similar set of teaching behaviors were identified as related to these children's success: providing positive feedback, giving sustaining feedback, responding supportively to students in general, responding supportively to low-ability students, responding supportively to learning problem behaviors, asking questions that receive correct responses, ensuring a high success rate, using time efficiently, manifesting a low rate of intervention for misbehavior, using punitive interventions infrequently, using few punitive responses, criticizing responses infrequently, disciplining students infrequently, using little time for student transitions, and having a low rate of off-task time (Larrivee, 1985).

Some special and general educators have stated that results of the teaching effectiveness literature should be used as a way of fostering successful mainstreaming. They maintain that if general education teachers would engage in more of these successful teaching behaviors, they could teach many of the disabled students who usually go to special or resource classes (Reynolds & Lakin, 1987; Wang, Reynolds, & Walberg, 1986). Although this may be true, a careful analysis of what would be required of general educators if they were to take responsibility for teaching most or all students with mild disabilities suggests that very substantial changes would have to occur. Most teachers would need to alter their instructional and behavior management strategies dramatically (Carnine & Kameenui, 1990; Lloyd, Keller, Kauffman, & Hallahan, 1988).

USING TEACHER CONSULTANTS. Although most states do not offer certification in **teacher consultation,** there has been since the early 1980s an ardent group of professionals from around the country who are its advocates (Friend, 1988; Idol, 1988). A variety of personnel can provide consultation to the general education teacher, but resource teachers or school psychologists most often deliver such services. Teacher consultation may address the problems of slow learners or those considered at risk, but it may be defined specifically for special education as follows:

> Special education consultation is a process of providing special education services to students with special needs who are enrolled in general education programs. Special

Mainstreaming in Reverse

Traditionally, most people think of mainstreaming in terms of placing a few disabled children in classes primarily made up of nondisabled students. Some professionals, however, have advocated what has come to be called **reverse mainstreaming**—that is, the placement of a few nondisabled children in classes primarily made up of disabled children. McCann, Semmel, and Nevin (1985) have presented the following arguments for the potential benefits of reverse versus traditional mainstreaming:

> Many of the conditions which characterize reverse mainstreaming appear more conducive to prosocial peer interaction than do those typical of traditional mainstreaming:

> Handicapped students are clearly not minority group members identified as "different" in special education classrooms. They do not lose their group affiliation, and they are not placed in the position of entering extant social groups when nonhandicapped peers are brought into the special class. The burden of achieving social acceptance is shifted to the nonhandicapped student, and teachers have discretion in selecting socially appropriate students to send to special classes. The ratio of handicapped to nonhandicapped students favors intergroup social interaction, since the majority of available peers are handicapped. Special education teachers are more likely to be aware of the need for and methods of providing special programming to facilitate positive social interaction, e.g., cooperative learning activities. Visits to special classes may reduce nonhandicapped students' fears and ignorance of these classes, with concomitant reductions in stigma associated with them. Further, reverse mainstreaming may provide opportunities for handicapped students to establish friendships with nonhandicapped students which may become critical sources of social acceptance when the handicapped student is mainstreamed in regular classes.

Although the rationale for reverse mainstreaming is well articulated, further research is needed to answer certain questions. So far there are few data available on its effectiveness. We do not even know how widespread reverse mainstreaming is. In addition, research is lacking on such things as the optimum length of time for integration and the optimum blend of characteristics (for disabled and nondisabled alike) such as age, sex, and types of disabilities.

One fear raised is that nondisabled children will be harmed by reverse mainstreaming because it might expose them to inappropriate models. Although more research is needed on this topic, one study found no negative influence of reverse mainstreaming on nondisabled preschoolers (Odom, Deklyen, & Jenkins, 1984). The nondisabled preschoolers were integrated with mildly and moderately disabled preschoolers at a ratio of 1 to 2. The researchers found no differences between an integrated group and a nonintegrated group on measures of intelligence, communication, and social development. Noting the small-scale nature of their study, however, they did caution that to "understand further the developmental effect of integrated special education on nonhandicapped children, replications in different settings, possibly with different proportions of handicapped children and different curriculum models, are recommended" (p. 47).

education teachers, general education teachers, other school professionals, and/or parents collaborate to plan, implement, and evaluate instruction conducted in the general classroom for the purpose of preventing or ameliorating students' academic or social behavior problems as they occur in the general school program. (Idol, 1988, p. 48)

Idol lists these advantages of the consultation approach: (1) It has been shown to be effective; (2) it uses special and general teachers' expertise more efficiently; (3) general teachers learn to assist many students with problems, not just those considered disabled; (4) it is cost efficient in that it expands special teachers' caseloads and develops general teachers' ability to prevent problems; (5) it actively and directly involves professionals and parents; (6) it is highly flexible; (7) it results in close monitoring of students' progress; (8) it can reduce referrals to special programs; (9) it can foster mutual understanding of and sharing by professionals; (10) it assists in identification of staff development needs; (11) it enables services to be provided in the least restrictive environment.

Research suggests that teacher consultation is a promising approach to meeting the needs of many students with disabilities in general education settings. Consultation *can* have many of the advantages suggested by its proponents. Nevertheless, much remains unknown about what makes consultation effective and the circumstances under which it is insufficient to meet students' needs (Lloyd, Crowley, Kohler, & Strain, 1988). We do not know precisely what is required for successful consultation or exactly how to define the role of the teacher consultant.

ESTABLISHING PREREFERRAL TEAMS. Closely aligned with the notion of teacher consultation is the practice of using **prereferral teams (PRTs).** Both involve professionals helping general education teachers deal with students who have problems in their classrooms. There are three essential ways in which they differ, however. First, teacher consultants are individuals, and PRTs are groups. Second, as indicated by their title, PRTs try to keep students from being formally referred for special education services. Although teacher consultants can and do often serve the same purpose, they put less stress on the notion of limiting referrals and usually do work with students identified as exceptional. Third, teacher consultants are usually not general education teachers, whereas some believe that general educators are the essential members of PRTs.

The role of the PRT is to work with classroom teachers to recommend different strategies for working with children exhibiting academic and/or behavioral problems.

One of the primary goals is to establish "ownership" of these types of children by general and not special educators. In other words, PRTs try to keep referrals to special education down by stressing that general educators need to try as many alternative strategies as possible before deciding that difficult-to-teach students need to become the primary responsibility of special educators.

Because of this emphasis on general education's ownership, some have maintained that general educators are the most important team members (Chalfant, Pysh, & Moultrie, 1979; Gerber & Semmel, 1985). A major justification for using classroom teachers to make decisions regarding referral to special education is that they may have information on individual children that is even more important than the usual standardized test data: "Teachers observe tens of thousands of discrete behavioral events during each school day. Formal tests of ability and achievement are based on analysis of only small samples of student behavior. Clearly teachers have available to them, if they choose to use it, a far richer and varied sample of student behavior than the typical 'test'" (Gerber & Semmel, 1984, p. 141).

There is very little research on the effectiveness of PRTs (Lloyd, Crowley, Kohler, & Strain, 1988). The few evaluations that have been done indicate two things: (1) They do cut down on the number of referrals to special education, and (2) team members and administrators report that they are effective (Schram et al., 1984).

Some who are interested in promoting new relationships between special and general education have combined the ideas of teacher consultation and PRTs into cooperative teaching, in which special and general educators are assumed to have equal expertise in meeting the needs of students with disabilities (Bauwens, Hourcade, & Friend, 1989; Johnson, Pugach, & Hammitte, 1988). The emphasis is on professionals working together as equal partners or team members to find different and successful ways of teaching and managing students who are not learning well. Research on the effectiveness of this type of working relationship is just beginning.

ENCOURAGING COOPERATIVE LEARNING. Much emphasis is placed on competition in the traditional regular class. This focus, some believe, is detrimental to the success of all students, especially those who are handicapped or of lower ability (Johnson & Johnson, 1986; Slavin, 1988). The Johnsons have found that **cooperative learning**—involving disabled and nondisabled peers in situations in which they must cooperate with one another—leads to better attitudes on the part of the nondisabled toward their disabled peers as well as better attitudes of disabled students toward themselves.

The Johnsons believe that cooperative situations foster differentiated, dynamic, and realistic views of group members, including the students with disabilities taking part in the cooperative venture. By *differentiated*, they mean that a child is viewed as possessing more attributes than just the stereotypic ones that accompany his or her label. And by *dynamic*, they mean that a child's attributes may not be viewed by other group members as relevant to all aspects of the task at hand. Once the teacher places disabled and nondisabled students in small, heterogeneous groups for the purpose of working toward a common goal, Johnson and Johnson state that a number of positive events will occur.

Although the Johnsons' use of cooperative learning has led to positive changes in attitudes, they have been less successful in affecting achievement. They have looked at achievement in only a few of their studies, and the results have been mixed. An investigator who has designed cooperative learning situations that have led to achievement gains, however, is Robert Slavin.

Although only a few of Slavin's studies have included formally identified students with disabilities, he has used cooperative learning with low-ability students. For there to be positive effects on achievement, he concludes that cooperative learning must involve two elements: (1) There must be group incentives, and (2) there must be individual accountability. What should be avoided are situations in which the group's solution to a problem can be found by just one or two members. One way of doing this is to base rewards on the group's average so that each individual's score contributes to the total score of the group.

USING PEER TUTORS. Yet another recommended method of integrating students with disabilities into the mainstream is **peer tutoring** (Jenkins & Jenkins, 1987), defined as one student tutoring another. Professionals have advocated using disabled children as tutors as well as tutees. When a child with a disability assumes the role of tutor, the tutee is usually a younger peer.

Research results on the effectiveness of peer tutoring are mixed (Scruggs & Richter, 1986). There is evidence suggesting that mildly disabled students can benefit academically when serving as tutor or tutee. There are few empirical data, however, to show that it improves self-concept.

It is important to remember that contrary to what some educators believe, peer tutoring does not save time (Gerber & Kauffman, 1981). A good peer-tutoring situation requires continuous organization and monitoring by the teacher.

USING CURRICULUM MATERIALS TO CHANGE ATTITUDES. Curriculum materials have been developed to enlighten regular education students about exceptional children. These materials often involve activities constructed to teach children about different aspects of disabilities, such as causes and characteristics, as well as to let students explore their feelings about children with disabilities. These materials range from full-blown curricula such as *Accepting Individual Differences* (Cohen, 1977) and *What If You Couldn't? An Elementary School Program about Handicaps* (Children's Museum of Boston, 1978) to individual books such as *Don't Feel Sorry for Paul* (Wolf, 1974). Many of these approaches involve a variety of media, as well as a variety of activities. One especially creative approach is *Kids on the Block*, a puppet show, with Muppet-like puppets that have different kinds of disabilities (e.g., mental retardation, cerebral palsy, emotional disturbance, and visual impairment). It comes with scripts designed to explain basic concepts about exceptional children and a variety of curriculum suggestions.

Another approach to curriculum designed to improve pupils' attitudes toward their peers who have disabilities is the use of simulations. Wesson and Mandell (1989) describe how teachers can promote understanding of adaptations to disability by using *simulated* handicaps in and out of school. Limitations in hearing, seeing, understanding, and moving or performing physical tasks are often much better understood—and attitudes toward people with limitations may be improved—through activities designed to impose disabilities temporarily. Walking through the school while blindfolded, wearing glasses smeared with petroleum jelly, or trying to button clothing with hands covered with thick socks, for example, may help students understand and appreciate the abilities of their peers who have limited vision or mobility.

Although more and more schools are using materials that purportedly teach children in regular education about exceptional students, very few efforts have been made to evaluate these curricular modifications systematically.

The Regular Education Initiative

Beginning in the mid-1980s, some special educators began to suggest that special education, especially for students with mild disabilities, was too separate from

Kids on the Block, Inc., produces handicapped puppets who perform in scripts designed to entertain young elementary school children as well as inform them about different kinds of handicaps. (The Kids on the Block, Inc., Alexandria, VA)

general education. Their arguments came to be known as the **regular education initiative** (*REI*, sometimes also known as the *general education initiative*, or *GEI*). In essence, the goal of the REI is to make general educators more responsible for the education of students who have special needs in school, including those who are economically or socially disadvantaged and those who are bilingual, as well as those who need special education. This goal, proponents of the REI believe, can be achieved only if general and special education are "restructured" so that few students, if any, are taught outside the regular classroom for any part of the school day. Massive changes in educational policy would be required if such restructuring were to take place.

The REI is a proposal for radical change in policies governing the education of exceptional students. These policy proposals are generally thought to have originated with President Reagan's primary political appointee in special education, former Assistant Secretary of Education Madeleine C. Will, through influential speeches and articles (Will, 1984, 1986). Will made very general suggestions for increased cooperation between special and general education. Other proponents of the REI have called for a total merger of special and general education (Stainback & Stainback, 1984). Some have referred to special education and other compensatory programs for children with special needs as a discriminatory "second system" (Wang, Reynolds, & Walberg, 1988) or described special education as a burden or "yoke" to be broken (Gartner & Lipsky, 1989). All agree that a dramatic shift toward mainstreaming should occur.

The proposed policy changes known as the REI became a controversy in special education because researchers, administrators, teachers, and parents of students with disabilities disagree about the answers to important questions such as these:

1. How effective is special education?
2. How effective are the alternatives to special education?
3. How can general education teachers effectively deliver special services for students with special needs?
4. If special and general education are merged, how will funds and services for exceptional children be channeled and monitored?
5. How ready is general education to assume more responsibility for students with disabilities?
6. How damaging are special education labels, and can labeling be avoided?
7. Is going to a special class for part of the school day more damaging to a student's self-esteem than receiving special help in the regular classroom?

Regulations and guidelines governing the education of exceptional children—including where and with whom they are to be taught—are based on what policymakers believe are the best answers to these and other questions. The REI involves many complex theoretical and practical issues, and some organizations and individuals have questioned whether the proposed changes in policy will serve the best interests of students with disabilities (Carnine & Kameeuni, 1990; Hallahan, Kauffman, Lloyd, & McKinney, 1988). Chalfant (1989, p. 398) reached the following conclusions:

> The Regular Education Initiative holds promise for the future education of many students with learning problems, but special education and regular education are at a turning point. There is too much at stake to make radical and revolutionary policy changes without first considering the evidence supporting each policy alternative. There are more opinions than there are reliable data and facts.

In the last decade of the twentieth century, some of the most intriguing questions facing the field of special education involve mainstreaming. Few doubt that mainstreaming is desirable, that it has resulted in better conditions for many exceptional children, and that it can still be improved. Many questions remain, however, regarding how we should implement it, especially in relation to the role and responsibility of general education teachers. Whether and in what ways general and special educators can create a partnership that results in better educational opportunities for *all* children will be a formidable challenge for the future.

Hal's Pals, a collection of handicapped dolls, is available from For Challenged Kids, a not-for-profit corporation. (Mattel, Inc., 5150 Rosecrans Ave., Hawthorne, CA 90250)

Summary

Integration means people with disabilities living, working, playing, and going to school with nondisabled people. Deinstitutionalization and mainstreaming are two aspects of integration that have been important issues since the 1960s. Deinstitutionalization requires not only moving people out of institutions but also having specific plans to integrate them into more normal community residences. Mainstreaming is the integration of students with disabilities into general education classes. For decades, arguments for mainstreaming were centered on research showing that special classes are ineffective. Today, arguments for mainstreaming tend to focus on ethical issues. Common strategies for implementing mainstreaming are effective teaching practices in general education, teacher consultants, prereferral teams, cooperative learning, peer tutors, and curricula designed to change attitudes toward people with disabilities. Since the mid-1980s, the regular education initiative has been a matter of controversy—how and to what extent can special and general education work together for students with disabilities? To a great extent, integration involves embracing the idea that diversity is desirable. We now turn to a consideration of the role of cultural diversity in special education.

CULTURAL DIVERSITY

Since the civil rights movement of the 1960s, educators have been increasingly aware of the extent to which differences among cultural and ethnic groups affect children's schooling. Gradually, educators are coming to understand that the cultural diversity of our society demands multicultural education. Progress in multicultural education has been slow, in part because of the way all cultural groups tend to view themselves as the standard against which others should be judged. Rogoff and Morelli (1989, p. 341) note that in the United States this view has led to a focus on minority cultures.

> The United States, like many modern nations, is an aggregate of peoples of many cultural backgrounds. However, the role of culture is most noticeable when any of us view the practices of some other group than our own, and so the study of culture has generally focused on minorities in the United States and on people of other nations. It is easy for dominant cultural groups to consider themselves as standard and other groups as variations. (Think of the number of people who comment on other people's accents and insist that they themselves do not have one.)

Education that takes full advantage of the cultural diversity in our schools and the larger world requires much critical analysis and planning. In fact, multicultural education is now a specialized field of study, and its full exploration is far beyond the scope of our discussion here. In this section of the chapter we discuss three areas in which cultural diversity presents particular challenges: assessment, instruction, and socialization. Before highlighting these challenges, we summarize some of the major concepts about education and cultural diversity that apply to special education.

Education and Cultural Diversity: Concepts for Special Education

The United States has long been known as a melting pot, an amalgam of various nationalities, cultures, races, classes, religions, and persons with varied abilities. One strength of our nation has been the diversity of its citizens. Paradoxically, another strength has been the melding of this diversity into a single, uniquely American identity. The crux of the problem of multicultural education is the management of tension between two competing ideas: (1) Cultural diversity is to be valued, and (2) common cultural values hold our society together. To understand the implications of cultural diversity for special education, we must first consider the definition of culture and how it is related to the educational needs of students.

Culture has many different definitions. As Banks (1988) points out, however, "most contemporary social scientists view culture as consisting primarily of the symbolic, ideational, and intangible aspects of human societies" (p. 73). Banks suggests six major components or elements of culture: values and behavioral styles, languages and dialects, nonverbal communication, awareness (of one's cultural distinctiveness), frames of reference (normative world views or perspectives), and identification (feeling part of the cultural group). These elements may together make up a national or shared culture, sometimes referred to as a **macroculture.** Within the larger macroculture are **microcultures**—smaller cultures that share the common characteristics of the macroculture but have their unique values, styles, languages and dialects, nonverbal communication, awareness, frames of reference, and identity. An individual may identify with the macroculture and also belong

Special educators must be increasingly attentive to cultural diversity of students. (Victoria Beller-Smith)

to many different microcultures, as shown in Figure 2.1. The variety of microcultures to which a person belongs affects his or her behavior.

Macroculture in the United States consists of certain overarching values, symbols, and ideas, such as justice, equality, and human dignity. Microcultures within the U.S. macroculture may share these common values but differ among themselves in many additional ways. The number of microcultures represented in U.S. schools has increased in recent decades because of the variety of immigrants from other countries, particularly Southeast Asia. Duke (1990) notes that "these newcomers contribute to a diversity of cultures and languages that probably has not characterized American society since the turn of the century" (pp. 69–70). Students from some microcultures in U.S. society do extremely well in school, but others do not. The factors accounting for the school performance of microcultural minoritries are complex, and social scientists are still searching for the attitudes, beliefs, behavioral styles, and opportunities that foster the success of specific microcultural groups (Jacob & Jordan, 1987).

The general purposes of multicultural education are to promote understanding of microcultures different from one's own and foster positive attitudes toward cultural diversity. These purposes cannot be accomplished unless students develop an understanding and appreciation of their own cultural heritage, as well as an awareness and acceptance of cultures different from their own. Understanding and appreciation are not likely to develop automatically through unplanned contact with members of other microcultures. Rather, teachers must plan experiences that teach about culture and provide models of cultural awareness and acceptance and the appreciation of cultural diversity.

The microcultures of particular importance for special education are ethnic groups and exceptionality groups. Banks (1988) defines an ethnic group as "a group that shares a common ancestry, cutlure, history, tradition, and sense of people-hood and that is a political and economic interest group" (p. 81). An ethnic group may be a majority or a minority of people in a given country or region. We define an exceptionality group as a group sharing a set of specific abilities or disabilities that are especially valued or that require special accommodation within a given microculture. Thus a person may be identified as exceptional in one ethnic group (or other microculture defined by gender, social class, religion, etc.) but not in another. Being unable to read or speak standard English, for example, may identify a student as having a disability in an Anglo-dominated microculture, although the same student is not considered disabled in a microculture in which English-language skills are unimportant. In certain cultures children avoid direct eye contact with adults in positions of authority. A child who does not look directly at the teacher may mistakenly be assumed to be inattentive or oppositional by adults from cultures in which eye contact between the teacher and pupil is expected. This child could be inappropriately identified as having a disability requiring special education.

Ethnicity and exceptionality are distinctly different concepts. In fact, multicultural special education must focus on two primary objectives that go beyond the general purposes of multicultural education:

1. Ensuring that ethnicity is not mistaken for exceptionality
2. Increasing understanding of the microculture of exceptionality and its relationship to other microcultures

Ethnicity may be mistaken for exceptionality when one's own ethnic group is viewed as setting the standard for all others. For example, patterns of eye contact, physical contact, use of language, and ways of responding to persons in positions of authority may vary greatly from one ethnic group to another. Members of each ethnic group must realize that what they see as deviant or unacceptable in their own group may be normal and adaptive in another ethnic group. That is, we must

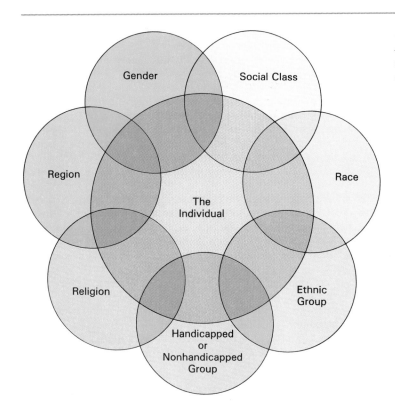

Figure 2.1. *Individuals Belong to Many Different Microcultural Groups*

SOURCE: J. A. Banks, *Multiethnic Education: Theory and Practice*, 2nd ed. (Boston: Allyn & Bacon, 1988), p. 79.

not mistakenly conclude that a student is handicapped or gifted just because he or she is different.

Members of minority ethnic groups are more apt to be identified as disabled because their differences are not well understood or valued by others. In part, this higher risk may be a result of prejudice—unreasonable or irrational negative attitudes, feelings, judgments, or behavior based on ignorance or misunderstanding. Prejudice may cause individuals to be judged as deviant or disabled on the basis of characteristics that are typical for their ethnic group or from stereotyping. That is, an individual's identity as a member of an ethnic group may result in the automatic assumption that he or she will behave in certain ways.

People with certain exceptionalities can develop their own microcultures. Those with severe hearing impairments, for example, are described by some as belonging to a "deaf subculture" that is not well understood by most normally hearing people and that results in feelings of isolation or separation from people with normal hearing (Martin, 1987). An important aspect of multicultural special education is developing an increased awareness, understanding, and appreciation of cultural differences involving disabilities. The box below contains Martin's suggestions for reducing prejudice and stereotyping and increasing understanding among deaf and normally hearing students. Similar strategies may be needed to overcome prejudice and stereotyping involving other disability groups.

Multicultural special education is not merely a matter of overcoming students' prejudice and stereotyping. It is also a matter of educating ourselves as teachers

---

Activities for Improving Understanding and Acceptance Among Deaf and Hearing Students

1. Provide multiple opportunities for deaf and hearing students to interact on a regular basis, preferably on joint projects or activities.
2. Give deaf and hearing children the opportunity to discuss openly why they react positively or negatively toward each other.
3. Encourage children to express in what ways their own culture might appear strange to a person from the other group. For example, hearing children should imagine which aspects of spoken language might appear bizarre to a deaf person.
4. Discuss the fundamental ways in which *all* human groups are similar (kinship, division of tasks, language, prolonged childhood dependency, belief system, use of symbols, tool systems, etc.). Deaf and hearing people are equally "human" because each group has established its own specific responses to those *same* needs.
5. Teach children about the processes by which humans develop stereotypes and have them list the ways in which they have seen themselves follow those processes in judging or misjudging deaf or hearing children.
6. Teach students that there is a wide variation of behavior *within* any culture; thus, stereotyping is bound to be false (e.g., some deaf people use sign language, while others do not).
7. Point out some nonstereotypic behaviors of both groups. For example, numerous deaf persons today have earned Ph.D.'s and teach in universities.
8. Teach about the positive contributions to human life by both groups. For example, focus on well-known deaf actors or athletes.
9. Help students to create and analyze a written description of a model culture in order to develop their thinking tools for understanding the deaf or hearing culture.

SOURCE: David S. Martin, "Reducing Ethnocentrism," *Teaching Exceptional Children*, Vol. 20(1) (Fall 1987), 7–8. Copyright 1987 by the Council for Exceptional Children.

to improve methods of assessment, provide effective instruction, and foster appropriate socialization. We now turn to specific problems in assessment, instruction, and socialization involving microcultural groups, including students with exceptionalities.

Assessment

Assessment is a process of collecting information about individuals or groups for the purposes of making decisions. In education, assessment ordinarily refers to testing, interviewing, and observing students. The results of assessment should help us decide whether problems exist in a student's education and, if problems are identified, what to do about them. Ysseldyke and Marston (1988) have discussed several characteristics of assessment that are important in the U.S. macroculture: "Assessment is a practice integral to making decisions about people. In our society there is a fundamental concern for accuracy, justice, and fairness in making decisions about individuals" (p. 21).

Unfortunately, the accuracy, justice, and fairness of many educational assessments, especially those involving special education, are open to question. Particularly when ethnic microcultures are involved, traditional assessment practices have frequently violated the U.S. ideals of fairness and equal opportunity regardless of ethnic origin, gender, or disability. That is, the assessment practices of educators and psychologists have frequently come under attack as (1) biased, resulting in misrepresentation of the abilities and disabilities of ethnic minorities and exceptional students, and (2) useless, resulting only in labeling or classification rather than improved educational programming (Council for Children with Behavioral Disorders, 1989; Reschly, 1987).

The problems of assessment of students for special education are numerous and complex, and there are no simple solutions. Many of the problems are centered on traditional standardized testing approaches to assessment that have serious limitations: (1) They do not take cultural diversity into account, (2) they focus on deficits in the individual alone, and (3) they do not provide information useful in teaching. Although these problems have not been entirely overcome, awareness of them and the use of alternative assessment strategies are increasing.

Standardized tests may be biased because most of the test items draw on specific experiences that students from different microcultures may not have had. Tests may, for example, be biased toward experiences likely to have been had by white middle-class students; be couched in language unfamiliar to members of a certain microculture; or be administered in a way that penalizes a student with impaired vision, hearing, or ability to answer in a standard way. Because test scores are often the basis for deciding that a student qualifies for special education, many scholars suspect that test bias accounts for the disproportionate representation of certain groups in special education, especially males and children of color (Chinn & Hughes, 1987).

At best, test scores represent a sample of an individual's ability to respond to a standard set of questions or tasks; they do not tell us *all* the important things an individual has learned or how much a student *can* learn. Controversy over the biases inherent in standardized tests and the search for "culture-free" and "culture-fair" tests continue (Reschly, 1987; Ysseldyke & Marston, 1988). Three cautions are in order:

1. Tests give only *clues* about what a student *has* learned.
2. Test scores must be interpreted with recognition of the possible biases the test contains.

3. Testing alone is an insufficient basis for classifying a student or planning an instructional program.

Traditional assessment procedures focus on the student, not on the environment in which the student is being taught. Critics of traditional assessment have decried the assumption that any deficit identified will be a deficit of the student. In addition to assessing the student's behavior or performance, many educators are now suggesting an assessment of the instructional environment (Bender, 1988; Ysseldyke & Christenson, 1987). Assessment of the instructional environment may involve classroom observation and interviews with the student and teacher. It focuses on such items as whether instruction is presented clearly and effectively, the classroom is effectively controlled, the teacher's expectations are appropriate, appropriate curriculum modifications are made, thinking skills are being taught, effective motivational strategies are used, the student is actively engaged in academic responding and is given adequate practice and feedback on performance, and progress is directly and frequently evaluated. The purpose of assessment of the instructional environment is to make sure that the student is not mistakenly identified as the source of the learning problem. An underlying assumption is that this approach will decrease the likelihood that cultural differences will be mistaken for disabilities.

Traditional assessment procedures result in test scores that *may* be useful in helping to determine a student's eligibility for special education or other special services. These testing procedures do not, however, typically provide information that is useful in planning for instruction. An alternative approach that emerged in the 1980s is *curriculum-based assessment* (Deno, 1985; Howell & Morehead, 1987). This method of assessment contrasts sharply with traditional testing, in which students are tested infrequently and may never before have seen the specific items on the test. Curriculum-based assessment involves students' responses to their usual instructional materials; it entails direct and frequent samples of performance from the curriculum in which students are being instructed. For example, the teacher may ask students to read aloud for one minute (perhaps three times a week) from a passage in their usual reader. The teacher then records their reading rates (words read correctly per minute and/or errors per minute) and compares them to those of other students in the same school using the same curriculum. Curriculum-based assessment is thought to be more useful for teachers than traditional testing and to decrease the likelihood of cultural bias.

Instruction

A major objective of multicultural education is ensuring that all students are instructed in ways that do not penalize them because of their cultural differences and that, in fact, capitalize on their cultural heritage. The methods used to achieve this objective are among the most controversial topics in education today. All advocates of multicultural education are concerned with the problem of finding instructional methods that help to equalize educational opportunity and achievement for all microcultural groups, methods that break down the inequities and discrimination that have been part of our public education system. But the question "What instructional methods are most effective in achieving this goal?" is highly debatable.

The controversy regarding instruction is generated by what Minow (1985) calls "the dilemma of difference." The dilemma is that either ignoring or recognizing students' linguistic or cultural differences can perpetuate them and maintain inequality of social power and opportunity among ethnic or other microcultural groups. If students' differences are ignored, the students will probably be given instruction that is not suited to their cultural styles or needs. They are then likely to fail to learn many skills, which in turn denies them power and opportunity in the dominant culture. For example, if we ignore non-English-speaking students' language and cultural heritage and force them to speak English, they may have great difficulty in school. "This story [of the harm children experience when their language and cultural differences are not recognized] manifests one half of the difference dilemma: nonacknowledgment of difference reiterates difference . . ." (p. 838).

However, the answer to this problem is not necessarily recognition of students' differences, for instruction geared to the students' cultural style may teach only skills valued by the students' microculture. Because the dominant culture does not value these skills, the students' difference is perpetuated. For example, if non-English-speaking students are taught in their native language and are not required to learn English, their progress in the English-speaking society will be slowed.

> Here . . . is the other side of the dilemma; acknowledgment of difference can create barriers to important aspects of the school experience and delay or derail successful entry into the society that continues to make that difference matter. Both sides of the dilemma appear and reappear in the history of education for students who are not native English speakers. (Minow, 1985, p. 384)

Should a student who speaks no English be forced to give up his or her native language in school and learn to use only English (ignoring the cultural-linguistic difference)? Or should we use the students' native language as the primary vehicle of instruction, while teaching English as a second language (acknowledging the cultural-linguistic difference)? We could pose similar questions for students with severe hearing impairments: Should we teach them by using primarily sign language or spoken language? And the same dilemma of difference appears in providing instruction for students with other disabilities: To what extent should they be treated as different and provided with special accommodations, and to what extent should they be treated just like everyone else?

To a great extent, the controversy over the dilemma of difference has to do with how students fare in society after their school years, not just how they are treated in school. Delpit (1988, p. 291) examines a variety of perspectives on the problem of multicultural education, including the following position:

> *Children have the right to their own language, their own culture. We must fight cultural hegemony and fight the system by insisting that children be allowed to express themselves in their own language and style. It is not they, the children, who must change, but the schools.*

Delpit's response to this perspective acknowledges both the benefit of recognizing and valuing different cultural styles and the necessity of accepting the realities of the society in which we live.

> I believe in diversity of style, and I believe the world will be diminished if cultural diversity is ever obliterated. Further, I believe strongly . . . that each cultural group should have the right to maintain its own language style. When I speak, therefore, of the culture of power, I don't speak of how I wish things to be but of how they are.
>
> I further believe that to act as if power does not exist is to ensure that the power status quo remains the same. To imply to children or adults . . . that it doesn't matter how you talk or how you write is to ensure their ultimate failure. I prefer to be honest with my students. Tell them that their language and cultural style is unique and·wonderful but that there is a political power game that is also being played, and if they want to be in on that game there are certain games that they too must play. . . . They [my colleagues] seem to believe that if we accept and encourage diversity within classrooms of children, then diversity will automatically be accepted at gatekeeping points. . . .

> I believe that will never happen. What will happen is that the students who reach the gatekeeping points . . . will understand that they have been lied to and react accordingly. (1988, p. 292)

The gatekeeping points to which Delpit refers are admission to higher education and employment.

Hilliard (1989) also notes the necessity of taking students' cultural styles into account in teaching, and the equal necessity of good teaching that prepares students of all cultural groups for the demands of the larger society.

> There is something we can call style—a central tendency that is characteristic of both individuals and groups. This style is cultural—learned. It is meaningful in the teaching and learning interaction. Students' style is not, however, to be used as an excuse for poor teaching or as an index of low capacity. (p. 69)

Clearly, the problem of instruction in multicultural education is not easily resolved, especially for bilingual students in special education. Most authorities now agree, however, that accepting and fostering cultural diversity must not be used as an excuse for not teaching students the skills they need to survive and prosper in the larger context of American macroculture (Delpit, 1988; Hilliard, 1989).

Socialization

Academic instruction is one of two primary purposes of education; the other is socialization. Socialization involves helping students to develop appropriate social perceptions and interactions with others and to learn how to work for desirable social change.

Destructive and stereotypic social perceptions and interactions among differing microcultural groups are long-standing problems in schools and communities in the United States. The most obvious examples involve racial discrimination, although sex discrimination and discrimination against people of differing religions and disabilities are also common in our society. Teachers must become keenly aware of their own cultural heritage, identity, and biases before they can help their students deal with cultural diversity in ways that enhance democratic ideals, such as human dignity, justice, and equality (Banks, 1988). Becoming comfortable with one's own identity as a member of microcultural groups is an important objective for both teachers and students. Depending on the cultural context, accepting and valuing one's identity can be quite difficult. In the box on page 73, Ved Mehta (1989) describes his feelings of discomfort with his identity as a member of two microcultural groups—East Indians and persons who are blind.

Teaching about different cultures and their value may be important in reducing racial and ethnic conflict and promoting respect for human differences. Equally important, however, is structuring classroom interactions to promote the understanding and appreciation of others. One of the most effective ways of breaking down prejudice and encouraging appropriate interaction among students with different characteristics is cooperative learning (D. W. Johnson & R. Johnson, 1986; Slavin, 1988). In cooperative learning, students of different abilities and cultural characteristics work together as a team, fostering interdependence. In *Among Schoolchildren*, Tracy Kidder describes this approach to socialization as it was used by a fifth-grade teacher, Chris Zajac:

> Then came fifteen minutes of study, during which teams of two children quizzed each other. Chris paired up good spellers with poor ones. She also made spelling an exercise in socialization, by putting together children who did not seem predisposed

Difference in Identity: The Struggle for Acceptance

In the following passage from one of his autobiographical books, Ved Mehta describes his feelings—during his college years—of social isolation and contempt for his identity as a person who is blind and from an Eastern culture. How might his college classmates and instructors have enhanced his feelings of self-worth as a member of these two microcultural groups?

Mandy went home most weekends. At first, I worried that she never invited me to go with her and meet her family. She never even offered to give me her home address or telephone number. But here, again, far from condemning her behavior, I came to condone it, thinking I should be grateful to her for protecting me from her family's ire. Putting myself in her father's place, I reflected that if I had a daughter who had got herself involved with a handicapped person I would vigorously oppose the romance and try to persuade her not to consider throwing away her life on a handicapped person out of some misguided notion that she could make up for the magnitude of his problems. (Coming from a country with practically no tradition of romantic love, I assumed that dating was tantamount to marriage.) Moreover, I told myself that I was not only handicapped but also a foreigner, who, no matter how superficially Westernized, could never have the same grasp of the English language and American customs that an American had. Just as living in a sighted society was making me contemptuous of everything to do with being blind, studying in America was making me contemptuous of everything to do with being Indian. As a freshman in college, I had taken courses in the history of Western civilization, the philosophy of Western civilization, and the classical music of Western civilization. In Berkeley, I was studying Western economics and American history. (Similar courses in Indian civilization were unheard of.) In the light of this Western education, everything Indian seemed backward and primitive. I remember once listening to a record of Mozart and being awed by the dozens of instruments magically playing in harmony, and then listening to a record of a sitar and being filled with scorn for the twang-twang of the gut.

SOURCE: Ved Mehta, *The Stolen Light* (New York: W. W. Norton & Co., 1989), p. 260.

to like each other. She hoped that some would learn to get along with classmates they didn't think they liked. At least they'd be more apt to do some work than if she paired them up with friends. Her guesses were good. Alice raised her eyes to the florescent-lit ceiling at the news that she had Claude for a spelling partner. Later she wrote, "Today is the worst day of my life." Clarence scowled at the news that he had Ashley, who was shy and chubby and who didn't look happy either. A little smile collected in one corner of Chris's mouth as she observed the reactions. "Now, you're not permanently attached to that person for the rest of your life," she said to the class. (1989, pp. 28–29)

Finally, we note that education should not merely socialize students to fit into the existing social order. The goals of multicultural education include teaching students to work for social change (Banks, 1988), which entails helping students who are members of oppressed minorities to become advocates for themselves and other members of their microcultures.

Summary

Education for cultural diversity involves managing tension between microcultural diversity on the one hand and common macrocultural values on the other. Many microcultures are found in the U.S. macroculture, which values justice, equality, and human dignity. Microcultures include ethnic and exceptionality groups, but ethnicity and exceptionality are discrete concepts. The general purposes of multicultural education are to promote understanding of microcultures—one's own and others—and to foster positive attitudes toward cultural diversity. Multicultural education also is intended to ensure that ethnicity is not mistaken for exceptionality, and it should increase our understanding of the microculture of exceptionality and its relationship to other microcultures. Assessment, instruction, and socialization present particular problems for the education of culturally diverse students, including those with exceptionalities.

SUMMARY

Special education has changed dramatically during its history, and the field appears poised for more changes. Three major issues that provide the basis for change are normalization, integration, and cultural diversity.

The philosophical belief that every exceptional individual should be provided with an education and living environment as close to normal as possible—normalization—has been the focus of advocacy for people with disabilities since the 1970s. It served, for example, as an underpinning of the concept of *least restrictive environment*, which was included in PL 94-142. The principle has been used by special educators to examine a number of ideas and practices, such as the antilabeling movement, disability rights movement, society's attitudes toward disabled newborns, applications of technology, and treatment of disabilities by the popular media.

The antilabeling movement arose out of fear that labeling students for special education stigmatizes them and makes them feel unworthy. Research on the effects of labeling indicates that labels do have a biasing effect on how others perceive disabled people, and the effects seem to depend on the other information one has about them. Labels are still used because they (1) are used to channel federal and state funds for special education, (2) help professionals communicate about children with disabilities, (3) would probably be replaced by other labels were they to be abandoned (labels may, in fact, be unavoidable), (4) provide a public spotlight for the problems of those with disabilities, and (5) appear to provide a justification for the differences of disabled people that increases tolerance for differences among the general public.

The disability rights movement has been strong since the late 1970s. Believing that society promotes biases they refer to as *handicapism* (analogous to *racism*), activists have sought goals similar to those of other civil rights movements—equal opportunity, freedom to choose, dignity, and freedom from stereotyping. Although gaining momentum, the disability rights movement has not achieved the same degree of visibility and societal change as other civil rights movements for several reasons: (1) the conservative political climate of the 1980s, (2) differences between disability and ethnicity or gender, (3) disagreements among activists themselves, (4) heterogeneity of the disabled population, and (5) lack of a sense of pride in the identity of being disabled.

Another topic related to normalization is the treatment of newborns with disabilities. Advances in neonatal treatment have resulted in the ability to preserve the lives of many newborns who previously would have died. Many people are now struggling with the complex ethical issues involved in defining quality of life and are questioning the way decisions are made about giving or withholding treatment to infants with severe disabilities.

Technology has undoubtedly contributed to normalization by allowing greater independence and making it possible for more people with disabilities to take part in activities that were previously impossible. Personal computers have probably been the single most important technological development enhancing the normalization of disabled persons. Some have cautioned, however, that disabled people might in certain instances come to rely on technology to help them do things they could do on their own.

Researchers and activists have raised questions about how the media portray disabilities, objecting, for example, that television and movies often portray disabled people in stereotypical ways—as evil or as superheros. These stereotypical roles tend to maintain prejudicial views of people with disabilities. Print media, including journalism and literature, also tend to stereotype the disabled person. However, the media appear to be making progress in presenting more accurate and nonstereotypical representations.

Integration is the normalization of where and with

whom people with disabilities live, work, play, and go to school. It involves the movement of people from institutions into homes in the community and the movement of students from special schools and classes into neighborhood schools and regular classrooms. Two aspects of integration that have been important issues since the 1960s are deinstitutionalization and mainstreaming.

Deinstitutionalization is part of the trend to move people with disabilities into closer contact with the community and home so that they can enjoy as normal a life as possible. Group homes, or community residential facilities (CRFs), are increasingly being used for severely disabled individuals, who in years past would have been placed in large institutions. Successful adjustment of CRF residents is related to their personal characteristics, such as good vocational skills and mild (as opposed to severe) behavior problems, and environmental factors, such as appropriate social support and clinical services. Deinstitutionalization alone will not necessarily improve the quality of life for people with disabilities, and placement in group homes will not necessarily make their lives more normal. Making sure that appropriate services are available and working to ensure acceptance of the CRF by the community are essential if the CRF is to provide a more normalized experience.

Mainstreaming—the integration of exceptional students into classes with their nonexceptional peers—is viewed by many as the primary way in which schools can foster normalization. From about 1950 until about 1980, advocates of mainstreaming tended to base their arguments on reports that students with mild disabilities learn more (or at least as much) in regular classes as in special classes. Most studies have produced mixed results: Regular classes produce more academic learning, but special classes produce more social acceptance.

Since the early 1980s attention has been focused on the ethical reasons for mainstreaming, especially the argument that it is unacceptable to separate any child from the peer group unless the benefits of special classes have been demonstrated. At the same time, researchers have been searching for ways to make mainstreaming more successful through effective teaching and the use of teacher consultants, prereferral teams, cooperative learning, peer tutoring, and curriculum materials designed to teach all students about those with disabilities. Although all these strategies for mainstreaming seem promising, more research supporting their effectiveness is needed.

Beginning in the mid-1980s, some special educators started the regular education initiative (REI). Advocates of the REI state that general education should take primary or total responsibility for most or all students with disabilities. Many theoretical and practical issues involved in implementing the REI remain unanswered, and a few professional organizations as well as individuals have questioned whether its implementation would serve the best interests of most students with disabilities.

Multicultural education is necessary to address the cultural diversity of students in U.S. schools. A strength of U.S. society is the diversity of its citizens, yet another strength is the melding of diverse groups into a common cultural identity.

Culture includes values and behavioral styles, languages and dialects, nonverbal communication, awareness (of one's cultural distinctiveness), frames of reference (normative world views or perspectives), and identification (feeling part of the cultural group). Within a national macroculture are found many microcultures, such as ethnic, racial, gender, religious, exceptionality, and other groups. A person may belong to a variety of microcultures that affect his or her behavior.

The general purposes of multicultural education are to promote understanding of microcultures and foster positive attitudes toward cultural diversity. Ethnic and exceptionality groups are particularly important microcultures in special education. Multicultural education should ensure that ethnicity and exceptionality are not confused. It should also promote understanding of the microculture of exceptionality and its relationship to other microcultures. Educators should design activities to reduce prejudice and stereotyping of multicultural groups other than one's own. Assessment practices, instructional programs, and socialization are particular problems in education for cultural diversity.

Traditional approaches to assessment, such as standardized testing, do not take cultural diversity into account, focus on the deficits of the individual, and provide little useful information for teaching. Alternatives to traditional approaches include assessing the instructional environment and curriculum-based assessment. In designing effective instruction for members of microcultural groups, we are faced with the dilemma of difference—the problem of perpetuating inequities if difference is acknowledged and also if it is not. Authorities now recognize the importance of acknowledging students' cultural styles while providing effective instruction in the skills that will enable them to be successful in the dominant culture. Socialization involves helping students become comfortable with their identification with microcultural groups, avoid destructive and stereotypic social perceptions and interactions, and become advocates for themselves and other members of their microcultures. Teachers must become comfortable with their own microcultural identification and provide classroom activities that encourage understanding and appreciation of others.

ALL MY HOUSEMATES
Camille Holvoet, Creative Growth Art Center

Mental Retardation

Everywhere, however, we hear talk of sameness. "All men are created equal" it is declared. And at the ballot box and the subway rush, in Hiroshima and Coney Island it almost seems that way. Moreover, coming back from Staten Island on the ferry, as you see an unkempt bootblack lift his head to gaze at the Manhattan skyline—you know these words of Jefferson are not mere snares for votes and popularity. But standing on the same boat with the hand of your idiot son in one of yours—with mingled love and distaste placing a handkerchief against his drooling mouth—you know that Jefferson's words are not easy to understand.

There is a difference in sameness. Perhaps the days of our years are for the bootblack. But assuredly the nights are for our idiot son.

(*Richard H. Hungerford, "On Locusts"*)

*T*here is considerable danger in relying on Hungerford's portrayal (p. 77) for our only view of what it is like to have a retarded child. Such children may be heartbreakingly different from the children next door in some ways, but also like them in others. More and more research evidence indicates that retardation is quantitative rather than qualitative. In many areas, it seems, the retarded child functions like a nondisabled child—but a nondisabled child at a younger chronological age. Even the differences that do exist need not cause parents a lifetime of constant heartache. Hungerford's statement is valuable because it presents honest feelings. Unlike the romanticized portraits found in many TV dramas, movies, and books, retarded children can evoke agony, hatred, sorrow, and frustration, as well as love, in their parents.

The Hungerford quote, published in 1950, points up something else as well. It reflects the once-popular stereotype of the retarded person as a clumsy, drooling, helpless creature. Today we know this is simply not true. First, most children classified as mentally retarded are *mildly* retarded and look like the hypothetical average child living next door. Second, it can be misleading to characterize even the more severely retarded as helpless. With advanced methods of providing educational and vocational training, we are finding that retarded people are capable of leading more independent lives than was previously thought possible. Given appropriate preparation, many are able to live and work with relatively small amounts of help from others.

The field of mental retardation has undergone a number of other exciting changes since the time Hungerford wrote. At one time, for example, minority children who functioned poorly in school were almost automatically labeled mildly retarded. The fact that they belonged to a cultural subgroup had much to do with this labeling. The trend today is to "de-label" such children.

Much of this change in attitude has come from changes in the definition of retardation. In this chapter we shall discuss the movement toward applying more stringent criteria when identifying retarded children. The wave of criticism of labeling has also had an effect on other aspects of the education of retarded children. Terminology, for example, is changing. Whereas at one time the use of the label "idiot" would have been acceptable, today we use words that are less stigmatizing. Delivery of services, too, has changed. No longer is institutionalization the norm for severely retarded individuals. More and more retarded children are attending neighborhood schools and being mainstreamed into general education classes.

DEFINITION

Today, professionals are much more reluctant to apply the label of mental retardation than they once were because they fear that the stigma of such a diagnosis can have harmful consequences for the individual. They also recognize that to a certain extent, mental retardation is a socially constructed condition. For example, the sociologist Jane Mercer (1973) holds that it is the individual's social system that determines whether he or she is retarded. She notes that most mentally retarded children, particularly those who are higher functioning, do not "officially" become retarded until they enter school. The school as a social system has a certain set of expectations some children do not meet.

AAMR Definition

The more conservative climate is reflected in the definition of retardation, currently accepted by most authorities, of the American Association on Mental Retardation

MISCONCEPTIONS
ABOUT PERSONS WITH MENTAL RETARDATION

Myth	*Fact*
Once diagnosed as mentally retarded, a person remains within this classification for the rest of his or her life.	The level of mental functioning does not necessarily remain stable, particularly for those in the mild classification.
In most cases, we can identify the cause of retardation.	In most cases (especially within the mild classification), we cannot identify the cause. For many of the children in the mild classification, it is thought that poor environment may be a causal factor. However, it is usually extremely difficult to document.
Most mentally retarded children look different from nondisabled children.	The majority of mentally retarded children are mildly retarded, and most mildly retarded children look like nondisabled children.
If a person achieves a low score on an IQ test, this means that his or her adaptive skills are also sure to be subnormal.	It is possible for a person to have a tested subnormal IQ and still have adequate adaptive skills. Much depends on the individual's training, motivation, experience, social environment, etc.
Most mental retardation can be diagnosed in infancy.	Because the majority of retarded children are mildly retarded, because infant intelligence tests are not as reliable and valid as those used in later childhood, and because intellectual demands on the child greatly increase upon entrance to school, most children eventually diagnosed as retarded are not so identified until they go to school.
Retarded individuals go through different learning stages compared to nondisabled individuals.	Many studies indicate that the learning characteristics of retarded individuals, particularly those classified as mildly retarded, do not differ from those of nondisabled people. That is, retarded people go through the same stages, but at a slower rate.
Children classified as moderately retarded (once called "trainable") require a radically different curriculum from that appropriate for children classified as mildly retarded (once called "educable").	Although academic subjects are generally stressed more with mildly retarded students, and vocational skills are stressed more with moderately and severely and profoundly retarded students, there is actually a great deal of overlap in curricular goals for all retarded students.
When a worker with mental retardation fails on the job it is usually because he or she does not have adequate job skills.	There is substantial research indicating that when mentally retarded workers fail on the job, it is more often because of poor job responsibility (e.g., poor attendance and lack of initiative) and social competence (e.g., not interacting appropriately with co-workers) than because of competence in task production.
Transition programming for students with mental retardation begins in secondary school.	Although the degree of emphasis should be greater for older students, most authorities agree that transition programming for students with mental retardation should begin in elementary school.
Severely retarded people are helpless.	With appropriate educational programming, many severely retarded people can lead relatively independent lives. In fact, with appropriate professional support, some can live in the community and even enter competitive employment.

(AAMR) (formerly known as the American Association on Mental Deficiency): "**Mental retardation** refers to significantly subaverage intellectual functioning resulting in or associated with impairments in adaptive behavior and manifested during the developmental period" (Grossman, 1983, p. 11). A very important element of this definition is that a person must be well below average in both measured intelligence and adaptive behavior to be classified as retarded. Whereas at one time it was common practice to diagnose individuals as retarded solely on the basis of an IQ below 85, today they must have deficits in adaptive behavior and an IQ below 75 or 70.

It is also noteworthy that the AAMR definition, in contrast to some earlier definitions of mental retardation (e.g., Doll, 1941), makes no mention of incurability. We no longer view retardation as a lifelong condition, especially for those whose degree of retardation is relatively mild. We now believe that people can, through appropriate educational efforts, improve to the point where they are no longer considered retarded. Furthermore, authorities now hold that early educational programming can prevent some children from being so diagnosed.

Adaptive Behavior

The AAMR definition emphasizes the role adaptive behavior plays in determining whether a person is retarded. A child can score low on a standardized intelligence test but have adequate adaptive skills; he or she may do poorly in school but still be "streetwise"—able to cope, for example, with the subway system, with an after-school job, with peers. Much of the AAMR definition's emphasis on adaptive behavior can be traced to the 1970 report of the President's Committee on Mental Retardation entitled "The Six-Hour Retarded Child." It held that some children may function in the retarded range while they are in school for six hours of the day but behave normally—adjust and adapt competently—once they return to the home community for the other eighteen hours.

Adaptive behavior, however, encompasses more than the ability to survive outside school. Adaptive skills are age- and situation-specific. They are different for the preschooler and the adult. The inner-city teenager may need to be streetwise, but the teenager in a rural community requires a very different set of abilities. The AAMR specifies that in infancy and early childhood, sensory-motor, communication, self-help, and socialization skills are important. In middle childhood and early adolescence, adaptive behavior makes use of abilities involving learning processes and interpersonal social skills. In late adolescence and adulthood, vocational skills and social responsibilities are important.

Intellectual Functioning

The words "subaverage general intellectual functioning" in the AAMR definition refer to scores more than two standard deviations below the mean on a standardized test of intelligence. One commonly used IQ is the Wechsler Intelligence Scale for Children–Revised [WISC–R]. On this test, a score of 70 would be two standard deviations below the mean, or average, of 100.* In the AAMR manual, however, it does state that the score of 70 should be treated as a guideline and a cutoff of 75 might be warranted in some cases.

---

* *Standard deviation* is a measure of the amount by which an individual test score differs from the mean (average) score. Standard deviations are statistical constructs that divide a normal distribution into areas, making it possible to predict the percentage of the distribution that falls above or below a score. *One* standard deviation refers to the range of IQ points that constitute one of these areas (see Figure 3.1).

Adaptive behavior for preschoolers includes self-help skills, such as the ability to dress themselves. (© Suzanne Szasz/Photo Researchers)

CLASSIFICATION

Most professionals classify retarded individuals according to the severity of their problems. The most generally accepted approach is to consider retardation as existing on a continuum or scale of severity. The two most common systems are that of the AAMR and the one used primarily by educators.

The AAMR System

The AAMR system is depicted in Table 3.1. There are three reasons why most professionals agree that the AAMR system is the most useful.

1. The terms used—**mild, moderate, severe,** and **profound retardation**— do not carry the degree of negative stereotyping of earlier descriptions ("idiot," "feebleminded"). They are adjectives commonly applied to a vast array of other things or conditions besides retardation.
2. The terms used emphasize the level of functioning of the individual.
3. The use of bands of IQ scores—for example 50–55 as the cutoff between mild and moderate retardation—leaves some room for clinical judgment and recognizes that IQ scores are not perfect predictors of a person's level of retardation. As the AAMR manual states, "Thus, someone whose Full Scale Wechsler IQ is 53 might be diagnosed as either mild or moderate, depending on other factors, such as the relative difference in Performance and Verbal IQ or results of other tests." (Grossman, 1983, p. 13).

TABLE 3.1 *Level of Retardation Indicated by IQ Range Obtained on Measure of General Intellectual Functioning*

Term	IQ Range for Level
Mild mental retardation	50–55 to approx. 70
Moderate mental retardation	35–40 to 50–55
Severe mental retardation	20–25 to 35–40
Profound mental retardation	Below 20 or 25
Unspecified	

SOURCE: H. J. Grossman (Ed.), *Classification in Mental Retardation* (Washington, DC: American Association on Mental Deficiency, 1983), p. 13. Reprinted with permission.

The Educators' System

Anyone who has been around school systems has no doubt heard of classes for "educable" and "trainable" retarded children. **Educable mentally retarded (EMR)** individuals are those with IQs between 75 or 70 (more and more school systems are now using 70, whereas previously they used 75) and 50. **Trainable mentally retarded (TMR)** persons have IQs between 50 and 25. Since the passage of PL 94-142, schools have been obligated to serve children with IQs below 25, and these individuals are commonly referred to as **severely and profoundly handicapped (SPH).** The use of the terms educable and trainable have survived over the years among educators because they describe, albeit grossly, the educational needs of retarded children. In general, persons classified EMR can learn some basic academic subjects. The curriculum for individuals classified TMR, on the other hand, concentrates more on functional academic subjects, with emphasis on self-help and vocational skills.

One disadvantage of this system is that some educators have at times taken the categories too literally. Some children labeled TMR were denied access to academic subject matter within their intellectual reach. Likewise, students classified EMR need to learn self-help and vocational skills. Intelligence test scores are not reliable and valid enough to be used to determine entirely different educational objectives for one child with an IQ of 51 (classified as educable) and another with an IQ of 49 (classified as trainable).

PREVALENCE

The average (mean) score on an IQ test is 100. Theoretically, we expect 2.27 percent of the population to fall two standard deviations (IQ = 70 on the WISC–R) or more below this average. This expectation is based on the assumption that intelligence, like so many other human traits, is distributed along a "normal curve." Figure 3.1 shows the hypothetical normal curve of intelligence. This curve is split into eight areas by means of standard deviations. On the WISC–R, where one standard deviation equals 15 IQ points, 34.13 percent of the population scores between 85 and 100. Likewise, 2.14 percent scores between 55 and 70, and 0.13 percent

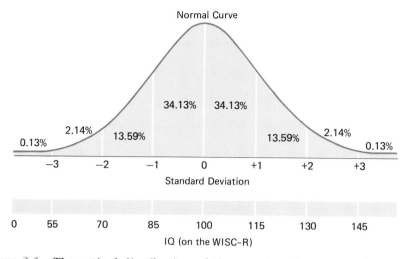

Normal Curve

34.13%   34.13%

2.14%   13.59%   13.59%   2.14%

0.13%   0.13%

−3   −2   −1   0   +1   +2   +3

Standard Deviation

0   55   70   85   100   115   130   145

IQ (on the WISC-R)

Figure 3.1   Theoretical distribution of IQ scores based on normal curve.

scores below 55. Thus it would seem that 2.27 percent should fall between 0 and 70.

In keeping with the figure of 2.27 percent, the federal government for years estimated the prevalence of retardation to be 2.3 percent. The U.S. Department of Education (1989), however, has reported that for 1987–1988, 1.21 percent of the population from six to seventeen years of age was identified as mentally retarded by the public schools. Authorities have pointed to three possible sources for the discrepancy between 2.3 and 1.21 percent. First, the fact that retarded children must now meet the dual criteria of low IQ *and* low adaptive behavior may have resulted in fewer children being identified. Second, litigation focusing on the improper labeling of minority students as mentally retarded may have made school personnel more cautious about identifying these children as retarded. Third, parents and school officials may be more likely to label children as learning disabled rather than mentally retarded because it is perceived as a less stigmatizing label.

CAUSES

Many experts estimate that we are able to pinpoint the cause of mental retardation in only about 6 to 15 percent of the cases. Although there is some overlap, for the most part the set of causal factors for mild retardation differs from that for more severe levels of retardation.

Mild Retardation

Most individuals identified as retarded are classified as mildly retarded. They typically do not differ in appearance from their nonhandicapped peers, and they are usually not diagnosed as mentally retarded until they enter school and begin to fall behind in schoolwork. In addition, in the vast majority of cases we are unable to specify the exact cause of retardation. Although there are no definitive data, the estimate of 6 to 15 percent for identifiable causes of all retardation is undoubtedly even lower when considering only mildly retarded persons.

Professionals often refer to mildly retarded individuals as having **cultural-familial retardation.** Some professionals use this term to refer to a person with a mild degree of retardation who has (1) no evidence of brain damage, (2) at least one parent who is retarded, and (3) at least one retarded sibling (if he or she has siblings) (Heber, 1959). The assumption is that the retardation is due to genetic and/or social environmental factors. The latter presumably cause retardation because they produce such effects as inadequate learning opportunities and poor nutrition. Just which ingredient—heredity or environment—is the culprit has been the subject of debate for years.

The Nature Versus Nurture Controversy

In the early part of this century proponents of the viewpoint that genetics determines intellectual development largely held sway. The classic study of Skeels and Dye (1939), however, did much to strengthen the position of the environmentalists. Skeels and Dye investigated the effects of stimulation on the development of infants and young children, many of whom were classified as mentally retarded, in an orphanage. One group of children remained in the typical orphanage environment, whereas the other group was given stimulation. For the latter group, nurturance was provided by retarded teenage girls who were institutionalized. The effects were clear-cut: Average IQs for members of the group given stimulation increased, whereas the other children's IQs decreased. Even more dramatic were the results of Skeels's follow-up study, done twenty-one years later:

> In the adult follow-up study, all cases were located and information obtained on them, after a lapse of 21 years. . . .

> All 13 children in the experimental group were self-supporting, and none was a ward of any institution. . . . In the contrast group of 12 children, one had died in adolescence

Although it is difficult to pinpoint the environment as a cause of retardation, most authorities believe that poor social-environment conditions can lead to mild retardation. Mild retardation presumed to be caused by poor environmental conditions is sometimes referred to as cultural-familial retardation. (C. Vergara/Photo Researchers)

following continued residence in a state institution for the mentally retarded, and four were still wards of institutions, one in a mental hospital, and the other three in institutions for the mentally retarded.

In education, disparity between the two groups was striking. The contrast group completed a median of less than the third grade. The experimental group completed a median of the 12th grade. Four of the subjects had one or more years of college work, one received a B.A. degree and took some graduate training.

Marked differences in occupational levels were seen in the two groups. In the experimental group all were self-supporting or married and functioning as housewives. The range was from professional and business occupations to domestic service, the latter the occupations of two girls who had never been placed in adoptive homes. In the contrast group, four (36 percent) of the subjects were institutionalized and unemployed. Those who were employed, with one exception, were characterized as "hewers of wood and drawers of water.". . .

Eleven of the 13 children in the experimental group were married: nine of the 11 had a total of 28 children, an average of three per family. On intelligence tests, these second generation children had IQs ranging from 86 to 125, with a mean of 104. In no instance was there any indication of mental retardation or demonstrable abnormality. . . .

In the contrast group, only two subjects had married. One had one child and subsequently was divorced. Psychological examination of the child revealed marked mental retardation. . . . Another male subject had a nice home and a family of four children, all of average intelligence. (Skeels, 1966, pp. 54–55)

By the 1960s there was a sizeable number of proponents of the nurture position. It was during this time, for example, that the federal government established the Head Start program. Head Start was based on the premise that the negative effects of poverty could be reduced through educational and medical services during the preschool years.

For many years theoreticians tended to view the nature-nurture issue from an either-or perspective—either you believed that heredity held the key to determining intellectual development or you held that the environment was the all-important factor. By the 1980s, however, most authorities believed that both genetics and the environment are critical determinants of intelligence. They have arrived at this judgment on the basis of several studies, but perhaps the most convincing was that conducted by Capron and Duyme (1989), who compared the IQs of four groups of adopted children: (1) children whose biological and adoptive parents were both of high socioeconomic status (SES), (2) children whose biological parents were of high SES but whose adoptive parents were of low SES, (3) children whose biological and adoptive parents were both of low SES, and (4) children whose biological parents were of low SES but whose adoptive parents were of high SES. The average IQs of the four groups were 119.60, 107.50, 92.40, and 103.60, respectively. Confirming the importance of the environment, the average IQ of the adoptees was about 12 points higher (111.60 versus 99.95) when they were raised by parents of high (groups 1 and 4) rather than low SES (groups 2 and 3). Confirming the importance of heredity, the average IQ of the adoptees was about 16 points higher (113.55 versus 98.00) when their biological parents were of high SES (groups 1 and 2) compared to low SES (groups 3 and 4).

The more scientists study genetic and environmental determinants of intelligence, the more they realize how complex the influence of these factors is. For example, scientists are far from being able to specify the exact way in which the environment influences intellectual development. They do not know, for example, whether the effect of SES "is related to access to quality education, the variety and complexity of intellectual stimulation in the home, the parents' press for scholastic achievement, or some other factor that differentiates between high- and low-SES homes" (McGue, 1989, p. 507). Further complicating the issue, there is considerable evidence that the environment is far from static, even within families (Plomin, 1989; Rowe & Plomin, 1981). Traditionally, investigators viewed the environmental influence of being raised in a particular family as equally distributed across family members. Researchers now believe, however, that different siblings in the same family experience different environments. The following scenario provides an example of how within-family variations can occur:

> Suppose a family with 16-year-old and 9-year-old boys visits the Space Center in Florida. The experience might have no effect whatsoever on the older child, who is heavily committed to basketball and dating. However, the younger boy, while showing aptitude in mathematics, has never really blossomed academically. He finds the Space Center fascinating. When he returns home he discovers his neighbor is a pilot, who shows the youngster about planes and takes him up for a ride. This ignites the child's interest in aviation. A unit on flight in a science class later that year reinforces it, and the child shows a marked increase in mental performance with this surge of motivation. (McCall, 1983, p. 414)

It should be obvious from the foregoing discussion that the study of the differential effects of heredity and environment on intellectual development has become more complex over the years. In other words, although we are now closer to an understanding of the potential effects of both environment and heredity, in individual cases we are far from knowing the exact contribution of each.

More Severe Retardation

Causes of retardation in individuals classified as moderately retarded through profoundly retarded are more easily determined than for those in the mild range of retardation. MacMillan (1982) divides causes for more severely retarded persons into two general categories—genetic factors and brain damage.

Genetic Factors

There are a number of genetically related causes of mental retardation. These are, generally, of two types—those that result from some damage to genetic material, such as chromosomal abnormalities, and those that are due to hereditary transmission. We discuss three conditions—Down syndrome, which results from chromosomal abnormality, and PKU (phenylketonuria) and Tay-Sachs disease, both of which are inherited.

Estimated to account for approximately 10 percent of all moderate and severe cases of retardation, **Down syndrome** is sometimes, but less acceptably, referred to as *mongolism* because of the facial characteristic of thick epicanthal folds in the corners of the eyes, making them appear to slant upward slightly. Other common physical characteristics include small stature; decreased muscle tone (hypotonia); hyperflexibility of joints; speckling of the iris of the eye; small oral cavity, which results in protruding of the tongue; short and broad hands with a single palmar crease; and a wide gap between the first and second toes (Batshaw & Perret, 1986; Blackman, 1984a).

Individuals with Down syndrome frequently have a number of other physical problems. For example, they are at greater risk than nondisabled persons to have

Persons with Down Syndrome are usually identifiable by their facial characteristics. (Richard Hutchings/Photo Researchers)

congenital heart defects and to develop visual impairments, upper respiratory infections, and leukemia, all of which reduce their life expectancy well below that of nondisabled persons (Patterson, 1987). Researchers have discovered an interesting link between Down syndrome and Alzheimer's disease, the exact meaning of which is still being investigated (Allore et al., 1988; Patterson, 1987). The neurons in the brains of individuals with Down syndrome over the age of thirty-five are characterized by the same abnormalities as those of people with Alzheimer's. In addition, people with Down syndrome are at greater than average risk to develop the behavioral symptoms of Alzheimer's disease. Researchers are coming closer and closer to discovering the exact gene or genes that cause Down syndrome.

The degree of retardation varies widely, most individuals falling in the moderate range. More children with Down syndrome than was once the case are achieving IQ scores in the mildly retarded range because of intensive preschool programming.

There are basically three different types of Down syndrome. In children with the **trisomy 21** type (by far the most common) there is an extra chromosome.* In this type the twenty-first set of chromosomes is a triplet rather than a pair, causing a condition called *trisomy*. The second type, **mosaicism,** results when because of faulty development some of the individual's cells have this extra chromosome and others do not. In **translocation,** the third type, all or part of the extra chromosome of the twenty-first pair becomes attached to another of the chromosome pairs.

The likelihood of having a child with Down syndrome depends to a great extent on the age of the mother: More such children are born to women under twenty and, especially, over forty. For example, a woman between the ages of twenty

* The nucleus of a normal human cell contains twenty-three pairs of **chromosomes,** making a total of forty-six chromosomes altogether. Chromosomes are composed of the essential genetic material—**genes.** Each gene within twenty-two of the chromosome pairs has a duplicate gene on the "matching" chromosome; the twenty-third pair is sex-linked, and its genes may be identical (XX for females) or different (XY for males).

Prenatal Diagnosis of Birth Defects

Beginning in the mid-1970s, there has been a dramatic increase in the availability of techniques for diagnosing defects in the unborn fetus. Three such methods are **amniocentesis, chorionic villus sampling (CVS),** and **sonography.**

AMNIOCENTESIS

In amniocentesis, the physician inserts a needle through the abdominal wall and into the amniotic sac of the pregnant woman and withdraws about one ounce of amniotic fluid from around the fetus. Fetal cells are separated from the fluid and allowed to grow in a culture medium for two to three weeks. The cells are then analyzed for chromosomal abnormalities. Although a variety of genetic disorders can be detected through amniocentesis, it is most often used to detect Down syndrome. In addition, amniocentesis allows one to analyze the amniotic fluid itself. Such analysis can detect about 90 percent of cases of spina bifida, a condition in which the spinal column fails to close during fetal development. In the fetus with spina bifida, certain proteins leak out of the spinal fluid into the surrounding amniotic sac. The elevation of these proteins enables this defect to be detected (see Chapter 9 for further discussion of spina bifida). Physicians most often perform amniocentesis at sixteen to eighteen weeks after the woman's last menstrual period.

CHORIONIC VILLUS SAMPLING

In chorionic villus sampling (CVS), the physician inserts a catheter through the vagina and cervix and withdraws about $\frac{1}{2000}$ of an ounce of villi, structures which will later become the placenta. Although first results are often available in two or three days, final verification takes two to three weeks. CVS can detect a variety of chromosomal abnormalities. The major advantage of CVS over amniocentesis is that it can be performed much earlier, between the ninth to eleventh week of pregnancy. If the woman then elects to have an abortion, she can have it with less risk. Some physicians are more hesitant to conduct CVS, however, because, being a newer procedure, less is known about it. In addition, although neither amniocentesis nor CVS is risky, the incidence of miscarriage after CVS is higher than it is after amniocentesis.

SONOGRAPHY

In sonography, high-frequency sound waves or ultrasound are converted into a visual picture of the fetus. This technique can be used to detect some major physical malformations such as spina bifida.

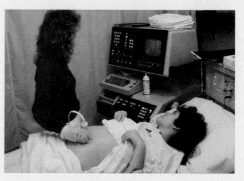

Sonography can be used to detect some major physical malformations, such as spina bifida, in the fetus. (© Russ Kinne/Photo Researchers)

KEEPING PRENATAL TESTING IN PERSPECTIVE

There is little doubt that rapid advances in the field of prenatal testing are now allowing people to detect a number of heretofore unavoidable birth defects. As amazing as this technology is, however, it is well to keep in mind that it in no way guarantees a perfect baby. Many disabilities cannot be detected by any available technique. In addition, as Pat Schnatterly, a genetic counselor in the University of Virginia's Department of Pediatrics, states,

> Prenatal testing is most appropriate when you know ahead of time what it is you're looking for. Thus, it is offered to couples who have specific known risks. This would include, for example, women 35 years of age and over, who have a higher risk for giving birth to a baby with Down syndrome. It would also include couples (for example, those of Ashkenazi Jewish descent who would be at risk for having a child with Tay-Sachs) whose ethnic backgrounds indicated they were at risk.

SOURCES: M. L. Batshaw and Y. M. Perret, *Children with Handicaps: A Medical Primer*, 2nd ed. (Baltimore: Paul H. Brookes, 1986); and M. Chitwood, "What's Past Is Prologue," *Helix*, *4*(2) (1986), 4–7. The interested reader is encouraged to consult these sources for further information.

---

and thirty has a 1 in 1,300 chance of having a Down syndrome baby, a woman between thirty and thirty-four has a 1 in 600 chance, a woman between thirty-five and thirty-nine has a 1 in 300 chance, and a woman between forty and forty-four has a 1 in 80 chance (Hansen, 1978). There are tests available whereby Down syndrome and some other birth defects can be diagnosed in the fetus during pregnancy. (See the box on pp. 88–89.) Physicians sometimes recommend such tests for older pregnant women because they are at higher risk for having a baby with Down syndrome.

Researchers are pointing to variables in addition to the age of the mother as possible causative factors in Down syndrome. Some of the factors being cited as potential causes are the age of the father, exposure to radiation, and exposure to some viruses (MacMillan, 1982).

PKU (phenylketonuria) involves the inability of the body to convert a common dietary substance—phenylalanine—to tyrosine; the accumulation of phenylalanine results in abnormal brain development. Babies can undergo a screening test for PKU in the first few days after birth, and many states require that they be performed before an infant leaves the hospital. Unless a baby with PKU starts a special diet controlling the intake of phenylalanine in infancy and continues it into middle childhood, the child will usually develop severe retardation (Guthrie, 1984). Because some studies have shown that if the diet is stopped at middle childhood a decrease in IQ occurs, many authorities believe the diet should be maintained indefinitely (Batshaw & Perret, 1986). In addition to treating PKU once it has been detected, more and more emphasis is being placed on screening parents to determine if they are possible carriers of the PKU gene. Even though chances are slim (about 1 in 3,600) of two carriers marrying, if this does occur, genetic counseling is highly advised.

Tay-Sachs disease, like PKU, can appear when both mother and father are carriers. It results in progressive brain damage and eventual death. It occurs almost exclusively among Ashkenazi Jews—that is, those of East European extraction. Public health personnel have used genetic screening programs to identify carriers. Also, the disease can be detected *in utero*.

Brain Damage

Brain damage can result from a host of factors that fall into two general categories—infections and environmental hazards.

INFECTIONS. Infections that may lead to mental retardation can occur in the mother-to-be or the infant or young child after birth. **Rubella** (German measles), **syphilis, and herpes simplex** in the mother can all cause retardation in the child. Rubella is most dangerous during the first trimester (three months) of pregnancy. The veneral diseases, syphilis and herpes simplex, present a greater risk at later stages of fetal development (Hetherington & Parke, 1986). (Herpes simplex, which shows as cold sores or fever blisters, is not usually classified as a veneral disease unless it affects the genitals.)

Three examples of infections of the child that can affect mental development are meningitis, encephalitis, and pediatric AIDS. **Meningitis** is an infection of the covering of the brain that may be caused by a variety of bacterial or viral agents. Resulting more often in retardation and usually affecting intelligence more severely is **encephalitis,** an inflammation of the brain. **Pediatric AIDS** is the fastest growing infectious cause of mental retardation. In fact, researchers have projected that it may soon become the leading cause of mental retardation and brain damage (Diamond & Cohen, 1987). The vast majority of children with pediatric AIDS have obtained their infection during birth from their mothers, who used intravenous drugs or were sexually active with infected men (Baumeister, Kupstas, & Klindworth, 1990).

Infections, as well as other causative factors, can also result in microcephalus or hydrocephalus. **Microcephalus** is a condition characterized by a small head with a sloping forehead. It can be caused by infections such as rubella or AIDS (Rubinstein, 1989) or by a genetic disorder. Retardation usually ranges from severe to profound. **Hydrocephalus** results from an accumulation of cerebrospinal fluid inside or outside the brain. Blockage of the circulation of the fluid, which results in a buildup of excessive pressure on the brain and enlargement of the skull, can occur for a variety of reasons—encephalitis, meningitis, malformation of the spine, or tumors. The degree of retardation depends on how early it is diagnosed and treated. Treatment consists of surgical implacement of a shunt (tube) that drains the excess fluid away from the brain and into a vein behind the ear or in the neck.

ENVIRONMENTAL HAZARDS. Examples of environmental hazards that can result in mental retardation are a blow to the head, poisons, radiation, malnutrition, prematurity or postmaturity, and birth injury. Although we are discussing these potential causal agents in this section, which deals with the causes of more severe forms of retardation, there is considerable evidence that in their milder forms each of these factors can result in mild retardation.

It should be obvious that a blow to a child's head can result in mental retardation. The obviousness of this connection, in fact, has served as an impetus for many of the mandatory laws pertaining to the use of child restraints in automobiles. Besides the usual accidents that can lead to brain damage, more and more authorities are citing child abuse as a cause of brain damage that results in mental retardation and other disabilities (see Chapter 9).

Poisoning resulting in mental retardation can occur in the expectant mother or in the child. We are now much more aware of the harmful effects of a variety of substances, from obvious toxic agents such as cocaine and heroin to more subtle

Expectant mothers who consume large amounts of alcohol are at risk of giving birth to infants with fetal alcohol syndrome, a condition characterized by physical disabilities and mental retardation. (© Rhoda Sidney/Monkmeyer Press)

potential "poisons" such as tobacco, alcohol, caffeine, and even food additives. In particular, research has shown that pregnant women who smoke and/or consume alcohol have a greater risk of having babies with behavioral and physical problems. For example, women who are heavy smokers are more likely than nonsmokers to have premature babies (Hetherington & Parke, 1986). And premature babies are at risk for a variety of developmental disabilities (see below).

Researchers have exposed **fetal alcohol syndrome (FAS)** as a significant health problem for expectant mothers who consume large quantities of alcohol and for their unborn children (Hetherington & Parke, 1986; F. R. Schultz, 1984); see also Chapter 9. Occurring in about one-third of the babies of pregnant alcoholic women, children with FAS are characterized by a variety of physical deformities as well as mental retardation.

Although pregnant women who drink moderately may not risk having children with FAS, there is evidence that even their infants will differ behaviorally from those born to women who do not drink during pregnancy. Among expectant mothers who drink moderately, there is evidence that the amount of alcohol they consume is related to their infants' arousal levels and central nervous system functioning (Streissguth, Barr, & Martin, 1983).

Some prescription drugs must also be avoided or used with caution by pregnant women. Research has linked some antibiotic, anticonvulsant, and anticancer medications to fetal malformations (Batshaw & Perret, 1986). And medication delivered to women during labor and delivery has also come under close scrutiny.

It is not always possible, of course, for expectant mothers to avoid using medication during pregnancy and labor. However, more and more authorities are questioning the high rates of drug ingestion by pregnant women; some studies have reported that expectant mothers in America ingest an average of six prescribed drugs and four over-the-counter drugs during their pregnancy. Given the potential for some of these drugs to be **teratogens**—substances that cause malformations in the fetus— many authorities have expressed caution about their use.

Although its use is now prohibited, infants still become poisoned by eating lead-based paint chips, particularly in slum areas. Lead poisoning varies in its effect on children; high levels can result in death. The federal government now requires that automobile manufacturers produce cars that use only lead-free gasoline.

We have recognized the hazards of radiation to the unborn fetus for some time. Physicians, for example, are cautious not to expose pregnant women to X-rays unless absolutely necessary. Since the mid- to late 1970s, however, the public has become even more concerned over the potential dangers of radiation from improperly designed or supervised nuclear power plants.

Retardation caused by improper nutrition can occur because the expectant mother is malnourished or because the child, once born, does not have a proper diet (Cravioto & DeLicardie, 1975; Hallahan & Cruickshank, 1973).

Disorders due to an abnormal length of pregnancy—either too short (prematurity) or too long (postmaturity)—can also result in retardation. The latter is not as likely to cause retardation, although it is possible that the fetus will suffer from poor nutrition if it is long overdue (Robinson & Robinson, 1976). Prematurity is sometimes defined by the length of the pregnancy and sometimes by the weight of the infant at birth (5.5 pounds or lower is often used as an index of prematurity). Both premature and small infants are candidates for a variety of physical and behavioral abnormalities, including retardation (Blackman, 1984b). Prematurity itself is associated with a number of factors—poor nutrition, teenage pregnancy, drug abuse, and excessive cigarette smoking.

Brain injury can also occur during delivery if the child is not positioned properly in the uterus. One problem that sometimes occurs because of difficulty during delivery is **anoxia** (complete deprivation of oxygen).

MEASUREMENT

Professionals measure two major areas to determine whether individuals are mentally retarded: intelligence and adaptive behavior. Even though intellectual capability and the ability to adapt are related to a moderate degree (it is expected, for example, that the more intelligent child will usually be better able to adapt to the environment), there is enough difference between the two concepts to make it necessary to measure each one separately, using different techniques.

Intelligence Tests

There are many types of IQ tests. Because of their accuracy and predictive capabilities, practitioners prefer individually administered tests over group tests. Individual tests are essential when used to diagnose a child for placement in a special education program. Two of the most common individual IQ tests for children are the Stanford-Binet and the Wechsler Intelligence Scale for Children–Revised (WISC–R). Both the Stanford-Binet and the WISC–R are verbal, although the WISC–R is intended to assess both verbal and performance aspects of intelligence. It has a verbal and a performance scale with a number of subtests. The verbal and performance IQ measures are sometimes compared to scores on the subtests for purposes of educational programming. The "full-scale IQ," a statistical composite of the verbal and performance IQ measures, is used when a single overall score for a child is needed.

Although not all IQ tests call for this method of calculation, one can get a rough approximation of a person's IQ by dividing **mental age** (the age level at which a person is functioning) by **chronological age** and multiplying by 100 (to eliminate the decimal point). For example, a ten-year-old child who performs on an IQ test as well as the *average* eight-year-old (and thus has a mental age of eight years) would have an IQ of 80.

Compared to most psychological tests, IQ tests such as the Stanford-Binet and the WISC–R are among the most reliable and valid. By *reliability*, we mean that a child will obtain relatively similar scores if given the test on two separate occasions that are not too close or far apart in time. *Validity* generally answers the question of whether the instrument measures what it is supposed to measure. A good indicator of the validity of an IQ test is its recognition as the best single index of how well a child will do in school. It is wise to be wary, however, of placing too much faith on any single score from a psychological test, even those as reliable and valid as the Stanford-Binet and WISC–R. There are at least four reasons for caution:

1. Even on very reliable tests an individual's IQ can change dramatically from one time to another (McCall, Applebaum, & Hogarty, 1973). Although it appears that this kind of shift is less likely with mentally retarded individuals (Robinson & Robinson, 1976), it nevertheless remains a possibility.
2. All IQ tests are culturally biased to a certain extent. Children from minority groups, largely because of differences in language and experience, are at a disadvantage in taking such tests.
3. The younger the child to whom the IQ test is administered, the less validity and reliability the test has. Infant intelligence tests are particularly questionable. However, as Robinson and Robinson (1976) point out, low scores on infant tests are much more valid than high scores. It is possible to identify retardation in infants, especially in the severe and profound ranges.
4. IQ tests are not the "be-all and end-all" when it comes to assessing an individual's ability to function in society. A superior IQ does not guarantee a successful life; a subnormal IQ does not doom a person to a miserable existence. Other variables are also important determiners of a person's coping skills in society (see the box on p. 94).

Systematic Attempts to Reduce Cultural Bias in Intelligence Tests

Many professionals are concerned that minority groups are at a disadvantage when taking intelligence tests. They claim that such tests assess what is important in the dominant white culture in the United States but do not test those abilities that are stressed in certain minority groups (e.g., blacks and Hispanics). Some psychologists recommend using the K-ABC (Kaufman Assessment Bettery for Children) with black children (Kaufman & Kaufman, 1983). The average score for black and white children is closer on the K-ABC than it is on the WISC–R or Stanford-Binet, and the K-ABC appears to be as good a predictor of achievement as the WISC–R and Stanford-Binet (Kamphaus & Reynolds, 1987).

Another reason the K-ABC is a relatively popular test is that it purports to be based on the most current theories of cognitive processing. The K-ABC is based

Keeping Tests in Perspective

Most professionals agree that tests, such as IQ tests and adaptive behavior instruments, are necessary. They can be helpful in making placement decisions and in evaluating program effectiveness. It is important to keep in mind, however, that they are far from perfect predictors about how a particular individual will function in the real world. The following excerpt from a case study of a mentally retarded woman makes this point nicely:

Superficially she *was* a mass of handicaps and incapacities, with the intense frustrations and anxieties attendant on these; at this level she was, and felt herself to be, a mental cripple—beneath the effortless skills, the happy capacities, of others; but at some deeper level there was no sense of handicap or incapacity, but a feeling of calm and completeness, of being fully alive, of being a soul, deep and high, and equal to all others. Intellectually, then, Rebecca felt a cripple; spiritually she felt herself a full and complete being.

When I first saw her—clumsy, uncouth, all-of-a-fumble—I saw her merely, or wholly, as a casualty, a broken creature, whose neurological impairments I could pick out and dissect with precision. . . .

The next time I saw her, it was all very different. I didn't have her in a test situation, "evaluating" her in a clinic. I wandered outside, it was a lovely spring day, with a few minutes in hand before the clinic started, and there I saw Rebecca sitting on a bench, gazing at the April foliage quietly, with obvious delight. Her posture had none of the clumsiness which had so impressed me before. Sitting there, in a light dress, her face calm and slightly smiling, she suddenly brought to mind one of Chekov's young women—Irene, Anya, Sonya, Nina—seen against the backdrop of a Chekovian cherry orchard. She could have been any young woman enjoying a beautiful spring day. This was my human, as opposed to my neurological, vision.

As I approached, she heard my footsteps and turned, gave me a broad smile, and wordlessly gestured. "Look at the world," she seemed to say. "How beautiful it is." And then there came out, in Jacksonian spurts, odd, sudden, poetic ejaculations: "spring," "birth," "growing," "stirring," "coming to life," "seasons," "everything in its time." I found myself thinking of Ecclesiastes: "To everything there is a season, and a time to every purpose under the heaven. A time to be born, and a time to die; a time to plant, and a time. . . ." This was what Rebecca, in her disjointed fashion, was ejaculating—a vision of seasons, of times, like that of the Preacher. . . . Why was she so de-composed before, how could she be so re-composed now? I had the strongest feeling of two wholly different modes of thought, or of organisation, or of being. The first schematic—pattern-seeing, problem-solving—this is what had been tested, and where she had been found so defective, so disastrously wanting. But the tests had given no inkling of anything *but* the deficits, anything, so to speak, *beyond* her deficits.

They had given me no hint of her positive powers, her ability to perceive the real world—the world of nature, and perhaps of the imagination—as a coherent, intelligible, poetic whole: her ability to see this, think this, and (when she could) live this; they had given me no intimation of her inner world, which clearly *was* composed and coherent, and approached as something other than a set of problems or tasks. . . . It was perhaps fortunate that I chanced to see Rebecca in her so-different modes—so damaged and incorrigible in the one, so full of promise and potential in the other—and that she was one of the first patients I saw in our clinic. For what I saw in her, what she showed me, I now saw in them all.

SOURCE: O. Sacks, *The Man Who Mistook His Wife for a Hat: And Other Clinical Tales* (New York: Summit Books, 1985, pp. 170–173.) © 1970, 1981, 1983, 1984, 1985 by Oliver Sacks. Reprinted by permission of Summit Books, a division of Simon & Schuster, Inc.

on the notion that cognitive tasks can be categorized primarily as requiring either simultaneous or sequential processing of information. Subtests are thus designated as tapping simultaneous or sequential processing abilities. There is, however, considerable debate about whether the theoretical rationale for the K-ABC is valid.

Assessing Adaptive Behavior

Numerous adaptive behavior measures are available. Two of the most commonly used are probably the AAMD Adaptive Behavior Scale-School Edition (Lambert & Windmiller, 1981) and the Adaptive Behavior Inventory for Children (ABIC) (Mercer & Lewis, 1977). The AAMD scale has two sections, one for daily living skills and one for personality and behavior. The ABIC assesses adaptive behavior in six areas—family, community, peer relations, nonacademic school roles, earner-consumer, and self-maintenance. In the area of family, for example, the examiner asks the parent such things as how well the child gets along with brothers and/or sisters. For the community section, the child's relationships with people and events in the community are assessed. For peer relations, the interviewer asks questions regarding the student's ability to get along with peers. In the area of nonacademic roles, the child's degree of involvement with the school is assessed. In the earner/consumer section, the examiner asks questions about the child's degree of knowledge about money and its management. In the area of self-maintenance, the questions address the ability to take care of daily living needs.

PSYCHOLOGICAL AND BEHAVIORAL CHARACTERISTICS

We base our statements about the psychological and behavioral characteristics of mentally retarded children on research studies comparing *groups* of intellectually subaverage children with nonretarded children. We cannot stress too strongly that *individual* mentally retarded children may not display all the characteristics mentioned. There is a great deal of variability in the behavior of retarded students, and we must consider each retarded person as a unique and separate individual. In this section we discuss both the cognitive and personality characteristics of retarded individuals.

Cognitive Characteristics

The most obvious characteristic of retardation is a reduced ability to learn. There are a number of ways in which persons who are retarded may exhibit cognitive problems. Research has documented that retarded students are likely to have difficulties in at least four areas related to cognition* —attention, memory, language, and academics.

Attentional Abilities

The importance of attention for learning is critical. A child must be able to attend to the task at hand before he or she can learn it. For years researchers have posited that we can attribute many of the cognitive problems of retarded individuals to attentional problems (e.g., Brooks & McCauley, 1984; Zeamon & House, 1963).

---

* *Cognition* refers to the process of thinking.

Often attending to the wrong things, many retarded people have difficulty allocating their attention properly. As Brooks and McCauley state,

> Perhaps in older or more intelligent people some of the basic processes become automatic in much the same way as some motor skills such as bicycle riding or typing may become automatic. If a particular process is automatic one does not have to devote effort to directing or monitoring it. Attention not being used for some processes is then available to be focused on other cognitive activities.
>
> Younger or less intelligent people would then be investing all of their attention on the simpler more basic processes, leaving less for more difficult or complicated processes. Thus, when asked to tell an examiner in what way a grape and an apple are alike, retarded people may not retrieve category information that they have available because they are expending so much of their attentional effort trying to keep the given examples in mind.
>
> Other possibilities, again, with attention as the culprit, include the theory that retarded individuals simply have less attention to allocate to different processes or the theory that retarded people cannot (or do not) efficiently assign the proper amount or quality of attention to the various aspects of a task. (pp. 481–482)

Memory

One of the most consistent findings in comparisons of the learning abilities of nondisabled and retarded individuals is that when the latter are asked to remember a list of words or sounds or a group of pictures presented a few seconds previously, they do more poorly than the nondisabled (Borkowski, Peck, & Damberg, 1983; Brown, 1974; Estes, 1970). Many authorities have conceptualized these memory problems within a theoretical framework that stresses the depth of processing that an individual must perform to remember certain material (Craik & Lockhart, 1972; Craik & Tulving, 1975). They maintain that we process incoming stimuli at various levels of analysis. At shallow levels we process only perceptual features, whereas at deeper levels we process semantic features of the incoming stimuli. For example, asking an individual to make judgments about whether a word just seen was in capital letters is an example of relatively shallow processing. Asking the person if the word would fit into a sentence that was presented just before the word is an example of deep processing (Craik & Tulving, 1975).

Research has demonstrated that the deeper the level of processing required, the larger the likelihood that mentally retarded individuals will have greater memory problems than their nonretarded peers (E. E. Schultz, 1983). In other words, the more complicated the memory task, the more likely it is that a retarded individual will have difficulties with it.

LEARNING STRATEGIES AND EXECUTIVE CONTROL PROCESSES (METACOGNITIVE PROCESSES). One of the primary reasons retarded individuals have problems on more complicated memory tasks is that they have difficulty using efficient learning strategies such as mediation and organization (Borkowski & Wanschura, 1974; Bray, 1979; Brown, 1974). An example of a mediation strategy is *rehearsal*. When given a list of words to remember, most individuals will rehearse the list aloud or to themselves in an attempt to "keep" the words in memory. Retarded students generally do not use rehearsal spontaneously (Borkowski & Cavanaugh, 1979).

One example of an organizing strategy is *clustering*. An example of clustering is the strategy of rehearsing serially presented items in groups. For instance, in trying to remember the digits 1, 7, 8, 5, 3, 4, it is easier to rehearse them in two

Developmental Versus Difference Theories of Cultural-Familial Retardation

There are two basic views of how culturally-familially retarded individuals differ from the nonretarded on cognitive tasks. Those who take a "difference" position (e.g., Ellis, 1982) maintain that retarded people learn in a way that is qualitatively different from that of the nonretarded. Some of these theorists attribute this different performance to structural defects in the retarded individual's brain.

Developmental theorists maintain that culturally-familially retarded individuals do not differ qualitatively from the nonretarded (Estes, 1970; Zigler & Balla, 1982). They believe that their differences are quantitative in nature in that they are slower to acquire knowledge or skills. They posit that culturally-familially retarded individuals go through the same stages of learning as do nonretarded persons, but at a slower rate.

Although far from conclusive, the evidence tends to favor the developmental position. For thorough coverage of the developmental versus difference debate, see Zigler and Balla's *Mental Retardation: The Developmental-Difference Controversy* (Hillsdale, NJ: Erlbaum, 1982).

clusters—178 and 534. There is a tendency, however, for retarded individuals not to do this spontaneously.

Many authorities have attributed retarded students' inefficient use of learning strategies such as rehearsal and clustering to the fact that their executive control processes are less well developed (Brown, 1974; Justice, 1985; Sternberg & Spear, 1985). **Executive control processes,** also called **metacognitive processes,** "are used to plan how to solve a problem, to monitor one's solution strategy as it is being executed, and to evaluate the results of this strategy once it has been implemented" (Sternberg & Spear, 1985, p. 303). Research has demonstrated that when confronted with learning problems, retarded individuals frequently have trouble picking the best strategies to use, monitoring the use of the strategies (keeping track of their own performance), and evaluating the use of strategies (knowing whether the strategies are working).

But even though retarded individuals have been found to be deficient in the spontaneous use of learning strategies and executive control processes, research has shown they can be taught to use such processes successfully (Glidden, 1985). More and more, teachers are emphasizing the use of executive control processes in working with retarded students.

Language Development

Many mentally retarded individuals have language and speech problems, for example, articulation errors. The greater the degree of retardation, the more severe the difficulties. In general, the language of retarded persons, especially those classified as mildly retarded, follows the same developmental course as that of nonretarded individuals. Their language development progresses at a slower rate, however.

Academic Achievement

Because of the strong relationship between intelligence and achievement, it is not surprising that retarded students lag well behind their nonretarded peers in all areas of achievement. They also tend to be underachievers in relation to expectations based on their intellectual level (MacMillan, 1982).

The self concepts of children with mental retardation are influenced by their friendships with peers. (Mark Downey)

Personality Characteristics

Mentally retarded individuals are candidates for a variety of social and emotional problems. In particular, they often have problems making friends (Luftig, 1988; Zetlin & Murtaugh, 1988) and have poor self-concepts (Leahy, Balla, & Zigler, 1982). There are at least two reasons why this may be so. First, some of their behavior may "turn off" their peers. For example, they engage in higher rates of inattention and disruptive behavior than their nonretarded classmates. Second, their nonretarded peers may shun them simply because they do not want to associate with people who are disabled. In either case, they end up having problems in social interactions with others. (See the box below, The Importance of Friendship.)

The Importance of Friendship

Professionals often overlook the importance of an area as fundamental as friendship. The following extract highlights the important role friendship can play in the lives of retarded people.

A sense of belonging, of feeling accepted, and of having personal worth are qualities brought to life through friendship. Friendship creates an alliance and a sense of security. It is a vital human connection.

Mentally retarded people want and need friendship like everyone else. Yet they are often denied opportunities to form relationships or to develop the skills necessary to interact socially with others. Their exposure to peers may be limited because they live and work in sheltered or isolated environments. They typically lack a history of socializing events such as school clubs, parties, or sleepovers that help to develop or refine personal skills. They may not know how to give of themselves to other people and may be stuck in an egocentric perspective. Retarded persons may also respond inappropriately in social situations unless instructed otherwise. Many people shun retarded individuals who freely hug or kiss strangers when greeting them. Some retarded persons have speech problems, making communication difficult. Other factors may further hinder their ability to attract and keep friends. Mildly retarded individuals often avoid associating with other retarded persons for fear of emphasizing their own stigma. The normal community, however, may be reluctant to incorporate these retarded individuals within their smaller social circles, given what are often real differences in interests.

With few contacts and opportunities, retarded persons may attempt to befriend strangers or unwitting individuals. Many attempt to become social acquaintances with their professional contacts. In their effort to maintain those contacts and relationships they have developed, some retarded individuals will overcompensate: calling their friend too many times, talking too long on the phone, demanding attention, and not being able to let up. Unfortunately, these behaviors tend to make people uncomfortable and hesitant to interact with retarded persons for fear that they will have to "hurt their feelings" at some later date. Some mentally retarded persons have also been victimized or exploited by some "friends"—a situation which unfortunately may be a normal risk.

A friend can play a vital role in the adjustment of a retarded individual to community living, by providing emotional support and guidance through the exigencies of daily life. Certain organizations have begun to address the mentally retarded adult's need for friends by constructing social opportunities with realistic peer groups. Examples of these include the Mohawks and Squaws, a social club for retarded adults in which members plan their own parties and projects, and Citizen Advocacy programs which sponsor one-to-one relationships between a community volunteer and a retarded individual for the purpose of aiding adjustment. Researchers in behavior training have also begun to devise strategies for teaching retarded individuals appropriate social skills, such as how to address strangers, initiate conversations, and respond in various social situations.

SOURCE: J. R. Patton and J. L. Spears, "Adult and Community Issues," in J. R. Patton, J. S. Payne, and M. Beirne-Smith (Eds.), *Mental Retardation*, 2nd ed. (Columbus, OH: Chas. E. Merrill, 1986, pp. 470–471). © 1986 Merrill Publishing Company. Reprinted by permission.

In addition to social-emotional problems, and perhaps to some degree because of these difficulties, many persons who are retarded have motivational problems (Balla & Zigler, 1979; Zigler & Balla, 1982). They tend to lack confidence in their own abilities. Believing that they have little control over what happens to them and that they are primarily controlled by other people or events, they have a tendency to give up easily when faced with challenging tasks.

EDUCATIONAL CONSIDERATIONS

Although there is some overlap, in general the focus of educational programs varies according to whether the students are mildly, moderately, or severely and profoundly retarded. For example, the lesser the degree of retardation, the more the teacher emphasizes academic skills, and the greater the degree of retardation the more stress there is on self-help, community living, and vocational skills. You need to keep in mind, however, that this distinction is largely a matter of emphasis; in practice, all teachers of retarded students, no matter what their severity level, need to teach academic, self-help, community living, and vocational skills.

The similarity between the educational needs of mildly and moderately retarded students is particularly evident. Although at one time there was more of a difference between the two populations, many authorities have noted that those who are identified as mildly retarded today tend to have greater disabilities than those of

Collaboration: A Key to Success

BRUCE G. WOJICK   *THEONE THOMAS HUG*

BRUCE: I see about seventy students daily, a few more boys than girls. They range in age from thirteen to sixteen; forty are white, twenty-eight are black, and two are Native American. Their handicapping conditions include mental retardation, learning disabilities, and emotional disturbance. Their reading grade equivalents range from 1.5 to 3.8; math from 3.0 to 5.2.

THEONE: I teach different groups of seventh- and eighth-grade students for ten weeks at a time. I see approximately 100 students daily and have four separate preparations per day just for the regular classes. My students range in age from twelve to sixteen. Classes include basic, average, and merited (gifted) abilities. I usually have one to three mainstreamed students per class who have mental retardation, learning disabilities, or behavioral disorders. For one ten-week period per year, I teach a self-contained class of no more than twelve students who have mental retardation and behavioral disorders. My classes have about the same ethnic composition as Bruce's. As a teacher with very little background in exceptional education, most of my learning has come from actual experience and trial and error. I find it extremely important that special education teachers give me a background on each student. I'm eager for their suggestions and find good communication and mutual backup and support a necessity for the student's success.

BRUCE: We've decided to describe our work with a student we'll call Cindy. Cindy was fourteen, an eighth-grader who was tall, was overweight, and had poor hygiene. She had poor gross motor coordination but adequate fine motor skills. Her reading and math were lower

than second-grade level. She had very poor social skills and was basically non-verbal. She started the school year with only one close friend, also nonverbal. She had a very limited attention span and a negative self-image, and she tended to daydream a lot. Her large stature, battle with adolescent skin problems, and unkempt hair contributed to the little effort her classmates made to befriend her. It was obvious she came from a poor background, where dress and neatness were unimportant.

THEONE: Cindy was introverted in her speech and social skills. She wouldn't volunteer, and she'd never bring any attention to herself. She always sat alone in the cafeteria. But she was cooperative with adults. She really tried her best to complete assignments. She always tried to contribute when we called on her, even though she wasn't always correct. She was very helpful and seemed to like being in school. Her attendance was good. In terms of learning, she was very slow and required extremely clear and repetitive instructions. Her total lack of self-esteem and extremely quiet nature made it necessary for her teachers to recognize when she needed help, as she wouldn't solicit any.

BRUCE: We immediately recognized that Cindy needed as much positive reinforcement as we could give her. She also needed to fit in with her peers in both our classes. So, as a team we decided that we would praise every effort she made, every response she gave. We made sure that we communicated about her work and efforts so that we could really just about double the positive reinforcement she would get.

THEONE: As a regular classroom teacher I make a special effort with every mainstreamed child to make him or her feel comfortable—an important part of my class. I start out by carefully planning an assignment that I'm almost certain the student can complete successfully, and I give this assignment the first few days the special student is in my class. When Cindy came to my class, I gave the entire class instructions about a project. Then, while they were working, I went around the room and repeated the instructions to several students, spending extra time with Cindy. Once I got her started and she seemed comfortable, I reminded her frequently to keep working and keep up the good effort. Then, after she completed the project, I used hers as an example for the rest of the class of what we were trying to achieve. This encouraged other kids in the class to accept her—they recognized her personal success. Of course, this raised her self-esteem, too. And I told Bruce about her success so that he could give her additional praise. I felt it was really important to build up Cindy's confidence. Once she got some confidence, I felt we'd see improvement in her academic work.

BRUCE: This kind of teamwork doesn't just happen. You see, once a student's schedule is completed by the special education department, I wait for at least a week to let the student get acquainted with each regular classroom teacher. Then I ask the student how he or she feels about each class and each teacher. It's really important that the student feel comfortable with the teacher I choose to team up with. The teachers who seem to show more interest in the students are the ones I always tend to work with on a closer basis. I want lots of positive reinforcement—praise, recognition for good behavior and achievement—to always be available from the regular teacher as well as from me. I believe that from the beginning Cindy felt fairly comfortable in both of our classes because of the positive reinforcement we agreed to give her. She got praise and encouragement from both of us, repeated over and over in and out of our classrooms.

THEONE: Yes, we felt we could work well together as teachers. But we were really frustrated by the lack of concern on the part of Cindy's parents. They did come to parent conferences, but it seemed to us that otherwise they didn't seem to care very much how Cindy was doing.

BRUCE: Any assignments or projects we gave Cindy to take home were always completed in school with our help. We're not saying that Cindy's parents never helped her, but on the other hand there wasn't much evidence that they did. Cindy was the type of student who needed constant praise and attention to overcome her difficulties. And as far as we could tell the only place she got this was in school. Our working with Cindy during the school day just wasn't enough. Every new week with Cindy was a fresh start on building up her self-esteem—it seemed like it just disappeared every weekend and holiday.

THEONE: Even so, we saw some really fantastic progress in Cindy in school. At the end of eight weeks in my class I gave an assignment to write a paper about a chosen career. Cindy chose baby-sitting. Students were supposed to find two pages worth of information, set it up in outline form, and eventually share it with the class as an oral report. This was a really, really big challenge for Cindy. Bruce and I both felt that our work had paid off when Cindy—well prepared, without hesitation—stood in front of the class and presented her report. She even looked at the class while she spoke! She had good information, and even showed pictures of babies and baby-sitters she had cut and mounted from magazines. Along with the pictures, she shared a photograph of herself as a baby with the rest of the class.

BRUCE. The most rewarding aspect of working together as colleagues is being able to share the simple smiles and accomplishments of the student. Actually to see the results of our efforts is reward in itself. Sharing always makes the reward doubly nice.

> I want lots of positive reinforcement . . . from the regular teacher as well as from me.

THEONE: I agree. And aside from the student-generated personal rewards is the professional reward. We both agree that being able to work with a colleague who is flexible, interested, and willing to communicate new ideas makes the work atmosphere more productive and enjoyable. Being able to work with a colleague who takes the time to listen, make suggestions, and honestly evaluate joint efforts promotes personal gratification through student successes. After years of teaching, this kind of cooperative experience renews your eagerness to be more effective.

BRUCE: Right. But it isn't easy to make this happen. Finding time during the school day for teachers to get together is next to impossible. The time the special student spends with the regular teacher is often the only break the special teacher has during the day. Theone and I agree that this problem of time or scheduling is the greatest barrier to working together.

THEONE: As a regular classroom teacher, I find I am often forgotten when it comes to giving me information about a mainstreamed student. Unfortunately, in the past the lack of communication has set up situations in which I didn't even know that students were being mainstreamed until several weeks after they came into my class! The way a special education teacher can help me most is to take the time to identify and give me a quick background on each student he or she is mainstreaming into my class.

BRUCE: I believe that it is my responsibility as the special education teacher to inform each receiving teacher of the student's potential, capabilities, idiosyncrasies, and so on. It's also my responsibility to acquaint myself with the mainstreamed class so that I can more realistically prepare an intelligent and rational IEP for the student.

THEONE: Sometimes there is an unfortunate tendency for the special education teacher to claim "sole ownership" of students. This can impair effective, cooperative working relationships and build impenetrable barriers.

BRUCE G. WOJICK:
Middle school special education teacher, Niagara Falls (New York) Public Schools; B.S.Ed., Exceptional Education (Mental Retardation) State University College of New York at Buffalo; M.S. Ed., Niagara University

THEONE THOMAS HUG:
Middle school home/career skills teacher; B.S.Ed., Home Economics Education, State University College of New York at Buffalo; M.S.Ed., Home Economics Education, State University College of New York at Buffalo

previous years (Epstein, Polloway, Patton, & Foley, 1989; Forness & Kavale, 1984; MacMillan, 1988; MacMillan & Borthwick, 1980; Polloway, 1985). This is particularly true of those who are taught in self-contained classes. There are at least three reasons for this shift to a more disabled population of mildly retarded students. First, the IQ cutoff score was changed from 85 to 75 or 70 in 1973. Second, there is now a greater hesitancy to label students mildly retarded because of the fear that the label will stigmatize the individual. Third, with the emphasis on mainstreaming as many disabled children as possible into general education classrooms, the ones who remain in self-contained settings tend to have relatively severe problems.

Because the educational programs for mildly and moderately retarded students are so similar, we choose to discuss the two together. We now review some of the major features of educational programs for (1) mildly and moderately retarded students and (2) severely and profoundly retarded students. Our focus here is on the elementary school level. We discuss preschool and secondary programming in later sections.

Education for Mildly and Moderately Retarded Students

Early elementary education is heavily oriented toward providing mildly and moderately retarded children with **readiness skills,** abilities that are prerequisites for later learning. They include such things as the ability to

1. Sit still and attend to the teacher
2. Discriminate auditory and visual stimuli
3. Follow directions
4. Develop language
5. Increase gross- and fine-motor coordination (e.g., hold a pencil or cut with a pair of scissors)
6. Develop self-help skills (e.g., tying shoes, buttoning and unbuttoning, zipping and unzipping, using the toilet)
7. Interact with peers in a group situation

The teacher provides instruction in language and concept development. In addition, the teacher needs to help these children in the rudiments of socialization. Programs are available for training socially adaptive behaviors. An example is ACCEPTS (A Curriculum for Children's Effective Peer and Teacher Skills) (Walker et al., 1983), a tightly structured and sequenced set of activities designed to teach children to get along with their peers.

In the later elementary years, there is greater emphasis on academics. The academics frequently taught, however, are what are known as functional academics. Whereas the nonretarded child is taught academics, such as reading, in order to learn other academic content, such as history, the retarded child is often taught reading in order to learn to function independently. In **functional academics** the child learns academics in order to do such things as read a newspaper, read the telephone book, read labels on goods at the store, make change, and fill out job applications.

Although emphasized much more in high school, moderately and even many mildly retarded children often need to learn the rudiments of community and vocational living skills in later elementary school (Hasazi & Clark, 1988). This is especially true of those students with mental retardation whose level of functioning is such that they must be taught in self-contained classes rather than mainstreamed settings (Epstein, Polloway, Patton, & Foley, 1989; MacMillan, 1988). The idea is that the lower the level of functioning, the longer it will take for the individual to learn particular skills; therefore, at the least, it is best to start acquainting mildly retarded students with these skills as early as elementary school.

Education for Severely and Profoundly Retarded Students

Most authorities agree that the following features should characterize educational programs for severely and profoundly retarded students:

1. Age-appropriate curriculum and materials
2. Functional activities
3. Community-based instruction
4. Integrated therapy
5. Interaction with nondisabled students
6. Family involvement

Age-Appropriate Curriculum and Materials

In the past there was a tendency to "baby" even older severely and profoundly retarded persons because of their intellectual limitations. Authorities now agree that this is not only demeaning but also educationally harmful (Bates, Renzaglia, & Wehman, 1981). Using infantile materials works against the goal of fostering as much independent behavior as possible.

Functional Activities

Because so much of educational programming for severely and profoundly retarded students is focused on preparing them to live as independently as possible, activities need to be practical (Bates, Renzaglia, & Wehman, 1981; Wehman, Moon, Everson, Wood, & Barcus, 1988). Learning to dress oneself by practicing on a doll, for example, is not as effective as practice with one's own clothes. Some severely and profoundly retarded students can learn some academic skills. Because teaching them basic reading and math is very time-consuming, it is important to teach only what they will need and can learn (Snell, 1988).

Community-Based Instruction

In keeping with the notion of functional skills, educational programs for students who are severely and profoundly retarded need to take place in the community as much as possible (Snell, 1988). Because many of the skills they learn are for use in settings outside the classroom, such as public transportation or the grocery store, instruction in such activities has proved more effective when done in those settings (Sailor et al., 1986). The teacher may wish to use simulated experiences in the classroom, by creating a "mini-grocery store" with a couple of aisles of products and a cash register, for example, to prepare students before they go to a real store. But such simulations by themselves are not enough. Severely and profoundly retarded students need the experience of going into those settings in which they will need to use the skills they are learning.

Integrated Therapy

Many severely and retarded persons have multiple disabilities, necessitating the services of a variety of professionals, such as speech, physical, and occupational therapists. In keeping with the notion of functional activities, many authorities believe it better that these professionals integrate what they do with students into the overall educational program rather than meeting with them alone in a

Appropriate vocational instruction for persons with mental retardation should take place in community settings. (MacPherson/Monkmeyer Press)

therapy room (Bates, Renzaglia, & Wehman, 1981; Snell, 1988). For example, they point out that it would be better to teach students how to walk up and down the actual stairs in the school they attend instead of using the specially made stairs that are traditionally placed in therapy rooms for this purpose (Snell, 1988).

Interaction with Nondisabled Students

Most authorities agree that it is beneficial for both severely and profoundly retarded students and their nondisabled peers to interact. One method some schools are trying involves having nondisabled students act as tutors or classroom helpers in classes for severely and profoundly retarded students.

Family Involvement

As we discuss in Chapter 11, family involvement is important for the success of educational programming for disabled students of all types and severity levels. It is particularly important for severely and profoundly disabled students, however, because many of the skills they are being taught will be used in their homes (Bates, Renzaglia, & Wehman, 1981). The involvement can range from simply informing parents about the progress of their children to having them act as classroom aides.

Using Applied Behavior Analysis to Teach Retarded Students

Although teachers use applied behavior analysis with all types of disabled students, it is particularly applicable with mentally retarded students, especially those with more severe learning problems. **Applied behavior analysis** is the application and evaluation of principles of learning theory in teaching situations. According to Wolery, Bailey, and Sugai (1988) it consists of six steps (See Table 3.2). First, the teacher identifies the overall goal. This usually consists of a skill area the student needs more work in or an inappropriate behavior that he or she needs to decrease. Second, further information is obtained on the identified skill area or behavior by taking a baseline measurement. The **baseline** measurement tells at what level the student is currently functioning; the teacher can later compare the student's perfor-mance after instruction with the original baseline performance. Third, the teacher decides on a specific learning objective; that is, he or she breaks down the overall goal into specific skills the child is to learn. Fourth, the teacher implements an

TABLE 3.2 Applied Behavior Analysis Teaching Model

Step	Procedures	Example 1	Example 2
1	Identify overall goals by us-ing broad problem state-ments.	Laura is behind in her math skills.	Lorenzo has trouble staying in his chair.
2	Gather specific information about the problem.	Laura can add single-digit problems with sums to 10, but cannot carry.	Lorenzo gets out of his seat an average of 15 times per hour.
3	Specify learning objectives.	Laura will add numerals with sums to 30, at a rate of at least 5 correct solutions per minute.	Lorenzo will stay in his seat for at least 10 minutes before getting up.
4	Plan and implement an in-tervention program.	Drill and practice first on sums to 20, no carry-ing required; then teacher instruction and modeling for carrying procedure. Bonus free choice during recess for 90% correct or better on daily work sheets.	Lorenzo loses 5 minutes of recess each time he gets out of his seat with-out permission.
5	Monitor student perfor-mance.	Teacher keeps daily record of accuracy on worksheets. Every Fri-day teacher conducts a 1-minute timing to de-termine rate of perfor-mance.	Teacher counts Lo-renzo's out-of-seat behavior during routinely selected periods, for a total of 20 minutes of ob-servation per day.
6	Evaluate student perfor-mance.	Teacher charts accu-racy and speed data weekly and uses infor-mation to decide whether or not a change is necessary.	Teacher keeps a daily chart of out-of-seat behavior. If Lor-enzo goes 3 days without any im-provement, she makes a change in consequences.

SOURCE: M. Wolery, D. B. Bailey, & G. M. Sugai, *Effective Teaching: Principles and Procedures of Applied Behavior Analysis with Exceptional Students* (Boston: Allyn & Bacon, 1988), p.24.

intervention designed to increase needed skills or decrease inappropriate behavior, for example, a drill and practice routine for math problems or a reward system for good behavior. Fifth, the child's progress is monitored by measuring performance frequently, usually daily. Sixth, the teacher evaluates the effects of the intervention, usually by charting the student's performance during intervention and comparing it with the baseline performance. Based on this evaluation, the teacher decides whether to continue, modify, or end the intervention.

Administrative Arrangements

We have already mentioned most of the kinds of administrative placements for mentally retarded children. The most common types are regular classes, resource rooms, special classes, special day schools, and residential facilities. The degree of retardation has a lot to do with which situation is most appropriate. Generally, this list is ordered from the least to the most severe. For example, mildly retarded children are more likely than severely retarded students to be found in resource rooms or regular classes.

As is true for the other areas of special education, resource room placement for retarded children is becoming more and more common. In this type of arrangement the child is in the regular classroom for part of the day or week and goes to a resource teacher for the rest of the time. For the most part, the resource room has been used with children in the mildly retarded range. Some instruction may take place in community settings, especially for older students.

Because the academic program of the typical moderately retarded child is generally restricted, it is uncommon to place children at that level or below in a resource room. Integration for moderately retarded students is usually in nonacademic activities such as physical education, music, or art. Probably the most common placement for these students is the special class. As with mildly retarded students, it is common for moderately retarded students to receive some instruction in the community. Although becoming more and more uncommon, a few moderately retarded children are also found in residential facilities. Residential placement for the moderately retarded child may be appropriate when other handicaps (such as deafness) are present and severe or when the family situation is undesirable.

For years, the traditional placement for the severely and profoundly retarded individual was the institution. With increased sophistication in dealing with the special problems of severely retarded individuals and the growing public commitment to their education, more and more of these children are being kept in the home, and large institutions are being depopulated.

The Community Residential Facility or Group Home

One administrative arrangement growing in popularity is the **community residential facility (CRF)** or group home. With the movement toward depopulation of large residential institutions, many formerly institutionalized individuals are now placed in small groups (three to ten people) in houses under the direction of house parents. The level of retardation of individuals in these homes ranges from mild to severe. Group homes have been established to accommodate children, adolescents, and adults, with each home focused on a specific age range. Placement in a CRF can be permanent or, with higher-functioning individuals, a temporary living arrangement to prepare the person for independent living (Sitkei, 1980). In either case, the purpose of the CRF is to teach independent living skills in a more normal setting. For many parents of retarded individuals, the CRF provides a positive and less stigmatized alternative to institutional placement.

EARLY INTERVENTION

We can categorize preschool programs for mentally retarded children as those whose purpose is to prevent retardation and those designed to further the development of children already identified as retarded. In general, the former address children who are at risk for mild retardation and the latter are for children who are moderately or severely and profoundly retarded.

Early Childhood Programs Designed for Prevention

The 1960s witnessed the birth of infant and preschool programs for at-risk children and their families. Since the late 1970s, when many of the young children placed in these programs were reaching their teenage years, we have been able to assess the effects of these programs. Investigators from twelve such projects decided to pool their data in 1976 when their original children ranged in age from nine to nineteen years (Lazar & Darlington, 1982). In 1984 a further follow-up study was done of one of the twelve projects, the Perry Preschool Project (Berrueta-Clement, Schweinhart, Barnett, Epstein, & Weikart, 1984). Begun in the early 1960s, the Perry Preschool Project was designed to answer the question "Can high-quality early childhood education help improve the lives of low-income children and their families and the quality of life of the community as a whole?" A sample of 123 three- and four-year-old black children, from impoverished backgrounds and having IQs between 60 and 90, were randomly assigned to an experimental group that received two years of a cognitively oriented curriculum or to a control group that received no preschool program. When studied again at nineteen years of age, a number of differences favored those who had received the preschool program over those who had not:

- They scored significantly higher on a test designed to measure skills needed for educational and economic success.
- They were more likely to complete high school and almost twice as likely to attend college or receive other postsecondary training (38 versus 21 percent).
- They were less likely to have been classified as handicapped, especially mentally retarded (15 versus 35 percent).
- They were more likely to be employed (50 versus 32 percent).
- They had a median annual income three times higher.
- They were more likely to report high levels of job satisfaction (42 versus 26 percent).
- They had a lower teenage pregnancy rate.
- They were less likely to be receiving welfare (19 versus 32 percent).

One of the best-known infant stimulation programs among those started more recently is the Abecedarian Project (Ramey & Campbell, 1984). Potential participants were identified before birth by selecting a pool of pregnant women living in poverty. For example, the typical child in this study came from a home headed by a single twenty-year-old black woman who had less than a high school education and no earned income. After birth, half of the identified infants were randomly assigned to a day-care program and half were not. The program provided them with experiences to promote perceptual-motor, intellectual, language, and social development. The families were also given a number of social and medical services. Results reported through second grade of the Abecedarian Project indicate that preschool educational programming can improve the IQ and achievement test scores of children at risk for eventually being identified as mildly retarded.

Early Childhood Programs Designed for Furthering the Development of Identified Mentally Retarded Children

Unlike preschool programs for at-risk children, in which the goal is to prevent retardation from developing, programs for moderately and severely and profoundly retarded infants and preschoolers are designed to help them achieve as high a cognitive level as possible. These programs place a great deal of emphasis on language and conceptual development. In addition, because these children often have multiple disabilities, other professionals—for example, speech therapists and physical therapists—are frequently involved. Also, many of the better programs include opportunities for parent involvement. Parents can reinforce through practice with their children some of the skills that teachers are working on. Parents of infants with physical disabilities, such as cerebral palsy, can learn from physical therapists the appropriate ways of handling their children to further their physical development, and from speech therapists they can learn appropriate feeding techniques.

TRANSITION

For many years there was relatively little programming for mentally retarded adults. Beginning in the late 1970s, however, there began to be a significant change in philosophy. The increased emphasis on integrating persons with retardation into the community, even those classified as severely and profoundly retarded, has resulted in much more attention to the needs of adults who are mentally retarded. In the mid-1980s the U.S. Department of Education made transition programming a priority.

Transition programming for individuals with mental retardation involves two related areas—community adjustment and employment. Most authorities agree that although the degree of emphasis on transition programming should be greater for older than for younger students, such programming should begin in the elementary years. Table 3.3 depicts some examples of curriculum activities across the school years pertaining to domestic, community living, leisure, and vocational skills.

One of the keys to effective transition programming is to include an individualized transition plan (ITP) as part of the student's individualized educational program (IEP). For an **individualized transition plan** to be effective, it should (1) be drawn up by school personnel as well as professionals from service agencies (e.g., Association for Retarded Citizens, vocational rehabilitation, and social services) who will be involved in implementing the plan once the student leaves school, (2) be drawn up at least by the time the student is sixteen years old, and (3) include longitudinal goals for community and vocational adjustment (Wehman, Moon, Everson, Wood, & Barcus, 1988).

Community Adjustment

For persons with mental retardation to adjust to living in the community, they need to acquire a number of skills, many of which are in the area of self-help. Researchers have found, for example, that successful living in the community depends on such things as the ability to manage money, prepare meals, maintain a clean house, and keep one's clothing and oneself groomed (Schalock & Harper, 1978; Schalock, Harper, & Carver, 1981). In addition, the degree of family involvement

TABLE 3.3 **Examples of Curriculum Activities Across the School Years for Domestic, Community Living, Leisure, and Vocational Skills**

Elementary School Student: Tim

Skill Areas

Domestic	Community	Leisure	Vocational
Picking up toys	Eating meals in a restaurant	Climbing on swing set	Picking up plate, silverware, and glass after a meal
Washing dishes	Using restroom in a local restaurant	Playing board games	Returning toys to appropriate storage space
Making bed	Putting trash into container	Playing tag with neighbors	Cleaning the room at the end of the day
Dressing	Choosing correct change to ride city bus	Tumbling activities	Working on a task for a designated period (15–20 minutes)
Grooming	Giving the clerk money for an item he wants to purchase	Running	
Eating skills		Playing kickball	
Toileting skills			
Sorting clothes			
Vacuuming			

Junior High School Student: Mary

Skill Areas

Domestic	Community	Leisure	Vocational
Washing clothes	Crossing streets safely	Playing volley ball	Waxing floors
Cooking a simple hot meal (soup, salad, and sandwich)	Purchasing an item from a department store	Taking aerobic classes	Cleaning windows
Keeping bedroom clean	Purchasing a meal at a restaurant	Playing checkers with a friend	Filling lawn mower with gas
Making snacks	Using local transportation system to get to and from recreational facilities	Playing miniature golf	Hanging and bagging clothes
Mowing lawn		Cycling	Bussing tables
Raking leaves	Participating in local scout troop	Attending high school or local college basketball games	Working for 1–2 hours
Making a grocery list	Going to neighbor's house for lunch on Saturday	Playing softball	Operating machinery (such as dishwasher, buffer, etc.)
Purchasing items from a list		Swimming	Cleaning sinks, bath tubs, and fixtures
Vacuuming and dusting living room			Following a job sequence

TABLE 3.3 (continued)

High School Student: Sandy

Skill Areas

Domestic	Community	Leisure	Vocational
Cleaning all rooms in place of residence	Utilizing bus system to move about the community	Jogging	Performing required janitorial duties at J. C. Penney
Developing a weekly budget	Depositing checks into bank account	Archery	Performing house-keeping duties at Days Inn
Cooking meals	Using commu-nity depart-ment stores	Boating	Performing grounds-keeping duties at VCU campus
Operating thermostat to regulate heat or air condi-tioning	Using commu-nity restau-rants	Watching college basketball	Performing food ser-vice at K St. Cafeteria
Doing yard maintenance	Using commu-nity grocery stores	Video games	Performing laundry duties at Moon's Laundromat
Maintaining personal needs	Using commu-nity health facilities (phy-sician, phar-macist)	Card games (UNO)	Performing photogra-phy at Virginia Na-tional Bank Head-quarters
Caring for and maintaining clothing		Athletic club swim-ming class	
		Gardening	
		Going on a vacation trip	

SOURCE: Adapted from P. Wehman, M. S. Moon, J. M. Everson, W. Wood, & J. M. Barcus, *Transition from School to Work: New Challenges for Youth with Severe Disabilities* (Baltimore: Paul H. Brookes, 1988), pp. 140–142.

is important for the community adjustment of retarded individuals (Schalock & Lilley, 1986). Successful community placement is easier when the family of the person with retardation becomes actively involved in the integration process. In general, research has shown that attempts to train community survival skills can be successful, especially when the training occurs within the actual setting in which the individuals are to live.

One of the keys to being able to live in the community is ensuring that the citizenry is prepared to accept persons with retardation. Even those individuals who are able to live independently (i.e., not in a community residential facility) may require some special accommodations. Although there are not a lot of data available, one survey of landlords renting to individuals with mental retardation indicated that a substantial number of landlords do have some problems (Salend & Giek, 1988). Examples of these problems were independent living difficulties, such as failing in the upkeep of the property and overdependence on the landlord, and deviant behavior, such as playing the television too loudly. Fortunately, most of these kinds of problems could be avoided by providing landlords with a modest degree of information and assistance before they rent to the retarded tenant.

Employment

Traditionally, the employment figures for retarded adults have been appalling (Hasazi, Collins, & Cobb, 1988; Hasazi et al., 1985; Wehman, Moon, Everson, Wood & Barcus, 1988). One statewide survey, for example, found that of retarded students who had graduated from high school between 1980 and 1984, only 41 percent were employed full or part time in the competitive job market and 82 percent were living with their families (Hasazi et al., 1985).

Even though employment statistics for retarded workers have been pessimistic, most professionals working in this area are very optimistic about the potential for providing training programs that will lead to meaningful employment for mentally retarded people. Research indicates that with appropriate training, retarded workers can hold down jobs with a good deal of success, as measured by such things as attendance, employer satisfaction, and length of employment (Brown et al., 1986; Martin, Rusch, Tines, Brulle, & White, 1985; Rusch, Martin, & White, 1985; Stodden & Browder, 1986).

When retarded adults do fail on the job, they do so because they have problems related to job responsibility, task production competence, and/or social competence (Salzberg, Lignugaris/Kraft, & McCuller, 1988). Table 3.4 illustrates behaviors commonly associated with each of these problems. Contrary to popular opinion, there is considerable evidence suggesting that job responsibility and social competence are more important than task production competence as reasons for job termination of mentally retarded workers (Greenspan & Shoultz, 1981; Salzberg, Lignugaris/ Kraft, & McCuller, 1988).

There are a variety of vocational training and employment approaches for individuals with mental retardation. Most of these are subsumed under two very different kinds of arrangements—the sheltered workshop or the nonsheltered work environment, or competitive employment.

Professionals and students alike recognize the importance of transition programming—preparing handicapped students to move from high school to the workforce. (Mimi Forsyth/ Monkmeyer Press)

Sheltered Workshops

The traditional job-training environment for mentally retarded adults, especially those classified as moderately or more severely retarded, has been the sheltered workshop. A **sheltered workshop** is a structured environment where a retarded person receives training and works with other disabled workers on jobs requiring relatively low skills. This can be either a permanent placement or a transitional placement before a person obtains a job in the competitive job market.

Although they remain a relatively popular placement, more and more authorities are voicing their dissatisfaction with sheltered workshops (Wehman, Moon, Everson, Wood, & Barcus, 1988). Among their criticisms, they cite the following:

1. Clients only make between one and five dollars per day. Sheltered workshops rarely turn a profit. Usually managed by personnel with only limited business management expertise, they rely heavily on charitable contributions.
2. There is no integration with nondisabled workers. This restricted setting makes it difficult to prepare retarded workers for working side by side with nondisabled workers in the competitive work force.
3. They offer only limited job-training experiences. A good workshop should provide opportunities to learn a variety of new skills. All too often, however, the work is repetitive and does not make use of current industrial technology.

TABLE 3.4   Summary of Behaviors Commonly Related to Involuntary Termination

Job Responsibility	Task Production Competence	Social-Vocational Competence	
		Task-related Social Competence	Personal-Social Competence
1. Poor attendance	1. Low rate of work	1. Not following and/or clarifying instructions	1. Bizarre, emotional, and aggressive behavior
2. Poor punctuality	2. Low quality of work	2. Not responding appropriately to criticism	2. Inappropriate conversation
3. Not attending consistently to job tasks	3. Lack of independent performance	3. Not interacting appropriately with co-workers and supervisors	3. Loud, vulgar, or sexually explicit behavior
4. Not calling in when late or absent	4. Inability to learn new tasks	4. Not requesting assistance when needed	4. Inappropriate dress, grooming, or eating
5. Stealing	5. Inability to perform diversity of tasks	5. Not requesting information when needed	5. Dirty appearance or excessive body odor
6. Lack of initiative		6. Not cooperating with co-workers	6. Absence of or excessive verbalizing
7. Lack of motivation			7. Emotional response to teasing or job pressure
8. Walking off the job			

SOURCE: C. L. Salzberg, B. Lignugaris/Kraft, & G. L. McCuller, *Research in Developmental Disabilities*, 9 (1988), 168.

Competitive Employment

In contrast to sheltered employment, **competitive employment** is a job that provides at least the minimum wage in a workplace in which most of the workers are nondisabled. Although the ultimate goal for some adults with mental retardation may be competitive employment, many will need supported competitive employment for a period of time or even permanently. In **supported competitive employment,** the retarded worker has a competitive employment position but receives ongoing assistance, often from a job coach.

THE ROLE OF THE JOB COACH. The major responsibilities for the **job coach**

> may include job identification and development, vocational assessment and instruction, transportation planning, and interactions with parents, employers, Social Security, and other related service agencies. Job coaches provide on-site training to clients which addresses not only actual job tasks, but also social skill development and independent living skills. They monitor employee progress through performance observation and communication with employers and coworkers. (Berkell, 1988, pp. 164–165)

OVERCOMING DEPENDENCE ON THE JOB COACH. One potential problem with the supported competitive employment model is that the client can become too dependent on the support provided by the job coach (Lagomarcino, Hughes, & Rusch, 1989). If they are to move into a competitive employment setting, retarded workers must learn to function independently, and even if they stay in a supported situation, it is important that they develop as much independence as possible.

To combat overdependence on the job coach, authorities have recommended that professionals teach retarded employees to use self-management techniques (Lagomarcino, Hughes, & Rusch, 1989; Rusch & Hughes, 1988; Rusch, Martin, & White, 1985; Wheeler, Bates, Marshall, & Miller, 1988). Rusch and his colleagues have noted that four self-management procedures are particularly effective in helping persons with mental retardation become more independent on the job: (1) picture cues, (2) self-instruction, (3) self-monitoring, and (4) self-reinforcement.

Picture cues provide a visual prompt to workers to help them perform work tasks. For example, on an assembly task the worker might prearrange the various parts on corresponding pictures in the order in which they are to be assembled. There is some evidence suggesting that picture cues are not as effective with severely and profoundly retarded persons as they are with mildly and moderately retarded workers (Martin, Mithaug, & Burger, 1990).

Self-instruction involves saying aloud that which one is about to do. For example, the job coach might teach the worker to say aloud each major step in performing a task before he or she does it.

Self-monitoring involves workers observing their own performance and then recording it. For example, they might observe and record the number of times they are late for work per week.

Self-reinforcement entails workers rewarding themselves for appropriate performance. For example, a person might reward himself or herself with a night at the movies for having gone two consecutive weeks without being late for work.

Teachers have also successfully used self-instruction, self-monitoring, and self-reinforcement in classroom instruction with a variety of exceptional children. In particular, teachers have used them with learning-disabled children (see Chapter 4).

Prospects for the Future

Although current employment figures for mentally retarded adults may look bleak, there is reason to be optimistic about the future. Surveys indicate that although the sheltered workshop remains the most common work environment for retarded adults, placement into competitive employment is increasing (Schalock, McGaughey, & Kiernan, 1989). With the development of innovative transition programs, many persons with mental retardation are achieving levels of independence in community living and employment that were never thought possible.

It is important to keep in mind, however, that in most cases the family still remains an extremely important source of support for the adult with retardation who lives in the community (Zetlin, Turner, & Winik, 1987). (See Chapter 11 for more discussion on the importance of the family.) They often play a critical role in helping the mentally retarded person find a job, for example (Hasazi, Collins, & Cobb, 1988). Furthermore, families can lend a hand in domestic and community living as the need arises. Through the joint supportive efforts of professionals and families, then, persons with retardation are enjoying greater and greater levels of independence in their living and working environments.

SUGGESTIONS FOR TEACHING STUDENTS WITH MENTAL RETARDATION IN GENERAL EDUCATION CLASSROOMS

What to Look for in School

Although children with moderate and severe and profound mental retardation are identified before entering school, children who are mildly retarded typically are identified during the school years. Like children with learning disabilities, mildly retarded students experience difficulties in attention, language, and memory. For example, they may have difficulty beginning assignments promptly and staying on task. They also develop motor, language, social, and independent skills more slowly than most students in a class. In addition, many students with mild mental retardation have short-term memory problems and do not know how to use learning strategies that nondisabled students seem to use spontaneously.

Furthermore, mildly retarded students usually have difficulty learning in all academic areas, and they acquire new skills at a slower rate than nondisabled students. However, teachers can help them master many of the concepts and skills presented in elementary school if they

- Divide learning materials into small segments or steps
- Carefully sequence these steps from simplest to most difficult
- Use concrete examples and experiences to teach concepts
- Teach learning strategies
- Provide much drill and practice to promote mastery
- Give consistent feedback and reinforcement.

How to Gather Information

If you think one of your students may be mentally retarded, collect several examples of his or her work in arithmetic, reading, and writing. Show these samples along with your observations of the student's motor, language, and social behaviors to the special educator, counselor, or administrator in your building who manages the child study committee. This committee considers the persistent problems of individual students in school and suggests modifications that may promote their learning and/or appropriate school behavior. If these modifications do not result in improvement, the committee may recommend the student receive a full educational, medical, sociological, and psychological evaluation for special education. Student work samples, your records, and your observations will provide necessary information to the child study committee.

Teaching Techniques to Try

To give the repeated practice and individual help mentally retarded students need in a large, heterogeneous class, you may decide to use peer tutoring, a technique that under certain conditions has been shown to benefit both tutor and tutee academically, behaviorally, and socially. In student tutoring programs teachers typically provide instruction to all class members. Then students in the class (peer tutors) or older students (cross-age tutors) who have mastered the learning assist those individuals who require additional instruction and practice during regularly scheduled tutorial sessions. Tutors can take on a variety of responsibilities such as reviewing lessons, directing and monitoring the performance of newly learned skills, and providing feedback and reinforcement. Planning, supervising, and evaluating a peer tutoring program, however, requires careful planning and supervision by the teacher. Several studies and reviews (Gerber & Kauffman, 1981; Jenkins & Jenkins, 1985; Knapczyk, 1989) indicate that the following conditions are necessary if peer tutoring is to be effective:

1. Tutor training includes such skills as understanding the instructional objective(s), discrimination between correct and incorrect responses, delivery of corrective feedback and reinforcement, monitoring progress and record keeping, and appropriate interpersonal skills.
2. Well-defined behavioral objectives reflect the regular class curriculum.
3. Instructional steps are carefully sequenced and clearly outlined in a lesson format so that tutors can follow easily.
4. Instruction continues in a single skill or concept until the tutee has mastered that learning.
5. Easily identifiable tutee responses are required that tutors can consistently recognize and then correct or reinforce.
6. Tutors monitor and record tutee performance on instructional objectives during each session.
7. Teachers actively monitor both tutor and tutee performance frequently.
8. Teachers deliver frequent reinforcement consistently to the tutor and the tutee contingent on their appropriate performance.
9. Tutorial sessions are scheduled at least two or three times each week, each meeting lasting approximately fifteen to thirty minutes.
10. Tutors provide examples from all settings in which tutees are to use the learning.

To start a student tutoring program, Jenkins and Jenkins (1985) suggest that you first identify those students who require additional instruction and then pinpoint the curricular objectives in which they need extra help. After designing a lesson format that is instructionally sound and easily implemented by the tutors, you will want to select tutors, making parents aware of the program and obtaining their permission. Once parents and tutors have agreed, training that provides information on the purpose and specific obligations of being a tutor can begin. Training may include such topics as these (Jenkins & Jenkins, 1985, p. 11):*

- Responsibilities of tutors, which can serve as the criteria for later tutor evaluation
- Class attendance and grading policies
- Individual differences
- Active listening
- Nonverbal messages
- Instructional techniques
- Behavior management techniques
- Goal setting
- Motivation
- Monitoring progress
- Critical attributes of a good tutor

---

* Specific training information is available from Joseph Jenkins, director of the Experimental Education Unit, Child Development and Mental Retardation Center, University of Washington, Seattle.

After the training is completed and tutorial sessions have begun, it is important for you to monitor the first lessons carefully and to schedule debriefing sessions with the tutors in which you provide feedback on their performance. As the student tutors become more proficient you can reduce the frequency of the debriefing sessions. Scheduling additional brief weekly meetings in which tutors check on the assignments and the progress of their tutee gives them needed information and an opportunity to ask for suggestions and to discuss problems. Offering this support to tutors along with your personal attention not only improves the quality of the tutoring but also helps maintain tutors' interest in the program.

Educators (Asselin & Vasa, 1983) have suggested several ways in which you can evaluate the effectiveness of your student tutoring program. Systematic observations, for example, provide information about students' attitudes and performance. Developing a checklist or rating scale that compares the tutor's role description with the tutor's performance gives you data regarding the specific responsibilities each tutor is fulfilling. A time log completed by the tutor following each session provides further information about the tutoring activities that can be used both to give feedback to the students and to plan and prepare instructional materials. Asselin and Vasa further suggest considering the following questions in your evaluation (p. 82):

1. Is the role description accurate for the tutor?
2. Is the tutor training program effective?
3. How has the attitude of the student being tutored been affected by the tutoring?
4. Is the student being tutored maintaining and improving skills?
5. What effect has the program had on the tutor?
6. How has the tutoring program affected the teacher's preparation and instruction time?
7. What are the attitudes of teachers toward the program?

Reverse Mainstreaming

Another educational arrangement in which students help other students is reverse mainstreaming. As you know from reading Chapter 2, this program involves a few nondisabled students participating in some of the activities conducted in special education classrooms. Their participation helps disabled students learn appropriate behaviors such as social and language skills while promoting within the nonhandicapped children an awareness of special education students and classes (Dean & Nettles, 1987; McCann, Semmel, & Nevin, 1985). Although teachers are using reverse mainstreaming with increasing frequency, to date they have implemented it most often during play activities in preschool classes (Fitzgerald, 1985; McCann, Semmel, & Nevin, 1985; Odom, Deklyen, & Jenkins, 1984). Typically teachers select nondisabled student volunteers who demonstrate socially appropriate behaviors. After obtaining the permission of their parents and, in some cases, after giving introductory information about special needs children, teachers invite these volunteers into special education classes during play periods.

In one reverse mainstreaming program, Project Special Friend, volunteers interacted with severely retarded children in such activities as fingerpainting, putting puzzles together, and playing ball for as long as thirty minutes a day (Poorman, 1980). As in student tutoring programs, teachers and aides carefully monitored the interaction between special friends, "modeling procedures, answering questions, and keeping control of the activity" (p. 141).

As you can see, implementing successful peer tutoring or reverse mainstreaming programs requires careful teacher planning and consistent monitoring and adjusting. Therefore, these programs must be judged by the teacher to be appropriate and effective alternatives to other types of instruction for all students (Gerber & Kauffman, 1981). Alternative teaching techniques discussed in the Suggestions for Teaching in General Education Classrooms sections in this book include such methods as behavior modification, strategy training, and cooperative learning.

Helpful Resources

School Personnel

The special educator who also teaches your mentally retarded student may provide additional instructional suggestions that have been successful in improving performance. This teacher also can recommend, and perhaps obtain, learning materials that are designed for special education students and suggest ways in which regular class materials can be adapted for retarded students. In addition, he or she can recommend books on a variety of subjects that are of high interest to older students and written at lower reading levels. Finally, this teacher and the school psychologist are good resources for specific cognitive and behavioral information about your student.

Instructional Methods

Fowler, G. L., & Davis, M. (1985). The storyframe approach: A tool for improving reading comprehension. *Teaching Exceptional Children, 17,* 296–298.

Horton, S. (1983). Delivering industrial arts instruction to mildly handicapped learners. *Career Development for Exceptional Individuals, 6,* 85–92.

Isaacson, S. (1988). Teaching written expression; directed reading and writing; self-instructional strategy training; and computers and writing instruction. *Teaching Exceptional Children, 20,* 32–39.

Jenson, W. R., Sloane, H. N., & Young K. R. (1988). *Applied behavior analysis in education: A structured teaching approach.* Englewood Cliffs, NJ: Prentice-Hall.

O'Shea, L., & O'Shea, D. (1988). Using repeated readings. *Teaching Exceptional Children, 20,* 26–29.

Polloway, E. (1989). *Strategies for teaching retarded and special needs learners* (4th ed.). Columbus, OH: Chas. E. Merrill.

Robinson, G. A., & Polloway, E. A. (Eds.). (1987). *Best practices in mental disabilities. Volume One.* Des Moines: Iowa State Department of Education, Bureau of Special Education.

Schloss, P. J., & Sedlak, R. A. (1982). Behavioral features of the mentally retarded adolescent: Implications for mainstreamed educators. *Psychology in the Schools, 19,* 98–105.

Curricula

Carnine, D., Silbert, J., & Kameenui, E. J. (1990). *Direct instruction reading.* Columbus, OH: Chas. E. Merrill.

Dixon, B., & Engelmann, S. (1979). *Corrective spelling through morographs.* Chicago: Science Research Associates.

Engelmann, S., & Bruner, E. (1974). *DISTAR reading.* Chicago: Science Research Associates.

Engelmann, S., & Bruner, E. C. (1983): *Reading mastery.* Chicago: Science Research Associates.

Engelmann, S., Carnine, D., Johnson, G., & Meyers, L. (1988). *Corrective reading: Decoding.* Chicago: Science Research Associates.

Engelmann, S., Carnine, D., Johnson, G., & Meyers, L. (1989): *Corrective reading: Comprehension.* Chicago: Science Research Associates.

Silbert, J., & Carnine, D. (1981). *Direct instruction mathematics.* Columbus, OH: Chas. E. Merrill.

Literature About Mentally Retarded Individuals

ELEMENTARY: AGES 5–8 AND 9–12

Carrick, C. (1985). *Stay away from Simon!* New York: Carion. (Ages 8–11)

Clifton, L. (1980). *My friend Jacob.* New York: E. P. Dutton. (Ages 6–10)

Gillham, B. (1981). *My brother Barry.* London: A. Deutsch. (Ages 9–12)

Rabe, B. (1988). *Where's Chimpy?* Berkeley, CA: Gray's Book Company. (Ages 4–7)

Shyer, M. F. (1988). *Welcome home, Jellybean.* New York: Aladdin.

Wright, B. R. (1981). *My sister is different.* Milwaukee, WI: Raintree. (Ages 5–8)

SECONDARY: AGES 13–15

Hill, D. (1985). *First your penny.* New York: Atheneum.

Hull, E. (1981). *Alice with golden hair.* New York: Atheneum.

Miner, J. C. (1982). *She's my sister.* Mankato, MN: Crestwood House. (Reading levels: grades 3–4; interest level: grades 7–12)

Slepian, J. (1980). *The Alfred summer.* New York: Macmillan.

Software

Bobo's Park, Academic Technologies, Inc.; (609) 778–4435 (life skills).

Coinsnkeys, Castle Special Computer Services, Inc., 9801 San Gabriel N.E., Albuquerque, NM 87111; (505) 293–8379 (coin recognition and counting).

Comparative Buying Series, MCE, 157 S. Kalamazoo Mall, Suite 250, Kalamazoo, MI 49007.

Computer CUP, Amidon Publications, 1966 Benson Avenue, St. Paul, MN 56116; (612) 690–2401. (Nine discs teach basic concepts such as "right-left," "as many," "beginning.")

Financing a Car, MECC, 3490 Lexington Avenue N., St. Paul, MN 55112.

First Day on the Job, MECC, 3490 Lexington Avenue N., St. Paul, MN 55112.

Job Success Series, MCE, 157 S. Kalamazoo Mall, Suite 250, Kalamazoo, MI 49007.

Language L.A.B., Specialsoft, P.O. Box 1983, Santa Monica, CA 90406; (800) 421–6534.

Library and Media Skills, Educational Activities, 1937 Grand Avenue, Baldwin, NY 11510.

Library Skills, Micro Power & Light Company, 12820 Hillcrest Road, Suite 219, Dallas, TX 75230.

Spell It!, Davidson & Associates, 6069 Groveoak Place, Suite 12, Rancho Palos Verdes, CA 90274.

Telling Time, Random House, 400 Hahn Road, Westminister, MN 21157.

Vocabulary Challenge, Learning Well, 200 S. Service, Roslyn Heights, NY 11577.

Vocabulary Game, J & S Software, 140 Reid Avenue, Port Washington, NY 11050.

Ways to Read Words, Intellectual Software, 798 North Avenue, Bridgeport, CT 06606.

Whole Brain Spelling, SubLogic, 713 Edgebrook Drive, Champaign, IL 61820.

Work Habits for Job Success, MEC, 157 S. Kalamazoo Mall, Suite 250, Kalamazoo, MI 49007.

World of Work, Computer Age Education, 1442A Walnut Street, Suite 341, Berkeley, CA 94709.

Organizations

American Association on Mental Retardation, 1719 Kalorama Road, N.W., Washington, DC 20009; (202) 387–1968.

Association for Children with Retarded Mental Development, 162 Fifth Avenue, 11th floor, New York, NY 10010; (212) 741–0100.

Association for Retarded Citizens, P.O. Box 6109, Arlington, TX 76005; (817) 640–0204.

Mental Retardation Division of the Council for Exceptional Children, 1920 Association Drive, Reston, VA 22091; (703) 620–3660.

Bibliography for Teaching Suggestions

Asselin, S. B., & Vasa, S. F. (1983). The use of peer tutors in vocational education to assist mildly handicapped students. *Career Development for Exceptional Individuals, 6*, 75–84.

Dean, M., & Nettles, J. (1987). Reverse mainstreaming: A successful model for interaction. *The Volta Review, 89*, 27–34.

Fitzgerald, N. B. (1985, March). Competencies and contexts of friendship development in a reverse mainstreamed preschool. Paper presented at the Annual Meeting of the American Educational Research Association, Chicago (ERIC Document Reproduction Service No. ED 262 876).

Gerber, M., & Kauffman, J. M. (1981). Peer tutoring in academic settings. In P. S. Strain (Ed.), *The utilization of classroom peers as behavior change agents* (pp. 155–187). New York: Plenum Press.

Jenkins, J., & Jenkins, L. (1985). Peer tutoring in elementary and secondary programs. *Focus on Exceptional Children, 17*, 1–12.

Knapczyk, D. R. (1989). Peer-mediated training of cooperative play between special and regular class students in integrated play settings. *Education and Training in Mental Retardation, 24*, 255–264.

McCann, S. K., Semmel, M. I., & Nevin, A. (1985). Reverse mainstreaming: Nonhandicapped students in special education classrooms. *Remedial and Special Education, 6*, 13–19.

Odom, S. L., Deklyen, M., & Jenkins, J. R. (1984). Integrating handicapped and nonhandicapped preschoolers: Developmental impact on nonhandicapped children. *Exceptional Children, 51*, 41–48.

Poorman, C. (1980). Mainstreaming in reverse with a special friend. *Teaching Exceptional Children, 12*, 136–142.

SUMMARY

Professionals are generally more cautious about identifying students as retarded than they once were. The definition of the American Association on Mental Retardation reflects this concern. The AAMR definition posits that *both* intellectual and adaptive behavior are important; indeed, if there is adequate adaptive behavior, a person is not considered retarded.

The most commonly accepted approach to classification is to consider retarded people along a continuum of degree of severity. Most professionals favor using the AAMR classification system, which uses the terms *mild, moderate, severe,* and *profound.* These terms help minimize negative stereotyping. Some educators also use the classifications *educable, trainable,* and *severely and profoundly* retarded.

From a purely statistical-theoretical viewpoint, 2.27 percent of the population should score low enough on an IQ test (below about 70) to qualify as retarded. Most recent figures indicate, however, that 1.21 percent of the population from six to seventeen years of age is identified as retarded by the public schools. The discrepancy may be due to three factors. First, low adaptive behavior as well as low tested IQ is needed to consider an individual retarded. Second, school personnel tend to be cautious about labeling minority children. Third, parents and school professionals may prefer to have children labeled "learning disabled" rather than "mentally retarded" because they perceive it as less stigmatizing.

A variety of factors can cause mental retardation, but in very few cases, especially among the mildly retarded population, can we actually specify the cause. Most people with mild retardation are considered culturally-familially retarded, a term professionals use to include causes related to poor environmental and/or hereditary factors. Although the nature-nurture debate has raged for years, most authorities now believe that *both* heredity and the environment are important factors in determining intelligence. We can categorize causes of moderately to severely retarded individuals as due to genetic factors or brain damage. Down syndrome, PKU, and Tay-Sachs disease are all examples of genetic causes. Brain damage can be the result of infectious diseases—for example, meningitis, encephalitis, rubella, and pediatric AIDS—or environmental hazards, such as poisons (e.g., cocaine and alcohol) and excessive radiation. Premature birth can also result in mental retardation. With amniocentesis, chorionic villus sampling, or sonography, physicians are now able to detect a variety of defects in the unborn fetus.

Although there are now tests that purportedly minimize cultural bias—for example, the SOMPA and K-ABC—the Wechsler Intelligence Scale for Children–Revised (WISC–R) and the Stanford-Binet continue to be the two that psychologists most commonly use. These cautions regarding use and interpretation of IQ tests are in order: (1) An individual's IQ score can change. (2) IQ tests are culturally biased to a certain extent. (3) The younger the child, the less reliable the results. (4) A person's ability to live a successful and fulfilling life does not depend solely on his or her IQ. In addition to IQ tests, several adaptive behavior scales are available.

Individuals with mental retardation have learning problems related to attention, memory, language, and academics. Two important concepts when considering cognitive problems are depth of processing and executive control or metacognitive processes. Depth of processing refers to how much cognitive activity a person has to undergo to perform a task. Individuals with retardation process information at a shallower level than nonretarded people. Executive control or metacognitive processes refer to ability in planning, monitoring, and evaluating one's own performance. Individuals with retardation have problems with executive control processes. In addition to cognitive problems, mentally retarded students often have behavioral and personality problems. For example, they often have trouble making friends, poor self-esteem, and difficulties with motivation.

Educational goals for mildly and moderately retarded students are quite similar. At younger ages there is an emphasis on readiness skills, and at the older ages there is more emphasis on functional academics and vocational training. Functional academics are academics for the purpose of enabling the person to function independently. Educational programs for severely and profoundly retarded students are characterized by (1) age-appropriate curriculum and materials, (2) functional activities, (3) community-based instruction, (4) integrated therapy, (5) interaction with nondisabled students, and (6) family involvement. Applied behavioral analysis—the application and evaluation of principles of learning theory—is often the method of choice for teachers working with retarded students.

Depending to a large extent on the degree of retardation, schools may place students in general education classrooms, resource rooms, special classes, special day schools, or residential facilities. Although mildly and moderately retarded children are usually placed in special classes, more and more of them, especially those classified as mildly retarded, are being educated in resource rooms and general education classrooms. The deinstitutionalization movement has resulted in many more severely and profoundly retarded students attending self-contained classes in public schools.

Preschool programming differs in its goals according to whether the program is aimed at preventing retardation or furthering the development of children already identified as retarded. For the most part, the former types of programs are aimed at children at risk to develop mild retardation, whereas the latter are for moderately, severely, and profoundly retarded children.

Transition programming for individuals with mental retardation has mushroomed. Curricular goals related to transition include activities in domestic, community living, leisure, and vocational skills. Although the emphasis on transition programming increases with age, authorities recommend that such efforts begin in elementary school. The employment picture for workers with retardation is changing. Although sheltered work environments remain popular, authorities have pointed out their weaknesses: (1) Wages are very low. (2) There is no integration with nondisabled workers. (3) They only offer limited job-training experiences. Placement of retarded workers in supported competitive employment is becoming more and more prevalent. In supported competitive employment the worker (1) receives at least a minimum wage, (2) works in a setting with mostly nondisabled workers, and (3) receives assistance from a job coach. Many authorities are advocating the use of self-management techniques (e.g., picture cues, self-instruction, self-monitoring, and self-reinforcement) to help retarded workers function more independently. Although employment figures are discouraging, the growth in innovative transition programs gives reason to be optimistic regarding the future of community living and employment for the adult retarded population.

FLOWER GARDEN
Eleanor Hackett, Creative Growth Art Center

4

Learning Disabilities

and report cards I was always afraid to show
Mama'd come to school
and as I'd sit there softly cryin'
Teacher'd say he's just not tryin'
Got a good head if he'd apply it
but you know yourself
it's always somewhere else

I'd build me a castle
with dragons and kings
and I'd ride off with them
As I stood by my window
and looked out on those
Brooklyn roads

(*Neil Diamond, "Brooklyn Roads"*)

eil Diamond's "Brooklyn Roads" (see page 121) expresses the frustrations often felt by the learning-disabled child. Such children, as usually defined, have learning problems in school even though they may be no less intelligent than their nondisabled classmates. They have difficulty in one or more academic areas. Reading, in particular, looms as a major stumbling block. Learning-disabled children are also apt to be hyperactive and inattentive. In the early school years their parents may see them as simply overenergetic. Later this unconcern may turn to desperation when, unlike their playmates, these children fail to outgrow their ungovernable ways and poor school performance.

It is such desperation that has led many parents of children with learning disabilities to seek miracle cures. Professionals also sometimes fall for what seem to be quick and easy solutions to the array of problems presented by the learning-disabled child. In no other area of special education have so many fads been so intensely embraced. But the field of learning disabilities is unusual because it is a blend of the old and the new. Even though it is the most recent formal category of special education, its roots lie deep in other areas of the field, particularly mental retardation. It is for this reason that the discipline of learning disabilities has often served as a testing ground for new ideas and a battleground for old wars. Issues debated years ago concerning other exceptionalities have frequently resurfaced in slightly different forms. It has been encouraging to see the renewal of some of these controversies, for they have taught us something; and it is refreshing to see a positive response to innovation. Though many of the methods and approaches introduced to the field of learning disabilities have eventually been discarded as unworkable, others have not.

The lyrics of Diamond's song might well apply to children in other categories of exceptionality, particularly behaviorally disordered children, with whom learning-disabled children have much in common. This recalls the old chicken-and-egg dilemma: Does the learning disability cause behavioral disorders or vice versa? How realistic *is* it to attempt to determine causes? How can we tell whether a child really has a learning problem or is "just not tryin'"? It is to the critical question of definition that we turn first.

DEFINITIONS

The field of learning disabilities is the newest category of special education. It was at a parents' meeting in New York City in the early 1960s that Samuel Kirk proposed this term as a compromise because of the confusing variety of labels then being used to describe the child with relatively normal intelligence who was having learning problems. Such a child was likely to be referred to as being *minimally brain injured*, a *slow learner*, *dyslexic*,* or *perceptually disabled*. However, many parents as well as teachers believed the label *minimal brain injury* to be problematic. **Minimal brain injury** refers to individuals who show behavioral, but not neurological, signs of brain injury. They exhibit behaviors (e.g., distractibility, hyperactivity, and perceptual disturbances) similar to those with real brain injury, but their neurological examinations are indistinguishable from those of nondisabled individuals. The diagnosis of minimal brain injury was sometimes dubious because it was based on questionable behavioral evidence rather than more solid neurological data. Also, the label often carried with it the notion of irreversibility, leading some professionals to give up on trying to change such children's behavior. Moreover,

---

* **Dyslexia** refers to a severe impairment of the ability to read.

MISCONCEPTIONS
ABOUT PERSONS WITH LEARNING DISABILITIES

Myth	*Fact*
All learning-disabled children have brain damage.	Although more learning-disabled children show solid evidence of damage to the central nervous system than their nondisabled peers, many of them do not. Many authorities now refer to learning-disabled children as having central nervous system *dysfunction,* which indicates a malfunctioning of the brain rather than actual tissue damage. Some professionals hold that even the use of the term *dysfunction* is problematic because its diagnosis is not exact.
It is valuable for the teacher to know whether the child's learning disability is due to brain damage.	Although the diagnosis of brain injury may be important for the medical professional, educators gain no useful information from it.
A child who is mixed-dominant (e.g., right-handed, left-eyed, left-footed, and right-eared) will have a learning disability.	Although there is a slight *tendency* for mixed dominance to occur more frequently in learning-disabled children, many children who are mixed-dominant learn normally.
All learning-disabled children have perceptual problems.	Although perceptual problems are more frequent in learning-disabled children, many do not have them.
Hyperactive children's most serious problem is excessive motor activity.	Although hyperactive children do exhibit excessive motor activity, most authorities now believe their most fundamental problems lie in the area of inattention.
Using drugs to control hyperactivity is simply a matter of the physician prescribing the right pill.	To use drugs effectively is a highly complex affair. The parents, physician, teacher, and child must maintain close communication to monitor the drug's effects.
Professionals and parents need not be concerned about learning-disabled children's social and emotional well-being because their problems are in learning, not social adjustment.	Many children with learning disabilities also develop problems in the social-emotional area. We may have a tendency to overlook this fact because of our emphasis on the learning problems of learning-disabled children. Programming for these students also needs to address their social adjustment.
Learning-disabled students exhibit disorders of language, reading, and writing much more than problems in math.	Math problems are more prevalent than was once thought. It has been estimated that two out of three learning-disabled children receive special instruction in math and one out of four receives special education services primarily because of math problems.
Perceptual and perceptual-motor training will automatically lead to academic gains (e.g., in reading).	There is very little research to support the notion that such training will automatically lead to academic gains. The most that can be said, and the research is equivocal even on this, is that perceptual training may increase perceptual skills, which can then serve as the basis for academic remediation.
Most learning-disabled children outgrow their disabilities as adults.	Most learning-disabled adults still have some learning difficulties, especially in reading and spelling. With intensive and long-term intervention, however, many learning-disabled adults lead successful and productive lives. More and more learning-disabled students are attending college.

it was not an educationally meaningful label because such a diagnosis offered little real help in planning and implementing treatment. The term *slow learner* described the child's performance in some areas but not in others—and besides, intelligence testing indicated that the *ability* to learn existed. *Dyslexic*, too, fell short as a definitive term because it described only reading disabilities, and many of these children had problems in other academic areas such as math. To describe a child as *perceptually disabled* just confused the issue further, for perceptual problems might be only part of a puzzling inability to learn. So it was finally around the educationally oriented term *learning disabilities* that the New York parents' group rallied to found the Association for Children with Learning Disabilities, now known as the Learning Diabilities Association of America. Following the lead of the parents, a few years later the professionals officially recognized the term by forming the Division for Children with Learning Disabilities, now called the Division for Learning Disabilities, of the Council for Exceptional Children, the major professional organization concerned with the education of exceptional children.

The interest in learning disabilities evolved as a result of a growing awareness that a large number of children were not receiving needed educational services. Because they were within the normal range of intelligence, these children did not qualify for placement in classes for retarded children. In addition, although many of them did show inappropriate behavior or personality disturbances, some of them did *not*. Thus it was felt that placement in emotionally disturbed classes was inappropriate. Parents of children who were not achieving at their expected potential—*learning disabled* children—wanted their children's *academic achievement* problems corrected.

Factors to Consider in Definitions of Learning Disabilities

Eleven different definitions of learning disabilities have enjoyed some degree of acceptance since the field's inception in the early 1960s (Hammill, 1990). Created by individual professionals and committees of professionals and lawmakers, each definition provides a slightly different slant. There are four factors—each of which is included in some definitions, but not all—that have historically caused considerable controversy:

1. IQ—achievement discrepancy
2. Presumption of central nervous system dysfunction
3. Psychological processing disorders
4. Learning problems not due to environmental disadvantage, mental retardation, or emotional disturbance

We discuss these factors briefly and then present the two most commonly used definitions.

IQ–Achievement Discrepancy

An **IQ–achievement discrepancy** means that the child is not achieving up to potential as measured, usually, by a standardized intelligence test. The child with an IQ–achievement discrepancy or *academic* retardation, then, is one who fails to achieve at the level of his or her intellectual abilities. For many years, most professionals agreed that an IQ–achievement discrepancy was the least debatable characteristic of learning-disabled children. Recently, however, some have begun to question the notion of such a discrepancy, especially with respect to how one measures it.

"Your feelings of insecurity seem to have started when Mary Lou Gurnblatt said, 'Maybe I don't have a learning disability—maybe you have a teaching disability.'"
SOURCE: J. H. Crouse and P. T. McFarlane, "Monopoly, Myth, and Convivial Access" to the Tools of Learning, *Phi Delta Kappan*, 56(9)(1975), 593. Drawn by Tony Saltzman.

Environmental Factors

Environmental causes are difficult to document. There is much evidence showing that environmentally disadvantaged children are more prone to exhibit learning problems. It is still not certain if this is due strictly to inadequate learning experiences or to biological factors such as brain damage or nutritional deprivation (Cravioto & DeLicardie, 1975; Hallahan & Cruickshank, 1973).

Another factor that has been named as a possible environmental cause of learning disabilities is poor teaching (Engelmann, 1977; Lovitt, 1977). Some believe that if teachers were better prepared to handle the special learning problems of children in the early school years, some learning disabilities could be avoided.

MEASUREMENT

It is now a commonly accepted idea that psychological and educational testing must be oriented toward providing relevant information for educational program-ming. Scores on a test are meaningless unless they can be translated into educational recommendations. This "diagnosis for teaching" rather than for identification is sometimes referred to as *prescriptive teaching* (Peter, 1965). Prescriptive teaching, then, is the writing of an educational prescription in the form of educational tasks on the basis of diagnostic information gained from testing and observing the child.

Four methods of testing are popular in the field of learning disabilities:

1. Standardized achievement tests
2. Process tests
3. Informal reading inventories
4. Formative evaluation methods

Standardized Achievement Tests

The most common test for learning-disabled children is the standardized achieve-ment test because achievement deficits are the primary characteristic of these children. The fact that the test is standardized means it has been administered to a large group of children so that any one child's score can be compared to the norm, or average. Most of these tests are relatively easy and inexpensive to administer. Standardized achievement tests can be designed to assess either multiple areas or just one area of achievement.

One limitation to most standardized tests is that you cannot use them to gain insight into the "whys" of a student's failure. Teachers and clinicians primarily use standardized achievement tests to identify students with learning problems and to provide gross indicators of academic strengths and weaknesses. After using a standardized test, teachers sometimes administer a process test, or even more often they use an informal reading inventory or a formative evaluation method. As we discuss, these measurement procedures provide much more specific information regarding a student's strengths and weaknesses, thus making them more usable for educational programming.

Process Tests

The use of tests of psychological processes to diagnose underlying processing* deficiencies is one of the innovations brought to the field of special education by the discipline of learning disabilities. Some have not viewed this practice as a blessing. *Process testing* is the assessment of those psychological (usually perceptual or linguistic) processes, one or more of which the tester assumes is (are) the cause(s) of the child's academic problem. With this approach, the child with a reading difficulty is not treated simply for his or her reading problems. Tests are given to identify the particular psychological process in which the child is deficient. Remediation is then planned accordingly. That is, the educational program focuses on the underlying process problem rather than directly on the reading problem.

Opponents of process testing note that these tests tend to be low in their predictive validity for academic failure. Predictive validity here refers to whether one can predict the score a child will obtain on an achievement test on the basis of his or her score on the process test. It is obviously important for a test to have good predictive validity if it is to be educationally useful. Reviews of the literature (e.g., Hallahan & Cruickshank, 1973; Hammill & Larsen, 1974) indicate that some of the most popularly used instruments in this area have *not* been demonstrated to be good predictors of academic achievement.

Two typical process tests are the Illinois test of Psycholinguistic Abilities (ITPA) (Kirk, McCarthy, & Kirk, 1961, 1968) and the Marianne Frostig Developmental Test of Visual Perception (DTVP) (Frostig, Lefever, & Whittlesey, 1964). Samuel Kirk and his colleagues developed the ITPA on a psycholinguistic model that includes *channels, levels of mental organization*, and *processes*. The test features subtests covering (1) auditory-vocal and visual-motor channels; (2) representational (meaningful) and automatic (nonmeaningful) levels of organization; and (3) receptive, associative, and expressive representational processes as well as the automatic processes of memory and closure. Although research has not substantiated the predictive validity of the ITPA, its introduction had at least one positive impact on the field of special education. Kirk designed the ITPA primarily for the purpose of gathering educationally relevant information, and this notion of using assessment information to help design educational programming was a relatively novel idea in the early 1960s. The ITPA thus helped bring about an awareness that psychological and educational testing should be sensitive to the educational needs of the child.

---

* *Processing* refers to what takes place after an individual has perceived something through the senses—how he or she interprets or puts the perception to meaningful use intellectually.

Marianne Frostig and her colleagues designed the DTVP to assess various aspects of visual perception thought to be crucial to reading. Like the ITPA's attempt to evaluate different areas of psycholinguistic functioning, the DTVP purports to measure relatively specific facets of visual perception. The five areas it covers are eye-motor coordination, figure-ground discrimination, constancy of shape, position of objects in space, and spatial relationships of objects.

Informal Reading Inventories

A common method of assessment used by teachers in the area of reading is an informal reading inventory (IRI). An IRI is

> a series of reading passages or word lists graded in order of difficulty. A student reads from the series of lists or passages, beginning with one that the teacher thinks is likely to be easy. As long as the reading does not become too difficult, the student continues to read from increasingly harder lists or passages. As the student reads, the teacher monitors performance and may record the kinds of reading errors a student makes (e.g., omitted word, mispronunciation, reversal). When an IRI is made up of passages, the teacher may ask questions after each one to help estimate the student's comprehension of the material. Depending on the student's accuracy in reading and answering questions, various levels of reading skill can be ascertained. . . . In general, the kind of material that a student can read with a certain degree of ease is considered to be at his or her *independent, instructional*, or *frustration level*. (Hallahan, Kauffman, & Lloyd, 1985, p. 210)

Because of the growing disenchantment with formal, or standardized, tests, particularly those that are process oriented, there has been a trend toward the greater use of informal inventories. The major drawback to IRIs is that their reliability and validity depend on the skills of the teachers constructing them. In the hands of a skilled teacher, however, they can be invaluable for determining what level of reading material the student should be working on as well as for pinpointing specific reading deficits.

Formative Evaluation Methods

Although some authorities have espoused them since the 1960s, formative evaluation methods began receiving a great deal of attention in the 1980s (e.g., Deno, 1985; Fuchs, 1986; Fuchs & Fuchs, 1986; Germann & Tindal, 1985; Marston & Magnusson, 1985; White & Haring, 1980). **Formative evaluation methods** directly measure a student's behavior to keep track of his or her progress. Formative evaluation is less concerned with how the student compares with other students and more concerned with how the student compares with himself or herself. Although there are a variety of different formative evaluation models, at least five features are common to all of them:

1. The assessment is usually done by the child's teacher rather than a school psychologist or diagnostician.
2. The teacher assesses behaviors directly relevant to classroom functioning. Whereas process testing concerns behaviors that are purported to be related to behaviors relevant to classroom success, formative evaluation involves observation and recording of such behaviors directly. For instance, if the teacher is interested in measuring the child's pronunciation of the letter *l*, he or she

looks at that particular behavior and records whether the child can pronounce that letter.

3. The teacher observes and records the child's behavior frequently and over a period of time. Most other kinds of tests are given once or twice a year at the most. In formative evaluation performance is measured at least two or three times a week.

4. The teacher uses formative evaluation to assess the child's progress toward educational goals. After an initial testing, the teacher establishes goals for the child to reach in a given period of time. For example, if the child can orally read 25 words correctly in one minute out of a certain book, the teacher may set a goal, or criterion, of being able to read 100 words correctly per minute after one month. This aspect of formative evaluation is sometimes referred to as **criterion-referenced testing.**

5. The teacher uses formative evaluation to monitor the effectiveness of educational programming. For instance, in the preceding example, if after a few days the teacher realizes that it is unlikely that the child will reach the goal of 100 words, the teacher can try a different educational intervention.

Curriculum-Based Assessment

Curriculum-based assessment (CBA) is a particular model of formative evaluation. Although drawing heavily on earlier research, CBA was largely developed by Deno and his colleagues (Deno, 1985; Fuchs, Deno, & Mirkin, 1984).

Because it is a type of formative evaluation, CBA has the five features just listed. In addition, it has two other distinguishing characteristics. First, it is designed to measure children's performance on the particular curriculum to which they are exposed. In spelling, for example, a typical CBA assessment strategy is to give children two-minute spelling samples, using dictation from a random selection of words from the basal spelling curriculum, the number of words or letter sequences correctly spelled serving as the performance measure. In math, the teacher may give the children two minutes to compute samples of problems from the basal text and record the number of digits computed correctly. Proponents of CBA state that this reliance on the curriculum is an advantage over commercially available standardized achievement tests, which are usually not keyed to the curriculum in any particular school.

Second, CBA compares disabled children's performance to that of their peers in their own school or school division. Deno and his colleagues advocate that the teacher take CBA measures on a random sample of nondisabled students so that this comparison can be made. Comparison with a local reference group is seen as more relevant than comparison with national norming groups used in commercially developed standardized tests.

Research on the Effectiveness of Formative Evaluation

Research indicates that formative evaluation results in positive changes for both teachers and learning-disabled students. Teachers who use CBA (1) have more specific goals for monitoring progress, (2) have more objective information for assessing whether students are meeting their goals, and (3) are more likely to introduce instructional modifications than are teachers who do not use CBA (Fuchs, Fuchs, & Strecker, 1989).

Several studies indicate that students make more progress when their teachers use CBA. These studies also demonstrate that the effectiveness of CBA is enhanced if the teacher (1) uses prescribed rules for deciding when to change a student's educational program because it is not working, (2) measures performance at least twice weekly, (3) writes goals for students that promote task persistence, and (4) writes goals that focus on **generalization** and **maintenance** (Fuchs, 1986). Generalization refers to being able to demonstrate in one situation or setting (e.g., Ms. Kirk's class) that which one has learned in another situation or setting (e.g., Mr. Cruickshank's class). Maintenance refers to being able to demonstrate something that one learned some time ago (e.g., two or three months ago). Both generalization and maintenance, especially the former, are very difficult for learning-disabled students.

PSYCHOLOGICAL AND BEHAVIORAL CHARACTERISTICS

A variety of characteristics have been attributed to learning-disabled children. A national task force, recognizing the proliferation of terms and labels in this area, found ninety-nine characteristics reported in the literature (Clements, 1966). The ten most frequently found symptoms were these:

1. Hyperactivity
2. Perceptual-motor impairments
3. Emotional lability (frequent shifts in emotional mood)
4. General coordination deficits
5. Disorders of attention (short attention span, distractibility, preservation)
6. Impulsivity
7. Disorders of memory and thinking
8. Specific academic problems (reading, arithmetic, writing, spelling)
9. Disorders of speech and hearing
10. Equivocal neurological signs and EEG irregularities

We cover most of these characteristics in the following discussion, but for purposes of organization we group similar ones together.

It is important to keep in mind that not all these characteristics are found in every learning-disabled child; any individual student is likely to exhibit only a few. The broad range of disabilities makes it exceedingly difficult for practitioners and researchers alike to work with and study learning-disabled children. Researchers are beginning to make progress, however, in breaking this heterogeneous population into discrete subgroups (see the box on p. 134).

Perceptual, Perceptual-Motor, and General Coordination Problems

Studies indicate that some children with learning disabilities exhibit visual and/or auditory perceptual disabilities (Hallahan, 1975). These problems are not the same as visual and auditory acuity problems evidenced by blind or deaf individuals. Rather these are disturbances in organizing and interpreting visual and auditory stimuli. A child with visual perceptual problems might, for example, have trouble solving puzzles or seeing and remembering visual shapes. A child with auditory perceptual problems might have difficulty discrimininating between two words that sound alike (e.g., *fit* versus *fib*) or reciting poetry.

Teachers and parents have also noted that some learning-disabled children have

Coping with the Heterogeneity of Persons with Learning Disabilities: The Search for Subtypes

For years the wide range of problems displayed by learning-disabled students has stymied teachers and researchers. Teachers have found it difficult to plan educational programs for the diverse group of children they find in their classrooms; and the heterogeneity of the learning-disabled population has produced nightmares for researchers, who worry about whether inconsistent results from study to study are indeed real or are caused by variations in children selected for one study versus another.

Since the inception of the learning disabilities field, investigators have searched for the existence of subgroups, or subtypes (e.g., Bateman, 1968; Boder, 1973; Ingram, 1969; Johnson & Myklebust, 1967; Kinsbourne & Warrington, 1963). The research of these early investigators, who relied on clinical intuition to direct their research efforts, was methodologically limited, but it did provide the impetus for more objective endeavors (McKinney, 1987a).

Using more sophisticated statistical techniques, researchers began in the late 1970s to make progress on documenting subtypes of learning disabilities. There are now a number of research teams focused on the task of discovering the most useful ways to subtype learning-disabled children. Perhaps the most fruitful of all these teams has been the one led by James D. McKinney (e.g., McKinney & Feagans, 1984; McKinney, Short, & Feagans, 1985; McKinney & Speece, 1986; Speece, McKinney, & Applebaum, 1985).

McKinney has continued to follow a sample of sixty-three first- and second-graders who were first identified as learning disabled in 1978. As part of the project, investigators have documented the existence of subtypes within three different domains: (1) perceptual-cognitive, (2) language, and (3) behavioral. Thus far, most of their research has focused on subtypes within the behavioral area. Using teachers' ratings on four bipolar dimensions (task orientation/distractibility, independence/dependence, introversion/extroversion, and considerateness/hostility), they have found evidence for seven different behavioral subtypes:

- *Subtype 1: Attention Deficit.* This subtype is characterized by inattention and dependent behavior. It is also the largest group, representing about 29 percent of the sample.
- *Subtype 2: Normal Behavior.* Although this subtype has slightly elevated ratings on considerateness and introversion, all behaviors are within normal limits. This subtype comprised about 25 percent of the sample.
- *Subtype 3: Conduct Problems.* Representing about 14 percent of the sample, this subtype is characterized by mild attention deficits and high hostility and distractibility.
- *Subtype 4: Withdrawn Behavior.* Made up mostly of girls, this subtype exhibits dependent and introverted behavior. Eleven percent of the sample falls into this subtype.
- *Subtype 5: Normal Behavior.* Although this subtype has slightly elevated ratings on hostility, like subtype 2 all of the ratings are within the normal range. It contains about 10 percent of the sample.
- *Subtype 6: Low Positive Behavior.* Children in this subtype are characterized by low ratings on all of the positive behaviors—that is, task orientation, independence, extroversion, considerateness—but without high ratings on the negative counterparts of those behaviors—that is, distractibility, dependence, introversion, hostility. This subtype contains about 6 percent of the sample.
- *Subtype 7: Global Behavior Problems.* Representing only about 5 percent of the sample, this subtype is characterized by extremely negative ratings on all the behaviors.

McKinney and his colleagues have come up with a number of educationally relevant findings relative to these subtypes. Two of their most important findings are these:

1. There was some movement in classification from one subtype to another. However, if a child was originally classified in one of the maladaptive subtypes, he or she was five times more likely to be classified still in a maladaptive subtype than to move into an adaptive one. One of the most important trends was for children in the attention deficit subtype to move into one of the problem behavior subtypes.
2. Although children in the various subtypes did not differ from each other in achievement at the beginning of the study when they were in the first and second grades, over the next two years there were different achievement outcomes based on subtype membership. Students in the normal behavior and withdrawn subtypes progressed well academically, but those in the attention deficit subtype and the behavior problem subtypes (3, 6, and 7) deteriorated academically.

These findings hold promise for helping educators plan educational programs for learning-disabled children. For example, McKinney (1989) speculates that because all of the learning-disabled students in the sample were receiving resource room services over the course of the two years, this type of placement may not be appropriate for those with attention deficits and behavior problems. They may require more intensive services. There is also the related question of whether particular types of teaching approaches, for example, those emphasizing behavioral principles, are more or less effective with certain behavioral subtypes. McKinney and his colleagues are currently designing research to answer questions related to whether certain subtypes are more or less responsive to different educational strategies.

difficulty in physical activities involving motor skills. They describe some of these children as having "two left feet" or "ten thumbs." The problems involve both fine-motor (small motor muscles) and gross-motor (large motor muscles) skills. Fine-motor skills often involve the coordination of the visual and motor systems.

Several of the early theorists in the learning disabilities field believed that there is a causal link between perceptual problems and learning disabilities, especially reading disabilities. They believed that by training visual perceptual skills, for example, learning-disabled students would read better. However, research has shown that perceptual training does not improve the reading skills of learning-disabled students.

Disorders of Attention and Hyperactivity

Numerous studies have documented the existence of attention problems and hyperactivity in a large percentage of learning-disabled children. These estimates have ranged from as low as 33 percent to as high as 80 percent (Shaywitz & Shaywitz, 1987). Even the lowest estimates suggest that attention disorders and hyperactivity are frequently encountered problems in learning-disabled students. Similarly, although a child can have attention problems and hyperactivity without also having a learning disability, the prevalence of learning disabilities is considerably higher among children who are inattentive and hyperactive.

The Relationship between Attentional Problems and Hyperactivity

Professionals and laypeople alike often use the terms *attentional problems* and *hyperactivity* interchangeably. They do so with good reason, for research has shown

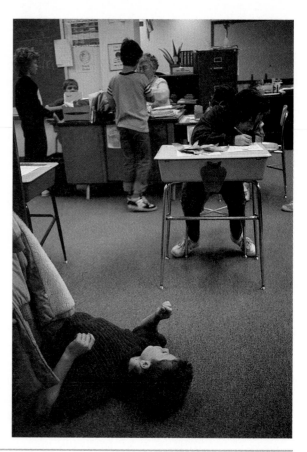

Hyperactivity is one of the most frequently mentioned characteristics of children with learning disabilities. Most experts agree that attentional problems are at the heart of most hyperactive children's problems. (Grant LeDuc/Monkmeyer Press)

that the relationship between the two is a strong one. In addition, most authorities agree that attentional problems are more basic than hyperactivity problems (Hallahan, Kauffman, & Lloyd, 1985; Henker & Whalen, 1989; Shaywitz & Shaywitz, 1987). In other words, the major problems of most children labeled "hyperactive" lie more in the area of attention difficulties than in the area of excessive motor activity.

The psychiatric profession also recognizes the prominence of attentional problems in hyperactive children. Its members do not clinically refer to children as "hyperactive" without also attaching the label "attention deficit," and they refer to such individuals as having an attention-deficit hyperactivity disorder (ADHD) (American Psychiatric Association, 1987). In addition to attentional problems and hyperactivity, the American Psychiatric Association also includes impulsivity as a feature of those identified as having ADHD. Not surprisingly, substantial research documents the existence of impulsive rather than reflective thinking in learning-disabled students (Hallahan, Kauffman, & Ball, 1973; Heins, Hallahan, Tarver, & Kauffman, 1976). The American Psychiatric Association lists fourteen behaviors that indicate ADHD. The threads of *inattention, hyperactivity,* and *impulsivity* are woven throughout these diagnostic criteria:

(1) often fidgets with hands or feet or squirms in seat (in adolescents, may be limited to subjective feelings of restlessness)
(2) has difficulty remaining seated when required to do so
(3) is easily distracted by extraneous stimuli

(4) has difficulty awaiting turn in games or group situations

(5) often blurts out answers to questions before they have been completed

(6) has difficulty following through on instructions from others (not due to oppositional behavior or failure of comprehension), e.g., fails to finish chores

(7) has difficulty sustaining attention in tasks or play activities

(8) often shifts from one uncompleted activity to another

(9) has difficulty playing quietly

(10) often talks excessively

(11) often interrupts or intrudes on others, e.g., butts into other children's games

(12) often does not seem to listen to what is being said to him or her

(13) often loses things necessary for tasks or activities at school or at home (e.g., toys, pencils, books, assignments)

(14) often engages in physically dangerous activities without considering possible consequences (not for the purpose of thrill-seeking), e.g., runs into street without looking (pp. 52–53)

To be diagnosed as ADHD a child must (1) display at least eight of the preceding criteria, (2) exhibit these criteria much more frequently than most people of the same mental age, (3) show the onset of these criteria before seven years of age, and (4) have had the criteria for at least six months.

Disorders of Memory and Thinking

Memory

Many learning-disabled children demonstrate memory deficits for both auditory and visual stimuli (Hallahan, 1975; Swanson, 1987; Torgesen, 1988; Torgesen & Kail, 1980). Joseph Torgesen has been one of the most active researchers in this area. Based on his work, we can make two important generalizations about learning-disabled children who have memory problems:

1. They are deficient in using *strategies* that nondisabled children use in situations requiring memory. For example, most children, when presented with a list of words to memorize, will rehearse the names to themselves. They will also make use of categories by rehearsing words in groups that go together. Learning-disabled children, however, do not generally use these strategies spontaneously.

2. They find it especially difficult to remember verbal material because they have particular problems with phonological information. **Phonology** refers to the sounds, or phonemes, that make up words.

Thinking

Thinking can be defined in a number of ways. Among other things, thinking involves the ability to solve problems and to conceptualize. The ability to think, broadly considered, is what is generally thought of as "intelligence." So it is not surprising that very little consideration was originally given to the thought processes of learning-disabled children because they are commonly regarded as being of normal intelligence.

Metacognition is an extremely important aspect of thinking, and many learning-disabled students are particularly deficient in metacognitive abilities (see Hallahan, Kneedler, & Lloyd, 1983; Hallahan, Lloyd, Kauffman, & Loper, 1983; Kneedler &

Hallahan, 1984; Short & Weissberg-Benchell, 1989 for reviews of this literature). **Metacognition** has two components:

(1) An awareness of what skills, strategies, and resources are needed to perform a task effectively and (2) the ability to use self-regulatory mechanisms to ensure the successful completion of the task, such as planning one's moves, evaluating the effectiveness of one's ongoing activities, checking the outcomes of one's efforts, and remediating whatever difficulties arise. (Baker, 1982, pp. 27–28).

An example of learning-disabled students' difficulties with the first component—awareness of skills, strategies, and resources—was evident in a study conducted by Torgesen (1977) in which he asked children how they would go about remembering different things. When asked such questions as "Suppose you lost your jacket while you were at school, how would you go about finding it?" learning-disabled students could not produce as many strategies as their nondisabled peers.

Some examples of the second component of metacognition—ability to self-regulate—are contained in the box below. These examples focus on a particular type of self-regulation—comprehension monitoring. **Comprehension monitoring** refers to metacognitive abilities employed while one reads and attempts to comprehend textual material.

Social Adjustment

Emotional lability—frequent changes in mood—can be viewed as a particular aspect of personality and social maladjustment. Laypeople, and even some professionals,

Comprehension Monitoring

How often have you been reading along in a novel, a magazine, or some other material and suddenly realized that for the past few seconds, maybe even minutes, you've not really been comprehending it? Perhaps thoughts of tomorrow's meeting with the principal intruded. Or maybe you were thinking of more important matters, such as whether or not you should go to a movie this evening. Or maybe you weren't thinking of anything in particular—your mind just wandered. You needn't be overly concerned if you have experienced these lapses of concentration. Even the best readers tune out on occasion. Actually, the very fact that you recognize that you're not comprehending is a strong indication that you are a good reader. By catching yourself in the act of not paying attention, you are displaying a skill that researchers are finding of utmost importance in reading comprehension. You are demonstrating *comprehension monitoring skills.* The learning disabled, however, are apparently more susceptible than most of us to those stray thoughts of what movie to watch tonight. Researchers believe their problem is due to their lack of a repertoire of skills that help them organize their approach to the task of reading.

CRITICAL COMPREHENSION MONITORING SKILLS PINPOINTED

In the last few years there has been an explosion of interest in comprehension monitoring. The results of recent studies (by individuals from a wide geographical range such as Thomas Anderson and Ann Brown at the University of Illinois, Linda Baker at the University of Maryland, Candace Bos at the University of Arizona, Scott Paris at the University of Michigan, and Bernice Wong at Simon Fraser University in Canada) have led to a number of important conclusions regarding the comprehension monitoring skills needed to be a good reader. These researchers have summarized their findings with the following points:

—*Clarifying the Purposes of Reading*. Before efficient readers begin to read, they have a mind-set regarding the general purpose of their reading. They approach reading to obtain the gist of a news article with a different mind-set than the one they use for reading to gain information from a textbook on which they will be tested. Learning-disabled children, however, are not as adept at adjusting their reading style to fit the purpose or the difficulty level of the reading material.

—*Focusing Attention on Important Parts of Text*. Learning-disabled children have problems in picking out the main idea of a paragraph. Good readers spend more time and effort focusing on the major ideas contained in the text they read.

—*Monitoring One's Level of Comprehension*. It isn't yet known exactly what tips them off, but efficient readers can sense when it is that they are not understanding what they're reading. Timing is apparently a key. They pick up quickly, before they've covered a lot of material, that something's not quite right, that they're losing the meaning.

—*Rereading and Scanning Ahead*. So what do efficient readers do when they realize that they're not comprehending? Researchers have identified a couple of strategies used by good readers, but not by poor ones. These strategies are neither mysterious nor complex. Good readers often stop and reread portions of the passage and/or scan ahead looking for clues that will help them understand what they're reading.

—*Consulting External Sources*. Another way in which good readers have a leg up on the learning-disabled is that they know when to use external sources for help; they realize that they can use the written language system to their advantage. For example, they realize that consulting a dictionary, asking others for help, and using contextual cues are good ways of helping them figure out specific words that give them difficulty.

SUCCESSFUL TEACHING TECHNIQUES IDENTIFIED

Investigators are just beginning to devise teaching techniques designed to short-circuit comprehension monitoring difficulties. One of the most active researchers in this area has been Dr. Bernice Wong of Simon Fraser University in Canada. In one of her studies, she tested the effects of a set of teaching procedures that are designed to help learning-disabled children improve their reading comprehension. Before each paragraph of a story the children were reading, the teacher read aloud questions pertaining to the main ideas of the paragraph. The same questions were printed in the children's copies of the stories. This simple and straightforward procedure resulted in the students recalling more of the story on a subsequent test. In particular, they improved their comprehension of the most thematically important ideas in the story.

In another investigation, Wong developed an even more streamlined instructional procedure. She improved the comprehension of learning-disabled students by having them:

—ask themselves, "What am I studying the passage for?";

—find the main ideas and underline them;

—think of a question about the main idea and write it;

—look back at questions and answers to see how they provide them with more information.

The development of instructional techniques for attacking the comprehension monitoring deficits of learning-disabled students is still in its infancy. The future holds great promise for the development of yet other teaching strategies. One of the striking aspects of curriculum development in this area is that it is so "commonsensical." The teaching techniques developed by Wong and others are, at once, powerful and simple—simple in the sense that their rationale can be easily understood by learning-disabled students themselves. It's a good bet that the inherent understandability of these techniques is what makes them work so well.

SOURCE: *Special Education Today*, November 1983, pp. 4–5. Reprinted with permission.

tend to neglect the fact that many learning-disabled children have social-emotional problems. We emphasize the learning problems of these children so much that we sometimes forget that they can also have serious difficulties in social adjustment. There are at least four sources of evidence for the notion that learning-disabled individuals demonstrate signs of social maladjustment—ratings by peers, teachers, parents, and learning-disabled children themselves (Bryan, 1974; Chapman, 1988; Epstein, Cullinan, & Lloyd, 1986; Gottlieb, Gottlieb, Berkell, & Levy, 1986; McConaughy & Ritter, 1986).

Possible Explanations for Socialization Problems

Authorites have given several explanations for why learning-disabled children have such difficulties in social situations. According to Bryan and Bryan (1986), as many as five different areas have been suggested as possible causes of social problems for learning-disabled children: (1) social norm violation, (2) social cognition, (3) role-taking skills, (4) referential communication, and (5) classroom behavior.

SOCIAL NORM VIOLATION. Even though learning-disabled students are aware of social norms, some of them are more willing than nondisabled peers to violate them. For example, they admit to being more willing to commit antisocial acts (Bryan, Werner, & Pearl, 1982), and they tend to use inappropriate ways of getting others to like them (Bryan, Sonnefeld, & Greenberg, 1981).

SOCIAL COGNITION. Some learning-disabled children elicit negative reactions from others because they lack social comprehension skills (Horowitz, 1981; Weiss, 1984; Wong & Wong, 1980). They often exhibit difficulties in reading social cues and may misinterpret the feelings and emotions of others. For example, one study compared them to their nondisabled peers in ability to judge the feelings of soap opera characters (Pearl & Cosden, 1982). Segments of soap operas were chosen because they are often laden with emotion. The learning-disabled group's understanding of the social interchanges was less accurate than that of the nondisabled group.

ROLE-TAKING SKILLS. Some learning-disabled students have difficulty understanding and taking the perspective of others. This is not surprising because being able to put oneself in another's shoes is a complex cognitive-affective task.

REFERENTIAL COMMUNICATION. The learning-disabled child's tendency to have trouble communicating with others, both as a listener and a speaker, puts that child at risk for social difficulties. One can readily imagine how easy it would be to misinterpret inattentiveness in a social interchange as disinterest or negativism.

CLASSROOM BEHAVIOR. Although teachers *rate* learning-disabled children as engaging in a variety of negative behaviors, researchers who have directly observed classroom interactions have not been able to discover exactly what it is the children actually do to evoke these negative ratings. One interesting hypothesis is that their nonverbal behavior contributes in some way to negative reactions. In one clever laboratory study, adults were shown brief videotapes of learning-disabled and nondisabled children (Bryan & Perlmutter, 1979). After just a few minutes of exposure to the tapes, adults judged the learning-disabled child as less socially desirable than the nondisabled child. What is even more amazing, adults were able to make these judgments even when the sound was turned off! The particular nonverbal behaviors that elicit such immediate negative reactions remain a mystery, although a subsequent study suggests it may be that learning-disabled children do not make appropriate eye contact with other people in conversations (Bryan, Sherman, & Fisher, 1980).

Motivational Difficulties

Another source of social adjustment problems for learning-disabled students is their motivation, or feelings about their own abilities to deal with life's many problems. Many learning-disabled individuals exhibit motivational problems (Deci & Chandler, 1986). They appear content to let events occur without attempting to take charge of their own destinies. Learning-disabled individuals may demonstrate their motivational problems in three interrelated ways: (1) external locus of control, (2) negative attributions, and (3) learned helplessness.

EXTERNAL LOCUS OF CONTROL. **Locus of control** refers to one's view of being controlled by either internal or external factors. People with an internal locus of control believe that they are essentially in control of what happens to them whereas those with an external locus of control believe that they are controlled by external factors such as luck or fate. Learning-disabled individuals are much more likely to exhibit an external rather than an internal locus of control (Hallahan, Gajar, Cohen, & Tarver, 1978; Short & Weissberg-Benchell, 1989). For example, when asked a question such as "Suppose you did a better than usual job in a subject at school. Would it probably happen (1) because you tried harder or (2) because someone helped you?" the learning-disabled child is more likely to choose (2). In other words, these children view themselves as controlled by external rather than internal factors.

NEGATIVE ATTRIBUTIONS. Closely related to the work on locus of control is research on **attributions,** which refer to what people think are the causes of their successes and failures. The findings on attributions of learning-disabled children are consistent with what one would expect, given their propensity for an external locus of control. Bryan and Bryan (1986, p. 203) provide the following summary of attribution research:

> Across ages, then, learning-disabled children and adolescents are unlikely to take pride in their successes and are particularly prone to minimize or discount whatever successes they achieve. They are not so reluctant, however, to minimize their responsibilities for failure. Further, they appear to be more pessimistic than nondisabled peers with regard to future success.

LEARNED HELPLESSNESS. Given the motivational profile of an external locus of control and pessimistic attributions, it is no wonder that authorities have also tagged learning-disabled children as being at risk for developing **learned helplessness,** a person's belief that his or her efforts will not result in desired outcomes (Seligman, 1975). These people learn to expect failure no matter how hard they try; therefore, they tend to "give up" or to lose motivation. Learning-disabled children tend to devalue effort, to believe that no amount of effort on their part will help them achieve. They tend to view themselves as helpless in the academic situation (Schunk, 1989).

Whether the learned helplessness causes the academic problems of the learning-disabled child or vice versa is an unanswerable question at this point. It is logical to assume, however, that there is a kind of vicious circle: The learning-disabled child who exhibits problems in certain areas learns to expect failure in any new situation. This expectancy of failure, or learned helplessness, may cause the child to give up readily in the face of a task that is not easily solvable. The result is failure. A child who has experienced years of this failure–expectancy of failure–failure chain will probably need to be taught coping strategies for dealing with failure (Pearl, Bryan, & Donahue, 1980).

The Child with Learning Disabilities as an Inactive Learner with Strategy Deficits

Many of the psychological and behavioral characteristics we have described can be summed up by saying that the learning-disabled child is a passive individual who lacks strategies for attacking academic problems (Hallahan & Bryan, 1981; Hallahan & Reeve, 1980; Torgesen, 1977). Specifically, research points to the learning-disabled child as one who does not believe in his or her own abilities (learned helplessness), has an inadequate grasp of what strategies are available for problem solving (poor metacognitive skills), and is unable to produce appropriate learning strategies spontaneously. *The picture we get is of a child who does not actively involve himself or herself in the learning situation.*

But there is a bright side to the generalization that many learning-disabled children are inactive, passive learners: This inactivity can be overcome. Given appropriate experiences, learning-disabled children can be taught to use appropriate task-approach strategies. (We discuss this topic in more detail in the section on cognitive training.)

Academic Achievement

There is little disagreement among professionals concerning the presence of academic deficits in learning-disabied children. Indeed, such deficits are the hallmark of learning disabilities. In fact, by definition, if there is no academic problem, a learning disability does not exist. Some children have deficits in all scholastic areas—reading, spoken language, written language, and mathematics; others have problems in only one or two academic subjects.

Spoken Language Problems

Many learning-disabled individuals have significant problems with the *mechanical* and *social uses of language*.

MECHANICS OF LANGUAGE. Numerous authorities have documented the fact that many learning-disabled children have trouble with the mechanical, or structural, aspects of language (Mann, Cowin, & Schoenheimer, 1989; Vellutino, 1987; Vogel, 1977; Wiig, Semel, & Abele, 1981). In addition to having problems with **syntax** (grammatical aspects of language) and **semantics** (meaningful aspects of language), learning-disabled students have particular difficulty with phonology. **Phonology** is the study of how individual sounds make up words. Learning-disabled individuals frequently encounter problems both in breaking down words into their component sounds and in blending individual sounds together to make words.

SOCIAL USES OF LANGUAGE. **Pragmatics** refers to the child's knowledge of how to use language in social settings. It deals less with the mechanics of language and more with how individuals use language to communicate. Studies indicate that learning-disabled children often have problems in the use of language in social situations (Bryan & Bryan, 1986; Bryan, Donahue, & Pearl, 1981; Bryan, Donahue, Pearl, & Sturm, 1981, Mathinos, 1988). These deficiencies are manifested both in the production of language and in listening to the language of others.

Many learning-disabled children are unskilled conversationalists. They are unable to engage in the mutual give and take that conversations require between individuals. When conversing with others, they are often agreeable and cooperative, but they tend to be unpersuasive and deferential. Their conversations are frequently marked by long silences because they do not use the relatively subtle strategies that their nondisabled peers do to keep conversations going. They are not skilled at responding to others' statements or questions and have a tendency to answer their own questions before their companion has a chance to respond. They tend to make task-irrelevant comments and make uncomfortable those with whom they are talking. In one often-cited study, for example, learning-disabled and nondisabled children took turns playing the role of host in a simulated television talk show (Bryan, Donahue, Pearl, & Sturm, 1981). Analysis of the verbal interactions revealed that in contrast to nondisabled children, learning-disabled children playing the host role allowed their nondisabled guests to dominate the conversation. Also, their guests exhibited more signs of discomfort during the interview than did the guests of nondisabled hosts.

Reading Problems

The academic area that poses the most difficulty for most learning-disabled students is reading. One of the most popular explanations for this problem is related to the deficient language skills of learning-disabled children, in particular, phonology (Foorman & Liberman, 1989; Mann, Cowin, & Schoenheimer, 1989; Vellutino, 1987). It is easy to understand why problems with phonology would be at the heart of many reading difficulties. If a child has trouble recalling the sounds of words or has problems breaking words into their component sounds, for example, it is logical that he or she will have trouble learning to read.

Written Language Problems

Written language can be divided into handwriting, spelling, and composition. Learning-disabled students often have difficulties in one or more of these areas.

HANDWRITING. Although even the best students can have less than perfect handwriting, the kinds of problems manifested by some learning-disabled students are much more severe. Their written products are frequently illegible, and in addition, learning-disabled students are sometimes very slow writers.

SPELLING. Spelling involves the ability to learn the correspondence between phonemes (sounds) and graphemes (written letters), a skill poorly developed in some learning-disabled children (Carpenter & Miller, 1982; Gerber & Hall, 1981). The high prevalence of spelling problems is no doubt related to the fact that the English language consists of a wide variety of graphemes for individual phonemes.

COMPOSITION. Problems in composition range from grammatical errors to stylistic deficiencies (Englert et al., 1988; Lynch & Jones, 1989; Morris & Crump, 1982; Thomas, Englert, & Gregg, 1987). According to Englert and colleagues there are three types of difficulties. First, learning-disabled students are not aware of the basic purpose of writing—an act of communication; rather, they approach writing as a test-taking task. Second, their writing lacks fluency in that they write shorter sentences and stories. Third, they do not adequately understand writing strategies, such as planning, organizing, drafting, and editing.

Mathematical Problems

Although disorders of language, reading, and writing have traditionally received more emphasis than problems in mathematics, the latter are now gaining a great deal more attention. For example, it is estimated that two out of three learning-disabled students receive special instruction for arithmetic disabilities and more than one in four get special education services primarily because of problems in math (McLeod & Armstrong, 1982).

Learning-disabled students who exhibit problems in math do so for a variety of reasons. Some of their problems are caused indirectly by difficulties in other, related areas, such as attention and reading. Learning-disabled children have particular difficulty in solving "story problems." There is considerable evidence, however, that many children also exhibit computational errors, usually the result of applying incorrect problem-solving strategies (Rivera & Smith, 1988).

EDUCATIONAL CONSIDERATIONS

There are several possible orientations for planning treatment programs for learning-disabled children. The following seven categories reflect what the majority of professionals recognize as the major approaches:

- Process training
- Multisensory approaches
- Structure and stimulus reduction
- Medication
- Cognitive training
- Behavior modification
- Direct instruction

In practice, one often finds a combination of two or more of these approaches. With the possible exceptions of process training and behavior modification or process training and direct instruction, which seem mutually exclusive, it is not uncommon to find a blend of several.

Process Training

At one time there were numerous advocates of the idea that we must consider underlying psychological processes in planning educational programs for learning-disabled students. Although not as abundant as they were several years ago, there are still proponents of process training. They assume we can specify the underlying processes involved in learning academic subjects. We then train the children's processes themselves rather than working directly on academic materials. For example, a child believed to have reading problems because of difficulties in visual perception would receive visual perception training before any reading instruction.

A number of programs have been developed for training visual and visual-motor skills (e.g., Frostig & Horne, 1964; Getman, Kane, & McKee, 1968; Kephart, 1971, 1975) as well as psycholinguistic processes (Kirk & Kirk, 1971; Minskoff, Wiseman,

& Minskoff, 1974). Many of these programs were devised specifically to be used with information from process tests. The teacher is to use Frostig's program in conjunction with the Frostig DTVP test; and Kirk and Kirk and Minskoff and colleagues designed their materials for use with the ITPA.

Kephart's (1971, 1975) approach is a representative example of process training. Kephart's contention that in the course of normal human maturation, motor development precedes visual development led him to devise training activities that first stress motor skills. Many developmental psychologists have disagreed (Hetherington & Parke, 1986). They maintain that visual development occurs chronologically before motor skills.

In addition to concerns about the theoretical underpinnings of Kephart's approach, critics have also questioned his methods and other process training programs on the grounds that they have not documented their effectiveness (Hallahan & Cruickshank, 1973; Hammill & Larsen, 1974). It is largely on the basis of these criticisms that process training is not as popular as it once was.

Multisensory Approaches

Although they include some of the same activities found in process training, programs classified as multisensory are more likely to emphasize working with academic materials directly (Fernald, 1943; Gillingham & Stillman, 1956). Multisensory methods use a combination of the child's sensory systems in the training process. The assumption is that the child will be more likely to learn if more than one sense is involved in learning experiences.

The prototype of most multisensory approaches is Fernald's VAKT method (*V* stands for visual, *A* for auditory, *K* for kinesthetic, and *T* for tactual). In the first step the child tells the teacher a story. The teacher writes down the words of the story, which serves as the material as the child learns to read. (Advocates point out that using a student's own story is a particularly good motivator, especially for older children.) In learning the words, the child first sees the word (visual), then hears the teacher say the word (auditory). Next the child says the word (auditory), and finally, the child traces the word (kinesthetic and tactual).

Structure and Stimulus Reduction for Hyperactivity and Distractibility

William Cruickshank developed an educational program for learning-disabled students with attentional problems and hyperactivity (Cruickshank, Bentzen, Ratzeburg, & Tannhauser, 1961). Based on earlier work with mentally retarded children (Strauss & Kephart, 1955; Strauss & Lehtinen, 1947), Cruickshank's approach included three principles:

1. Structure
2. Reduction of environmental stimulation
3. Enhancement of intensity of teaching materials

Basically, a **structured program** is one that is almost totally teacher directed— that is, most activities are determined by the teacher. The rationale for this approach is that the hyperactive and distractible child cannot make his or her own decisions until carefully educated to do so.

Because of the child's susceptibility to distraction, irrelevant stimuli are reduced.

Collaboration: A Key to Success

JULIE TELLER JAYNE

JOYCE SEYMOUR

■ **JULIE:** My caseload consists of children in grades K–3. This includes youngsters from a transitional readiness classroom. All of them have average or above intelligence, but they all have specific learning disabilities or difficulties which impede their academic achievement. They come to me for help with reading/decoding, written language and cursive handwriting, reading and math readiness skills, and fine motor and visual motor skills. I see some children in the resource room (ranging from twice a week for thirty minutes to five times per week for an hour) and some children in their regular classrooms as part of our school's Generic Teaching model.

■ **JOYCE:** My class consists of eighteen third-graders, ages eight and nine. Three of my students are LD and spend most of their day in the resource room; the other fifteen (eight girls, seven boys) range from low average to above average in academic achievement. I have three reading groups: four students in reading level 2.2, four in a 3.0 level, and eight in a 4.0 level. I taught second grade last year, so I know most of my students well; four are spending their second year with me.

■ **JULIE:** We've worked together closely with Charlie. He's a bright, engaging third-grader with a high-average to superior IQ. He demonstrates high-level thinking skills and a verbal capacity that is superior for his age. In class, he frequently makes perceptive comments. He's well liked by his peers and gets along very well with adults. But in second grade, he started making frequent letter and number reversals and having difficulty finishing written assignments. Also, he had difficulty in word recognition, word attack, and any assignment involving silent reading. So, Charlie was referred for testing, and we found he had significant deficiencies in reading and written language.

In September—in third grade—Charlie started receiving special education. His IEP specified resource room five times per week for thirty minutes. Three of these were to be used for developing and strengthening reading and written language skills. The other two were to be used for improving handwriting skills.

■ **JOYCE:** I worried that Charlie would resent leaving my room to go to the resource room, but Charlie took an immediate liking to Julie and really looked forward to seeing her. Certain aspects of his IEP didn't seem quite right to me, though. I knew he was getting excellent one-on-one support from Julie and that she was following my weekly plans, but he was leaving the class during reading time, which ironically caused him to fall behind in his own reading group's assignments.

■ **JULIE:** Charlie seemed to enjoy the small-group learning environment. He thrived on the positive reinforcement and extra attention I gave him. But he became very dependent on the resource room support. One day he said, "I wish I had you for a whole hour each day. I really need you!" When I discussed this with Joyce, she was concerned that Charlie was starting to see himself as a "resource room kid"—someone who couldn't function in an average classroom. At this point we decided to implement our Generic Teaching model. Because of his visual-motor weaknesses, we decided to continue the resource room twice a week for cursive handwriting instruction.

■ **JOYCE:** At that time, Julie and I attended an in-service that caused us to take another look at what was going on with Charlie. The in-service introduced us to the Generic Teaching model, a way to bring special education into the regular education classroom. In this model, special education teachers come into the regular classroom to work with LD students. One benefit is the fact that LD students receive direct help with material presented in class without having to leave the classroom. Another benefit is that special needs students aren't stigmatized. And the special education teacher can help all students in the classroom, not just the child with the IEP. Julie and I decided this sounded right for Charlie, so we developed the following schedule:

Mon.—Cursive handwriting in resource room.
Tue.—9:15: I introduce vocabulary for the weekly basal reader story and begin reading the story with Charlie's group.
9:30: The group moves to Julie's table, where she provides a brief phonics lesson and vocabulary exercise.
Wed.—9:15: I finish reading the story with Charlie's group and discuss it.
9:30: Julie assigns a creative writing task incorporating the basal reader story's theme and vocabulary. She works with the group on brainstorming ideas for their stories and guides the children through writing.
Thur.—9:15: I work on skills related to the basal reader story.
9:30: Children read stories they wrote on Wednesday to Julie and me, then work on supplementary workbook pages with Julie.
Fri.—Cursive handwriting in resource room.

JULIE: So far, our experience has been very encouraging. I'm now helping four children instead of one. The children I'm working with are all below grade level, and otherwise they wouldn't receive any special services. Also, Charlie's group is getting immediate reinforcement of the lesson they just finished with Joyce. They're still getting the remedial instruction they need, but with relevant materials that are pertinent to their classroom instruction. Another big advantage is the old adage "two heads are better than one." Joyce and I not only share ideas and brainstorm solutions to problems but also, because we're working in the same room, we often overhear one another and get new ideas.

However, we did run into several unanticipated problems. One problem was Charlie's reaction when I explained that he wouldn't be coming to resource every day. I explained to him that because he was doing so well, Joyce and I felt that instead of coming to resource for reading, he was ready to have reading in his own classroom. I went on to explain that I'd be coming into his classroom and working with his entire group. I made it clear to Charlie that no one would need to know that I was there for him.

Charlie was apprehensive and unhappy about this. He told me he loved coming down to the resource room and would miss it. But I persuaded him to give it a try. The first week was an adjustment for everyone. The other three children in the group quickly adapted to the new model. The frustration of independent seatwork was gone, and in its place was increased direct instruction and lots of positive reinforcement. Charlie started acting out in group, though, making errors that I knew were purposeful. His plan, we think, was to convince us that he needed the resource room support. We let it go for a week, but when his behavior began to escalate I spoke with him after group one day and told him I thought he was angry at me. He denied it at first but eventually admitted he was upset because he could only come to resource twice a week. After a long talk, we compromised: If he behaved appro-

> . . . she was concerned that Charlie was starting to see himself as a "resource room kid". . .

priately and put forth maximum effort in class all week, I'd let him come to the resource room for half an hour on Friday afternoon. Each week, he could choose his own activity. This plan seems to be working so far. Charlie's behavior has improved dramatically and the entire reading group has made significant gains.

JOYCE: The rewards became apparent as soon as we began this plan. Charlie's whole reading group benefitted from Julie's instruction. Interestingly, I had more time to devote to my two higher reading groups; before, Charlie's group had dominated my time because they required the most direct instruction. Also, I noticed that having another teacher in my room was helping me. Often, I found myself listening to Julie and getting ideas for my own teaching. For instance, one day I overheard her telling her group that they could earn extra credit points for each vocabulary word that they used

in their stories. Since then, I've been using the same technique with my middle and high groups, and with lots of success.

JULIE: We think the Generic Teaching model has great possibilities, but it is unlikely to replace the resource room as a tool for remediation. Some skills are best taught outside the regular classroom, and some children require a resource room setting in order to learn. A case in point is Charlie's specialized handwriting program, which is unavailable in the regular classroom. Furthermore, many aspects of this model are potentially negative. For one, it depends on the compatibility of the teachers involved. To work effectively, the teachers have to establish a rapport. Without that rapport, the model is worthless. Realistically, this rapport isn't always possible. Also, the success of this model depends on open channels of communication. The teachers have to be able to give and receive suggestions from each other and maintain a high level of honesty. Then too, at times this model can be distracting to the students. If one teacher is doing a particularly interesting lesson with her group, others may be more interested in watching it than in doing their own assignments. For certain groups of students, the presence of two teachers in the room at once may be too much to handle. Some teachers accustomed to traditional settings may feel uncomfortable having another teacher in their classroom. But in spite of the potentially negative aspects of this model, we think it can sometimes be an excellent alternative to the resource room.

JULIE TELLER JAYNE:

LD resource teacher; B.A., Elementary Education, Boston College; Pursuing M.Ed., Special Education, University of New Hampshire

JOYCE SEYMOUR:

Third-grade teacher; B.A., English, Colby College; M.Ed., Curriculum and Instruction, University of Lowell

What the teacher wants the child to attend to is increased in intensity (often through the use of bright colors). **Stimulus reduction** is achieved by some of the following modifications:

- Soundproofed walls and ceilings
- Carpeting
- Opaque windows
- Enclosed bookcases and cupboards
- Limited use of bulletin boards
- Use of cubicles and three-sided work areas

Research on the effectiveness of Cruickshank's stimulus reduction methods has been mixed (Hallahan & Kauffman, 1975). In general, researchers have found that the approach leads to greater attending skills in children but does not automatically result in achievement gains. This result has led some practitioners to suggest using stimulus reduction techniques as a way of readying the inattentive child for instruction.

The Use of Medication with Hyperactive Children

There has been considerable controversy about the use of drugs to control attention problems and hyperactivity in children (see the box below). Claims have been made, for example, that the use of drugs represents a conspiracy of the middle class to keep the lower class docile and oppressed, and that drug usage in childhood will automatically lead to drug abuse in the teenage years.

There is very little question about the effectiveness of drugs in changing the behavior of many learning-disabled children (Henker & Whalen, 1989). Medication, particularly stimulant drugs such as Ritalin, is often successful in reducing hyperactive behavior and increasing attending skills. The concern many have is that teachers and parents will come to rely too heavily on drugs. As one parent has said, parents and teachers can also become "addicted" to Ritalin. Drugs cannot substitute for good teaching. Another fear is that drugs may be given to children who do not really need them. It is not always an easy matter to determine when the overactivity warrants medication. When drugs are prescribed, it is important that physician, teacher, parent, and child be in close communication to monitor the dosage. Side effects are not uncommon and determination of the proper dosage requires medical expertise.

The Use and Misuse of Drugs for Hyperactivity: What the Research Tells Us

Of all the controversies in the area of learning disabilities (and there are many), the issue of whether drugs should be used to help control hyperactivity is one of the most hotly debated. Questions of possible drug abuse, harmful side effects, hidden plots to control the behavior of America's youth, and inappropriate advertising practices have been raised. Although physicians have prescribed a variety of drugs to control hyperactive and inattentive behavior, the three most commonly recommended are the psychostimulants Ritalin, Dexedrine, and Cylert. As one might expect in such a highly controversial area, research has not yet provided many definitive answers. Comprehensive reviews (Gadow, Torgesen, Greenstein, & Schell, 1986; Henker & Whalen, 1980, 1989;

Kauffman & Hallahan, 1979; Pelham, 1983; Pelham & Murphy, 1986; Shaywitz & Schay-witz, 1987; Stroufe, 1975; Whalen & Henker, 1980) of the available research, however, point to the following ten cautions:

1. Psychostimulants produce inconsistent effects on intelligence and achievement test scores—some studies have found gains, others have not.
2. Possibly related to the first point is the conclusion that drugs do not appear to have much, if any, effect on the child's acquisition of new skills but do influence academic productivity—the child's ability to produce more of the kind of academic work with which he or she is already familiar.
3. The time course for many of these drugs is relatively brief, meaning that optimal response to the medication may last only a few hours.
4. Side effects are common. The most frequent are a decrease in appetite and an increase in sleeplessness.
5. Psychostimulants do not affect all children in the same way. Some experience side effects; others do not. Researchers estimate that around 60 to 70 percent who receive psychostimulants show improvement on teachers' ratings of their behavior. The remainder either do not improve or actually get worse.
6. There are little data to support the long-term benefits of psychostimulant use. Although some have speculated that there may be a causal relationship between psychostimulant use in childhood and later substance abuse, researchers have not yet conducted definitive studies on this possibility.
7. There is the possibility that the taking of medication leads to undesirable motiva-tional changes. Children may come to rely on the medicine rather than themselves to change their behavior.
8. The medication of children may also lead to motivational changes on the part of adults. It may be that in some cases drugs are too effective in the sense that they appear to offer an apparently quick and easy solution to a problem that needs to be approached on a variety of fronts. Drugs may, for example, afford an easy excuse for teachers to shirk their duties.
9. Teachers need to be aware that dosage levels that lead to a lessening of motor activity may be so high as to lead to impaired performance on cognitive tasks. The result can be a situation in which, although the child's behavior seems better to the teacher, he or she is actually on too high a dosage level to gain any benefits in academic performance.
10. Medication alone is rarely, if ever, enough. A child whose behavioral problems are severe enough to warrant the administration of psychostimulants will almost always also need to be provided with strong educational programming. Some clinicians believe that a combination of drug therapy with behavior or cognitive training is better than either one alone. Research on this matter thus far, however, is inconclusive.

Does this list of cautions mean that drugs should never be used with hyperactive children? No. But professionals should keep all these cautions in mind before administering drugs, and should never forget that these drugs are powerful substances. Again, this does not mean that one should never prescribe drugs. *Many authorities recommend that when educational efforts alone have failed, one may want to attempt drug therapy in combination with educational programming.* Research does indicate that for many hyperactive and distractible children, psychostimulants lead to improvements in goal-directed and attentional behavior. When drugs are used, however, it should be obvious from the preceding ten points that they must be monitored extremely closely. To reap the maximum benefit of the drugs and to reduce any harmful side effects, it is essential that close communication be maintained among parents, physician, teacher, and child.

Cognitive Training

Traditional behavior modification focuses on modifying overt behavior. The focus of **cognitive training** is on changing covert thoughts. Pioneered by Donald Meichenbaum, cognitive training has gained widespread popularity as an intervention approach for learning-disabled students (Borkowski, Estrada, Milstead, & Hale, 1989; Hallahan, Kneedler, & Lloyd, 1983; Kneedler, 1980; Kneedler & Hallahan, 1984; Lloyd, 1988; Pressley, Symons, Snyder, and Cariglia-Bull, 1989; Swanson, 1989). Authorities give at least three reasons why cognitive training is particularly appropriate for learning-disabled children:

1. It stresses self-initiative by involving the child as much as possible as his or her own teacher. In this way, it is aimed at helping the child overcome motivational problems of passivity and learned helplessness.
2. It provides the child with specific learning strategies for solving problems.
3. Many of the techniques appear particularly well suited for attentional and impulsivity problems.

Cognitive training is sometimes given different names, largely depending on the particular orientation of the practitioner or researcher. Some have used the term **cognitive behavior modification** to stress the distinction between *cognitive* versus *behavior* modification. Others have used the term **metacognitive strategy instruction** to emphasize providing the child with strategies for understanding and regulating thought processes. Although there are sometimes some distinctions in practice among these approaches, they are often so subtle that we can use the terms *cognitive training*, *cognitive behavior modification*, and *metacognitive strategy instruction* synonymously.

A variety of specific techniques fall under the heading of cognitive training. The box on page 151 lists characteristics common to many successful cognitive training approaches. Here we present four techniques that are particularly useful

Inattention comes in many forms, such as daydreaming.
(Bob Adelman/Magnum)

Eight Principles of Effective Cognitive Training Programs

Many specific techniques fall under the rubric of cognitive training. Because of this diversity it is sometimes difficult for teachers to know which strategies are most likely to be successful. Pressley and colleagues, however, after examining several effective cognitive training programs, arrived at a list of eight common features (Pressley, Symons, Snyder, & Cariglia-Bull, 1989; Symons, Snyder, Cariglia-Bull, & Pressley, 1989). A teacher can use them as a guide when choosing among cognitive training options.

1. *Teach a few strategies at a time.* Rather than bombarding children with a number of strategies all at once, it is better to teach them just a few. In this way, there is a better chance that the students can learn the strategies in a comprehensive and not a superficial fashion.
2. *Teach self-monitoring.* It is helpful if students keep track of their own progress. When checking their own work, if they find an error, they should be encouraged to try to correct it on their own.
3. *Teach them when and where to use the strategies.* Many learning-disabled students have problems with the metacognitive ability of knowing when and where they can use strategies that teachers have taught. Teachers must give them this information as well as extensive experience in using the strategies in a variety of different settings.
4. *Maintain the students' motivation.* Students need to know that the strategies work. Teachers can help motivation by consistently pointing out the benefits of the strategies, explaining how strategies work, and charting students' progress.
5. *Teach in context.* Students should learn cognitive techniques as an integrated part of the curriculum. Rather than using cognitive training in an isolated manner, teachers should teach students to employ cognitive strategies during academic lessons.
6. *Do not neglect a nonstrategic knowledge base.* Sometimes those who use cognitive training become such avid proponents of cognitive strategies that they forget the importance of factual knowledge. The more facts children know about history, science, math, English, and so forth, the less they will need to rely on strategies.
7. *Engage in direct teaching.* Because the emphasis in cognitive training is on encouraging students to take more initiative in their own learning, teachers may feel that they are less necessary than is actually the case. Cognitive training does not give license to back off from directly teaching students. Students' reliance on teachers should gradually fade. In the early stages, teachers need to be directly in control of supervising the students' use of the cognitive strategies.
8. *Regard cognitive training as long term.* Because cognitive training often results in immediate improvement, there may be a temptation to view it as a panacea or a quick fix. To maintain improvements and have them generalize to other settings, however, students need extensive practice in applying the strategies they have learned.

with learning-disabled students: self-monitoring, mnemonic keyword method, self-instruction, and reciprocal teaching. We discuss another cognitive training approach, the Learning Strategies Curriculum, in the section on secondary educational programming.

Self-Monitoring

Self-monitoring refers to procedures that require the individual to keep track of whether he or she engages in particular behaviors. For example, Hallahan and colleagues have taught learning-disabled children to self-monitor when they are displaying attentive behaviors (Hallahan, Lloyd, Kosiewicz, Kauffman, & Graves, 1979; Lloyd, Hallahan, Kosiewicz, & Kneedler, 1980). The procedure is a simple one. The teacher places a tape recorder near the child. While the child is engaged in some kind of academic activity, a tape containing tones (the time between tones varies randomly) is played. Whenever he or she hears a tone, the child is to stop work and ask, "Was I paying attention?" He or she then records on a separate score sheet a "Yes" or "No" depending on his or her own assessment of attentional behavior. This technique has been successful in aiding learning-disabled children to increase attentive behavior and academic productivity. Presumably, it helps children to become more aware of and in control of their own attentional processes. Here is a set of sample instructions:

> "Johnny, you know how paying attention to your work has been a problem for you. You've heard teachers tell you, 'Pay attention,' 'Get to work,' 'What are you supposed to be doing' and things like that. Well, today we're going to start something that will help you help yourself pay attention better. First we need to make sure that you know what paying attention means. This is what I mean by paying attention." (Teacher models immediate and sustained attention to task.) "And this is what I mean by not paying attention." (Teacher models inattentive behaviors such as glancing around and playing with objects.)

> "Now you tell me if I was paying attention." (Teacher models attentive and inattentive behaviors and requires the student to categorize them.) "Okay, now let me show you what we're going to do. While you're working, this tape recorder will be turned on. Every once in a while, you'll hear a little sound like this:" (Teacher plays tone on tape.) "And when you hear that sound quietly ask yourself, 'Was I paying attention?' If you answer 'yes,' put a check in this box. If you answer 'no,' put a check in this box. Then go right back to work. When you hear the sound again, ask the question, answer it, mark your answer, and go back to work. Now, let me show you how it works." (Teacher models entire procedure.) "Now, Johnny, I bet you can do this. Tell me what you're going to do every time you hear a tone. Let's try it. I'll start the tape and you work on these papers." (Teacher observes student's implementation of the entire procedure, praises its correct use, and gradually withdraws her presence.) (Hallahan, Lloyd, & Stoller, 1982, p. 12)

Mnemonic Keyword Method

Margo Mastropieri and Thomas Scruggs have developed the **mnemonic keyword method,** a way of helping children with memory problems remember information. Learning-disabled students have used it for remembering content in a variety of subjects, such as English, history, science, and foreign languages (e.g., Mastropieri & Scruggs, 1988; Mastropieri, Scruggs, & Fulk, in press). The keyword method is a way of modifying curriculum materials so that abstract information is made more concrete. For example,

> To learn that Eddie Rickenbacker was a World War I flying ace who shot down many German airplanes, the learner is first provided with a keyword for Rickenbacker. In this case, "linebacker" is a good keyword because it sounds like "Rickenbacker" and is easily pictured. A picture is then provided of the reconstructed keyword and the response in an interactive picture or image, here, a picture of a linebacker shooting down German planes over a football field. When asked, then, who Rickenbacker was, learners can think of the keyword "linebacker," think back to the picture of the line-backer, and describe the relevant information (that is, Rickenbacker was a flying ace who shot down German airplanes). (Mastropieri & Scruggs, 1988, pp. 17–18)

Self-Instruction

The idea of self-instruction is to bring behavior under verbal control by having children talk about the various stages of problem-solving tasks while they are performing them (Meichenbaum, 1975; Meichenbaum & Goodman, 1971). This is usually done gradually. Typically, the teacher first models the use of the verbal routine while solving the problem; then he or she closely supervises the children using the verbal routine while doing the task, and then the children do it on their own.

Kosiewicz, Hallahan, Lloyd, and Graves (1982) provide an example of the successful use of self-instruction. They found that a self-instructional routine improved the handwriting performance of a learning-disabled boy. The particular steps the teacher taught the child to use were these:

1. The child said the word to be written aloud.
2. He said the first syllable of the word.
3. He named each of the letters in the syllable three times.
4. He said each letter as he wrote it.
5. He repeated steps 2 through 4 for each succeeding syllable.

Several investigators have used *self-questioning* as a particular form of self-instruction (Billingsley & Wildman, 1988; Griffey, Zigmond, & Leinhardt, 1988; Wong, 1979). They typically instruct the children to ask themselves questions before and/or while they are working on academic material such as reading or math.

Reciprocal Teaching

An approach that includes self-questioning, as well as several other cognitive training techniques, is reciprocal teaching. Developed by Ann Brown and Annemarie Palincsar, **reciprocal teaching** focuses on metacognitive skills for fostering and monitoring reading comprehension.

Reciprocal teaching is based on the Soviet psychologist Vygotsky's theory of the importance of social context in children's learning. Vygotsky's theory states that children learn from their elders in ways that are similar to apprentices who learn their craft from masters. In translating this theory to the teaching situation, Brown and Palincsar believe that in good teaching the teacher provides a structure, or "scaffolding," with which children can gradually learn. In other words, the teacher at first structures the teaching situation but then gradually gives more and more responsibility to the students. This method requires teachers to monitor a child's level of understanding so that they can judge how much structure to provide. The teaching situation is called "reciprocal" because there is a dialogue between teacher and students "for the purpose of jointly constructing the meaning of the [reading] text" (Palincsar, 1986, p. 119).

Here is an example of reciprocal teaching in action:

> The adult teacher assigned a segment of the passage (usually a paragraph) to be read and either indicated that it was her turn to be the teacher or assigned one of the students to teach that segment. The adult teacher and the students then read the assigned segment silently. After reading the text, the teacher (student or adult) for that segment summarized (reviewed) the content, discussed and clarified any difficulties, asked a question that a teacher or test might ask on the segment, and, finally, made a prediction about future content. All of these activities were embedded in as natural a dialogue as possible, with the teacher and other students giving feedback to one another. (Brown & Campione, 1984, p. 174)

Behavior Modification

For years, practitioners have used behavior modification successfully to work with inattention and hyperactivity (Hallahan & Kauffman, 1975) as well as with specific academic behaviors (Kauffman, 1975; Lovitt, 1975a,b). Lovitt, for example, has used behavior modification to improve arithmetic performance and linguistic skills.

Direct Instruction

Direct instruction is similar to behavior modification. It differs, however, in that it focuses specifically on the instructional process. Advocates of direct instruction stress a logical analysis of the concept to be taught, rather than the characteristics of the student. A variety of direct instruction programs are available for reading, arithmetic, and language. These programs consist of precisely sequenced, fast-paced lessons taught to small groups of four to ten. There is a heavy emphasis on drill and practice. The teacher teaches from a script and pupils follow the lead of the teacher, who often uses hand signals to prompt participation. The teacher offers immediate corrective feedback for errors and praise for the correct responses.

Two of the most popular direct instruction programs are *Corrective Reading: Decoding* (Engelmann, Carnine, Johnson, & Meyers, 1988) and *Corrective Reading: Comprehension* (Englemann, Carnine, Johnson, & Meyers, 1989). There is a wealth of research evidence supporting the effectiveness of direct instruction programs. Not only do they result in immediate academic gains but also there are indications that they lead to long-term academic gains (see Lloyd, 1988, for a review of this research).

Administrative Arrangements

Although residential programs and special classes are sometimes used with learning-disabled children, the resource room is the most common arrangement. Because the learning-disabled child, as usually defined, is of at least near-normal intelligence and may have deficits in only a few areas of academic achievement, he or she is often seen as a good candidate for such placement.

The resource room is not the solution for all the ills of special education. A major consideration is how capable the regular class teacher is and how well equipped he or she is to deal with the special needs of the exceptional child. That we should always be striving toward reintegrating the learning-disabled child into the regular class is seen in the following anecdote related by Hewett (1974, p. 397):

> The patient was having delusions about people tapping his telephone and hiding tape recorders in his room. The therapist continually called the patient's attention to the fact that these beliefs were unlikely to be true and that they were simply not reality. After many sessions during which he heard the term, reality, over and over again the patient angrily confronted the therapist with, "Tell me, Doc, what's so good about this reality?" The therapist looked him straight in the eye and calmly stated, "I never said it was good. I only said it was there." Whatever else the contemporary American public school regular classroom may be, it most certainly is "there."

EARLY INTERVENTION

There is very little preschool programming for learning-disabled children because of the difficulties in identifying them at such a young age. When we talk about testing the learning-disabled preschool child, we are really talking about prediction rather than identification (Keogh & Glover, 1980). In other words, because preschool children do not ordinarily engage in academics, it is not possible, strictly speaking, to say that they are behind academically. Unfortunately, all other things being equal, prediction is always less precise than identification.

At least two factors make prediction at preschool ages of later learning disabilities particularly difficult:

1. In many cases of learning disabilities, we are talking about relatively mild problems. Many of these children seem bright and competent until faced with a particular academic task such as reading or spelling. Unlike many other disabled children, learning-disabled children are not so immediately noticeable.

2. It is often difficult to determine what is a true developmental delay and what is merely a maturational slowness (Mercer, Algozzine, & Trifiletti, 1979). Many nondisabled children show slow developmental progress at this young age, but they soon catch up with their peers.

Although most professionals hesitate to program for learning-disabled children at the preschool level, ideally it would be good to do so. Thus we greatly need research on better predictive tests at the preschool level. At present we know that the most accurate predictors are preacademic skills (Mercer, Algozzine, & Trifiletti, 1979). **Preacademic skills** are behaviors that are needed before formal instruction can begin, such as identification of letters, numbers, shapes, and colors.

The most accurate predictors of later academic problems are preacademic skills, such as counting. (Richard Hutchings/Photo Researchers)

Note-taking during lectures poses problems for many college students with learning disabilities. (Ulrike Welsch/Photo Researchers)

TRANSITION

Until the late 1970s and early 1980s there was relatively little educational programming for learning disabilities that extended beyond the elementary school years. This attitude of benign neglect probably emanated from the mistaken impression that children with learning disabilities would outgrow their disabilities or learn to compensate for them in some way. Although more positive than for children with some other disabilities (e.g., behavior disorders and mental retardation), the long-term prognosis for some learning-disabled individuals is not rosy. In an extensive review of the long-term effects of learning disabilities, Kavale (1988, p. 337) concluded that the child with learning disabilities "is likely never to lose the feeling that reading and spelling are areas of difficulty." How any particular child will fare as an adult is extremely difficult to predict and depends on a variety of factors. In addition to parental attitudes and the individual's motivation, one of the most important factors in determining the individual adult's adjustment is whether he or she received intensive and long-term educational intervention (Kavale, 1988). Fortunately, we now have numerous secondary programs for learning-disabled students, and there is a blossoming of programs at the college level.

Secondary Programming

There are a variety of approaches to educating learning-disabled students at the secondary level. Zigmond and Sansone (1986) note that these models differ in (1) how much time students spend with the special versus general education teachers and (2) the degree to which their curriculum is "special," or different from the general curriculum. Models can differ on each of these two dimensions. At the one extreme are those approaches, used with students with relatively mild learning disabilities, in which the student spends little or no time with special educators and does not have a special curriculum. For example, the special education teacher may consult with the general education teachers to help them adjust their teaching to accommodate learning-disabled students, or he or she may tutor learning-disabled students on subjects in which they are having difficulties.

At the other extreme of the two dimensions are approaches designed for students with very severe learning disabilities. They require intensive involvement with special educators and a different type of curriculum. For example, similar to what we often use with mildly retarded students (see Chapter 3), these programs may combine a **functional academics** curriculum with a **work-study program.** Functional academics refers to the teaching of academics, such as reading, for the purpose of gaining practical, independent living skills (e.g., reading newspapers, job applications, telephone books, and so forth) rather than attaining other academic content. Work-study programs involve on-the-job training. These more intensive approaches are oriented more toward preparing students for the job market than toward achieving higher levels of academic preparation.

There are a number of learning-disabled adolescents whose problems are neither so mild nor so severe that the preceding approaches are appropriate. We can best serve these students with programs having a modest amount of special educator involvement, up to about two hours per day, and some use of different curricula. An example is the Learning Strategies Curriculum.

Learning Strategies Curriculum

Donald Deshler, Jean Schumaker, and their colleagues have developed a curriculum for secondary learning-disabled students called the Learning Strategies Curriculum (Deshler & Schumaker, 1986; Ellis, Deshler, & Schumaker, 1989). The idea behind this approach is that learning-disabled adolescents need strategies to learn how to learn more than they need specific subject content.

The organization of the Learning Strategies Curriculum is determined by the major demands of the secondary curriculum. It therefore comprises three strands. One is devoted to helping students acquire information from written materials. It includes strategies for such things as word identification, reading comprehension, and interpretation of diagrams and charts. A second strand helps students remember important information and facts. It contains strategies for such things as taking notes and using mnemonics. A third strand helps to improve written expression. It includes strategies for such things as writing sentences and paragraphs. Another feature of this strand is that it includes strategies for completing assignments on time and taking tests.

Multipass is an example of one set of the strategies used in the strand designed for getting information from written materials (Schumaker, Deshler, Alley, Warner, & Denton, 1982). Based on the SQ3R method (Robinson, 1946), Multipass has the student make many "passes" (hence the name) through the reading material. The three major passes are the Survey, the Size-Up, and Sort-Out. These three

Learning Disabilities and Juvenile Delinquency: Is There a Causal Connection?

There is a higher prevalence of learning disabilities among juvenile delinquents than is ordinarily found in the general population. A review of prevalence studies (Murphy, 1986) found that although the particular prevalence rates vary widely from a low of 9 percent to a high of 36.5 percent, even the most conservative figures contrast sharply with what is usually found in the population at large.

The reason for the high rate of learning disabilities among juvenile delinquents has been a topic of debate for years. There are several feasible explanations for the association between the two categories, some of which specify a direct causal link between the two and some of which do not. In a review of this literature funded by the U.S. Department of Justice's Office of Juvenile Justice and Delinquency Prevention, Keilitz and Dunivant (1986) found five theoretical explanations. The first three theories are causal; the last two are not:

CAUSAL THEORIES

1. *School failure theory*: This theory posits that learning disabilities directly result in school failure, which then results in juvenile delinquency. There are five hypothesized ways in which this can happen. These students may
   a. Become angry at their inability to learn and "strike back at society in anger and retaliation" (p. 19)
   b. Be influenced by other delinquency-prone students with whom they are grouped in school, for example, behavior-disordered children
   c. Because of their school failure become disenchanted with teachers and other symbols of the school as an institution, and this disenchantment may diminish their commitment to socially accepted behavior
   d. Perceive that their academic failure will prohibit them from obtaining a job leading to adequate financial resources and prestige, and this, in turn, leads them to try to obtain money and prestige through illegal means
   e. Because of their lack of success in school blame others rather than themselves for negative events
2. *Susceptibility theory*: According to this theory, learning-disabled children have certain personality and cognitive attributes that make them susceptible to delinquent behavior. These characteristics include such things as poor impulse control, problems in reading social cues, and suggestibility.
3. *Differential treatment theory*: This theory posits that there may not actually be any difference in how often learning-disabled and nondisabled children commit delinquent acts. Instead, there is a difference in whether they are caught for their delinquent acts and/or how they are treated by the juvenile justice system. This theory has three hypotheses:
   a. *Differential arrest hypothesis*: This hypothesis holds that learning-disabled students are more likely than nondisabled students to be apprehended by the police for the same activities. Differential arrest rates may occur for a variety of reasons—for example, learning-disabled students' inability to use strategies for not being caught or their inability to talk their way out of arrest.
   b. *Differential adjudication hypothesis*: This hypothesis posits that learning-disabled youths, after being arrested, are more likely to have their cases settled judicially. A variety of explanations for this higher incidence of adjudication have been forwarded—for example, their lack of self-control and social ineptness may cause the authorities to bring them to trial.
   c. *Differential disposition hypothesis*: For some of the same reasons noted under

a and b, this hypothesis holds that learning-disabled youths receive harsher treatment by the juvenile court.

NONCAUSAL THEORIES

4. *Sociodemographic characteristics theory*: This theory holds that learning disabilities and juvenile delinquency frequently occur together because they are both caused by social factors such as parents' education level and socioeconomic status.
5. *Response bias theory*: This theory holds that learning-disabled adolescents do not commit more delinquent acts than their nonhandicapped peers. However, when asked in surveys or questionnaires to reveal their delinquent behaviors, they are less likely to conceal them.

If we look at these five theories and some of the subtheories, it should be apparent just how complicated the relationship between learning disabilities and juvenile delinquency is. No wonder there has been so much debate about whether there is a causal connection. Although we need more research on this issue, Keilitz and Dunivant (1986) have conducted two large-scale studies that support the three preceding causal theories. From these results, they have concluded,

Generally, the data are consistent with causal theories that describe the contribution learning disabilities makes to delinquent behavior. Of course, LD is only one among many causes of delinquency. Only a relatively small proportion of the youth population is affected by LD. Within this group, however, learning disabilities appear to be one of the important causes of delinquency (p. 24)

passes are embedded in a context of highly individualized programming and a heavy reliance on ensuring that the child achieves certain performance goals before moving on to the next stage. Here is a description of Multipass:

The purpose of the Survey Pass was to familiarize the student with main ideas and organization of the chapter. Thus, this previewing pass required the student to: (a) read the chapter title, (b) read the introductory paragraph, (c) review the chapter's relationship to other adjacent chapters by perusing the table of contents, (d) read the major subtitles of the chapter and notice how the chapter is organized, (e) look at illustrations and read their captions, (f) read the summary paragraph, and (g) paraphrase all the information gained in the process.

The Size-Up Pass was designed to help students gain specific information and facts from a chapter without reading it from beginning to end. This pass required the student to first read each of the questions at the end of the chapter to determine what facts appeared to be the most important to learn. If the student was already able to answer a given question as a result of the Survey Pass, a check mark ($\sqrt{}$) was placed next to the question. The student now progressed through the entire chapter following these steps: (a) look for a textual cue (e.g., bold-face print, subtitle, colored print, italics); (b) make the cue into a question (e.g., if the cue was the italicized vocabulary word *conqueror*, the student asked, "What does conqueror mean?"; if the cue was the subtitle "The Election of 1848," the student might ask, "Who won the election of 1848?" or "Why was the election of 1848 important?"; (c) skim through the surrounding text to find the answer to the question; and (d) paraphrase the answer to yourself without looking in the book. When the student reached the end of the chapter using these four steps for each textual cue, he/she was required to paraphrase all the facts and ideas he/she could remember about the chapter.

The Sort-Out Pass was included to get students to test themselves over the material presented in the chapter. In this final pass, the student read and answered each question at the end of the chapter. If the student could answer a question immediately, he/she placed a checkmark next to it. If the student was unable to answer a question, however, the answer was sought by (a) thinking in which section of the chapter the answer would most likely be located, (b) skimming through that section for the answer, (c) if the answer was not located, thinking of another relevant section, and (d) skimming that section, and so on until the student could answer the question. A checkmark was then placed next to the question, and the student moved on to answer the next question. (Schumaker, Deshler, Alley, Warner, & Denton, 1982, pp. 298–299)

Postsecondary Programming

Postsecondary programs include vocational and technical programs as well as community colleges and four-year colleges and universities. More and more individuals with learning disabilities are enrolling in colleges and universities, and more and more universities are establishing special programs and services for learning-disabled students. Although there is as yet no consensus on how best to arrange college programs for learning-disabled individuals, we are making headway in describing the specific needs of these students. One of the major difficulties for the learning-disabled student in the transition from high school to college is the decrease in the amount of guidance provided by adults (Siperstein, 1988). Many learning-disabled students find this greater emphasis on self-discipline particularly difficult. The greater demands on writing skills (Gajar, 1989) and note taking also present major problems for many college students with learning disabilities.

> For many LD [learning-disabled] adults, the task of taking notes in lectures is overwhelming, nor is it any wonder. Note-taking requires simultaneous listening, comprehending, and synthesizing and/or extracting main ideas while retaining them long enough to formulate a synopsis and write it down. The writing act, in turn, requires automaticity and speed in letter formation and sufficient legibility and spelling ability to decipher what has been written at a later time. (Vogel, 1987, p. 523)

Siperstein (1988), believing in a long-range view of programming for college-bound learning-disabled students, has conceptualized service delivery as consisting of three transitions: (1) high school to college, (2) during college, and (3) college to employment. During the first stage, high school to college, Siperstein recommends that teachers and counselors develop what he refers to as *individualized college plans* (ICPs) for students akin to their individualized educational plans (IEPs). A major goal of the ICP would be to foster awareness of what college options are available. Because of their frequent experiences with failure, many learning-disabled students do not aspire to education beyond high school. The ICP would also concentrate on preparing students for making the right choice of colleges as well as delineating what types of accommodations they will need in their programs. Parents and students need to consider the unique characteristics of the student as well as those of different colleges and their programs in matching the student with the appropriate institution (McGuire & Shaw, 1987). During this stage, pupils and their families may take advantage of published guides to college programs for learning-disabled students—for example, *A Guide to Colleges for Learning-Disabled Students* (Liscio, 1986) and *Lovejoy's Four-Year College Guide for Learning-Disabled Students* (1985). Also students can be made aware of the special accommodations available for learning-disabled students taking the Scholastic Aptitude Test (SAT) and the American College Test (ACT).

The second stage, which covers the time period during college, focuses on

Some authorities are now pointing to previously unrecognized learning disabilities as a possible cause of college failure. (Michael Philip Manheim/Southern Light)

enhancing the chances of successfully earning a degree. It includes support services for both academic and social functioning. For example, in addition to tutoring, the college can provide such services as note taking, transcription of taped lectures, and study skills workshops. The administration can modify program standards by waiving certain requirements (e.g., a foreign language) (Vogel, 1987), and the faculty can alter their usual teaching and evaluation activities by, for example, making themselves more available for student consultation and allowing untimed tests. An important resource in programming are the learning-disabled college students themselves. Third- and fourth-year students with learning disabilities can help establish peer support systems.

The third stage, transition from college to employment, is important because even if they survive the rigors of college, many learning-disabled individuals have difficulties obtaining appropriate employment in the competitive job market. According to Siperstein (1988), institutions of higher education can alleviate these problems by helping college graduates plan ahead for their transition to employment. He recommends workshops for career awareness, job-search strategies, and job-maintenance skills.

There is little doubt that much of what we need to know to program effectively for learning-disabled individuals at the postsecondary level remains to be learned. The field, however, has made great strides in opening windows of opportunity for learning-disabled young adults. Authorities have noted that many learning-disabled college applicants attempt to hide their learning disability for fear they will not be admitted (Shaywitz & Shaw, 1988). If the burgeoning interest in postsecondary programming for learning-disabled individuals continues, we may in the near future see the day when students and colleges routinely collaborate to use information concerning the students' learning disability in planning their programs.

LEARNING DISABILITIES

SUGGESTIONS FOR TEACHING STUDENTS WITH LEARNING DISABILITIES IN GENERAL EDUCATION CLASSROOMS

What to Look for in School

All students who are learning disabled, by definition, have near-average, average, or above-average intelligence. They learn some academic skills easily, while they acquire other skills with great difficulty. In addition to underachievement in some school subjects, individuals with learning disabilities exhibit behaviors that may help you identify them in your classrooms. In primary grades, learning-disabled children may appear to be immature, delayed in language, motor, and readiness skills. They may have general coordination problems and appear clumsy or have difficulties with specific motor skills such as cutting with scissors, coloring within lines, and writing. Their use of language also may lag behind their classmates. Speaking in an immature or "babyish" way and having difficulty expressing themselves in conversation and group discussions may be additional clues. Sometimes children with learning disabilities do not demonstrate reading readiness skills such as right-left and up-down orientations, spatial relationships, and eye-hand coordination.

In intermediate grades students who are learning disabled may seem not to listen to oral directions and instruction or may have difficulty reading written materials. They may be constantly "on the move" and find sitting or working on one activity for even a few minutes difficult. In addition, they may be ineffective learners who do not know how to plan their work or how to remember information from one day to the next.

Many learning-disabled students in middle and high school, appear to be unmotivated, rarely beginning independent work without extra prodding and completing homework assignments inconsistently. In addition, acting before thinking may result in their turning in "careless," incomplete papers and getting in trouble for interacting and reacting impulsively with other students. Individuals with learning disabilities are also often disorganized. They frequently lose or misplace books, pencils, and homework. Furthermore, they may be easily frustrated with tasks that are too difficult and mask their problems in doing assignments by saying they "had better things to do" or "didn't feel like it." The social problems that some learning-disabled students experience at all ages may be increasingly apparent as they mature. Frequently they say and do the wrong thing unknowingly and misread social situations.

Although these behavior clues may exist at any age, the fact that they may be more obvious only at some ages can make recognizing learning-disabled students difficult. The wide range of academic and social problems learning-disabled persons exhibit further complicates identification. A discrepancy between ability, as estimated by IQ tests, and actual achievement is a key factor in determining whether a student has a learning disability. Although trained professionals administer and interpret intelligence tests, you can be a key person in identifying students with learning disabilities by collecting achievement information and by recording observations of their social-emotional behaviors and giving this information to the special education teacher or counselor in your school.

How to Gather Information

There are a variety of materials and procedures you can use to gather information about your students' achievement. A student's cumulative folder provides information about past school performance that may indicate whether the problems you are observing are new or part of a pattern exhibited in different grades. This folder also contains attendance and retention data and group achievement test results, which provide a comparison of your student's achievement with that of other students in the same grade. Former teachers may provide additional information about your student's ability to meet regular class demands, necessary instructional modifications, and social adjustment.

To gather current information, you can conduct any of several informal assessment procedures, such as informal inventories (see p. 131) and criterion referenced tests (see p. 132), or analyze samples of your student's work for error patterns and inconsistent use of skills. Another effective procedure is curriculum-based assessment (CBA) (see p. 132). In addition to providing guidelines for grouping students and for placing them in curricular materials that are appropriate to their skill level, CBA identifies specific skills students have not yet mastered. To determine these skills, Blankenship (1985) recommends constructing and giving CBA measures for different subject areas by following these steps:

1. List the skills presented in the instructional materials you are using. For example, if you were interested in evaluating reading skills, you would note all the skills presented in the basal reader your student is reading. Some textbooks provide a scope and sequence chart that is useful in making this list.
2. Review the list to see whether all important skills are included and if they are arranged in logical order.
3. Write an instructional objective for each skill on the list. In some states, objectives are included in state guidelines or standards of learning.
4. Prepare items to test each of the skills. Each CBA measure consists of a few items specified by your objectives. You will give several of these short tests, each of which contains similar items, throughout the year. For example, to learn what sight words a student can read, you might develop several tests from a list of all the sight words that appear in the child's reader.
5. Prepare testing materials for each skill to give to the students. For example, when giving a CBA reading measure, teachers often print two copies of a test: one from which the student reads and the other on which the teacher records the student's responses. Although teachers usually give oral reading measures individually, several students can complete CBA measures for reading comprehension, spelling, and math at one time.
6. Give one CBA immediately before beginning instruction on a topic.
7. Study the results to determine if students have mastered the material, have the necessary prerequisite skills but have not mastered the material, or do not have the necessary preskills. These results will guide your instructional plans for your students.
8. Readminister different CBA tests during and after instruction. Again you will examine the results to learn whether students are making sufficient progress but require more practice or instruction, are not making sufficient progress and require a modification in instruction, or have mastered the skill.
9. Readminister these CBA measures periodically throughout the year to determine the student's long-term retention.

CBA measures indicate students who do not have prerequisite skills and who may be having academic difficulties. These measures coupled with your observation of the student's behaviors may suggest a learning disability.

Teaching Techniques to Try

Self-Regulatory Strategies

Once identified as having a learning disability, students must learn to manage a wide range of learning problems. One of the most common difficulties they face is not knowing how to plan, monitor, and check their work or how to remediate their problems in learning. Teachers can help them to learn needed strategies that include

1. Attention strategies (see p. 145)
2. Self-instruction strategies (see p. 153)
3. Self-questioning strategies (see p. 139)
4. Self-monitoring strategies (see p. 151)

Academic Strategies

Educators have designed strategies for specific academic areas. You will notice that most of them include components designed to teach students both specific skills and the self-regulation procedures they need to use them successfully.

HANDWRITING. Blandford and Lloyd (1987) formulated important instructional features of handwriting into questions that prompted students both to think about correct handwriting and to evaluate their writing. When using this procedure, you may decide to tape models of correct letter formations (letter lines) to students' desks. Ask them to write the following questions on a card:

1. a. Am I sitting correctly?
    b. Is my paper positioned correctly?
    c. Am I holding my pencil correctly?
2. a. Are all my letters sitting on the line?
    b. Are all my tall letters touching or nearly touching the top line?
    c. Are my short letters filling only half of the space?
3. Am I leaving enough, but not too much, space between words?

COMPOSITION. Harris and Graham (1985) developed a strategy to help students increase the number of action words they use in their compositions. This process also requires students to evaluate the quality of their work and to think of ways in which they could increase the number of action words they included. If you decide to use this strategy, the authors recommend preparing a chart of several pictures selected from magazines. They gave their students these directions:

Look at this picture and write a story to go with it. Use everything that you have learned about writing stories to help you. Please remember that I cannot help you write the story. However, if you do not know how to spell a word, I will write it out for you. (p. 29)

Once you have given your students directions, they follow these steps:

1. Look at the picture and write down good action words.
2. Think of a good story idea to use my words in.
3. Write my story—make sense and use good action words.
4. Read my story and ask—Did I write a good story? Did I use action words?
5. Fix my story—Can I use more good action words?

READING COMPREHENSION. To facilitate students' understanding of the text, you may choose to use the following strategy, which reminds students to find the main ideas and prompts them to think about their purpose in reading, to generate questions about the important ideas, and to evaluate whether their questions and answers provide additional information (Wong & Jones, 1982) by following five steps:

1. Think what you are studying this passage for.
2. Find the main ideas in the passage and underline them.
3. Think of a question about the main idea you underlined.
4. Learn the answers to your questions.
5. Always look back at your questions and answers to see how each successive question and answer provides you with more information.

ARITHMETIC. Cullinan, Lloyd, and Epstein (1981) devised the following strategy to help students solve basic multiplication problems:

1. Read the problem. (Student reads "$3 \times 7 = .$")
2. Point to the number you know how to count by. (Student points to 3.)
3. Make the number of marks indicated by the other number. (Student writes *///////.*)
4. Begin counting by the number you know how to count by and count up once for each mark, touching that mark. (Student says, "3, 6, 9. . . .")
5. Stop counting when you've touched the last mark. (Student counts "12, 5, 18, 21.")
6. Write the last number you said in the answer space. (Student writes "21.")

Currently educators are developing and evaluating a strategy, called SUCCESS, that is designed to help adolescents with learning disabilities recognize a problem, solve it by developing their own strategy, monitor the effectiveness of the strategy, and make the needed modifications (Ellis, Deshler, & Schumaker, 1989). Although teachers can easily use any strategy in their mainstreamed classes, those that teach learning-disabled students to regulate their use of strategies and to develop their own strategies will not only increase the independence of the learners but also require a minimum of time and supervision.

From reading the chapter, you know there are many teaching techniques you can use to improve the achievement of students with learning disabilities. Some of these methods are also useful in remediating the learning difficulties of other disabled students and are discussed in greater detail in the Suggestions for Teaching in General Education Classrooms sections throughout this text.

Helpful Resources

School Personnel

As indicated in other chapters, several people in your school system can help you identify and manage the special education students in your classroom. The resource teacher who also teaches your mainstreamed students has information about individual learning problems that you will find helpful. This teacher also may be able to suggest specific materials and methods that will help your learning-disabled students learn. Regularly scheduled meetings with the resource teacher may facilitate the exchange of information about your students' progress and develop and coordinate the instructional programs you both are implementing.

Instructional Methods

Baroody, A. J. (1987). *Children's mathematical thinking*. New York: Harcourt Brace Jovanovich.

Bos, C. S., & Vaughn, S. (1988). *Strategies for teaching students with learning and behavior problems*. Boston: Allyn & Bacon.

Carnine, D., & Silbert, J. (1979). *Direct instruction reading*. Columbus, OH: Chas. E. Merrill.

Devine, T. G. (1987). *Teaching study skills: A guide for teachers*. New York: Allyn & Bacon.

Duffy, G. G., & Roehler, L. R. (1986). *Improving classroom reading instruction: A decision-making approach*. New York: Random House.

Mastropieri, M. A. (1988). Using the keyboard methods. *Teaching Exceptional Children, 20*, 1–8.

Mercer, C. (1989). *Teaching students with learning problems*. Columbus, OH: Chas. E. Merrill.

Palincsar, A. S., & Brown, A. L. (1984). Reciprocal teaching of comprehension-fostering and monitoring activities. *Cognition and Instruction, 1*, 117–175.

Wallace, G., & Kauffman, J. M. (1986). *Teaching students with learning and behavior problems*. Columbus, OH: Chas. E. Merrill.

Curricula

Charles, R. I., & Lester, F. K., Jr. (1984). An evaluation of a process-oriented instructional program in mathematical problem solving in grades 5 and 7. *Research in mathematics education, 15*, 15–34. (The Mathematic Problem Solving, MPS, program).

Engelmann, S., & Bruner, E. C. (1983). *Reading mastery*. Chicago: Science Research Associates.

Dixon, B., & Engelmann, S. (1979). Corrective spelling through morographs. Chicago: Science Research Associates.

Engelmann, S., & Bruner, E. (1974). *DISTAR reading*. Chicago: Science Research Associates.

Engelmann, S., Carnine, D., Johnson, G., & Meyers, L. (1988). *Corrective reading: Decoding*. Chicago: Science Research Associates.

Engelmann, S., Carnine, D., Johnson, G., & Meyers, L. (1989). *Corrective reading: Comprehension*. Chicago: Science Research Associates.

Paris, S. G., Cross, D. R., & Lipson, M. (1984). Informed strategies for learning: A program to improve children's reading awareness and comprehension. *Journal of Educational Psychology, 76*, 1239–1252.

Silbert, J., & Carnine, D. (1981). *Direct instruction mathematics*. Columbus, OH: Chas. E. Merrill.

University of Kansas, Institute for Research on Learning Disabilities. P.O. Box 972, Lawrence, KS 66045. The Kansas IRLD has several strategy packages available that concentrate mainly on study skills and reading comprehension and written language skills.

Literature about Individuals with Learning Disabilities

ELEMENTARY: AGES 5–8 AND 9–12

Aiello, B., & Shulman, J. (1988). *Secrets aren't (always) for keeps*. Frederick, MD: Kids on the Block.

Avi (1980). *Man from the sky*. New York: Knopf. (ages 9–12)

Cassedy, S. (1987). *M. E. and Morton*. New York: Crowell.

Gibson, J. (1980). *Do bananas chew gum?* New York: Lothrop, Lee & Shepard. (ages 9–12)

Hall, L. (1988). *Just one friend*. New York: Collier Books.

Lasker, J. (1980). *Nick joins in*. Chicago: Albert Whitman. (ages 5–8)

Levinson, M. (1985). *And don't bring Jeremy*. New York: Holt, Rinehart & Winston.

Pevsner, S. (1977). *Keep stompin' till the music stops*. New York: Bradbury. (ages 9–12)

Wolff, V. E. (1988). *Probably still Nick Swansen*. New York: Holt, Rinehart & Winston.

Software

Bank Street Speller, Computer Aids, 20417 Nordhoff Street, M5, Chatsworth, CA 91311.

Captain's Log: Cognitive Training System Network Services, 1915 Huguenot Road, Richmond, VA 23235; (804) 379-2253.

The Complete Spelling Program, Special Learning Education Software; (612) 926-5820.

Core Reading and Vocabulary Development, Educational Activities, Inc.; (516) 223-4666.

Create-Spell It, Hartley Courseware, Inc., 133 Bridge Street, Box 419, Dimondale, MN 48821.

DLM Math Fluency Program, DLM Teaching Resources, One DLM Park, Allen, TX 75002; (800) 527-5030.

Explore-a-Science, D. C. Heath & Company, 125 Spring Street, Lexington, MA 02173; (617) 860-1847.

Explore-a-Story, D. C. Heath & Company, 125 Spring Street, Lexington, MA 02173; (617) 860-1847.

Following Directions, Laureate Learning Systems, Inc., 110 East Spring Street, Winoski, VT 05404; (802) 655-4755.

Goofy's Word Factory, Sierra On Line—Disney Software, P.O. Box 85, Coarsegold, CA 93614.

Haunted House, Tandy Corporation, 1400 One Tandy Center, Fort Worth, TX 76102.

Newsroom, Scholastic, Inc., 730 Broadway, Department J.S., New York, New York, 10003; (800) 325-6149.

Ollie Series, C. C. Publications, Inc.; (800) 547-4800 (features basic skills/concepts such as matching upper- and lowercase letters; matching beginning and ending letters; discrimination of objects, letters, and short words).

Processing Power Program, Instructional Communications Technology, Inc., 10 Stepar Place, Huntington Station, New York 11746; (800) 225-5428.

Quiet Duck Learning Series, Computer Talk; (818) 331-0413.

Special Education Collection, Humanities Software, P.O. Box 590727, San Francisco, CA 94415; (415) 759-9324.

Word Processing Programs:
  No graphics:
    Bank Street Writer II, Scholastic, Inc., 730 Broadway, Department J.S., New York, N.Y. 10003; (800) 325-6149.
    Magic Slate II, Sunburst Communications, Inc., Pleasantville, NY 10570; (800) 431-1934.
    Talking Textwriter, Scholastic, Inc., 730 Broadway, Department JS, New York, NY 10003; (800) 325-6149.
  Graphics:
    Bank Street Story Book, Mindscape, Inc., 3444 Dundee Road, Northbrook, IL 60062; (312) 480-7667.

Videodiscs

Earth Science, Systems Impact, Inc., 200 Girard Street, Suite 214, Gaithersburg, MD 20877; (301) 869-0400.

Mastering Decimals and Percents, Systems Impact, Inc.

Mastering Equations, Roots, and Exponents, Systems Impact, Inc.

Mastering Fractions, Systems Impact, Inc.

Mastering Ratios and Word Problem Strategies, Systems Impact, Inc.

Understanding Chemistry and Energy, Systems Impact, Inc.

Organizations

Council for Exceptional Children, Division of Learning Disabilities, 1920 Association Drive, Reston, VA 22091; (703) 620-3660.

Council for Learning Disabilities, P.O. Box 40303, Overland Park, KS 66204; (913) 492-8755.

Foundation for Children with Learning Disabilities, 99 Park Avenue, 6th Floor, New York, NY 10016; (212) 687-7211.

Learning Disabilities Association of America, 5255 Grace Street, Pittsburgh, PA 15236; (412) 341-1515.

Orton Dyslexia Society, 724 York Road, Towson, MD 21204; (301) 296-0232.

Bibliography for Teaching Suggestions

Blandford, B. J., & Lloyd, J. W. (1987). Effects of a self-instructional procedure on handwriting. *Journal of Learning Disabilities*, *20*(6), 342–346.

Blankenship, C. S. (1985). Using curriculum-based assessment data to make instructional decisions. *Exceptional Children*, *52*, 233–238.

Cullinan, D., Lloyd, J., & Epstein, M. (1981). Strategy training: A structured approach to arithmetic instruction. *Exceptional Education Quarterly*, *2*, 41–49.

Ellis, E. S., Deshler, D. D., & Schumaker, J. B. (1989). Teaching adolescents with learning disabilities to generate and use task-specific strategies. *Journal of Learning Disabilities*, *22*, 108–119.

Griffey, Q. L., Zigmond, N., & Leinhardt, G. (1988). The effects of self-questioning and story structure training on the reading comprehension of poor readers. *Learning Disabilities Research*, *4*, 45–51.

Harris, K., & Graham, S. (1985). Improving learning disabled students' composition skills: Self-control strategy training. *Learning Disabilities Quarterly*, *8*, 27–36.

Lloyd, J., & deBettencourt, L. (1982). *Academic strategy training: A manual for teachers*. Charlottesville: University of Virginia Research Institute.

Wong, B. Y., L. & Jones, W. (1982). Increasing metacomprehension in learning disabled and normally achieving students through self-questioning training. *Learning Disability Quarterly*, *5*, 228–239.

SUMMARY

In the early 1960s parents and professionals advocated a new category of special education—learning disabilities—to describe individuals who in spite of normal or near-normal intelligence have a puzzling array of learning problems. What prompted the creation of this newest area was the realization that many children with learning problems were not receiving needed educational services.

The four most common factors in definitions of learning disabilities are IQ–achievement discrepancy, presumption of central nervous system dysfunction, psychological processing problems, learning problems not due to environmental disadvantage, mental retardation, and emotional disturbance. The most commonly used definition, that of the federal government, includes all four of these factors. Another popular definition, that of the National Joint Committee for Learning Disabilities, does not include psychological processing problems.

The prevalence of students identified as learning disabled has increased dramatically. During the 1987–1988 school year, 4.41% of the population from 6 to 17 years of age received such services.

Causal factors for learning disabilities fall into organic and biological, genetic, and environmental. More and more evidence is accumulating that many learning disabled individuals have brain, or central nervous system, dysfunction. Also, more and more evidence is accumulating that genetic factors are at the root of some learning disabilities. Environmental causes have been more difficult to pinpoint, although some professionals believe that poor teaching can lead to learning disabilities.

Practitioners use tests of several different types to measure learning disabilities: standardized achievement tests, process tests, informal reading inventories, and formative evaluation methods. Process tests, designed to assess underlying psychological processes (e.g., visual perception) presumed to cause academic difficulties, are not as popular as they once were. There is growing interest in curriculum-based assessment, a particular type of formative evaluation with five features: (1) The teacher usually does the assessment, (2) the focus is on behaviors directly relevant to classroom performance, (3) the teacher measures the child's behavior frequently and over a period of time, (4) the assessment is used in conjunction with the setting of educational goals and, (5) the teacher uses the assessment information to decide whether the educational program for an individual student is effective.

The variety of psychological and behavioral characteristics attributed to learning-disabled individuals underscores the heterogeneity of this population; that is, not all learning-disabled people are alike. Some learning-disabled students exhibit perceptual, motor, or perceptual-motor problems. However, there is little evidence that these problems cause academic problems such as difficulty in reading.

There is a higher prevalence of attention-deficit hyperactivity disorder (ADHD) among learning-disabled children. Children with ADHD exhibit excessive motor activity, impulsivity, and inattention.

Many learning-disabled individuals demonstrate memory deficits. They have problems using memory strategies, such as rehearsal, and they find it especially difficult to remember verbal material because of their problems with phonology, the sounds that make up words.

Problems in metacognition interfere with the learning-disabled student's awareness of learning strategies and the ability to regulate their use. These metacognitive difficulties, in turn, impede the child's academic performance.

Ratings by peers, teachers, and parents are consistent in demonstrating that learning-disabled children are not well liked. The children, themselves, have poor self-esteem, especially regarding their academic abilities. Frequently they are poorly motivated, showing signs of external rather than internal sources of motivation. In the area of attributions, they fail to acknowledge that their own efforts can lead to success, but they are quick to attribute their failures to their own inabilities. These pessimistic attributions put them at risk for developing "learned helplessness," a perception that no matter what they do, they will still fail.

Needless to say, all learning-disabled students have scholastic difficulties. Reading disabilities, especially severe reading difficulties, are often related to problems with phonology. The students have problems in breaking words into their component sounds and in blending individual sounds together to make words. Although their most frequent difficulties are in reading, the possibility of math problems should not be ignored.

Some authorities believe that a composite of the preceding characteristics indicates that many learning-disabled children are passive rather than active learners. Many of their problems may be caused by this inactive learning style.

Given the great heterogeneity of behavioral characteristics, some researchers are trying to document subtypes of learning disabilities. One research team, for instance, suggests that learning-disabled children in an attention deficit subtype and subtypes characterized by behavioral problems are at risk to decline over time academically.

There are many approaches to educating learning-disabled students. In process training, such elements as visual and auditory perception and psycholinguistic processes are the focus of instruction rather than academics per se. Although once quite popular, fewer teachers now use process training because research has not documented its effectiveness in increasing achievement.

Multisensory approaches attempt to remedy learning problems by using a combination of the sensory systems in training. In the VAKT method, the child uses his or her visual, auditory, kinesthetic, and tactile senses. Cruickshank's approach is built on the notion that

inattentive and hyperactive children need a reduction in irrelevant stimuli and a great deal of structure. Classroom activities are strongly teacher-directed.

Medication can be highly effective in increasing the concentration of some, but not all, children with attentional problems. Because the drug is powerful, with some possible side effects, teachers, parents, and physicians need to work together to monitor its effects.

Cognitive training focuses on changing thought processes. Many professionals advocate cognitive training because it (1) stresses self-initiative, (2) provides specific learning strategies, and (3) appears particularly well suited for attentional and impulsivity problems. In self-monitoring the individual evaluates and records his or her own behavior. In the keyword method, students use pictures and keywords to help remember concepts from content areas such as history or science. In self-instruction individuals talk about what they are doing, perhaps asking themselves questions before and during a reading assignment. In reciprocal teaching, the teacher gently structures the learning situation so that students gradually take over more and more responsibility for their own instruction.

Behavior modification has been used effectively with learning-disabled students. In this procedure, the teacher specifies goals, carefully monitors behavior, and reinforces successful performance.

Direct instruction is similar to behavior modification, but it focuses more on what the teacher should be doing during instruction. Research on its effectiveness has been very positive.

The resource room is the most common placement for learning-disabled students. The goals of such an arrangement are to move the child back into the general education classroom for more and more of the day and to gear teaching methods to the needs of the individual student.

Most professionals are cautious about establishing programs for learning-disabled preschoolers because it is hard to predict at that age which children will develop later academic difficulties. We do know that certain pre-academic skills such as letter, number, shape, and color recognition are the best predictors of later academic learning.

The importance of educational programming at the secondary level and beyond is underscored by evidence that learning-disabled individuals do not automatically outgrow their problems as adults. In particular, reading and spelling frequently remain problems, and without intensive and long-term intervention significant learning difficulties are likely to remain. There is evidence of a higher prevalence of learning disabilities among juvenile delinquents. Although the connection between the two is complex, many authorities believe learning disabilities cause delinquent behavior in some way.

Secondary programs vary in two ways: (1) how much time students spend with the special versus general education teacher and (2) the degree to which the curriculum is "special," or different from the general curriculum. Many learning-disabled students fall in the middle on these criteria, needing a modest amount of special educator involvement and some use of different curricula.

Postsecondary programs include vocational and technical schools as well as community colleges and four-year colleges. More and more universities and colleges are establishing programs and services for learning-disabled students. One way of conceptualizing services for the college-bound, learning-disabled student has three transition stages: high school to college, during college, and college to employment. Such a model stresses the need to consider programming from a long-range viewpoint.

MAJESTIC TIGER

Robert Lauricella, Creative Growth Art Center

If schools are to address the educational problems of delinquent and antisocial children and youths, the number served by special education will have to be increased dramatically.

CAUSES

The causes of E/BD have been attributed to four major factors: biological disorders and diseases, pathological family relationships, negative cultural influences, and undesirable experiences at school. Although in the vast majority of cases there is no conclusive empirical evidence that any of these factors is directly responsible for disordered behavior, it is apparent that some may give a child a predisposition to exhibit problem behavior, and others may precipitate or trigger it. That is, some factors, such as genetics, influence behavior over a long period of time and increase the likelihood that a given set of circumstances will trigger maladaptive responses. Other factors (e.g., observing one parent beating the other) may have a more immediate effect and may trigger maladaptive responses in an individual who is already predisposed to problem behavior.

Another concept important in all theories of E/BD is the idea of *contributing factors.* It is extremely unusual to find a single cause that has led directly to disordered behavior. Usually several factors together contribute to the development of a problem. In almost all cases the question of what specifically has caused a child to have a behavioral disorder cannot be answered; no one really knows.

Biological Factors

Behavior may be influenced by genetic, neurological, or biochemical factors, or by combinations of these. Certainly there is a relationship between body and behavior, and it would therefore seem reasonable to look for a biological causal factor of some kind for certain emotional/behavioral disorders. The fact is, though, that only rarely is it possible to demonstrate a relationship between a specific biological factor and E/BD. Many children with E/BD have no detectable biological flaws that could account for their actions, and many behaviorally normal children have serious biological defects. For most children with E/BD, there simply is no real evidence that biological factors alone are at the root of the problem. For those with severe and profound disorders, however, there is evidence to suggest that biological factors may contribute to the condition (Prior & Werry, 1986).

All children are born with a biologically determined behavioral style, or **temperament.** Although children's inborn temperaments may be changed by the way they are reared, some believe that children with "difficult" temperaments are predisposed to develop E/BD (Thomas & Chess, 1984). There is no one-to-one relationship between temperament and E/BD, however. A "difficult" child may be handled so well or a child with an "easy" temperament so poorly that the final outcome is quite different from what one might predict on the basis of initial behavioral style. Other biological factors besides temperament—disease, malnutrition, and brain trauma, for example—may predispose children to develop emotional problems (Baumeister, Kupstas, & Klindworth, 1990; Lozoff, 1989). Substance abuse also may contribute to serious emotional and behavioral problems (Newcomb & Bentler, 1989). However, except in rare instances it is not possible to determine that these factors are direct causes of problem behavior.

As is the case in mental retardation, there is more often evidence of a biological cause among severely and profoundly disabled children. Psychotic (autistic or schizophrenic) children frequently, but not always, show signs of neurological defects (Prior & Werry, 1986). There is convincing evidence that genetic factors contribute to schizophrenia (Plomin, 1989), although even when there is severe and profound disturbance, the role of specific biological factors often remains a mystery (Kauffman, 1989; Prior & Werry, 1986). It is now generally accepted that autism is a neurological disorder, but the nature and causes of the neurological defect are unknown.

Family Factors

Mental health specialists have been tempted to blame behavioral difficulties primarily on parent-child relationships because it is obvious that the nuclear family—father, mother, and children—has a profound influence on early development. In fact, some advocates of psychoanalysis believe that almost all severe problems of children stem from early negative interactions between mother and child. However, empirical research on family relationships indicates that the influence of parents on their children is no simple matter, and that deviant children may influence their parents as much as the parents influence them. It is increasingly clear that family influences are interactional and transactional and that the effects of parents and children on one another are reciprocal (Patterson, DeBaryshe, & Ramsey, 1989). Even in cases of severe and profound E/BD, it is not possible to find consistent and valid research findings that allow the blame for the children's problem behavior to be placed primarily on their parents (Sameroff, Steifer, & Zax, 1982).

The outcome of parental discipline depends not only on the particular techniques used but also on the characteristics of the child (Rutter, 1985). Generalizations about the effects of parental discipline are difficult to make, for as Becker (1964) commented long ago, "There are probably many routes to becoming a 'good parent' which vary with the personality of both the parents and children and with the pressure in the environment with which one must learn to cope" (p. 202). Nevertheless, sensitivity to children's needs, love-oriented methods of dealing with misbehavior, and reinforcement (attention and praise) for appropriate behavior unquestionably tend to promote desirable behavior in children. Parents who are generally lax in disciplining their children but are hostile, rejecting, cruel, and inconsistent in dealing with misbehavior are likely to have aggressive, delinquent children. Broken, disorganized homes in which the parents themselves have arrest records or are violent are particularly likely to foster delinquency and lack of social competence.

In discussing the combined effects of genetics and environment on behavioral development, Plomin (1989) warns against assuming that the family environment will make siblings similar. "Environmental influences do not operate on a family-by-family basis but rather on an individual-by-individual basis. They are specific to each child rather than general for an entire family" (p. 109). Thus although we know that some types of family environments (abusive, neglectful, rejecting, and inconsistent, for example) are destructive, we must also remember that each child will experience and react to family relationships in his or her unique way.

Cultural Factors

Children and their families are embedded in a culture that influences their behavior (Rogoff & Morelli, 1989). Aside from family and school, many environmental conditions affect adults' expectations of children and children's expectations for themselves and their peers. Values and behavioral standards are communicated to children through a variety of cultural conditions, demands, prohibitions, and models. Several specific cultural influences leap to mind: the level of violence in the media (especially television and motion pictures), the use of terror as a means of coercion, the

How parents deal with their children's exasperating behavior may contribute to behavior disorders; however, parental discipline alone is not the cause of most behavior problems. (Bill Binzen/Photo Researchers)

availability of recreational drugs and the level of drug abuse, changing standards for sexual conduct, religious demands and restrictions on behavior, and the threat of nuclear accidents or war.

Undoubtedly, the culture in which children are reared exerts an influence on their emotional, social, and behavioral development. Case studies of rapidly changing cultures bear this out.

Other studies suggest cultural influences on anxiety, depression, and aggression (Chivian et al., 1985; Goldstein, 1983; Hawton, 1986). The fear of nuclear holocaust contributes to depression for some children and youths. The level of violence depicted on television and in movies is almost certainly a contributing factor in the increasing level of violence in our society. Particularly troubling is the finding that television violence seems more "real" to disturbed than to nondisturbed children. This finding suggests that disturbed children may be more likely than others to perform aggressive acts after watching televised violence (Sprafkin, Gadow, & Dussault, 1986).

In short, social and cultural conditions or changes may have a marked effect on children's behavior. As Morse (1985, pp. ix–x) observes,

> Sexual mores have changed, placing new responsibilities on adolescents. The consequence of these and many other societal changes are reflected in more than half-a-million teenage mothers each year; the increase in depression and suicide; and the prevalence of delinquency, alcoholism, and drug abuse. Currently, a million youths run away each year. Although youth violence is a mirror image of adult behavior, it has reached epidemic proportions in some schools. . . . It is a sad commentary that over half of the robberies and assaults on youngsters actually occur in school!

Garmezy (1987) and Baumeister, Kupstas, & Klindworth (1990) also note the changing cultural conditions in the United States during the 1980s that predispose children to develop E/BD and a variety of other handicapping conditions. Among these are dramatic increases in the number of children living in poverty. There have also been substantial increases in the number of children born to teenage mothers and to mothers who have abused crack, cocaine and other substances. At the same time, medical and social services available to poor children and their families have been cut substantially. In short, the Reagan era was a period of enormous affluence for some Americans but also a period in which poverty and related problems grew rapidly. Neglect of the problems of poor children and their families have led some to question the importance of the health and welfare of children in U.S. culture (see also Rogoff & Morelli, 1989).

School Factors

Some children already have E/BD when they begin school; others develop behavioral or emotional disorders during their school years, perhaps in part because of damaging experiences in the classroom itself. Children who exhibit E/BD when they enter school may become better or worse according to how they are managed in the classroom. School experiences are no doubt of great importance to children; but like biological and family factors, we cannot justify many statements regarding how such experiences contribute to the child's behavioral difficulties. A child's temperament and social competence may interact with classmates' and teachers' behavior in contributing to emotional/behavioral problems. When a child with an already difficult temperament enters school lacking the skills for academic and social success, he or she is likely to get negative responses from peers and teachers.

There is a very real danger that such a child will become trapped in a spiral of negative interactions in which he or she becomes increasingly irritating to and irritated by teachers and peers. The school can contribute to the development of emotional problems in several rather specific ways. Teachers may be insensitive to children's individuality; they may require a mindless conformity to the rules and routines. Educators and parents alike may hold too high or too low expectations for the child's achievement or conduct, and they may communicate to the child who disappoints them that he or she is inadequate or undesirable.

Discipline in the school may be too lax, too rigid, or inconsistent. Instruction may be offered in skills for which the child has no real or imagined use. The school environment may be such that the misbehaving child is rewarded with recognition and special attention (even if that attention is criticism or punishment), whereas the child who behaves is ignored. Finally, teachers and peers may be models of misconduct—the child may misbehave by imitating them (Kauffman, 1989).

IDENTIFICATION

It is much easier to identify disordered *behaviors* than it is to define and classify types and causes of E/BD. Most children with E/BD do not escape the notice of their teachers. Occasionally a child will not be a bother to anyone and thus be "invisible," but it is usually easy for experienced teachers to tell when a child needs help. The most common type of E/BD—conduct disorder—attracts immediate attention, so there is seldom any real problem in identification. Immature children and those with personality problems may be less obvious, but they are not difficult to recognize. Children with E/BD are so readily identified by school personnel, in fact, that few schools bother to use systematic screening procedures. Also, special services for children with E/BD lag far behind the need. There is not much point in screening children for problems when there are no services available to treat them.

Children with psychoses (or pervasive developmental disorders) are easily recognized. In fact, the parents of children with autism frequently report that soon after their child's birth they noticed that he or she was strange or different from most children—unresponsive, rigid, or emotionally detached, for example. Children with schizophrenia are seldom mistaken for those who are developing normally. Their unusual language, mannerisms, and ways of relating to others soon become matters of concern to parents, teachers, and even many casual observers. But children with psychotic disorders are a small percentage of those with E/BD, and problems in their identification are not usually encountered.

However, it should not be thought that there is never any question about whether or not a child has an E/BD. The younger the child, the more difficult it is to judge whether or not that child's behavior signifies a serious problem. And some children with E/BD are undetected because teachers are not sensitive to their problems or because they do not stand out sharply from other children in the environment who may have even more serious problems. Furthermore, even sensitive teachers sometimes make errors of judgment. Finally, some children with E/BD do not exhibit problems at school.

Formal screening and accurate early identification for the purpose of planning educational intervention are complicated by the problems of definition already discussed. In general, however, teachers' informal judgment has served as a fairly valid and reliable means of screening children for emotional/behavioral problems (as compared with judgments of psychologists and psychiatrists). When more formal procedures are used, teachers' ratings of behavior have turned out to be quite accurate (Edelbrock & Achenbach, 1984). Children's ratings of their peers and their own behavior have also proved helpful (Bower, 1981).

Walker and his colleagues have devised a screening system for use in elementary schools based on the assumption that a teacher's judgment is a valid and cost-effective though greatly underused method of identifying children with E/BD (Walker et al., 1988). Although teachers tend to overrefer students who exhibit externalizing behavior problems (those with conduct disorders), they tend to underrefer students with internalizing problems (those who are characterized by anxiety-withdrawal). To make certain that children are not overlooked in screening, but that a lot of time and effort is not wasted, a three-step process is used.

First, the teacher lists and rank-orders students with externalizing and internalizing problems. Those who best fit descriptions of students with externalizing problems and those who best fit descriptions of those with internalizing problems are listed. Then they are rank-ordered from most like to least like the descriptions. Second, the teacher completes two checklists for the three highest-ranked pupils on each list. One checklist asks the teacher to indicate whether or not each pupil exhibited specific behaviors during the past month (such as "steals," "has tantrums," "uses obscene language or swears"). The other checklist requires the teacher to judge how often (never, sometimes, frequently) each pupil shows certain characteristics (e.g., "follows established classroom rules," or "cooperates with peers in group activities or situations"). Third, pupils whose scores on these checklists exceed established norms are observed in the classroom and on the playground by a school professional other than the classroom teacher (a school psychologist, counselor, or resource teacher).

Classroom observations indicate the extent to which the pupil meets academic expectations; playground observations assess the quality and nature of social behavior. These direct observations of behavior, in addition to teachers' ratings, are then used to decide whether or not the child has problems that warrant classification for special education. Such carefully researched screening systems may lead to improved services for children with E/BD. Systematic efforts to base identification on teachers' judgment *and* careful observation should result in services being directed to those most clearly in need.

PSYCHOLOGICAL AND BEHAVIORAL CHARACTERISTICS

Describing the characteristics of children and youths with E/BD is an extraordinary challenge because disorders of emotions and behavior are extremely varied. The box on pages 187–188 provides profiles of children and families in need of mental health services, in which, in most cases, special education is an important part. As you read the description of psychological and behavioral characteristics, remember that we are attempting to provide a general picture of these children; individual children may vary markedly in intelligence, achievement, life circumstances, and emotional/behavioral characteristics.

Intelligence and Achievement

The idea that children with E/BD tend to be particularly bright is a myth. Research clearly shows that the average child with E/BD has an IQ in the dull-normal range (around 90) and that relatively few score above the bright-normal range. Compared to the normal distribution of intelligence, more children with E/BD fall into the slow-learner and mildly retarded categories. Although children with autism are often untestable, those who can be tested are likely to have IQs in the retarded range; the average for these children is about 50. On the basis of a review of the research on the intelligence of children with E/BD, Kauffman (1989) hypothesized distributions of intelligence as shown in Figure 5–1. Of course, we have been referring to children with E/BD as a group. Some children who have E/BD are extremely bright and score very high on intelligence tests.

There are pitfalls in assessing the intellectual characteristics of a group of children by examining the distribution of the IQs. Intelligence tests are not perfect instruments for measuring what we mean by "intelligence," and it can be argued that emotional/behavioral difficulties may prevent children from scoring as high as they could. That is, it might be argued that intelligence tests are biased against children with E/BD and that their "true" intelligence is higher than the test scores indicate. Still, the lower-than-normal IQs for these children do indicate lower ability to perform tasks other children can perform successfully, and the lower scores are consistent with impairment in other areas of functioning (academic achievement and social skills, for example). IQ is a relatively good predictor of how far a child will progress academically and socially, even in cases of severe and profound disorders.

Most children with E/BD are also underachievers at school, as measured by standardized tests (Kauffman, 1989). A child with E/BD does not usually achieve at the level expected for his or her mental age; it is relatively seldom that one finds such a child to be academically advanced. Many children with severe disorders lack even the most basic reading and arithmetic skills; and the few who seem to be competent in reading or math are often unable to apply their skills to everyday problems. Some children with severe disorders do not even possess basic self-care or daily living skills, such as using the toilet, grooming, dressing, and feeding.

Profiles: Children and Families in Need of Mental Health Services

Following are examples of children and youths with emotional/behavioral characteristics indicating a need for mental health services. Note that these brief profiles often indicate problems of families and communities, teachers and schools, and social agencies as well.

Infant

Willie's muscles were more tense at birth than those of most babies. His mother, who had been abandoned as a baby and beaten as a young child, was sure Willie was rejecting her. She became nervous, then angry. When Willie cried, she ignored him. By the time he was one month old, Willie was avoiding his mother's gaze, and she was suspicious and guarded.

Fortunately, Willie's mother was referred to a special clinic where one therapist was assigned to work with her, another to work with Willie. Willie's therapist, a pediatric nurse trained to work with babies, devised a game. Since Willie ignored real faces, she drew a face on cardboard and got him to watch that. Then she would lower the cardboard face to reveal her own. Willie found this interesting and played the game tirelessly. In a few weeks he preferred a human face to the cardboard one. But his mother was still moody and unpredictable. Some days she would not let Willie's therapist into the house. It was several months before she played the face game with Willie herself.

Preschool Child

Alissa is three years eight months old and already in serious trouble. She is overly active and disobedient at home, demanding and clingy with adults, bites her nails, cannot sleep, and wets her bed nightly. At her day care center she is aggressive and uncontrollable. She actually injured several children, and parents are insisting she be dismissed.

School-Aged Child

Jerry is a small, wiry, very sad third grader. He is performing just below grade level, although an early IQ test suggests he is gifted. For the past two years, Jerry's world has been falling apart. Early in first grade, Jerry's favorite grandfather died, and his mother suffered a miscarriage. During the second grade, his parents were divorced. Concerned about dramatic changes in Jerry's behavior, Jerry's parents sought help, and Jerry began to see a therapist at a local mental health clinic. Although Jerry's parents first were told that the school would pay for therapy, the school refused because academically Jerry was doing all right. The parents had some insurance coverage, but it was used up by the time Jerry was in third grade. So Jerry was told he could not see his therapist any more. Jerry was very attached to the therapist. When he faced the prospect of another loss, his school work began to deteriorate rapidly. One day he was found riding his bike in the middle of a heavily trafficked street. His parents again approached the school. This time officials agreed that Jerry needed help and suggested assigning him to an intern who was doing field work as an elementary school counselor. They refused to pay for Jerry to continue with his own therapist.

Adolescent

Daryl is a 14-year-old who was enrolled in the Positive Education Program's day treatment center . . . after going two years without receiving any educational or treatment services. He had been expelled from school for his constant use of abusive language, his inability to stay in his seat for more than three or four minutes, his destruction of school property, and his frequent use of weapons, pipes, bats, and other dangerous objects. Before coming to the day treatment program, he was rejected by ten residential treatment services.

In day treatment Daryl's behavior was initially violent and disruptive. Academically he functioned at a second or third grade level. Gradually, he began to improve, responding to the support of one teacher-counselor and to the incentive of going on camping trips if he worked hard. In the past Daryl's mother had avoided all discussions regarding her son with schools, courts, and mental health personnel. With the aid of another parent in the day treatment program, she became part of the helping team. After one and one-half years in the program, Daryl's behavior was so improved he was able to return to his home school, although serious academic problems remain. (Cited with permission from the Positive Education Program.)

Hospitalized Child

Ruth has had severe mental health problems since age two. Now she is 12. She is agitated and miserably unhappy, imagines everyone is against her, and strikes out at others at random. In fifth grade she was suspended from school for hitting a teacher and breaking her foot. Since then Ruth has been in and out of residential placements and psychiatric hospitals. She runs away from most placements and once fled in the winter without coat or shoes. Other places push her out. Last fall she was immediately discharged from a private psychiatric hospital when she assaulted a physician. More recently, she was evicted from another inpatient setting where she was described as "dramatically aggressive." Now Ruth is at home and her behavior is deteriorating rapidly. Her parents feel helpless. They alternate between overprotecting Ruth and rejecting her. The programs to which Ruth has been referred recently do not believe their staff can protect both her and the other children in their care. They claim to lack the resources required to provide Ruth the intensive services she needs. Ruth could benefit from long-term care, delivered by staff trained to work with children like herself. No such program has appeared, and Ruth may well end up on the adult ward of a state psychiatric hospital before one comes along. (Ruth's state has no adolescent units.)

Child in State Custody

Cheryl was 14 years old and sexually active when the elderly aunt she lived with refused to have anything to do with her. The aunt committed Cheryl to a local community mental health center as an adolescent inpatient. She petitioned the court to declare Cheryl "incorrigible." This would have made Cheryl a ward of the court, transferring responsibility for her to the child welfare system. Cheryl liked this idea because it meant a chance to live in a foster home. For three months while she waited for the court's decision, Cheryl was a model patient. Then everything fell apart. The court decided not to make Cheryl its ward and refused to provide any services for her through the child welfare agency. So Cheryl remained in the hospital for three years. Her behavior worsened dramatically; she became combative and hostile. Her cognitive skills deteriorated so badly that an IQ test found her retarded. Ironically, at that point the court decided to declare Cheryl its ward and, at taxpayers' expense, sent her to an out-of-state facility in a rural area 2,000 miles from home. Cheryl ran away, back to her own city. Shortly after, Cheryl, now 18, was picked up as a prostitute, sent to jail, and released. Her behavior became increasingly bizarre. Ultimately, she was placed in the state psychiatric hospital on a ward for chronic schizophrenics.

Minority Child

Pablo is an adolescent whose father died young. Pablo's stepfather, with whom he is very close, was recently disabled. Now Pablo has begun to fight with other children and is increasingly fresh to his teachers. School personnel say he is a "discipline problem." At home he is often depressed, cries easily, and is readily angered. He lives in a city rich in psychiatric resources. But he primarily speaks Spanish, and a search for a Spanish-speaking male therapist has proved futile. An educational advocate trying to help Pablo said bitterly, "No one sees them until they learn English."

SOURCE: J. Knitzer. *Unclaimed Children: The Failure of Public Responsibility to Children and Adolescents in Need of Mental Health Services* (Washington, DC: Children's Defense Fund, 1982), pp. ix–7.

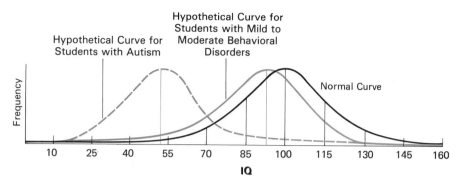

Figure 5.1   Hypothetical frequency distributions of IQ for students with mild to moderate disorders and students with autism compared to normal frequency distribution.

SOURCE: J. M. Kauffman, *Characteristics of Behavior Disorders of Children and Youth,* 4th ed. (Columbus, OH: Charles E. Merrill, 1989), p. 183. Reprinted with permission.

Social and Emotional Characteristics

Previously we described two major dimensions of disodered behavior based on analyses of behavior ratings: externalizing and internalizing. The externalizing dimension is characterized by aggressive, acting-out behavior; the internalizing dimension is characterized by anxious, withdrawn behavior. Our discussion here will focus on the aggressive and withdrawn types of behavior typically exhibited by children with E/BD.

Although both aggressive and withdrawn behaviors are commonly seen in most children with E/BD, we will discuss the characteristics of severe and profound disturbance in a separate section. These children may be qualitatively as well as quantitatively different from others, for certain behavioral features set them apart. Remember, too, that a given child might, at different times, show both aggressive and withdrawn behaviors.

At the beginning of this chapter we said that most children with E/BD are not well liked by their peers. Studies of the social status of students in regular elementary and secondary classrooms have indicated that those who are identified as having E/BD are seldom socially accepted. Given what we know about the behavioral characteristics of students with E/BD and the behavioral characteristics that support social acceptance, this should come as no surprise: "The research indicates that children—whether normal or exceptional—who are in frequent conflict with authority, who fight or bother others a great deal, and who demonstrate verbal aggression are rarely the objects of social acceptance" (Drabman & Patterson, 1981, p. 53). Children who show these characteristics are actively rejected, not just neglected, by their peers.

Aggressive, Acting-Out Behavior (Externalizing)

As noted earlier, conduct disorders are the most common problems exhibited by children with E/BD. Hitting, fighting, teasing, yelling, refusing to comply with requests, crying, destructiveness, vandalism, extortion—these behaviors, if exhibited often, are very likely to earn a child the label "disturbed." Normal children cry, scream, hit, fight, become negative, and do almost everything else disturbed children do, only not so impulsively and so often. Children of the type we are discussing here drive adults to distraction. They are not popular with their peers either, unless they are socialized delinquents who do not offend other social deviants. They typically do not respond quickly and positively to well-meaning adults who care about them and try to be helpful.

Some of these children are considered hyperactive or brain-injured; some are called **sociopathic** because they appear to hurt others deliberately and without any sense of doing wrong. Their behavior is not only extremely troublesome but also appears to be resistant to change through typical discipline. Often they are so frequently scolded and punished that punishment means little or nothing to them. Because of adult exasperation and their own deviousness, they get away with misbehavior a lot of the time. We are talking about children who behave horribly not once in a while but so often that the people they must live with or be with cannot stand them. Of course, aggressive, acting-out children typically cannot stand the people they have to live and be with either, and often for good reason. Such children are screamed at, criticized, and punished a lot. The problem, then, is not just the child's behavior. What must be examined if the child or anyone else is to be helped is the *interaction between the child's behavior and the behavior of other people in his or her environment.*

Aggression has been analyzed from many different viewpoints. The analyses that have the strongest support in empirical research are those of social learning theorists such as Bandura (1973) and behavioral psychologists such as Patterson (Patterson, DeBaryshe, & Ramsey, 1989). Their studies take into account the child's experience and his or her motivation, based on the anticipated consequences of aggression. In brief, they view aggression as *learned* behavior, and they assume that it is possible to identify the conditions under which it will be learned. The following statements about learned aggression are supported by research.

Aggressive children are frequently in conflict with others. Fighting, teasing, or causing pain and discomfort for no socially acceptable purpose are aggressive behaviors. (Ken Gaghan/Jeroboam, Inc.)

Children learn many aggressive behaviors by observing parents, siblings, play-mates, and people portrayed on television and in movies. Individuals who model aggression are more likely to be imitated if they are high in social status and are observed to receive rewards and escape punishment for their aggression, especially if they experience no unpleasant consequences or obtain rewards by overcoming their victims. If children are placed in an unpleasant situation and they cannot escape from the unpleasantness or obtain rewards except by aggression, they are more likely to be aggressive, especially if this behavior is tolerated or encouraged by others.

Aggression is encouraged by external rewards (social status, power, suffering of the victim, obtaining desired items), vicarious rewards (seeing others obtain desirable consequences for their aggression), and self-reinforcement (self-congratu-lation or enhancement of self-image). If children can justify aggression in their own minds (by comparison to the behavior of others or by dehumanizing their victims), they are more likely to be aggressive. Punishment may actually increase aggression under some circumstances: when it is inconsistent or delayed, when there is no positive alternative to the punished behavior, when it provides an example of aggression, or when counterattack against the punisher seems likely to be successful.

Teaching aggressive children to be less obnoxious is no simple matter, but social learning theory and behavioral research do provide some general guidelines. In general, research does not support the notion that it is wise to let children "act out" their aggression freely. The most helpful techniques include providing examples (models) of nonaggressive responses to aggression-provoking circumstances, helping the child rehearse or role-play nonaggressive behavior, providing reinforcement for nonaggressive behavior, preventing the child from obtaining positive conse-quences for aggression, and punishing aggression in ways that involve as little counteraggression as possible (using "time-out" or brief social isolation rather than spanking or yelling).

The seriousness of children's aggressive, acting-out behavior should not be under-estimated. As noted, it has been a popular idea for decades that although these children cause a lot of trouble, they are not as seriously disturbed or handicapped as children who are shy, anxious, neurotic types. Research has exploded this myth. When combined with school failure, aggressive, antisocial behavior in childhood generally means a gloomy future in terms of social adjustment and mental health, especially for boys. Neurotic, shy, anxious children are much more likely to be able to get and hold a job, overcome their emotional problems, and stay out of jails and mental hospitals than are adults who were conduct problems and delinquent as children (see Kazdin, 1987).

Of course, there are exceptions to the rule. But there is a high probability that the aggressive child who is a failure in school will become more of a social misfit as an adult than the withdrawn child. When we consider that conduct disorders and delinquency are highly correlated with school failure, the importance of meeting the needs of acting-out and underachieving children is obvious.

Immature, Withdrawn Behavior (Internalizing)

In noting the seriousness of aggressive, acting-out behavior, we do not intend to downplay the handicaps of immaturity and withdrawal. In their extreme forms, withdrawal and immaturity are characteristics of the severe and profound disorders known as childhood schizophrenia and infantile autism. Such disorders (sometimes called childhood psychoses) are not only extremely damaging to individuals in their childhood years but also carry a very poor prognosis for adult mental health. The child whose behavior fits a pattern of immaturity and withdrawal cannot develop the close and satisfying human relationships that characterize normal development. Such a child will find it difficult to meet the pressures and demands of everyday life.

All children exhibit immature behavior and act withdrawn once in a while. Children who fit the withdrawn, immature description, however, are typically infantile in their ways or reluctant to interact with other people. They are social isolates who have few friends, seldom play with children their own age, and lack the social skills necessary to have fun. Some retreat into fantasy or daydreaming; some develop fears that are completely out of proportion to the circumstances; some complain constantly of little aches and pains and let their "illness" keep them from participating in normal activities; some regress to earlier stages of development and demand constant help and attention; and some become depressed for no apparent reason (see Klein & Last, 1989; Kovacs, 1989).

As in the case of aggressive, acting-out behavior, withdrawal and immaturity may be interpreted in many different ways. Proponents of the psychoanalytic approach are likely to see internal conflicts and unconscious motivations as the underlying causes. Behavioral psychologists tend to interpret such problems in terms of failures in social learning. This view is supported by more empirical research data than other views (see Kauffman, 1989). A social learning analysis attributes withdrawal and immaturity to an inadequate environment. Causal factors may include overrestrictive parental discipline, punishment for appropriate social responses, reward for isolate behavior, lack of opportunity to learn and practice social skills, and models (examples) of inappropriate behavior. It is possible to teach immature or withdrawn children the skills they lack by arranging opportunities for them to learn and practice appropriate responses, showing models engaging in appropriate behavior, and providing rewards for improved behavior.

A particularly important aspect of immature, withdrawn behavior is depression. Only very recently have mental health workers and special educators begun to realize that depression is a widespread and serious problem among children and adolescents (Forness, 1988; Klein & Last, 1989; Kovacs, 1989). Today the consensus of psychologists is that the nature of depression in children and youths is quite similar to that of depression in adults. The indications of depression include disturbances of mood or feelings, inability to think or concentrate, lack of motivation, and decreased physical well-being. A depressed child or youth may act sad, lonely, and apathetic; exhibit low self-esteem, excessive guilt, and pervasive pessimism; avoid tasks and social experiences; and/or have physical complaints or problems in sleeping, eating, or eliminating. Sometimes depression is accompanied by such problems as bed-wetting (nocturnal enuresis), fecal soiling (encopresis), extreme fear of or refusal to go to school, failure in school, or talk of suicide or suicide attempts.

Suicide has increased dramatically during the past decade among those between the ages of fifteen and twenty-four; is is now among the leading causes of death in this age group (Hawton, 1986). Depression, especially when it is severe and accompanied by a sense of hopelessness, is linked to suicide and suicide attempts. Therefore it is important for all those who work with young people to be able to recognize the signs (Guetzloe, 1987). Substance abuse is also now a major problem among children and teenagers and may be related to depression (Newcomb & Bentler, 1989).

Depression sometimes has a biological cause, and antidepressant medications have at times been successful in helping depressed children and youths overcome their problems. In many cases, however, no biological cause can be found. Depression

Depression, which often includes social withdrawal in various forms, is now recognized as a frequent and serious problem of youth. (Richard Hutchings/Photo Researchers)

can also be caused by environmental or psychological factors, such as the death of a loved one, separation of one's parents, school failure, rejection by one's peers, or a chaotic and punitive home environment. Interventions based on social learning theory—instructing children in social interaction skills and self-control techniques and teaching them to view themselves more positively, for example—have often been successful in such cases.

Special Characteristics of Children with Psychotic Disorders

Children whose behavior is grossly different from normal are generally considered psychotic, severely retarded, or in some other way severely or profoundly disabled. We have avoided using a particular label such as autistic for these children because there is still confusion about exactly what the common labels mean. We know that these children are extremely different, but diagnosticians often disagree about the most appropriate label in the individual case. Generally, however, **schizophrenia** refers to psychotic behavior manifested by loss of contact with reality, bizarre thought processes, and extremely inappropriate behavior. **Autism** is characterized by extreme social withdrawal, self-stimulation, cognitive deficits, and language disorders that are apparent before the age of thirty months. Childhood schizophrenia typically does not manifest itself until the child is at least five years old, and the onset often occurs in later childhood or adolescence, whereas autism (sometimes called *early infantile autism*) is a disorder beginning before the child is two and one-half years old.

We will describe briefly the types of behavior that set these children apart from those having less severe disorders. Remember that not every child with a severe disorder exhibits all these characteristics (Durand & Carr, 1988; Prior & Werry, 1986; Rutter & Schopler, 1987).

Lack of Daily Living Skills

One of the reasons children with severe E/BD and children with mental retardation are often confused is that both frequently lack basic self-care skills. They may be unable to dress and feed themselves and not be toilet trained at the age of five or even ten years. Unable to communicate with others and take care of their daily needs, they present a picture of helplessness characteristic of infancy. Adolescents may have basic self-care skills but be unable or unwilling to engage in activities that are typical for youths in their age group.

Perceptual Deviations

Children with severe E/BD are sometimes mistakenly thought to be deaf or blind. They may seem deaf or blind to the casual observer because at first they appear to be oblivious to what is going on around them: They ignore people and do not seem to be affected by conversation or loud noises or bright lights. In short, they are not responsive to visual and auditory stimuli in the same way as ordinary children with vision and hearing. Yet closer observation shows that such a child does respond to some auditory and visual stimuli, perhaps sights and noises that are insignificant or uninteresting to most children. It is as if the child cannot make sense of what he or she sees and hears. Some may have hallucinations, seeing imaginary people, objects, or events.

Cognitive Deficits

Some children with severe E/BD are untestable. Those who can be given intelligence and achievement tests frequently score in the mentally retarded range. Some of these children may seem intellectually competent because they can carry on a conversation. But after a while it is obvious that there is only one topic they can converse about, or their conversation soon turns to meaningless jargon and bizarre statements or questions. Many severely disturbed children "look" intelligent and some can perform amazing feats of memory or computation, but their "intelligence" is deceptive—they cannot apply their skills or seeming brilliance to everyday tasks.

Unrelatedness to Other People

One of the most disconcerting aspects of the behavior of children with severe E/BD is that they tend to react to other people, including their parents and siblings, as physical objects. Often these children ignore or resist their parents and others who are trying to show love and affection. They do not adapt their posture to the parents' when they are being held and they do not develop an anticipatory posture when being picked up. There is no exchange of warmth and gratification between adults and such children. Adolescents may be overly dependent on others or maintain extremely distant or bizarre relationships.

Language and Speech Deviations

Some children with severe E/BD do not speak at all or do not seem to understand language. Some show **echolalia**—that is, they parrot back whatever they hear but do not say anything else (see Chapter 6). Misuse of pronouns (*he* or *you* for *I* or *her* for *you*) and meaningless jargon are common. Some of these children have an extremely strange vocal quality (such as extraordinarily low- or high-pitched voice) or repeat questions or statements incessantly. Some talk about their delusions—what they describe bears little or no resemblance to reality.

Self-Stimulation

Behavior that is stereotyped, repetitive, and useful only for obtaining sensory stimulation is common in children with severe E/BD. Such self-stimulation can take a nearly infinite variety of forms (swishing saliva, twirling an object, patting one's cheeks, flapping one's hands, staring at lights). These children often exhibit such behavior so constantly that it is extremely difficult to engage them in any other activity.

Self-Injurious Behavior

Some children with severe E/BD injure themselves purposely and repeatedly to such an extent that they must be kept in restraints so they will not multilate and/ or slowly kill themselves. They seem impassive to the self-inflicted pain. The ways such children can injure themselves include biting, scratching, poking, bumping, or scraping various parts of their bodies.

Aggression Toward Others

It is common for children with severe E/BD to throw severe temper tantrums in which they strike out at others or to treat others in calculatedly cruel ways. Biting, scratching, and kicking others are common characteristics of these children. Adolescents may strike out because of delusions that others are persecuting them or are "out to get them."

Self-stimulation may range from relatively mild forms, such as thumb-sucking, to stereotypic behaviors that are incompatible with normal activity and learning. (Marion Bernstein)

Prognosis Without Early Intensive Intervention

The undesirability of these characteristics is obvious. Not so obvious is the fact that the prognosis for these children is poor. Many are likely to function at a retarded level and require supervision and care even after years of the most effective treatment known today, unless the intensive treatment is begun while they are still very young. Recent research has shown that if intensive treatment (forty hours or more of one-to-one teaching per week) is begun before three and one-half years of age, about 50 percent of these children may recover completely—that is, become indistinguishable from other children by the time they are in the first or second grade (Lovaas, 1987). With less intensive treatment and when treatment is started later, the prognosis is much more guarded. The children are likely to continue showing severely handicapping behaviors, and many of them will probably be considered psychotic as adults (Petty, Ornitz, Michelman, & Zimmerman, 1984).

EDUCATIONAL CONSIDERATIONS

Coherent, comprehensive descriptions of educational programs for students with E/BD are rare. The few program descriptions one can find often lack adequate details about such critical elements as guiding philosophy, goals, definition of the students to be served, criteria for entry into and exit from the program, and educational methods (Grosenick & Huntze, 1983). The lack of good program descriptions means that teachers and administrators have relatively little guidance in establishing, operating, and evaluating programs. One of the greatest needs in the field today is for an adequate literature to guide program development and improvement.

If you ask special educators and mental health professionals how children with E/BD should be educated, you will get many different answers—partly because the general category of E/BD embraces so many different behavior problems, ranging from aggression to withdrawal, and degrees of disability, ranging from mild to profound. But the major reason for differing views goes back to something first mentioned in the discussion of definition—the problem of different conceptual models or theories.

Conceptual Models and Education

Conceptual models are just theories until they are used to guide educational practices; then the essential differences among models can be tested empirically. The differences among recommended practices and their outcomes, therefore, should provide the basis for evaluation of conceptual models. But although it would seem to be relatively simple to compare them, the job is actually quite difficult because it is not always apparent whether a difference between practices is a real one or just a matter of terms. For example, is the difference between the "planned ignoring" technique (a practice associated with the psychoeducational model) and "extinction" (a practice associated with the behavioral model) a real one? Does the teacher actually do different things? In reading the statements of those who propose different theoretical models, one gets the impression that the differences are often more words than deeds.

Of course, there are some real differences between conceptual models. For example, the proponents of a psychoanalytic model purposely encourage acting-out behavior in some circumstances, on the assumption that the child must work through underlying conflicts before more desirable behavior can be expected. In contrast, behaviorists discourage misbehavior because they believe it only makes the problem worse. They consistently try to suppress inappropriate behavior and reward desirable responses. The real differences between some conceptual models may make them incompatible, for under some circumstances they suggest directly opposite actions and cannot be used in combination.

Our purpose here is merely to point out that there are many different views regarding the education of children with E/BD and to provide brief sketches of the major features of several different approaches (see Table 5.1). McDowell, Adamson, & Wood (1982) provide a more detailed analysis of various approaches and their theoretical underpinnings. Some concepts are common to several approaches, and in practice we seldom find a really "pure" single viewpoint. But as pointed out, the ideas of one model can be incompatible with those of another. There is a limit to the extent to which a teacher can pick and choose techniques without it becoming self-defeating (Kauffman, 1989).

The Psychoanalytic Approach

This particular approach to education was formuated primarily by psychiatrists and clinical psychologists who believe that the guiding principles of **psychoanalysis** can be used in education. The problem of E/BD is viewed as a pathological imbalance among the dynamic parts of the mind: id, ego, and superego. Educational practices

TABLE 5.1   Approaches to Educating Children with E/BD

	Psychoanalytic Approach	Psychoeducational Approach	Humanistic Approach	Ecological Approach	Behavioral Approach
The Problem	A pathological imbalance among the dynamic parts of the mind (id, superego, ego)	Involves both underlying psychiatric disorders and the readily observable misbehavior and underachievement of the child	Belief that the child is out of touch with his or her own feelings and can't find fulfillment in traditional educational settings	Belief that the child interacts poorly with the environment; child and environment affect each other reciprocally and negatively	Belief that the child has learned inappropriate responses and failed to learn appropriate ones
Purpose of Educational Practices	Use of psychoanalytic principles to help uncover underlying mental pathology	Concern for unconscious motivation/underlying conflicts *and* academic achievement/positive surface behavior	Emphasis on enhancing child's self-direction, self-evaluation, and emotional involvement in learning	Attempts to alter entire social system so that it will support desirable behavior in child when intervention is withdrawn	Manipulates child's immediate environment and the consequences of behavior
Characteristics of Teaching Methods	Reliance on individual psychotherapy for child and parents; little emphasis on academic achievement; highly permissive atmosphere	Emphasis on meeting individual needs of the child; reliance on projects and creative arts	Use of nontraditional educational settings in which the teacher serves as resource and catalyst rather than as director of activities; nonauthoritarian, open, affective, personal atmosphere	Involves all aspects of a child's life, including classroom, family neighborhood, and community, in teaching the child useful life and educational skills	Involves measurement of responses and subsequent analyses of behaviors to change them; emphasis on reward for appropriate behavior

Collaboration: A Key to Success

JAY SHIPMAN

BOB RABOIN

■ **JAY:** We'll describe our work with Todd, a fifth-grader. Todd was small but strong, and a good runner. He had dark hair, somewhat protruding blue eyes, and enough braces on his teeth to rechrome a '58 Buick. He rarely spoke to anyone, and when he did it was almost impossible to hear him. He typically did not respond to adults or children who talked to him, and he didn't look at them either. Todd was capable of above-average academic work in all areas, but he did so little that it took a long time to figure out what he knew. If I asked him to correct a mistake, no matter how gently I phrased it, he would deny he had made a mistake and call me a liar. Then he might sneer and swear, turn over his desk, throw his books, and make loud noises or bark like a dog for two or three hours. This scenario was repeated three or four days a week. Todd acted this way anytime he was asked to do something he didn't care to do at the moment. His tantrums could take place anytime I asked him to sit down or use a pencil instead of a pen. He would hit me or punch other students and teachers when things didn't go his way. For example, once he got his book bag tangled up with another boy's as they were getting on the bus. Todd was instantly furious, thrashing like a wild animal caught in a net. When he was free, he slugged a boy—who just happened to be standing in front of him—in the back of the head. He threw his tray at the woman who served the school lunches and called her a "fucking bitch" because she wouldn't give him a second helping. He seemed to have missed the fact that there wasn't any food left. The first three months of the year Todd rarely left my room. He had no friends and was still trying to see if we would let him be the person in charge. I saw him as fearful, withdrawn, and furious.

■ **BOB:** You get the idea we weren't dealing with a typical fifth-grader here!

■ **JAY:** My first job as the special education teacher was to reduce Todd's aggression and increase his compliance. I talked with Todd's parents and concluded that the major factors contributing to Todd's behavior were manipulative behaviors he had learned in the family. His mother seemed concerned but helpless. Todd could manipulate her easily. His father appeared unconcerned and condescending, as though *I* had a problem. It wasn't hard to see why Todd was used to getting his own way and felt that others should do his bidding or there was something wrong with *them*. I started very early to make sure that he knew I was in charge. I set up a program with his parents: We would make rules and stick to them. Todd could throw tantrums all he wanted—we really couldn't stop him—but that wouldn't change the consequences. We wanted to show him that he had the power to choose how he reacted to the rules, but he did not have the power to change or make the rules. Home and school tried to accentuate the positive and withhold what he liked when he made poor choices. We tried to keep the consequences logical: You don't go out for recess when you don't work; you don't go to the movies when you swear at your mother. The point with Todd wasn't to punish him—that only would have made things worse. He simply needed to know that eleven-year-olds don't tell adults what to do. My job was to ride out his tantrums calmly so he would be left with the consequences of his choices. If I got upset, then he would get more reinforcement for being manipulative and aggressive.

■ **BOB:** My first contact with Todd was when Jay introduced me to him in the hall. I tried to make casual conversation. This wasn't easy because Todd didn't talk to me, but I kept it up. I ran into Todd on the playground, usually to pry his hands off some other kid's throat. I don't think this made him a big fan of mine, but I'm not sure it did much damage either. Todd was so turned in on himself that I don't think he even remembered me when he came to my class in December. He came to my special project class at first. We do string art and woodworking and macramé, among other things. Todd came as a reward for doing well in the special education class. By December Todd would have done anything to get away from Jay, and he liked the stuff we did. My job was to be as aware as possible of what Jay and Todd had gone through so far. Jay and I do not teach the same way; we don't need to be alike. I did need to make sure that the consequences were the same for Todd, even if our rules and personal styles were different. Jay sends me a rating slip for every class. I teach the way I normally do, and Todd takes the rating slip back to Jay after every class. Todd gets the same consistent consequences; I don't have to design an individual reward system, and the changes are kept to a minimum for Todd. My part of the bargain is to teach fifth grade, and I need to provide the best possible environment for Todd to see and practice appropriate social behavior. I talk a lot with my students about the individual needs of various students. We learn to tolerate differences and eventually respect them. Jay and I talk when we need to, sometimes three times a day and sometimes not for a week. Todd gradually participated in more and more classes. We had minor problems but nothing major. Jay's job is to get the kid to the point of being able to handle a class in my room. He should show up in my room with the right materials and follow the rules. I make individual adjustments for most of my students when I can. If the students cannot meet my minimum standards over a period of time, they go back to Jay's room for awhile. Jay's never questioned that. Good teachers do what's best for a student, but we all have limits. Knowing your limits isn't a sign of weakness; it shows insight and respect for others.

JAY: The most challenging aspect of teamwork is the communication. This is hard when you have a violent student in your room that you cannot leave alone. Talking confidentially about a mainstreamed student is hard when you're holding onto one of them. The major challenge I faced with Todd was a private issue for me. I had to find reasons to want to work with and for Todd. He insulted me verbally, lashed out at me physically, and was the most rude and cruel student I had worked with in years. I wasn't sure Todd would last five days

in Bob's class. I told Bob I had this boy who was usually extremely withdrawn but could, without apparent provocation, jump on some kid and start crushing his windpipe. Bob said that Todd sounded fine and he anticipated no major problems. I knew that meant that Todd was welcome and we would take it one day at a time, one class at a time. I think Todd saved most of his major acting out for times when he wasn't in Bob's room. He couldn't break the habits of ten years in three months, but he had lots of respect for Bob and worked very hard to do well and not "let him down." We wanted not to shield Todd from consequences and gradually to transfer the responsibility for applying those consequences to Bob.

> *. . . we would take it one day at a time, one class at a time.*

BOB: My challenges as a fifth-grade teacher were different. I had to get to know Todd. I had to get accurate information from Jay on what I could reasonably expect academically and behaviorally. I also had to try to predict how Todd was going to affect and be affected by the other students in my class. I had to make sure I filled out the rating slips after every class so Jay could apply the proper consequences and help Todd get any late work done. This seems like a small thing, but with about thirty students it isn't always easy to remember to do it. I had one more person to teach, one more batch of papers to correct, and one more child to show that I cared about him and respected him. These are things I think any student should take for granted. My point is that they take time.

JAY: Many of the students we work with have been badly damaged through the malice or ignorance of others. It is extremely gratifying to see a student who was chronically depressed or angry finally become happy much of the time. Most people have given up on our students. We get a chance to experience

the joy of watching a boy discover that life can be a gift as well as a burden. This is what makes teaching a wonderful profession.

BOB: I think collaboration is primarily a product of the desire to work together and the amount of time and resources available.

JAY: I think my primary responsibility is to make sure that the situation is productive and successful for the student and the regular teacher. A big part of my time is devoted to establishing and maintaining good working relationships with other teachers. I have to earn the respect of secretaries, custodians, teachers, bus drivers, and the principal. If you do not find it easy to get along with a wide variety of people, being a teacher of disturbed children will be very difficult. You have to be aware of personal and classroom stress and plan accordingly. You think about who has the time and the personality that will work for a given child. The most common mistake in mainstreaming is placing a student who isn't ready or picking a poor placement.

BOB: My teaching doesn't change much when I have a student with an emotional/behavioral disorder. I've been told what to expect, but I've never been told to change what I do. Jay has asked me to make adjustments for a given child, and we've always at least worked out a compromise. I have the hardest time when I don't think I have the resources that a student needs. There are times when the numbers or group chemistry just make it impossible to give a student the attention he or she may need.

JAY SHIPMAN:

Teacher of emotionally disturbed students, grades K–6, Coolidge School, Neenah, Wisconsin; B.A. History, St. Norbert College; M.Ed., Special Education, University of Wisconsin–Oshkosh

BOB RABOIN:

Fifth-grade teacher; B.S.Ed., University of Wisconsin–Superior are designed to help uncover the underlying mental pathology in an effort to improve psychological functioning, as well as behavior and achievement.

The emphasis is on building a teacher-pupil relationship in which the child feels accepted and free to act out his or her impulses in a permissive environment. The primary concern of the teacher is to help the child overcome underlying mental conflicts, not to change the surface behavior or to teach academic skills. Usually the child and the parents receive therapy, and the psychotherapist is relied on to help the child "work through" problems in therapy sessions.

The Psychoeducational Approach

Those who developed the psychoeducational approach have tried to interweave psychiatric and educational concerns. Since the problems of children with E/BD are assumed to involve both underlying psychiatric disorders and observable misbehavior and underachievement, there is a balance between therapeutic goals and goals for achievement in the recommended educational practices. Unconscious motivation and underlying pathology are taken into account, but there is also concern for the management of surface behavior and academic achievement. There is emphasis on meeting the individual needs of children, and teaching often involves projects or the creative arts (music, art, dance).

The Humanistic Approach

The humanistic approach to educating children with E/BD grew out of humanistic psychology (Maslow, 1962; Rogers, 1969), the open education movement, and the revolt against traditional concepts of education beginning in the late 1960s. The basic problem, as humanistic educators see it, is that children with E/BD are out of touch with their own feelings and cannot find meaning and self-fulfillment in traditional educational settings. The recommended educational practices are designed to enhance children's self-direction, self-evaluation, and emotional involvement in learning in nontraditional settings. The teacher functions as a resource and catalyst for children's learning rather than as a director of activities. Children and teachers work together as learners, pursuing areas of interest to themselves and sharing information. *Nonauthoritarian*, *self-directed*, *self-evaluative*, *affective*, *open*, and *personal* are words used to describe humanistic education for disturbed children.

The Ecological Approach

Proponents of the ecological approach believe that the problem of E/BD is one of the child in interaction with the various elements of the environment (school, family, community, and social agencies). The child is viewed as a *disturber* of the environment, and his or her behavior is considered as disturbing as it is disturbed. Borrowing concepts from biological ecology and ecological psychology, these theorists suggest that educational practices must be part of a strategy to alter the entire social system in which the child is enmeshed. The goal of this approach is not just to invervene in the child's behavior but also to change the environment enough so that it will continue to support desirable behavior once the intervention is over. There is concern not only for effective teaching of the child in the classroom but also for work with the child's family, neighborhood, and community agencies. The ecological approach requires teachers who are able to teach children specific, useful skills (including academics, recreation, and everyday living skills) and to work with adults in the child's environment.

The Behavioral Approach

In the 1960s Hewett (1968) and others presented an approach to the education of children with E/BD based on the principles of operant and respondent conditioning. The assumption was that behavioral problems represent inappropriate learning and that children can be helped when their observable behavior is modified. Modification of behavior can be accomplished by manipulation of the child's immediate environment—the classroom and the consequences of the child's behavior. Since it is the child's behavior that is the focus of concern, recommended educational practices include precise measurement of the child's responses. Because behavior is assumed to be learned, educational practices are clearly specified and analyzed for their effects on the behaviors being measured. The focus of the behavioral approach, then, is on precise definition and measurement of the observable behaviors that are a problem and manipulation of the consequences of these behaviors in order to change them.

Current Syntheses of Conceptual Models

Within the past decade, psychologists of all theoretical persuasions have placed new emphasis on the self. Morse (1985) describes a "metamorphosis" in psychologists' thinking about why individuals behave and perceive things as they do: "This metamorphosis is a result of the blending of developmental and learning psychology with a balanced attention to both the affective and cognitive aspects, which is sometimes called social cognition" (p. 4). The synthesis of developmental and learning perspectives is called **individual psychology** by Morse and other writers. **Cognitive-behavior modification** is not exactly the same as individual psychology, but it is also an attempt to blend learning theory with concern for the individual's thoughts, feelings, and perceptions (Harris, Wong, & Keogh, 1985; Meichenbaum, 1977; see also Chapter 4).

People change their behavior, most psychologists now agree, for multiple reasons. They do not change simply because they obtain new understandings about themselves or because they resolve their troubled feelings. Neither do they change simply because someone arranges different consequences for their behavior or shows them appropriate behavioral models. The most effective methods of changing behavior typically require attention to the child as a thinking, feeling person *and* to the consequences of the child's behavior. Attempts to blend learning and developmental theories often result in involving the child in self-management. This may mean self-monitoring (keeping track of one's own behavior), self-instruction (talking one's way through a problem), self-evaluation (judging one's own performance), self-reinforcement (complimenting oneself or allowing oneself a reward for good performance), and so on.

Setting goals for oneself is an example of a behavior change strategy involving self-control. Such a strategy may be used in conjunction with other behavior modification techniques. The outcome of an experimental study involving goal setting is shown in Figure 5.2. Lyman (1984) worked with six boys, aged eleven to thirteen, who were considered emotionally disturbed and attended a school in a residential treatment facility. The boys exhibited conduct disorders, including such problem behaviors as noncompliance with teachers' directions, aggression, truancy, and de-

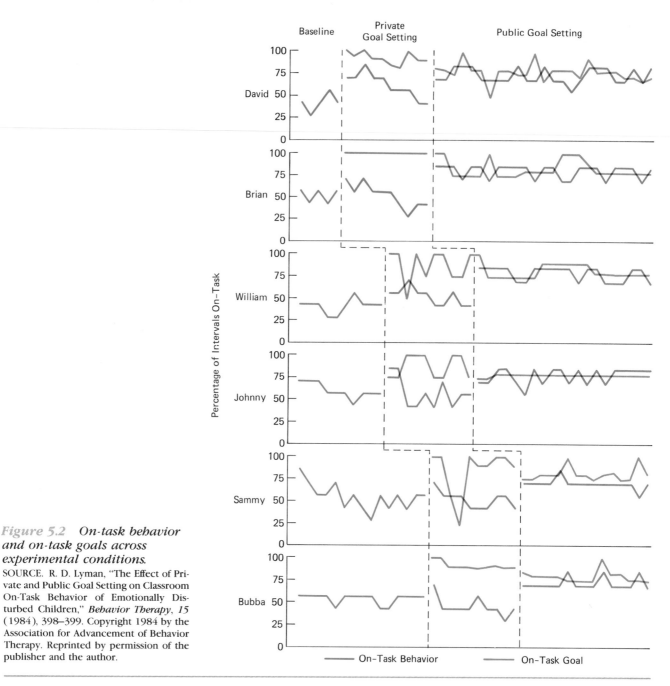

Figure 5.2   On-task behavior and on-task goals across experimental conditions.

SOURCE. R. D. Lyman, "The Effect of Private and Public Goal Setting on Classroom On-Task Behavior of Emotionally Disturbed Children," *Behavior Therapy, 15* (1984), 398–399. Copyright 1984 by the Association for Advancement of Behavior Therapy. Reprinted by permission of the publisher and the author.

struction of property. All of them were considerably behind their age-mates academically and had difficulty staying on task in the classroom. Lyman defined "on-task" behavior as looking at one's workbook or paper, asking a question related to the assigned work, or listening to the teacher. Each student's on-task behavior was observed systematically during one hour of the school day, and the percentage of time each student was observed to be on task was recorded and plotted on a graph, as shown in Figure 5.2. After obtaining observational data under baseline conditions in which specific goals were not set by the students, Lyman experimented with the effects of private and public goal setting. In the private goal-setting phase each student was called to the teacher's desk and given the following instructions individually:

> We're going to try something to help you work better in class. I want you to pick a goal for yourself for a percentage of time you're going to work for the next hour. Working means looking at your workbook or response sheet, asking a question about your work, or listening to the teacher. This should be a level that you can try for and that you think is a fair goal for yourself. Try to challenge yourself but don't set a goal that would be unfair to you. Now I want you to pick a percent of time for your goal. I'll write it down on this card and give it to you to remind you of your goal. (p. 398)

In the public goal-setting phase the teacher gave students the same individual instructions, but instead of saying "'I'll write it [the goal] down on this card and give it to you to remind you of your goal,' the teacher said, 'I'll write it down on this card and put it up here on this chart to remind you of your goal'" (p. 298). The student's card was then placed beside his or her name on a bulletin board at the front of the class under the heading "Work Goals." As shown in Figure 5.2, the students all performed better (i.e., spent more time on task) when their goal setting was public than when it was private. Note that the private and public goal-setting phases were started at different times for pairs of students to show that the goal setting, not some other uncontrolled factor, was responsible for the observed changes in behavior.

Administrative Arrangements

A relatively small percentage of children and youths with E/BD are officially identified and receive any special education or mental health services at all (Institute of Medicine, 1989). Consequently, the children who do receive special education tend to be those with severe problems, although most (along with those who have mild mental retardation or learning disabilities) have typically been assumed to have only "mild" disabilities. That is, the problems of the typical student with E/BD who is identified for special education may be more serious than many people have assumed. "Severe" does not apply only to the disorders of autism and schizophrenia; a child can have a severe conduct disorder, for example, and its disabling effects can be extremely serious and persistent (Kazdin, 1987; Wolf, Braukmann, & Ramp, 1987).

A higher percentage of students with E/BD than of students with most other disabilities are educated outside regular classrooms and schools, probably in part because students with E/BD tend to have more serious problems before they are identified. Because E/BD inlcudes so many different types of behavioral and emotional problems, it is hard to make generalizations about the way programs are administered. Programs for students with psychotic disorders and for juvenile delinquents tend to be administered differently from those for students with other types of problems, so we shall discuss them under different headings.

Programs for Students with Psychotic Disorders

Many children with autism must be taught individually at first. They simply do not learn in a group without having had intensive individual instruction first because of their great difficulty in paying attention, responding, and behaving appropriately in a group. After they have learned some of the basic skills required for instruction, they may be taught in small groups. Eventually, if intensive early intervention is provided, large-group instruction may be feasible and many children can be integrated into regular schools and classrooms. Students with schizophrenia vary widely in the behavior they exhibit and the learning problems they have. Some may need hospitalization and intensive treatment. Others may remain at home and attend regular public schools. The trend today is away from placement in institutions or special schools and toward inclusion in regular public schools. In many cases, children with psychotic disorders who attend regular schools are enrolled in special classes.

Teachers of children with psychotic disorders must have more than empathy and a desire to help. Unless teachers are equipped with specific teaching skills, the time they spend with these children will amount to little more than custodial care. A permissive environment maintained under the fiction of "therapy" is not likely to be effective and may in fact be detrimental to the child's progress. Empathy and humanistic concern are to be encouraged, but skill in using behavior modification techniques is essential for teachers who work with such children.

The curriculum for most children with autism must be basic in the early stages of education—a lot like curriculum for most children with severe mental retardation. It may involve teaching daily living skills, language, and preacademic skills. Teachers who work with these children must be willing to spend countless hours of patient labor to achieve small gains. Moreover, they must be ready to persist in working with children whose behavior is extremely unpleasant and who will often reject efforts to help them (see Bower, 1989; Durand & Carr, 1988; Koegel, Rincover, & Egel, 1982).

Programs for Juvenile Delinquents

Educational arrangements for juvenile delinquents are hard to describe in general terms because delinquency is a legal term, not an educational distinction, and because programs for extremely troubling youths are so varied from state to state and among localities. Special classes or schools are sometimes provided for youths who have a history of threatening, violent, or disruptive behavior. Some of these classes and schools are administered under special education law, but others are not because the pupils assigned to them are not considered "seriously emotionally disturbed." In jails, reform schools, and other detention facilities housing children and adolescents, wide variation is found in educational practices (Nelson, Rutherford, & Wolford, 1987). Education of incarcerated handicapped children and youths is governed by the same laws that apply to those who are not incarcerated, but the laws are not always carefully implemented. Many incarcerated children do not receive assessment and education appropriate for their needs because of lack of resources, poor cooperation among agencies, and the attitude that delinquents and criminals are not entitled to the same educational opportunities as law-abiding citizens (Leone, Price, & Vitolo, 1986; Nelson, Rutherford, & Wolford, 1987).

Programs for Students with Other Disorders

The trend in programs for students with other types of disorders is toward integration into regular schools and classrooms. When children are placed in separate schools and classes, educators hope for reintegration into the mainstream. Integration of these students is typically difficult and requires intensive work on a case-by-case basis (Fuchs, Fuchs, Fernstrom, & Hohn, 1989; Lloyd, Kauffman, & Kupersmidt, 1990).

The academic curriculum for most students with E/BD parallels the curriculum for most children. The basic academic skills have a great deal of survival value for any child in our society who is capable of learning them; failure to teach a child to read, write, and perform basic arithmetic deprives such a child of any reasonable chance for successful adjustment to the everyday demands of life. Children who do not acquire academic skills that allow them to compete with their peers are likely to be socially rejected (Kauffman, 1989; Patterson, Kupersmidt, & Griesler, 1989). Students with E/BD may need specific instruction in social skills as well. We emphasize two points: First, effective methods are needed to teach basic academic skills to students with E/BD; second, social skills and affective experiences are as crucial as academic skills. How to manage one's feelings and behavior and how to get along with other people are essential features of the curriculum for many children with E/BD. These children cannot be expected to learn such skills without instruction, for the ordinary processes of socialization obviously have failed.

Teachers of students with E/BD must be able to tolerate a great deal of unpleasantness and rejection without becoming counteraggressive or withdrawing. Most of the students they teach are rejected by others: If kindness and concern were the only things required to help these children, they probably would not be considered handicapped. The teacher cannot expect caring and decency always to be returned. Teachers must be sure of their own values and confident of their teaching and living skills. They must be able and willing to make wise choices for children when the children choose to behave unwisely.

EARLY INTERVENTION

Early identification and prevention are basic goals of intervention programs for any category of handicap. For students with E/BD these goals present particular difficulties—yet they hold particular promise. The difficulties are related to definition and measurement of E/BD, especially in young children; the particular promise is that young children's social-emotional behavior is quite flexible, so preventive efforts seem to have a good chance of success.

As mentioned previously, defining E/BD in such a way that children can be reliably identified is a difficult task. Definition and identification of preschool children with E/BD are complicated by several additional factors. First, the developmental tasks that young children are expected to achieve are much simpler than those expected of older children, so the range of normal behaviors to be used for comparison is quite restricted. Infants and toddlers are expected to eat, sleep, perform relatively simple motor skills, and respond socially to their parents. School-age children must learn much more varied and complex motor and cognitive skills and develop social relations with a variety of peers and adults. Second, there is wide variation in the child-rearing practices of good parents and in family expectations for preschool children's behavior in different cultures, so we must guard against inappropriate norms used for comparison. "Immature," "withdrawn," or "aggressive" behavior in one family may not be perceived as such in another. Third, in the preschool years children's development is rapid and often uneven, making it difficult to judge what spontaneous improvements might occur.

Fourth, the most severe types of E/BD often are first observed in the preschool years. But it is frequently difficult to tell the difference between E/BD and other conditions, like mental retardation or deafness. Often the first signs of E/BD are difficulty with basic biological functions (e.g., eating, sleeping, eliminating) or social responses (e.g., responding positively to a parent's attempts to offer comfort or "molding" to the parent's body when being held). Difficulty with these basic areas or in achieving developmental milestones like walking and talking indicate that the child may have an emotional/behavioral disability. But these difficulties may also be indicators of other conditions such as mental retardation, sensory impairment, or physical disability.

The patterns of behavior that signal problems for the preschool child are those that bring them into frequent conflict with or keep them aloof from their parents or caretakers and their siblings or peers. Infants or toddlers who exhibit a very "difficult temperament"—who are irritable; have irregular patterns of sleeping, eating, and eliminating; have highly intense responses to many stimuli and negative reactions toward new situations—are at risk for developing serious behavior problems unless their parents are particularly skillful at handling them. Children of preschool age are likely to elicit negative responses from adults and playmates if they are much more aggressive or much more withdrawn than most children their age. (Remember the critical importance of same-age comparisons. *Normal* toddlers frequently grab what they want, push other children down and throw things and kick and scream when they don't get their way; *normal* toddlers do not have much finesse at social interaction and often hide from strangers.)

Because children's behavior is quite responsive to conditions in the social environment and can be shaped by adults, the potential for *primary prevention*—preventing serious behavior problems from occurring in the first place—would seem to be great. If parents and teachers could be taught effective child management skills, perhaps many or most cases of E/BD could be prevented. Furthermore, one could imagine that if parents and teachers had such skills, children who already have E/BD could be prevented from getting worse (*secondary prevention*). But as Bower (1981) notes, the task of primary prevention is not that simple. For one thing, the tremendous amount of money and personnel needed for training in child management are not available. For another, even if the money and personnel could be found, professionals would not always agree on what patterns of behavior should be prevented or on how undesirable behavior could be prevented from developing (see Kazdin, 1987).

If overly aggressive or withdrawn behavior has been identified in a preschooler, what kind of intervention program is most desirable? Our experience and reading of the literature lead us to the conclusion that behavioral interventions are most effective. A behavioral approach implies defining and measuring the child's behaviors and rearranging the environment (especially adults' and other children's responses to the problem child) to teach and support more appropriate conduct. In the case of aggressive children social rewards for aggression would be prevented. For example, hitting another child or throwing a temper tantrum might result in brief social isolation or time out instead of adult attention or getting one's own way.

Researchers are constantly seeking less punitive ways of dealing with problem behavior, including aggression. The best way of handling violent or aggressive play or play themes, for example, would be one that effectively reduces the frequency of aggressive play yet requires minimum punishment. In one study with children between the ages of three and five, violent or aggressive theme play (talk or imitation of weapons, destruction, injury, etc.) was restricted to a small area of the classroom defined by a carpet sample (Sherburne, Utley, McConnell, & Gannon, 1988). Children engaging in imaginative play involving guns, for example, were merely told by the teacher, using a pleasant tone of voice, "If you want to play guns, go over on

All preschoolers engage in behavior that could be considered emotionally disturbed or behaviorally disordered in older children or adults. Young children must be taught socially appropriate ways of interacting with their peers and adults. (Suzanne Szasz/Photo Researchers)

the rug" (p. 169). If violent theme play continued for more than ten seconds after the teacher's warning, the child or children were physically assisted to the rug. They were not required to stay on the rug for a specific length of time, merely to go there if they wanted to engage in aggressive play. This simple procedure was quite effective in reducing violent and aggressive themes in the children's play.

In all cases of aggression, attention and other rewards for desirable, nonaggresive behavior must be provided. Sometimes prompts for appropriate behavior and models of good conduct are also needed. Socially withdrawn preschoolers have responded well to several behavioral techniques: providing peer models (either live or filmed) of social interaction, training peers to initiate social interactions, and encouraging preschoolers to play games in which affectionate behaviors are shown (Strain & Fox, 1981). Early intervention with preschoolers, whether they are aggressive or withdrawn, has the potential to make many such children "normal"—that is, indistinguishable from their peers—by the time they are in the elementary grades (Lovaas, 1987; Strain, Steele, Ellis, & Timm, 1982). Nevertheless, "the long-term effectiveness of behavioral therapy for autism remains much in question, at times sparking intense debate even among investigators using it" (Bower, 1989, p. 312).

TRANSITION

The programs designed for adolescents with E/BD have varied widely in aims and structure (Kerr, Nelson, & Lambert, 1987). Nelson and Kauffman (1977) described the following types and commented on the effectiveness of each: regular public high school classes, consultant teachers who work with the regular teacher to provide individualized academic work and behavior management, resource rooms and special self-contained classes to which students may be assigned for part or all of the school day, work-study programs in which vocational education and job experience are combined with academic study, special private or public schools that offer the regular high school curriculum in a different setting, alternative schools that offer highly individualized programs that are nontraditional in both setting and content, and private or public residential schools.

Incarcerated E/BD youths are an especially neglected group in special education (Nelson, Rutherford, & Wolford, 1987). One suspects that the special educational needs of many (or most) E/BD teenagers who are in prisons are neglected because incarcerated youths are defined as "socially maladjusted" rather than "seriously emotionally disturbed." The current federal definition appears to allow the denial of special education to a very large number of young people who exhibit extremely serious misbehavior and have a long history of school failure.

One of the reasons it is difficult to design special education programs for students with E/BD at the secondary level is that this category of youths is so varied. Adolescents categorized for special education purposes as "seriously emotionally disturbed" may have behavioral characteristics ranging from autistically withdrawn to aggressively delinquent, intelligence ranging from severely retarded to highly gifted, and academic skills ranging from preschool to college level. Therefore it is hardly realistic to suggest that any single type of program or model will be appropriate for all such youths. In fact, youths with E/BD, perhaps more than any other category of exceptionality, need a highly individualized, creative, and flexible education. Programs may range from teaching daily living skills in a sheltered environment to advanced placement in college, from regular class placement to institutionalization, and from the traditional curriculum to unusual and specialized vocational training.

Transition from school to work and adult life is particularly difficult for adolescents with E/BD. Many of them lack basic academic skills necessary for successful employment. In addition, they often behave in ways that prevent them from being accepted, liked, and helped by employers, co-workers, and neighbors. It is not surprising that they are among the students most likely to drop out of school and among the most difficult individuals to train in transition programs (Edgar, 1987; Neel, Meadows, Levine, & Edgar, 1988).

Many children and youths with E/BD grow up to be adults who have real difficulties in leading independent, productive lives. The outlook is especially grim for children and adolescents fitting two classifications: psychotic and conduct disordered. With today's typical treatment, many psychotic children, whether labeled autistic or schizophrenic, are likely to be considered bizarre as adults, and some will be institutionalized. Some will make a successful adjustment to community living and hold jobs that allow them to be self-sufficient. But as follow-up studies show, the majority are unlikely ever to get rid of all the troublesome characteristics they showed during the developmental period (Petty, Ornitz, Michelman, & Zimmerman, 1984).

Contrary to popular opinion, the child or youth who is shy, anxious, or neurotic is not the most likely to have psychiatric problems as an adult. It is, rather, the conduct-disordered (hyperaggressive) child or youth whose adulthood is most likely to be characterized by socially intolerable behavior (Kazdin, 1987). About half the children who are hyperaggressive will have problems that require legal intervention or psychiatric care when they are adults.

One of the frustrating things about the prognosis for children with E/BD is that it is impossible to predict which psychotic or hyperaggressive children will make a successful adult adjustment and which will not. That is, we can only predict a *percentage* of cases that will improve, not point to the *individuals* who will improve. Painstaking research will be required to find out what characteristics of individual children and their treatments or environments make the critical difference in adult outcomes.

SUGGESTIONS FOR TEACHING STUDENTS WITH EMOTIONAL/BEHAVIORIAL DISORDERS IN GENERAL EDUCATION CLASSROOMS

What to Look for in School

Recognizing students with emotional or behavioral disorders (E/BD) is sometimes easy and sometimes complex. Some children and adolescents with E/BD are aggressive. They act out in ways that are obviously inappropriate for school. For example, they may physically provoke others to frequent fights, or they may verbally annoy others by constantly criticizing or teasing. Their aggressive, overt behavior quickly suggests potentially serious behavior problems.

On the other hand, some students with E/BD are withdrawn. They exhibit more subtle behaviors, which in the context of a busy classroom, may be difficult to identify. In the early elementary grades, they may whine or cry in situations that usually don't cause such responses. They also may be dependent, asking others for help to complete work they can do on their own. They may be alone, without friends, or sad or depressed much of the time.

The key to identifying both the aggressive and the withdrawn types of E/BD is the persistence and severity of the behaviors. To be considered serious these behaviors must be shown to a marked degree over a long period of time in a variety of settings.

How to Gather Information

If you suspect any of your students may have serious emotional or behavioral problems, you can help identify them in several ways. Record the specific behaviors you observe, the approximate time of the day and the date, the context in which the behavior occurred, and the consequences. For example, you might note that Alan slapped and kicked Sam after a softball game during recess on Monday, November 2 and describe the circumstances provoking the incident as well as the consequences for Alan.

Noting the exact times of more subtle behavior problems may be difficult. Recording your observations at the end of the day or during a planning period is helpful. For example, you might report that Laura was alone while other students talked together before school in class, during lunch in the cafeteria, and at recess outdoors on Tuesday, October 30. This log will provide an important record of the frequency, severity, and circumstances surrounding the behaviors, which may help you and the school psychologist, counselor, or special education teacher identify the exact nature of the problem.

Describing particularly serious events in greater detail is also helpful. The student's comments regarding these events and the consequences of the behavior provide valuable information. For example, one teacher reported,

David started a fire in the art storage area adjacent to the art room after school on Friday, December 11. He said he did it to get back at the art teacher, who sent him to the principal's office during class that day for splattering paint on another student's holiday project for parents. His parents were called and came to school immediately. Following a discussion of the seriousness of his behavior and the potential legal ramifications, David was suspended for 10 days. No charges were filed.

Noting relevant information from parents, such as descriptions of the student's behavior at home or treatment he or she is receiving outside of school, is also important.

Samples of the student's work in different subjects and a record of what specific skills the student has or does not have will provide needed information regarding learning difficulties, which often accompany serious emotional or behavioral disorders. It is helpful also to note activities, such as oral reports, projects, and small-group discussions, that seem to improve motivation for this student. Gathering this kind of information not only will be helpful to other school personnel in identifying students with E/BD but also will be useful to you in managing these students in your classrooms because the most effective interventions are those based on specific information.

Teaching Techniques to Try

Although there are several approaches to the treatment of children and adolescents with E/BD, one that teachers often use identifies the factors in school that contribute to the students' inappropriate behaviors and the factors in school that can be altered to change those behaviors. Interventions include helping students to increase appropriate behaviors, decrease inappropriate ones, and learn behaviors they do not know already.

To manage students' behaviors Lewis and Doorlag (1987) suggest that teachers follow a step-by-step process:

1. Stating the behavioral expectations for all students in the class
2. Determining whether students who meet these expectations are receiving reinforcement so they will continue to meet the expectations.
3. If there are students who do not meet the expectations, determining whether they understand the expectations and whether they have the needed skills to perform the behaviors
4. For students who use inappropriate behaviors, identifying a behavior to change
5. Deciding how you will observe and gather information on this behavior
6. After reviewing the information you have collected, determining whether the behavior needs to be increased, decreased, or learned
7. Choosing a strategy that is positive rather than punishing
8. While using the strategy, collecting information on the student's behavior
9. Reviewing this information to decide whether this strategy should be continued, modified, or stopped
10. When the student performs the behavior at the desired level, continuing to monitor and returning to step 4 if the student has other behaviors that require intervention

Increasing Appropriate School Behaviors

One strategy to increase a student's appropriate behavior involves rewarding that behavior when the student exhibits it. The reward can take many forms. For example, it may be a point or token exchangeable at a later time for a special privilege or a positive comment, such as "Good work, Tony. I liked the way you worked by yourself on the math problems." However, not all students like the same rewards. You will want to find the one that works with a particular student or groups of students. Some examples of rewards teachers often find effective are being a team leader, having extra computer time, and eating lunch with a friend.

The timing of the reward is key to its impact. It is important to reward students as soon as you observe them demonstrating the appropriate behaviors. For example, if you are trying to increase the number of assignments a student completes, reward the student at the time he or she turns in a completed paper. Waiting until you have graded and returned the assignment will not be as effective.

Once the student exhibits the desirable behavior regularly, you can begin gradually to decrease the frequency of the reward until the student continues to use the behavior at the specified level with less frequent rewards. The following example illustrates how one teacher used positive reinforcement to increase her student's assignment completion:

Sara is a thirteen-year-old behavior-disordered student of average intelligence who rarely turns in her class assignments. Her teacher, Ms. Ellenon, wanted to increase to 80 percent the percentage of class assignments she handed in daily, after noting that Sara completed only one out of five assignments (20 percent) each day for a week. Ms. Ellenon also observed that during seat work, Sara often became very upset and then cried. When this happened Ms. Ellenon immediately comforted her by talking individually with her until the crying stopped. In reviewing these observations, Ms. Ellenon suspected her individual attention to Sara was reinforcing the crying, and she decided to use that attention to reward Sara each time she turned in an assignment. The first day she used the reward strategy, Sara completed three out of five assignments (60 percent), and Ms. Ellenon talked privately with her after she handed in each paper. She did not give Sara attention for crying. Sara did so well that on the third day, with Sara's consent, Ms. Ellenon reduced the reward to one individual talk after Sara completed two assignments and then only after she finished three assignments. By the eleventh day Sara reached the 80 percent criterion level Ms. Ellenon established.

Decreasing Inappropriate School Behaviors

Just as some students, like Sara, need help in increasing appropriate behaviors, others require help in reducing behaviors that are not appropriate for school. Although several techniques are effective in decreasing dangerous behaviors, many of them involve types of punishment that must be carefully administered by trained professionals. Because punishment is defined as any consequence that results in a reduction in the frequency or strength of a specific behavior, however, teachers' mild reprimands, purposeful ignoring of a student's behavior, and withholding other rewards are mild punishment strategies (Kauffman, 1989). Although these strategies, combined with positive rewards when students use appropriate behaviors, are effective, they must be managed carefully and used consistently as suggested by the ten-step process already discussed.

Another strategy teachers use is to reinforce a desirable behavior that is incompatible with the one they want to decrease. For example, if you want to decrease talking out in class and promote raising one's hand, you would reward hand raising by calling on only students who have raised their hands.

Still another technique, called a behavioral contract, systematizes the use of reinforcement. This written agreement between adult(s) and student is often called a contingency contract because it specifies what rewards and consequences will result from, or be contingent on, the student's performance of a specific behavior.

Like any contract, its contents are negotiated and all participants must agree to its terms. A contract states the

- Behavior to be performed
- Condition under which the behavior will be performed
- Criterion for successful performance of the behavior
- Reward for performing the behavior
- Consequences for failing to perform the behavior
- Signatures of the participants
- Date (Teachers who plan to use several contracts to improve a student's behaviors also often include the number of the contract.)

The following is an example of a contract negotiated by Ms. Randolph, Bill, and Bill's parents to decrease his arguing and fighting.

BEHAVIORAL CONTRACT
written on September 21

Ms. Randolph will check a Good Play card for Bill each time he plays during recess without fighting or arguing with any student. When Bill has earned 10 checks from Ms. Randolph and has had his card signed by his parents, he may use the computer for 15 minutes.

Signed: _____ (Student) _____ (Teacher) _____ (Parents)

Prevention of Inappropriate Behaviors

Because using even mild forms of punishment is less desirable than using positive strategies, teachers may reduce the need to use punishing techniques by preventing many behavior problems. Lewis and Doorlag (1987) recommend several preventive measures:

1. Make rules and routines positive, concrete, and functional, relating them to the accomplishments of learning and order in the classroom (e.g., "work quietly at the learning centers" rather than "don't talk when working").
2. Design rules and routines to anticipate potential classroom problems and to manage these situations. For example, teachers may want students to raise their hands when they need help rather than calling out or leaving their seat to locate the teacher.
3. Establish classroom rules and routines at the beginning of the school year by introducing them the first day.
4. Demonstrate or model the rules and routines and continue to provide opportunities for students to practice them until the students have mastered them.
5. Associate rules and routines with simple signals that tell students when they are to carry out or stop specific activities and behaviors.
6. Monitor how students follow rules and routines, rewarding students for appropriate behaviors.

Although many behavior management strategies, such as those just discussed, are teacher-directed, other effective strategies are managed by the student or, in part, by other students. One peer-mediated intervention used frequently is cooperative learning.

Helpful Resources

School Personnel

In addition to the school personnel listed in previous chapters, the school psychologist may be helpful in understanding and managing students with serious emotional and behavioral disorders. Like the special education teacher, psychologists can provide specific information about a student's problems based on their individual evaluation, and they may recommend teaching methods and materials.

School counselors are helpful in building resources. They not only provide course and vocational guidance based on students' interests, abilities, and skills but also may help when students have behavioral crises. In addition, they are an important link between the classroom teacher and parents and can provide frequent reports of students' progress and coordinate home and school plans to improve the students' behavior and performance.

Instructional Methods

Buckley, N. K., & Walker, H. M. (1978). *Modifying classroom behavior: A manual of procedures for classroom teachers*. Champaign, IL: Research Press.

Cartledge, G., & Milburn, J. F. (1986). *Teaching social skills to children*. New York: Pergamon Press.

Center, D. B. (1989). *Curriculum and teaching strategies for students with behavioral disorders*. Englewood Cliffs, NJ: Prentice-Hall.

Charles, C. M. (1985). *Building classroom discipline: From models to practice*. White Plains, NY: Longman.

Kerr, M. M., & Nelson, C. M. (1983). *Strategies for managing behavior problems in the classroom*. Columbus, OH: Chas. E. Merrill.

Long, J. D., & Frye, V. H. (1985). *Making it till Friday: A guide to successful classroom management*. Princeton, NJ: Princeton Book Company.

Smith, D. D. (1984). *Effective discipline*. Austin, TX: Pro-Ed.

Walker, H. M. (1987). *The antisocial child in school: Strategies for remediating aggressive and disruptive child behavior*. Austin, TX: Pro-Ed.

Curricula

Goldstein, A. P., Sprafkin, R. P., Gershaw, N. J., & Klein, P. (1980). *Skillstreaming the adolescent: A structural learning approach to teaching prosocial skills*. Champaign, IL: Research Press.

Hazel, J. S., Schumaker, J. B., Sherman, J. A., & Sheldon-Wildgen, J. (1981). *ASSET: A social program for adolescents*. Champaign, IL: Research Press.

Jackson, N. F., Jackson, D. A., & Monroe, C. (1983). *Getting along with others*. Champaign, IL: Research Press.

McGinnis, E., Goldstein, A. P., Sprafkin, R. P., & Gershaw, N. J. (1984). *Skillstreaming the elementary school child: A guide for teaching prosocial skills*. Champaign, IL: Research Press.

Stokes, T. F., & Baer, D. M. (1988). *The Social Skills Curriculum*. Circle Pines, MN: American Guidance Service.

Walker, H., McConnell, S., Holms, D., Todis, B., Walker, J., & Golden, N. (1983). *The Walker social skills curriculum: The ACCEPTS program*. Austin, TX: Pro-Ed.

Weisgerber, R., Appleby, J., & Fong, S. (1984). *Social solution curriculum*. (Developed at American Institute for Research, Palo Alto, CA.) Burlingame, CA: Professional Associated Resources.

Literature About Individuals with Emotional/Behavioral Disorders

ELEMENTARY

Berger, T. (1979). *I have feelings, too*. New York: Human Sciences Press.

Sheehan, C. (1981). *The colors that I am*. New York: Human Science Press.

Simon, N. (1974). *I was so mad!* Chicago: A. Whitman Middle School.

Hamilton, V. (1971). *The planet of Junior Brown*. New York: Macmillan.

Platt, K. (1968). *The boy who could make himself disappear*. New York: Dell.

ADULT

Greenfeld, J. (1978). *A place for Noah*. New York: Washington Square Press.

Greenfeld, J. (1986). *A client called Noah*. San Diego: Harcourt Brace Jovanovich.

Software

Little Computer People, Triton Products Company, P.O. Box 8123, San Francisco, CA 94128; (800) 227-6900.

Videodisc

Interactive Videodisc Social Skills (IVSS) Program, Ron Thorkildsen, Department of Special Education, Utah State University, Logan, UT 84322-6500; (801) 750-1999.

Organizations

Council for Children with Behavioral Disorders, 1920 Association Drive, Reston, VA 22091.

Federation of Families for Children's Mental Health, 1021 Prince St., Alexandria, VA 22314.

National Society for Children and Adults with Autism, 621 Central Avenue, Albany, NY 12206.

Bibliography for Teaching Suggestions

Kauffman, J. M. (1989). *Characteristics of behavior disorders of children and youth* (4th ed.). Columbus, OH: Chas. E. Merrill.

Lewis, R. B., & Doorlag, D. H. (1987). *Teaching special students in the mainstream* (2nd ed.). Columbus, OH: Chas. E. Merrill.

SUMMARY

An emotional/behavioral disorder (E/BD) involves inappropriate social interactions and transactions between the child and the social environment. E/BD is not simply a problem of undesirable behavior or inappropriate social circumstances. Most children with E/BD are isolated from others because they either withdraw from social contact or behave in an aggressive, hostile way and others withdraw from them.

Many different terms have been used for children's emotional and behavioral disorders. We use *E/BD* to designate those children and youths called "seriously emotionally disturbed" in PL 94-142 because the terminology of the field is in transition.

For several reasons no one definition of E/BD is widely accepted. Defining E/BD is particularly difficult because we lack an adequate definition of mental health, people conceptualize the problem in many different ways, measuring emotions and deviant behavior is difficult, the relationship between E/BD and other handicapping conditions is often unclear, and different social agencies and professions have different purposes for defining the problem. Nevertheless, it is generally agreed that E/BD refers to behavior that goes to an extreme, is unacceptable because of social or cultural expectations, and is chronic.

The current federal definition lists five characteristics, one or more of which may indicate that a child is "seriously emotionally disturbed" if it is exhibited to a marked extent and over a long period of time and has an adverse effect on educational performance: (1) inability to learn that cannot be explained by intellectual, sensory, or health factors; (2) inability to build or maintain satisfactory relationships with peers and teachers; (3) inappropriate behavior or feelings under normal conditions; (4) a pervasive mood of unhappiness or depression; and (5) physical symptoms, pains, or fears associated with personal or school problems. Such characteristics obviously include children with autism or schizophrenia, although children with autism have been excluded from the category of seriously emotionally disturbed and those with schizophrenia have been explicitly included in federal regulations. Children who are "socially maladjusted but not seriously emotionally disturbed" are also excluded. This exclusion presents great problems in determining who is eligible for special education, and some professional organizations have called for its elimination.

Determining subcategories of E/BD is also difficult. Many authorities today agree that psychiatric categories are of little value for educational purposes and recommend reliance on individual assessment of each child's behavior and situational factors. Dimensional classification describes clusters of interrelated behaviors. Two broad, pervasive dimensions are externalizing (aggression, acting out) and internalizing (immaturity, withdrawal). Six dimensions frequently found in research are conduct disorder, socialized aggression, attention problems-immaturity, anxiety-withdrawal, psychotic behavior, and motor excess. All children may exhibit behavior characteristic of one or more of these dimensions to some degree, but children with E/BD tend to exhibit this behavior to an extreme degree.

Children with psychotic or pervasive developmental disorders exhibit quantitatively and qualitatively different behavior than normal children. Autism is a severe developmental disorder that begins before the child is thirty months old and is characterized by lack of responsiveness to people, problems in communication, peculiar speech, peculiar interests, and stereotyped behavior. Schizophrenia is a disorder of thinking and is characterized by delusions and hallucinations.

Estimates of the prevalence of E/BD vary greatly because of the absence of a standard definition. Most estimates are in the range of 6 percent to 10 percent, but only about 1 percent of the school-aged population is currently identified as having E/BD for special education purposes. Most children so identified are boys, and most exhibit externalizing behavior. About 3 percent of U.S. youths are referred to juvenile court in any given year.

A single, specific cause of E/BD can seldom be identified. In most cases it is possible only to identify causal factors that contribute to the likelihood that a child will develop a disorder or that predispose a child to developing a disorder. Major contributing factors are found in biological conditions, family relationships, cultural influences, and school experiences. Possible biological factors include genetics, temperamental characteristics, malnutrition, brain trauma, and substance abuse. Family disorganization, parental abuse, and inconsistent discipline are among the most important family factors contributing to E/BD. However, it is inappropriate to conclude that parenting is always or solely responsible for children's problems. Family factors appear to affect each individual family member in a different way. Cultural factors contributing to E/BD include the influences of the media, values and standards of the community, the peer group, and social services available to children and their families. School factors that may contribute to E/BD are insensitivity to children's individuality, inappropraite expectations, inconsistent or inappropriate discipline, unintentional rewards for misbehavior, and undesirable models of conduct. Efforts to prevent E/BD are concentrated on identifying and teaching the social skills that help children make and keep friends and get along with adults as well as on reducing risk factors such as neglect, abuse, family conflict, and school failure.

Most children with E/BD, especially those who have a conduct disorder or a psychotic disorder, are easily recognized by teachers. Few schools use systematic screening procedures, partly because services would be unavailable for the many children likely to be identified. The most effective identification procedures use a combination of teachers' rankings and ratings and direct observation of students' behavior. Peer rankings or ratings are often used as well.

The typical student with E/BD has an IQ in the dull-normal range, although some are very intelligent. Most children with autism test in the moderately to severely retarded range of intelligence. Most children with E/BD lack, in varying degrees, the ability to apply their knowledge and skills to the demands of everyday living.

Those who express their problems in aggressive, acting-out behavior are involved in a vicious cycle. Their behavior alienates others, so that positive interactions with adults and peers become less and less likely. Children whose behavior is consistently aggressive have less chance of learning to make social adjustments and of achieving mental health in adulthood than do those who are shy, anxious, or neurotic.

Children with severe or profound disorders usually lack basic self-care skills, may appear to be perceptually handicapped, and have serious cognitive deficits. Especially evident and important is their inability to relate to other people. In addition, deviations in speech and language abilities, self-stimulation or self-injurious behavior, and the tendency to injure others deliberately combine to give these children a poor prognosis. Some of them function permanently at a retarded level and require continued supervision and care, although recent research brings hope that many may make remarkable progress with early intensive intervention.

Good descriptions of special educational programs for children with E/BD are seldom found, and there are many different views. The psychoanalytic approach is characterized by a high degree of permissiveness, little emphasis on academic achievement, and reliance on individual psychotherapy for the child and parents to resolve the underlying causes of the problem. The psychoeducational approach recognizes the existence and importance of underlying causes but also stresses academic achievement and learning to cope with the realities of everyday living. In the humanistic approach, children with E/BD are considered to be out of touch with their own feelings and unable to find meaning and self-fulfillment in traditional education. Educational practices are characterized by a nonauthoritarian atmosphere in which the teacher functions as a resource and catalyst rather than as a director of activities. Those who subscribe to the ecological approach see E/BD as a problem of the child in interaction with the various elements of the environment. Educational intervention is aimed at altering the child's relationship with school, family, community, and social agencies. The behavioral approach sees E/BD as representing inappropriate learning. The focus of this approach is on observation and measurement of maladaptive behavior and manipulation of the consequences of behavior to change it. Today, a synthesis of conceptual models, variously termed *individual psychology* or *cognitive-behavior modification*, is often suggested. These current approaches, which blend developmental and learning theories, place new emphasis on enhancing the child's self. Behavior change strategies intended to teach self-control are now commonly suggested.

A relatively small percentage of children and youths with E/BD receive special education and related services. Only those with severe problems are likely to be identified, and as a consequence many are educated outside regular classrooms and schools. Psychotic disorders may require individual instruction until the child has learned basic skills required for instruction in small groups. There is a trend toward educating children with psychotic disorders in regular schools and classes. Programs for juvenile delinquents are extremely varied, and the educational needs of many delinquents are not addressed. The academic curriculum for students with other disorders tends to parallel the curriculum for most children but should include instruction in social skills as well.

Early identification and prevention are goals of early identification programs. These goals hold particular promise because children's behavior is quite flexible, but they pose particular difficulties because E/BD is so hard to define precisely in preschoolers and because different conceptual models suggest different goals and intervention methods. Behavioral approaches to early intervention appear to be particularly effective. Researchers are seeking more effective and less punitive ways of dealing with the problem behavior of young children, including aggression.

Programs of special education for adolescents and young adults with E/BD are extremely varied and must be highly individualized because of the wide differences in intelligence, behavioral characteristics, and achievements of the students involved. Transition from school to work and adult life is particularly difficult for students with E/BD, and they are among those most likely to drop out of school. The outlook for adulthood is particularly poor for children and youths who have psychotic disorders or are highly aggressive.

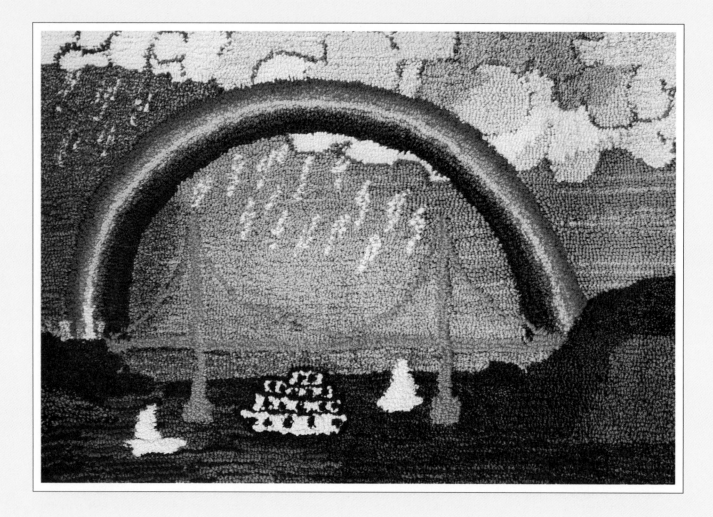

GOLDEN GATE BRIDGE
William Tyler, Creative Growth Art Center

6

Communication Disorders

I said goodbye and turned to go, but she wrapped her purple-green arms around my neck, kissed my cheek, and said, "I love you, Jeremy."

"I'll miss you so much."

"I really, truly love you with all my soul," she said.

"My Dad's waiting. I better go."

She took her arms off me and stepped back, straightened her smock. Then she said, "I've already told you I love you, Jeremy. Can't you say, 'I love you, Faith'?"

"I love you," I said.

" 'I love you, *Faith*,' " she insisted.

This little scene in the garage occurred only a few months after my futile attempt to say *Philadelphia* in the living room. Stutterers have a tendency to generalize their fear of one word that begins with a particular sound to a fear of all words that begin with the same sound. In the space of the summer I'd effectively eliminated every *F* from my vocabulary, with the exception of the preposition, "for," which for the time being was too small to incite terror. A few weeks later, my fear of *F* ended when another letter—I think it was *L*—suddenly loomed large. But at the moment, early October 1962, in Faith's garage, I was terrified of *F*s. I simply wasn't saying them. I hadn't called Faith by her first name for nearly a month and had, instead, taken to calling her Carlisle, as if her patronymic had become a term of jocular endearment.

"I can't," I said. "I can't say that."

(*David Shields*, Dead Languages)

ommunication is such a natural part of our everyday lives that we seldom stop to think about it. Social conversation with families, friends, and casual acquaintances is normally so effortless and pleasant that it is hard to imagine anyone having difficulty with it. Most of us have feelings of uncertainty about the adequacy of our speech or language only in stressful or unusual social situations, such as talking to a large audience or being interviewed for a job. If we always had to worry about communicating we would worry about every social interaction we had.

Not all communication disorders involve disorders of speech. Some **speech disorders** are not so handicapping in social interactions as **stuttering,** nor is stuttering the most common disorder of speech. The problem Shields describes (see p. 217) affects only about one person in a hundred, and then usually just during childhood. But stuttering is a mystery. Its causes and cures remain largely unknown, although for many years it captured a large share of speech-language pathologists' attention. In one sense, then, stuttering is a poor example to use in introducing a chapter on communication disorders. It is not the most representative disorder, it is difficult to define precisely, its causes are not fully understood, and few suggestions about how to overcome it can be made with confidence. But in another sense stuttering is the best example. When people think of speech and language disorders, they tend to think first of stuttering (Owens, 1986). It is a disorder we all have heard and recognized (if not experienced) at one time or another, the social consequences are obvious, and it *appears* to be a simple problem with obvious "logical" solutions ("Just slow down"; "Relax, don't worry"; "Think about how to say it"); but these seemingly commonsense approaches do not work.

Our points here are simply these: First, all communication disorders carry social penalties. Second, communication is among the most complex human functions, and disorders of this function do not always yield to intuitive or commonsense "solutions."

DEFINITIONS

Speech and language are tools used for purposes of communication. Communication requires *encoding* (sending in understandable form) and *decoding* (receiving and understanding) messages. Communication always involves a sender and a receiver of messages, but it does not always involve language. Animals communicate through movements and noises, for example, but their communication does not qualify as a true language. We are concerned here only with communication through language.

Language is the communication of ideas through an arbitrary system of symbols used according to certain rules that determine meaning. When people think of language, they typically think of the oral language most of us use. **Speech**—the behavior of forming and sequencing the sounds of oral language—is the most common symbol system used in communication between humans. Some languages, however, are not based on speech. For example, American Sign Language does not involve speech sounds; it is a manual language used by many people who cannot hear speech. Moreover, **augmentative communication** for people with disabilities involving the physical movements of speech may consist of alternatives to the speech sounds of oral language.

The American Speech-Language-Hearing Association provides definitions of disorders of communication, including **speech disorders, language disorders,** and variations in communication (differences or dialects and augmentative systems) that are not disorders (see the box on p. 220). Note that language disorders include problems in the comprehension and use of language for communication, regardless

MISCONCEPTIONS
ABOUT PERSONS WITH COMMUNICATION DISORDERS

Myth	*Fact*
Children with language disorders always have speech difficulties as well.	It is possible for a child to have good phonology, voice, and speech flow and yet not make any sense when he or she talks; however, most children with language disorders have speech disorders as well.
Individuals with communication disorders are always emotionally disturbed or mentally retarded.	Some children with communication disorders are normal in cognitive, social, and emotional development.
How children learn language is now well understood.	Although recent research has revealed quite a lot about the sequence of language acquisition and led to theories of language development, exactly how children learn language is still unknown.
Stuttering is primarily a disorder of people with extremely high IQs. Children who stutter become stuttering adults.	Stuttering can affect individuals at any level of intellectual ability. Some children who stutter continue stuttering as adults; most, however, stop stuttering before or during adolescence with help from a speech-language pathologist. Stuttering is primarily a childhood disorder, and it is found much more often in boys than in girls.
Disorders of phonology (or articulation) are never very serious and are always easy to correct.	Disorders of phonology can make speech unintelligible; it is sometimes very difficult to correct phonological or articulation problems, especially if the individual is retarded, disturbed, or has cerebral palsy.
A child with a cleft palate always has defective speech.	The child born with a cleft palate may or may not have a speech disorder, depending on the nature of the cleft, the medical treatment given, and other factors such as psychological characteristics and speech training.
There is no relationship between intelligence and disorders of communication.	Communication disorders tend to occur more frequently among individuals of lower intellectual ability, although it is possible for these disorders to occur in individuals who are extremely intelligent.
There is not much overlap between language disorders and learning disabilities.	Problems with verbal skills—listening, reading, writing, speaking—are often a central feature of a learning disability. The definitions of learning disability and language disorder are overlapping.

of the symbol system used (spoken, written, or other). The *form, content,* and/or *function* of language may be involved. The form of language includes sound combinations **(phonology),** construction of word forms such as plurals and verb tenses **(morphology),** and construction of sentences **(syntax).** The content of language refers to the intentions and meanings people attach to words and sentences **(semantics).** Language function is the use to which language is put in communication, and it includes nonverbal behavior as well as vocalizations that form the pattern of language use **(pragmatics).**

Definitions of the American Speech-Language-Hearing Association

COMMUNICATIVE DISORDERS

A. A SPEECH DISORDER is an impairment of voice, articulation of speech sounds, and/or fluency. These impairments are observed in the transmission and use of the oral symbol system.

1. A VOICE DISORDER is defined as the absence or abnormal production of voice quality, pitch, loudness, resonance, and/or duration.

2. An ARTICULATION DISORDER is defined as the abnormal production of speech sounds.

3. A FLUENCY DISORDER is defined as the abnormal flow of verbal expression, characterized by impaired rate and rhythm which may be accompanied by struggle behavior.

B. A LANGUAGE DISORDER is the impairment or deviant development of comprehension and/or use of a spoken, written, and/or other symbol system. The disorder may involve (1) the form of language (phonologic, morphologic, and syntactic systems), (2) the content of language (semantic system), and /or (3) the function of language in communication (pragmatic system) in any combination.

1. Form of Language
   a. PHONOLOGY is the sound system of a language and the linguistic rules that govern the sound combinations.
   b. MORPHOLOGY is the linguistic rule system that governs the structure of words and the construction of word forms from the basic elements of meaning.
   c. SYNTAX is the linguistic rule governing the order and combination of words to form sentences, and the relationships among the elements within a sentence.

2. Content of Language
   a. SEMANTICS is the psycholinguistic system that patterns the content of an utterance, intent and meanings of words and sentences.

3. Function of Language
   a. PRAGMATICS is the sociolinguistic system that patterns the use of language in communication which may be expressed motorically, vocally, or verbally.

COMMUNICATIVE VARIATIONS

A. COMMUNICATIVE DIFFERENCE/DIALECT is a variation of a symbol system used by a group of individuals which reflects and is determined by shared regional, social, or cultural/ethnic factors. Variations or alterations in the use of a symbol system may be indicative of primary language interferences. A regional, social, or cultural/ethnic variation of a symbol system should not be considered a disorder of speech or language.

B. AUGMENTATIVE COMMUNICATION is a system used to supplement the communicative skills of individuals for whom speech is temporarily or permanently inadequate to meet communicative needs. Both prosthetic devices and/or nonprosthetic techniques may be designed for individual use as an augmentative communication system.

SOURCE: American Speech-Language-Hearing Association, *Definitions: Communicative Disorders and Variations, ASHA,* 24, (1982) 949–950.

The voice must be modulated according to the demands of a given situation. But disorders of voice sometimes involve inappropriate use, such as speaking in a voice much louder or softer than necessary. Prolonged abuse of the vocal mechanism, such as screaming at an athletic competition, can result in temporary or permanent problems in voice production. (Bill Weems/Woodfin Camp & Associates)

SPEECH DISORDERS

As we noted at the beginning of the chapter, speech disorders include disorders of voice, articulation, and fluency. Remember that an individual may have more than one disorder of speech and that speech and language disorders sometimes occur together.

Voice Disorders

People's voices are perceived as having pitch, loudness, and quality. Changes in pitch and loudness are part of the stress patterns of speech. Vocal quality is related not only to production of speech sounds but also to the nonlinguistic aspects of speech. Together, the three dimensions of voice are sufficient to reveal a person's identity, and often a good deal about the individual's physical and emotional status as well. *Voice disorders,* though difficult to define precisely, are characteristics of pitch, loudness, and/or quality that are abusive of the **larynx;** hamper communication; or are perceived as markedly different from what is customary for someone of a given age, sex, and cultural background. Voice disorders that involve a dysfunction within the larynx are referred to as *disorders of phonation.* Disorders having to do with the dysfunction of the oral and nasal air passageways are called *disorders of* **resonance**.

Estimates of the prevalence of voice disorders depend on what age group is surveyed and what criteria are used to define abnormalities. Children in the lower grades tend to have more voice problems than older children (Moore, 1986),

TABLE 6.1   Summary of Six Theories of Language Classified by Basic Language Disorders, Assessment, and Intervention

	Neuropsychological Theory	Behavioral Theory	Information Processing Theory
Basic focus	Language is derived from brain function. Specific language behaviors relate to specific areas of the brain.	Language is learned behavior resulting from antecedents and consequences of language behavior.	Language is described by a serial relation between input (sensation, perception, etc.) and output (encoding, imitation, etc.) processes.
Language development	Language unfolds during the brain's maturational process.	The learners are taught language. It is trained and shaped by the environment.	Language develops as each component in the input and output serial process develops.
Language disorders	The degree and type of language impairment is related to the degree and type of brain dysfunction. Therefore, there are different kinds of language disorders.	The difference between the language behavior of a child and that of adult models constitutes a disorder. Variations in the nature, cause, and characteristics of disorders are irrelevant.	Deficits in the function of any of the processes in the sequence of decoding and encoding impair performance of subsequent processes. Different kinds of language disorders result and such differences are determined by comparison with age peers.
Assessment	The purpose of assessment is to describe and separate language deficits due to brain dysfunction from that due to other causes. This is termed *differential diagnosis*.	The purpose of assessment is to identify differences between what a child does and what he or she should be doing by adult standards.	Assessment involves the analysis of each process in the decoding and encoding sequence. Comparison is made between processes within the child and with other children by means of normative data.
Intervention	Intervention is directed to the strengthening of or compensation for skills impaired in brain dysfunction by instruction using activities that require repetition.	Intervention uses a basic stimulus/response/reinforcement paradigm to train behaviors that a child does not perform.	Intervention is directed to improve weak processes or compensate for them. Emphasis is placed on using child's learning style to instruct.

SOURCE: E. Carrow-Woolfolk, *Theory, Assessment and Intervention in Language Disorders: An Integrative*

Focus, Language Development,

Linguistic Theory	Cognitive Organization Theory	Pragmatic Theory
Language is a system of abstract rules from which an individual can generate an infinite number of utterances.	Language is one of many similar cognitive tasks that are instances of skill acquisition and are based on common cognitive knowledge and processes.	Language's primary function is communication, and its basic unit is the speech act that occurs in a context that helps to determine its form.
Language rules are induced by a child whose own system controls the selection of rules and their internal construction. The process has universal characteristics.	The cognitive ability to learn rules and skilled behavior and to solve problems is responsible for the child's acquisition of language rules and his or her performance of language.	Language is acquired through interaction with the environment. The environment helps to shape the direction of acquisition.
Differences between a child and peers are judged on developmental indices. Problems are judged to be a result of a child's failure to induce rules. Cause of difference is not considered relevant to intervention.	Language deficits and related cognitive problems are a result of basic problems in the learning system. The impairment may be in the rule-learning area or in the area of performance and skill behavior.	Language disorders are a result of a breakdown in the interaction process in communication. This breakdown may be related to problems in the child's system or in the environment.
Assessment involves detailed description of child's production of language structure by means of analysis of language samples and comparison with developmental data.	Assessment involves the evaluation of basic cognitive abilities (symbolic behavior, storage, retrieval, etc.) and the determination of their relation to the learning of cognitive skills, including language.	Assessment involves the description of the child's pragmatic skills observed in naturalistic settings.
Emphasis in intervention is on providing exemplars of target rules in a naturalistic setting and thereby facilitating rule induction.	Intervention is through teaching cognitive skills that may improve general learning. Modification of materials is provided to make rule induction easier, and repetition is used for improving performance.	Intervention is provided in naturalistic settings for developing pragmatic skills. The environment is used to make target behaviors more salient.

Approach (Philadelphia: Grune & Stratton), pp. 25–26.

The Speech-Language Pathologist

A speech-language pathologist is a highly trained professional capable of assuming a variety of roles in assisting persons who have speech and language disorders. Entering the profession requires rigorous training and demonstration of clinical skills under close supervision. Certification requires completion of a master's degree in a program approved by the American Speech-Language-Hearing Association (ASHA). You may want to write to ASHA, 10801 Rockville Pike, Rockville, MD 20852 for a free booklet, *Careers in Speech-Language Pathology and Audiology*.

Because of the emphasis on *least restrictive environment* or mainstreaming (see Chapters 1 and 2), speech-language pathologists are doing more of their work in regular classrooms and are spending more time consulting with classroom teachers than they have in the past. The speech-language pathologist of the future will need more knowledge of classroom procedures and the academic curriculum, especially in reading, writing, and spelling, and will be more involved in the overall education of children with communication disorders. More emphasis will be placed on working as a team member in the schools to see that handicapped children obtain an appropriate education. Because of legislation and changing population demographics, speech-language pathologists of the future will also probably be more involved with preschool children and those with learning disabilities and severe, multiple disabilities. There will be broader concern for the entire range of communication disorders, including both oral and written communication.

and one would expect to find more voice problems among children with other disabilities than among the general population. Moore estimates that voice problems affect 6 percent of children of school age.

Voice disorders can result from a variety of biological and nonbiological causes. Growths in the larynx (such as nodules, polyps, or cancerous tissue), infections of the larynx (laryngitis), damage to the nerves supplying the larynx, or accidental bruises or scratches on the larynx can cause disorders. Misuse or abuse of the voice also can lead to a voice that is temporarily abnormal. High school cheerleaders, for example, frequently develop temporary voice disorders (Campbell, Reich, Klockars, & McHenry, 1988). Disorders resulting from misuse of abuse can damage the tissues of the larynx. Sometimes a person has psychological problems that lead to a complete loss of voice (aphonia) or to severe voice abnormalities. Voice disorders having to do with resonance may be caused by physical abnormalities of the oral cavity (such as *cleft palate*) or damage to the brain or nerves controlling the oral cavity. Infections of the tonsils, adenoids, or sinuses can also influence how the voice is resonated. Most people who have a severe hearing loss typically have problems in achieving a normal or pleasingly resonant voice. Finally, sometimes a person simply has not learned to speak with an appropriately resonant voice. There are no biological or deep-seated psychological reasons for the problem; rather, it appears that the person has learned faulty habits of positioning the organs of speech (Moore, 1986; Starkweather, 1983).

When children are screened for speech and language disorders, the speech-language pathologist is on the lookout for problems in voice quality, resonance, pitch, and loudness. If a problem is found, referral to a physician is indicated. A medical report may indicate that surgery or other treatment is needed because of a growth or infection. Aside from the medical evaluation, the speech-language pathologist will evaluate when the problem began and how the individual uses his or her voice in everyday situations and under stressful circumstances. Besides looking for how voice is produced and structural or functional problems, the pathologist looks for signs of infection or disease that may be contributing to the disorder and signs of serious illness.

Articulation Disorders

Distinctions between articulation disorders and phonological disorders are sometimes difficult to make. *Phonology* refers to the study of the rules for using the sounds of language. When a person has difficulty communicating because he or she does not use speech sounds according to standard rules, the disorder is phonological. *Articulation* refers to the "movements of the articulators in production of the speech sounds that make up words of our language" (McReynolds, 1986, p. 142). The distinction between articulation and phonological disorders is a technical one, and even speech-language pathologists may disagree about how a given individual's problem should be classified.

Articulation and phonological disorders involve errors in producing words. Word sounds may be omitted, substituted, distorted, or added. Lisping, for example, involves a substitution or distortion of the [s] sound (e.g., *thunthine* or *shunshine* for *sunshine*). Missing, substituted, added, or poorly produced word sounds may make a speaker difficult to understand or even unintelligible. Such errors in speech production may also carry heavy social penalties, subjecting the speaker to teasing or ridicule.

When are articulation or phonological errors a disorder? Deciding that errors represent a disorder really depends on a clinician's subjective judgment. That judgment will be influenced by the clinician's experience, the number and types of errors, the consistency of these errors, the age and developmental characteristics of the speaker, and the intelligibility of the person's speech.

Young children make many errors in speech sounds when they are learning to talk. Many children do not master all the phonological rules of the language and learn to produce all the speech sounds correctly until they are eight or nine years old. Furthermore, most children make frequent errors until after they enter school. The age of the child is thus a major consideration in judging the adequacy of articulation. Another major consideration is the phonological characteristics of the child's community because children learn speech largely through imitation. A child reared in the deep South may have speech that sounds peculiar to residents of Long Island, but that does not mean that the child has a speech disorder.

Detailed information about the prevalence of articulation and phonological disorders in children is not readily available. Estimates are that about 10 percent of the population has some type of problem communicating and that about 75 percent of these problems involve articulation or phonology (Newman, Creaghead, & Secord, 1985). The number of children having difficulty in producing word sounds decreases markedly during the first three or four years of elementary school. Among children with other disabilities, especially mental retardation and neurological disorders like cerebral palsy, the prevalence of articulation disorders is higher than in the general population.

Lack of ability to articulate speech sounds correctly can be caused by biological factors. For example, brain damage or damage to the nerves controlling the muscles used in speech may make it difficult or impossible to articulate sounds. Furthermore, abnormalities of the oral structures, such as a cleft palate, may make normal speech difficult or impossible. Relatively minor structural changes, such as loss of teeth, may produce temporary errors. Delayed phonological development may also result from a hearing loss. But most children's articulation disorders are not the result of biological factors. Nor can one say with confidence that they are the result of perceptual-motor problems or psychosocial factors. There simply is no satisfactory explanation for the fact that some children whose development appears to be normal in every other way persist in making articulation errors (McReynolds, 1986).

Parents of preschool children may refer their child for assessment if he or she has speech that is really difficult to understand. Most schools screen all new pupils for speech and language problems, and in most cases a child who still makes many articulation errors in the third or fourth grade will be referred for evaluation. Older children and adults sometimes seek help for themselves when their speech draws negative attention. A speech-language pathologist will assess not only phonological characteristics but also social and developmental history, hearing, general language ability, and speech mechanism. Assessment of articulation may involve giving commercially perpared tests and/or using materials the clinician has devised. Testing to compare the child's phonology to that of others is done by having the child say words, count, name or describe pictures, and so on. Judgment of whether or not a particular sound is correctly articulated rests with the trained ear of the pathologist.

The decision about whether or not to include the child in an intervention program will depend on the child's age, other developmental characteristics, and the type and consistency of the articulatory errors. The decision will also depend on the pathologist's assessment of the likelihood that the child will self-correct the errors and of the social penalties, such as teasing and shyness, the child is experiencing. If the child misarticulates only a few sounds but does so consistently and suffers social embarrassment or rejection as a consequence, an intervention program is usually called for.

Intervention for a child who has severely delayed speech usually begins in the preschool or early elementary grades. Children who have a developmental phonological disorder—one not known to be caused by or associated with other developmental problems—may not be included in an intervention program until the middle grades. The speech-language pathologist will teach the child the auditory, visual, and tactile cues involved in producing sounds correctly by providing models, giving instructions, having the child listen to differences in sounds, and helping the child understand the movements of the tongue and lips in producing sounds.

Once sounds are reliably produced correctly in a clinical setting, the focus of intervention shifts to transfer of the training to the everyday environment (McReynolds, 1986). To make it likely that the child will articulate the correct sounds in ordinary conversation, the clinician may enlist the aid of parents and teachers. Parents and teachers may give the child reminders, provide special practice sessions, or be asked to change the ways they respond to the child's errors and correct sound productions. In some cases, children are taught to monitor their own articulation (Koegel, Koegel, Voy, & Ingham, 1988).

Fluency Disorders

Normal speech is characterized by some interruptions in speech flow. All of us occasionally get speech sounds in the wrong order (*revalent* for *relevant*), speak too fast to be understood, pause at the wrong place in a sentence, use an inappropriate pattern of stress, or become *disfluent*—that is, stumble and backtrack, repeating syllables or words, and fill in pauses with *uh* while trying to think of how to finish what we have to say. It is only when the speaker's efforts are so intense or the interruptions in the flow of speech are so frequent or pervasive that they keep the speaker from being understood or draw extraordinary attention that they are considered disorders. Besides, listeners have a greater tolerance for some types of disfluencies than others. Most of us will more readily accept speech-flow disruptions we perceive as necessary corrections of what the speaker has said or is planning to say than disruptions that appear to reflect the speaker's inability to proceed with the articulation of what he or she has decided to say.

The most frequent type of fluency disorder is stuttering. About 1 percent of children and adults are considered stutterers. More boys than girls stutter. Most stutterers are identified by at least age five (Andrews et al., 1983). However, parents sometimes perceive their child as stuttering as early as twenty to thirty months of age (Yairi, 1983). The majority of stutters begin to show an abnormal speech pattern between two and five years of age. Many children outgrow their childhood disfluencies. These children generally use regular and effortless disfluencies, appear to be unaware of their hesitancies, and have parents and teachers who are unconcerned about their speech patterns (Shames & Rubin, 1986).

A child who is thought to stutter should be evaluated by a speech-language pathologist. Early diagnosis is important if the development of chronic stuttering is to be avoided. Unfortunately, many educators and physicians do not refer potential stutterers for in-depth assessment because they are aware that disfluencies are a normal part of speech-language development. But nonreferral is extremely detrimental to children who are at risk to stutter. If their stuttering goes untreated, it may result in a lifelong disorder that affects their ability to communicate, develop positive feelings about self, and pursue certain educational and employment opportunities (see Meyers, 1986; Shames & Rubin, 1986).

Speech Disorders Associated with Orofacial Defects

A wide variety of abnormalities of the mouth and face can interfere with speech and language (McWilliams, 1986). Nearly all of these defects are present at birth. A few are acquired through accident or disease in which part of the facial tissues must be removed surgically. The defects can involve the tongue, lips, nasal passages, ears, teeth and gums, and **palate.** Any defect in the mechanisms of hearing and speaking can affect the development and use of speech and language. By far the most common orofacial defect in children is an orofacial cleft—a rift or split in the upper part of the oral cavity or the upper lip. (Cleft lip is sometimes referred to inappropriately by uninformed or insensitive individuals as "harelip.") We discuss only orofacial clefts, although all types of craniofacial abnormalities may have implications for speech and language.

The prevalence of clefts varies from one racial group to another. It is about 1 in 750 to 1,000 births for Caucasians, but about 1 in 500 for Orientals and about 1 in 2,000 or 3,000 for persons of African descent. More boys than girls are born with clefts (McWilliams, 1986). Orofacial clefts may result from genetic inheritance, mutant genes, abnormalities in chromosomes, or damage to the embryo during development. Regarding causes and characteristics, Shprintzen (1988) notes that children with cleft palates are "a hodgepodge of children who have their clefts in common but little else" (p. 147). Therefore careful individualized assessment is crucial.

Clefts of the palate (roof of the mouth) may cause the child to have difficulty eating because the food escapes into the nasal passage when he or she tries to swallow. Because the function of the **eustachian tube** (the tube connecting the

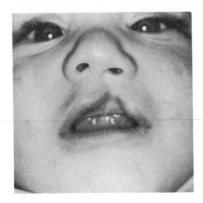

(a)

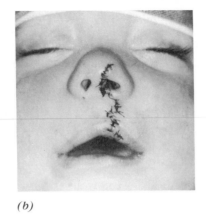

(b)

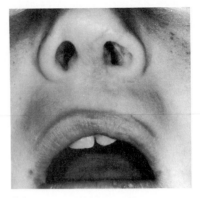

(c)

Figure 6.1 Preoperative and postoperative photos of a unilateral cleft lip. The preoperative photo (a) shows the unrepaired cleft and an associated asymmetry of the nose. The postoperative photos (b) and (c) show the extent to which the cleft was closed and the nose made symmetrical.

SOURCE: Courtesy of Dr. Milton T. Edgerton, Chairman, Department of Plastic Surgery, University of Virginia School of Medicine.

middle ear and the throat) is usually impaired when there is a cleft in the palate, the child may be prone to impaired hearing. By far the most important consideration for speech, however, is the difficulty the child with a cleft palate has in building up sufficient air pressure in the oral cavity and in preventing air from escaping through the nasal cavity while articulating most sounds. If too much air is allowed to escape through the nasal cavity during speech, the speaker will probably be perceived as having a speech disorder. The speech disorders associated with clefts are primarily disorders of articulation and voice (especially resonance).

Clefts are virtually always correctable by surgery; such repair usually is made soon after birth. Figure 6.1 shows how effective surgery can be in repairing a cleft lip. Children who are much more severely disfigured by clefts than the one shown here can be restored to almost normal appearance.

Surgery and clinical correction of defective speech have made great advances in recent years. But they are not yet so advanced that speech problems can be eliminated in all cases. Whether or not a child will have a speech defect depends on much more than the presence or absence of certain speech structures or the condition of these structures. General intelligence, hearing acuity, environmental stimulation, and dental characteristics affect the adequacy of speech (McWilliams, 1986).

Assessment of orofacial defects and their implications for speech and language requires an interdisciplinary team of specialists. Intervention, too, must be an interdisciplinary effort. A pediatrician and a plastic surgeon are typically involved from the beginning. Frequently a child with an orofacial defect has health problems requiring consultation with other medical specialists. Dentists, audiologists, psychologists, and speech-language pathologists are part of the team required for adequate assessment and intervention.

The work of the speech-language pathologist with a child who has an orofacial defect is similar in many respects to work with children who have articulation, voice, or other disorders but no defect of the speech mechanism. That is, the goal is to teach the child how to use appropriate voice, articulate sounds so that they can be understood, and use language skillfully. The difference is that in working with the child who has an orofacial defect it is necessary to collaborate closely with other specialists. In cases in which the defect prevents normal articulatory movement, the pathologist must teach the child alternative ways of making speech sounds.

Speech Disorders Associated with Neurological Damage

The muscles that make speech possible are under voluntary control. When there is damage to areas of the brain controlling these muscles or to the nerves leading to them, there is a disturbance in the ability to speak normally. These disorders may involve articulation of speech sounds (**dysarthria**) or selecting and sequencing speech (**apraxia**). The difficulties in speaking are due to the fact that the muscles controlling breathing, the larynx, the throat, the tongue, the jaw, and/or the lips cannot be controlled precisely. Depending on the nature of the injury to the brain, perceptual and cognitive functions may also be affected; the individual may have a language disorder in addition to a speech disorder (Blosser & DePompei, 1989; LaPointe, 1986; Mysak, 1986).

In Chapter 9 we discuss the many possible causes of brain injury. Among them are physical trauma, oxygen deprivation, poisoning, diseases, and strokes. Any of these can be the cause of dysarthria or apraxia. Probably the condition that most frequently accounts for dysarthria and apraxia in children is *cerebral palsy*—brain injury before, during, or after birth that results in muscular weakness or paralysis. Vehicular accidents are a frequent cause of brain injury in adolescence and young adulthood.

The speech-language pathologist will assess the neurologically impaired individual's ability to control breathing, phonation, resonation, and articulatory movements by listening to the person's speech and inspecting the speech mechanism. Medical, surgical, and rehabilitative specialists in the treatment of neurological disorders also must evaluate the person's problem and plan a management strategy. As in the case of orofacial disorders, surgical or mechanical interventions may be possible. Even after all possible medical-surgical treatment has been exhausted, the speech-language pathologist is still called on to aid the person in learning or relearning more intelligible speech. In cases in which the neurological impairment makes the person's speech unintelligible, alternative communication systems may be required.

LANGUAGE DISORDERS

There has been a shift in concern among speech-language pathologists away from speech disorders. Much more interest is now shown in the disorders of language. Estimates are that today 50 to 80 percent of the children seen by speech-language pathologists have language disorders (Wiig, 1986).

The primary reason for the shift in focus from speech to language is the recognition that disorders of language are much more debilitating—they are much more at the center of difficulties in communication. The distinction between speech and language disorders is significant. It is possible for a child to have normal speech—to have acceptable voice, articulation, and fluency—yet not make sense when talking or misinterpret the meaning of what is heard or read. Speech has to do with intelligible vocal encoding of messages; language has to do with the formulation and interpretation of meaning. Language involves listening and speaking, reading and writing, technical discourse, and social interaction. Language problems are basic to many of the disabilities discussed in this text, especially hearing impairment, mental retardation, and learning disability.

Prevalence

No trustworthy estimates of the prevalence of language disorders in children and youths are available. Estimating prevalence is extremely difficult because the procedures for definition and assessment still lack precision. Moreover, language disorders typically occur in combination with other handicapping conditions, such as hearing impairment, learning disability, cerebral palsy, emotional/behavioral disorders, and mental retardation. If this overlap is considered and if language is defined to include speaking, listening, reading, and writing, probably 5 to 10 percent of the child population could be considered to have a language disorder.

Classification of Language Disorders

Language disorders can be classified according to several criteria. The ASHA definitions on page 220 provide a classification scheme involving five subsystems of language; *phonology* (sounds), *morphology* (word forms), *syntax* (word order and sentence structure), *semantics* (word and sentence meanings), and *pragmatics* (social use of language). Difficulty with one of these dimensions of language is virtually certain to be accompanied by difficulty with one or more of the others. However, children with language disorders often have particular difficulty with one dimension. Language disorders involving these subsystems are illustrated in the box below.

Disorders of the Five Subsystems of Language

Oral language involves communication through a system of sound symbols. Disorders may occur in one or more of five subsystems of oral language: *phonology* (sounds and sound combinations), *morphology* (words and meaningful word parts), *syntax* (sequences and combinations of words), *semantics* (meanings or content), and *pragmatics* (use for communication). The following interactions illustrate disorders in each of these subsystems. Note that a given illustration may involve more than a single subsystem.

PHONOLOGY

Alvin has just turned 6. He is in kindergarten, but has been receiving speech therapy for 2 years. At 4, his parents sought assistance when his speech and language remained unintelligible and he did not appear to be "growing out" of his problem. He has two older siblings whose speech and language are well within the normal range. Alvin substitutes and omits a number of speech sounds, and in addition, he has difficulty with other subsystems of language as shown in the example below:

Clinician: I'd like you to tell me about some words. Here's something that you may have for breakfast: orange juice. What's orange juice?
Alvin: I doh noh. [I don't know.]
Clinician: See if you can guess. What color is orange juice?

Alvin: Ahnge. N you dink i. [Orange. And you drink it.]
Clinician: That's good. Tell me some more about orange juice.
Alvin: Doh noh.
Clinician: Let's try another. What's sugar? Tell me what sugar is.
Alvin: Yukky.
Clinician: Yukky? Why?
Alvin: Cah i wahtuns yer tee. ['Cause it rottens your teeth.]

MORPHOLOGY

Children with language disorders in the morphological realm will exhibit difficulty in either understanding or producing morphological inflections. These include the ability to add -*s* to change a word from singular to plural; to include *'s* to make a word a possessive; -*ed* to change the tense of a word from present to past; or to use other inflectional endings to differentiate comparatives and superlatives, among others.

Children with morphological difficulties will use inappropriate suffixes. . . . Here are a few . . . examples, taken from the test protocols of school-age children:

Examiner: Anna, say this after me: *cow*.
Anna: (age 6) Cow.
Examiner: Good. Now say *boy*.
Anna: Boy.
Examiner: Now put them together. Say *cowboy*.
Anna: Boy.

Examiner: Frank, find two little words in this big word: *outside*.
Frank: (age 7) Outside.
Examiner: Not quite right. We need *two* words.
Frank: (Shrugs and looks around the room)
Examiner: Well, if one word is *side*, the other would be . . .?
Frank: Be?

Examiner: Jamie, can you tell me a story?
Jamie: (age 8) I can't think of none.
Examiner: What if the story began, "One night I walked into a dark haunted house . . . and . . .
Jamie: I met a ghost. He wanted to kill me. But he couldn't. I ran very, very fastest. And all of a sudden I saw a coffin. I hides in there. And all of a sudden there a ghostes inside there. And I sent out of the coffin. And then there weres a guy named Count. And then he tried to suck my blood. And then he couldn't find me because I hided. And then I met a mummy. And then he wanted to tie me up . . . and . . . that's all.

SYNTAX

Marie is 8 years old and in a special first-grade class. Her syntactical difficulties are demonstrated in the following story-telling event:

Clinician: Marie, I want you to listen carefully. I am going to tell you a story; listen, and when I'm done, I want you to tell me the story.
Marie: (interrupting) I don't know.
Clinician: I haven't told you the story yet. Remember, listen carefully to my story. When I'm done, you are to tell me everything you can remember about the story.
One day Mr. Mouse went for a walk. As he was walking, he saw a cat lying in the road. The cat had a stone in his paw so he couldn't walk. Mr. Mouse pulled the stone out of the cat's paw. The cat thanked Mr. Mouse for helping him. They shook hands and walked down the road together.

Marie: Uh, uh, uh . . . Cat was on the road and Mr. Mouse taken out the stone his paw, and then they walked down together the hill and they said thanks, and they walk on the hill, and the mouse chase him.

This task of retelling a story reveals that Marie has difficulty not only in syntax but in the ordering of events and in accurate recall. Indeed, Marie seems unaware that she has modified the story considerably, including giving the story a new ending.

SEMANTICS

Clinician: Burt, tell me about birthday parties.
Burt: (age 6) Sing "Happy Birthday," blow away candles, eat a birthday cake, open your presents.
Clinician: All right, now listen to this story and then say it back to me . . . tell me the whole story: "One day, a little boy went to school. He went up the steps of the school and opened the door. The boy went into his classroom and started playing with his friends. The teacher said, 'Time to come to circle.' The boy put away his toys and sat down on the rug."
Burt: A teacher . . . a boy played with a teacher's toys . . . time for us to come to circle . . . and it's the end.

You will note that Burt does not "blow out" candles; rather, his retrieval of information from semantic memory provides the response "blow away." In addition, it is clear that even the immediate retelling of a story, which in reality represents a string of events well within Burt's everyday experience, is very difficult for Burt. The pauses noted reflect the period of time during which Burt attempted to recall the necessary information.

PRAGMATICS

. . . Greg, age 7, interacts with his special education teacher. Greg is in a self-contained classroom for mentally retarded children and is one of the more verbal children in the class. Assessment by the speech-language pathologist indicates difficulties in phonology, syntax, morphology, and semantics. He has been identified as suffering from a significant language delay. On most language tests, he functions between 2:7 and 3:6 years of age. His teacher, who has visited his home many times, notes that there are no toys, no books, no playthings, and that there appears to be little communication between Greg and his mother, a single parent. The teacher is eager to draw Greg into conversation and story-telling, and has arranged a "talking and telling time" as part of the daily activities with the seven children who comprise her class.

Teacher: Greg, I'd like you to tell me a story. It can be about anything you like.
Greg: No me.
Teacher: Go ahead, it's your turn.
Greg: (having had previous instruction on "taking turns") No, s'yer turn.
Teacher: You do it. It's your turn.
Greg: I can't. I forget.
Teacher: I bet you can tell me a story about school.
Greg: You eat snack. What we have for snack?

Greg's teacher praises his contribution to the conversation and moves on to another student. She grins to herself; she and Greg have had a running joke about "turns." She feels that Greg tends to use "it's your turn" (when it is inappropriate) to delay the necessity to respond. This time she has enticed him into contributing to the conversation by requesting that he recall something that happens frequently within the school context. Greg attempts to comply, recalling from memory a favored episodic event. A small victory for both Greg and his teacher.

SOURCE: K. G. Butler, *Language Disorders in Children* (Austin, TX: Pro-Ed, 1986), pp. 13–14, 16–17, 19, 23, 28–29.

A second scheme for classifying language disorders is by comparison to the normal developmental schedule and sequence (Leonard, 1986). The child with a language disorder may follow the same sequence of development as most children but achieve each skill or milestone at a later age. Some children whose language development is delayed will catch up and achieve all the language characteristics of nonhandicapped children, but at a later age. Others reach a final level of development significantly below that of their nonhandicapped peers. Still other children are generally delayed in language development but show great discrepancies in the rate at which they acquire certain features of language. Differences in the development of a child with a language disorder and a normally developing child are outlined in Table 6.2. Notice that, in general, the sequence of development is similar for the two children, but the child with the language disorder shows slower development. Careful examination of the table reveals, however, that the children

TABLE 6.2 Pattern of Development Shown by a Child with a Language Disorder and a Nonhandicapped Child

Child with Language Disorder			Nonhandicapped Child		
Age	Attainment	Example	Age	Attainment	Example
27 months	First words	this, mama, bye bye, doggie	13 months	First words	here, mama, bye bye, kitty
28 months	50-word vocabulary		17 months	50-word vocabulary	
40 months	First two-word combinations	this doggie more apple this mama more play	18 months	First two-word combinations	more juice here ball more T.V. here kitty
48 months	Later two-word combinations	Mimi purse Daddy coat block chair dolly table	22 months	Later two-word combinations	Andy shoe Mommy ring cup floor keys chair
52 months	Mean sentence length of 2.00 words		24 months	Mean sentence length of 2.00 words	
55 months	First appearance of -ing	Mommy eating		First appearance of -ing	Andy sleeping
63 months	Mean sentence length of 3.10 words		30 months	Mean sentence length 3.10 words	
66 months	First appearance of is	The doggie's mad		First appearance of is	My car's gone!
73 months	Mean sentence length of 4.10 words		37 months	Mean sentence length of 4.10 words	
79 months	Mean sentence length of 4.50 words First appearance of indirect requests	Can I get the ball?		First appearance of indirect requests	Can I have some cookies?
			40 months	Mean sentence length of 4.50 words	

SOURCE: L. Leonard, "Early Language Development and Language Disorders," in G. H. Shames and E. H. Wiig (Eds.), *Human Communication Disorders*, 2nd ed. (Columbus, OH: Charles E. Merrill, 1986), p. 294. © 1986 Charles E. Merrill Publishing Company. Reprinted by permission of the publisher.

show different relationships among certain linguistic features. For example, the normally developing child uses the suffix *-ing* when the mean length of her sentences is 2.00 words, but the child with the language disorder does not use *-ing* when her average sentences are the same length.

A third way of classifying language disorders is based on the presumed cause or related conditions. Leonard (1986) notes that during the previous twenty years efforts have been made to describe the language characteristics of children with mental retardation, autism, hearing impairments, and various other conditions. This classification scheme has not worked very well because the language problems of children with different diagnostic labels are often similar, and the problems of those in a given diagnostic category are often extremely varied.

Yet another classification scheme has been suggested by Naremore (1980), who relies on description of the language and related behaviors of a child. It is important to know (1) what language and nonlanguage behaviors the child imitates because much language learning is based on imitation, (2) what the child comprehends because receptive language is important in early learning, and (3) what language the child produces spontaneously because communication is the ultimate goal. With this in mind, we discuss four general types of language disorders (see Table 6.3):

1. The child has not developed any verbal language.
2. The child's language is qualitatively different from normal language.
3. The child's language follows normal pattern of development but is delayed.
4. The child's language development is interrupted.

Absence of Verbal Language

Some children three years of age or older show no signs that they understand language and do not use language spontaneously. They may make noises, but they use these for communication in only the most primitive way (e.g., by grunting, crying, or screaming to get what they want). Often these children are clearly disabled in other ways besides their lack of language. Some of them are known to be deaf or deaf and blind; some are developmentally disabled in obvious ways (i.e., profoundly retarded or brain damaged and/or physically disabled); some show bizarre patterns of behavior characteristic of childhood psychosis. A few of the children who fall into this category are normal in physical development, relate to other people in normal ways except for lack of language, and are alert to visual stimuli. These children seem to have a problem in processing or making sense of auditory stimuli. The reason for their disability is not clear, but the suspicion is that they have suffered neurological damage.

Children who have little or no useful language by the time they are three years old are usually considered severely mentally retarded or severely emotionally disturbed (unless they are deaf). Teaching these children to speak is one of the first goals in their education. Without functional language, they cannot become truly social beings (Lane, 1976). Because nonverbal children are often severely retarded or disturbed, teachers of these children must have a working knowledge of how speech and language skills can be taught. The task is not one that can be made the sole responsibility of the speech-language pathologist.

In the 1960s and 1970s, systematic efforts to teach language to nonverbal children consisted of the use of operant conditioning methods. That is, a step-by-step sequence of behaviors approximating functional language was established, and the child's

TABLE 6.3 *Types of Language Disorders*	
Type	Commonly Suspected Causative Factors or Related Conditions
No Verbal Language Child does not show indications of understanding or spontaneously using language by age 3.	Congenital or early acquired deafness Gross brain damage or severe mental retardation Childhood psychosis
Qualitatively Different Language Child's language is different from that of nonhandicapped children at any stage of development—meaning and usefulness for communication are greatly lessened or lost.	Inability to understand auditory stimuli Childhood psychosis Learning disability Mental retardation Hearing loss
Delayed Language Development Language follows normal course of development, but lags seriously behind that of most children who are the same chronological age.	Mental retardation Experiential deprivation Lack of language stimulation Hearing loss
Interrupted Language Development Normal language development begins but is interrupted by illness, accident, or other trauma; language disorder is acquired	Acquired hearing loss Brain injury due to oxygen deprivation, physical trauma, or infection

SOURCE: Summarized from R. C. Naremore, "Language Disorders in Children," in T. J. Hixon, L. D. Shriberg, and J. H. Saxman (Eds.), *Introduction to Communication Disorders* (Englewood Cliffs, NJ: Prentice-Hall, 1980).

responses at each step in the sequence were rewarded. The rewards typically consisted of praise, hugs, and food given by the teacher immediately following the child's performance of the desired behavior. At the earliest step in the sequence the child might be reinforced for establishing eye contact with the teacher. The next step might be making any vocalization while looking at the teacher, next making a vocalization approximating a sound made by the teacher, then imitating words spoken by the teacher, and finally replying to the teacher's questions. Of course, this description is a simplification of the procedures that were employed, but through such methods nonverbal children were taught basic oral language skills (Devany, Rincover, & Lovaas, 1981; Koegel, Rincover, Egel, 1982).

A major problem of early research on these methods was that few of the children acquired truly functional language, even after intensive and prolonged training. Their speech tended to have a stereotyped, mechanical quality and often was used for a restricted range of purposes. A current trend in language training for nonverbal children is to try to make their language *functional*. The goal is to give the child a tool for communication—a means of influencing and interacting with the environment. Instead of training the child to imitate words in isolation or to use syntactically

TABLE 6.4 Differences Between the Analogue and the Natural Language Paradigm Conditions

	Analogue Condition	NLP Condition
Stimulus items	a. Chosen by clinician	a. Chosen by child
	b. Repeated until criterion is met	b. Varied every few trials
	c. Phonologically easy to produce, irrespective of whether they were functional in the natural environment	c. Age-appropriate items that can be found in child's natural environment
Prompts	a. Manual (e.g., touch tip of tongue, or hold lips together)	a. Clinician repeats item
Interaction	a. Clinician holds up stimulus item; stimulus item not functional within interaction	a. Clinician and child play with stimulus item (i.e., stimulus item is functional within interaction)
Response	a. Correct responses or successive approximations reinforced	a. Looser shaping contingency so that attempts to respond verbally (except self-stimulation) are also reinforced
Consequences	a. Edible reinforcers paired with social reinforcers	a. Natural reinforcer (e.g., opportunity to play with the item) paired with social reinforcers.

SOURCE: R. L. Koegel, M. C. O'Dell and L. C. Koegel. "A Natural Language Teaching Paradigm for Nonverbal Autistic Children," *Journal of Autism and Developmental Disorders, 17* (1987), p. 191. Copyright © 1987 by Plenum. Reprinted by permission.

and grammatically correct forms, we might train him or her to use a language structure to obtain a desired result. For example, the child might be taught to say, "I want juice" (or a simplified form: "juice" or "want juice") in order to get a drink of juice. The goal is to train the child to use language in a functional way in social contexts—to train *communicative competence* (McCormick & Schiefelbusch, 1984).

The first consideration in such training is the arrangement of an environment that will give the child many opportunities to use language and that will provide immediate reinforcement for steps toward communication. This requires parents and teachers to work closely with a communication specialist. A second consideration in training is how to combine structure, content, and function—what is said and what is talked about or intended. Training in the structure of language is of little value without training in how to use language for communication. But the uses of language cannot be taught successfully without attention to its structure.

Today, efforts to teach nonverbal children to speak emphasize building natural acts of communication. Earlier intervention programs depended primarily on the use by an adult of highly structured, tightly controlled lessons in which the child was taken through a developmental sequence analogous to that of normal language development. Differences between the analogue and natural teaching methods used by Koegel, O'Dell, and Koegel (1987) are summarized in Table 6.4. Note that under the natural language paradigm (NLP) conditions the emphasis is on pragmatics—using language in social interactions.

Qualitatively Different Language

Some children can make speech sounds with no difficulty and acquire an extensive oral vocabulary. The way they use words, however, is very different from normal speech. These language-impaired children do not use speech effectively in communication. We give a few examples of qualitative differences in language that impair its value for communication.

Some children are echolalic (they repeat, parrotlike, what they've heard). An attempted conversation with an echolalic child might go like this:

Adult:	Are you Johnny?
Child:	Johnny?
Adult:	Yes.
Child:	Yes.
Adult:	I'm Jim.
Child:	Jim.
Adult:	Right.
Child:	Right.
Adult:	What's your name?
Child:	Your name?
Adult:	No, *your* name.
Child:	*Your* name.
Adult:	Johnny.
Child:	Johnny.
Adult:	I'm Jim.
Child:	I'm Jim.
Adult:	No, *I'm* Jim.
Child:	*I'm* Jim.
Adult:	. . . Forget it.
Child:	Forget it.

Other children may speak jargon or nonsense words that fail to meet the demands of social situations. Sometimes we find that a child understands what is said to him or her but almost never imitates speech or spontaneously produces it. Or when asked to imitate a sentence, a child may not be able to convey its meaning, as most children could. Naremore (1980, p. 156) gives this example: "When asked to repeat the sentence, 'The little boy's dump truck is broken,' a nonhandicapped two-year-old said, 'Dump truck broke,' whereas a language-impaired six-year-old responded with, 'Boy is break.' " The nonhandicapped child did not imitate precisely but chose words that preserved the meaning of the sentence. The language-impaired child, however, could not convey the meaning.

The qualitative differences we have mentioned so far are most frequently associated with severe emotional/behavioral disorder or mental retardation. Recently there has been interest in the language disorders of children with learning disabilities (see Chapter 4). The research to date has not pinpointed the ways in which the language of learning-disabled children is different from other children's language, but it appears that these children are less capable than nonhandicapped children of making themselves understood (Hallahan, Kauffman, & Lloyd, 1985). They do not seem to comprehend language well or be able to adapt their language usage to the social context so that meaning is communicated. In talking to younger children, for example, they may fail to make their language appropriately simple.

They may not understand instructions or the meaning of another person's statements. They may say things in social situations that most children would know are inappropriate. Finally, they may fail to understand or produce written language, even though their oral language skills are adequate (see Butler, 1986a).

Language is always embedded in a social context. Its meanings and nuances can easily be lost by the producer or interpreter so that no communication takes place. Qualitative differences in language can seriously distort or obscure meaning or pragmatic value. These differences often occur in the language abilities of children whose social behavior and academic achievement are impaired. In fact, language disabilities appear to be closely connected with learning disabilities of all types. The implications of qualitative differences in language for remediation strategies are not presently clear. However, it is likely that an emphasis on the *functions* of language and *strategies* for comprehension and production will be most helpful in this area (Fey, 1986; Lahey, 1988).

Delayed Language

A child may progress through the stages of language development with one principal exception: He or she does so at a significantly later age than most children. Many of the children whose language development is delayed show a pervasive developmental lag. Frequently they are diagnosed as mentally retarded or "developmentally disabled." Sometimes they come from environments where they have been deprived of many experiences, including language stimulation from adults, required for normal development.

It may be difficult in some cases to tell the difference between delayed and qualitatively different language because not much is known about the normal development of language and because qualitative differences may be very subtle. Usually, children with delayed language learn language in the same way most children do, and their level of language learning approximates their level of general intellectual ability.

Language learning may be delayed for a variety of reasons. This child's learning of oral language is delayed because of her hearing impairment. A special teaching program is necessary to help her learn to produce the sounds of oral language. (Irene Boyer/Monkmeyer Press)

Interrupted Language Development

Children can *acquire* a language disorder after a period of normal development if their hearing or brain functioning is seriously damaged. Deprivation of oxygen, accident, or infection, for example, can result in damage to the mechanisms of hearing or to the brain (see Chapters 7 and 9). The specific effects of acquired hearing loss or brain injury depend not only on the nature and extent of the loss or injury but also on the age of the child when the loss or injury occurs. A child deafened before he or she learns oral language will not learn language as easily as one who has learned language before the deafness was acquired; and the more language experience a child has acquired before deafened, the better his or her communication skills are likely to be. On the other hand, damage to the brain generally has more serious consequences when it occurs later in the development of language. The younger child's nervous system is generally more "plastic"—it compensates more easily for loss of or damage to its tissues.

Children whose language development has been interrupted by an illness or accident that damaged the brain are sometimes said to have **acquired aphasia** (Leonard, 1986). The terms *severely language impaired* and *severe language disability* are also used to designate the disabilities of children who have extreme difficulties in acquiring or using language, especially when the disabilities are known or thought to be the result of brain damage. Head injury is an increasingly common cause of language disorders, and language disorders resulting from head injury frequently complicate a student's return to school following physical recuperation (Blosser & DePompei, 1989).

Strategies for Assessment and Intervention

We have already mentioned some of the considerations for assessing and correcting various types of language disorders. Here we provide a thumbnail sketch of the general features of language assessment and intervention. Only a brief sketch is possible because the assessment, classification, and treatment of language disorders are complex and changing rapidly. Although much research is under way, relatively little is understood about the disorders of this most complex of all human activities.

Two general strategies of language assessment are to determine in as much detail as possible what the child's current language abilities are and to observe the ease and speed with which the child learns new language skills. The first strategy typically involves standardized testing, nonstandardized testing, use of developmental scales, and behavioral observations. Standardized testing has many dangers and is not always useful in planning an intervention program. But it can sometimes be helpful in making crude comparisons of the child's abilities in certain areas. Development scales are ratings or observations that may be completed by direct observation or based on memory or records of developmental milestones. Nonstandardized tests and behavioral observations are nonnormative in nature, but they may yield the most important assessment information. As Schiefelbusch and McCormick (1981) point out, the subjective judgment of an experienced clinician based on observation of the child's language in a variety of environments and circumstances may provide the most useful basis for intervention. Because language disorders vary widely in nature and are seen in individuals ranging from early childhood through old age, assessment and intervention are never simple and are always idiosyncratic.

An intervention plan must take into consideration the content, form, and use of language (Fey, 1986). That is, one must consider (1) what the child talks about and should be taught to talk about, (2) how the child talks about things and how he or she could be taught to speak of those things more intelligibly, and (3) how the child uses language and how his or her use of it could be made to serve the purposes of communication and socialization more effectively. In arranging a training sequence, one might base instruction on the normal sequence of language development. Other sequences of instruction might be more effective, however, since language-disordered children obviously have not learned in the normal way and since research suggests that different sequences of learning may be more effective (Devany, Rincover, & Lovaas, 1981). It is more and more apparent that effective language intervention must occur in the child's natural environment and involve parents and classroom teachers, not just the speech-language pathologist (Bernstein & Tiegerman, 1989; Lahey, 1988; Spradlin & Siegel, 1982).

Educational Considerations

Helping children overcome speech and language disorders is not the responsibility of any single profession. Identification is the joint responsibility of the classroom teacher, the speech-language pathologist, and the parents. The teacher can carry out specific suggestions for individual cases. By listening attentively and empathetically when children speak, providing appropriate models of speech and language for children to imitate, and encouraging children to use their communication skills appropriately, the classroom teacher can help not only to improve speech and language but also to prevent disorders from developing in the first place.

Role of the Teacher in Language Use (Pragmatics)

The primary role of the classroom teacher is to facilitate the *social use of language*. Phonology, morphology, syntax, and semantics are certainly important. Yet the fact that a student has a language disorder does not necessarily mean that the teacher or clinician must intensify efforts to teach the student about the form, structure, or content of language. Rather, language must be taught as a way of solving problems by making oneself understood and making sense of what other people say.

The classroom offers many possibilities for language learning. It should be a place in which there are almost continuous opportunities for students and teachers to employ language and obtain feedback in constructive relationships. Language is the basic medium through which most academic and social learning takes place in school. Nevertheless, the language of schools, including that found in classrooms and textbooks, is often a problem for both students and teachers (Butler, 1986b; Wallach & Miller, 1988).

School language is more formal than the language many children use at home and with playmates. It is structured discourse in which listeners and speakers or readers and writers must learn to be clear and expressive, to convey and interpret essential information quickly and easily. Without skill in using the language of school, a child is certain to fail academically and virtually certain to be socially unsuccessful as well.

The box on page 245 illustrates a problem in using language in school. Helping students like Tom learn to use language as a tool for academic learning and social relations is particularly difficult, because their language disorders seem to reflect basic problems in cognition—understanding or thinking. Teachers must use their own cognitive and language skills to divise ways to help such children learn more effective use of language.

Language Learning in the Classroom

Observing group instruction within the later elementary classrooms can be most instructive. In the classroom described below, children's linguistic understanding is tested, and misunderstandings are resolved. (Note the importance of context. A different response might have been anticipated if the request had occurred in an obstetrician's office.)

Teacher:	Okay, Tom. What's a contraction?
Tom:	It's like when . . . a contraction . . . you contract stuff.
Teacher:	Yes, but what does *contraction* mean?
Tom:	(No response.)
Several students:	(overlapping comments) I know! I know!
Teacher:	(shifting her gaze to another student) Okay, Susan.
Susan:	It's when you make something smaller.
Tom:	Yeah. When the road contracts, it gets broken up. Our driveway got contracts and broken up.
Lisa:	You mean "cracks up."
Teacher:	But what about the kind of contraction we learned about yesterday?
Robert:	Oh, a "word contraction."
Teacher:	Yes. What is a word contraction?
Susan:	It's when you make a word smaller.
Tom:	The word . . . it gets broken up.
Teacher:	Right. Excellent.

A commendation is also in order for this teacher, who skillfully manipulates the questioning so that Tom, who initially appears to be having considerable difficulty, is able to semantically map the correct meaning of the word and to not only gain insight, but share that insight with the remainder of the group. This interactive sequence of mutual discovery is an important step on the way to language success and truly literate students.

SOURCE: K. G. Butler, *Language Disorders in Children* (Austin, TX: Pro-Ed, 1986), pp. 40–41.

Teachers need the assistance of speech-language specialists in assessing their students' language disabilities and in devising interventions. Part of the assessment and intervention strategy, however, must examine the language of the teacher. Problems in classroom discourse involve how teachers talk to students as well as how students use language. Learning how to be clear, relevant, and informative and how to hold listeners' attention is not only a problem for students with language disorders—it's also a problem for their teachers.

One example of the role of the teacher's language in classroom discourse is in asking questions. Blank and White (1986) note that teachers often ask students questions in areas of their identified weakness. For example, a teacher might ask a preschooler who does not know colors to identify colors repeatedly. Unfortunately, teachers may not know how to modify their questions to teach a concept effectively, so their questions merely add to the child's confusion.

The following exchange between a teacher and a child diagnosed as having difficulties with problem solving and causal reasoning illustrates this point.

Teacher:	How could grass in a jungle get on fire?
Child:	'Cause they (*referring to animals*) have to stay in the jungle.

Collaboration: A Key to Success

ARDELL FITZGERALD   *ELLEN BRUNO*

■ **ARDELL:** My caseload includes twenty-nine children from kindergarten to fifth grade, both in regular education and a special education classroom. The speech and language disorders I work with include articulation, stuttering, voice, language/learning disabilities, developmental apraxia, and hearing impairment. I'm responsible for evaluation, diagnosis, and remediation. I also team-teach four days a week in a special education kindergarten class (eight children with a teacher and an aide) and pull out children in small groups who have been identified as having communication disorders from fifteen regular classrooms. I also meet with the school support team weekly to discuss interventions for children who are having problems in regular classrooms. I screen children referred by teachers, parents, and the support team and help make decisions about the necessity for diagnostic testing.

■ **ELLEN:** Before assuming my present position as a special education kindergarten teacher, I taught children with hearing impairments for seven years, kids with behavior disorders for four years, and students with communication disorders for five years. Now I'm teaching five- to seven-year-olds who are more than two years below age level in at least one of the following developmental areas: cognitive, psychomotor, speech/language, or social/emotional. The SEED classroom has a maximum of eight children with special needs who are integrated with a group of sixteen "normal" children in a morning kindergarten program. An early childhood educator, two educational aids, and I team-teach all twenty-four children.

■ **ARDELL:** We'll describe our work with Sara, a seven-year-old.

■ **ELLEN:** I met Sara at the very beginning of the school year. I was pleased to have a second-grade girl in my all-boy class and excitedly asked about her summer. She beamed and rambled on and on. I had no idea what she was saying but politely nodded and commented, "Gee, that sounds like fun!"

■ **ARDELL:** Sara's severely disordered articulation and language interfered with communication. Because of her developmental apraxia (difficulty planning and sequencing motor movements), she was almost 90 percent unintelligible to the unfamiliar listener. She produced many of her sounds in the back of her mouth, substituting /k/ and /g/ for the tongue-tip sounds. Not only her speech sounds but also her sentence structure was disordered.

■ **ELLEN:** In the classroom, Sara was especially slow to tune into instructions. She needed to be alerted before she could take in information. Because of her low muscle tone and trunk support, she was unable to sit at her desk or on the floor for an activity longer than ten minutes. She was weak in understanding basic concepts. She had difficulty sequencing, retelling a simple story, following directions, predicting, and telling

why. These problems were common to many of my communication-disordered students. Academically, Sara was on a readiness level in reading and on a first-grade level in math.

■ **ARDELL:** Sara had many strengths. Her intelligence was normal. Her ability to understand language was better than her expressive ability. She was pleasant, cooperative, and willing to try a task several times. In spite of her communication problems, she readily initiated conversation with peers and teachers. At the beginning of the school year, Ellen and I discussed what we had learned about Sara from reports, individual assessments, and classroom observation. I shared information about Sara's speech patterns and disordered language structures. We decided that I could best address these areas in individual sessions in my room, but that I would keep Ellen and others informed about Sara's progress so they could reinforce phonological skills in the classroom. For example, during reading sessions Ellen would know which words Sara could pronounce correctly. We also involved Sara's parents. I set up a weekly time for her mother to join our therapy session; she was very conscientious about participating in the sessions. Sara's father had severe cerebral

SPECIAL EFFECTS

Client: A five-year-old male with an unknown cognitive level but suspected moderate mental retardation was placed in a preschool program for children with multiple handicaps. He had no previous computer experience.

Communication characteristics: Mostly single word with occasional two-word utterances previously observed by his teachers and clinician. Attention to task during most school activities was reported to be poor, with minimal successful interaction with peers or adults.

Computer application: *Muppet Learning Keys* (Koala Technologies, 1984) is an alternative keyboard for children, which plugs into the gameport of the host computer. It consists of a large (18″ by 18″) tablet covered with colorful touch-sensitive control pads. The control pads, or "keys," represent the alphabet, primary colors, numbers from 0 to 9, and some specialized keys including a STOP key and a GO key. Accompanying software makes use of this special keyboard. During the Discovery Stage activity, for example, pressing the C causes a camel to appear on the screen. Pressing number 6 causes six camels to appear. Pressing the GO key causes the camels to prance on the screen (along with music), and pressing STOP will freeze this action. There is no prescribed order or directions to follow. If no keys are pressed, nothing happens. However, if *any* key is pressed, something happens.

Results: Much to the clinician's surprise, this child quickly assumed control of the *Muppet Keys* and maintained a high level of interest and attention to task throughout even his first 15–20-minute session with this program. He was able to shift his attention between the screen, the clinician, and the keys appropriately. Spontaneous two-word utterances and appropriate verbal imitations related to the activity were frequently observed, including appropriate verbal and nonverbal interaction with the clinician. He systematically explored the consequences of pressing the keys, quickly learning functions such as which ones would stop and start activity on the screen or change the color and number of items shown. His interaction with the clinician and the computer during this activity suggested better learning and adaptation skills than he had previously demonstrated during evaluations or instruction. Using this computer-based activity as a shared context, the clinician had a rich opportunity to address receptive and expressive language goals across several sessions.

SOURCE: G. L. Bull, P. S. Cochran, and M. E. Snell, "Beyond CAI: Computers, Language, and Persons with Mental Retardation," *Topics in Language Disorders*, 8(4) (1988), 68–69.

COMMUNICATIVE DIFFERENCES

An increasing concern of classroom teachers and speech-language clinicians is facilitating the communication of children whose cultural heritage or language patterns are not those of the professional's microculture (see Chapter 2 for a discussion of microculture). On the one hand, care must be taken not to mistake a cultural or ethnic difference with disorder; on the other hand, disorders existing in the context of a language difference must not be overlooked (Langdon, 1989). When assessing children's language, the professional must be aware of the limitations of normative tests.

Children who score below norms, not because they are speech and language impaired, but because they have language experiences that do not match those measured by most evaluation tools, must not be labeled as handicapped. On the other hand, children from diverse cultural communities who *have* true language disorders must be identifiable (Bernstein & Tiegerman, 1989, p. 426).

A child may not have a language disorder yet have a communicative difference that demands special teaching. Delpit (1988) and Foster (1986) have discussed the need for teaching children of nondominant cultures the rules for effective communication in the dominant culture while understanding and accepting the effectiveness of the children's "home" language in its cultural context. Failure to teach children the skills they need to communicate effectively according to the rules of the dominant culture will deny them many opportunities.

A major concern in both special and general education today is teaching the child who is learning English as a second language (ESL), who is non-English proficient (NEP), or who has limited English proficiency (LEP). Bilingual education is a field of concern and controversy because of the rapidly changing demographics in many American communities. Spanish-speaking children are a rapidly growing percentage of many school districts (Fradd, Figueroa, & Correa, 1989). Moreover, a large number of Asian/Pacific children have immigrated to the United States during the past decade (Cheng, 1989). Many of these children have no proficiency or limited proficiency in English. Some of them have disabilities as well. Bilingual special education is "an emerging discipline with a brief history" (Baca & Amato, 1989, p. 168). Finding the best way to teach children to become proficient in English, particularly when they have disabilities as well as language differences, is a special challenge for the 1990s (Baca & Amato, 1989; Baca & Cervantes, 1989).

EARLY INTERVENTION

Preschoolers who require intervention for a speech or language disorder typically have multiple handicaps. Their disabilities are sometimes severe or profound. Language is closely tied to cognitive development, so impairment of general intellectual ability is likely to have a retarding influence on language development. Because speech is dependent on neurological and motor development, any neurological or motor problem might impair ability to speak. Normal social development in the preschool years depends on the emergence of language, so a language-impaired child is at a disadvantage in social learning. Therefore it is seldom that the preschool child's language is the only target of intervention (Ensher, 1989; Fey, 1986).

Researchers have become increasingly aware that language development has its beginning in the earliest mother-child interactions. Concern for the child's development of the ability to communicate cannot be separated from concerns for development in other areas (Ensher, 1989). Therefore, speech-language pathologists are a vital part of the multidisciplinary team that evaluates a handicapped infant or young child and develops an Individualized Family Service Plan (IFSP). Early intervention programs inevitably involve training parents to facilitate the communication of their infants or young children. In fact, much of the language intervention activity for infants and young children involves playing the part of the good parent. This means a lot of simple play with accompanying verbalizations. It means talking to the child about objects and activities in the way most mothers talk to their babies. But it also means choosing objects, activities, words, and consequences for the child's vocalizations with great care so that the chances that the child will learn functional language are enhanced (McKnight-Taylor, 1989; McMorrow, Foxx, Faw, & Bittle, 1986).

Intervention in early childhood is likely to be based on assessment of the child's behavior related to the content, form, and especially the use of language in social interaction. For the child who has not yet learned language, assessment and intervention will focus on imitation, ritualized and make-believe play, play with objects, and functional use of objects. At the earliest stages in which the content and form of language are interactive, it is important to evaluate the extent to which the child looks at or picks up an object when it is referred to, does something with an object when directed by an adult, and uses sounds to request or refuse things and call attention to objects. When the child's use of language is considered, the earliest objectives involve the child's looking at the adult during interactions; taking turns in and trying to prolong pleasurable activities and games; following the gaze of an adult and directing the behavior of adults; and persisting in or modifying gestures, sounds, or words when an adult does not respond.

In the preschool, teaching **discourse** (conversation skills) is a critical focus of language intervention. In particular, emphasis is placed on teaching children to use the discourse that is essential for success in school. Children must learn, for example, to report their experiences in detail and to explain why something happened, not just add to their vocabulary. They must learn not only word forms and meanings but also how to take turns in conversations and maintain the topic of a conversation or change it in an appropriate way. Preschool programs in which such language teaching is the focus may include teachers' daily individualized conversations with children, daily reading to individual children or small groups, and frequent classroom discussions. In a program described by Roberts et al. (1989), "teachers were taught to use a high quality of interaction by modeling talk that was informative, reflective, and problem solving, and by responding to children in such a way as to acknowledge, comment on, question, and extend what they said" (p. 776).

Current trends are directed toward providing speech and language interventions in the typical environments of young children (Ensher, 1989). This means that classroom teachers and speech-language pathologists must develop a close working relationship, the specialist working directly with children in the classroom and advising the teacher about the aspects of intervention that he or she can carry out as part of the regular classroom activities. It is also likely to mean involving the handicapped child's peers in intervention strategies. Because language is essentially a social activity, its facilitation requires involvement of others in the child's social environment, peers as well as adults. Nonhandicapped peers have been taught to assist in handicapped children's language development by doing the following during playtimes: establishing eye contact; describing their own or others' play; and repeating, expanding, or requesting clarification of what the handicapped child says (Goldstein & Strain, 1989). Another intervention strategy involving peers is sociodramatic play. Children are taught in groups of three, including a handicapped child, to act out social roles such as those people might take in various settings (e.g., a restaurant or shoe store). The training includes scripts that specify what each child is to do and say, which may be modified by the children in creative ways. Goldstein and Strain (1989) reviewed research showing that such interventions have resulted in significant improvements in the quality of normally developing children's playtime interactions as well as advances in handicapped children's language development.

In summary, early intervention in speech and language disorders emphasizes the development of functional communication, not isolated skills. Communication is so intertwined with all areas of the child's development that intervention strategies must be made an integral part of the child's everyday world. Speech and language interventions for young children seldom involve activities that are best carried out in a clinic or separate setting. Rather, they are almost always interactions that must be programmed as part of the child's daily routines and typical interactions with peers and adults.

TRANSITION

In the past, adolescents and adults in speech and language intervention programs generally fell into three categories: the self-referred, those with other health problems, and the severely handicapped. Adolescents or adults may refer themselves to a speech-language pathologist because their phonology, voice, or stuttering is causing them social embarrassment and/or interfering with occupational pursuits. These are generally persons with problems of long standing who are highly motivated to change their speech and obtain relief from the social penalties their differences impose.

Those with other health problems have suffered damage to speech or language capacities as a result of disease or injury. They may have lost part of their speech mechanism through injury or surgical removal. Treatment of these individuals always demands an interdisciplinary effort. In some cases of progressive disease, severe neurological damage, or loss of tissues of the speech mechanism, the outlook for functional speech is not good. However, surgical procedures, medication, and prosthetic devices are making it possible for more people to speak normally. Loss of ability to use language is typically more disabling than loss of the ability to speak. Head injury may leave the individual with a seriously diminished capacity for self-awareness, goal setting, planning, self-directing or initiating actions, inhibiting impulses, monitoring or evaluating one's own performance, or problem solving (Ylvisaker & Szekeres, 1989). Recovering these vital language-based skills is a critical aspect of transition of the adolescent or young adult from hospital to school and from school to independent living.

Severely handicapped individuals may need the services of a speech-language pathologist to help them achieve more intelligible speech. They may also need to be taught an alternative to oral language or given a system of augmented communication. One of the major problems in working with severely handicapped adolescents and adults is setting realistic goals for speech and language learning. Teaching simple, functional language such as social greetings, naming objects, and making simple requests may be realistic goals for some severely handicapped adolescents and adults (McMorrow et al., 1986). A major concern of transition programming is ensuring that the training and support provided during the school years are carried over into adult life (Falvey, McLean, & Rosenberg, 1988). To be successful, the transition must include speech-language services that are part of the natural environment. That is, the services must be community based and be integrated into vocational, domestic, recreational, consumer, and mobility training activities. Speech language interventions for severely disabled adolescents and young adults must emphasize functional communication—understanding and making oneself understood in the social circumstances most likely to be encountered in everyday life. For example, Lord (1988) identified two primary goals for the communication of adolescents with autism: participating in age-appropriate social relationships outside the family and developing the ability to use language to pursue one's interests. Developing appropriate conversation skills (e.g., establishing eye contact, using greetings, taking turns, and identifying and staying on the topic), reading, writing, following instructions related to recreational activities, using public transportation, and performing a job are examples of the kinds of functional speech-language activities that may be emphasized.

Today much more emphasis is being placed on the language disorders of adolescents and young adults who do not fit into any of the categories just described. Many of these individuals were formerly seen as having primarily academic and social problems that were not language related, but now it is understood that underlying many or most of the school and social difficulties of adolescents and

By providing many opportunities for children to speak and listen, the classroom teacher can foster language development. Of primary importance is the child's understanding and mastery of the social uses of language.(Michal Heron/Woodfin Camp & Associates)

adults are basic disorders of language (Wallach & Miller, 1988). These language disorders are a continuation of difficulties experienced earlier in the person's development.

> There is strong evidence now . . . that many young language impaired children will continue to encounter difficulties in acquiring more advanced language skills in later years and that these problems will be manifested in both social and academic realms. Thus children's understanding of figurative language affects both their ability to use slang correctly with peers and their ability to recognize metaphors that appear in language arts or English literature texts. (Stephens, 1985, p. v)

Some adolescents and adults with language disorders are excellent candidates for *strategy training,* which teaches them how to select, store, retrieve, and process information (see Hallahan et al., 1985, and Chapter 4). Others, however, do not have the required reading skills, symbolic abilities, or intelligence to benefit from the usual training in cognitive strategies.

Whatever techniques are chosen for adolescents and older students, the teacher or speech-language pathologist should be aware of the principles that apply to intervention with these individuals. Larson and McKinley (1985) note the importance of understanding the theoretical basis of intervention and summarize several additional principles as follows:

> Clinicians must treat their adolescent clients like the maturing adults they are, engaging them as full partners committed to the intervention enterprise. Clinicians should recognize that many adolescents will need and will benefit from counseling regarding the impact of their language disorders on academic progress, personal and social growth, and the achievement of vocational goals. Finally, adolescents seem to function best in natural group settings, in which peers talk to peers and learn from each other. (p. 77)

SUGGESTIONS FOR TEACHING STUDENTS WITH COMMUNICATION DISORDERS IN GENERAL EDUCATION CLASSROOMS

What to Look for in School

Communication disorders encompass a wide variety of speech and language impairments, ranging from mild to severe. This section will focus on the communication problems of students of near-average or above intelligence who do not have sensory or orthopedic disabilities. For information about modifications for sensory-impaired and physically disabled students see Chapters 7, 8, and 9. Mild and moderate speech disorders may be easy to identify because they affect speech sounds. Common indicators of articulation problems (Cantwell & Baker, 1987) include

1. Omission of certain sounds from speech (e.g., *ca* for *car*)
2. Substitution of certain sounds for other sounds (e.g., *wabbit* for *rabbit*)
3. Reversal of the order of sounds within words (e.g., *aminal* for *animal*)
4. Difficulty in saying certain speech sounds (e.g., *sh/r/th*)
5. Frequent nonspeech vocalizations (e.g., clicks tongue, hums)
6. Difficulty performing oral movements (e.g., chewing, yawning, sticking out tongue)

Signals of fluency and voice impairments, other types of speech disorders (Cantwell & Baker, 1987), include

1. Constant congestion or nasality
2. Constantly harsh-sounding or breathy-sounding voice
3. Continual hoarseness
4. Speaking in a too-soft voice
5. Speaking in a sing-song voice
6. Speaking in monotone
7. Speaking too slowly or too fast
8. Unusually high or low voice pitch
9. Unusual pattern of stressing words in sentences
10. Struggling to say words (e.g., grimaces, blinks eyes, clenches fists)

In contrast to speech disorders, many language impairments are undiagnosed until children are in school. Here are some indicators of language problems (Wiig & Semel, 1984):

- Primary grades: Problems in following verbal directions; difficulty with preacademic skills (e.g., recognizing sound differences), phonics, word attack, structural analysis, and language used to learn new material
- Intermediate grades: Word substitutions; inadequate language processing and production that may adversely affect reading comprehension and achievement in academic areas
- Middle and high school: Inability to understand abstract concepts and multiple word meanings and to connect previously learned information to new material that must be learned on their own; widening gap in achievement compared to peers

In addition, poor speech and language skills may affect children's social interactions and interpersonal relationships at all grade levels. Wood (1982, p. 5) emphasizes the importance of using language in social interactions and identifies the following skills as essential:

- Carrying on a conversation, including turn taking and responding to another's utterances
- Communicating in a socially and situationally appropriate way
- Maintaining the topic of conversation
- Organizing and directing behavior

Teaching Techniques to Try

You can play an important role in assisting your students with speech and language disorders by arranging class instruction and activities that both facilitate learning and maximize communication. One such arrangement is cooperative learning. In cooperative learning, students work together in small groups to reach a common goal. They are accountable not only for their own achievement but also for the learning of other group members. This interdependence makes cooperative learning an especially effective technique to integrate students with disabilities into mainstream classes because it promotes learning, communication, and positive attitudes among diverse students.

To begin using cooperative learning in your classroom, form groups of four or five students who are heterogeneous in gender, race, handicapping condition, and academic skills. Plan to have students work together for a marking period so that they have sufficient time to develop and use cooperative skills with other members of their group.

Cooperative Learning Methods

Next, decide what type of cooperative learning method best meets your students' needs and your educational purposes. There are four types of cooperative learning programs, all of which involve small groups of heterogeneous students working together to complete a common task. They differ, however, in the way they structure these learning tasks and in the reinforcement students receive. Here is a summary of the types of cooperative learning methods.

LEARNING TOGETHER. This approach emphasizes building group members' interpersonal skills while students work together to complete a single assignment. Teachers evaluate these skills by observing students as they interact in their groups and provide feedback to individuals and to the group as a whole. Students also assess their cooperative skills during group processing, in which they discuss questions such as

- How many members believe they had a chance to share their ideas today?
- What did members do to help the group accomplish its goal? What cooperative skills did each member use today?

For more information about this method see *Circles of Learning: Cooperation in the Classroom* (Johnson, Johnson, Holubes, & Roy, 1984).

THE JIGSAW METHOD. This method, like the learning together approach, includes group-building exercises that facilitate group processes. However, instead of students all working on a single assignment, the teacher divides the instructional material into learning segments. For example, during a unit on animals, one teacher divided the subject of rabbits into four topics: characteristics, foods, habitats, and protective devices. In jigsaw puzzle fashion, each member learns one segment of the topic and then teaches this information to the other members in his or her home group. To assist students in becoming "experts" in their learning area, all class members who have been assigned the same topic meet in expert groups to help one another learn the material and to prepare for the presentation they will make to their home groups. Once members have presented their topics to their group, all students are responsible for knowing all the information and for completing a test on the topic. For specific details about implementing this type of cooperative learning, see *The Jigsaw Classroom* (Aronson, Blaney, Stephan, Skies, & Snapp, 1978).

GROUP INVESTIGATION. In this method members follow a six-step process that promotes higher-cognitive learning, investigative skills, and positive interpersonal attitudes:

Step 1: The teacher selects a general topic that can be divided into learning segments.

Step 2: Students cooperatively decide how to divide the subject further and then each group member chooses a subtopic that is of interest to him or her.

Steps 3 and 4: Students plan and conduct their investigations, collecting information from a variety of community and school resources.

Step 5: Group members then analyze and evaluate the information they have gathered and decide how to summarize it for the whole class in an interesting way.

Step 6: Students and the teacher evaluate each group's contribution to the work of the class.

To learn more about group investigation see *Small-Group Teaching* (Sharan & Sharan, 1976).

Student Team Learning. A final approach, student team learning, includes four different methods: Teams-Games-Tournaments (TGT), Student Teams Achievement Divisions (STAD), Team Accelerated Individualization (TIA), and Cooperative Integrated Reading and Composition (CIRC). The most frequently used method is STAD, which involves a structured schedule of instruction, including teacher presentation of new academic material in lecture or discussion; review/study of this material in teams; and a follow-up quiz. Individual team members' quiz scores form a team score and are based on improvement over past performance. Consequently, each member, regardless of his or her ability, can contribute equally to the team score. A weekly newsletter announces the teams and individuals who earned the highest scores. For specific instructions, sample worksheets, and scoring forms, see *Cooperative Learning* (Slavin, 1990).

Once you have decided on a specific cooperative learning method, you will want to organize your classroom by arranging the desks so members can talk together and share materials easily. Several educators recommend discussing the concept of cooperation and the ways in which group members can cooperate with one another before using any of the methods to teach specific school subjects.

Although every cooperative learning method has its own reinforcement and evaluation procedures, you will want to monitor the students' interactions. In groups in which students with speech and language disorders are members, encourage students to do the following (Oyer, Crowe, & Haas, 1987; Wood, 1982):

1. Model appropriate speech and language usage.
2. Reword statements that contain words with simple meanings or select other words.
3. Use simple rather than complex language structures.
4. Use nonverbal cues such as facial expressions, gestures, and body language, when appropriate.
5. Use direct and concrete statements and avoid subtleties and innuendoes.
6. Accept the contributions of all students.

In addition, it is important to ensure that students talk "with" and not "at" or "for" students with communication disorders.

Helpful Resources

School Personnel

Speech-language pathologists are responsible for providing therapy to students with communication disorders. For an example of the roles they play in the education of students see pages 246–247.

Instructional Methods

Bernstein, D. K., & Tiegerman, E. (1989). *Language and communications disorders in children* (2nd ed.). Columbus, OH: Chas. E. Merrill.

Cantwell, D. P., & Baker, L. (1987). *Developmental speech and language disorders*. New York: Guilford Press.

Cavallaro, C. C. (1983). Language interventions in natural settings. *Teaching Exceptional Children, 16,* 65–70.

Cole, M. L., & Cole, J. T. (1989). *Effective intervention with the language-impaired child* (2nd ed.). Rockville, MD: Aspen Publications.

Conant, S., Berdoff, M., & Hecht, B. (1983). *Teaching language-disabled children*. Cambridge, MA: Brookline Books.

Creaghead, N. A., Newman, P. W., & Secord, W. A. (1989). *Assessment and remediation of articulatory and phonological disorders* (2nd ed.). Columbus, OH: Chas. E. Merrill.

Fey, M. E. (1986). *Language intervention with young children*. San Diego, CA: College-Hill Press.

Hayes, J. R., & Flowers, L. S. (1987). On the structure of the writing process. *Topics in Language Disorders, 7,* 19–30.

Hurvitz, J. A., Pickert, S. M., & Rilla, D. C. (1987). Promoting children's language intervention. *Teaching Exceptional Children, 19,* 12–15.

Lindsfors, J. W. (1987). *Children's language and learning* (2nd ed.). Englewood Cliffs, NJ: Prentice Hall.

Lowenthal, B. (1985). Listening to the special student. *Academic Therapy, 21,* 51–54.

Norris, J. A. (1988). Using communication strategies to enhance reading acquisition. *The Reading Teacher, 47,* 668–673.

Norris, J. A. (1989). Providing language remediation in the classroom: An integrated language-to-reading intervention model. *Language, Speech, and Hearing Services in Schools, 20,* 205–217.

Oyer, H. J., Crowe, B. J., & Haas, W. H. (1987). *Speech, language, and hearing disorders: A guide for the teacher*. Boston: Little, Brown.

Panagos, J. M., & Griffith, P. L. (1982). Helping children talk by using discourse. *Academic Therapy, 18,* 37–42.

Reed, V. A. (Ed.) (1986). *An introduction to children with language disorders*. New York: Macmillan.

Sayre, J. M. (1984). *Helping the child to listen and talk: Suggestions for parents, teachers, speech-language pathologists, and others* (2nd ed.). Danville, IL: Interstate Printers and Publishers.

Wood, M. L. (1982). *Language disorders in school-age children*. Englewood Cliffs, NJ: Prentice Hall.

Curricular Materials

Bloomin' series provides activities to improve pragmatics by focusing on such areas as holidays, recipes, experiments, and language arts. LinguiSystems, 3100 Fourth Avenue, P.O. Box 747, East Moline, IL.

Flowers, A. M. (1986). *The big book of language through sounds* (3rd ed.). Danville, IL: Interstate Printers and Publishers.

Frimmer, B. (1986). Sounds and language: A work/play approach. Danville, IL: Interstate Printers and Publishers.

Help Series includes exercises in such areas as language processing, concepts, paraphrasing, problem-solving, and pragmatics. LinguiSystems, 3100 Fourth Avenue, P.O. Box 747, East Moline, IL.

Holloway, J. A. (1987). *Aunt Amada: On cloud nine and other idioms and expressions*. Danville, IL: Interstate Printers and Publishers.

Kagan, A. (1981). *"Teach 'n' reach" communicatively handicapped: Hearing impaired, language impaired* (Book 2 out of 4). La Mesa, CA: La Mesa-Spring Valley School District, Special Programs Department, 4750 Date Avenue, La Mesa, CA 92041.

Literature About Individuals with Communication Disorders

ELEMENTARY: AGES 5–8, 9–12

Arthur, R. (1985). *The three investigators in the mystery of the stuttering parrot.* New York: Random House. (Ages 9–12)

Brown, A., & Forsberg, C. (1989). *Lost boys never say die.* New York: Delacorte Press. (Ages 9–12)

Bunting, E. (1980). *Blackbird singing.* New York: Macmillan. (Ages 9–12)

Knopp, P. (1980). *Wilted.* New York: Coward, McCann & Geoghegan. (Ages 9–12)

Namovicz, G. I. (1987). *To talk in time.* New York: Four Winds Press. (Ages 9–12)

Rounds, G. (1980). *Blind Outlaw.* New York: Holiday House. (Ages 9–12)

Software

Basic Vocabulary Builder on Computer, Ballard & Tighe, Inc., 480 Atlas Street, Brea, CA 92621; (714) 321-4332.

Chatterbox Dictionary, Voice Learning Systems, 2265 Westwood Boulevard, Ste. 9, Los Angeles, CA; (213) 475-1036.

Chatterbox English, Voice Learning Systems, 2265 Westwood Boulevard, Ste. 9, Los Angeles, CA; (213) 475-1036.

Drills in Language Concepts, College-Hill Press, 4284 41st Street, San Diego, CA; (800) 854-2541.

I Can Talk, Soft Cole, 1804 Mississippi, Lawrence, KS 66044; (913) 842-6044.

Idioms in America, Communication Skill Builders, P.O. Box 42050, Tucson, AZ 85733; (602) 323-7500.

Language L.A.B., Specialsoft, P.O. Box 1983, Santa Monica, CA 90406; (800) 421-6534.

Natural Language Processing Program, Educational Audiology Programs, Inc., 1077 Gilpin Street, Denver, CO 80209; (303) 777-0740.

Paint with Words, MECC, 3490 Lexington Avenue North, St. Paul, MN 55126; (800) 228-350.

Rate Drill in Articulation, Language and Fluency, UNITED Educational Services, Inc., P.O. Box 605, East Aurora, NY 14052; (800) 458-7900.

Reading Around Words Program, Instructional/Communications Technology, Inc., 10 Stepar Place, Huntington Station, NY 11746; (800) CALL-ICT.

Study Buddy, Access Unlimited-Speech Enterprises, 9030 Katy Freeway, Ste. 414, Houston, TX 77024; (713) 461-0006.

Talk About a Walk, College-Hill Press, 4284 41st Street, San Diego, CA 92105; (800) 854-2541.

Talking Textwriter, Scholastic Software, Dept. JS, 730 Broadway, New York, NY 10003; (212) 505-3537.

Organizations

American Speech-Language-Hearing Association, 10801 Rockville Pike, Rockville, MD 20852; (301) 897-5700.

Division for Children with Communication Disorders, Council for Exceptional Children, 1920 Association Drive, Reston, VA 22091.

Bibliography for Teaching Suggestions

Aronson, E., Blaney, N., Stephan, C., Skies, J., & Snapp, M. (1978). *The jigsaw classroom.* Beverly Hills, CA: Sage Publications.

Cantwell, D. P., & Baker, L. (1987). *Developmental speech and language disorders.* New York: Guilford Press.

Johnson, D. W., Johnson, R. T., Holubes, E. J., & Roy, P. (1984). *Circles of learning: Cooperation in the classroom.* Washington, D.C.: Association for Supervision and Curriculum Development.

Oyer, H. J., Crowe, B., & Haas, W. H. (1987). *Speech, language, and hearing disorders: A guide for teachers.* Boston: Little, Brown.

Rousey, C. G. (1984). *A practical guide to helping children with speech and language problems.* Springfield, IL: Chas. C. Thomas.

Sharan, S., & Sharan, Y. (1976). *Small-group teaching.* Englewood Cliffs, NJ: Educational Technology Publications.

Slavin, R. E. (1980). Cooperative learning. *Review of Educational Research, 50,* 315–342.

Slavin, R. E. (1990). *Cooperative learning: Theory, research and practice.* Englewood Cliffs, NJ: Prentice Hall.

Wiig, E. H., & Semel, E. (1984). *Language assessment and intervention for the learning disabled* (2nd ed.). Columbus, OH: Chas. E. Merrill.

Wood, M. L. (1982). *Language disorders in school-age children.* Englewood Cliffs, NJ: Prentice Hall.

SUMMARY

Communication requires sending and receiving meaningful messages. Language is the communication of ideas through an arbitrary system of symbols that are used according to rules. Speech is the behavior of forming and sequencing the sounds of oral language. Communication disorders may involve language or speech or both. The prevalence of communication disorders is difficult to determine, but disorders of speech and language are among the most common disabilities of children.

Language development begins with the earliest mother-child interactions. The sequence of language development is fairly well understood, but relatively little is known about how and why children learn language. Many theories of language development have been proposed, including the following major ideas: Language learning depends on brain development and proper brain functioning (neuropsychological theory); language learning is affected by the consequences of language behavior (behavioral theory); language is learned from inputs and outputs related to information processing (information processing theory); language learning is based on linguistic rules (linguistic theory); language is one of many cognitive (thinking) skills (cognitive organization theory); language arises from the need to communicate in social interactions (pragmatic theory). Although research supports some aspects of all these theories, pragmatic theory is now widely accepted as having the most important implications for speech-language pathologists and teachers.

Children may have more than one type of speech disorder, and disorders of speech may occur along with language disorders. Voice disorders may involve pitch, loudness, and quality of phonation. Such disorders may be unpleasant to the listener, interfere with communication, or abuse the larynx. Articulation or phonological disorders involve omission, substitution, distortion, or addition of word sounds, making the individual's speech difficult to understand. The most common fluency disorder is stuttering, which may seriously hamper communication. Speech disorders associated with orofacial clefts (cleft palate or cleft lip) typically involve articulation and voice problems. Neurological damage can affect people's speech by making it difficult for them to make the voluntary movements required.

Today, more attention is given to language disorders than to speech disorders because the former are more debilitating. Language disorders may be classified in a variety of ways. One classification is based on the five subsystems of language: phonology, morphology, syntax, semantics, and pragmatics. Other classifications are based on comparisons between normal and delayed language or on the presumed causes of disorders or related conditions. Yet another system of classification includes the following categories: the child has not developed any verbal language; the child's language is qualitatively different from normal language; the child's language follows the normal pattern of development but is delayed; the child's language development is interrupted.

Assessment and intervention in language disorders require standardized testing and more informal clinical judgments. An intervention plan must consider what the child talks about and should talk about, how the child talks and should speak to become more intelligible, and how the child uses language for communication and socialization. Helping children learn to use language effectively is not the task of any single professional group. Speech-language pathologists now regularly work with classroom teachers to make language learning an integral part of classroom teaching. One of the teacher's primary roles must be to help children learn to use language effectively in the context of the classroom.

Augmentative communications systems must be devised for those whose physical or cognitive disabilities preclude oral language. These systems typically provide a way to select or scan an array of pictures, words, or other symbols. Advances in the power and availability of microcomputers are radically changing augmentative communication.

Differences in dialect or native language must not be mistaken for language disorders. At the same time, the language disorders of children with communicative differences must not be overlooked. A major concern today is teaching children who have little or no proficiency in English. Bilingual special education is an emerging discipline.

Children requiring early intervention for speech and language disorders typically have severe or multiple disabilities. It is now recognized that the young child's ability to communicate cannot be separated from other areas of development. Consequently, early language intervention involves all social interactions between a child and his or her caretakers and peers. Early intervention emphasizes functional communication in the child's natural environment, not isolated skills.

Adolescents and young adults with speech and language disorders may be self-referred, have health problems, or be severely handicapped. A major concern of transition programming has been providing for the carryover of training and support during the school years into adult life in the community. Emphasis today is on functional communication skills taught in naturalistic settings. Today it is also recognized that the language disorders of many young children are the basis for academic and social learning problems in later years.

A BEAR AND TWO BIRDS IN THE COUNTRY
America Sites, Courtesy Very Special Arts

7

Hearing Impairment

No deaf child who has earnestly tried to speak the words which he has never heard—to come out of the prison of silence, where no tone of love, no song of bird, no strain of music ever pierces the stillness—can forget the thrill of surprise, the joy of discovery which came over him when he uttered his first word. Only such a one can appreciate the eagerness with which I talked to my toys, to stones, trees, birds and dumb animals, or the delight I felt when at my call Mildred ran to me or my dogs obeyed my commands. It is an unspeakable boon to me to be able to speak in winged words that need no interpretation.

(*The Story of My Life,* Helen Keller)

lthough Helen Keller's achievements were unique in the truest sense of the word, the emotions she conveys here are not (see page 263). The deaf child who does acquire the ability to speak must certainly experience a "joy of discovery" similar to Keller's. Hearing impairment is a great barrier to the normal development of language. As we will see, even if the impairment is not severe enough for the child to be classified as "deaf," but rather as "hard of hearing," the hearing-impaired child is at a distinct disadvantage in virtually all aspects of language development. The importance of language in our society, particularly in school-related activities, is obvious. A significantly large group of educators of deaf individuals believe that many of the problems of hearing-impaired people related to social and intellectual development are primarily due to their deficiencies in language. We will explore this issue in some depth in this chapter.

Another related controversy inherent in Keller's words is the debate concerning whether the hearing-impaired child should be educated to communicate orally or through manual **sign language.** Keller's opinion is that the ability to speak offers a richer means of communication. But she was extraordinary; extremely few individuals who are deaf have attained her level of fluency. Furthermore, because for many years educators exclusively emphasized teaching deaf children to speak and actively discouraged their use of sign language, they unwittingly denied deaf children access to communication. Equal to the poignancy of Keller's breakthrough with verbal language was Lynn Spradley's discovery of communication after years of frustration with trying to speak:

"Tom! Bruce! Come quick!" . . .

I jumped up. In an instant we were in Lynn's room.

"Watch!" Louise said, tears streaming down her face. "She said it two times!" Lynn, legs crossed in front of her, sat at the head of her bed. Louise, sitting on the edge, turned back to Lynn.

"I—love—you," her voice came through the tears as she signed. She hugged Lynn, then sat back and waited.

Lynn, beaming, held up two tiny fists, crossed them tightly against her heart, then pointed knowingly at Louise. Without hesitating, she reached out and hugged Louise tightly. The room was blurred; fighting back tears, I picked up Lynn, pulled her close in a long embrace, then sat back on the edge of her bed.

"I—love—you," I signed slowly, my voice quivering as I spoke. I dropped my hands and waited.

"Love you," Lynn signed clearly, confidently, then reached out to hug me. I looked at Louise. There were tears in our eyes.

Bruce hugged his little sister. "I love you," he signed perfectly, a broad smile on his face.

"Love you," Lynn signed back, this time in a more definite exaggerated rhythm.

She had found her voice! (Spradley & Spradley, 1978, pp. 245–246)

The oral versus manual debate has raged for years. For many years there was no middle ground. Although some still debate the merits of each, many educators now have begun to use a method of "total communication," which involves a combination of both of these orientations.

MISCONCEPTIONS ABOUT PERSONS WITH HEARING IMPAIRMENT

Myth	Fact
Deafness leads automatically to inability to speak.	Even though hearing impairment, especially with greater degrees of hearing loss, is a barrier to normal language development, some deaf people can be taught some understanding of oral language and the ability to speak.
Deafness is not as great a handicap as blindness.	Although it is impossible to predict the exact consequences of a handicap on a person's functioning, in general deafness is a greater handicap than blindness. This is due to a large degree to the effects hearing loss can have on the ability to understand and speak oral language.
The deaf child is inherently lower in intellectual ability.	It is generally believed that unless they are born with additional handicaps, deaf infants have the same intellectual capacities as hearing infants. Deaf individuals, however, may perform more poorly on some tasks because of their difficulty in communicating with those who hear.
In learning to understand what is being said to them, deaf individuals concentrate on reading lips.	*Lipreading* refers only to visual cues arising from movement of the lips. Some deaf people not only learn to lipread but also learn to make use of a variety of other visual cues, such as facial expressions and movements of the jaw and tongue. They thus engage in what is referred to as *speechreading*, a term that covers all visual cues associated with speaking.
Teaching American Sign Language is harmful to a child and may hamper development of oral language.	Most authorities today recognize the value of American Sign Language as a means of communication.
American Sign Language is a loosely structured group of gestures.	American Sign Language is a true language in its own right with its own set of grammatical rules.
American Sign Language can only be used to convey concrete ideas.	American Sign Language can be used at any level of abstraction.
A hearing aid is of no use to a person with a sensorineural loss.	Although not as useful as with conductive hearing losses, hearing aids can help some people with sensorineural impairments.

DEFINITION AND CLASSIFICATION

There are many definitions and classification systems of hearing impairment. By far the most common division is between deaf and hard of hearing. This would seem simple enough, except that the two categories are defined differently by different professionals. The extreme points of view are represented by those with a physiological orientation and those with an educational orientation. Those maintaining a strictly physiological viewpoint are interested primarily in the *measurable degree* of hearing loss. Children who cannot hear sounds at or above a certain intensity (loudness) level are classified as deaf; others with a hearing loss are considered hard of hearing. Hearing sensitivity is measured in **decibels** (units of relative loudness of sounds). Zero decibels (0 dB) designates the point at which people with normal hearing can detect the faintest sound. Each succeeding number of decibels indicates a certain degree of hearing loss. Those who maintain a physiological viewpoint generally consider those with hearing losses of about 90 dB or greater to be deaf, those with less to be hard of hearing.

People with an educational viewpoint are concerned with how much the hearing loss is likely to affect the child's ability to speak and develop language. Because of the close causal link between hearing loss and delay in language development, these professionals categorize primarily on the basis of spoken language abilities. Following are the most commonly accepted set of definitions reflecting this educational orientation:

- *Hearing impairment*: A generic term indicating a hearing disability which may range in severity from mild to profound: it includes the subsets of *deaf* and *hard of hearing*.
- A *deaf* person is one whose hearing disability precludes successful processing of linguistic information through audition, with or without a hearing aid.
- A *hard of hearing* person is one who, generally with the use of a hearing aid, has residual hearing sufficient to enable successful processing of linguistic information through audition (Brill, MacNeil, & Newman, 1986, p. 67)

Educators are extremely concerned about the *age of onset* of the hearing impairment. Again, the close relationship between hearing loss and language delay is the key here. The earlier the hearing loss manifests itself in a child's life, the more difficulty he or she will have in developing language. For this reason, professionals working with hearing-impaired children frequently use the terms **congenitally deaf** (those who were born deaf) and **adventitiously deaf** (those who acquire deafness at some time after birth). Two other frequently used terms are even more specific in pinpointing language acquisition as critical: **Prelingual deafness** is "deafness present at birth, or occurring early in life at an age prior to the development of speech or language"; **postlingual deafness** is "deafness occurring at any age following the development of speech and language" (Brill, MacNeil, & Newman, 1986, p. 67). Experts differ regarding the dividing point between prelingual and postlingual deafness. Some believe it should be at about eighteen months, whereas others think it should be lower, at about twelve months or even six months (Meadow-Orlans, 1987).

The following hearing threshold classifications are common: mild (26–54 dB), moderate (55–69 dB), severe (70–89 dB), and profound (90 dB and above). These levels of severity according to loss of hearing sensitivity cut across the broad classifications of "deaf" and "hard of hearing." The broader classifications are not directly dependent on hearing sensitivity. Instead, they stress the degree to which speech and language are affected.

Some authorities object to following any of the various classification systems too strictly. These definitions, because they deal with events that are difficult to measure and that occur in variable organisms, are not precise. It is best not to form any hard-and-fast opinions about an individual's ability to hear and speak solely on the basis of a classification of his or her hearing disability.

PREVALENCE

Estimates of the numbers of children with hearing impairment vary considerably. Such things as differences in definition, populations studied, and accuracy of testing contribute to the varying figures. The U.S. Department of Education (1989) has reported that .12 percent of the population from six to seventeen years of age were identified as deaf or hard of hearing by the public schools for 1987–1988. Although the U.S. Department of Education does not report separate figures for the categories of deaf and hard of hearing, some authorities believe that many hard-of-hearing children who could benefit from special education are not being served.

ANATOMY AND PHYSIOLOGY OF THE EAR

The ear is one of the most complex organs of the body. The many elements that make up the hearing mechanism are divided into three major sections: the outer, middle, and inner ear. The outer ear is the least complex and least important for hearing; the inner ear is the most complex and most important for hearing. Figure 7.1 shows these major parts of the ear.

The Outer Ear

The outer ear consists of the auricle and the external auditory canal. The canal ends with the **tympanic membrane** (eardrum), which is the boundary between the outer and middle ear. The **auricle** is the part of the ear that protrudes from the side of the head. Although the auricle is the one part of the ear visible to all, it is the least important in terms of hearing (Martin, 1986). The part that the

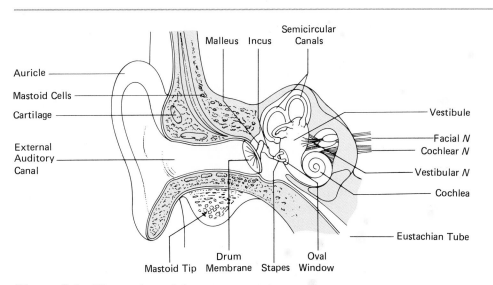

Figure 7.1 Illustration of the outer, middle, and inner ear.
SOURCE: H. L. Davis and S. R. Silverman (Eds.), *Hearing and Deafness,* 4th ed. (New York: Holt, Rinehart & Winston, 1978). Copyright © 1947, 1960, 1970, 1978 by Holt, Rinehart & Winston, Inc. Reprinted by permission.

outer ear plays in the transmission of sound is relatively minor. Sound is "collected" by the auricle and is funneled through the external auditory canal on to the eardrum, which vibrates, sending the sound waves on to the middle ear.

The Middle Ear

The middle ear comprises the eardrum and three very tiny bones (**ossicles**) called the **malleus** (hammer), **incus** (anvil), and **stapes** (stirrup) contained within an air-filled space. The chain of the malleus, incus, and stapes conducts the vibrations of the eardrum along to the **oval window,** which is the connecting link between the middle and inner ear. To prevent a significant loss of energy between the vibration of the eardrum and the vibration of the oval window, the chain of bones is constructed in such a way that it takes advantage of the physical laws of leverage. Because of this there is an efficient transfer of energy from the air-filled cavity of the middle ear to the dense, fluid-filled inner ear (Davis, 1978a; Martin, 1986).

The Inner Ear

About the size of a pea, the inner ear is an intricate mechanism of thousands of moving parts. Because it looks like a maze of passageways and because of its complexity, this part of the ear is often called a *labyrinth*. The inner ear is divided into two sections according to function: the **vestibular mechanism** and the **cochlea.** These sections, however, do not function totally independently of each other.

The vestibular mechanism, located in the upper portion of the inner ear, is responsible for the sense of balance. It is extremely sensitive to such things as acceleration, head movement, and head position. Information regarding movement is fed to the brain through the vestibular nerve.

By far the most important organ for hearing is the cochlea. Lying below the vestibular mechanism, this snail-shaped organ contains the parts necessary to convert the mechanical action of the middle ear into an electrical signal in the inner ear that is transmitted to the brain. In the normally functioning ear, sound causes the malleus, incus, and stapes of the middle ear to move. When the stapes moves, it pushes the oval window in and out, causing the fluid in the cochlea of the inner ear to flow. The movement of the fluid in turn causes a complex chain of events in the cochlea ultimately resulting in excitation of the cochlear nerve. With stimulation of the cochlear nerve, an electrical impulse is sent to the brain, and the sound is heard.

MEASUREMENT OF HEARING ABILITY

There are three different general types of hearing tests: pure-tone audiometry, speech audiometry, and specialized tests for very young children. Depending on the characteristics of the examinee and the use to which the results will be put, the audiologist* may choose to give any number of tests from any one or a combination of these three categories.

Pure-Tone Audiometry

Pure-tone audiometry is designed to establish the individual's threshold for hearing at a variety of different frequencies. (Frequency, measured in **Hertz (Hz) units,**

---

* **Audiology** is the science of hearing impairments, their detection, and their correction.

Testing with a pure-tone audiometer. The child is indicating by raising her hand that she hears the tone. (David R. Frazier/Photo Researchers)

has to do with the number of vibrations per unit of time of a sound wave; the pitch is higher with *more* vibrations, lower with *fewer*.) A person's threshold for hearing is simply the level at which he or she can first detect a sound; it refers to how *intense* a sound must be before the person can detect it. Intensity is measured in units known as decibels (dB).

Pure-tone audiometers present tones of various intensities (dB levels) at various frequencies (Hz). Audiologists are usually concerned with measuring sensitivity to sounds ranging from 0 to about 110 dB. A person with average-normal hearing is barely able to hear sounds at a sound-pressure level of 0 dB. The zero-decibel level is frequently called the zero hearing-threshold level (HTL) or **audiometric zero.**

Hertz are usually measured from 125 Hz ("low" sounds) to 8,000 Hz ("high" sounds). Sounds below 125 Hz or above 8,000 Hz are not measured because most speech does not fall within this range. (The whistle designed to call dogs, for example, has a frequency too high to be heard by human beings.) Frequencies contained in speech range from 80 to 8,000 Hz, but most speech sounds have energy in the 500 to 2,000 Hz range.

The procedure for testing a person's sensitivity to pure tones is relatively simple. Each ear is tested separately. The audiologist presents a variety of tones within the range of 0 to about 110 dB and 125 to 8,000 Hz until he or she establishes at what level of intensity (dB) the individual can detect the tone at a number of frequencies—125 Hz, 250 Hz, 500 Hz, 1,000 Hz, 2,000 Hz, 4,000 Hz, and 8,000 Hz. For each of these frequencies there is a measure of degree of hearing impairment. A 50-dB hearing loss at 500 Hz, for example means the individual is able to detect the 500-Hz sound when it is given at an intensity level of 50 dB, whereas the normal person would have heard it at 0 dB.

Speech Audiometry

Because the ability to detect and understand speech is of prime importance, a technique called **speech audiometry** has been developed to test a person's detection and understanding of speech. Speech detection is defined as the lowest level (in dB) at which the individual can detect speech without understanding. More important is the determination of the dB level at which one is able to *understand* speech. This is known as the **speech reception threshold (SRT).** One way to measure SRT is to present the person with a list of two-syllable words, testing each ear separately. The dB level at which he or she can understand half the words is often used as an estimate of SRT level.

Tests for Young and Hard to Test Children

A basic assumption for pure-tone and speech audiometry is that the person being tested understands what is expected of him or her. The individual must be able to comprehend the instructions and to show with a head nod or raised hand that he or she has heard the tone or word. He or she must also be cooperative. None of this may be possible for very young children (under about four years of age) or for children with other handicaps.

Play Audiometry

One uses this technique to establish rapport with the child and to motivate him or her to respond. The examiner sets up the testing situation as a game. Using pure tones or speech, the examiner teaches the child to do various activities whenever he or she hears a signal. The activities are designed to be attractive to the young child. For example, the child may be required to pick up a block, squeeze a toy, or open a book.

Reflex Audiometry

Infants normally possess some reflexive behaviors to loud sounds, which are useful for the testing of hearing by **reflex audiometry.** Present at birth is the *Moro reflex*, which is defined as a movement of the face, body, arms, and legs and a blinking of the eyes (Davis, 1978b). Another response that may be used to determine hearing ability is the *orienting response*. This response is evident when the infant turns his or her head and body toward the source of a sound.

Evoked-Response Audiometry

Another method of measuring hearing in a person unable to make voluntary responses is **evoked-response audiometry.** This technique involves measuring changes in brain-wave activity by using an electroencephalograph (EEG). All sounds heard by an individual result in electrical signals within the brain, so this method has become more popular with the development of sophisticated computers. Although very expensive and difficult to interpret, evoked-response audiometry has certain advantages. It can be used during sleep, and the child can be sedated and thus not be aware that he or she is being tested.

School Screening

Although children with severe hearing losses are easily identified, those with mild losses are likely to be undetected for years without some routine screening procedures (Newby, 1971). Schools, therefore, are frequently involved in screening for hearing problems.

Screening tests are administered either individually or in a group. In the group setting the examiner may present pure tones to children one at a time or to more than one child at a time. Each child has a pair of earphones and is instructed to keep his or her eyes closed and to raise his or her hand upon hearing a tone.

As with any kind of testing, group tests are less accurate than individual tests. Thus individual tests are generally preferred, even though this means the testing will be more time-consuming. The most common individual screening test is the **sweep test** performed with a portable audiometer (Newby, 1971). The examiner presents each child with a tone at about 20 to 25 dB for the frequencies of 500 Hz, 1,000 Hz, 2,000 Hz, 4,000 Hz, and 6,000 Hz. Children with problems detected in this procedure are referred for more extensive evaluation.

CAUSES

Conductive, Sensorineural, and Mixed Impairments

The most common way to classify the causes of hearing loss is on the basis of the location of the problem within the hearing mechanism. There are three major classifications: conductive hearing losses, sensorineural hearing losses, and mixed hearing losses (a combination of the first two). A *conductive loss* refers to impairments that interfere with the transfer of sound along the conductive pathway of the ear. Anatomically, conductive losses are the result of problems of the outer and/or middle ear. *Sensorineural impairments* involve problems confined to the inner ear.

One of the most important functions of the audiologist is to determine the specific site of the hearing loss. The first problem to be solved is whether the impairment is conductive, sensorineural, or mixed. The first clue may be the severity of the hearing loss. A general rule of thumb is that any hearing loss greater than 60 or 70 dB involves some inner-ear malfunctioning. Audiologists, by administering and interpreting the results of a pure-tone test, can more precisely categorize the location of the hearing impairment. They often convert the results of their testing to an **audiogram**—a graphic representation of the weakest (lowest dB) sound that the individual can hear at each of several frequency levels.

Impairments of the Outer Ear

As indicated earlier, the auricle and external auditory canal of the outer ear are less important than the middle and inner ear for hearing. This does not mean, however, that problems associated with the outer ear cannot cause real educational difficulties. Several conditions of the outer ear, particularly the external auditory canal, can cause the child to be hard of hearing.

In some children, for example, the external auditory canal does not form, resulting in a condition known as **atresia.** Children are also subject to hearing losses produced by the presence of foreign objects in the external ear. They may also suffer from **external otitis,** or "swimmer's ear," an infection of the skin of the external auditory canal. Tumors of the external auditory canal, if large enough, are another source of impairment. Excessive buildup of cerumen, or earwax, can result in hearing problems. Finally, perforation of the eardrum, resulting from any of a number of causes, ranging from a blow to the head to excessive pressure in the middle ear, also produces hearing impairment.

Impairments of the Middle Ear

Hearing losses resulting from abnormalities of the middle ear are generally more serious than those of the external ear. But middle-ear problems rarely result in deafness; children with impairments arising from middle-ear problems are usually classified as hard of hearing. Another factor that makes middle-ear impairments less devastating than inner-ear problems is that most of them are correctable with medical or surgical treatment. Most middle-ear hearing losses occur because the mechanical action of the ossicles is interfered with in some way.

Probably the most common problem of the middle ear is **otitis media**—an infection of the middle-ear space. Although otitis media can affect individuals of any age, it is primarily a disease of childhood, occurring most commonly in children under the age of two years (Pelton & Whitley, 1983). Estimated to occur in about 5 percent of all children before the age of ten (Martin, 1986), otitis media is even more common among children with Down syndrome or cleft palate. The reason for the high incidence among children with these congenital conditions is linked to physical abnormalities of the eustachian tube (Castiglia, Aquilina, & Kemsley, 1983), where the infection usually begins before spreading to the middle ear. Otitis media can result in a temporary conductive hearing loss and, if left untreated, can eventually lead to rupture of the tympanic membrane.

More subtle in its effects, but still a childhood middle-ear problem of some significance, is **nonsuppurative otitis media.** This condition, which can occur without infection, also usually results from a disruption of the functioning of the eustachian tube such that negative pressure occurs in the middle ear, which causes the blood serum of the middle-ear lining to be "sucked" into the middle-ear cavity. Nonsuppurative otitis media is generally preceded by a bout with infectious otitis media. In addition, some authorities hold that allergies, by leading to eustachian tube malfunctioning, can cause nonsuppurative otitis media (Castiglia, Aquilina, & Kemsley, 1983).

Besides the more common problems resulting from otitis media, there are a number of other, less frequent middle-ear disorders. **Otosclerosis,** which occurs rarely in children, is a disease of the bone that causes the stapes to become abnormally attached to the oval window. Tumors may also interfere with the mechanism of the middle ear, and a blow to the head is also obviously a potential cause of middle-ear malfunction. Middle-ear problems may also be the result of congenital defects.

Impairments of the Inner Ear

The most severe hearing impairments are associated with the inner ear. Unfortunately, inner-ear hearing losses present the greatest problems for both education and medicine. Troubles other than those related to loss of threshold sensitivity are frequent. For example, sound distortion often occurs. Disorders of the inner ear can result in problems of balance and vertigo along with hearing loss. Also, some individuals with inner-ear impairments may hear roaring or ringing noises.

Causes of inner-ear disorders can be hereditary or acquired. The most frequent cause of childhood deafness is heredity (Schildroth, Rawlings, & Allen, 1989). Acquired hearing losses of the inner ear include those due to bacterial infections (such as meningitis, the second most frequent cause of childhood deafness), prematurity, viral infections (such as mumps and measles), anoxia (deprivation of oxygen) at birth, prenatal infections of the mother (such as maternal rubella, congenital syphilis, and cytomegalovirus), Rh incompatibility (which can now usually be prevented with proper prenatal care of the mother), blows to the head, unwanted side effects of some antibiotics, and excessive noise levels.

Congenital cytomegalovirus (CMV) has, beginning in the late 1970s and early 1980s, received a great deal of attention as a potential cause of hearing impairment as well as other handicapping conditions (Hanshaw, 1982). CMV is the most fre-

Cochlear Implants

A new surgical procedure now allows some profoundly deaf individuals to hear previously unheard sounds. An internal electromagnetic coil, with an electrode that runs into the cochlea of the inner ear, is placed in the mastoid bone behind the ear. An external coil is fitted on the skin right over the internal coil. Sounds are picked up by a microphone worn on the clothing and are sent on to the cochlear nerve in the inner ear by way of the external coil, internal coil, and electrode in the inner ear.

Although the implant allows deaf individuals to hear a number of environmental sounds such as ringing phones and car horns, Paul Lambert, an otolaryngologist at the University of Virginia who has done the surgery, notes its limitations. It does not automatically enable a patient to understand speech, although it does make speechreading easier and the speech of the deaf person more understandable. After the surgery the patient needs to be seen by a therapist in order to learn how to differentiate the sounds he or she is now hearing for the first time.

SOURCE. Helix, Winter 1983. Drawing by F. J. Kabir. Reprinted with permission.

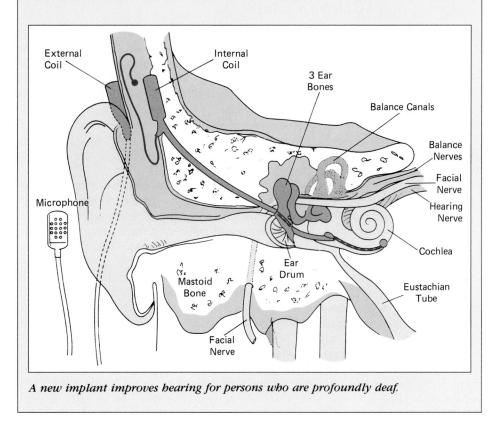

A new implant improves hearing for persons who are profoundly deaf.

quently occurring congenital virus among newborns, but it is difficult to know precisely how many cases of deafness are caused by CMV because it is often difficult to diagnose (Schildroth, Rawlings, & Allen, 1989).

More attention has also been given to noise as a possible contributor to hearing loss. With overcrowded living conditions, individuals are exposed for longer periods of time to loud noises; also playing portable cassette players with headphones at loud levels can lead to hearing problems.

There is a relationship between the cause of the hearing impairment and the degree of hearing loss. The most devastating losses occur because of meningitis, maternal rubella, and hereditary factors (Karchmer, Milone, and Wolk, 1979).

PSYCHOLOGICAL AND BEHAVIORAL CHARACTERISTICS

Hearing loss can have profound consequences for some aspects of a person's behavior and little or no effect on other characteristics. Everyone knows the question "If you were forced to choose, which would you rather be—blind or deaf?" On first impulse most of us choose deafness, probably because we rely on sight for mobility and because many of the beauties of nature are visual. But in terms of functioning in a language-oriented society, the deaf person is at a much greater disadvantage. Let us see why.

Language and Speech Development

By far the most severely affected areas of development in the hearing-impaired person in the United States are the comprehension and production of the *English* language. We stress here the fact that it is the English language because that is the predominant language in the United States of those who can hear. In other words, hearing-impaired people are generally deficient in the language used by most people of the "hearing" society in which they live. The distinction is important because hearing-impaired people can be expert in their own form of language. The current opinion is that hearing-impaired individuals who use manual sign language are taking part in the production and comprehension of a true language. We return to this point later in this chapter.

Regarding English, however, it is an unfortunate but undeniable fact that hearing-impaired individuals are at a distinct disadvantage. This is true in terms of language comprehension, language production, and speech. With regard to speech, for example, teachers have reported that 23 percent of students with hearing impairment have speech that is not intelligible, 22 percent have speech that is barely intelligible, and 10 percent are unwilling to speak in public. Speech intelligibility is linked to degree of hearing loss, with 75 percent of profoundly deaf children having nonintelligible speech but only 14 percent of children with less than severe hearing loss having nonintelligible speech (Wolk & Schildroth, 1986). In addition, it is much more difficult for prelingual deaf children to learn to speak than those who have acquired their deafness, mainly because they do not receive auditory feedback from the sounds they make. In addition, they have not heard an adult language model. An interesting research finding is that infants born deaf enter the babbling stage at the same time as hearing infants but soon abandon it (Ling & Ling, 1978; Schow & Nerbonne, 1980; Stoel-Gammon & Otomo, 1986). By as early as eight months of age, and possibly earlier, hearing-impaired babies babble less than hearing infants. And the babbling they do is of a qualitatively different nature (Stoel-Gammon & Otomo, 1986). It is thought that these differences occur because hearing infants are reinforced by hearing their own babbling and by hearing the verbal responses of adults. Deaf children, unable to hear either themselves or others, are not reinforced.

The lack of feedback has also been named as a primary cause of deaf children's poor speech production. As Fry (1966) states, hearing children learn to associate the sensations they receive when they move their jaws, mouth, and tongue with the auditory sounds these movements produce. Hearing-impaired children are obvi-

TABLE 7–1 Relationship of Degree of Impairment* to Understanding of Language and Speech

Average of the Speech Frequencies in Better Ear	Effect of Hearing Loss on Understanding of Language and Speech
Slight 27–40 dB (ISO)	May have difficulty hearing faint or distant speech. May experience some difficulty with language arts subjects.
Mild 41–55 dB (ISO)	Understands conversational speech at a distance of 3–5 feet (face to face). May miss as much as 50 percent of class discussions if voices are faint or not in line of vision. May exhibit limited vocabulary and speech anomalies.
Marked 56–70 dB (ISO)	Conversation must be loud to be understood. Will have increased difficulty in group discussions. Is likely to have defective speech. Is likely to be deficient in language usage and comprehension. Will have limited vocabulary.
Severe 71–90 dB (ISO)	May hear loud voices about 1 foot from the ear. May be able to identify environmental sounds. May be able to discriminate vowels but not all consonants. Speech and language defective and likely to deteriorate.
Extreme 91 dB or MORE (ISO)	May hear some loud sounds but is aware of vibrations more than tonal patterns. Relies on vision rather than hearing as primary avenue for communication. Speech and language defective and likely to deteriorate.

SOURCE: Adapted from *Report of a Committee for a Comprehensive Plan for Hearing-Impaired Children*, May 1968, Office of the Superintendent of Public Instruction, Title VI, Elementary and Secondary Education Act, and the University of Illinois, Division of Services for Crippled Children.
* Medically irreversible conditions and those requiring prolonged medical care.

ously handicapped in this process. In addition, they have a difficult time hearing the sounds of adult speech, which other children hear and imitate, so they are deprived of an adequate adult model.

Table 7–1 gives general examples of the effects various degrees of hearing loss may have on English language development. This is only a general statement of these relationships since many factors interact to influence language development in the hearing-impaired child.

Intellectual Ability

The intellectual ability of hearing-impaired children, particularly those classified as deaf, has been a subject of much controversy over the years. For many years, professionals believed that the conceptual ability of deaf individuals was deficient because of their deficient language. They assumed that one can equate language with cognitive abilities. The Soviet psychologist Vygotsky (1962), for instance, theorized that the early speech of children becomes interiorized as inner speech, and inner speech is the equivalent of cognitive thought. Not only have some investigators questioned whether language is the equivalent of cognitive thought, but also, in the case of deaf individuals who cannot speak, they have pointed out that one should not assume that such individuals do not have any language because they do not have *English* language. More and more professionals are recognizing that manual sign language is a true language with its own rules of grammar (Baker & Battison, 1980; Klima & Bellugi, 1979; Meadow, 1980; Wilbur, 1979). Problems hearing-impaired children may have on conceptual tasks are due to the relative lack of communication between them and the "hearing" society, which uses only standard spoken English (Liben, 1978).

Intelligence Testing

Besides experimental investigations of concept development, there is also a long tradition of controversy over results of intelligence testing of children with hearing impairment. Years ago, the prevailing opinion was that hearing impairment led to lower intelligence scores. These notions, however, were based on studies using IQ tests that were heavily verbal. Today, most authorities agree that if nonverbal intelligence tests are used, and especially if these tests are administered by sign language, hearing-impaired students are not intellectually retarded (Sullivan, 1982).

Academic Achievement

Unfortunately, hearing-impaired children are frequently handicapped in varying degrees in educational achievement. Reading ability, which relies heavily on language skills and is probably the most important aspect of academic achievement, is the most affected. A number of surveys over the years, taken as a whole, paint a gloomy picture of the academic progress of hearing-impaired students, particularly deaf students. A large-scale survey conducted in the 1970s, for example, found that by age twenty, only about half of the students with hearing impairment were able to read at a mid-fourth-grade level, that is, barely at a newspaper literacy level (Trybus & Karchmer, 1977). In addition, in arithmetic, a subject that is one of the highest achievement areas for hearing-impaired students, less than half of the students were able to work at an eighth-grade level by age twenty. Although these data are several years old, most authorities agree that there is little reason to believe the situation has improved much. Most authorities also believe, however, that this does not mean that students with hearing impairment are inherently incapable of achieving much higher levels than they ordinarily do. It is fair to say that hearing-impaired students are in need of much more intensive instruction, especially in academics, than they typically receive in order to make up for the disadvantage of their hearing loss (Moores, 1990). For example, a three-year program of intensive and systematic instruction for profoundly hearing-impaired children, begun when they were six to eight years of age, resulted in the students being only one year behind their hearing peers in reading achievement (Moog & Geers, 1985).

Several research studies have demonstrated that deaf children of deaf parents have higher reading achievement than do deaf children of hearing parents (Kampfe & Turecheck, 1987). Authorities often speculate that this result is due to the ability of deaf parents to communicate better with their children through the use of sign language.

Social Adjustment

Social and personality development in the general population depends heavily on communication. Social interaction, by definition, is the communication of ideas between two or more people. In the hearing population, language is by far the most common way messages move between people. Because of society's heavy dependence on language, it is no wonder that many investigators have found hearing-impaired individuals to have personality and social characteristics different from those of people who have normal hearing ability (Meadow, 1975, 1984). The personality problems to which we refer are not severe. Severe emotional disturbance is no more prevalent in deaf individuals than in those with hearing. There is also some evidence suggesting that it is the 20 to 40 percent of deaf children who have additional handicaps—for example, visual impairment and learning disabilities—who are likely to exhibit social maladjustment (Meadow, 1984).

Whether a hearing-impaired child will develop behavioral problems depends on how well those in the child's environment accept the disability (Hoemann & Briga, 1981; Moores, 1982). Just as with other physical and sensory impairments, it is not the hearing impairment itself but how individuals in the child's environment—particularly parents—respond that largely determines whether the child will show behavioral problems. As Hoemann and Briga point out, the family climate is critical:

> When there is only one deaf child among the family of hearing persons, it often happens that the deaf child is excluded from the affairs of the family. It is tedious for a hearing member of the family to explain things to the deaf child, and it is easy to leave the deaf child out of family discussions and decision making. Meanwhile, hearing children not only hear, they overhear much of what goes on in the home, even the fights that their parents have and their telephone conversations with personal and business associates. The deaf child does not benefit from this informal education about the affairs of living, and such an experiential deficit can have long-lasting effects on the child's social adjustment and development of social competence (p. 232)

Because they are frequently cut off from communicating with the population at large, hearing-impaired children can grow up in relative isolation. They sometimes have difficulty making friends and are perceived by readers as excessively shy (Loeb & Sarigiani, 1986). This tendency toward withdrawn behavior can be even more pronounced if they do not have hearing-impaired parents or peers with whom they can interact nonverbally.

It is probably the need for social interaction and acceptance that is most influential in leading many hearing-impaired individuals to associate primarily with other hearing-impaired persons. Hard-of-hearing and, especially, deaf individuals, more than any other handicapped group, tend to mix socially with people who have the same handicap.

The Deaf Culture

In the past, many professionals viewed this isolation from the hearing community on the part of some deaf persons as a sign of social pathology. More and more professionals, however, are agreeing with the many deaf individuals who believe in the value of having their own deaf culture. They view this culture as a natural condition emanating from the common bond of sign language. Many deaf people can communicate only with other deaf persons, and they do this through sign language. The following depicts just how strong the deaf culture can be:

> To the hearing world the deaf community must seem like a secret society. Indeed, deafness is a culture every bit as distinctive as any an anthropologist might study. First, there is the language, completely separate from English, with its own syntax, structure, and rigid grammatical rules. Second, although deaf people comprise a minority

More than any other disabled population, deaf people tend to socialize with others who share the same disability. This is due to the special role that communication plays in social interaction. (Bob Nickelsberg/Monkmeyer Press)

group that reflects the larger society, they have devised their own codes of behavior. For example, it's all right to drop in unannounced, because many people don't have the special TTY telephone hookups. How else could they contact their friends to let them know they're coming? If a deaf person has a job that needs to be done—from electrical wiring to accounting—he's expected to go to a deaf person first. The assumption is that deaf people won't take advantage of each other and that they need to support their own kind. The deaf world is a microcosm of hearing society. There are deaf social clubs, national magazines, local newspapers, fraternal organizations, insurance companies, athletic competitions, colleges, beauty pageants, theater groups, even deaf street gangs. The deaf world has its own heroes, and its own humor, some of which relies on visual puns made in sign language, and much of which is quite corny. Because deafness is a disability that cuts across all races and social backgrounds, the deaf world is incredibly heterogeneous. Still, deafness seems to take precedence over almost everything else in a person's life. A deaf person raised Catholic will more likely attend a Baptist deaf service than a hearing mass. (Walker, 1986, p. 22)

EDUCATIONAL CONSIDERATIONS

The problems facing the educator of children with hearing impairments are formidable. As one would expect, one major problem is communication. Teachers of hearing-impaired pupils face the challenge of communicating with their students and teaching them how to communicate.

Dating back to the sixteenth century, there has been a raging debate concerning how deaf individuals should converse (Lane, 1984). This controversy is sometimes referred to as the oralism-manualism debate to represent two very different points of view—one of which advocates teaching deaf people to speak and the other, the use of some kind of manual communication. Manualism was the preferred method until the middle of the nineteenth century, when oralism began to gain predominance. Currently, most educators advocate the use of both oral and manual methods in what is referred to as a **total communication approach.** About two-thirds of all deaf children are now taught by total communication and one-third are taught by an oral approach (Jordan & Karchmer, 1986).

We first discuss the major oral techniques that make up the oral approach and the oral portion of the total communication approach, and then we take up total communication.

Oral Techniques—Auditory Training and Speechreading

Auditory training is the procedure of teaching the deaf or hard-of-hearing child to make use of what hearing he or she possesses. Advocates claim that all but a very few totally deaf children are able to benefit from auditory training. The benefits of auditory training have been augmented by rapid technological advances in the development of hearing aids.

Speechreading—sometimes inappropriately called lipreading—involves teaching hearing-impaired children to use visual information to understand what is being said to them. *Speechreading* is a more accurate term than *lipreading* because the latter refers only to the use of visual cues arising from movement of the mouth in speaking. Other visual stimuli in the environment, however, can help the hearing-impaired person to understand spoken messages.

There is a controversy among those advocating the oral approach about how much to stress auditory training versus speechreading. One popular view is that the teacher should first concentrate on getting the hearing-impaired child to use his or her residual hearing (Sanders, 1982). Accordingly, visual cues associated with speechreading should not be ignored, but the teacher should focus attention on them only when the student needs more information than can be gained from auditory stimulation alone.

Auditory Training

Auditory training frequently involves three major goals:

1. Development of awareness of sound.
2. Development of the ability to make gross discriminations among environmental sounds.
3. Development of the ability to discriminate among speech sounds.

DEVELOPMENT OF AWARENESS OF SOUND. The first task in auditory training is to be sure the child knows that there is a variety of sounds, including speech, in the environment. Those children who have not used hearing aids since early infancy

More and more authorities are now recognizing that sign language is a true language. (Victoria Beller-Smith)

Collaboration: A Key to Success

KEN ALEXANDER *LYNN POTT*

KEN: The eight students I currently teach range in age from eight to eleven. They have severe to profound bilateral sensorineural hearing losses and are placed in my total communication class at Bellerive Elementary. (Total communication, which utilizes the simultaneous methods of speech, lip-reading, amplification, and sign language, is one of two types of programs offered by our special district; the other is auditory/oral, which emphasizes understanding and using spoken language.) Two of my students have deaf parents, and three have one or more deaf siblings. Although all the students are encouraged to use their best speech, only two of the eight have good to excellent conversational speech. The other six are generally unintelligible to those unfamiliar with the speech of deaf persons. Three of these students have transferred from oral programs at age eight or older. Seven of the eight have excellent signed communication skills. Five of the eight have good written English-language skills (this means they have generally good written English for deaf children: For instance, the structure of the language may be correct, but they may have problems in verb conjugation). The other three have concepts and ideas to express in writing but have great difficulty with basic English patterns.

LYNN: My fifth-grade class of twenty-eight is a heterogeneous group. The average academic level is above national norms, but my students have a wide range of ability—third-grade to seventh-grade reading levels. I teach all subject areas.

KEN: We'll describe our work with Beth, a twelve-year-old. Her father is a fluent signer and knowledgeable of deaf culture. Her mother is also a skilled communicator in sign language. Picture an artistic, creative student who is continuously struggling with perfection. She is eager to learn English and its relationship to American Sign Language. She is equally enthusiastic about reading and expressing herself in written English. She is above average in intelligence, a charming student with an amiable manner, but one whose emotions are usually kept in check. She's a visual-manual learner who relies on an interpreter to facilitate communication in the mainstream. A profoundly deaf child, she has a good sense of communication and languages, and therefore is remarkable in her communicative skills, although her speech intelligibility is only fair. She's a student who feels responsible for her own destiny. In short, you can see that she's the cat's pajamas!

LYNN: Beth is an achiever. She wants to be sure her assignments are completed correctly and neatly. During her first month in my class she didn't ask any questions, but she answered questions through the interpreter. Beth is a listener and an observer. She watches everything that goes on in the classroom. Because she is so attentive, she has become a leader among her three hearing-impaired classmates. She knows what's going on and clarifies concepts for the other hearing-impaired students. Sometimes she gets frustrated with them. I've learned to watch her facial expressions and the forcefulness in her signing. I can tell when she's frustrated. At first, she didn't want to call attention to herself, so she'd save her questions and ask for Ken's help when she returned to his classroom. By the second semester she'd lost much of her shyness and would ask questions. As she grew more confident in my classroom, she began to speak as she signed. Some of her speech could be understood, but with difficulty.

KEN: Beth was mainstreamed for science, social studies, and language at the fifth-grade level. As the teacher for the deaf, I was responsible for any preteaching, reviewing, and additional explanations to ensure success. Sometimes, specific vocabulary for science and social studies needed to be invented, based on concepts of American Sign Language and consistent with signs already in existence. I taught these in my classroom to facilitate speedy and appropriate interpreting while Beth was in hearing classes.

LYNN: As a classroom teacher I was responsible for presenting the curriculum content, giving the assignments, and testing for understanding. At the beginning of the year I needed to understand Beth's capabilities and what I could expect of her.

KEN: I recall one instance that was a particular problem—beginning note taking. Fifth grade introduces note taking as part of beginning outline skills and conceptualization of content. I had decided not to use a note taker and the usual paper. I knew that outlining skills were more important. I took the time to explain to Beth that in sixth grade note takers would be used, but that in the fifth grade it was more important to write a simple outline. She needed to learn specialized techniques to develop memory skills. I helped her learn techniques to use at home during independent study. Her parents were also involved in the various study techniques. All this helped her learn to discriminate important information from what was less important. Another challenging aspect of our teamwork, unrelated to her academic skills, was her overall social development—as a deaf person with a deaf peer group coexisting within a larger hearing society. Another matter requiring immediate attention was parental denial. One of her parents felt that her academic successes meant that she was ready to be totally mainstreamed with the necessary support. This was a denial of her deafness. The fact is that Beth's hearing peers could never know her as a person, although they could admire her for her abilities or academic skills. She didn't seek out deep, meaningful communication with hearing peers; therefore, they had virtually no sense of her as a person. Through discussion in our classroom, as well as guided discussion groups led by a counselor for the deaf, we were able to help Beth come to grips with this issue. She came to accept these realities as she saw them: She was deaf; she enjoyed socializing primarily with her deaf peers or within the deaf community; she could learn more content being mainstreamed with an interpreter and be more challenged intellectually within a larger, hearing-student classroom. In the final analysis, she had a strong self-identity as a deaf person existing within a larger hearing society.

LYNN: I definitely needed Ken's help. I had never had hearing-impaired students in my classroom before, and I had twenty-eight other students. Ken kept me informed of any concerns or problems that Beth was having. He was similar to a private tutor to Beth. Rather than burden me with reteaching, he would clarify concepts and strategies so Beth would have confidence in the regular classroom. It worked. As the year progressed, Beth began volunteering on a regular basis. He was the link that helped connect the integrated classroom to the comfortable, but isolated, deaf/hard-of-hearing classroom.

> A rewarding outcome . . . was that we saw Beth come to accept herself better within the larger mainstream.

KEN: During the course of Beth's fifth-grade year I saw attitude changes because of the way Lynn and I worked as a team. In the beginning of the year, Beth was concerned about how she would be perceived by her hearing peers. She was afraid they would reject her because of her speech skills or that they might equate her poor speech production with lower IQ. Instead, her hearing peers began to see her as a well-functioning fifth-grader. We worked within a framework that facilitated relaxed integration in academic areas as well as nonacademic areas. This allowed her hearing peers to see her during work and play, and it also helped her to develop more self-confidence about her abilities compared to those of her hearing peers. Consequently, she acquired a strong, healthy self-concept outside of her small group of deaf peers. A rewarding outcome of my collaboration with Lynn was that we saw Beth come to accept herself better within the larger mainstream.

LYNN: There were other rewards, too. As the students in my classroom began to understand Beth's feelings, they grew to respect and admire her for her abilities. She became their classmate and friend. I also grew as a teacher. I learned from Ken and Beth to watch people so that I can understand them—all people, not just those with handicaps. I remember Ken saying how significant facial expressions and body language are to his students. As a class, we talked about this. We all became more aware of the different aspects of communication. My students began to learn sign language so they could communicate with Beth.

KEN: I guess the major barrier that keeps special and general education teachers from working together are the intense and often acrimonious feelings associated with ethnocentric identity. These attitudes often include an "us-them" mentality, denigration of American Sign Language, the feeling that speech is all important, low expectations of people with disabilities, and a focus on disability rather than ability.

LYNN: Classroom teachers need to be aware of their own feelings and the feelings that deaf students experience. It is so important to have a teacher of hearing-impaired children who truly understands the frustrations of the students and is patient with the classroom teacher. If that special teacher doesn't provide input, a barrier could materialize. Perhaps this is why some mainstreaming programs are not successful.

KEN ALEXANDER:
Teacher of the deaf/hard-of-hearing, total communication, Special District of St. Louis County; B.A., Education and Psychology, Webster University; M.Ed., Education of the Deaf, Western Maryland College

LYNN POTT:
Fifth-grade teacher, Bellerive Elementary School, and instructor, Washington University; B.S., Elementary Education, University of Missouri; M.Ed., Maryville College; doctoral student, St. Louis University

may have great difficulty adjusting to them (Sanders, 1982). The sounds they are hearing for the first time may seem so overwhelming that they learn to "tune them out." Thus, most advocates of auditory training stress the importance of introducing hearing aids as early as possible.

GROSS DISCRIMINATIONS OF ENVIRONMENTAL SOUNDS. Once the child is aware of sound, the process of teaching gross discriminations of environmental sounds begins. This training sometimes requires children to match prerecorded environmental sounds with their corresponding pictures.

DISCRIMINATION AMONG SPEECH SOUNDS. The discrimination of speech sounds requires much more sophisticated learning on the part of the child than does the discrimination of gross environmental sounds. One of the reasons speech discrimination training is so complicated is that everyday speech frequently occurs among a variety of factors, referred to as "noise," which can reduce the discriminability of speech sounds. **Noise** used in this sense has a broader meaning than mere audible noise. Noise can occur within the speaker, the environment, or the listener. An example of noise within the environment is sound reverberation; within the listener, his or her high distractibility (Sanders, 1982). Thus, although speech discrimination training in the early stages should take place under ideal, low-noise conditions, the child must gradually learn to cope with discriminating speech under more natural conditions, which are relatively high in noise.

Speechreading

Sometimes referred to as lipreading, speechreading involves using visual information to understand what is being said. There are three general kinds of visual information that speechreaders try to take advantage of (Sanders, 1982):

1. Stimuli from the environment
2. Stimuli associated with the message but not part of speech
3. Stimuli directly connected with the production of speech

ENVIRONMENTAL STIMULI. Speechreading depends greatly on the ability to pay attention to and obtain meaning from the environment. Good speechreaders are able to anticipate certain kinds of messages in certain situations.

Figure 7.2 Differentiation among vowels is made on the basis of jaw opening and lip shaping. The contrast between /a/ (as in father*) and /i/ (as in* he*) is shown here.*
SOURCE: D. A. Sanders, *Aural Rehabilitation*, 2nd ed. (Englewood Cliffs, NJ: Prentice Hall, 1982). p. 128.

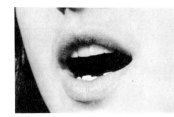

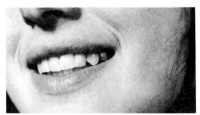

[ɑ]   [i]

NONVERBAL STIMULI RELATED TO THE SPEAKER. Training in this area involves teaching the child that some actions of the speaker are more likely to be connected with certain messages. Facial expressions are a good example. It would, for instance, be unlikely that a person would be smiling while talking about a serious accident he or she had seen.

SPEECH STIMULI. The most important aspect of speechreading is the ability to discriminate among the various speech sounds by relying on visual cues from the lips, tongue, and jaw. For example, to learn to discriminate among vowels, the speechreader concentrates on cues related to the degree of jaw opening and lip shaping (see Figure 7.2).

Unfortunately, speechreading is extremely difficult, and good speechreaders are rare. A number of factors make speechreading so hard; for one thing, many sounds are produced with little obvious movement of the mouth. Also, there are many **homophenes,** different sounds that are identical in terms of how they look. For example, the speechreader cannot distinguish among the pronunciation of [p], [b], or [m]. There is great variability among speakers in how they visibly produce sounds. Furthermore, as the following account by an experienced speechreader indicates, a number of environmental factors can greatly stretch the capabilities of even the best speechreaders:

> The success of speech and lipreading depends on many factors. Fatigue, not knowing the topic under discussion, or lack of interest can contribute to lipreading difficulties. Many factors such as poor lighting, people walking in front of the talker, poor or very tight lip movement, covering the lips with paper or other objects, rapid speaking, and talkers turning their heads can be beyond the individual's control. Even when we look at television or the movies, there are offstage voices, shadows, tight lip movement (try reading the characters on "Miami Vice"!), and talkers' backs turned to the viewer. In these cases, lipreading just does not work. Jacobs (1982) provided many excellent strategies for lipreading, but they cannot always be used. For example, at a meeting of 100 people one cannot stand up and tell the talker to slow down or please trim his beard. (Menchel, 1988, p. 13)

Total Communication

The shift that occurred in the 1970s from oral-only instruction to total communication, the use of oral and manual methods, was brought about by two factors (Moores & Maestas y Moores, 1981):

1. A number of research studies found that deaf children of deaf parents who had been exposed to manual methods, when compared to deaf children of hearing parents who had not been so exposed, were superior in English skills, academic achievement, writing, reading, and social maturity. In addition, there were no differences in speech between the two groups.
2. There was a growing dissatisfaction with the effectiveness of oral-only methods, particularly at the preschool level.

Signing English Systems

Signing English systems are the type of manualism most often used in the total communication approach. **Fingerspelling,** the representation of letters of the English alphabet by finger positions, is also used occasionally to spell out certain words, such as proper nouns. (See Figure 7.3) **Signing English systems** refer to signing systems that have been devised for the express purpose of teaching deaf people to communicate. There are several such systems, for example, Signing Exact English (Gustason, Pfetzing, & Zawolkow, 1972) and Signed English (Bornstein, Hamilton, & Saulnier, 1983).

It is important to know that signing English systems are not the same thing as true sign languages, such as American Sign Language (ASL). Although some ASL signs are used in signing English systems, the basic difference is that ASL is a true language (see the box on p. 285). Whereas signing English systems are invented by one or a few people in a short period of time, true sign languages such as ASL have evolved over several generations of users. One of the most important differences between the two for practitioners is that signing English systems follow the same word order as spoken English, thus making it possible to sign and speak at the same time (Stedt & Moores, 1990).

There is as yet a small, but growing, movement to use ASL instead of signing English systems in classrooms with deaf students (Lane, 1987; Padden & Humphries, 1988; Sacks, 1989). Advocates of ASL assert that ASL is the natural language of deaf people and that it should be fostered because it is the most natural and efficient

Figure 7.3 Fingerspelling alphabet.
SOURCE: L. J. Fant, Jr., *Say It With Hands* (Silver Springs, MD: National Association for the Deaf, 1971), pp. 1–2.

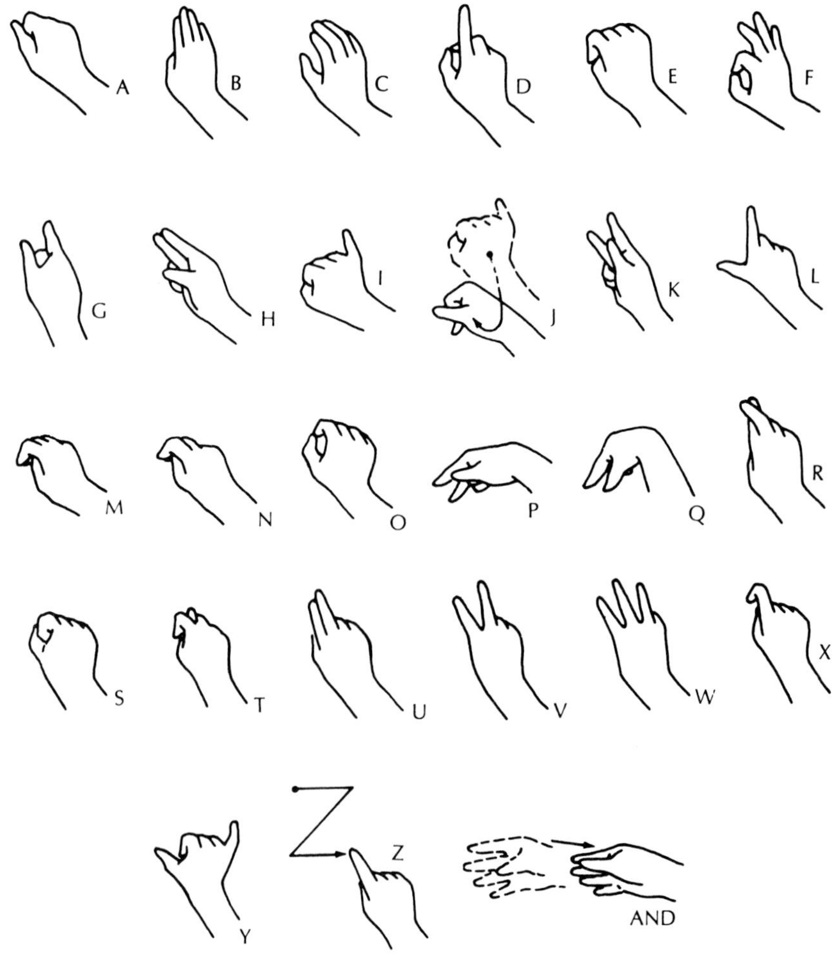

American Sign Language Is a True Language

Many people, even some of those working in the area of deaf education, have the misconception that ASL and other sign languages are not true languages. (There is no universal sign language; ASL is only one among many. Most of them are nearly as different from each other as the spoken languages of the world.) Some believe ASL is merely a loosely constructed system of gestures, and some believe that the signs are so highly pictorial in nature that they limit ASL to the representation of concrete rather than abstract concepts. Research has demonstrated that ASL's detractors are wrong on both counts.

ASL HAS ITS OWN GRAMMAR

Far from a disorganized system, ASL has its own, very complicated grammar. It was the linguist William Stokoe who first submitted that analogous to the phonemes of spoken English, each sign in ASL consists of three parts: handshape, location, and movement (Stokoe, 1960; Stokoe, Casterline & Croneberg, 1976). He proposed that there are nineteen different handshapes, twelve locations, and twenty-four types of movements. Scoffed at by his colleagues when he first advanced his theory, Stokoe has come to be regarded as a genius for his pioneering work on the structure of ASL (Sacks, 1989).

ASL CAN BE USED TO CONVEY ABSTRACT IDEAS

The misconception that ASL transmits primarily concrete ideas probably comes from the belief held by many that signs are made up mostly of pictorial, or iconic, cues. Actually, the origin of some signs is iconic. But over time, even many of these iconic signs have lost their pictorial qualities (Klima & Bellugi, 1979). Sacks (1989) notes that it is the duality of sign—the use of the abstract and the concrete—that contributes to its vividness and aliveness. The following description captures the beauty of sign:

> The creativity can be remarkable. A person can sculpt exactly what he's saying. To sign "flower growing," you delicately place the fingertips at each side of the nose as if sniffing the flower, then you push the fingertips of one hand up through the thumb and first finger of the other. The flower can bloom fast and fade, or, with several quick bursts, it can be a whole field of daffodils. In spoken English, most people would seem silly if they talked as poetically as some supposedly illiterate deaf people sign. With one handshape—the thumb and little finger stretched out, the first finger pointing forward—you can make a plane take off, encounter engine trouble and turbulence, circle an airport, then come in for a bumpy landing. That entire signed sentence takes a fraction of the time that saying it aloud would. (Walker, 1986, p. 48)

way for deaf students to learn about the world. They believe that not only are signing English systems awkward but also they are very difficult to use because they put such a heavy strain on a person's memory (Sacks, 1989). It will be interesting to see over the next several years how successful ASL proponents are in replacing signing English systems.

Administrative Arrangements

We find hearing-impaired students in settings ranging from general education classrooms to residential institutions. With the passage of PL 94–142, more and more hearing-impaired children are attending general education classes. According to

A total communication approach is a blend of oral and manual methods. (Melissa Grimes-Guy/Photo Researchers)

the U.S. Department of Education, however, only about 20 percent are primarily in regular classes.

The major reason professionals and parents are hesitant to mainstream large numbers of students with hearing impairments is the great difficulty they have with the English language. Whereas most people with disabilities have embraced the notion of mainstreaming, a sizable number of deaf people vociferously oppose placing deaf children in general education classrooms. Residential facilities have been a major influence in fostering the concept of a deaf community or culture. Many deaf persons want to preserve this deaf culture, especially the use of ASL, which defines it. Some believe mainstreaming for deaf children is not feasible:

> The object of mainstreaming is to integrate handicapped children into the larger society of children during their school years, and give them the opportunity to make friends. But deaf children find few friends outside the resource rooms. They cannot communicate with hearing children: they cannot hear them, they cannot speak. The hearing children do not sign. Deaf children are transported to their schools from widely scattered areas, and the likelihood of any two living in the same neighborhood is almost nil. After school, they ride the bus home, and lead solitary lives. Their social contacts are restricted to those with whom they can communicate at home, and to those with whom they can communicate in the resource room—often their only friends.
>
> Instead of restricting deaf children to the buildings, grounds, and playing fields of a residential school, mainstreaming often restricts them to a single room in a public school. Without speech and hearing, their participation in the world of hearing children is essentially unchanged, and their needs remain unfulfilled. (Neisser, 1983, pp. 150–151).

The objections raised by some to mainstreaming deaf children are by no means universal. The prevailing philosophy among educators at this time is still to try to mainstream as much as possible. Table 7.2 provides guidelines for integration—first drawn up in 1975 and endorsed again in 1986 (Brill, MacNeil & Newman, 1986)—that are held by many educators of deaf students.

A movement that is gaining in popularity is the use of residential institutions as resource centers for parents and local schools (Schildroth, 1986). They provide such things as parent-child programs and summer sessions for the community. In addition, more and more residential institutions are enrolling day students, that is, students who return to their homes each day.

Technological Advances

A number of technological advances have made it easier for hearing-impaired individuals to communicate with the hearing world. This explosion of technology has taken place primarily in four areas: computer-assisted instruction, television, telephone, and hearing aid.

Table 7–2 Guidelines for Integration of Hearing-Impaired and Normal-Hearing Peers

Hearing Threshold Levels (ISO)	Probable Impact on Communication and Language	Present-Day Implications for Educational Settings	
		Type*	Probable Need
Level I** 26–54 dB	Mild	Full integration Partial integration Self-contained	Most frequent Frequent Infrequent
Level II 55–69 dB	Moderate	Full integration Partial integration Self-contained	Frequent Most frequent Infrequent
Level III 70–89 dB	Severe	Full integration Partial integration Self-contained	Infrequent Most frequent Frequent
Level IV 90 dB and above	Profound	Full integration Partial integration Self-contained	Infrequent Frequent Most frequent

SOURCE: Report of the Ad Hoc Committee to Define Deaf and Hard of Hearing, *American Annals of the Deaf, 120* (1975), 510. Reprinted with permission.
* *Full integration* means hearing-impaired children are totally integrated into regular classes for hearing students, with special services provided under the direction of specialists in educational programs for the deaf and hard of hearing. *Partial integration* means the children take all classes in a regular school, some on an integrated basis and some on a self-contained basis. *Self-contained* means the children attend classes exclusively with other deaf and/or hard-of-hearing classmates in regular schools, special day schools, or special residential schools.
** It is assumed that these decibel scores were obtained by a qualified audiologist using an average of scores within the frequency range commonly considered necessary to process linguistic information.

The availability of captions now makes television more accessible to deaf people. (Closed Caption Institute)

Computer-Assisted Instruction

Many professionals are pointing to microcomputers as an excellent means of instructing hearing-impaired students. For example, one team of researchers has developed a program for teaching reading, writing, and sign language (Prinz & Nelson, 1985; Prinz, Pemberton, & Nelson, 1985). This program allows the child to type a sequence of words, or a sentence, that appears on the screen, along with a picture of the sentence and the appropriate signs. Researchers are also working on computers that will display in visual form the speech produced by individuals. Although still a long way from being widely applicable (Boothroyd, 1987), visual displays of speech have the potential of helping deaf students learn to speak better. Work is also being done on developing interactive videodisc systems to help hearing people learn sign language (Slike, Chiavacci, & Hobbis, 1989).

Television Captioning and Teletext

There are two types of television captions—open and closed. **Open captions,** used with certain programs in the 1970s, were seen on all television screens. Their use was short-lived, primarily because the general viewing audience complained that they were distracting. In the 1980s **closed captions** became available. These captions are visible only on television sets equipped with a special decoder. There has been a dramatic increase in the number of closed caption programs. Approximately 200 hours of programs per week are now available, and nearly every type of program is represented (Carney & Verlinde, 1987).

Some hearing-impaired individuals are also taking advantage of teletext, which provides access to such information as news, cultural calendars, and community announcements through television.

Telephone Adaptations

Hearing-impaired individuals have traditionally had problems using telephones because of acoustic feedback, noise from the closeness of the telephone receiver to their hearing aids, and the fact that speechreading cues cannot be used. The development of the **teletypewriter (TTY),** which connects with a telephone, has thus been welcomed. The TTY allows the hearing-impaired person to communicate through type with anyone who also has a TTY.

One of the TTY's major drawbacks is that it limits the deaf person's opportunity to communicate with hearing individuals. Even though research has demonstrated that deaf and hearing individuals are capable of communicating with one another by means of TTYs (Geoffrion, 1982), very few people other than those who are deaf have reason to own one. Work is currently under way to enable an individual with a TTY to communicate with those who do not have one. The **Superphone,** for instance, can be used by a deaf person to communicate with anyone who has a pushbutton phone (Stoker, 1982). The Superphone changes the typed message into an electronic voice for the hearing person. The hearing individual can then "type" back a message by pushing the touch-tone buttons. The resulting message shows up on the deaf individual's TTY.

Hearing Aids

Hearing aids differ in size, cost, and efficiency. The various kinds range from wearable hearing aids to group auditory training units, which can be used by a number of children at the same time. The wearable hearing aid—the type most familiar to the general public—comes in a number of models. Some are inserted within the external auditory canal, some are built into glasses and some are placed behind the ear. The most powerful kind of wearable aid consists of a unit worn on the clothing with an attached earpiece. In general, the more inconspicuous the hearing aid, the less powerful it is. With recent advances in the manufacture of miniature transistors, however, the efficiency of very small units has increased dramatically. This has resulted in a marked increase in the use of in-the-ear and behind-the-ear aids, especially the former. With continuing rapid advances in hearing aid technology, most authorities predict that these smaller hearing aids will become even more popular in the years to come.

Group auditory trainers are used in school situations in which it is desirable to provide amplification for a group of children. Group trainers, because they do not need to be small enough to wear, are usually more powerful and give better sound quality than the most advanced individual aids. For a long time a major limitation of the group unit was that it confined the movements of both teacher and children. The teacher's microphone and the children's headphones were plugged into the auditory unit. Although still seen occasionally today, these "hard-wire" systems have rapidly given way to wireless FM systems that allow greater mobility (Niemoeller, 1978).

Although hearing aids are an integral part of educational programming for many students with hearing impairments, some deaf children cannot benefit from them because of the severity and/or kind of their hearing impairment. Generally, hearing aids make sounds louder, not clearer, so if a person's hearing is distorted, a hearing aid will merely amplify the distorted sound.

For those who can benefit from hearing aids, it is critical for the child, parents, and teachers to work together to ensure the maximum effectiveness of the aid. This means that the teacher should be familiar with the operation and maintenance of the instrument. It is also important for the teacher to monitor the child's use of the hearing aid closely to make sure that he or she is using the aid consistently and that it is operating appropriately.

*Hearing aids come in a variety of sizes and shapes, and effective
teachers of hearing-impaired students will learn as much
as possible about the functioning of different kinds of hearing
aids.* (Suzanne Szasz/Photo Researchers)

EARLY INTERVENTION

Starting in the 1970s there has been a sharp increase in public school and state-supported residential school involvement in preschool programming for hearing-impaired children. Previously, preschool programs were usually not "educational"; few teachers of deaf students were involved in them, and social, cognitive, and linguistic concerns were largely ignored. Moores (1987) cites three factors that impelled the increase in educational programming for the preschool hearing-impaired child:

1. Many professionals were concerned about the poor academic performance of hearing-impaired children in the elementary grades. It was their hope that earlier intervention would reduce poor school performance.
2. The movement in general education toward compensatory education (e.g., Head Start) also influenced educators of hearing-impaired children to look to preschool education as a way to solve a variety of academic problems.

Gallaudet U. Selects First Deaf President

BOARD CHIEF RESIGNS; STUDENT DEMANDS MET

In a landmark decision aimed at fulfilling the dreams of the deaf community, Irving King Jordan was selected last night as the first deaf president of Gallaudet University, culminating a historic weeklong struggle for deaf civil rights.

Jordan, 44, who has been dean of the college of arts and sciences at Gallaudet for two years and has been on the faculty for 15 years, replaces Elisabeth Ann Zinser, a hearing president who resigned late Thursday after less than a week in the position.

University officials also announced that board chairman Jane Bassett Spilman, whose role in Zinser's selection angered many in the Gallaudet community, had resigned from the Board of Trustees. The news set off a jubilant victory party at the Northeast Washington campus, which houses the world's only liberal arts college for the deaf.

"We will never let deafness stop us again," student leader Bridgetta Bourne told more than 400 students gathered in the fieldhouse to celebrate. They screamed, hugged each other and poured foaming bottles of beer on each other in a frenzied release of happiness.

The developments concluded a remarkable week in which a group of deaf students and other members of the deaf community seized control of the federally mandated, federally funded university and transformed their protest into a national campaign for deaf rights.

With the support of deaf and hearing people, including members of Congress, the campus group—which calls itself the Deaf President Now Council—declared that it would keep the university shut down until four demands had been met.

The council called for a deaf president, Spilman's resignation, a deaf majority on the board and no reprisals against demonstrators.

"We got five demands, not just four," student body president Greg Hlibok said after the board's announcement.

The bonus, Hlibok said, was that the board now had a deaf chairman—Philip W. Bravin, who was chosen last night to replace Spilman.

Shortly after 8 P.M yesterday the Board of Trustees, which had been meeting in emergency session all day at the Embassy Row Hotel near Dupont Circle, took a recess to announce its decisions.

Spilman, chairman of the board for six years and a target of student protests, said she had submitted her resignation "willingly."

"In some minds, I have become an obstacle for the future of the university," said Spilman, 56. "Because I care deeply about Gallaudet's future, I am removing that obstacle."

Smiling as she has throughout the crisis that erupted a week ago, Spilman added: "The board was not simply called upon to select a president, but to aid in the consummation of a dream, the elevation of a deaf person to the presidency of the greatest educational institution of the deaf and the hearing-impaired world."

Bravin, the new chairman, said the board has established a task force to study its bylaws and the composition of its 20-member board, which includes four deaf members.

Student leaders were notified of the board's actions about a half-hour before the formal announcement.

As Bravin spoke with Hlibok on a TTY—an adapter that allows two people to send printed messages to each other through the telephone—more than 50 demonstrators crowded into the ground floor offices of the Alumni Association, which had served as the students' command post during the weeklong protest.

Using sign language, Hlibok told the group gathered around him of each of the concessions made by the board. With each gesture, Hlibok passed the news. The excitement mounted, then swept across campus as students dashed out to tell others, waving their hands frantically to convey the news.

Hlibok said in his conversation with Bravin that the students had agreed to relinquish control of the university immediately.

In a prepared statement, Jordan said he was "thrilled to accept the invitation of the Board of Trustees" to become the president of Gallaudet. "It is an historic moment for deaf people around the world."

Jordan is the eighth person to head the school since it was authorized in 1864 by President Lincoln.

Jordan is married and has two children, King, 17, and Heidi, 15. His three degrees in psychology include a bachelor's degree from Gallaudet and a master's and a PhD from the University of Tennessee.

Jordan was one of three finalists when the board selected a new president last week. The others were Harvey Corson, superintendent of the Louisiana School for the Deaf in New Orleans, and Zinser, the vice chancellor for academic affairs at the University of North Carolina at Greensboro.

Despite the intense pressure from the deaf community for a deaf president, the board selected Zinser, the only one of the three finalists with normal hearing. Zinser, 48, does not know sign language and had no background in deaf culture.

After assuming her position within days of her selection, she resigned Thursday, saying. "I have responded to this extraordinary social movement of deaf people."

Jordan had waffled in his support for Zinser. He supported the board's selection of Zinser on Wednesday, then reversed his position a day later.

Last night, Jordan praised "the students of Gallaudet for showing us all exactly how, even now, one can seize an idea with such force of argument that it becomes a reality."

SOURCE: Molly Sinclair and Carlos Sanchez, *Washington Post*, March 14, 1988.

3. The measles epidemic of 1964–1965 produced more hearing-impaired children, many of whom had additional handicaps. In anticipation of their entrance into elementary school in the early 1970s, educators set up preschool programs to help these children.

Given that professionals have made a commitment to preschool programming for hearing-impaired children, the question remains of what types of programs are the most effective. The same debate regarding oral versus manual communication that is evident at older age levels is also alive at the preschool level. In fact, it is even more controversial at the preschool age because this is the time when much of the foundation for later language development is rapidly being laid. In general, the most effective preschool programs are those that (1) provide academic and cognitive training, (2) emphasize parental involvement, and (3) use both oral and manual techniques (Goppold, 1988; Moores, 1987). For individual children, the degree of emphasis on oral versus manual instruction should vary according to the way in which they benefit.

TRANSITION

Before the mid-1960s the only institution established specifically for the postsecondary education of hearing-impaired students was Gallaudet College (now Gallaudet University). Except for this one institution, hearing-impaired individuals were left with no choice but to attend traditional colleges and universities. These programs, of course, were generally not equipped to handle the special needs of hearing-impaired students, so it is little wonder that a study by Quigley, Jenne, and Phillips (1968) was able to identify only 224 hearing-impaired graduates of regular colleges and universities in the United States between 1910 and 1965. It is also not surprising that the occupational status of hearing-impaired individuals is not at a par with that of the hearing population (Boatner, Stuckless, & Moores, 1964; Moores, 1969; Schein & Delk, 1974). Although hearing-impaired individuals can make good employees, many are unemployed and a large proportion are overqualified for the jobs they hold. They are overrepresented in the manual trades and underrepresented in professional and managerial positions.

It was findings such as these that led to the expansion of postsecondary programs. The government, through the allocation of federal money, has funded a wide variety of postsecondary programs for hearing-impaired students. Starting in 1965, the National Technical Institute for the Deaf (NTID) (established at the Rochester Institute of Technology) was founded. The NTID program, emphasizing training in technical fields, complements the liberal arts orientation of Gallaudet University. At NTID some of the hearing-impaired students also attend classes with hearing students at the Rochester Institute of Technology. Research has indicated that this mainstreaming is related to better academic achievement and future career adjustment (Saur, Coggiola, Long, & Simonson, 1986).

Following the establishment of NTID, there was an explosion of postsecondary programs. A college and career guide for deaf students published by Gallaudet University and NTID lists 145 postsecondary programs in the United States and Canada for hearing-impaired students (Rawlings, Karchmer, DeCaro, & Egelston-Dodd, 1986). By law, Gallaudet and NTID are responsible for serving students from all fifty states and territories. Some of the others serve students from several states, from one state only, or from a specific district only.

Programs at universities that specialize in courses of study for hearing-impaired students frequently provide a variety of special services as well (Rawlings, Trybus, & Biser, 1978). Some of these special provisions are sign language interpreters, training in manual communication for students and instructors, note-taking services, tutoring, and vocational counseling and placement programs. And since the late 1970s and early 1980s, universities that have not traditionally provided programs for hearing-impaired students have begun to provide special services for such students (Flexer, Wray, & Black, 1986).

In addition to the need for normal schooling, some hearing-impaired adults may need counseling to help them cope with potential problems related to such things as work and family life. With regard to the latter, for example, counseling may be particularly helpful for those deaf parents who have hearing children. Research indicates that deaf parents need not fear that their hearing children will have spoken English language problems if the children can hear enough good spoken language models (Schiff-Myers, 1982).

Although we have made much progress in improving postsecondary programming for and occupational status of hearing-impaired adults, there is still considerable room for improvement. The level of unemployment and the number of individuals who are over-qualified for their jobs are too high. Despite the expansion of postsecondary programs for hearing-impaired persons, many of them are limited to short-term vocational training or two-year associate-of-arts courses. The availability of programs at four-year institutions of higher education are much more limited (Moores, 1987). If more postsecondary opportunities become available, many more persons with a hearing impairment can take their place in the work force.

SUGGESTIONS FOR TEACHING STUDENTS WITH HEARING IMPAIRMENT IN GENERAL EDUCATION CLASSROOMS

What to Look for in School

Children with mild hearing losses can attend school for several years before their impairments are identified. Although they may have learned to compensate for their hearing difficulties in many school situations, they are at a disadvantage when compared academically to their nondisabled classmates and at risk to become frustrated learners and socially isolated from other students. For these reasons, it is important to be aware of the following indicators of a possible hearing loss:

1. Difficulties in understanding spoken language and/or in speaking
2. Frequent absences because of ear aches, sinus congestion, allergies, and related conditions
3. Inattention and daydreaming
4. Disorientation and/or confusion, especially when noise levels are high
5. Difficulties in following directions
6. Frequent imitation of other students' behaviors in the classroom

How to Gather Information

If these signs occur consistently, contact the speech and language specialist assigned to your school, who can administer tests to determine whether or not there is a hearing loss. If your student is found eligible for special education, support will be available to you. The exact type of assistance will depend on the student's specific needs and the services provided by your school system. It is important that you understand both the services your student will receive and the complete educational plan he or she will follow. For example, you may want to ask the special education teacher the following questions (White, 1981);

- Do I have the information I need to plan an effective educational program in all subjects I teach? Do I have appropriate materials to carry out this program?
- How should I schedule and group students to maximize educational and social opportunities?
- What amplification equipment will be used by the student? By me?
- Who is responsible for demonstrating the use of this equipment and for maintaining it?
- Whom do I contact and what procedures do I follow to request assistance if a problem arises?

Teaching Techniques to Try

Students who are mainstreamed can be expected to follow the regular curriculum (Ross, 1982). Some students with hearing losses, however, may require modifications of the physical, instructional, and social environments to benefit fully from mainstreamed education. Modifications of the physical environment may involve simple changes in seating, such as moving students away from such sources of background noise as open windows and doors and noisy heating and cooling systems (Ross

1982). Adapting seating arrangements (students are located in the front of the room with their chairs or desks turned slightly so that they can see the faces of all the other students), permitting free movement around the classroom (students can reduce the distance between themselves and the speakers), and using flexible seating arrangements (students can change seats as activities change) also promote understanding and participation in class activities (Ross, 1982). Positioning speakers so that their faces are illuminated even when the room is darkened for slides, videotapes, and films further facilitates speechreading.

Kampfe (1984) summarizes other adaptations to the physical environment that require more extensive planning and expense, including: reducing classroom noise by carpeting floors, draping windows, and covering walls with materials that absorb extraneous noise (such as corkboard or Styrofoam sheets); locating the classroom away from high traffic and noise areas (such as gyms, cafeterias, and playgrounds); and minimizing class activities in large echoing rooms.

Instructional modifications can also enhance the learning of your hearing-impaired students. Using teaching formats that include exhibits, demonstrations, experiments, and simulations provide hands-on experiences that tend to promote understanding and are easier to follow than lectures and whole-class discussions. Writing directions in short, simple sentences and using pictures to illustrate the procedure or process supplement the oral explanations you give during demonstrations (Waldron, Diebold, & Rose, 1985).

When you use lecture and discussion formats, you may decide to pretutor students by having them read ahead or work with another student to become familiar with the new concepts and information that will be discussed. Identifying and defining important vocabulary words and providing lecture notes may further enhance comprehension (Newton, 1987). Other techniques you can use to promote understanding during lectures and discussions (Kampfe, 1984; Palmer, 1988; Ross, 1982) include the following:

- Using an overhead projector to note important points so that you can face students while lecturing
- Avoiding moving around the room while speaking so that students can see your face
- Shortening and simplifying verbalizations
- Repeating main points
- Providing nonverbal cues and using facial expressions, body movements, and gestures
- Calling speakers' names to reduce the time spent in locating the source of speech
- Requiring students to raise their hands to reduce the noise and confusion that results from several people talking at once

Garwood (1987, p. 449) suggests a mnemonic device to improve oral instruction with hearing-impaired students:

S = State the topic to be discussed
P = Pace your conversation at a moderate speed with occasional pauses to permit comprehension
E = Enunciate clearly, without exaggerated lip movements
E = Enthusiastically communicate, using body language and natural gestures
CH = CHeck comprehension before changing topics.

In addition to modifying oral communication, educators (Reyolds & Booher, 1980; cited in Waldron, Diebold, & Rose, 1985) also emphasize the importance of modifying written materials by using graphic-pictorial forms such as diagrams, pictures, graphs, and graphic outlines. They indicate that the "best instructional format with deaf students . . . is predominantly pictorial with some . . . verbal information" (Waldron, Diebold, & Rose, 1985, p. 40). Adapting materials in this way reduces the language and reading demands and the amount of content that may be difficult for hearing-impaired students to cover, especially students who are enrolled in high school classes in which the reading requirements are substantial.

Regardless of the teaching format you use, it is advisable to follow a preview, teach, and review cycle (Ross, 1982). Student tutors can assist in this process, and hearing-impaired students may benefit socially as well as academically from tutoring by a classmate. For example, peer tutors can preview materials by pointing out main points and new vocabulary before the lesson is presented. After you present the lesson, the student tutor can review the material, providing additional examples, practice, and clarification, as needed. For additional information about peer tutoring see the Suggestions for Teaching section of Chapter 3.

Teachers can create other opportunities for social and academic interactions by using the buddy system. In this arrangement a normally hearing student sits next to a student who has a hearing loss to clarify explanations, directions, page numbers, and other oral communications (Robinson, 1984). Buddies may also share class notes, so that hearing-impaired students can concentrate on the speaker, and alert students to warning signals, such as fire alarms. Both peer tutoring and buddy arrangements encourage increased communication and social interactions between students.

The desire to improve communication led administrators, teachers, and students at Apollo High School in St. Cloud, Minnesota, to establish another means of facilitating social contact between normally hearing and hearing-impaired students. They developed a Sign Language Communication and Deafness elective course (Redding, 1986). Although the primary focus of the class was on learning the skills to communicate, the teacher of hearing-impaired students and an interpreter who team-taught the class also included information related to deaf awareness on topics such as hearing aids and telecommunication devices, problems of deaf adolescents, and communication modes. Students in the class were encouraged to participate in social activities outside of school, such as going out to dinner and attending after-school sports events. Sociodiagrams of normally hearing and hearing-impaired students' interactions at the start and conclusion of the class indicated that by the end of the semester course most students had become friends rather than acquaintances.

Helpful Resources

School Personnel

In many school systems, special education services are provided to hearing-impaired students by hearing specialists who work in several schools. Typically, they work with students in each building one day or one-half day a week on such skills as communication, auditory training, listening, and reading (Dilka, 1984). They are good resources for information about hearing impairments, amplification equipment, and instructional modifications. They may also adapt instructional materials for your mainstream class.

Some school divisions employ resource clinicians who are located in each building and provide supplemental and tutorial help to hearing-impaired students at regularly scheduled times each day. In addition to teaching language skills to students, they usually provide services to classroom teachers, such as reviewing difficult lessons with students and suggesting ways in which teachers can adapt classrooms and instruction to promote the learning of hearing-impaired students (Dilka, 1984).

Instructional Methods

Berg, F. S. (1987). *Facilitating classroom listening: A handbook for teachers of normal and hard of hearing students.* San Diego, CA: College Hill/Little, Brown.

Bolte, A. (1987). Our language routine: Reading together and loving it. *Perspectives for Teachers of the Hearing Impaired, 5,* 3–5.

Davis, M. B. (1985). Food for thought: Dishing up math in ways students find appealing. *Perspectives for Teachers of the Hearing Impaired, 4,* 8–9.

Dreher, B., & Duell, E. (1987). Videotapes make storybooks come alive. *Perspectives for Teachers of the Hearing Impaired, 5,* 18–20.

Dunn, L. S. (1988). Let me "read" you a story. *Perspectives for Teachers of the Hearing Impaired, 7,* 14–16.

Easterbrooks, S. R. (1985). On prepositions. *Perspectives for Teachers of the Hearing Impaired, 4,* 15–17.

Ewoldt, C., & Hammermeister, F. (1986). The language experience approach to facilitating reading and writing for hearing-impaired students. *American Annals of the Deaf, 13,* 271–274.

Gelzer, L. (1988). Developing reading appreciation in young deaf children. *Perspectives for Teachers of the Hearing Impaired, 6,* 13–16.

Heathman, M. D., & LeBuffe, J. R. (1988). Three steps in developing high school students' notetaking skills. *Perspectives for Teachers of the Hearing Impaired, 7,* 9–12.

Hull, R. H., & Dilka, K. I. (Eds.). (1984). *The hearing-impaired child in school.* Orlando, FL: Grune & Stratton.

Kelly, L. P. (1987). Writing assignments can be an invitation to learning. *Perspectives for Teachers of the Hearing Impaired, 6,* 21–23.

Lucker, J. L. (1987). Strategies for building your students' self-esteem. *Perspectives for Teachers of the Hearing Impaired, 6,* 9–11.

Marcine, T. (1983). Ten basic materials for the elementary classroom. *Perspectives for Teachers of the Hearing Impaired, 1,* 13–14.

Moores, D. F. (1987). *Educating the deaf* (3rd ed.). Boston: Houghton Mifflin.

Miller, E. (1988). A pop-up, cut-and-paste, knock out approach to creative writing. *Perspectives for Teachers of the Hearing Impaired, 7,* 5–7.

Nussbaum, D. (1988). Questions and answers about deafness: Introducing hearing loss to students. *Perspectives for Teachers of the Hearing Impaired, 6,* 18–21.

Stern, R. C. (1980). Adapting media to meet your students' needs. *American Annals of the Deaf, 12,* 861–865.

Sunal, D. W. (1984). Without reinventing the wheel. *Perspectives for Teachers of the Hearing Impaired, 2,* 16–18.

Sunal, D. W., & Burch, P. E. (1982). School science programs for hearing impaired students. *American Annals of the Deaf, 127,* 411–417.

Wray, D., Hazlett, J., & Flexer, C. (1988). Strategies for teaching writing skills to hearing-impaired students. *Language, Speech, and Hearing Services in Schools, 19,* 182–190.

Curricular Materials

Curricular materials designed for hearing-impaired students are available for several areas from the bookstore at Gallaudet University. For a free catalogue of current offerings write or call Gallaudet Bookstore, Kendall Green, P.O. Box 103, Washington, DC 20002; (202) 651-5380.

Captioned films that address subjects such as business, English, mathematics, and career education are available from Modern Talking Picture Service, Captioned Films Division, 500 Park Street, St. Petersburg, FL 33709; (800) 237-6213.

Fitz-Gerald, M. (1986). *Information on sexuality for young people and their families.* (ERIC Document Reproduction Service No. ED 294 407). Washington, DC: Gallaudet College.

Gillespie, S. (1988). *Science curriculum guide; Kendall Demonstration Elementary School* (2nd ed.). (ERIC Document Reproduction Service No. ED 298 741). Washington DC: Gallaudet College.

Introduction to communication (1986). (ERIC Document Reproduction Service No. ED 298 746). Washington, DC: Outreach, Pre-College Programs, Gallaudet College.

Pucciarelli, C. S. (Ed.). (1987). *Curriculum for mainstreamed preschool children who are hearing impaired.* (ERIC Document Reproduction Service No. ED 299 778). Westbury, NY: Nassau County Board of Cooperative Educational Services.

Social studies: Kendall Demonstration Curriculum Guide Series (2nd ed.). (ERIC Document Reproduction Service No. ED 298 742). Washington, D.C.: Gallaudet College.

Sunal, D. W. & Sunal, C. S. (1981). *Teachers guide for science—Adapted for the hearing impaired: Introduction and Levels 3–7.* (ERIC Document Reproduction Service No. ED JUNRIE). Morgantown: West Virginia University.

Literature About Hearing-Impaired Individuals

ELEMENTARY: AGES 5–8 AND 9–12

Aseltine, L., & Mueller, E. (1986). *I'm deaf and it's okay.* New York: Albert Whitman. (Ages 5–8)

Bridges, C. (1980). *The hero.* Northridge, CA: Joyce Media, Inc.

Crowley, J. (1981). *The silent one.* New York: Knopf. (Ages 9–12)

Guccione, L. D. (1989). *Tell me how the wind sounds.* New York: Scholastic. (Ages 9–12)

Hess, L. (1985). *The good luck dog.* New York: Scribner.

Levi, D. H. (1989). *A very special friend.* Washington, DC: Kendall Green Publications.

Pollock, P. (1982). *Keeping it secret.* New York: Putnam. (Ages 9–12)

Riskind, M. (1981). *Apple is my sign.* Boston: Houghton Mifflin. (Ages 9–12)

Zelonky, J. (1980). *I can't always hear you.* Milwaukee, WI: Raintree. (Ages 5–8)

SECONDARY: AGES 13–18

Clark, M. G. (1980). *Who stole Kathy Young?* New York: Dodd, Mead. (Ages 13–15)

Levinson, N. S. (1981). *World of her own.* New York: Harvey House. (Ages 13–15)

Morganroth, B. (1981). *Will the real Renie Lake please stand up?* New York: Atheneum. (Ages 13–15)

Ray, N. L. (1981). *There was this man running.* New York: Macmillan. (Ages 13–15)

Rosen, L. (1984). *Just like everyone else.* New York: Harcourt Brace Jovanavich. (Ages 13–15)

Software

Academic Skills and Drill Builder Program in Language Arts, Developmental Learning Materials, One DLM Park, Allen, TX 75002; (800) 527-5030.

Create with Garfield, Developmental Learning Materials, One DLM Park, Allen, TX 75002; (800) 527-5030.

Lessons in Syntax, Dormac, Inc., P.O. Box 270459, San Diego, CA 921228-099983; (800) 547-8032.

Micro Labs, Laureate Learning Systems, 110 East Spring Street, Winoski, VT 05404; (802) 655-4755.

Spellicopter, DesignWare, 185 Berry Street, San Francisco, CA 94107.

Spelling Tutor, Nibble, P.O. Box 325, Lincoln, MA 01773.

Stickybear Reading, Weekly Reader Family Software, 245 Long Hill Road, Middletown, CT 05457.

Walt Disney Comic Strip Maker, Apple Scribe, DMP, 666 Fifth Avenue, New York, NY 10103.

Word Find, Nibble, P.O. Box 325, Lincoln, MA 01773.

Word Invasion, Developmental Learning Materials, One DLM Park, Allen, TX 75002; (800) 527-5030.

Organizations

Alexander Graham Bell Association for the Deaf, 3417 Volta Place, N.W., Washington, DC 20007; (202) 337-5220.

American Society for Deaf Children, 814 Thayer Avenue, Silver Springs, MD 20910; (301) 585-5400.

National Association for the Deaf, 814 Thayer Avenue, Silver Springs, MD 20910; (301) 587-1788.

National Foundation for Children's Hearing Education and Research, 928 McLean Avenue, Yonkers, NY 10704; (914) 237-2676.

Self-Help for Hard of Hearing People, 7800 Wisconsin Avenue, Bethesda, MD 20814; (301) 657-2248.

Bibliography for Teaching Suggestions

Dilka, K. L. (1984). The professions and others who work with the hearing-impaired child in school. In R. H. Hull & K. L. Dilka (Eds.), *The hearing-impaired child in school* (pp. 69–82). Orlando, FL: Grune & Stratton.

Garwood, V. P. (1987). Audiology in the public school setting. In F. N. Martin (Ed.), *Hearing disorders in children* (pp. 427–467). Austin, TX: Pro-Ed.

Kampfe, C. M. (1984). Mainstreaming: Some practical suggestions for teachers and administrators. In R. H. Hull & K. L. Dilka (Eds.), *The hearing-impaired child in school* (pp. 99–112). Orlando, FL: Grune & Stratton.

Newton, L. (1987). The educational management of hearing-impaired children. In F. N. Martin (Ed.), Hearing disorders in children (pp. 321–359). Austin, TX: Pro-Ed.

Palmer, L. (1988). Speechreading as communication. *The Volta Review, 90,* 33–42.

Redding, J. (1986). Three cheers for sign language class. *Perspectives for teachers of the hearing impaired, 4,* 21–23.

Robinson, E. B. (1984). Hamilton P.S.: An alternative that's working. *Perspectives for teachers of the hearing impaired, 3,* 11–12.

Ross, M. (1982). *Hard of hearing children in regular schools.* Englewood Cliffs, NJ: Prentice-Hall.

Waldron, M. B., Diebold, T. J., & Rose, S. (1985). Hearing impaired students in regular classrooms: A cognitive model for educational services. *Exceptional Children, 52,* 39–43.

White, N. A. (1981). The role of the regular classroom teacher. In V. J. Froehlinger (Ed.), *Today's hearing-impaired child: Into the mainstream of education* (pp. 108–127). Washington, DC: Alexander Graham Bell Association for the Deaf.

SUMMARY

In defining hearing impairments, professionals with an educational orientation are concerned primarily with the extent to which the hearing loss affects the ability to speak and understand spoken language. The time of onset is therefore important. Those who are deaf at birth or before spoken language develops are referred to as having *prelingual deafness*, and those who acquire their deafness after spoken language starts to develop are referred to as having *postlingual deafness*. Professionals favoring a physiological viewpoint define *deaf* children as those who cannot hear sounds at or above a certain intensity level; they call others with hearing impairments *hard of hearing*. The generally accepted definition reflects a more educational orientation: A deaf person is unable to process language through audition, with or without a hearing aid, whereas a hard-of-hearing person *can* do this.

The U.S. Department of Education reports that .12 percent of the population from six to seventeen years of age are identified as deaf or hard-of-hearing by the public schools.

The three most commonly used types of tests for hearing acuity are pure-tone audiometry, speech audiometry, and specialized tests for very young and hard-to-test children. In determining hearing ability, the examiner uses pure tones or speech to find the intensity of sound (measured in decibels) the person can hear at different frequency levels (measured in hertz). Very young children, as well as those who may have difficulty understanding what is expected of them or in voluntary responding, must often be tested in other ways.

Professionals often classify causes of hearing loss according to the location of the problem within the hearing mechanism. *Conductive* losses are impairments that interfere with the transferral of sound along the conductive pathway of the ear. *Sensorineural* problems are confined to the complex inner ear and are apt to be much harder to treat.

Impairments of the outer ear are caused by such things as infections of the external canal, objects put into the ear by children, buildup of earwax, or perforation of the eardrum. Usually middle-ear troubles occur because of some malfunction of one or more of the three tiny bones, or ossicles, in the middle ear—the malleus, incus, and stapes. Otitis media, allergy problems that cause the eustachian tube to swell, otosclerosis, and tumors are among problems that can occur in the middle ear, otitis media being the most common. The most common causes of inner-ear troubles are linked to hereditary factors. Acquired hearing losses of the inner ear include those due to bacterial infections (such as meningitis), viral infections (such as mumps and measles), prenatal infections of the mother (such as cytomegalovirus, maternal rubella, and syphilis), and deprivation of oxygen at birth.

Impairment of hearing ability can have a profound effect on people, largely because of the language and academic orientation of American society. The earlier the hearing loss occurs, the greater the English language deficit. Also, there is evidence that early hearing loss begins to exert an effect on language at a very early age: Babies born deaf begin to exhibit less babbling by as early as eight months of age.

In the past, because they held to the notion that language is the equivalent of thought, professionals believed that deaf individuals were intellectually inferior. Researchers are now questioning the theory that thought is dependent on language. Furthermore, most authorities now recognize that sign language is as true a language as spoken language. Research supports the position that hearing impairment does not necessarily lead to cognitive problems. Using nonverbal rather than verbal tests of intelligence, investigators have generally found that hearing-impaired students score in the normal range of intelligence.

Academic achievement of hearing-impaired students does suffer. Surveys show that only about one-half of hearing-impaired students by age twenty are able to read at the mid-fourth-grade level. Even in arithmetic, one of their better academic areas, they demonstrate severe underachievement. Several studies have shown that deaf children of deaf parents have higher reading achievement than deaf children of hearing parents, probably because deaf parents are able to communicate with their children through sign language.

The primary determinant of whether the hearing-impaired individual will develop behavioral problems is the degree to which others accept his or her disability. Although deaf individuals may have personality and social characteristics that are different from hearing people, they do not have a higher prevalence of serious emotional problems. There is a strong inclination for people with hearing impairment to stay within a societal subgroup of their own. Some authorities believe that this tendency toward a deaf culture is positive.

For many years there were two basic approaches to teaching hearing-impaired students. The oralists believed it was crucial for the deaf child to learn to develop his or her remaining hearing ability and to learn to communicate orally. The manualists held that very few people considered deaf have enough hearing ability to be able to communicate orally, so they emphasized such methods as sign language. Today, however, most deaf educators favor *total communication*, a blend of oralism and manualism. Most educators who use total communication stress auditory training and speechreading and employ signing English systems, which are different from American Sign Language. Signing English systems are not true languages and follow the same word order of spoken English. There is controversy over whether ASL should be used instead of signing English systems in educating deaf students.

Hearing-impaired pupils can be found in a variety of settings, ranging from general education classrooms to residential settings. Mainstreaming of hearing-impaired students is growing in popularity, but only about 20 percent of hearing-impaired students are placed primarily in regular classrooms. A growing minority believes that mainstreaming is not appropriate for deaf students. The language problems exhibited by many hearing-impaired students is a major deterrent to widespread integration into general education classrooms.

Numerous technological advances are helping persons with hearing losses. These innovations are occurring primarily in the areas of computer-assisted instruction, television, telephones, and hearing aids.

There are now many programs for hearing-impaired preschoolers. Research indicates that in general, the more successful programs focus on increasing cognitive development and academic achievement, involve parents, and use both oral and manual techniques.

Until the mid-1960s there was very little special provision for the postsecondary education of hearing-impaired students. This relative neglect was responsible for their overrepresentation in manual trades. Since the establishment of more and better postsecondary programs, the employment picture has been slowly improving. There are now several postsecondary programs for hearing-impaired students; Gallaudet and the National Technical Institute for the Deaf are two of the major institutions serving the hearing-impaired population.

NIGHT BALLOONS
William Tyler, Creative Growth Art Center

Visual Impairment

JILL: God, I can't find anything in my place. The ketchup usually winds up in my stocking drawer and my stockings are in the oven. If you really want to see chaos, come and look at . . . (*She catches herself, self-consciously*), I mean . . . I meant . . .

DON: I know what you mean. Relax. I'm no different from anyone else except that I don't see. The blindness is nothing. The thing I find hard to live with is other people's reactions to my blindness. If they'd only behave naturally. Some people want to assume guilt—which they can't because my mother has that market cornered—or they treat me as though I were living in some Greek tragedy, which I assure you I'm not. Just be yourself.

JILL: I'll try . . . but I've never met a blind person before.

DON: That's because we're a small, very select group—like Eskimos. How many Eskimos do you know?

JILL: I never thought blind people would be like you.

DON: They're not all like me. We're all different.

JILL: I mean . . . I always thought blind people were kind of . . . you know . . . spooky.

DON: (In a mock-sinister voice) But, of course. We sleep all day hanging upside-down from the shower rod. As soon as it's dark, we wake up and fly into people's windows. That's why they say, "Blind as a bat."

(*Leonard Gershe*, Butterflies Are Free)

ot unlike anyone with a disability, the blind person wants to be treated like everyone else. Most blind people do not seek pity or even unnecessary help. Although they may need assistance in some situations, in the main they prefer to be independent. They appreciate the sensitivity of others, but they want to be reminded of their similarities rather than their differences.

Jill's discomfort with Don's blindness in the opening dialogue (see p. 301) is not that unusual. Visual impairments seem to evoke more awkwardness than most other disabilities. Why are we so uncomfortably aware of blindness? For one thing, blindness is *visible*. We often do not realize that a person has impaired hearing, for example, until we actually talk to that person. Many mentally retarded individuals are indistinguishable from others on the basis of physical appearance. However, the visually impaired person has a variety of symbols—white cane, thick or darkened glasses, a guide dog.

Another possible contributor to our awkwardness around blind people is the role that eyes play in social interaction. Poets, playwrights, and songwriters have long recognized how emotionally expressive the eyes can be. We all know how uncomfortable it can be to talk with someone who does not make eye contact with us. Think of how often we have heard someone say, or have ourselves said, that we prefer to talk "face to face" on an important matter rather than over the telephone. It is logical to assume that in social interactions we rely to a great degree on the expressiveness of people's eyes to judge how they are responding to what we are saying, and the lack of such feedback could contribute to our discomfort around visually impaired individuals. That such discomfort is due primarily to unfamiliarity with blind people is evidenced by the fact that sighted people who work with visually impaired individuals apparently do not have these feelings.

Also, research has shown that most of us have a special fear of blindness (Conant & Budoff, 1982). One reason may be that our eyes seem so vulnerable. The organs of hearing and thinking, for example, feel safely tucked away; eyes, on the other hand, seem dangerously exposed. So despite the fact that blindness is by far the least prevalent of all disabilities, we dread it. Another reason we fear loss of vision is that the sense of sight is linked so closely with the traditional concept of beauty. We derive great pleasure from our sight. Our feelings about others are often based largely on physical characteristics that are visually perceived. It is not until we talk with or read about a blind person's appreciation of sounds, smells, and touch that we begin to realize that sight is not the only sense that enables us to enjoy beauty.

One other point made in the introductory dialogue should be underscored. As Don says, "We're all different." In this chapter we hope to change the idea that visually impaired children are all alike in some odd way. We start by presenting a fact most people do not know: The majority of blind people can actually see.

DEFINITION AND CLASSIFICATION

The two most common ways of describing visual impairment are the legal and educational definitions. The former is the one laypeople and those in the medical professions use; the latter is the one educators favor.

Legal Definition

The legal definition involves assessment of visual acuity and field of vision. A **legally blind** person has visual acuity of 20/200 or less in the better eye even with correction

MISCONCEPTIONS
ABOUT PERSONS WITH VISUAL IMPAIRMENT

Myth	*Fact*
Legally blind people have no sight at all.	Only a small percentage of those who are legally blind have absolutely no vision. The majority have a useful amount of functional vision.
Most legally blind people use Braille as their primary method of reading.	The majority of legally blind individuals use print (even if it is in large type) as their primary method of reading. In addition, a recent trend shows that more blind people who cannot benefit from the use of print are now using aural methods (listening to tapes or records) rather than Braille.
Blind people have an extra sense that enables them to detect obstacles.	Blind people do not have an extra sense. They can develop an "obstacle sense" provided they have the ability to hear.
Blind people automatically develop better acuity in their other senses.	Through concentration and attention, blind individuals learn to make very fine discriminations in the sensations they obtain. This is not automatic but rather represents a better use of received sensations.
Blind people have superior musical ability.	The musical ability of blind people isn't necessarily any better than that of sighted people. Apparently many blind individuals pursue musical careers because this is one way in which they can achieve success.
Blind people are helpless and dependent.	With a good attitude and favorable learning experiences, a blind person can be as independent and possess as strong a personality as a sighted person.
If people with low vision use their eyes too much, their sight will deteriorate.	Only in rare conditions is this true; visual efficiency can actually be improved through training and use. Wearing strong lenses, holding books close to the eyes, and using the eyes as much as possible cannot harm vision.
Blind children automatically develop superior powers of concentration that make them good listeners.	Good listening is primarily a learned skill. Although many visually impaired individuals do develop good listening skills, this is the result of work on their part because they depend on these skills for so much of the information they gain from the environment.
Guide dogs take blind people where they want to go.	The guide dog does not "take" the blind person anywhere; the person must first know where he or she is going. The dog is primarily a safeguard against unsafe areas or obstacles.
The long cane is a simply constructed device that is easy to use.	The National Academy of Sciences has drawn up specifications for the manufacture of the long cane, and to use it properly, most visually impaired individuals require extensive instruction from mobility specialists.

(e.g., eyeglasses) or has a field of vision so narrow that its widest diameter subtends an angular distance no greater than 20 degrees. The fraction 20/200 means that the person sees at 20 feet what a person with normal vision sees at 200 feet. (Normal visual acuity is thus 20/20.) The inclusion of a narrowed field of vision in the legal definition means that a person may have 20/20 vision in the central field but severely restricted peripheral vision. Legally blind individuals qualify for certain legal benefits, such as tax advantages and money for special materials.

In addition to this medical classification of blindness, there is also a category referred to as partially sighted. **Partially sighted** individuals, according to the legal classification system, have visual acuity falling between 20/70 and 20/200 in the better eye with correction.

Educational Definition

Many professionals, particularly educators, have found the legal classification scheme inadequate. They have observed that visual acuity is not a very accurate predictor of how people will function or use whatever remaining sight they have. Although a small percentage of legally blind individuals have absolutely no vision, the vast majority are able to see. For example, an extensive study of legally blind students found that only 18 percent were totally blind (Willis, 1976). Furthermore, this study also indicated that most individuals classified as legally blind see well enough to read large- or regular-print books.

Many of those who recognize the limitations of the legal definition of blindness and partial sightedness favor the educational definition, which stresses the method of reading instruction. For educational purposes, blind individuals are so severely impaired they must learn to read Braille or use aural methods (audiotapes and records). (**Braille,** a system of raised dots by which blind people "read" with their fingertips, consists of quadrangular cells containing from one to six dots whose arrangement denotes different letters and symbols.) Educators often refer to those visually impaired individuals who can read print, even if they need magnifying devices or large-print books, as having **low vision.**

PREVALENCE

Blindness is primarily an adult disability. Most estimates indicate that blindness is approximately one-tenth as prevalent in school-age children as in adults. The U.S. Department of Education (1989) has indicated that for the 1987–1988 school year the public schools identified .05 percent of the population ranging from 6 to 17 years of age as visually impaired. This makes visual impairment one of the least prevalent disabilities in children.

ANATOMY AND PHYSIOLOGY OF THE EYE

The anatomy of the visual system is extremely complex, so our discussion here will focus just on basic characteristics. Figure 8.1 shows the functioning of the eye. The physical object being seen becomes an electrical impulse sent through the optic nerve to the visual center of the brain, the occipital lobes. Before reaching the optic nerve, light rays reflecting off the object being seen pass through several structures within the eye. The light rays:

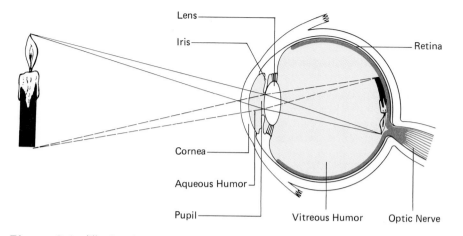

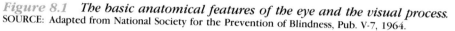

Figure 8.1 **The basic anatomical features of the eye and the visual process.**
SOURCE: Adapted from National Society for the Prevention of Blindness, Pub. V-7, 1964.

1. Pass through the **cornea** (a transparent cover in front of the iris and pupil), which performs the major part of the bending (refraction) of the light ray so that the image will be focused
2. Pass through the **aqueous humor** (a watery substance)
3. Pass through the **pupil** (the contractile opening in the middle of the **iris,** the colored portion of the eye that contracts or expands depending on the amount of light striking it)
4. Pass through the **lens,** which refines and changes the focus of the light rays before they pass through the **vitreous humor** (a transparent gelatinous substance)
5. Come to a focus on the **retina** (the back portion of the eye containing nerve fibers connected to the optic nerve)

MEASUREMENT OF VISUAL ABILITY

Visual acuity is most often measured with the **Snellen chart,** which consists of rows of letters (for individuals who know the alphabet) or *E*s (for the very young and for those who cannot read). In the latter case, the *E*s are arranged in various positions, and the person's task is to indicate in what direction the "legs" of the *E*s are facing. Each row corresponds to the distance at which a person with normal vision can discriminate the direction of the *E*s. (There are eight rows, one corresponding to each of the following distances: 15, 20, 30, 40, 50, 70, 100, and 200 feet.) People are normally tested at the 20-foot distance. If they can distinguish the direction of the letters in the 20-foot row, they are said to have 20/20 central visual acuity for far distances. If they can distinguish only the much larger letters in the 70-foot row, they are said to have 20/70 central visual acuity for far distances.

There are at least two reasons why the Snellen chart is not very useful for predicting the ability to read print. First, it measures visual acuity for distant, but not near, objects—which is why it is necessary to report the results in terms of central visual acuity for *far* distances. Many educational activities, particularly reading, require visual acuity at close distances, and there are a variety of methods available for measuring it (Carter, 1983). The results of some of these methods can be used to estimate what kinds of reading material the visually impaired person will be able to read, for example, store catalogs, children's books, or high school texts.

Second, the Snellen chart is not very appropriate for predicting ability to read print because visual acuity does not always correspond with visual efficiency. **Visual efficiency** refers to the ability, for example, to control eye movement, discriminate objects from their background, and pay attention to important details. Barraga and colleagues have developed the **Diagnostic Assessment Procedure (DAP)** to assess visual efficiency (Barraga, 1983; Barraga & Collins, 1979) accompanied by a 150-lesson curriculum.

There are screening procedures less time-consuming than the DAP but more thorough then the Snellen (Rathgeber, 1981). Using these screening tests, teachers can identify children in need of a more complete eye exam. Unfortunately, some schools use only the Snellen chart as a screening procedure. Because it does not pick up all possible types of visual problems, teachers should be alert to other signs that a child might have a visual impairment. The National Society for the Prevention of Blindness (1972) has listed a number of signs of possible eye problems (see the box on page 307).

CAUSES

The most common visual problems are the result of errors of refraction. **Myopia** (nearsightedness), **hyperopia** (farsightedness), and **astigmatism** (blurred vision) are all examples of refraction errors that affect central visual acuity. Although each can be serious enough to cause significant impairment (myopia and hyperopia are the most common impairments of low vision), usually glasses or contact lenses can bring vision within normal limits.

Myopia results when the eyeball is too long. In this case, the light rays from the object in Figure 8.1 would be in focus in front of rather than on the retina. Myopia affects vision for distant objects, but close vision may be unaffected. When the eyeball is too short, *hyperopia* (farsightedness) results. In this case, the light rays from the object in the diagram would be in focus behind rather than on the retina. Hyperopia affects vision for close objects, but far vision may be unaffected. If the cornea or lens of the eye is irregular, the person is said to have *astigmatism*. In this case, the light rays from the object in the figure would be blurred or distorted.

Among the more serious impairments are those caused by glaucoma, cataracts, and diabetes. They occur primarily in adults, but each of them, particularly the latter two, can occur in children. **Glaucoma** is a condition in which there is excessive pressure in the eyeball. Left untreated, the condition progresses to the point at which the blood supply to the optic nerve is cut off and blindness results.

The cause of glaucoma is presently unknown (although it can be caused secondarily by other eye diseases), and its onset can be sudden or very gradual. Because its incidence increases dramatically after age thirty-five and because it can be prevented if detected early, it is often strongly recommended that *all* adults have periodic eye examinations after age thirty-five. A common complaint during early stages of glaucoma is that lights appear to have halos around them (Thomas, 1985). **Cataracts** are caused by a clouding of the lens of the eye, which results in blurred vision. In children the condition is called *congenital cataracts*, and distance and color vision are seriously affected. Surgery can usually correct the problems caused

Symptoms the Regular Classroom Teacher Should Watch For

BEHAVIOR
- Rubs eyes excessively
- Shuts or covers one eye, tilts head, or thrusts head forward
- Has difficulty in reading or in other work requiring close use of the eyes
- Blinks more than usual or is irritable when doing close work
- Holds books close to eyes
- Is unable to see distant things clearly
- Squints eyelids together or frowns

APPEARANCE
- Crossed eyes
- Red-rimmed, encrusted, or swollen eyelids
- Inflamed or watery eyes
- Recurring styes

COMPLAINTS
- Eyes itch, burn, or feel scratchy
- Cannot see well
- Dizziness, headaches, or nausea following close eye work
- Blurred or double vision

by cataracts. Diabetes can cause **diabetic retinopathy,** a condition resulting from interference with the blood supply to the retina.

Several other visual impairments primarily affect children. Visual impairments of school-age children are often due to prenatal causes, many of which are hereditary. We have already discussed congenital (meaning present at birth) cataracts and glaucoma. Another congenital condition is **coloboma,** a degenerative disease in which the central and/or peripheral areas of the retina are not completely formed, resulting in impairment of the visual field and/or central visual acuity. Another prenatal condition is **retinitis pigmentosa,** a hereditary disease resulting in degeneration of the retina. Retinitis pigmentosa causes the person's field of vision to narrow. Also included in the prenatal category are infectious diseases that affect the unborn child, such as syphilis and rubella.

One of the most dramatic medical discoveries in the causes of blindness involved a condition now referred to as **retinopathy of prematurity (ROP)** (previously called *retrolental fibroplasia*). ROP, which results in scar tissue forming behind the lens of the eye, began to appear in the 1940s in premature infants. In the 1950s, researchers determined that excessive concentrations of oxygen often administered to premature infants was causing blindness. The oxygen was necessary to prevent brain damage, but it was often given at too high a level. Since then, hospitals have been careful to monitor the amount of oxygen administered to premature infants. We have not been able to eliminate cases of ROP, however. With medical advances many more premature babies are surviving, but they need very high levels of oxygen.

We can group together two other conditions resulting in visual problems because both are caused by improper muscle functioning. **Strabismus** is a condition in which the eye(s) is (are) directed inward (crossed eyes) or outward. Left untreated, strabismus can result in permanent blindness because the brain will eventually reject signals from a deviating eye. Fortunately, most cases of strabismus are correctable with eye exercises or surgery. **Nystagmus** is a condition in which there are rapid involuntary movements of the eyes, usually resulting in dizziness and nausea. Nystagmus is sometimes a sign of brain malfunctioning and/or inner ear problems.

PSYCHOLOGICAL AND BEHAVIORAL CHARACTERISTICS

Language Development

Most authorities believe that lack of vision does not alter very significantly the ability to understand and use language. They point to the many studies that show that visually impaired students do not differ from sighted ones on verbal intelligence tests. They also note that studies comparing visually impaired with sighted children have found no differences with regard to major aspects of language (McGinnis, 1981; Matsuda, 1984). Because auditory more than visual perception is the sensory modality through which we learn language, it is not surprising that studies have found blind people to be relatively unimpaired in language functioning. The blind child is still able to hear language and may even be more motivated than the sighted child to use it because it is the main channel through which he or she communicates with others.

However, there are a few subtle differences in the way in which language usually develops in visually impaired children compared to sighted children (Andersen, Dunlea, & Kekelis, 1984; Warren, 1984). Blind children's early language tends to be somewhat restricted by their lack of visual experiences. For example, whereas their language tends to be more self-centered, sighted children use language more readily to refer to activities involving other people and objects. Although such differences are relatively subtle and do not indicate that the blind individual will lead a linguistically deficient existence, it is a good idea to provide blind children with as rich an exposure to language as possible at as young an age as possible (Warren, 1984).

Intellectual Ability

Performance on Standardized Intelligence Tests

Samuel P. Hayes was the pioneer in the intelligence testing of blind individuals (Hayes, 1942, 1950). He took the verbal items from one of the commonly used IQ tests of his period—The Stanford-Binet—to assess the intelligence of blind individuals. The rationale was that these items should provide a true reflection of a blind person's intelligence because they do not rely on vision as much as some of the more performance-related items.

Since the work of Hayes, professionals have continued to use verbal IQ tests to test the intelligence of blind individuals. In addition, they have developed tests that are less verbal in nature. The Blind Learning Aptitude Test (BLAT) (Newland, 1979) is one of the most popular of the performance tests for blind individuals. One of its features is that in contrast to verbal IQ tests, it assesses the tactual sense—an ability required for reading Braille.

Whether using verbal or performance tests, one must be extremely cautious in attempting to compare the intelligence of blind and sighted individuals. It is virtually impossible to get a direct comparison between the two groups because it is so difficult to find comparable tests (Warren, 1984). Using a verbal test is not entirely satisfactory because many authorities think of intelligence as comprising more than just verbal facility. Some have used performance tests with blind and sighted groups while requiring the latter to wear blindfolds, but this method is problematic because sighted individuals are not accustomed to doing performance tasks without using their vision. From what we do know, however, we can conclude that there is no reason to believe that blindness results in lower intelligence.

Conceptual Abilities

The same problems have also hindered research that involved laboratory-type tasks of conceptual ability. A number of investigators have concluded that visually impaired children lag behind their sighted peers in conceptual development (e.g., Davidson, Dunn, Wiles-Kettenmann, & Appelle, 1981; Gottesman, 1976; Stephens & Grube, 1982). Many of these studies have compared the performance of blind children to sighted children, using conceptual tasks developed by the noted Swiss psychologist, Jean Piaget. Warren (1984) points out, however, that these comparisons are questionable because, like comparisons on IQ tests, it is virtually impossible to find equivalent tasks for sighted and blind individuals.

Nevertheless, there are some important differences between blind and sighted individuals' conceptual development, most of which are due to the difference between tactual and visual experiences.

TACTUAL VERSUS VISUAL EXPERIENCE. The tactual sense is primarily how the blind child acquires a variety of concepts that the sighted child usually acquires through the visual sense. There are two different kinds of tactual perception: synthetic touch and analytic touch (Lowenfeld, 1971).

Synthetic touch refers to a person's tactual exploration of objects small enough to be enclosed by one or both hands. Most physical objects are too large for synthetic touch to be useful, and analytic touch must be used. **Analytic touch** involves the touching of various parts of an object and then mentally constructing these separate parts. The sighted person is able to perceive different objects or the parts of one object *simultaneously*; the blind person must perceive things *successively*. A good example of the restricted nature of touch is that of a woman trying to find something in the depths of her handbag. She may well have to grope for quite a while, touching objects successively, before she finds what she wants.

As Warren (1981, pp. 195–196) noted, blind people are at a distinct disadvantage because they are unable to use sight to help them develop integrated concepts:

> Further, vision plays a vital role in the consolidation of various perceptual attributes into a single, integrated concept. The child can hear a dog barking or panting, can feel the texture of the dog's coat or can experience contact with the dog if one of them runs into the other, and can smell the dog's odor. If he or she has sight of the dog as well, then vision informs him or her that all of these perceptual attributes are parts of the same event. Thus vision serves as an effective bridge among the other experiences, and the growth of the integrated concept of dog is facilitated. If vision is impaired, the task of acquiring the integrated concept is much more difficult.

Another critical difference between sight and touch is that touch requires a great deal more conscious effort. As Lowenfeld (1973b, p. 36) has observed,

The sense of touch generally functions only if it is actively employed for the purpose of cognition, whereas vision is active as long as the eyes are open and hearing functions continually unless its organ is obstructed. Therefore, blind children must frequently be encouraged to apply touch for the purpose of cognition. In our society where something like a "touch taboo" prevails from infancy on, encouragement to apply touch is often prevented by a need to avoid social disapproval felt by parents and sometimes by educators.

As E. P. Scott (1982, p. 34) puts it,

For the sighted child, the world meets him halfway. What he sees encourages him to move further out into his environment and to explore it. He learns literally hundreds of thousands of things from observation, imitation, and identification, without any effort on his part or on the part of his parents or teachers. The visually impaired child is dependent on others to organize, explain, and interpret the strange and confusing world around him.

Little is known about the tactual sense of the blind child and how best to develop it. We do know, however, that good tactual perception, like good visual perception, relies on being able to use a variety of strategies (Berlá, 1981; Griffin & Gerber, 1982). The blind child who compares a pencil and a ruler, for example, by using such strategies as comparing the length of each to body parts and listening to differences in pitch when each is banged against a table will have an advantage in understanding the differences and similarities between these two objects. One general strategy that is especially important for tactual development is the ability to focus exploration on the most important stimulus features (Davidson, 1972)—those parts of the object that make it what it is. Research has also demonstrated that the earlier the blind child is trained in the use of such strategies, the more beneficial the training will be for tactual development (Berlá, 1981).

IMPORTANCE OF AGE AT ONSET AND DEGREE OF IMPAIRMENT FOR CONCEPT DEVELOPMENT. Just how different from a sighted child the conceptual development of any particular visually impaired child will be depends greatly on two factors—the degree of the visual impairment and the age at its onset. Children who are able to gain some visual experience before losing their sight will be able to rely on these experiences to some degree. Children who are blind from birth will generally rely more on their tactual sense to learn about their environment than those who acquire their blindness later. Likewise, children who are totally blind will depend more on the tactual sense for concept development than will those with low vision.

Mobility

Probably the most important ability for the successful adjustment of most visually impaired individuals is their mobility—their skill in moving about in their environment. Mobility skills depend to a great extent on spatial ability. Authorities have delineated two ways in which the visually impaired person can process spatial information—as a sequential route or as a map depicting the general relation of various points in the environment (Dodds, Howarth, & Carter, 1982; Fletcher, 1981; Herman, Chatman, & Roth, 1983; Rieser, Guth, & Hill, 1982). The latter method, referred to as **cognitive mapping,** is preferable because it offers more flexibility in navigating an environment. Consider three sequential points—*A*, *B*, and *C*. A sequential mode of processing spatial information restricts a person's movement so that he or she can move from *A* to *C* only by way of *B*. But a person with a cognitive map of points *A*, *B*, and *C* can go from *A* to *C* directly without going through *B*.

No matter which conceptualization of space—sequential or map—visually impaired individuals have, there is little doubt that they are at a distinct disadvantage in mobility relative to their sighted peers. For one thing, they are less able, or unable altogether, to rely on visual imagery. In addition, visually impaired travelers must rely much more on memory for their representation of space than sighted people do (Hollyfield & Foulke, 1983).

You have no doubt observed blind people who move relatively easily through crowded city streets; you may also have seen others so disoriented that they actually endanger themselves and others merely by walking down a quiet street. Determining what makes one blind person's mobility skills better than another's is not easy. For example, common sense seems to tell us that mobility would be better among those who have more residual vision, but this does not appear to be the case. *Motivation* to become mobile is believed to be the most important factor. Warren and Kocon (1974) cite studies that suggest that individuals with low vision have greater attitude problems than those who are blind. Possibly the former are more frustrated because they can see a little, but not enough to be completely at ease in moving about. This frustration may lead them to give up and become dependent on others. Blind individuals, on the other hand, are more likely to be motivated to learn as many cues as possible because they know they cannot rely on any visual help.

We might also expect early loss of vision to be more harmful to mobility than later loss. Although it is generally the case that those who lose their vision early are at a greater disadvantage in mobility than those who lose it later, age at the onset of visual impairment does not predict perfectly an individual's mobility skills (McLinden, 1988). Again, Warren and Kocon (1974) note that those who become visually impaired later in life may have greater adjustment difficulties. With proper motivation, however, these people should be able to profit from a visual frame of reference acquired through previous experiences (Warren, Anooshian, & Bollinger, 1973). They can relate their new reliance on nonvisual modalities to previous visual perceptions. In addition, they have an advantage over those who have been blind from birth because they have been able to develop the rudiments of mobility, such as learning to walk as infants.

"Obstacle Sense"

A large part of a blind person's skill in mobility is the ability to detect physical obstructions in the environment. A blind person walking along the street often seems to be able to "sense" an object in his or her path. This ability has come to be known as the "obstacle sense"—an unfortunate term because many laypeople, and some professionals, have taken it to mean that blind people somehow develop an extra sense. This is not true. A number of experiments have shown that blind people can become very proficient at picking up cues in their surroundings (Warren & Kocon, 1974). With practice, they are able to detect subtle changes in the pitch of high-frequency echoes as they move toward objects. Actually, they are taking advantage of the **Doppler effect,** a physical principle that says the pitch of a sound rises as a person moves toward its source. There is nothing special about being blind that allows one to develop this sense.

Although the obstacle sense can be important for the mobility of a blind person, by itself it will not make its user a highly proficient traveler. It is merely an aid.

Stevie Wonder at the keyboard. It is a misconception that being blind automatically results in superior musical ability. Blind people frequently follow musical careers because hearing is a sense they can use to achieve success. (Emerson/NARAS/Sygma)

Extraneous noises in the environment (traffic, speech, rain, wind) can make the obstacle sense unusable. Also, it requires walking at a fairly slow speed to be able to react in time.

The Myth of Sensory Acuteness

Along with the myth that blind people have an extra sense is a general misconception that with the loss of sight, blind people automatically develop better acuity in their other senses. This is not true. For example, they do not have lowered thresholds for sensation in touch and hearing. What they are able to do is make better use of the sensations they obtain. Through concentration and attention, they learn to make very fine discriminations. Another common belief that has been found to be a misconception (Pitman, 1965) is that blind people are superior in musical ability. Apparently they frequently follow musical careers, and some become accomplished musicians, because music is an avenue through which they can achieve success.

Academic Achievement

There have been very few studies of the academic achievement of visually impaired children and sighted children. Many professionals agree that direct comparisons are questionable, primarily because the two groups must be tested under such different conditions. For example, there are Braille and large-type forms of some achievement tests. But because reading Braille is an inherently slower process than reading print and because most visually impaired children who do read print read at a slow speed, the visually impaired child is usually allowed to take a longer time on the tests.

Despite these problems, some gross generalizations can be made from the research that has been done. There is some evidence to suggest that both low vision and blind children are behind their sighted peers (Bateman, 1963; Suppes, 1974). Another generally accepted conclusion is that the academic achievement of visually impaired children is not affected as greatly as that of hearing impaired children. Hearing is evidently more important for school learning than seeing. Many authorities believe that an increase in the use of auditory sources in instruction for blind students in recent years has resulted in less academic impairment than was once the case.

Social Adjustment

There is a great deal of conflicting evidence on whether visually impaired individuals are less well adjusted than their sighted peers. Because the research does not show visually impaired children to be generally maladjusted, we can conclude that personality problems are not an inherent condition of blindness. Cutsforth (1951) was among the first to stress that if maladjustment does occur in a blind person, it is more than likely because of the way society has treated that person. In essence, it is society's reaction to the blind person that determines adjustment or lack of it.

When visually impaired individuals are not accepted by those who are nondisabled, many professionals believe it is because some of them have difficulty attaining certain social skills, such as exhibiting appropriate facial expressions. Teaching visually impaired students social skills can be a very challenging task because such skills are traditionally acquired through modeling and feedback, using sight (Farkas, Sherick, Matson, & Loebig, 1981; Stewart, Van Hasselt, Simon, & Thompson, 1985; Van Hasselt, 1983). However, a number of investigators have been successful in teaching social skills to visually impaired students through behavioral principles (Van Hasselt, 1983).

Stereotypic Behaviors

An impediment to good social adjustment for a few visually impaired individuals is **stereotypic behaviors** or **stereotypies.** These are repetitive, stereotyped movements such as rocking or rubbing the eyes. For many years the term **blindisms** was used to refer to these behaviors because it was thought that they were manifested only in blind people, but they are also sometimes characteristic of severely retarded and disturbed children who have normal sight. *Stereotypic behaviors* and *stereotypies* are more appropriate terms because they stress the *repetitiveness* of the behaviors, which is the main point.

Very little research data support the notion that visually impaired individuals have an inordinate number of personality problems. Most are capable of normal community and social adjustment. (Bodhan Hrynewych/ Southern Light)

America's Boswell Drives Into the Dark

DUDLEY DOUST ON A REMARKABLE PLAYER

After he had stooped to feel the texture of the grass, and finger the edge of the cup, Charley Boswell paced with his caddie across the green to his ball. He counted as he went . . . 48, 49, 50 feet. "It's mostly downhill," said his caddie, crouching to line up the face of Boswell's putter. "Take off about 10 feet, and putt it like a 40-footer."

Boswell stroked the ball. It sped across the green, climbed and fell, curved, slowed down and dropped with a rattle into the hole. Boswell grinned: "Did you see that one?" Yes, I had seen it. But he hadn't. Charley Boswell is blind. In fact, he is one of the most remarkable blind sportsmen in the world and playing off a handicap as low as 12, he has won the United States Blind Golfers' Association Championship 17 times.

Putting, oddly enough, is one of Boswell's strong departments. Given, of course, the fact that his caddie reads the putt, his execution is immaculate. "A tip that we blind golfers can pass on to the sighted player," he said, "I don't worry about the breaks on a green. Don't try to curb your putt because, as Bobby Jones always said, every putt is a straight putt and let the slopes do the work."

A few weeks ago I met Boswell in California, where he was playing a benefit match for the Braille Institute of America. He had come up from Alabama, where he is the State Commissioner in the Department of Revenue, a remarkable enough job, and now he was walking to the second tee on a course in the lush Coachelle Valley. A wind blew down from the mountains. "Funny thing," he said, "wind is really the only thing that bothers me. It affects my hearing, and that ruins my sense of direction."

On the second tee his caddie, who is his home professional back in Alabama, lined up the face of Boswell's driver and stepped away. Boswell, careful not to lose this alignment, did not waggle his clubhead. He paused, setting up some inner rhythm, and swung with the certainty of a sighted player. He groaned as the ball tailed off into a slice.

"There are two ways I can tell if I hit a good shot," he said, frowning. "I can feel it through the clubhead and, more important, I finish up high on my follow-through. Come on, let's walk. I can't stand golf carts—they bother my judgment of distance."

Boswell has been walking down darkened fairways since shortly after the Second World War. Blinded when a German antitank gun scored a direct hit on his vehicle in the Ruhr, he was sent back to an American hospital for rehabilitation. A former gridiron footballer and baseball player, Boswell did not take easily to pampered, supervised sport.

"I tried swimming, and it bored me. I tried horseback riding until I rode under a tree and got knocked off. I tried ten-pin bowling, and that wasn't any good either—I fell over the ball-track." He laughed, idly swinging his club as he walked. "Then one day this corporal came in and suggested we play golf. I told him to get the hell out of my room."

Boswell had never swung a golf club in his life but, a few days later, aged 28, he gave it a try: "He handed me a brassie. I took six practice swings, and then he teed one up and I hit it dead centre, right out of the sweet spot. I tell you, I was lucky. If I'd missed the ball that first time I would have quit golf." There are no false heroics about Boswell.

Some holes later he, or rather we, found his ball in a bunker. The bunker shot was clearly the most difficult shot in Boswell's bag. Playing it required him to break two Rules of Golf: he not only needed his usual help from someone to line up his club but, to avoid topping the ball, or missing it altogether, he had to ground his club in the sand. "Also, I can't get fancy and cut across the ball," he said. "I have to swing square to the line of flight. I have to play it like an ordinary pitch."

These handicaps, he later pointed out, were in part counterbalanced by the actual advantages of being blind on a golf course. Boswell, for instance, is never tempted to play a nine-iron when a seven-iron will do the job. "In a match blind players play the course, not their opponents, because we can't see what they're doing anyway," he said, on the way to a score of 91 which, for him, was neat but not gaudy. "You know, I was once playing with Bob Hope, and he said: 'Charley, if you could see all the trouble on this golf course, you wouldn't be playing it.' And I suppose he was right."

SOURCE: Dudley Doust, *Sunday Times*, London, February 6, 1977. Reprinted by permission.

There are three major competing theories regarding the causes of stereotypic behaviors:

1. *Sensory deprivation*. Children with low levels of sensory stimulation, such as blind children, attempt to make up for this deprivation by stimulating themselves in other ways. Thurrell and Rice (1970) present a strong case for this position. They found a greater frequency of eye rubbing among children with minimal vision compared to those with a higher degree of vision or no vision at all. They believe that children with minimal vision are able to gain stimulation from neural impulses through pressure applied to the eyes. Totally blind children cannot.
2. *Social deprivation*. Even with adequate sensory stimulation, social isolation can cause individuals to seek added stimulation through stereotypic behaviors (Warren, 1981, 1984). Some studies with animals suggest that social isolation, even within a relatively rich sensory environment, can lead to stereotypic behaviors (Berkson, 1981).
3. *Retreat to familiar patterns of behavior under stress*. Arguing that even sighted children sometimes regress to less mature patterns of behavior, a number of researchers (Knight, 1972; Smith, Chethik, & Adelson, 1969) hold that stereotypic behaviors may be the child's way of retreating to "safer ground" to cope with stressful situations.

We have no conclusive evidence that any one of these three explanations is a single causal theory of stereotypic behaviors. It is safest to assume, therefore, that some combination of the three provides the best explanation for their occurrence.

EDUCATIONAL CONSIDERATIONS

Lack of sight can severely limit a person's experiences because a primary means for obtaining information from the environment is not available. What makes the situation even more difficult is that educational experiences in the typical classroom are frequently visual. Nevertheless, most experts agree that we should educate visually impaired students in the same general way as sighted children. Teachers need to make some modifications, but they can apply the same general educational principles. The important difference is that visually impaired will have to rely on other sensory modalities to acquire information.

The student with little or no sight will possibly require special modifications in four major areas: (1) Braille, (2) use of remaining sight, (3) listening skills, and (4) mobility training. The first three pertain directly to academic education, particularly reading; the last refers to skills needed for everyday living.

Collaboration: A Key to Success

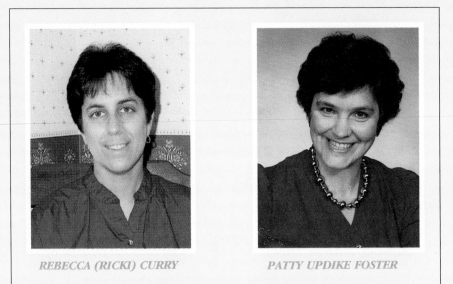

REBECCA (RICKI) CURRY   *PATTY UPDIKE FOSTER*

RICKI: My caseload varies from year to year as children move into the area served by the regional program. During the year Pat and I worked together, my caseload included sixteen children over a four-county area. Of these, three were totally blind and the others had varying degrees of visual impairment. Most of my partially sighted students were in regular classes receiving weekly itinerant services. They ranged from preschool through high school. Two of my blind students were in self-contained classes for moderately handicapped children, and one (John) was based in a class for learning-disabled students and mainstreamed into Pat's class for a large part of the school day.

PAT: I teach twenty-six students ranging from two mainstreamed special education students who read on a first-grade level to gifted children who read on a fifth- or sixth-grade level. They're nine- and ten-year-olds. We'll describe our work with nine-year-old John.

RICKI: John has been blind from birth. He functions very independently and learns quickly. He never needs coaxing to work or to learn and has an amazingly long attention span for academic work. He is socially aware and has a really on-target sense of humor. He doesn't work or move very quickly, though, and we're always trying to "hurry him up." Someone who observed him described him as a "little tank"—he keeps plugging away and gets where he's going but his pace is steady, not speedy.

PAT: I see John as a generally cheerful boy who likes meeting and getting to know people. He's usually cooperative and eager to learn new things. He shares his experiences willingly, always expecting to be accepted by his peers and teachers. He has a great sense of humor and uses that to play jokes on others. At first, he didn't understand that we could see certain actions. For instance, he would sneak a snack out of his desk before it was snack time and not realize that I could see him eating it. He has a terrific memory and easily identifies his associates by voice. He's very flexible and trusting, which enables him to work well with anyone, and he's willing to try new things. For example, he often opts to have a "new" person as his sighted guide because, as he puts it, "I haven't gotten to know them yet." Sometimes he's moody—very silent. Sometimes he's lazy, pretending he can't find his place in his Brailled text.

RICKI: Pat and I worked together to integrate John into her class. John moved to our region the summer before he entered third grade, and it was decided that for his first year in the school system he would be best served with a "home base" in a special education class so that we could assess his skills and needs in a protected environment. John's previous placement had been in a special class for visually impaired students in a university lab school, so he really had no experience in a typical public school setting.

At the same time, we wanted to give him the opportunity to learn to function socially and academically in the mainstream, so he had reading and math in the special class and other things in Pat's class.

PAT: I had John in my class for science, social studies, P.E., snack, silent reading time, and lunch. My primary responsibility was John's socialization and academic development in science and social studies. I chose and planned activities and decided when they would need adaptation for John. When this was necessary I asked Ricki to come up with methods and materials—usually a visual aid, but certainly not limited to that. I evaluated the content of his work and gave grades. Sometimes I had Ricki evaluate the Brailling skills John used and help me grade the work from a language arts perspective. I chose sighted guides for John and generally helped integrate him socially. I also helped John communicate daily assignments to his parents.

RICKI: Pat took complete responsibility for John while he was with her class. I was not in the building during these times. Before the school year started Pat and I discussed the adaptations that John would need and the materials and services I could provide. Throughout the year, Pat gave me print handouts to Braille for John, and I provided him with his science and social studies books in Braille. I spent the first week of school following John around so that I could identify times during the day when he needed help and orient him to various routines and locations. Ricki and I problem-solved getting him through the lunch line independently, out to recess, through a P.E. class with a sighted buddy. Pat and I worked out a rotating group of student sighted guides from her class. At the beginning of a month, Pat would give me a list of four or five students who would be John's sighted guides for that month. I took them out of class for a short training session and then Pat assigned John a sighted guide each day. His sighted guide was responsible for being his lunch companion (John sometimes needed help finding his seat after going through the line) and his P.E. buddy (to guide him out to the playground for recess and back into the building after recess, but not to spend recess playing with him).

> It was very exciting to have a colleague to share John's triumphs with.

■ PAT: For me, the most demanding part of all this was the need for advance planning so that materials could be obtained or made on time. Scheduling was a problem because Ricki was not full time at our school and therefore not always there when I needed Brailling or advice. John's parents were very cooperative and undemanding, but I felt that perhaps special education parents are accustomed to more regular feedback than they usually get in a regular education classroom. We lacked materials on certain topics, especially local interest units. Sometimes there was a lapse between assignments being completed in Braille and encoded back into print because Ricki's an itinerant teacher.

■ RICKI: Finding enough common time

in our schedules to discuss programming and materials was the most difficult and frustrating thing for me. As an itinerant teacher, I was always on the run; as a classroom teacher, Pat was always involved with a group of students. After school we both often had meetings. So we managed by "catching" each other and talking in snips of time. I often felt that I wasn't providing Pat with what she needed because of this lack of shared planning time.

■ PAT: The most rewarding aspect was the challenge of adapting the classroom routine to meet John's need without altering it so that the other students suffered. It was very exciting to have a colleague to share John's triumphs with. Ricki was extremely willing to help in any way needed and there were many materials available in Braille. Ricki was quite willing to research any availability and order what we needed. One of the most heart-warming results was the effect on the other students. Because of John's very pleasant personality he made many friends, and all the students liked and admired him. They learned compassion and that true friendships could be formed with a handicapped student. We also had students with other mild handicaps in our class. One student had always been quite uncoordinated. As a result she had problems relating socially and was very shy. John's presence helped the students recognize in a very real way that we all have the same needs for friendship and understanding regardless of our capabilities or handicaps. I saw a lot of growth in compassion toward this student, and I attribute this to their friendship with John. This helped to put other handicaps into perspective also.

■ RICKI: For me, seeing how a master teacher can integrate a blind child into her classroom without major adaptations was a real inspiration. Pat's classroom was a "real world" situation, and with very little help from me, she and John and the other students established the necessary routines and relationships that made it possible for him to be part of the class. Because this kind of integration is always the goal of a special education teacher, I felt lucky to be involved in such a success. It made me more hopeful

for integration of my other students who may not yet be as capable as John. Pat also gave me a model to refer to when trying to identify other mainstreaming teachers.

■ PAT: The greatest barrier to working together is lack of extra planning time to address the child's special needs. Classrooms sometimes have to be physically rearranged to accommodate a special needs student. The teacher may also be fearful of what she might expect from the student emotionally and physically and how that might affect her classroom. Classroom teachers feel already burdened and are reluctant to take on another, somewhat demanding student. Another hindrance is the unclear definition of responsibilities of resource and classroom teacher. Also, the two personalities of the teachers must be compatible, and there must be a workable trust level between the two.

■ RICKI: I think our different perspectives and responsibilities cause many misunderstandings and lack of appreciation for each other's problems. I have the luxury of zeroing in on one student at a time, but a classroom teacher has to look at the big picture and be responsible for many individuals at once. Asking a classroom teacher to give one special student a larger slice of time is definitely an imposition—one that some classroom teachers can tolerate better than others.

RICKI CURRY:

Itinerant teacher for the visually impaired, Piedmont Regional Education Program; A.B., Experimental Psychology, Brown University; M.Ed., Special Education for the Visually Impaired, University of Virginia

PATTY UPDIKE FOSTER:

Third-grade teacher, Hollymead Elementary School, Charlottesville, Virginia; B.S.Elem.Ed., Radford University; graduate work in early childhood education, University of Virginia

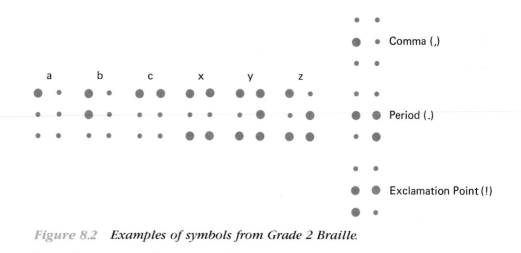

Figure 8.2   Examples of symbols from Grade 2 Braille.

Braille

In nineteenth-century France Louis Braille, himself blind, introduced the basic system of writing for blind people that is used today. Braille actually based his alphabet on a system that had been developed by a French officer, Charles Barbier, for writing messages that could be read at night. The Braille method was offered as a replacement for raised-line letters. In 1932 Standard English Braille was established as the standard code (Lowenfeld, 1973a). This made it possible for all Braille readers to read, no matter who had trained them.

The basic unit of Braille is a quadrangular "cell" containing anywhere from one to six dots. The different forms of Braille vary primarily in the number of contractions used. Grade 1 Braille, for example, contains no contractions; Grade 2 Braille, on the other hand, makes considerable use of contractions and the shortened forms of words. Grade 1 Braille is easier to learn because it is more literal. But Grade 2 Braille is the popular choice because it requires much less space and can be written and read much faster (see Figure 8.2).

Two means of writing in Braille are the Perkins Brailler and the slate and stylus. The **Perkins Brailler** (Figure 8.3) has six keys, one for each of the six dots of the cell. The keys, when depressed simultaneously, leave an embossed print on the paper. More portable than the Perkins Brailler, but more difficult to use, is the **slate and stylus** (Figure 8.4). The stylus must be pressed through the openings of the slate, which holds the paper between its two halves. The slate and stylus is also slower because the stylus makes an indentation in the paper, so the Braille cells have to be written in reverse order.

A number of factors diminish the utility of reading Braille. First, it is difficult to learn, much more difficult than learning to read print, for example. In addition to the fact that the contractions do not correspond to phonetic rules, reading Braille relies on memory to a great extent. Because the perceptual unit is the single cell, readers are forced to perceive the material much more sequentially. Also, because they cannot perceive a number of words at once, as can sighted persons reading print, Braille readers read much more slowly. Another factor that limits the usefulness of Braille is that the books are very large and take up a great deal of storage space. It is difficult to obtain some reading material in Braille, even though the American Printing House of the Blind and the Library of Congress provide extensive services.

Because of Braille's limitations and because of advances in technology in other

Figure 8.3   A Perkins Brailler in use. (Eunice Harris/ Photo Researchers)

Figure 8.4   A slate and stylus in use. (Dan Hallahan)

areas, fewer blind people rely on Braille than once was the case. A survey conducted by the American Printing House for the Blind (1985) indicated that only about 15 percent of the blind population reads primarily by Braille. In addition to a variety of technological devices (see the section on special instructional aids, pp. 328–330), those who have little or no sight are turning more and more to auditory materials for their reading, and more and more individuals with low vision are reading regular- and large-print materials.

Use of Remaining Sight

Because of the many problems associated with reading Braille and because the vast majority of visually impaired children have quite a bit of useful vision, many professionals believe that teachers should encourage visually impaired children to use their sight as much as possible. Hanninen (1975), for instance, believes that most visually impaired students should read print because of the greater speed of reading print, the ability to portray pictures and diagrams, and the greater accessibility of reading material.

For many years there was a great deal of resistance to having visually impaired children use their sight in reading and some other activities. There have been

Braille markings make many activities possible for people who are blind. (Eunice Harris, Science Source/Photo Researchers)

This is an example of 18-point type.

Figure 8.5

many myths about this issue. Among the most common are these: (1) Holding books close to the eyes harms the eyes, (2) strong lenses hurt the eyes, and (3) using the eyes too much injures them (Hanninen, 1975). At one time classes for partially sighted, or low vision, students were called "sight conservation" or "sight-saving" classes, reflecting the popular assumption that using the eyes too much causes them to deteriorate. It is now recognized that only in very rare conditions is this true. In fact, studies have shown that teachers can actually train visually impaired students to use what visual abilities they do have to better advantage (Barraga & Collins, 1979; Collins & Barraga, 1980).

The two general methods of aiding visually impaired children to read print are large-print books and magnifying devices. Large-print books are simply books printed in larger-size type. This text, printed primarily for sighted readers, is printed in 10-point type. Figure 8.5 shows print in 18-point type. Type sizes for visually impaired readers range up to 30-point type, but 18-point is one of the most popular.

The major difficulty with large-type books is that a great deal of space is required to store them. In addition, they are of limited availability, although, along with the American Printing House for the Blind, a number of commercial publishers are now publishing and marketing large-print books (see the box below).

Magnifying devices range from glasses and hand-held lenses to closed-circuit television scanners that present enlarged images on a TV screen. These devices can be used with normal-size type or large-type books.

Large-Print Publishing: The Eyes Have It

You may have noticed in your local bookstore a section devoted to large-print books. Though sales of individual titles remain small—4,000 is a best seller for a large-print book—more and more such titles are appearing every month and there is now a book club for readers of large-print books.

The guru of the large-print book in the United States is a third-generation San Franciscan named Lorraine Marchi, who is founder and head of the National Association for the Visually Handicapped (NAVH). Her interest in the subject began in the early 1950s when she discovered that there was no reading material available for her son who had just entered the first grade. . . .

"There are 498,000 legally blind people, and they are served by 800 agencies," says Lorraine Marchi. "But there are close to 11 million people who are visually handi-capped, which means that even with the best correction, the vision in their better eye is less than normal. . . ." It was for this group, and for the 90 percent of legally blind people who had some usable vision, that Mrs. Marchi set up the NAVH.

Among the organization's first aims was to make school-related textbooks available in large print for the visually handicapped. The first four large-print books it published in San Francisco in the 1950s included a fifth-grade speller and three social studies books for the third grade. The NAVH now has a backlist of about 200 books. . . .

The concept of "large print" has different interpretations, but the NAVH has a list of standards that make 16-point type a desideratum. A point equals $1/72$ of an inch.

Normal book type generally runs from 9 to 11 points, and Book Report is printed in 8.5 point type. "But," says Mrs. Marchi, "point size is only one factor. The amount of white space between lines, the blackness of the type, and the color of the paper are among other important considerations."

Though large-print books are only a small part of its overall business, the biggest name in the field is G. K. Hall, a Boston publisher that is strong in the library market. Probably its best-known division is Twayne, which does critical and biographical works aimed at college students. Hall began to do large-print books in 1970—buying rights from other publishers—and now issues 200 titles a year, primarily fiction. According to Janice Meagher, who has been Hall's executive editor for large-print titles since Jan. 1, the company's best-selling title in the area is probably the *Merriam-Webster Dictionary for Large-Print Users*, first issued in 1975. . . .

The other two major publishers in the large-print field are both run by people who once worked for G. K. Hall—Phillips Treleaven, who was president of Hall and now heads the Thorndike Publishing Company, and John Curley, a former marketing man with Hall who is boss of John Curley & Associates.

Thorndike is located in the town of Thorndike, Maine, which has a population of 500—"more cows than people," as Phillips Treleaven describes it. The company publishes 88 titles a year, plus 36 romances imported from the British arm of Harlequin Books, Mills & Boone. Its best-seller so far has been *Lake Wobegon Days* by Garrison Keillor, but it also has high hopes for its recently published edition of Jean Auel's *The Mammoth Hunters*. Because of the larger type size involved, the book was published in two volumes. . . .

A lover of Cape Cod, John Curley used to commute into Boston from South Yarmouth, Massachusetts, when he worked for Hall. Now he runs his business from there and can go out for a swim or a game of golf whenever he wants. Curley does nothing but large-print books. The company does about 250 titles a year, including two romances, two mysteries and two westerns every month. Starting next January, the number of westerns will rise to three a month. According to John Curley's daughter, Mary, who works for the company, its best-selling author is probably Zane Grey. Titles on Curley's upcoming fall list include *The Patient Has the Floor* by Alistair Cooke, *Tefuga* by Peter Dickinson, John Hersey's *Hiroshima* and biographies of John Wayne and Ethel Merman.

Walker & Co., a mainstream New York publisher, concentrates on "inspirational classics" in its large-print line including *The Prophet* by Khalil Gibran, *Jonathan Livingston Seagull* by Richard Bach, *Strength to Love* by Martin Luther King and *The Power of Positive Thinking* by Norman Vincent Peale. Walker has 67 large-print books in its backlist.

A new entry in the large-print sweepstakes is Isis, a company based in Oxford, England. Its American marketing is handled out of Brooklyn, N.Y., by Allen Kleiman, a librarian specializing in services for the aging, and his wife Rhonda. Isis has done about 50 books so far, issuing three nonfiction titles and two fiction each month. Its best seller so far has been *Dr. Christiaan Barnard's Arthritis Handbook* and in the fall it will be publishing Barnard's *Your Healthy Heart*.

An important development in the large-print field is the establishment—as part of the Doubleday group of book clubs (which includes the Literary Guild) — of the Doubleday Large Print Home Library. The club gets its selections from books under contract to its fellow clubs in the Doubleday group. Current offerings include *I'll Take Manhattan* by Judith Krantz, *High Jinx* by William F. Buckley Jr., *Break In* by Dick Francis and *Murder at the FBI* by Margaret Truman. For information, write to the club in Garden City, N.Y. 11534–1104. The club also has an 800 number: 800–343–4300, ext. 355.

Another source for users of large-print books is the library maintained by the NAVH, 22 West 21st Street, New York 10010 (telephone 212–889–3141). Up to two large-print books can be checked out of the library at any given time and mailed anywhere in the country. The NAVH also provides vision information, book catalogs and a free newsletter.

The latest development in the large-print field harks back to the beginnings of the NAVH and Mrs. Marchi's frustration at not being able to obtain books for her son. G. K. Hall has begun to publish children's books in large type, including such classics as *Five on a Treasure Island* by Enid Blyton, *Mrs. Frisby and the Rats of NIMH* by Robert C. O'Brien and *Are You There God? It's Me, Margaret* by Judy Blume. And they are excited by their seven-volume edition of C. S. Lewis's *The Chronicles of Narnia*, due in the fall.

And a sign of the times. While marketing people at the large-print companies see their main audience as the growing population of older people, they think there may be a secondary audience in another group: younger people who work in front of computer screens all day and come home with very tired eyes.

SOURCE: Charles Monaghan, *Washington Post Book World*, June 29, 1986, pp. 15, 16. © The Washington Post.

Listening Skills

The importance of listening skills for blind children cannot be overemphasized. The less a child is able to rely on sight for gaining information from the environment, the more crucial it is that he or she become a good listener. Some professionals still assume that good listening skills will develop automatically in blind children. This belief is unfortunate, for it is now evident that blind children do not spontaneously compensate for poor vision by magically developing superior powers of concentration. In most cases, they must be taught how to listen. There are a variety of curriculum materials and programs available to teach children listening skills (e.g., Bischoff, 1979; Swallow & Conner, 1982).

Listening skills are becoming more important than ever because of the popularity of recorded material as a method of teaching visually impaired individuals, who now have access to records and tapes and a variety of recording devices. The American Printing House for the Blind and the Library of Congress are major sources for these materials.

The major advantage of using recordings rather than Braille or large-print books is that the person can cover the same material much more quickly in a variety of ways. For example, one can simply play the material at normal speed. Even this method, which results in a rate of about 150 to 175 words per minute, allows the person to "read" much faster than would be possible with Braille. By far the most satisfactory method in terms of efficiency is to use a compressed speech device which allows one to read at about 250 to 275 words per minute (Tuttle, 1974). The idea behind this method is to discard very small segments of the speech. Some of the more sophisticated compressed speech devices use a computer to eliminate those speech sounds that are least necessary for comprehension.

There are some disadvantages to using recordings. First, there is the danger that the student will come to rely too heavily on them and will not learn to use residual vision. Moreover, recordings are not available for everything, especially of such everyday materials as newspapers and street signs. Hanninen (1975) notes that listening to recordings requires a great deal of concentration. Any momentary lapse in attention will cause the student to miss what is being said.

Mobility Training

How well individuals cope with a visual disability depends to a great extent on how well they are able to move about. Whether a person withdraws from the

Impediments to Independent Travel for Visually Impaired People: Rapid Rail Transit as an Example

Most of us who are sighted do not stop to consider how difficult our environment can be for the independent travel of the visually impaired person. Some prime examples of society-made dangers can be found in our subways. Jackson, Peck, and Bentzen (1983) conducted a study of the rapid rail systems of Atlanta, Boston, and Philadelphia. Their findings were based on the experiences of visually impaired individuals as they traversed each of these systems, as well as on their own personal observations. The following indicates just a few of the many problems encountered within the station.

PROBLEMS EXPERIENCED BY VISUALLY IMPAIRED TRAVELERS ON RAPID RAIL TRANSIT TRIPS

Accessibility within the Station

Requirement: User must perceive and understand information about the correct platform, train, and direction.

Problems:

Some signs were located too high or in inconsistent locations.[a]

Some signs were poorly lit, which hindered attempts to read them.[a]

Some signs were dirty or defaced.[a]

Some signs had low contrast between print and background or had high color saturation.[a]

Some signs were written only in small print.[a]

There were no large print maps.[a]

Requirement: User must approach fare barrier or ticket booth.

Problems:

There was no standard location of the entry gate or turnstile, which made it difficult to locate the appropriate gate.[c]

There was no textured or otherwise tactually discernible path to gate that could be used consistently.[c]

There were narrow turnstiles that were difficult to pass through with dog guides.[c]

There was no standard location for information and change booths.[c]

There was no distinction between entry and exit turnstiles in some places.[c]

The "handicapped gate," which the user was supposed to push when the buzzer sounded, was texturally unmarked, and the traveler pushed on the area adjacent to the gate rather than on the gate itself.[d]

Requirement: User must manipulate currency or show "proof of payment."

Problems:

There were farecard machines in which the farecard had to be inserted in a unique manner.[c]

There were coin or token slots that had no contrast to the rest of the fare-collection device, which made finding the slot a matter of trial and error.[b]

Requirement: The user must travel along the platform to wait for the train.

Problems:

There were station platform edges marked with badly faded painted lines which were not sufficiently distinct from their adjacent area.[a]

There were station platform edges without guard rails.[b]

There were station platform edges with texture strips that were not of sufficient contrast to the adjacent area to serve as tactile warnings.[c]

Requirement: The user must be able to avoid hazards.

Problems:

There were cracks and breaks in the pavement that could cause falls.[c]

---

[a] Problem for legally blind individuals with some residual vision.
[b] Problem for all types of subjects.
[c] Problem for totally blind and for legally blind individuals with some residual vision.
[d] Problem for totally blind individuals

There were litter baskets in potential travel paths.[b]

There were newspapers and display racks in potential travel paths.[b]

There were poles and columns in potential travel paths.[b]

There were protruding telephone kiosks which did not project low enough to be detected by a cane.[c]

Requirement: The user must negotiate vertical movement.

Problems:

There were handrails that did not project beyond the top or bottom of stairs.[b]

There were cluttered and littered stairs.[c]

There were no clear visual or textural markings that indicated the top step, which in some cases was the sidewalk.[a]

There were breaks in handrails at landings, which caused confusion when staircases changed direction at landings.[b]

Requirement: The user must identify the correct train.

Problems:

There were no train announcements of destination in the station.[b]

There were trains that sat silently in the station, and they could not be recognized until their doors closed.[d]

Requirement: The user must observe and approach the train door area and enter the vehicle.

Problems:

There were open spaces between cars on trains which were mistaken for doors.[c]

The gap between the platform and train could cause one to stumble.[b]

[a] Problem for legally blind individuals with some residual vision.
[b] Problem for all types of subjects.
[c] Problem for totally blind and for legally blind individuals with some residual vision.
[d] Problem for totally blind individuals

SOURCE: Material from "Visually Handicapped Travelers in the Rapid Rail Transit Environment" by R. M. Jackson, A. F. Peck, and B. L. Bentzen, *Journal of Visual Impairment and Blindness*, Vol. 77, no. 10 © 1983 by American Foundation for the Blind Inc. and reproduced by kind permission of American Foundation for the Blind, 15 West 16th Street, New York, NY 10011.

social environment or becomes independent depends greatly on mobility skills. Visually impaired individuals have four general methods available to aid them in mobility: (1) human guides, (2) guide dogs, (3) the long cane, and (4) electronic devices.

Human Guides

The human guide undoubtedly enables the visually disabled person to have the greatest freedom in moving about safely, but this arrangement is not practical in most cases. Furthermore, too much reliance on another person causes a dependency that can be harmful.

Most blind people who travel unaccompanied do not need help from those around them. However, if we see a blind individual who looks like he or she needs assistance, we should first ask if help is wanted. It might be that only verbal directions are needed. If physical guidance is required, we should allow the blind person to hold onto our arm above the elbow and walk a half-step behind us. Sighted people have a tendency to want to grasp the arm of blind individuals and "push" them in the direction they are heading.

Guide Dogs

Contrary to popular notions, a guide dog is also not recommended very often. Extensive training is required to teach the visually impaired person how to use a guide dog properly. This extended training, as well as the fact that guide dogs are large and walk fast, make them particularly inappropriate for children. In addition, like any pet, they must be cared for. Another disadvantage—again, contrary to what most people think—is that a dog does not "take" the blind person anywhere. The blind person must first know where he or she is going; the dog is primarily a safeguard against walking into dangerous areas.

The Long Cane

Professionals most often recommend the long cane for those visually impaired individuals in need of a mobility aid. The visually impaired traveler sweeps the **long cane** in an arc, lightly touching the ground in front. Although it does not provide very good protection to the upper part of the body, the long cane has many other advantages:

> The long cane is the most effective and efficient mobility aid yet devised for safe, independent travel by the majority of visually impaired people. The scanning system in which the user operates the cane supplies echo-ranging cues and force-impact data that give vital information about immediate environment. It informs the traveler about the nature and condition of the surface underfoot, gives sufficient forewarning of downsteps or dropoffs to prevent falls or injury, and protects the lower part of the body from collision. The cane informs the user about various ground-surface textures which can be related to specific areas and destinations. It is a highly maneuverable aid that allows investigation of the environment without actual hand contact. The long cane is reliable, long lasting, and somewhat unaffected by unfavorable weather and temperature conditions. Most require no accessories, and virtually no maintenance except occasional replacement of a worn tip. The cane can be accommodated to most users' physical specifications and, in some instances, their disabilities. (Farmer, 1980, p. 359)

Although the long cane looks like a simple device, scientists, mobility specialists, and others working under the auspices of the National Academy of Sciences have drawn up specifications for its construction. In addition, although watching a skilled user of the long cane may give the impression that it is easy to manipulate, blind individuals usually require extensive training in its proper use.

Electronic Devices

Researchers have developed a number of sophisticated electronic devices for sensing of objects in the environment. Many of them are still experimental; most are quite expensive. Representative examples are the Laser cane and the Sonicguide. These devices operate on the principle that human beings, like bats, can learn to locate objects by means of echoes.

The **Laser cane** has the advantage of being used in the same way as the long cane or as a sensing device that emits three beams of infrared light (one up, one down, and one straight ahead), which are converted into sound after they strike objects in the path of the blind traveler. Farmer (1975) gives the following interesting description of a method of "navigating" under the difficult conditions presented by snowy weather. Although it is obvious that the narrator is an accomplished

The long cane has proved to be the most useful travel aid for most blind people. (Peter Glass/ Monkmeyer Press)

traveler, note the degree of complexity and precision needed to use the device properly.

> The following is from a taped interview with a Laser cane user: "The element in travel that requires probably the most understanding by the traveler is when there is a great deal of snow on the ground and you don't have any well-defined shoreline. The ability to utilize the long cane technique will get you from point A to point B, but you're not going to be able to know when to make your right-angle turn into your particular house. Now, in my situation, where there are two rows of townhouses facing each other with roughly 40 to 45 feet in between the two rows of houses, this would normally pose a tremendous problem in picking out the right house— that's assuming that . . . you don't count steps—that's a cop-out! Under these circumstances, you've got the Laser Cane and every other home has a gas lamp set back seven or eight feet from what would be a sidewalk if it weren't covered with snow. So it is admissible to find your way (and I do) from one lamp post to the next with the laser beam and obviously when I get to the third lamp post, that's mine.
>
> "Now the spindle or shaft on the lamp post is very thin, so it's possible under cold conditions to miss feeling the tactile stimulation that those narrow spindles present— and I've done this. When I come to the end of the road, there are ten shallow down stairs to a lower level. I've worked my way through this snow field clear to the end, on occasions, and missed every confounded lamp post and, after I didn't know what post I was processing, the sensible thing to do was to go all the way to the end and then work my way back; because when you're at the steps, you're oriented, you know exactly where you are and I have a landmark that I can trust. Now I work my way back using the only clues I have, the three lamp posts, and again the third one is mine.
>
> "What I've learned to do is to find a reference of seven feet on each side, then I know I'm in the middle of the sidewalk. If I've been lucky and it's freshly fallen snow, there is about an inch or two of slope down from the grass to where the sidewalk is because the grass will accumulate snow and hold it that much quicker than the sidewalk. The sidewalk takes about one to one-and-a-half inches of snowfall to cool down to the temperature to accumulate. Then it takes a hell of a lot of fine cane touching the snow to follow that shoreline. But with a combination of that and the Laser Cane reaching out to the lamp post, you're OK!" (From L. W. Farmer, "Travel in Adverse Weather Using Electronic Mobility Guidance Devices," *New Outlook for the Blind, 69,* (1975), 439–451. American Foundation for the Blind)

A number of researchers have worked on the development of the **Sonicguide,** and devices closely related to it, with visually impaired individuals ranging in age from infancy to adulthood (Bower, 1977; Kay, 1973; Strelow & Boys, 1979). Figure 8.6 shows the device being used with a seven-month-old infant who has been blind from birth. Although still very much in the experimental stages, this ultrasonic aid may eventually help blind infants gain awareness of their spatial environment and objects within it. The device, worn on the head, emits ultrasound and converts reflections from objects into audible sound. Depending on characteristics of the sound, such as its pitch and clarity, and its direction, the Sonicguide wearer can learn about such things as the distance, texture, and direction of objects in the environment.

Because the Sonicguide is still experimental, there are a number of unresolved issues relating to its use. With the infant model, for example, there is controversy over the optimum age at which infants should begin using it (Aitkin & Bower, 1982; Ferrell, 1980; Harris, Humphrey, Muir, & Dodwell, 1985; Sampaio, 1989; Strelow, 1983). Some believe the benefits of the device diminish substantially if it

Figure 8.6 **A blind baby, with the help of an ultrasonic device worn on the head, learns to locate an object held by an adult.** (Rick Gemel)

is introduced after the age of one year. Others believe that introducing the Sonicguide at too early an age may be a waste of time because young infants may not be developmentally ready for its use.

Another issue is whether devices like the Sonicguide might delay language development. Some have speculated that intensive exposure to the sound from the aid might interfere with perception of speech sounds. These are all issues that further research needs to address.

In considering electronic mobility devices, a word of caution is in order. Because of their amazing technology, it is easy to become too optimistic about these devices. There are at least five things to keep in mind in this regard. Electronic devices are:

1. Still experimental; we need to know a lot more about them.
2. Still very expensive; they are not available to everyone.
3. Not a substitute for more conventional techniques such as the long cane (except in the case of the Laser cane, which can be used like a long cane).
4. Not easily used; they require extensive training.
5. Not a substitute for spatial concepts (D. H. Warren, personal communication, 1989); the blind person needs a fundamental sense of his or her spatial environment.

The final point may be the most critical. Detection of obstacles may be necessary but not sufficient for good mobility. Electronic devices may aid in the perception of objects, but the blind person must use the perceptual information gained to form spatial concepts, or cognitive maps, of his or her environment.

How the child with visual impairment responds to mobility training depends to a great extent on attitude and previous learning experiences. Simply fitting a blind child with an appropriate mobility aid is not the answer. Training the child to develop orientation and mobility skills requires not only patience and specific teaching techniques but an insight into the personality of the individual child as well.

Technological and Special Aids

In recent years a technological explosion has resulted in new electronic devices for the use of visually impaired individuals (see the box below). Among the first of these was the **Optacon.** The user of this device passes a hand-held scanner over printed material with one hand, and the visual letters are converted by pins into tactile letters on the index finger of the other hand. There is also an Optacon II available that the blind person can use to scan computer screens (Brody, 1989). In addition to portability, a major advantage of the Optacon and Optacon II is that they make accessible many different kinds of materials, like magazines, newspapers, and computer screens. Major disadvantages are their expense, and the slow rate of reading they allow.

Another innovation, the **Kurzweil Reading Machine,** has an advantage over the Optacon in allowing a reading rate as fast as human speech. This small computer converts print into synthesized speech. The material is placed face down on a scanner and is "read" by an electronic voice. Expense (a unit costs about $50,000) has limited purchase of the Kurzweil Reading Machine to libraries and institutions. However, in the late 1980s the much smaller Kurzweil Personal Reader, selling for under $10,000, was introduced (Brody, 1989).

For those who still wish to use Braille as a medium for instruction, **VersaBraille** saves time and space. The blind person records Braille onto tape cassettes and plays them back on the machine's reading board. A big advantage over traditional Braille is that the recorded material takes up much less space. There is also a VersaBraille II Plus, which can be used to convert letters on a personal computer screen into Braille.

The PC is My Lifeline

Imagine yourself blindfolded with your ears plugged. No light, no sound. That's what it means to be deaf and blind. How would you be able to use a PC? Read the manuals that come with dBASE IV? Communicate with others? Hold a full-time job as a computer professional?

It's all possible.

I was born deaf and sighted and gradually lost my vision. Adaptive devices did not exist when I enrolled as a student at New York University, so I depended on my usable sight to complete the required reading; I received my bachelor's degree summa cum laude with a major in mathematics. When I was doing graduate work in statistics at NYU, I began using a VTEK magnification system, which I continued to use in my work as a computer programmer. The system enlarges printed material and displays it on a TV-like monitor.

Since then, my vision has deteriorated, and I use other devices in my work and in my life. I have worked for several high-tech companies and am currently a senior programmer/analyst at Wang Laboratories in Lowell, Massachusetts. I work as a telecommuter from home and make weekly trips to the office. Though I still rely on fingerspelling for face-to-face conversations, I use a variety of devices in my work.

Optacon gives me immediate and independent access to printed material—computer manuals, books, and magazines. It uses a handheld scanner to reproduce characters, symbols, and even simple graphic images on a bed of vibrating pins that I feel with my index finger, one character at a time.

With VersaBraille II Plus, I can operate the AT-compatible Wang PC280 that I use at home. A portable braille terminal that can stand alone or connect to a PC or mainframe, it provides a 20-character braille display, or window, of what is on the screen. Special software enables me to navigate a 25-line-by-80-character PC screen.

These devices allow me to use off-the-shelf MS-DOS software such as WordPerfect, Lotus 1-2-3, dBASE III Plus and dBASE IV, ProComm, and PC programming language compilers.

I write software and documentation on the PC in languages such as COBOL, C, and dBASE III Plus using a regular text editor (KEdit from Mansfield Software Group). I compile, test, and debug the programs on the PC. When I'm working on mainframe programs, I use a high-speed modem and a terminal emulator to turn the PC into a workstation that runs off the Wang mainframe in Lowell, several miles away. In this mode, my VersaBraille helps me navigate the mainframe menus and get access to the company's electronic mail system, Wang Office. Through electronic mail, I also discuss technical issues and exchange information with my colleagues.

But the PC is more than a professional device for me. With the PC, I can hold telephone communications with anyone else who has a PC and modem. I have met many people through nationwide computer services like Delphi and CompuServe. On Delphi, I participate in computer conferences several times a week, chat with other computer enthusiasts around the country, and use electronic mail to keep in touch with them at other times. I also get news and weather reports online and occasionally play games; my favorite is a word game called Scramble. Because my disabilities are not visible to other users online, they have been surprised, on the rare occasions when I mention it, to find out that I am deaf and blind.

Adaptive device technology is at a point now where it can help disabled people like myself to live constructive and productive lives. However, these sophisticated devices must keep up with changes in PC technology. Most devices work only on MS-DOS-based systems and do not address operating systems such as Unix and OS/2. Not all special software can tell the user where highlighted words appear on the screen; the PC community must consider putting graphics into a format accessible to those who can't see the screen. And the equipment must be made affordable.

But with all that remains to be done, the technology is helping people. Without the PC and adaptive devices, my life would be much more lonely and solitary. I could not read all the books I want to read, and I probably wouldn't be working in a field that interests me. I would have far fewer opportunities to communicate and joke with others. Optacon, VersaBraille, and the PC have enhanced my life professionally, socially, and intellectually.

—Barbara Wegreich

Barbara Wegreich is a senior programmer and analyst at Wang Laboratories.

SOURCE: H. Brody, "The Great Equalizer: PCs Empower the Disabled," *PC Computing*, July 1989, p. 87.

Equipped with closed circuit television systems, some classrooms can present material more effectively to low vision students (Genensky, Petersen, Clewett, & Yoshimura, 1978). With TV cameras and monitors at both the student's and the teacher's desks, the two can keep in constant visual contact. In this way, for example, the pupil can see an enlarged image of what the teacher is writing on the chalkboard.

A variety of other special aids is available for mathematics instruction, for example, talking calculators (Melrose & Goodrich, 1984). These devices "talk" to users by "saying" the numbers as they are punched and then "saying" the answer. Less exotic are tactually oriented procedures that have been used for years for sighted people. The **Cranmer abacus,** an adaptation of the Japanese abacus, is a small device consisting of beads that can be manipulated for math computations. Struve, Cheney, and Rudd (1980) advocate **Chisanbop,** a Korean method of using the fingers for calculating.

Administrative Arrangements

There are four major alternative educational placements for the visually impaired child: residential school, special class, resource room, and itinerant teacher. Variations of these arrangements exist, but these are the most common. The order of the list reflects the extent to which the child is integrated with regular classroom children. The residential facility is the most segregated and the itinerant teacher program the most integrated.

Most states operate residential institutions for visually impaired individuals. One advantage of these institutions is that given the very low prevalence of visually impaired children in the general population, they allow for the concentration of a number of specialized services in one place (Warren, 1981). Today, however, this kind of placement is much less popular than it once was. Whereas virtually all visually impaired children were educated in residential institutions in the early 1900s, now virtually all receive their education in public schools. Much of this shift away from residential placements took place after Public Law 94–142 was enacted in 1975; from 1971 to 1981, the visually impaired residential population dropped 16 percent, and the public school visually impaired population increased 105 percent (McIntire, 1985). Since the 1970s the trend has been not to place blind children in institutions unless they have additional limiting disabilities, such as mental retardation or deafness.

Also indicative of the prevailing philosophy of integrating exceptional with nondisabled children is the fact that many residential facilities have established cooperative arrangements with public schools (McIntire, 1985; Stewart, Van Hasselt, Simon, & Thompson, 1985). The staff of the residential facility usually concentrates on training independent living skills such as mobility, personal grooming, and home management whereas the public school personnel emphasize academics.

The special class plan is still a relatively popular placement. Within this framework the child, who lives at home, spends all instructional time in one class, separated from other children in the school. Resource and itinerant teacher arrangements are gaining favor today, and more visually impaired children stay in the regular classroom for a portion of the day. In keeping with this trend, resource and itinerant teacher strategies are increasing. The itinerant teacher does not have a classroom; he or she travels from school to school, working with children and consulting with regular teachers. Given the low prevalence of visually impaired children, this concept is quite popular, particularly in sparsely populated areas.

EARLY INTERVENTION

For many years psychologists and educators considered the normally sighted infant as almost totally lacking in visual abilities during the first half year or so of life. We now know, however, that the young sighted infant is able to take in a great deal of information about the environment (Hetherington & Parke, 1986). This fact makes it easy to understand why the visually impaired infant, particularly the totally blind child, can be at a distinct disadvantage as immediately as the first few weeks after birth. Special educators recognize the need to begin intensive intervention as early as possible to help visually impaired babies begin to explore their environment.

Most authorities agree that it is extremely important to involve the parents of the visually impaired infant in early intervention efforts. With appropriate training, parents can become actively involved in working at home with their young children, helping them with fundamental skills such as mobility and feeding. Parents, too, sometimes need support in coping with their reactions to having a visually impaired child. It is sometimes difficult for parents to adjust to the birth of a blind infant. There is often an overwhelming sense of grief. Professionals working in early intervention programs for blind infants often recommend that initial efforts focus on helping parents cope with their own reactions to having a blind child (Fraiberg, 1975; Fraiberg, Smith, & Adelson, 1969; Maloney, 1981).

An area of particular importance in early intervention for visually impaired children is motor development (Dubose, 1976; Palazesi, 1986). Some totally blind infants are late to crawl, and some authorities have speculated that this is because they have not learned that there is something "out there" in their environment worth pursuing (Fraiberg, 1977). They may not be as motivated as sighted infants to explore their extended environment because they are more engaged in examining

Opportunities for exploration of the environment are crucial for the preschool blind child. (Karen Rosenthal/ Stock, Boston)

things that are in close proximity to their bodies. By about six months of age, the sighted child spontaneously reaches out to visually perceived objects. Without specific training, the totally blind infant may not reach out to things he or she hears until late in the first year. Parents can sometimes contribute to blind children's relative lack of exploration. Some parents, concerned for the safety of their blind children, are reluctant to allow them to investigate their surroundings. It is often difficult for them to assess the proper amount of caution.

Unfortunately, for many years professionals did not begin training motor development and mobility until visually impaired children were in the early elementary grades. Today, most authorities agree that mobility training should begin in preschool. Palazesi (1986) recommends that about twenty minutes be set aside every day for structured movement training. Some preschool programs teach precane mobility skills. Although preschoolers may not yet be able to handle a long cane, other devices can be useful (Bosbach, 1988). For example, one recommendation is an ordinary hula hoop. While walking, the child pushes the hula hoop on the ground in front of his or her body.

TRANSITION

Two closely related major areas are difficult for some visually impaired adolescents and adults—independence and employment. Most authorities agree that some of the blind person's major impediments to securing an appropriate job lie in the area of independent living.

Independent Living

Perhaps the single most important thing to keep in mind when working with visually impaired adolescents or adults is that it is often a constant struggle for them to develop and maintain a sense of independence. A common mistake is to assume that such an individual is helpless. This feeling may be rooted in our own experiences. When we enter a dark room for the first time, we feel defenseless, fearful. Visually impaired people, however, have had many opportunities to become accustomed to seeing little. They are not at the same disadvantage as sighted people who suddenly find themselves in a situation in which there is little or no visibility.

Many people think of blindness in terms of street beggars selling pencils, and they feel pity for someone in this position (Lowenfeld, 1973b), although there are those who claim that blind beggars are in reality very independent and have exceptionally strong personalities (Cutsforth, 1951; R. A. Scott, 1969). In *The Making of Blind Men*, Scott blames the dependency of blind people on the numerous organizations, agencies, and programs created to serve them. He claims that blind people become dependent on the agencies for services and employment because they are *taught* to play a dependent role by these agencies. Of course, organizations for blind individuals vary in the degree to which they foster dependency. Scott's criticism should be kept in mind, however, for there is a real danger that some of these agencies may unwittingly be working against the very goals they espouse for disabled people.

There is little doubt that the public, by sometimes treating blind people in a stereotypical and demeaning manner, can be at fault for the dependency exhibited by some of them. Ved Mehta, the accomplished Indian author and frequent contributor to *The New Yorker* magazine, has written several autobiographical books dealing with his adjustment to blindness and going to school in the United States (Mehta, 1982, 1984, 1985, 1989). In the book dealing with his adolescent years at the Arkansas School for the Blind, he talks about experiences that blind people typically have to face, experiences that undoubtedly can foster dependence:

> I decided that I didn't like going to coffee shops. I had generally eaten at a table, either with my family or with students and staff at a school, and eating alone at a counter filled me with sadness. Moreover, there were always incidents in the coffee shops that would leave me shaken. The waitresses would shout out the menu to me as if I were half deaf, and so attract the attention of everyone in the coffee shop. Even when they got to know me and treated me normally, I would have to contend with customers who didn't know me. I remember that once when I asked for my bill the waitress said, "A man already took care of it."

> "I insist on paying for myself."

> The waitress refused to accept the money. "The man done gone," she said to the coffee shop. "What does the kid want me to do—take money twice for the same ham sandwich? He should be thankful there are nice people to pay for him." I felt anything but thankful, however. I thought that I'd been an object of pity.

> I remember that another time Tom took me to a new coffee shop. The waitress, instead of asking me for my order, turned to him and asked, "What does he want to eat?"

> "A ham sandwich," I said, speaking up for myself. She brought me the ham sandwich, but throughout lunch she ignored me, talking to Tom as if I weren't there. (Mehta, 1985, pp. 198–199)

Rickelman and Blaylock (1983) conducted a survey of blind persons in which, among other things, they were asked to indicate how sighted individuals might respond to them to decrease their dependent behavior. Following are their main suggestions:

1. *Respecting and encouraging the blind person's individuality, capabilities, and independence*: Do not assume that because you can do something more conveniently or quickly you should automatically do it for the blind person.

   Blind people often do not need help. Ask, "Can I be of assistance?" instead of initiating help. Do not feel embarrassed or rejected if a blind person declines your offer of assistance.

   Avoid being oversolicitous or overly protective. Blind people have the right to make mistakes, too.

   The qualities and characteristics of the blind are as individual as the sighted. Respect this individuality.

2. *Talking with the blind*: Feel free to approach and talk to a blind person. You have the right to ask any questions you wish. The blind person has the right to respond as he wishes.

   Identify yourself before beginning a conversation or offering assistance.

   Approach a blind person without embarrassment, fear, or pity.

   If you are uncomfortable being around or associating with a blind person, admit it openly to the person. Neither the sighted nor the blind profit from avoiding each other.

When you leave the presence of a blind person, always let him or her know that you are leaving.

Talk in a normal tone of voice. Do not assume deafness or other disability.

If your business is with a blind person, speak directly to the person rather than to sighted companions or relatives to get information.

3. *Becoming knowledgeable about guide techniques*: Let the blind person take your arm and walk slightly behind you. Never take his or her arm and push the blind person ahead of you. Walk at a normal pace.

Always go through a door ahead of a blind person, telling him or her which way the door opens.

4. *Miscellaneous*: If you work in security at an airport, realize that the canes many blind people use are made of fiberglass and will not set off the metal detector.

If you work with blind people in a dentist's or physician's office, always orient them to the waiting, examining, or treatment room. Explain what is expected of them and the steps of any procedures to be done.*

Although there may be disagreement among professionals about who exactly is to blame for the dependency of some visually impaired people, there is little disagreement that they present special problems for the teaching of daily living skills. It is extremely important that people with visual impairment, especially by adolescence, develop the independent living skills taken for granted by sighted people. Many things that sighted people learn incidentally we need to teach explicitly to visually impaired individuals, for example, how to work household appliances, eat at a table, or prepare food for cooking. In addition, visually impaired adolescents often lag behind their sighted peers in obtaining accurate sex information (Welbourne, Lifschitz, Selvin, & Green, 1983). Because the usual way in which we gain information about sex is through the sense of sight, the visually impaired person can be at a distinct disadvantage. The topic of how best to teach human sexuality (e.g., whether it should be done in the home or school) is a hotly debated issue. There is little doubt, however, that teaching sexual information to visually impaired individuals presents special challenges.

Employment

Many working-age blind adults are unemployed, and those who are working are often overqualified for the jobs they hold (Pfouts & Nixon, 1982). Most authorities agree that school personnel need to take an active role in helping visually impaired students develop appropriate career aspirations and job performance skills (Graves & Lyon, 1985). Many professionals also believe that although the emphasis on such preparation should be strongest in secondary school, it should begin in elementary school.

Authorities now also recognize that job training is more likely to succeed if it takes place in regular work settings rather than in simulated settings in the classroom (Gaylord-Ross, Forte, & Gaylord-Ross, 1986; Storey, Sacks, & Olmstead, 1985; Wink-

---

* B. L. Rickelman and J. N. Blaylock, "Behaviors of Sighted Individuals Perceived by Blind Persons as Hindrances to Self-reliance in Blind Persons," *Journal of Visual Impairment and Blindness*, Vol. 77, No. 1. © 1983 by the American Foundations for the Blind, Inc. and reproduced by the kind permission of the American Foundation for the Blind, 15 West 16th Street, New York, NY 10011.

ley, 1985). The advantages of community-based instruction are described by Storey, Sacks, and Olmstead, (1985, p. 481):

> The transfer of skills from a simulated environment (classroom) to an actual work environment (assembly line, clerical, or technical), for visually impaired students, might create . . . difficulties. For example, conditions such as industrial lighting and sound, physical obstacles, and social interactions with normally sighted adult co-workers cannot be simulated in a classroom environment. The community classroom model allows students to participate in real work settings with the supervision of a special education instructor. The purpose of the training is not only to teach specific job tasks but to give students a variety of real work experiences. In doing so, the students will be better prepared to make career decisions as adults. In addition, such an approach gives students the opportunity to develop generic work behaviors (i.e., punctuality, grooming, following directions, social skills) which will carry over to other work or community environments.

Although not as frequent as we would like to see, reports of blind individuals achieving successful independent living and employment are becoming more and more common. There is no doubt that visual impairment poses a real challenge for adjustment to everyday living, but we need to remember Don's comments in the introduction to this chapter (see p. 301). People with visual impairment share many similarities with the rest of society. Attesting to these similarities are the results of a survey in which visually impaired teenagers mentioned concerns and interests very similar to their sighted peers (Tobin & Hill, 1988). Special and general educators need to achieve the delicate balance between providing special programming for visually impaired students and treating them in the same manner as they do the rest of their students.

SUGGESTIONS FOR TEACHING STUDENTS WITH VISUAL IMPAIRMENT IN GENERAL EDUCATION CLASSROOMS

What to Look for in School

Children whose vision is severely impaired are usually diagnosed before they enter school, whereas students who have less severe visual problems often are identified during vision screenings conducted in schools. These routine examinations, however, are not foolproof. For example, they often do not measure near-point vision. Consequently the problems of students who can read at a far distance but who cannot read materials that are near may not be detected. In addition, some students develop visual problems after the primary grades, when schools usually stop screening. Other students may have changes in vision as they spend more time reading and as the formats of reading materials become more dense and detailed. Teachers have many opportunities to observe students reading under a variety of conditions and to provide a record of their observations by noting symptoms of vision problems (see p. 307).

How to Gather Information

Once you have recorded your observations, discuss them with the school nurse or the person who conducts the vision screenings in your school, who may want to observe the student. Share your observations and those of the nurse with the student's parents.

Teaching Techniques to Try

Adaptation of Educational Materials

From reading the chapter you know that the primary educational difference between students with low vision and students who are blind is their ability to read print. Students who have low vision can read print, although they may use magnifying devices and require materials written in large print. Individuals who are blind, however, must be instructed by using materials written in Braille and aural methods, including records and audiotapes. Therefore, one of the modifications visually impaired students who are mainstreamed require is adaptation of instructional materials. Although the itinerant or resource teacher will prepare or provide instructional materials written in Braille, you may find that tape-recording instructional lessons, assignments, and tests saves time and reduces the need for planning far in advance. In addition, several organizations such as the Library of Congress and the American Printing House for the Blind provide audiotapes and records of a variety of textbooks and materials for pleasure reading. Other organizations such as Recording for the Blind also make a large selection of books available to severely visually impaired students and have readers who will record especially requested materials.

In addition to adapted printed materials, there are a variety of other aids that your visually impaired students may find useful in your classroom:*

A. Geography aids
   1. Braille atlases
   2. molded plastic relief maps
   3. relief globes
B. Mathematical aids
   1. abacus
   2. raised clockfaces
   3. geometric area and volume aids
   4. Braille rulers
   5. talking calculators
C. Writing aids
   1. raised-line checkbooks
   2. signature guides
D. Miscellaneous aids
   1. audible goal locators, used as a goal, base, or object locator or a warning device
   2. Braille or large-type answer sheets
   3. science measurement kits (including such items as thermometers, spring balances, gram weights)
   4. sports-field kit (includes raised drawings of various sports' playing fields or courts)
   5. simple machine kits (including working models of pulleys, levers, plane, wheel, and axle)

---

* Gearheart, Weishahn, & Gearheart (1988), pp. 164–165.

Although students with low vision can read print, they also require adaptations of educational materials. Harley and Lawrence (1984) recommend the following modifications:

Written Materials

- Use purple dittoes as little as possible and then only when there is a clear, sharp copy that has been typed in large print. Avoid handwritten dittoes.
- Use black ink on white paper or soft lead pencils and fiber-tipped, black ink pens on unglazed light and tinted paper, and use good quality typewritter ribbons to enhance the legibility of written materials.
- Arrange written materials on the page so that they are not crowded.
- Use only one side of the paper.
- Outline dim areas of materials with a felt-tip pen.
- Select materials with nongloss surfaces and high contrast.
- Write clearly in large print when preparing printed materials or when writing on the chalkboard.
- Keep chalkboards clean and write with white chalk to enhance the contrast.
- Arrange for your visually impaired students to sit in areas of high illumination when they are using duplicated materials.

Instructional Adaptations

Besides adapting educational materials you can make other modifications that will help your mainstreamed students. For example, alternating activities that require close eye work with those that are less visually demanding and permitting additional time for blind and low-vision students to complete reading assignments and to take tests will increase the likelihood of their success in your classroom (Harley & Lawrence, 1984). Using concrete materials and hands-on learning may improve instruction for visually impaired students, who often do not have the same background experiences as nondisabled students (Gearheart, Weishahn, & Gearheart, 1988). Repeat information you write on the chalkboard aloud and allow students to examine closely demonstrations you and other students present in class (Ashcroft & Zambone-Ashley, 1984).

Adaptations in the Classroom Environment

When students who are visually impaired first enter your class they will require orientation to the physical arrangement of the room, including the location of materials, desks, activity areas, the teacher's desk, and exits. You may orient your students more rapidly if you familiarize them with these features from one focal point, such as their desk (Ashcroft & Zambone-Ashley, 1980). Once students are oriented to the classroom, they should become familiar with the school and surrounding grounds, learning the location of the gym, library, restrooms, cafeteria, water fountains, and playground. Keep students informed of changes in and additions to the classroom or school arrangements. Although you should encourage them to move about without the aid of sighted guides, you may want to assign a guide for special events and activities that occur outside of the classroom such as fire drills and assemblies (Craig & Howard, 1981).

Appropriate seating in class can also improve your students' visual opportunities. Encouraging pupils who have low vision to change their seats whenever they need more or less light will eliminate many difficulties. Generally, it is advisable to seat them so that the light falls on the materials they are reading, that is, so that they are not working in their shadows or facing the light. Arranging for them to sit close to the chalkboard or screen is also important (Harley & Lawrence, 1984). Position yourself and students who are demonstrating or sharing information so that you are not directly in front of the windows or other bright light source to help all students see the presentation better.

As educators have pointed out, students with visual impairment deserve the same instruction in all content areas as their nondisabled classmates. However, they also deserve instruction in skill areas required to meet their specific needs, such as social, sensory-motor, independent, daily living, and orientation and mobility training (Curry & Hatlen, 1988). Although other professionals will conduct this training, you can play an important role by being aware of when your mainstreamed students will receive instruction outside of your class and by scheduling, whenever possible, new learning and special events when all students are in your room.

Helpful Resources

Catalogs of Appliances, Aids, Books

American Foundation for the Blind, 15 West Sixteenth Street, New York, NY 10011.

American Printing House for the Blind, Inc., 1839 Frankfort Avenue, Louisville, KY 40206.

Carroll Center for the Blind, 770 Centre Street, Newton, MA; (617) 969-6200.

The Communicator; (703) 766-3869.

Books and Records

Braille Book Bank of the National Braille Associates, 422 Clinton Avenue South, Rochester, NY 14620.

Braille Institute of America, 741 North Vermont Avenue, Los Angeles, CA 00029.

Library Reproduction Service, The Microfilm Company of California, Inc., 1977 South Los Angeles Street, Los Angeles, CA 90011.

National Braille Press, Inc.; (617) 266-6160.

Oakmont Visually Handicapped Workshop, Oakmont Adult Community, 6637 Oakmont Drive, Santa Rosa, CA 94505.

Recording for the Blind, Inc., 20 Roszel Road, Princeton, NJ 08540.

Regional Libraries of the Library of Congress.

Taping for the Blind, 3935 Essex Lane, Houston, TX 77027; (713) 622-2767.

Vision Foundation, 818 Mt. Alburn Street, Watertown, MA 02172; (617) 926-4232.

Toys and Games

Touch toys and how to make them: For information: Eleanor Timburg, 3519 Porter Street, N.W., Washington, DC 20016. To order: Touch Toys, P.O. Box 2224, Rockville, MD 20852.

Gallagher, P. (1978). *Educational games for visually handicapped children.* Denver: Love Publishing Company.

Services

Associated Services for the Blind, 919 Walnut Street, Philadelphia, PA 19107; (215) 627-0600.

Blind Service Association, 22 West Monroe, 11th Floor, Chicago, IL 60603; (312) 236-0808.

The Carroll Center for the Blind; (617) 969-6200.

Center for Technology in Human Disabilities, Johns Hopkins University; (301) 338-8273.

Directory of services for blind and visually impaired persons in the United States (23rd ed.). American Foundation for the Blind, 15 West Sixteenth Street, New York, NY 10011.

Guide Dog Foundation for the Blind, 371 East Jericho Turnpike, Smithtown, NY 11787; (516) 265-2121.

Guiding Eyes for the Blind, 611 Granite Springs Road, Yorktown Heights, NY 10598; (914) 245-4024.

National Braille Press, Inc.; (617) 266-6116.

New York Lighthouse Low Vision Service, 111 East Fifty-ninth Street, New York, NY 10022.

Visions, Services for the Blind and Visually Impaired, 817 Broadway, 11th Floor, New York, NY 10003; (212) 477-3800.

Instructional Methods

Aiello, B. (1981). *The visually handicapped child in the regular class*, Washington, DC: Teachers Network for Education of the Handicapped.

Couvillon, L. A., & Tait, P. E. (1982). A sensory experience model for teaching measurement. *Journal of Visual Impairment and Blindness, 76,* 262–268.

Hoops, H. (1981). Tips for environmental education: Working with special audiences. *Nature-Study, 34,* 14–15.

Maron, S. S., & Martinez, D. H. (1980). Environmental alternatives for the visually handicapped. In J. W. Schifani, R. M. Anderson, & S. J. Odle (Eds.), *Implementing learning in the least restrictive environment* (pp. 149–198). Baltimore, MD: University Park Press.

Shallow, R. M., & Conner, A. (1982). Aural reading. In S. S. Mangold (Ed.), *A teacher's guide to the special educational needs of blind and visually impaired children.* New York: American Foundation for the Blind.

Scott, E. P. (1982). *Your visually impaired student: A guide for teachers.* Baltimore, MD: University Park Press.

Literature About Individuals with Visual Impairment

ELEMENTARY (AGES 5–8 AND 9–12)

Aiello, B. (1988). *Business is looking up.* Frederick, MD: Twenty-first Century Books. (juvenile)

Carrick, M. (1979). *"I'll get you!"* New York: Harper & Row. (ages 9–12)

Christian, M. B. (1986). *Mystery at Camp Triumph.* Niles, Il: Whitman. (juvenile)

Clifford, E. (1987). *The man who sang in the dark.* Boston: Houghton Mifflin. (juvenile)

Fine, A. (1978). *The summer-house lion.* New York: Crowell. (ages 5–7)

First, J. (1985). *The absolute, ultimate end.* New York: Watts. (ages 9–12)

Fort, P. (1988). *Redbird,* New York: Orchard Books.

Hall, L. (1988). *Murder at the spaniel show.* New York: Scribner's. (ages 9–12)

Herman, H. (1986). *Jenny's magic wand.* New York: Watts. (juvenile)

Holland, I. (1989). *The unfrightened dark.* Boston: Little, Brown. (ages 9–12)

Leggett, L. R., & Andrews, L. G. (1979). *The rose-colored glasses: Melanie adjusts to poor vision.* New York: Human Sciences. (ages 9–12)

Loreto, J. M. (1986). *A song for Susan.* Surry, ME: Special Children's Friends. (juvenile)

MacLochlan, P. (1980). *Through grandpa's eyes.* New York: Harper & Row. (ages 5–8)

Martin, B., & Archambault, J. (1987). *Knots on a counting rope.* New York: Holt, Rinehart & Winston. (juvenile)

Milton, H. (1980). *Blind flight.* New York: Watts. (ages 9–12)

Paterson, K. (1978). *The great Gilly Hopkins.* New York: Crowell. (ages 9–12)

Rounds, G. (1989). *The blind colt.* New York: Holiday House. (ages 9–12)

Thomas, W. E. (1980). *The new boy is blind.* New York: Julian Messner. (ages 9–12)

Yeatman, L. (1988). *Perkins: The cat who was more than a friend.* New York: Barron.

ADOLESCENT AND ADULT

Mark, J. (1979). *Divide and rule.* New York: Crowell. (ages 16–18)

Ure, J. (1985). *After Thursday.* New York: Delacourt Press. (ages 13–15)

Computer Software

Keyboarding for the Visually Limited, Educational Electronic Techniques, LTD., 1088 Wantagh Avenue, Wantagh, NY 11793; (800) 433-8872.

Keys to Success: Computer Keyboard Skills for Blind Children, Life Science Associates, 1 Fenimore Road, Bayport, NY 11705; (516) 472-2111.

MECC Software adapted for blind students, American Printing House for the Blind, 1839 Frankfort Avenue, Louisville KY 40206; (502) 895-2405.

Pix Cells, Raised Dot Computing, Inc., 408 South Baldwin Street, Madison, WI 53703; (605) 257-9595.

Speaking Speller, American Printing House for the Blind, P.O. Box 6085, Louisville, KY 40206; (502) 895-2405.

Word Processing Programs

Dr. Peet's Talkwriter, Hartley Courseware, Inc., P.O. Box 431, Dimondale, MI 48821; (517) 646-6458 or (800) 247-1380.

Talking Keys, Lehigh Valley Easter Seal Society, 2200 Industrial Drive, Bethlehem, PA 18017-2198; (212) 866-8092.

TEXTWRITER, AccessUnlimited-SPEECH Enterprises, 9039 Katy Freeway, Suite 414, Houston, TX 77024; (713) 461-0006.

Organizations

American Council of the Blind, 1010 Vermont Avenue, N.W., Suite 1100, Washington, DC 20005; (202) 393-3666.

American Foundation for the Blind, 15 West Sixteenth Street, New York, NY 10011.

Association for Education and Rehabilitation of the Blind and Visually Impaired, 206 North Washington Street, Alexandria, VA 22314.

Division for the Visually Handicapped, Council for Exceptional Children, 1920 Association Drive, Reston, VA 22091; (703) 620-3660.

National Federation of the Blind, 1800 Johnson Street, Baltimore, MD 211230.

Bibliography for Teaching Suggestions

Ashcroft, S. C., & Zambone-Ashley, A. M. (1980). Mainstreaming children with visual impairments. *Journal of Research and Development in Education, 13,* 22–35.

Craig, R., & Howard, C. (1981). Visual impairment. In M. L. Hardman, M. W. Egan, & D. Landau (Eds.), *What will we do in the morning?* (pp. 180–209). Dubuque, IA: William C. Brown.

Curry, S. A., & Hatlen, P. H. (1988). Meeting the unique educational needs of visually impaired pupils through appropriate placement. *Journal of Visual Impairment and Blindness, 82,* 417–424.

Gearheart, B. R., Weishahn, M. W., & Gearheart, C. J. (1988). *The exceptional student in the regular classroom* (4th ed.). Columbus, OH: Chas. E. Merrill.

Harley, R. K., & Lawrence G. A. (1984). *Visual impairment in the schools* (2nd ed.). Springfield, Il: Chas. C Thomas.

Scott, E. P. (1982). *Your visually impaired student: A guide for teachers.* Baltimore, MD: University Park Press.

SUMMARY

There are two definitions of visual impairment—the legal and the educational. The legal definition depends on the measurement of visual acuity and field of vision. A legally blind person has visual acuity of 20/200 or less in the better eye, even with correction, or has a very narrow (less than 20 degrees) field of vision. Partially sighted individuals have visual acuity between 20/70 and 20/200 in the better eye with correction. Educators, however, prefer to define blindness according to how well the person functions, especially in reading. For the educator, blind individuals are those who need to read by Braille or aural methods. Those who can read print, even though they may need magnifying devices or books with large print, are considered to have low vision.

The majority of those who are legally blind have some vision. It is important to know that many legally blind students are not educationally blind because they can read print (whether large print or magnified regular print).

Blindness is one of the least prevalent disabling conditions in childhood but is much more prevalent in adults.

The Snellen chart, consisting of rows of letters or of *E*s arranged in different positions, is used to measure visual acuity for far distances. There are also special charts for measuring visual acuity for near distances. Barraga's Diagnostic Assessment Procedure measures visual efficiency, for example, control of eye movements and ability to pay attention to visual details.

Most visual problems are the result of errors of refraction: Because of faulty structure and/or malfunction of the eye, the light rays do not focus on the retina. The most common visual impairments are myopia (nearsightedness), hyperopia (farsightedness), and astigmatism (blurred vision). Eyeglasses or contact lenses can usually correct these problems. More serious impairments include glaucoma, cataracts, diabetic retinopathy, coloboma, retinitis pigmentosa, retinopathy of prematurity, strabismus, and nystagmus. Most serious visual impairments in school-age students are due to hereditary factors.

Most authorities believe that visual impairment may result in a few subtle language differences but not in deficient language skills. Also, most investigators believe that blindness does not result in intellectual retardation. There are some differences in conceptual development because visually impaired individuals rely more on touch than on vision to learn about their world. Sight more easily allows one to perceive objects or parts of an object simultaneously; touch, on the other hand, results in successive perception of most objects and requires more conscious effort. Research has shown that early training in the use of strategies helps blind children use their touch more efficiently.

Many scientists believe that the most important ability for successful adjustment of visually impaired people is mobility. There is not a one-to-one relationship between the age at onset or the degree of impairment and mobility skills. Mobility is greatly affected by motivation, attitude, and learning experiences. The mobility of visually impaired people largely depends on their spatial ability. Those who conceptualize their environment as a cognitive map have better mobility skills than those who process their environment in a sequential way.

Blind people do not, as is commonly thought, have an inherent obstacle sense. They can develop it, however, provided they possess the vital mode of hearing. Another myth about blind people is that they *automatically* develop better acuity in other senses. What they actually do is become adept at picking up other sensory cues in their surroundings, thus making better use of their intact senses.

Methods of testing academic achievement of visually impaired students differ substantially from those used in testing sighted students. Evidence suggests that low vision and blind students are behind their sighted peers in achievement.

Personality problems are not an inherent condition of visual impairment. Any social adjustment problems a blind individual may have are primarily the result of society's reaction to the blind. The stereotypies (e.g., repetitive rocking) exhibited by a few blind individuals can be an impediment to social acceptance, but behavioral techniques can diminish their occurrence.

Educational experiences in regular classrooms are frequently visual. But with some modification in methods, teachers can apply the same general principles of instruction to both sighted and visually impaired students. Braille may be useful for those whose vision is so impaired that they cannot read even large type. More and more blind individuals are turning to audio tapes for their reading medium. The compressed-speech method, in particular, permits fast and efficient presentation of material. Also, there are a number of technological devices being developed for the visually impaired population; examples are the Optacon, the Kurzweil Reading Machine, and talking calculators.

Mobility training can involve the use of human guides, guide dogs, the long cane, and electronic devices such as the Sonicguide. Most mobility instructors recommend the long cane for the majority of blind people.

The four basic educational placements for visually impaired students are the residential school, special class, resource room, and itinerant teacher. More and more visually impaired students are in general education classrooms. Residential placement, at one time the most popular alternative, is now recommended infrequently. Residential institutions for blind individuals now have greater percentages than before of people who have other disabling conditions in addition to visual impairment. One trend is for integrated programming between residential and community-based facilities.

Without special attention, the visually impaired infant may lag behind the sighted infant in cognitive and motor development. Impaired vision may restrict the infant's interaction with the environment. Early intervention frequently focuses on parental interaction with the child and parental reaction to the child's disability.

Education for the adolescent and adult stresses independent living and employment skills. Independence is particularly difficult to achieve for some visually impaired individuals, but it is extremely important, especially for work adjustment, for them to be able to function independently. A contributing factor to dependency is society, which often mistakenly treats visually impaired people as helpless. Only about one-third of working-age blind adults are employed, and they are frequently overqualified for their jobs. Professionals are attempting to change this bleak employment picture with innovative approaches such as job training in regular work settings rather than simulated settings in classrooms.

MAIN STREET
Micky Doolittle, Courtesy Very Special Arts

9

Physical Disabilities

We thank you Lord, 'cause Freddie's walkin'
We thank you Lord, 'cause Freddie's walkin'
Freddie's wearin' a smile, and rightly so,
'cause now his feet know how to go
We thank you Lord, 'cause Freddie's walkin'

We thank you Lord, 'cause Freddie's walkin'
We thank you Lord, 'cause Freddie's walkin'
Freddie's steppin' out, holdin' his head up high,
with his pretty blue eyes lookin' toward the sky
Oh, thank the Lord, 'cause Freddie's walkin'.

(*Chuck Mangione, "Freddie's Walkin'"*)

*I*n Western culture people are almost obsessed with their bodies. They don't just want to be healthy and strong; they want to be beautiful— well formed and attractive to others. In fact, some people seem to be more concerned about the impression their bodies make than they are about their own well-being. They may even endanger their health in an effort to become more physically alluring. It is not really surprising, then, that those with physical disabilities must fight two battles—the battle to overcome the limitations imposed by their physical condition and the battle to be accepted by others.

Children with physical disabilities often face more than the problem of acceptance, however. For many, accomplishing the seemingly simple tasks of everyday living is a minor—or major—miracle. Learning to walk, for example, may call for special celebration, as Chuck Mangione's song indicates.

DEFINITION AND CLASSIFICATION

In this chapter we consider children whose primary distinguishing characteristics are nonsensory health or physical problems. For the purposes of this book, children with physical disabilities are defined as those whose nonsensory physical limitations or health problems interfere with school attendance or learning to such an extent that special services, training, equipment, materials, or facilities are required. Our definition excludes children whose *primary* characteristics are visual or auditory impairments, although some physically disabled children have these deficiencies as *secondary* problems. Children who have physical disabilities may also have mental retardation, learning disabilities, emotional disturbance, speech and language disorders, or special gifts or talents. Thus we consider in this chapter those children whose physical condition is the first and foremost concern but whose additional characteristics may be extremely varied. The child's physical condition is, of course, the proper concern of the medical profession—but when physical problems have obvious implications for education, teaching specialists must enter the scene.

The fact that the primary distinguishing characteristics of children with physical disabilities are medical conditions, health problems, or physical limitations highlights the necessity of interdisciplinary cooperation. There simply *must* be communication between physicians and special educators to maintain the child's health and at the same time develop whatever capabilities he or she has (see Verhaaren & Connor, 1981a).

There is a tremendous range and variety of physical disabilities. Children may have **congenital anomalies** (defects they are born with), or they may acquire disabilities through accident or disease after birth. Some physical disabilities are comparatively mild and transitory; others are profound and progressive, ending in total incapacitation and early death. So it is difficult to discuss physical disabilities in general. Most of the remainder of the chapter will be organized around specific conditions and diseases falling under one of several categories: neurological impairments, musculoskeletal conditions, congenital malformations, accidents and other conditions, and child abuse and neglect.

PREVALENCE AND NEED

The federal Department of Education for many years estimated that for special education purposes, approximately 0.5 percent of school-age children have physical disabilities. About half of the physically disabled population was assumed to have

MISCONCEPTIONS ABOUT PERSONS WITH PHYSICAL DISABILITIES

Myth	Fact
Cerebral palsy is a contagious disease.	Cerebral palsy is not a disease. It is a nonprogressive neurological injury. It is a disorder of muscle control and coordination caused by injury to the brain before or during birth or in early childhood.
Physical disabilities of all kinds are decreasing because of medical advances.	The number of children with severe disabilities is increasing because of new medical technology. The number of survivors of serious medical conditions who develop normally or have mild impairments such as hyperactivity and learning disabilities is also increasing.
The greatest educational problem involving children with physical disabilities is highly specialized instruction.	The greatest educational problem is teaching people without disabilities about what it is like to have a disability and how disabilities can be accommodated.
The more severely people are crippled, the less intelligence they have.	A person may be severely physically disabled by cerebral palsy or another condition but have a brilliant mind.
People with epilepsy are mentally ill.	People with epilepsy (seizure disorder) are not any more or less disposed to mental illness than those who do not have epilepsy.
Arthritis is found only in adults, particularly the elderly.	Arthritic conditions are found in people of any age, including young children.
People with physical disabilities have no need for sexual expression.	People with physical disabilities have sexual urges and need outlets for sexual expression.

cerebral palsy or another crippling condition; the other half was assumed to have chronic health problems or diseases of one sort or another that interfered with schooling. If the 0.5 percent prevalence estimate is correct, one would expect to find about 200,000 children with physical disabilities needing special education in the United States.

Figures from the U.S. Department of Education (1989) indicate that in the late 1980s about 150,000 students were being served under three special education categories related to physical disabilities: orthopedically handicapped (about 41,000), other health impaired (about 43,000), and multiply handicapped (about 63,000). The needs of many students with physical disabilities appear to be unmet for many reasons, including the fact that the population of children and youths with physical disabilities is growing but health programs are not.

An increase in certain physical disabilities during the past two decades has been reported (Batshaw & Perret, 1986). Part of this increase may be due to improvements in the identification of and medical services to children with certain conditions. Ironically, however, medical advances have not only improved the chances of preventing or curing certain diseases and disorders. They have also assured the survival of more children with severe medical problems. Many severely and profoundly handicapped children and those with severe, chronic illnesses who in the past would not have survived long today can have a normal life span. So declining mortality rates do not necessarily mean there will be fewer disabled individuals. And improvements in medical care may not lower the number of disabled individuals unless there is also a lowering of risk factors in the environment—factors such as accidents, toxic substances, poverty, malnutrition, disease, and interpersonal violence.

The needs of American children with chronic illnesses were highlighted in reports by Hobbs and his colleagues. Research indicates that 1 to 2 percent of the child population—that is, at least 1 million American children—suffer from *severe* chronic illnesses and "live out their lives in a twilight zone of public understanding" (Hobbs, Perrin, Ireys, Moynahan, & Shayne, 1984, p. 206). No doubt more children now suffer from such illnesses and lack of public understanding than a decade ago, in part because of cuts in social welfare programs during the 1980s (Baumeister, Kupstas, & Klindworth, 1990).

NEUROLOGICAL IMPAIRMENTS

One of the most common causes of physical disability in children is damage to or deterioration of the central nervous system—the brain or spinal cord. Damage to the brain may be so mild as to be undetectable as far as the child's functioning is concerned, or so profound as to reduce the child to a very low level of functioning. There may be focal brain damage (involving a very specific and delimited area, often with specific effects on the child's behavior) or diffuse brain damage (involving a large or poorly defined area, often with generalized behavioral effects).

A child with brain damage may show a wide variety of behavioral symptoms, including mental retardation, learning problems, perceptual problems, lack of coordination, distractibility, emotional disturbance, and speech and language disorders. (Of course, a child may show any of these behavioral manifestations and not have a damaged brain—see the discussion of brain damage and learning disabilities in Chapter 4.) Other symptoms that indicate brain damage or malfunction are impaired motor function, paralysis, and certain types of seizures.

Even though a person's brain may be intact and functioning properly, he or she may have neurological impairment because of damage to the spinal cord. Since nerve impulses are sent to and from the extremities by way of the spinal cord, damage to the cord may mean that the child will lose sensation, be unable to control movement, or be incapable of feeling or moving certain parts of the body.

Neurological impairments have many causes, including infectious diseases, hypoxia (oxygen depletion), poisoning, congenital malformations, and physical trauma because of accidents or abuse. Poliomyelitis (polio or infantile paralysis) is an example of an infectious disease that attacks the nerves in the spinal cord or brain and often causes paralysis. Spina bifida is an example of a congenital malformation of the spine usually resulting in paralysis. In many cases of brain damage it is impossible to identify the exact cause of the impairment. The important point is that *when children's nervous systems are damaged, no matter what the cause, muscular weakness or paralysis is almost always one of the symptoms.* And because these disabled children cannot move about like most children, their education typically requires special equipment, special procedures, or other accommodations for their disabilities. We turn now to some specific types of neurological impairments.

Neurological impairments such as cerebral palsy or seizure disorder, in which there is sometimes the danger of hard falls, may require special protective equipment, as the helmets these children are wearing. (J. W. Myers/ Uniphoto Picture Agency)

Cerebral Palsy

Cerebral palsy (CP) is not a disease in the usual sense of the word. It is not contagious, it is not progressive (except that improper treatment may lead to complications), and there are no remissions. Although it is often thought of as a motor problem associated with brain damage at birth, it is actually more complicated. Cerebral palsy can, for practical purposes, be considered part of a syndrome that includes motor dysfunction, psychological dysfunction, seizures, or behavior disorders due to brain damage. Some individuals show only one indication of brain damage, such as motor impairment; others may show combinations of symptoms. The usual definition of CP refers to a condition characterized by paralysis, weakness, incoordination, and/or other motor dysfunction because of damage to the child's brain before it has matured (Batshaw & Perret, 1986). Symptoms may be so mild that they are detected only with difficulty or so profound that the individual is almost completely incapacitated.

Causes

Anything that can cause brain damage during the brain's development can cause CP. Before birth, maternal infections, chronic diseases, physical trauma, or maternal exposure to toxic substances or X-rays, for example, may damage the brain of the fetus. During the birth process the brain may be injured, especially if labor or birth is difficult or complicated. Premature birth, hypoxia, high fever, infections, poisoning, hemorrhaging, and related factors may cause harm following birth. In short, anything that results in oxygen deprivation, poisoning, cerebral bleeding, or direct trauma to the brain can be a possible cause of CP. Although CP occurs at every social level, it is more often seen in children born to mothers in poor socioeconomic circumstances. Children of the poor have a greater risk of incurring brain damage because of such factors as malnutrition of the mother, poor prenatal and postnatal care, and environmental hazards during infancy (see Baumeister, Kupstas, & Klindworth, 1990).

Cases in which genetic (chromosomal) factors cause CP are rare. In some cases of genetically determined biochemical disorders associated with mental retardation, the child may show evidence of brain damage or CP. Although there are many possible causes of CP, the actual causes are often unknown. The cause can be identified in only about 60 percent of cases (Batshaw & Perret, 1986).

Types of Cerebral Palsy

It may seem reasonable to classify CP according to the time period during which brain damage occurred (prenatal, natal, or postnatal), but ordinarily it is impossible to pinpoint the exact time of the damage. Classification according to degree of involvement (severity) or the extent and nature of the damage to the brain has not been successful either because severity involves subjective judgments. Brain damage cannot be assessed precisely except by autopsy and recently developed technologies (Banker & Bruce-Gregorios, 1983). The two means of classification that have been most widely accepted specify the limbs involved and the type of motor disability.

Classification according to the extremities involved applies not just to CP but also to all types of motor disability or paralysis. The most common classifications and the approximate percentage of individuals with CP falling into each class may be summarized as follows:

- **Hemiplegia:** One-half (right or left side) of the body is involved (35 to 40 percent).
- **Diplegia:** Legs are involved to a greater extent than arms (10 to 20 percent).
- **Quadriplegia:** All four limbs are involved (15 to 20 percent).
- **Paraplegia:** Only the legs are involved (10 to 20 percent).

Classification according to type of brain damage and consequent type of motor disability includes *pyramidal*, *extrapyramidal*, and *mixed* types. These may be described as follows:

- **Pyramidal (spastic):** Individuals with this type have suffered damage to the motor cortex or to the pyramidal tract of the brain. This results in problems with voluntary movements and in spasticity—stiffness or tenseness of muscles and inaccurate voluntary movement. About 50 percent of cases show spasticity.
- **Extrapyramidal (choreoathetoid, rigid, and atonic):** Damage is outside the pyramidal tracts and results in abrupt, involuntary movements and difficulty maintaining posture (choreoathetoid), malleable rigidity or "lead pipe stiffness" (rigid), or floppy muscle tone (atonic). About 25 percent of cases show symptoms associated primarily with extrapyramidal damage.
- **Mixed:** Damage is to both pyramidal and extrapyramidal regions of the brain, and the child shows a mixture of effects (e.g., spasticity in the legs and rigidity in the arms). About 25 percent of cases are classified as mixed.

The regions of the brain that are damaged and the resulting paralysis for several types of CP are depicted in Figure 9.1. Emotional state and general activity level may affect a child's movements, the disorder becoming more apparent when the child is under stress and/or moving about than when he or she is at ease.

Although there is no "cure" for CP, advances in medical and rehabilitation technology offer increasing hope of overcoming disabilities imposed by neurological damage. Today, for example, intensive, long-term physical therapy in combination with a surgical procedure called selective posterior rhizotomy—in which the surgeon cuts selected nerve roots below the spinal cord that cause spasticity in the leg muscles—allow some children with spastic CP to better control certain muscles. Such treatment allows some nonambulatory children to walk and helps others to walk more normally (Dyar, 1988).

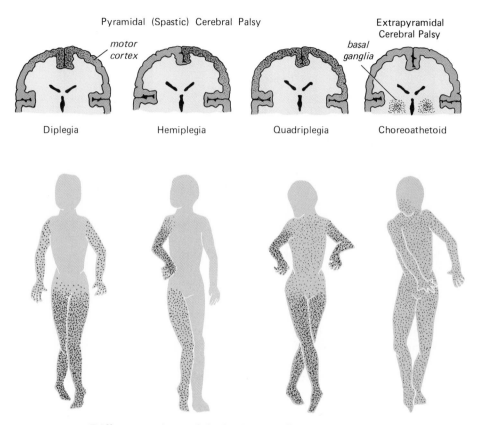

Pyramidal (Spastic) Cerebral Palsy

Extrapyramidal Cerebral Palsy

motor cortex

basal ganglia

Diplegia   Hemiplegia   Quadriplegia   Choreoathetoid

Figure 9.1 *Different regions of the brain are affected in various forms of cerebral palsy. The darker the shading, the more severe the involvement.*

SOURCE: M. L. Batshaw and Y. M. Perret, *Children with Handicaps: A Medical Primer*, 2nd ed. (Baltimore: Paul H. Brookes, 1986), p. 302.

Prevalence

The prevalence of CP is difficult to determine accurately. In the past a great deal of stigma was attached to the condition, and many parents hesitated to report their children's problems. Many cases occur among the poor and disadvantaged segment of the population and so may not be identified or receive medical treatment. In addition, prevalence estimates are confused by the many handicaps, such as mental retardation and emotional disorders, that can accompany CP. There are data indicating that CP occurs at a rate of approximately 1.5 per 1,000 live births— about 0.15 percent of the child population (Batshaw & Perret, 1986). A higher percentage of male than female and white than black children are affected.

Associated Disabilities and Educational Problems

Research during the past few decades has made it clear that CP is a developmental disability—a multihandicapping condition far more complex than a motor disability alone (Cruickshank, 1976; Batshaw & Perret, 1986). When the brain is damaged, sensory abilities, cognitive functions, and emotional responsiveness as well as motor performance are usually affected. A very high proportion of children with CP are found to have hearing impairments, visual impairments, perceptual disorders, speech

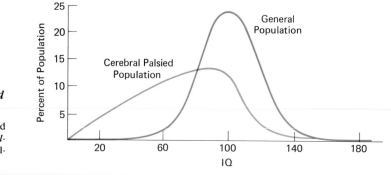

Figure 9.2 *Hypothetical curves showing distribution of IQs for general population and population with cerebral palsy.*

SOURCE: Data provided in T. W. Hopkins, H. V. Bice, and K. C. Colton, *Evaluation and Education of the Cerebral-palsied Child* (Arlington, VA: Council for Exceptional Children, 1954).

defects, behavior disorders, mental retardation, or some combination of several of these handicapping conditions in addition to motor disability. They may also exhibit such characteristics as drooling or facial contortions.

Some individuals with CP have normal or above-average intellectual capacity, and a few test within the gifted range. The *average* tested intelligence of children with CP, however, is clearly lower than the average for the general population (Batshaw & Perret, 1986). A comparison between the normal distribution of IQs and that for children with CP is shown in Figure 9.2. As Cruickshank and others point out, proper testing of these children requires a great deal of clinical sophistication since many intelligence tests or specific test items are inappropriate for children with multiple disabilities. Consequently, one must be cautious in interpreting test results for such children.

The educational problems of children who have CP are as multifaceted as their disabilities. Not only must special equipment and procedures be provided because the children have physical disabilities, but also the same special educational procedures and equipment required to teach children with vision, hearing, or speech and language disorders, learning disabilities, behavior disorders, or mental retardation are often needed. Careful and continuous educational assessment of the individual child's capabilities is particularly important. Teaching the child who has CP demands competence in many aspects of special education and experience in working with a variety of disabling conditions in a multidisciplinary setting (Verhaaren & Connor, 1981a, 1981b; Zadig, 1983).

Seizure Disorder (Epilepsy)

A person has a **seizure** when there is an abnormal discharge of electrical energy in certain brain cells. The discharge spreads to nearby cells, and the effect may be loss of consciousness, involuntary movements, or abnormal sensory phenomena. The effects of the seizure will depend on the location of the cells in which the discharge starts and how far the discharge spreads.

People with epilepsy have recurrent seizures. About 6 percent of the population will have a seizure at some time during life, but most of them will not be diagnosed as having epilepsy because they do not have repeated seizures (Batshaw & Perret, 1986).

Most seizures first occur before the individual is six years old or when he or she has reached old age; seizures are primarily a phenomenon of early childhood and old age (Hauser & Kurland, 1975). Seizures beginning before the age of two years are usually associated with developmental defects (Cavazzuti, Ferrari, & Lalla, 1984); those with onset after age twenty-five are usually a sign of organic brain disease. Seizures reflect abnormal brain activity, so it is not surprising that they occur more often in children with developmental disabilities (e.g., mental retardation or cerebral palsy) than in children without disabilities (Batshaw & Perret, 1986; Jacobs, 1983).

Causes

Seizures apparently can be caused by almost any kind of damage to the brain. The most common causes include lack of sufficient oxygen (hypoxia), low blood sugar (hypoglycemia), infections, and physical trauma. Certain conditions, like those named, tend to increase the chances that neurochemical reactions will be set off in brain cells (Batshaw & Perret, 1986). In many cases, the cause is unknown (Wolraich, 1984).

Types of Seizures

The International League Against Epilepsy suggests two major types of seizures: *generalized* and *partial*. A **generalized seizure** involves the discharge of cells in a large part of the brain; a **partial seizure** begins in a localized area, and only a small part of the brain is involved. Several subtypes of both generalized and partial seizures have been classified. The important point here is that seizures may take many forms. They may differ along at least the following dimensions:

- *Duration*: They may last only a few seconds or for several minutes.
- *Frequency*: They may occur as frequently as every few minutes or only about once a year.
- *Onset*: They may be set off by certain identifiable stimuli or be unrelated to the environment, and they may be totally unexpected or be preceded by certain internal sensations.
- *Movements*: They may cause major convulsive movements or only minor motor symptoms (e.g., eye blinks).
- *Causes*: They may be caused by a variety of conditions including high fever, poisoning, trauma, and other conditions mentioned previously; but in many cases the cause is unknown.
- *Associated disabilities*: They may be associated with other handicapping conditions or be unrelated to any other medical problem or disability.
- *Control*: They may be controlled completely by drugs, so that the individual has no more seizures, or only partially controlled.

Prevalence

Seizure disorders of all types (but not isolated seizures) occur in about 0.5 percent of the general population (Wolraich, 1984).

Educational Implications

About half of all children with seizure disorders have average or higher intelligence. Among those without mental retardation, however, one may expect to find a higher than usual incidence of learning disabilities (Batshaw & Perret, 1986). Although many children who have seizure disorders have other disabilities, some do not. Consequently, both general and special education teachers may be expected to encounter children who have seizures. Besides obtaining medical advice regarding

First Aid for Epileptic Seizures

A major epileptic seizure is often dramatic and frightening. It lasts only a few minutes, however, and does not require expert care. These simple procedures should be followed:
- REMAIN CALM. You cannot stop a seizure once it has started. Let the seizure run its course. Do not try to revive the child.
- If the child is upright, ease him to the floor and loosen his clothing.
- Try to prevent the child from striking his head or body against any hard, sharp, or hot objects; but do not otherwise interfere with his movement.
- Turn the child's face to the side so that saliva can flow out of his mouth.
- DO NOT INSERT ANYTHING BETWEEN THE CHILD'S TEETH.
- Do not be alarmed if the child seems to stop breathing momentarily.
- After the movements stop and the child is relaxed, allow him to sleep or rest if he wishes.
- It isn't generally necessary to call a doctor unless the attack is followed almost immediately by another seizure or the seizure lasts more than ten minutes.
- Notify the child's parents or guardians that a seizure has occurred.
- After a seizure, many people can carry on as before. If, after resting, the child seems groggy, confused, or weak, it may be a good idea to accompany him home.

Courtesy of Epilepsy Foundation of America.

management of the child's particular seizure disorder, teachers should know first aid for epileptic seizures (see the box above).

Seizures are primarily a medical problem and require primarily medical attention. Educators are called on to deal with the problem in the following ways: (1) General and special teachers need to help dispel ignorance, superstition, and prejudice toward people who have seizures and provide calm management for the occasional seizure the child may have at school. (2) Special education teachers who work with students with mental retardation or teach children with other developmental disabilities (especially institutionalized or severely and profoundly handicapped students) need to be prepared to manage children's seizures as well as to handle learning problems. The teacher should record the length of a child's seizure and the type of activity the child was engaged in before the seizure. This information will help physicians in diagnosis and treatment. If a student is being treated for a seizure disorder, the teacher should know the type of medication and its possible side effects.

Some children who do not have mental retardation but have seizures exhibit learning and behavior problems. Stores (1978) reported that learning and behavior problems associated with seizure disorders occur more often in boys than in girls and are most often seen in children who have persistent abnormal electrical discharges in the left temporal lobe of the brain. Learning and behavior problems may result from damage to the brain that causes other disabilities as well. The problems may also be the side effects of anticonvulsant medication or the result of mismanagement by parents and teachers. Teachers must be aware that seizures of any type may interfere with the child's attention or the continuity of education. Brief seizures may require the teacher to repeat instructions or allow the child extra time to respond. Frequent major convulsions may prevent even a bright child from achieving at the usual rate.

Research has shown that children with seizure disorders do have emotional and behavioral problems more often than most children (Freeman, Jacobs, Vining, & Rabin, 1984; Hoare, 1984). One must not, however, conclude that seizure disorders cause emotional and behavioral problems directly. The stress of having to deal with seizures, medications, and stigma, as well as adverse environmental conditions, is more likely to cause these problems. Moreover, Freeman and his research group have shown that the school adjustment of students with seizure disorders can be improved dramatically if they are properly assessed, placed, counseled, taught about seizures, and given appropriate work assignments.

Spina Bifida

During early fetal development the two halves of the embryo grow together or fuse at the midline. When the closure is incomplete, a congenital "midline defect" is the result. Cleft lip and cleft palate are examples of such midline defects (see Chapter 6). **Spina bifida** is a congenital midline defect resulting from failure of the bony spinal column to close completely during fetal development. The defect may occur anywhere from the head to the lower end of the spine. Because the spinal column is not closed, the spinal cord (nerve fibers) may protrude, resulting in damage to the nerves and paralysis and/or lack of function or sensation below the site of the defect. This is called a **myelomeningocele** (or **meningomyelocele**) (see Figure 9.3). A myelomeningocele is often accompanied by paralysis of the legs and of the anal and bladder sphincters because nerve impulses are not able to travel past the defect.

Surgery to close the spinal opening is performed in early infancy, but this does not repair the nerve damage. The mortality rate for children with spina bifida is being lowered, meaning that more severely impaired children are surviving and attending school (Korabek & Cuvo, 1986).

Cause and Prevalence

The cause of spina bifida is not known, although many factors are suspected (Batshaw & Perret, 1986). Prevalence is estimated at 0.1 percent, making it one of the most common birth defects causing physical disability.

Educational Implications

The extent of the paralysis resulting from myelomeningocele depends on the location of the spinal cord defect (how high or low on the spinal column it is). Some children will walk independently, some will need braces, and others will have to use a wheelchair. Some children will have acute medical problems, which may lead to repeated hospitalizations for surgery or treatment of infections. Among the other considerations for teachers are the following:

- Spina bifida is often accompanied by hydrocephalus, a condition in which there is excessive pressure of the cerebrospinal fluid, sometimes leading to an enlarged head or to attention disorders, learning disabilities, or mental retardation (see Chapter 3). Hydrocephalus is typically treated surgically by installing a shunt to drain the cerebrospinal fluid into a vein. Another possible complication of spina bifida is meningitis (bacterial infection of the linings of the brain or spinal cord).

- Damage to nerves along the spine may result in complications in which the child is likely to fracture bones in the lower extremities.

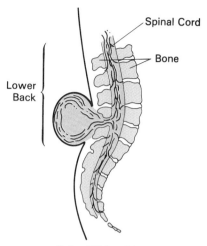

Spina Bifida with Meningomyelocele

Figure 9.3 *Spina bifida.*

SOURCE: *Spina Bifida: Hope Through Research*, PHS pub. no. 1023, Health Information Series No. 103, 1970.

Neurological or musculoskeletal conditions that impair ability to sit or stand require physical therapy. (Guy Gillette/Photo Researchers)

- Lack of sensation in certain areas of the skin may increase the risk of burns, abrasions, and pressure sores. The child may need to be positioned periodically during the school day and monitored carefully during some activities in which there is risk of injury.
- Lack of bowel and bladder control in some children will require periodic catheterization. Many children can be taught to do the procedure known as clean intermittent **catheterization** (CIT) themselves, but teachers should know what to do or obtain help from the school nurse.
- Spina bifida generally has no effect on a child's stamina, and most children with myelomeningocele can participate in a full day of school activities.

Other Neurological Impairments

In addition to these conditions, a variety of other rare diseases, disorders, hereditary syndromes, and accidents can result in neurological impairment. The effects of these impairments vary widely and include sensory, motor, emotional, and intellectual deficits. The educational needs of students with neurological impairments must be considered on a case-by-case basis.

An increasingly frequent cause of neurological impairment in children and youths is traumatic head injury. Savage (1988) refers to such injury, often the result of vehicular accidents, as a "pervasive epidemic in our children and young adults" (p. 2). Traumatic head injury results in brain injury, which may range from mild to profound and be temporary or permanent. The brain injury may affect emotional and social behavior as well as physical and cognitive functioning (National Head Injury Foundation, 1988; see the box on p. 355). Savage summarizes the educational implications of traumatic head injury as follows:

1. Transition from hospital (or rehabilitation center) to school requires involvement of both institutions; information must be shared to ensure a smooth transition.
2. Teachers need training about traumatic brain injury and its ramifications (materials are available from NHIF, 333 Turnpike Road, Southborough, MA 01772).
3. The school must use a team approach involving regular and special educators, other special teachers, the guidance counselor, administrators, and the student's family.

The Story of My Head Injury

I was 8-years-old when I got my head injury. I was riding my bike on the sandpit road when a high school kid came around the corner and hit me. I don't remember anything about it. My brother Ian was with me and he saw the car smack me and me fly over the car into the bushes. My bike got run over cause the kid that hit me was drinking. And he didn't even stop until he saw my brother and his friends up the road. That's all stuff that Ian told me because I was unconscious.

I don't remember the hospital much. I remember my mom holding me and rubbing my head. My leg hurt the most cause it got broke in the accident. My mom says I was unconscious for 16 days and nights. She says they had to feed me with tubes and I had another tube to help me breath. Mrs. R. had the kids in school send me cards. My mom read them to me over and over. I wanted to be back in school real bad. I missed our Halloween party.

After I got home a teacher worked with me. Then I went back to school. I only remember how happy I was to be back. I didn't remember where my desk was. I guess I cried the first day cause everything was so hard and the kids were way ahead of me. My mom says I cried all week. I had to take two medicines for my head injury. I don't know what they were.

Now I'm in the 5th grade and I am doing much better. I got 2 B's, and 3 C's on my last report card. My mom says to say that it is still hard for me to read and think for a long time. As for me, I hate spelling. But I hated it before my head injury too. It takes me a while to get things and sometimes I have to bring work to my special teacher Mr. M. He helps me every afternoon for 45 minutes. When I first went back to school I saw him all afternoon. He says cause of me he is a head injury expert—Ha, Ha.

One thing I remember in grade 3 is not being able to stay awake long. I was tired a lot. I even fell asleep in school. And I hated lunch, not the food. But I got mixed up cause everything was so loud. Mrs. R used to let me eat lunch with her. This was good except she made me practice my math as we ate lunch.

I am suppose to tell you about my friends too. Ian, my brother, is still my best friend. He helps me with my homework and he is teaching me his computer. He said to say that I also have friends like Tommy, Jason, Franky, and Mica. We are on the same baseball team. We ride our bikes almost every day. I got a new bike after a year. My dad sent it from New York. My mom wasn't too happy about it. But I told her not to worry.

Right now I feel very good. I only take one medicine for my head injury. I think I am the same but sometimes it is still hard for me to learn stuff like reading for ideas and stuff. My teacher says I have come a long ways. Next year will be better, I hope.

The End,
Bobby G.

SOURCE: National Head Injury Foundation, *An Educator's Manual: What Educators Need to Know About Students with Traumatic Head Injury* (Southboro, MA: Author, 1988), pp. 89–90.

4. The educational plan for the student must be concerned with cognitive, social/behavioral, and sensorimotor domains.
5. The student should be placed into an appropriate educational service category, usually "other health impaired."
6. Most students with traumatic head injury experience problems in focusing and sustaining attention for long periods, remembering previously learned facts and skills, and learning new things. They have difficulty with organization, abstraction, and flexible thinking. They often lose basic academic skills and learning strategies and experience high levels of frustration, fatigue, and irritability. They also have difficulty reestablishing associations with peers and controlling inappropriate social behavior.
7. Programs for students must emphasize the cognitive processes through which academic skills are learned as well as content.
8. The school needs to consider the student's long-term needs in addition to the annual IEP goals, but initial IEP goals should be reviewed at least every six weeks because rapid changes sometimes take place early in recovery.

MUSCULOSKELETAL CONDITIONS

Some children are physically disabled because of defects or diseases of the muscles or bones. Even though they are not neurologically impaired, their ability to move about is affected. Most of the time muscular and skeletal problems involve the legs, arms, joints, or spine, making it difficult or impossible for the child to walk, stand, sit, or use his or her hands. The problems may be congenital or acquired after birth, and the causes include genetic defects, infectious diseases, accidents, or developmental disorders. We will describe two of the most common musculoskeletal conditions: muscular dystrophy and arthritis.

Muscular Dystrophy

Some children are handicapped by a weakening and wasting away of muscular tissue. If there is neurological damage or the muscles are weak because of nerve degeneration, the condition is called **atrophy.** When there is no evidence of a neurological disease or impairment, the condition is called **myopathy.** The term **dystrophy** is applied to cases in which the myopathy is progressive and hereditary. Although there are many varieties of muscular atrophy and myopathy, some of the most common serious conditions of this type fall under the general heading of **muscular dystrophy,** a hereditary disease characterized by progressive weakness caused by degeneration of muscle fibers. The exact biological mechanisms responsible for muscular dystrophy are not known, nor is there at present any cure (Batshaw & Perret, 1986).

Two major types of muscular dystrophy are the pseudohypertrophic (Duchenne) form and the facioscapulohumeral (Landouzy-Dejerine) form. The pseudohypertrophic form is found only in boys. It is usually first noticed when the child is learning to walk, and it progresses throughout childhood. By early adolescence the child is often confined to a wheelchair. Pseudohypertrophy (literally false growth) of the muscles of the pelvic girdle, shoulder girdle, legs, and arms gives the child the outward appearance of health and strength, but the muscles are actually being replaced by fatty tissue. The individual seldom lives beyond young adulthood. Facioscapulohumeral muscular dystrophy is found in both boys and girls. The onset is usually in adolescence. Weakness of the shoulders and arms is more prominent than weakness of the legs, and the facial muscles are affected. The progression is slower than in the Duchenne form. Some individuals become totally disabled, although others live a normal life span and are hardly aware of the symptoms.

Problems associated with muscular dystrophy are impairment of physical mobility and the prospect of early total disability or death. In advanced cases complications involving the bones and other body systems are common. One of the primary considerations is maintaining as normal a pattern of activity as possible so that the deterioration or degeneration of muscle tissue is minimized. Although muscular dystrophy itself does not affect intellectual functioning, research indicates that children with the Duchenne form tend to have lower than average verbal IQs (Batshaw & Perret, 1986). Furthermore, when a child with muscular dystrophy has low intelligence, he or she tends to lose ambulation ability sooner, possibly because of lower motivation to continue exercise programs and use braces properly (Ziter & Allsop, 1976).

Arthritis

Pain in and around the joints can be caused by many factors, including a large number of debilitating diseases and conditions known as **arthritis.** Many people think of arthritis as a condition found exclusively in adults, especially the elderly. But arthritic conditions may be found in people of any age, including young children. **Rheumatoid arthritis,** the most common form, is a systemic disease with major symptoms involving the muscles and joints. The cause and cure are unknown, although in juvenile rheumatoid arthritis there are complete remissions in 75 to

Juvenile Rheumatoid Arthritis

"I feel more and more like a regular person these days," Amy Levendusky says. This is not the sort of thing a 9-year-old girl should have to say. But Amy has juvenile rheumatoid arthritis, which affects 71,000 children in this country. The disease gripped Amy at the age of 4 and spread from her feet to every joint in her body. "She'd be sitting there not able to move because it hurt so much," says her father, John. "I'd have to pick her up to take her from one place to another." Now a fourth grader, Amy attends a school outside her home district in Whitefish Bay, Wis., because it has an elevator. Most days she doesn't go outside for recess—even a bump might send a shock of pain through her whole body.

Still, Amy has shown signs of improvement in the last year. She has a daily regimen of joint exercises, and an anti-inflammatory drug called methotrexate seems to be helping. "There's not as much pain or stiffness most of the time," she says. "I can walk up the stairs normally now. Before, I had to pull myself up with my hands." She began piano lessons as therapy two years ago and discovered a love for the keyboard. "She just wants to be seen as a normal little girl," says her mother, Susan. But in one unexpected way the disease may have made Amy special. "I think she has developed a keener sensitivity," Susan says. "There will be times when she'll notice how beautiful things look outside and say, 'Let's take a walk.' Most kids her age wouldn't pay attention to things like that."

SOURCE: From Melinda Beck with Mary Hager and Vern E. Smith, "Living with Arthritis," *Newsweek,* March 20, 1989, p. 67.

TABLE 9.1	Additional Musculoskeletal Conditions
Condition	Description
Clubfoot	One or both feet are turned at the wrong angle at the ankle.
Scoliosis	There is abnormal curvature of the spine.
Legg-Calve-Perthes disease	There is flattening of the head of the femur or hipbone.
Osteomyelitis	There is bacterial infection of the bone.
Arthrogryposis	Muscles of the limbs are missing or smaller and weaker than normal.
Osteogenesis imperfecta	Bones are formed improperly and break very easily.

80 percent of the cases. More girls than boys are affected. Arthritis may vary greatly in severity, from relatively mild inflammation, swelling, and stiffness in the joints and connective tissues to extremely debilitating symptoms accompanied by atrophy and joint deformity. Sometimes there are complications such as fever, respiratory problems, heart problems, and eye infections. Educational considerations for children with arthritis consist of making the school experience as normal as possible (see the box on p. 357).

Among handicapped children, **osteoarthritis** is the most common form. The cartilage around the joint is damaged, the space between the bones becomes smaller and loses its lubrication, and movement becomes painful or impossible. Osteoarthritis is especially likely to occur when the child has a condition in which a joint has been dislocated. Children with cerebral palsy, for example, may have recurring dislocations and suffer from painful arthritis. Surgery to correct the dislocation may also involve repair of the joint to reduce the risk of arthritis (Batshaw & Perret, 1986).

Other Conditions

A wide variety of other congenital conditions, acquired defects, and diseases can affect the musculoskeletal system (see Batshaw & Perret, 1986; Blackman, 1984). Some of these are listed in Table 9.1. In all these conditions, as well as in cases of muscular dystrophy and arthritis, intelligence is unaffected unless there are additional associated handicaps. Insofar as the musculoskeletal problem itself is concerned, special education is necessary only to overcome the child's mobility deficit, to see that proper posture and positioning are maintained, to provide for education during periods of confinement to hospital or home, and otherwise to make the educational experience as normal as possible.

CONGENITAL MALFORMATIONS

Several of the conditions we have described are always congenital (spina bifida, for example); others are sometimes congenital and sometimes acquired after birth (e.g., cerebral palsy). Babies can be born with a defect or malformation of any body part or organ system; here we will give examples of only some of the more common or obvious ones. Congenital defects occur in about 3 percent of live births (Batshaw & Perret, 1986). Some congenital anomalies are not noticed at birth but discovered during the first year. Not all these defects are debilitating.

Common Malformations

Congenital malformations of the heart and/or blood vessels leading to or from the heart are particularly serious. More children with congenital heart defects are surviving as advances are being made in heart surgery. Today defects that once would have required an extremely sheltered or restricted life are being repaired so successfully that many children with congenital heart defects can look forward to a life of normal activity.

Congenital dislocation of the hip is a fairly common problem, occurring in about 1.5 of every 1,000 live births; eight times more females than males are affected. The defect appears to be genetically determined and tends to run in families. It can usually be corrected with the use of casts or braces until the hip socket grows properly.

Congenital malformations of the extremities may range from relatively minor abnormalities of the foot or hand (webbing of the fingers or an extra toe) to profound malformations of the legs and arms. Some babies are born with arms or legs completely or partly missing. Minor malformations of the extremities can ordinarily be corrected by plastic or reconstructive surgery; major malformations require the fitting of prosthetic (artificial) devices, perhaps in addition to corrective or reconstructive surgery, and instruction in how to make the best use of the existing extremities.

Congenital malformations of the head and face (craniofacial abnormalities) are serious not only because they are cosmetic defects but also because the brain, eyes, ears, mouth, and nose may be involved. In addition to bizarre appearance, the child may suffer brain damage, visual impairment, auditory impairment, no sense of smell or taste, or inability to eat or talk normally. Advances in medicine, especially in plastic and reconstructive surgery, have had two obvious consequences: First, more children with major craniofacial anomalies are surviving than previously; second, children who formerly had to go through life markedly deformed can now often be made quite normal in appearance and be given the ability to see, smell, taste, or eat more normally. The extent to which craniofacial deformities can be corrected is illustrated in the before and after pictures in Figure 9.4.

Congenital Malformations and Teratogens

Some children are born with malformed bodies because of a genetic defect—that is, they are destined to be malformed from conception because of the chromosomes contributed by the mother and/or father. Others are damaged at some time during fetal development. In some cases viruses, bacteria, radiation, or chemical substances—**teratogens**—damage the chromosomes of the parent(s) or interfere with normal fetal development. An almost endless list of diseases, drugs taken by the mother, and poisonous substances to which the mother may have been exposed during the course of pregnancy can cause a deformed fetus. Although in the vast majority of cases a specific teratogenic agent cannot be identified, the list of drugs, chemicals, and bacteria known to be capable of producing deformed fetuses is constantly growing.

A particular factor may be teratogenic *only* if the mother (and, indirectly, of course, the fetus) is exposed to it at a certain critical interval. In general, the first trimester is the crucial stage of fetal development. By the end of this first three

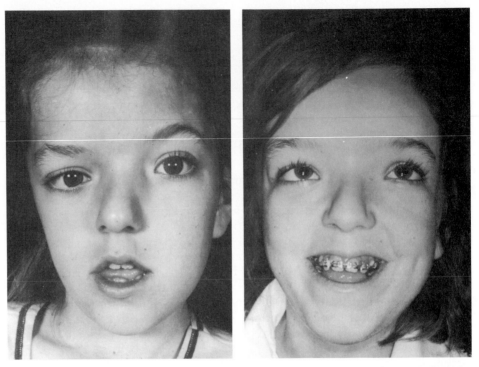

Figure 9.4 *Preoperative and postoperative photos of a girl with craniofacial defects. The preoperative photo (left) shows ocular hypertelorism (eyes abnormally far apart) with orbital dystopia (displacement of the eyes) and malalignment of the nose and facial bones due to a condition known as craniostenosis, in which the growth of the head and/or face is distorted. Notice that the right side of the face is smaller than the left. The postoperative photo (right) shows a much better alignment of the eyes and nose and improvement in facial symmetry.*

SOURCE: Courtesy of Dr. Milton T. Edgerton, chairman, Department of Plastic Surgery, University of Virginia School of Medicine.

months of pregnancy all the body parts have developed, although they have not completed their growth in size. For example, if a woman contracts **German measles (rubella)** during the first trimester, her baby may be born with a deformity. After this period maternal rubella ordinarily presents no danger to the fetus.

Perhaps the most dramatic, and infamous, teratogenic drug is thalidomide. This apparently "safe" sedative or antinausea drug, taken by many pregnant women in the late 1950s and early 1960s (especially in Europe), was responsible for the birth of thousands of babies with extremely deformed or missing limbs and other peculiar anomalies (Batshaw & Perret, 1986). "Thalidomide babies" typically showed a deformity that is called **phocomelia,** in which the limbs are extremely short or are missing completely, and the hands and feet are attached directly to the torso.

Not as dramatic and infamous, but probably the most frequently used teratogenic drug in contemporary life, is alcohol. Ethanol, the type of alcohol found in beer, wine, and liquor, is known to be capable of causing cancer, mutations, and birth defects (Wilsnack, Klassen, & Wilsnack, 1984). A pregnant woman who drinks alcohol excessively runs the risk of having a baby with **fetal alcohol syndrome** (or **alcohol embryopathy**). Fetal alcohol syndrome is now the most frequent teratogenic damage seen in humans. The syndrome can range from mild to severe and includes effects such as fetal and postnatal growth retardation, brain damage, mental retardation, hyperactivity, anomalies of the face, and heart failure.

ACCIDENTS AND OTHER PHYSICAL CONDITIONS

Falling, burning, poisoning, and mishaps involving bicycles, motorcycles, and automobiles are some of the ways children and youths acquire disabilities. Neurological impairments as well as disfigurement or amputation may result from such accidents; and the physical, psychological, and educational problems range from insignificant to profound. The problem of childhood accidents can hardly be overrated: More children die in accidents each year than are killed by all childhood diseases combined. Millions of children under the age of sixteen are injured in accidents each year. Spinal cord injury occurs at a particularly high rate in young persons fifteen to twenty-four years of age because of vehicular accidents (Rutledge & Dick, 1983). Sports injuries also contribute to temporary and permanent disabling conditions of children and youths (Vinger & Hoerner, 1986).

A variety of other physical conditions that may affect children's development and education are summarized in Table 9.2. This is not an exhaustive list; children are susceptible to many more disorders and diseases than those given here. The important thing to remember is that these conditions affect normal bodily functions— breathing, eating, digestion, growth, elimination, healing, or movement. And because these bodily functions are adversely affected, the child may lack vitality, require

TABLE 9.2 *Additional Physical Conditions*

Condition	Description
Asthma	Chronic respiratory condition characterized by repeated episodes of difficulty in breathing, especially exhalation
Cystic fibrosis	Inherited disease characterized by chronic respiratory and digestive problems, including thick, sticky mucus and glandular secretions
Diabetes	A hereditary or developmental problem of sugar metabolism caused by failure of the pancreas to produce enough insulin
Nephrosis and nephritis	Disorders or diseases of the kidneys due to infection, poisoning, burns, crushing injuries, or other diseases
Sickle-cell anemia	Severe, chronic hereditary blood disease (occurring primarily among black children) in which red blood cells are distorted in shape and do not circulate properly
Hemophilia	A rare, sex-linked disorder in which the blood does not have a sufficient clotting component and excessive bleeding occurs
Rheumatic fever	Painful swelling and inflammation of the joints (typically following strep throat or scarlet fever) that can spread to the brain or heart
Tuberculosis	Infection by the tuberculosis bacterium of an organ system, such as lungs, larynx, bones and joints, skin, gastrointestinal tract, genitourinary tract, or heart
Cancer	Abnormal growth of cells that can affect any organ system

special medical treatment or therapy, or be unable to participate in some ordinary school activities.

AIDS

Perhaps the most feared and controversial disease currently known is **Acquired Immune Deficiency Syndrome (AIDS).** The virus that causes the disease—HTLV-III—interferes with the body's immune system, leaving the individual vulnerable to chronic and ultimately fatal infections from a variety of microbes. As of 1990, there is no known cure for the disease, and no vaccine has yet been developed.

First described as a disease of homosexual men, AIDS was soon detected among Haitians, intravenous drug users, persons with hemophilia (see Table 9.2), others who had received blood transfusions, heterosexual prostitutes, and young children. Today it is known that the disease can be transmitted through intimate sexual contact with an AIDS patient or a carrier of the virus, through transfusions of blood from patients or carriers, and from contaminated hypodermic needles.

The seriousness of AIDS and the medical concern regarding its control can hardly be overemphasized. Church, Allen and Stiehm (1986) describe AIDS as a "devastating epidemic disorder of extraordinary morbidity and mortality" (p. 423). Both the U.S. Surgeon General and the National Academy of Sciences have called for massive education programs to prevent a worsening of the epidemic. However, AIDS education and the matter of education for students with AIDS are controversial for two reasons: (1) The disease is usually sexually transmitted, and therefore sex education is involved; (2) fear of the disease creates pressure to exclude infected children and adults from classrooms.

An Educator's Resource Guide

The following organizations and publications are good sources of information about AIDS. In addition, most states now operate hotlines and have agencies that produce their own materials on AIDS. Don't forget to contact your local parent/teacher organizations and health agencies for information, too.

ORGANIZATIONS

- **American Red Cross** has produced several publications on AIDS. For sample copies, contact your local office or write AIDS Education Office, 1730 D St. N.W., Washington, DC 20006. Ask for "AIDS and Children: Information for Parents of School Age Children" and "AIDS and Children: Information for Teachers and School Officials." Single copy free, bulk orders available.

- **Bureau of National Affairs** maintains a database in local, state and federal legislation, regulations, and guidelines and produces "AIDS in the Workplace: Data Report," which deals with employment relations. Subscribers may obtain the report from BNA PLUS, 1231 25th St. N.W., Washington, DC 20037. Ph. 800/452-7773 nationwide or 202/452-4323 in Washington, DC. BNA also produces "AIDS in the Workplace: Resource Material," which is available for $60 from BNA Customer Service, 9435 Key West Ave., Rockville, MD 20850.

- **Center for Attitudinal Healing,** 19 Main St., Tiburon, CA 94920, dispenses a variety of materials for those facing life-threatening illnesses. The poster reproduced in black and white on page K-2 is available in color for a $10 donation.

- **National Coalition of Hispanic Health and Human Services Organizations,** 1030 15th St. N.W., Suite 1053, Washington, DC 10005, assists those needing AIDS information in Spanish.
- **National Education Association** published a guide in August 1987 for its members, titled "The Facts About AIDS." Write for NEA AIDS Booklet, NEA Communications, 1201 16th St. N.W., Washington, DC 20036.
- **National School Boards Association** produces *AIDS and the Public School*, a 55-page report on a national conference sponsored by NSBA in February 1986 (priced at $15), and, for reporters, "Issue Briefs" on AIDS and the impact on schools (free). Both are available from NSBA, 1680 Duke St., Alexandria, VA 22314.
- **Sex Information and Education Council of the U.S.** produces "How to Talk to Your Children About AIDS," by Ronald Moglia and Ann Welcourne Moglia. Write New York University, SIECUS Library, 5th Floor, 32 Washington Place, New York, NY 10003. The first two copies are free; up to 50 copies are 60 cents each.
- **U.S. Centers for Disease Control,** 1600 Clifton Rd. N.E., Atlanta, GA 30333, distributes "AIDS: Recommendations and Guidelines" and "Information/Education Plan to Prevent and Control AIDS in the United States." Both are free of charge.
- **U.S. Department of Education** disseminates a 28-page set of guidelines, *AIDS and the Education of Our Children: A Guide for Parents and Teachers*. For free copies write to Consumer Information Center, Dept. ED, Pueblo, CO 81009.

BOOKS

A survey by *Publishers Weekly* last spring found 130 books and references about AIDS at that time, with more on the way. Below are a few selected examples.

- *AIDS: From the Beginning*, a compendium of articles on AIDS from the *Journal of the American Medical Association*, is a 450-page book in magazine format. It is available from the AMA's Book and Pamphlet Fulfillment Department, 535 N. Dearborn St., Chicago, IL 60610. Ph. 800/621-8335 outside Illinois or 312/645-4987 in Illinois. The price is $22.50.
- David Black, *The Plague Years, A Chronicle of AIDS, the Epidemic of Our Times* (Simon & Schuster, 1230 Ave. of the Americas, New York, NY 10020, 1986).
- Inge B. Corless and Mary Pittman-Lindenman, eds, *AIDS: Principles, Practices, and Politics* (Harper & Row, 2350 Virginia Ave., Hagerstown, MD 21740).
- Ann Guidici Fettner and William A. Check, *The Truth About AIDS: Evolution of an Epidemic* (Holt, Rinehart & Winston, 521 Fifth Ave., 6th Fl., New York, NY 10175, 1984). Revised in 1985.
- Eve K. Nichols, *Mobilizing Against AIDS, The Unfinished Story of a Virus* (Institute of Medicine/National Academy of Science/Harvard University Press, 79 Garden St., Cambridge, MA 02138, 1986). The price is $15.
- Chris Norwood, *Advice for Life: A Woman's Guide to AIDS Risks and Prevention* (Pantheon Books, 201 E. 50th St., New York, NY 10022, 1987).
- Randy Shilts, *And the Band Played On* (St. Martin's Press, 175 Fifth Ave., New York, NY 10010, 1987).
- Roberta Weiner, *AIDS: Impact on the Schools* (Special Report from the Education Research Group, 1101 King St., P.O. Box 1453, Alexandria, VA 22313, 1986).

CURRICULUM MATERIALS

- *Criteria for Evaluating an AIDS Curriculum*, National Coalition of Advocates for Students, CAS, 100 Boylston St., Suite 737, Boston, MA 02116; $2 postage and handling.

- Merrill Publishing Company published two booklets on AIDS for students in grades 5 through 12 emphasizing abstinence and adherence to parental rules. Write Merrill Publishing Co., 936 Eastwin Dr., Westerville, OH 43081. Ph. 614/890-1111. Free copies are available to school districts; otherwise single copies are $6, and bulk orders are $2.97 each.
- *Teaching AIDS* includes seven lesson plans, worksheets, and a resource listing. Published by ERT Associates, 1700 Mission St., P.O. Box 1830, Santa Cruz, CA 95061. The price is $14.95, plus $2.24 shipping.

VIDEOS

- "AIDS in the Workplace—A Three Hour Teleconference," available from PBS Video, 475 L'Enfant Plaza S.W., Washington, DC 20024; $395 for ¾″ (a set of three tapes); $345 for VHS and Beta.
- "AIDS: Profile of an Epidemic" is a videocassette of a one-hour program that aired in January 1986. Suitable for 11th- and 12th-grade use. Write AIDS-Update, Indiana University Audio-visual Center, Bloomington, IN 47405. The price is $180.
- "Beyond Fear," Modern Talking Picture Service, 5000 Park St., North St. Petersburg, FL 33709; free loan for adults and senior high school students.
- "National AIDS Awareness Test," a two-hour documentary sponsored by Metropolitan Life Insurance Company, includes an accompanying quiz and answer key. Write Corporate Communications, Area 12VW, Metropolitan Life Insurance Company, 1 Madison Ave., New York, NY 10010.

FOR KIDS ONLY

- "AIDS Prevention Program for Youth" is a new program for high school students from the American Red Cross. Materials include: "Letter from Brian," a video free on loan or available for purchase for $95; Teacher's Manual, $8.75 for five copies; Student Workbooks, $25 for 25 copies; Parents' Brochure, $4.50 for 100 copies. Order from American Red Cross, AIDS Education Office, 1730 D St. N.W., Washington, DC 20006.
- "AIDS: What Young Adults Should Know" is published by the American Alliance for Health, Physical Education, Recreation, and Dance. Teacher's guide, $8.95; student guide, $2.50. Write P.O. Box 704, Waldorf, MD 20601.
- "Sex, Drugs, and AIDS" is a 20-minute videotape (somewhat controversial because it is explicit). An alternative is "Subject Is: AIDS Is Abstinence." Both are produced by O.D.N. Productions, 74 Varick St., New York, NY 10013. Cost: $400 film, $325 video.
- "Teens & AIDS: Playing It Safe" is a free brochure published by the American Council of Life Insurance and the Health Insurance Association of America. Packages of 100 are available for $10 from 1001 Pennsylvania Ave. N.W., Washington, DC 20004.

AIDS HOTLINES

Most states and local communities now have hotlines with up-to-date information on AIDS. The following is a national hotline.
- The U.S. Public Health Service has a 24-hour, toll-free number. Call 1-800-342-AIDS for a recorded message.

SOURCE: S. Reed, "Children with AIDS: How Schools Are Handling the Crisis" (Kappan special report), *Phi Delta Kappan*, 69 (1988), K10–K11.

At this time, it appears that public officials and physicians are likely to maintain a cautious approach toward AIDS and take few risks of exposing children to the virus. Church, Allen, and Stiehm (1986) have noted that whether or not a child should be excluded from school depends on the individual case. If the child is extraordinarily sensitive to infection, school placement may be inappropriate; if the child shows only positive antibody tests, the child should not be excluded.

"In the 1990s AIDS will spare no school" (Merina, 1989; see the box on p. 362). The issue will involve teachers and other school personnel with AIDS, as well as pupils (Reed, 1988). The U.S. Centers for Disease Control estimate that by 1993, 450,000 cases of AIDS will have been diagnosed in the United States. AIDS will be a particular problem for special education because of the increasing number of infants and young children who are contracting the disease from their mothers and because the complications of AIDS, in addition to frequent infections, include a variety of cognitive, behavioral, and neurological symptoms (Crocker, 1989). As children born with AIDS survive longer, we will see an increasing number needing special medical and educational services. These services will be required not only because of the children's fragile and declining physical health but also because of other effects the disease may produce, including psychotic behavior, mental retardation, seizures, and neurological impairments similar to cerebral palsy.

Adolescent Pregnancy

Adolescent pregnancy cannot of course be considered a physical handicap, but to the extent that it interferes with a young person's schooling, special educational provisions are necessary. Furthermore, teenage mothers are ten times more likely than women over twenty to give birth to premature babies, to have babies with handicapping conditions, and to be abusive to their children. The problem is not just one of maternal health; it also involves prevention of handicapping conditions (Anastasiow, 1983; Baumeister, Kupstas, & Klindworth, 1990).

Each year over a million American girls between the ages of fifteen and nineteen become pregnant (about 10 percent of this age group). A large percentage of these pregnancies end in miscarriage or abortion. About 800,000 babies are born to teenage mothers annually (Delatte, Orgeron, & Preis, 1985). Clearly, massive efforts to educate teenagers about pregnancy and child care and to provide for the continued schooling of teenagers who are pregnant or mothers or fathers are needed. Federal law now disallows federal funds to any school system that does not include pregnant girls in its education programs.

Children Born to Substance-Abusing Mothers

We have already mentioned fetal alcohol syndrome, which results in disabilities acquired by children of mothers who abuse alcohol during pregnancy. In recent years, "crack babies," born to mothers who use crack cocaine during pregnancy, have increased dramatically in number. The effects of maternal cocaine addiction involve not only multiple physiological, emotional, and cognitive problems of newborns but a high probability of neglect and abuse by the mother after her baby is born. Many women who are intravenous drug users not only risk chemical damage to their babies but also give them venereal diseases such as syphilis, which can result in disabilities. As the number of substance-abusing mothers increases, the number of infants and young children with severe and multiple disabilities will increase as well. Many of these young children will enter the education system with problems that are now hard to predict precisely but that will undoubtedly demand extraordinary efforts on the part of schools and other social agencies. These children's problems may typically extend throughout their school careers and into adulthood.

Children Dependent on Ventilators

An increasing number of children are returning home from hospitalization able to breathe only with the help of a ventilator (a mechanical device forcing oxygen into the lungs through a tube inserted into the trachea). Many of these children are also returning to public schools, sometimes with the assistance of a full-time nurse. The conditions under which it is appropriate for children dependent on ventilators to attend regular classrooms are still a matter for debate. Educators and parents together must make decisions in the individual case, weighing medical judgment regarding danger to the child as well as the interest of the child in being integrated into as many typical school activities as possible with his or her peers.

CHILD ABUSE AND NEGLECT

Since the early 1960s there has been national interest among child health specialists in the **battered child syndrome.** Klein and Stern (1971) define the syndrome as "frank unexplained skeletal trauma or severe bruising or both, or such neglect as to lead to severe medical illness or immediate threat to life" (p. 15). Public Law 93-247, passed in 1974, defines child abuse and neglect as "physical or mental injury, sexual abuse, negligent treatment, or maltreatment of a child under the age of 18 by a person who is responsible for the child's welfare under circumstances which indicate that the child's health or welfare is harmed or threatened." Although the definition of child abuse is not simple and current prevalence estimates are not reliable, it is known that many thousands of children ranging in age from newborns to adolescents are battered or abused each year in the United States. They are beaten, burned, sexually molested, starved, or otherwise neglected or brutalized by their parents or other older persons.

The consequences of child abuse may be permanent neurological damage, other internal injuries, skeletal deformity, facial disfigurement, sensory impairment, or death. Psychological problems are an inevitable outcome of abuse. Evidence indicates that the abuse of children is increasing. Abuse and neglect by adults is now a leading cause of injury—both physical and psychological—and death among children. Unfortunately, congressional action to prevent abuse and provide services to abusive families has been weak (Chadwick, 1989).

Child abuse and neglect constitute one of the most complex problems confronting our society today. There is a need for better understanding of the nature and extent of the problem among both the general public and professionals. Education for parenting and child management, including family life education in the public schools, is an obvious need in our society. Without concerted effort on the part of all professionals, as well as a strong coalition of political constituencies, the problem will not be satisfactorily addressed. Since abuse and injury vary so greatly from case to case, the special educational provisions appropriate for abused and neglected children range from special attention by regular classroom teachers to residential or hospital teaching.

Teachers can play an extremely important role in detecting, reporting, and preventing child abuse and neglect because, next to parents, they are the people who spend the most time with children. It is therefore vital that teachers be aware of the indicators that a child is being abused or neglected at home (see the box below). Teachers must also be aware of the reporting procedures that should be followed when they suspect abuse or neglect. These vary from one area and state to another, but ordinarily the teacher is required to report suspected cases of child abuse or neglect to a school administrator or public health official. A professional who fails to report child abuse or neglect may be held legally liable.

Protecting Abused Kids

Q. Is child abuse still a problem in this country?
A. Emphatically, yes. We have succeeded in making the problem visible but not in reducing it. It remains a pervasive, debilitating societal problem that affects many, many children and adults.

Q. How common is child abuse?
A. A conservative estimate is that at least 30 percent of our population will be abused at some time during childhood. Every year two or three percent of all U.S. children are reported as having been abused or neglected.

Q. What are the various forms of abuse?
A. The usual classifications are neglect, physical abuse (causing physical injury), sexual abuse, and emotional abuse.

Q. Does abuse "run" in families?
A. Persons who have abused their children very often say they themselves were abused as children.

Q. Who abuses children? Is there a specific "abusing" personality?
A. That depends on the type of abuse. Generally, people who have already abused children are quite likely to do it again. The trick is finding out who has that kind of history.

Potential child abusers don't have any obvious physical or mental features that make them stand out in a crowd. When there's no available record of abuse, you need to know a lot of personal things about someone to recognize that potential.

Q. How can child abuse be detected? What kind of physical symptoms or injuries are present?
A. Teachers can learn to recognize signs of physical abuse. They should be concerned if a child repeatedly comes to class in the morning with swellings and bruises. Teachers also should be concerned if a child habitually wears long sleeves or layers of clothing even when the weather is warm. Some kids will tell a teacher they're being abused if the teacher just comes out and asks them.

School-based child abuse education programs emphasize the importance of telling someone about the abuse. Often a sexually abused child in such a program will tell someone about their situation. When you give children definitions of abuse—especially sexual abuse—they'll more clearly understand that what is happening to them is wrong, and they'll be more likely to report it.

Teachers also can pick up on abuse by keeping an eye out for behavioral problems. A kid who all of a sudden starts acting out or becomes violent could just be displaying something learned at home. Teachers should wonder, "Where did this child pick up this behavior? Where did he or she learn this violence?" Most likely it came from a parent.

Q. What should a teacher do who suspects a student is being abused?
A. Every state has a law requiring teachers to report cases of child abuse. So it's imperative

that teachers receive training on how to deal with the issue and how to handle the situation. Unfortunately, not enough of this kind of instruction is going on.

Q. What determines how much psychological damage an abused child suffers, and when is such damage likely to show up?
A. The amount of damage depends on how severe and intense the abuse is, how long it lasts, and when it starts. The earlier in life abuse begins, the worse effects it's likely to have later in life.

Abuse causes more psychological damage to children at certain ages than at others. But even those children who are abused at particularly vulnerable points in their development may not show any abnormality from abuse until later in life. Sexually abused children, for example, usually don't manifest problems until they're older, when they're beginning to develop and understand their own sexuality.

Q. Do some children withstand abuse better than others?
A. It appears that they do, but the exact reasons are hard to sort out. Some children survive severe abuse and emerge as successful, healthy adults; others become virtually disabled psychologically.

Genetic factors seem to play some role, but a lot of evidence indicates that the most important factor in "surviving" child abuse may be a long-term relationship with a supportive, healthy adult, perhaps a relative or a teacher, who stays interested and available.

Q. How can child abuse be prevented or at least reduced?
A. In-home services are quite effective in combatting either neglect or physical abuse—except for sexual abuse. Someone (usually a social worker from the school or a local social service agency) comes into the home on friendly terms with the family and provides any kind of support that's possible. This person teaches parents to be parents—often they don't know how—and serves as a role model.

This kind of friendly relationship with the family takes a long time to develop. In-home service people often drop in five or six times a day. They teach abusive parents to live for the next day. All too often, abusive people live only for today because they don't know whether there will be a tomorrow.

It's important to know that abuse is compulsive, repetitive behavior. It's habitual, like an addiction.

And, again like substance abusers, child abusers can find help and support in groups of people who share their problem. One group, "Parents Anonymous," has been around for over 30 years and has a chapter in almost every city. Its program's modeled after the 12-step Alcoholics Anonymous program.

Q. Has child abuse declined with the increase in education and publicity over the years?
A. In the '70s we did fairly well in managing the situation and preventing abuse, but in the '80s services for abused children and their families deteriorated dramatically. Although reporting of cases has improved and society's consciousness has been raised, little has been done in recent years to actually improve the situation for these children.

Q. Beyond reporting the problem, what role can school employees play in helping abused children?
A. School employees can play a crucial role. First, they can teach about abuse and prevention. In California, for example, school districts must provide every child with at least three child abuse education courses between kindergarten and high school.

Second, abused children lack a sense of security. We know that comfortable relationships with adults—and school employees can be very important adults in this respect—can make a big difference in abused children's health. Beyond recognizing the problems and getting help for the victims, that's a very important contribution school employees can make.

SOURCE: D. Chadwick, "Protecting Abused Kids," *NEA Today*, 8(5) (1989), 23.

Children who are already disabled physically, mentally, or emotionally are more at risk for abuse than are nonhandicapped children (Zirpoli, 1986). Because the disabled children are more vulnerable and dependent, abusive adults find them easy targets. The poor social judgment and limited experience of many handicapped children make them even more vulnerable to sexual abuse. Moreover, some of the characteristics of handicapped children are sources of additional stress for their caretakers and may be contributing factors in physical abuse—they often require more time, energy, money, and patience than nonhandicapped children. Parenting any child is stressful; parenting a child with a disability can demand more than some parents are prepared to give. It is not surprising that handicapped children are disproportionately represented among abused children and that the need for training is particularly great for parents of children with disabilities.

PSYCHOLOGICAL AND BEHAVIORAL CHARACTERISTICS

Academic Achievement

It is impossible to make many valid generalizations about the academic achievement of children with physical disabilities because they vary so widely in the nature and severity of their conditions. Many students with physical disabilities have erratic school attendance because of hospitalization, visits to physicians, the requirement of bed rest at home, and so on. Some learn well with ordinary teaching methods; others require special methods because they are mentally retarded or sensorily impaired in addition to being physically disabled. Because of the frequent interruptions in their schooling, some fall considerably behind their age-mates in academic achievement, even though they have normal intelligence and motivation. Some children with mild or transitory physical problems have no academic deficiencies at all; others have severe difficulties. Some students who have serious and chronic health problems still manage to achieve at a high level. Usually these high-achieving children have high intellectual capacity, high motivation, and teachers and parents who make every possible special provision for their education. Children with neurological impairments are, as a group, most likely to have intellectual and perceptual deficits and therefore to be behind their age-mates in academic achievement (see Batshaw & Perret, 1986; Verhaaren & Connor, 1981a, 1981b).

Personality Characteristics

Research does not support the notion that there is a "personality type" associated with any physical disability (DeLoach & Greer, 1981; Lewandowski & Cruickshank, 1980). Physically disabled children are as varied in their psychological characteristics as nondisabled children, and they are apparently responsive to the same factors that influence the psychological development of the average child. How they adapt to their physical limitations and how they respond to social-interpersonal situations greatly depends on how parents, siblings, teachers, peers, and the public react to them.

Public Reactions

Public attitudes can have a profound influence on how physically disabled children see themselves and on their opportunities for psychological adjustment, education, and employment. If the reaction is one of fear, rejection, or discrimination, they may spend a great deal of energy trying to hide their stigmatizing differences. If the reaction is one of pity and an expectation of helplessness, people with disabilities will tend to behave in a dependent manner. To the extent that other people can see children with physical handicaps as persons who have certain limitations but are otherwise just like everyone else, disabled children and youths will be encouraged to become independent and productive members of society.

Several factors seem to be causing greater public acceptance of people with physical disabilities. Professional and civic groups encourage support and decrease fear of handicapped people through information and public education. Government insistence on the elimination of architectural barriers that prevent handicapped citizens from using public facilities serves to decrease discrimination. Programs to encourage hiring of handicapped workers help the public to see those with physical disabilities as constructive, capable people. Laws that protect *every* child's right to public education are bringing more individuals into contact with severely and profoundly handicapped children. Public agencies are including physically disabled youths in their programs. For example, the National Park Service has begun a program in which young people with a variety of physical disabilities—including severe arthritis, cerebral palsy, multiple sclerosis, and spinal cord injuries—work as staff members during the summer (Satz, 1986). This program has not only benefited the disabled participants, but made the public and the Park Service more sensitive to the needs of disabled persons. All these changes are encouraging more positive attitudes toward handicapped children and adults (DeLoach & Greer, 1981). But there is no doubt that many children with physical disabilities are still rejected, feared, pitied, or discriminated against. The more obvious the physical flaw, the more likely it is that the person will be perceived in negative terms by the public.

Public policy regarding children's physical disabilities has not met the needs of most such children and their families (Baumeister, Kupstas, & Klindworth, 1990; Hobbs, Perrin, & Ireys, 1984; Hobbs, Perrin, Ireys, Moynahan, & Shayne, 1985). Particularly as successful medical treatment prolongs the lives of more and more children with severe chronic illnesses and other disabilities, issues of who should pay the costs of treatment and maintenance (which are often enormous) and which children and families should receive the limited available resources are becoming critical (Lyon, 1985).

Children's Reactions

As suggested earlier, children's reactions to their own physical disabilities are largely a reflection of the way they have been treated by others. Shame and guilt are learned responses; children will have such negative feelings only if others respond to them by shaming or blaming them (and those like them) for their physical differences. Children will be independent and self-sufficient (within the limits of their physical disability) rather than dependent and demanding only to the extent that they learn how to take care of their own needs. And they will have realistic self-perceptions and set realistic goals for themselves only to the extent that others are honest and clear in their appraisal of their condition.

However, certain psychological reactions are inevitable for the child with physical disabilities, no matter how he or she is treated. The wish to be nondisabled and participate in the same activities as most children, and the fantasy that the disability will disappear, are to be expected. With proper management and help, the child can be expected eventually to accept the disability and live a happy life, even though he or she knows the true nature of the condition (DeLoach & Greer, 1981). Fear and anxiety, too, can be expected. It is natural for children to be afraid when they are separated from their parents, hospitalized, and subjected to medical examinations and procedures that may be painful. In these situations, too, proper management can minimize emotional stress. Psychological trauma is not a necessary effect of hospitalization. The hospital environment may in fact be better than the child's home in the case of abused and neglected children.

Other important considerations regarding the psychological effects of a physical handicap include the age of the child and the nature of the disability (e.g., whether it is congenital or acquired, progressive or not). But even these factors are not uniform in their effects. A child with a relatively minor and short-term physical disability may become more maladjusted, anxious, debilitated, and disruptive than another child with a terminal illness because of the way the child's behavior and feelings are managed. Certainly understanding the child's and the family's feelings about the disability are important. But it is also true that managing the consequences of the child's behavior is a crucial aspect of education and rehabilitation.

It may seem reasonable to expect more frequent psychological depression and suicide attempts among physically disabled adolescents and young adults than among their nonhandicapped peers since disability does impose psychological stress. However, Bryan and Herjanic (1980) concluded that "the association between handicaps and depression, suicide attempts, and suicide has not been clearly established" (p. 64). It is true that a disabled youth must go through a difficult period of learning to accept a disability, its permanence, and its personal and social implications. It is equally true that adolescents without physical disabilities find the task of establishing an identity difficult.

PROSTHETICS, ORTHOTICS, AND ADAPTIVE DEVICES FOR DAILY LIVING

A **prosthesis** is an artificial replacement for a missing body part (an artificial hand or leg); an **orthosis** is a device that enhances the partial function of a part of a person's body (a brace or a device that allows a person to do something; see Figures 9.5 to 9.8). **Adaptive devices** for daily living include a variety of adaptations of ordinary items found in the home, office, or school that make performing the

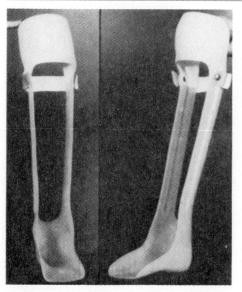

Figure 9.5 *Examples of thermoform leg braces. The braces are molded to fit the contour of the wearer's leg and hold the knee, ankle, and/or foot in a more correct or acceptable position. The orthoses are lighter in weight, more functional, and cosmetically more acceptable than older-style braces and can be worn with a variety of footwear.*

SOURCE: J. C. Drennan and J. R. Gage, "Orthotics in Cerebral Palsy," in G. H. Thompson, I. L. Rubin, and R. M. Bilenker (Eds.), *Comprehensive Management of Cerebral Palsy* (Orlando, FL: Grune & Stratton, 1983), pp. 206, 208. Reprinted by permission of Grune & Stratton, Inc.

Figure 9.6   A drinking cup equipped with a special handle can be used by someone who has little or no ability to grasp.

SOURCE: Photos 9.6 through 9.8 courtesy of Laura Vogtle, Children's Rehabilitation Center, University of Virginia.

Figure 9.7   Devices to assist a physically disabled person in eating. Notice that the plate is attached to the table with suction cups to keep it from moving. The metal rim around the plate (a "plate guard") keeps food from being accidentally pushed off the plate and provides help in getting food onto the utensil. The eating utensil shown is a "spork," a combination spoon and fork. With a spork, a person can both spear and scoop food without changing utensils. The band around the hand, with the fitting holding the spork, is a "universal cuff," a very simple, practical orthotic device. The cuff allows a person who has no grasp to hold and use common objects, such as eating utensils, pencils, paint brushes, and pointers.

Figure 9.8   A ball-bearing feeder in use. This orthotic device is counterbalanced so that a person who has use of the hand, but not the arm and shoulder, can perform tasks such as feeding. The arm and shoulder can be moved into position with almost no effort by using the feeder, allowing the person to grasp or manipulate objects with the fingers. This orthosis is often needed by individuals with muscular dystrophy or high spinal-cord injury.

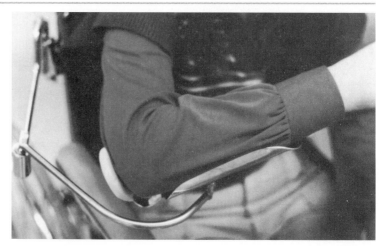

tasks required for self-care and employment easier for the person who has a physical disability, such as a device to aid bathing or handwashing or walking.

The most important principles to keep in mind are use of residual function, simplicity, and reliability. For example, an artificial hand is operated by the muscles of the arm, shoulder, or back. A person without legs must be taught to use his or her arms to move about in a wheelchair, or to use torso and arms to get about on artificial legs (perhaps using crutches or a cane in addition).

Two points regarding prosthetics, orthotics, and residual function must be kept in mind. First, residual function is often important even when a prosthesis, orthosis, or adaptive device is not used. For example, it may be crucial for the child with cerebral palsy or muscular dystrophy to learn to use the affected limbs as well as possible without the aid of any special equipment because using residual function alone will make the child more independent and may help to prevent or retard physical deterioration. Too, it is often more efficient for a person to learn not to rely completely on a prosthesis or orthosis as long as he or she can accomplish a task without it.

Second, spectacular technological developments often have very limited meaning for the immediate needs of the majority of physically disabled individuals. It may be years before expensive experimental equipment is tested adequately and marketed at a cost most people can afford, and a given device may be applicable only to a small group of individuals with an extremely rare condition (Moore, 1985). For a long time to come, common "standby" prostheses, orthoses, and other equipment adapted to the needs of the individual will be the most practical devices. A few common devices that are helpful to persons with various physical disabilities are shown in Figures 9.6 to 9.10. (See DuBose & Deni, 1980; Fraser & Hensinger, 1983; Verhaaren & Connor, 1981b, for additional illustrations of such devices.)

We do not mean to downplay the importance of technological advances for

Figure 9.9   *The head stick is a very useful device for individuals who cannot use their hands. It can be used for pointing, writing, dialing a phone, operating switches, etc., in addition to typing. The wand can be adjusted for angle and length and can be replaced with a pencil, paint brush, or other tool.* (George Bellerose, Stock, Boston.)

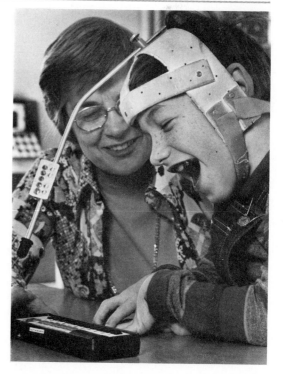

Figure 9.10 *Rehabilitation engineers are redesigning wheelchairs for use in off-the-street recreational and work environments. These all-terrain chairs allow disabled persons to engage in work and play that formerly were difficult or impossible for them.* (Rehabilitation Medical Center, Information Services, University of Virginia.)

physically disabled people. Our point here is that the greatest significance of a technological advance often lies in how it changes seemingly "ordinary" items or problems. For example, technological advances in metallurgy and plastics have led to the design of much more functional braces and wheelchairs. The heavy metal-and-leather leg braces—which were cumbersome, difficult to apply, and not very helpful in preventing deformity or improving function—formerly used by many children with cerebral palsy or other neurological disorders have been largely supplanted by braces constructed of thermoform plastic (see Figure 9.5). Wheelchairs are being built of lightweight metals and plastics and redesigned to allow users to go places inaccessible to the typical wheelchair (see Figure 9.10). And an increasing number of computerized devices are improving the movement and communication abilities of people with disabilities.

EDUCATIONAL CONSIDERATIONS

Too often we think of people who have physical disabilties as being helpless or unable to learn. It is easy to lower our expectations for them because we know that they are indeed unable to do some things. We forget that many people with physical disabilities can learn to do most or all of the things most nondisabled persons do, although sometimes they must perform these tasks in a different way (e.g., a person who does not have the use of the hands may have to use the feet or mouth). Accepting the limitations imposed by physical disabilities without trying to see how much disabled people can learn or how the environment can be changed to allow them to respond more effectively is an insulting and dehumanizing way of responding to physical differences.

Educating physically disabled students is not so much a matter of special instruction for the disabled children as it is of educating the nondisabled population. Physically disabled people solve many of their own problems, but their lives are often needlessly complicated because the nondisabled give no thought to what life is like for someone with specific physical limitations. Design adaptations in buildings, furniture, household appliances, and clothing can make it possible for someone with a physical disability to function as efficiently as a nondisabled person in a given environment, be it home, school, or community (see the box below and on page 378).

Behavior Modification Procedures

Some of the most effective teaching techniques that can be used with disabled children are derived from the principles of behavior modification. Basically, they are the same strategies used with other children: A sequence of steps is determined—beginning with what the child can already do and leading to an ultimate goal—and the child's performance of each successive step is rewarded. Such techniques are especially effective because they focus on specific behavioral responses and on maximizing motivation to perform (Hanson & Harris, 1986).

Individualized Planning

Students with complex physical disabilities typically require a wide array of related services as well as special education. The IEPs (individualized education programs)

Disability Doesn't Hamper Fashion Sense

THE ASSOCIATED PRESS

When actress and model Pamela Ann Martin suffered a disabling spinal stroke she spent a year in a hospital, flat on her back—but she still managed to get to a shopping mall on a stretcher to follow her passion for fashion.

"I was the only person shopping for clothes from a horizontal position," recalls the vivacious brunette, who graduated from California's Brooks College with a degree in fashion merchandising and design. . . .

Her modeling gigs have been mainly in behalf of Everest & Jennings, a California-based firm that produces "Avenues," a catalog line of fashionable clothing with hidden features to speed dressing for wheelchair users.

"People who are disabled deserve to have a positive fashion image," says Pamela, whose modeling endeavors began at the age of 6. "I did fashion shows for charity and social events throughout my schoolgirl and college days.

"Now the biggest difference between my ability and disability is that I model on wheels instead of in heels.

"Most people just jump in their clothes and—zip—they're off, but for me, getting dressed can be a major project."

Often, she points out, conventional clothing doesn't fit or look attractive on people who spend their day sitting. Jackets are too long and too binding when propelling a wheelchair. Slacks are too short and pockets are out of reach. Skirts drag and get caught in wheels.

Designers of clothes for wheelchair users should develop patterns which flatter the seated figure, according to clothing consultants. . . .

Research and testing indicate that such clothing should be cut with extra fabric in the seat and less in the front.

Other touches can include thigh pockets or hidden calf pockets for keeping glasses, keys and other items within easy reach. And some pants can have hidden ankle-to-knee zippers to speed dressing and accommodate braces.

SOURCE: Supplement to *The Daily Progress*, September 10, and to the *Progress Plus*, September 13, 1989.

Collaboration: A Key to Success

HELEN: I have six children in my self-contained class, five boys and a girl. They range in age from eight to eleven and in grade level from one to four. One is nonverbal, three have speech that is difficult to understand, one is on a respirator, and one has behavior problems. All of them are nonambulatory, and they're all mainstreamed for about 60 percent of the school day. They participate in whatever regular classes they can. The greatest handicap my students have is how other people see them. Too often, nonhandicapped people see wheelchairs, adaptive equipment, respirators, communication devices, and so on; their vision of someone with a disability ends there. My goal is to help nonhandicapped children see the kids I teach as regular kids who have some physical limitations. I've been a regular classroom teacher too, and I know that all children learn with and from other children. I want my students to participate in regular class activities, not just be physically present. I think you'll understand what I mean when we describe how we worked with Brett, an eight-year-old with spina bifida (myelomeningocele). He is nonambulatory and has poor expressive language. His speech is difficult to understand. He has good trunk control and is able to write with a pencil, cut with scissors, use a computer keyboard independently, and transfer himself from his wheelchair to other types of seating with minimal assistance. He's very shy and doesn't initiate conversations with strangers.

DENISE: At the beginning of the year, Helen and I discussed the possibility of mainstreaming Brett into my class of twenty-one students. We discussed the amount of time he'd spend in my class, the best time of day, appropriate instruc-

HELEN M. COYLE

DENISE PILGRIM

tion levels, and because Brett's in a wheelchair, space for movement in my classroom.

HELEN: Brett wasn't eager to go to Denise's class at first. Last year he developed confidence in me, though. We started planning for mainstreaming when we wrote his IEP for this year.

DENISE: We started mainstreaming Brett after the fourth week of school, first just in the morning during math when Helen could spend some time in my class. This made it a lot easier for him. At first, Brett was reluctant to participate in my class, but with Helen's encouragement and mine—and especially his new classmates'—his fear soon disappeared. Then we added language arts, which follows math. Helen would come into my classroom periodically to reassure Brett that he wasn't alone and to see what we were doing so she'd know what he was working on. Eventually, we dropped that support. Brett now comes to my classroom as soon as he gets to school so that he can interact with his classmates during free activity time and be with them during our initial activities of the day. This allows him to participate when I go over the day's schedule and

we do the calendar and sing our song for the month.

HELEN: Denise is responsible for Brett's academic learning only. He gets the same report card as the regular students, he's graded by the same criteria as others, he takes the same standardized tests, participates in class activities, and goes on class field trips. He goes to assembly programs, music, art, and library with the regular first-graders, as well as the academic classes Denise mentioned. For field trips, I arrange for the special bus and determine whether the place the class is going is wheelchair accessible. I provide the adaptive equipment Brett requires—a floor table and a computer, for example. Brett wears a body jacket to prevent further scoliosis. Because of this, spinal exercises such as stretching and twisting are imperative. He has to have some special therapies.

DENISE: Brett's special therapies cause him to miss some assignments in my room, which are made up as homework or in Helen's class. I don't alter my instruction or goals for Brett, but I do make adjustments that will enable him to complete his work and get the most out of instruction. For example, I place him in the front of the room when he's copying from the board and provide a pointer when he needs to point to words we're reading from the board or pocket chart. My aide and I had to learn how to lift Brett correctly to get him from his chair to the floor so he can work at his floor desk, which he prefers. The occupational therapist made large link letters that enable Brett to work on individual sight words. All this seems simple, but our success required shared responsibilities and understanding. It involved teamwork for follow-up, scheduling, and being aware of Brett's condition—his capabilities, strengths, and weaknesses.

HELEN: Time is a very important commodity in Brett's day, so I try to incorporate as much therapeutic movement into his regular activities as I can. When he's manipulating objects in math and working at his floor table, I put the materials behind him and to his right and left. This way he needs to twist and stretch to get the materials. Brett also needs to stand during the day. When time doesn't permit this in my classroom, I take his standing table into Denise's class. I'm responsible to see that Brett's required therapies are scheduled, that he's getting alternate positioning, and that his bathroom and eating needs are met. Denise doesn't need to take care of these concerns. She and I meet frequently during the week to discuss his needs, achievement, and goals. I look to Denise to meet his academic needs, and I try to reinforce the concepts she presents. I've made some materials that are easier for him to use, and I try to give him as much access to a computer as I can. Brett can write legibly with a pencil, but he can write faster with the computer. I try to have Brett develop his physical and mental abilities as much as possible. If he can do something without adaptive equipment, I encourage him to do that and not get used to equipment that would keep him dependent.

DENISE: The most difficult thing for me is not to allow Brett to just get by. Sometimes he doesn't finish work or gets tired and doesn't want the challenge. I had to make myself keep the expectations and goals the same as for other children. Helen kept reminding me that

Brett is here to learn and asking what she could do to help make it easier for me. You might think that Brett's poor speech and manual dexterity would have been issues, but they weren't. True, he might have to tell me something several times before I understand, and it takes him longer to complete an assignment. But I learned to be patient, and his difference doesn't interfere with the rest of the class.

> He's learning self-worth. What more important lesson can we teach our students?

HELEN: When Brett began going into Denise's class, the other children were very curious about why he had to be in a wheelchair. Denise arranged a time when I could speak to her class about Brett's physical condition. I brought in a plastic skeleton and a model of the brain and began to describe the nature of Brett's handicap and why he couldn't walk or feel his legs. The children accepted what they were able to understand, asked questions, and then accepted Brett as one of their group. They put no conditions on their friendship and didn't exclude him. The most difficult part of mainstreaming Brett doesn't have anything to do with Denise. It comes from other school personnel who are not used to having a physically handicapped child during regular activities. They're not used to having students like Brett participate in standardized testing, school performances, and so on. The more activities I can involve them in, the more the curtain of fear and disbelief is lifted and the easier it gets.

DENISE: I think the greatest barriers to special and general education teachers' working together are not having enough time to talk and plan and general education teachers' belief that they'll have to alter their instruction too much. I think we general educators tend to forget why we are doing what we're doing—forget that we're not here just for the general population but also for special

kids who may take a little longer to understand or complete a task. Kids in special education need to see what the "real world" is like, too, not experience just the special class with its small student-teacher ratio and teachers who are trained to meet their special needs. We general educators mustn't forget that we went into our profession to prepare all students to achieve whatever they can and that we must accept all students and what they bring to the classroom. Special education teachers have to find the right classroom teachers to make this work—those with the right personality, classroom setup, and a willingness to talk.

HELEN: The most rewarding aspect of our teamwork for me is Brett's progress. He now willingly goes to Denise's class and doesn't need me to be with him. He initiates and participates in conversations with other kids and adults. He's more outgoing and sociable, and he's beginning to read. He's excited about learning new things, and he's eager to share what he's learned with his family and me. It's almost like a metamorphosis. It's brought a lot of joy to his family. They see him now as capable, and their hopes are lifted. Brett is gaining pride in himself and his accomplishments. He's learning self-worth. What more important lesson can we teach our students?

DENISE: I agree with Helen. Another rewarding aspect of working with Brett is knowing that I have the support of the special education team and Brett's family. The other children cheer him on, and they're always willing to give a helping hand—sometimes too much so!

HELEN M. COYLE:
Teacher of multi-handicapped, Hollymead Elementary School, Charlottesville, Virginia; B.S., Education, State College at Fitchburg, Massachusetts

DENISE PILGRIM:
First-grade teacher, Hollymead Elementary School; B.S., Early Childhood, North Carolina A&T State University; M.Ed., Reading, University of Virginia

"Uncomplicated" Fashions Designed for Handicapped

Some days Teresa White's joints are so stiff that she cannot stand to pull on pants. She must lean against a wall. A social worker who worked in rehabilitation of the disabled and elderly, Mrs. White now knows—and lives—the daily frustrations of her former patients. She suffers from rheumatoid arthritis. . . .

Some 30 million disabled Americans share Mrs. White's frustrations. For the vast majority, fashionable clothing is out of the question. They search clothing racks for loose-fitting garments with large zippers and buttons or elasticized waists. If they are able to find easy-access clothing, it is often dowdy. But along came M. Dolores Quinn, a fashion design professor at Drexel University here, who has begun a quiet revolution. . . .

Four summers ago, Miss Quinn was planning a course for her students when she concluded that they should learn to work within limits. "Students hadn't been directing their thinking toward boundaries, that discipline we all apply on a daily basis," she recalled. So she assigned them a project of designing clothing for the physically handicapped.

Her able-bodied students taped their fingers together to experience the difficulty of dressing with limited hand motion, tried dressing with only one arm and confined themselves in other ways to understand the dressing limitations of a disabled person. They talked with handicapped people, nurses, and therapists. By the end of the summer the students had turned out garments that were not only comfortable and easily donned and doffed, but were stylish in design.

That summer course was the seed that grew into Miss Quinn's "Design Within Limits" project. With funds from Drexel, the National Endowment for the Arts, several foundations and private contributors, she opened a design laboratory from which have come attractive functional prototype clothes for men and women with physical limitations, including the following:

- Slacks that convert to shorts with horizontal zippers that make prosthesis fitting easier for an amputee.
- A wrap skirt, for easy access, with several pleats at the side. Its matching pleat-front vest has no buttons.
- A tissue-like navy nylon raincoat designed for wheelchair-bound women. Gathered across the bodice and trimmed in narrow blue and green piping, it features a hood that drops to become a cowl collar. People in wheelchairs told Miss Quinn that they do not like to sit on a lot of bulky fabric, so she designed the raincoat with a slit from the midback to the hem.
- Slacks with two diagonal zippers from the waist to the side seams, allowing the front panel to drop easily, useful for people who wear a catheter.
- Stretch denim jeans designed with horizontal pleats over a Lycra backing at the knee. This accordion-like design gives more stretch room at the knee and keeps pant legs from riding up for people in wheelchairs.
- Slacks with vertical zippers in each side seam from waist to ankle, which are useful for those who wear braces and need extra width in getting a foot into a pant leg.
- Pockets are handy for people in wheelchairs but the conventional placement of pockets, in side seams, is inconvenient and bulky. Miss Quinn designed pockets that can be attached to a waistband in front.

SOURCE: Martha Jablow, New York Times News Service. Copyright © 1981 by The New York Times Company. Reprinted with permission.

for such students tend to be particularly specific and detailed. The instructional goals and objectives often include seemingly minute steps, especially for young children with severe disabilities. Many of the children under the age of three years who need special education and related services are children with physical disabilities. These children are required by law (P.L. 99-457) to have **individualized family service plans (IFSPs)** rather than IEPs (see Chapters 1 and 11). These plans must specify how the family will be involved in intervention as well as what other services will be provided.

Educational Placement

Children with physical disabilities may be given an education in any one of several different settings, depending on the type and severity of the condition, the services available in the community, and the medical prognosis for the condition. If such children ordinarily attend regular public school classes but must be hospitalized for more than a few days, they may be included in a class in the hospital itself. If they must be confined to their homes for a time, a visiting or homebound teacher may provide tutoring until they can return to regular classes. In these cases, which usually involve accident victims or conditions that are not permanently and severely disabling, relatively minor, commonsense adjustments are required to continue the children's education and keep them from falling behind their classmates. At the other extreme, usually involving serious or permanent disabilities, the child may be taught for a time in a hospital school or a special public school class designed specifically for children with physical disabilities. Today most are being integrated into the public schools because of advances in medical treatment: new developments in bioengineering, allowing them greater mobility and functional movement; decreases in or removal of architectural barriers and transportation problems; and the movement toward public education for *all* children (Fraser & Hensinger, 1983).

Educational Goals and Curricula

It is not possible to prescribe educational goals and curricula for physically disabled children as a group because their limitations vary so greatly from child to child. Even among children with the same condition, goals and curricula must be determined after assessing the individual child's intellectual, physical, sensory, and emotional characteristics.

A physical disability, especially a severe and chronic one that limits mobility, may have two implications for education. The child may be deprived of experiences that nondisabled children have, and the child may find it impossible to manipulate educational materials and respond to educational tasks the way most children do. For example, a child with severe cerebral palsy cannot take part in most outdoor play activities and travel experiences and may not be able to hold and turn pages in books, write, explore objects manually, or use a typewriter without special equipment.

For children with an impairment that is only physical, curriculum and educational goals should ordinarily be the same as for nondisabled children: reading, writing, arithmetic, and experiences designed to familiarize them with the world about them. In addition, special instruction may be needed in mobility skills, daily living skills, and occupational skills. That is, because of their physical impairments, these children may need special, individualized instruction in the use of mechanical devices that will help them perform tasks that are much simpler for the nondisabled.

For children with other handicaps in addition to physical limitations, curricula will need to be further adapted (Hanson & Harris, 1986).

Educational goals for students with severe or profound disabilities must be related to their functioning in everyday community environments. Only recently have educators begun to address the problems of analyzing community tasks (e.g., crossing streets, using money, riding public transportation, greeting neighbors) and planning efficient instruction for severely handicapped individuals (Snell & Browder, 1986). Efficient instruction in such skills requires that teaching occur in the community environment itself.

Links with Other Disciplines

In the opening pages of this chapter we made two points: Physically disabled children have medical problems, and interdisciplinary cooperation is necessary in their education. It is important for the teacher to know what other disciplines are involved in the child's care and treatment, and to be able to communicate with professionals in these areas about the physical, emotional, and educational development of each child.

It goes almost without saying that knowing the child's medical status is crucial. Many physically disabled children will need the services of a physical therapist and/or occupational therapist. Both can give valuable suggestions about helping the child use his or her physical abilities to the greatest possible extent, continuing

Hospitalization, frightening and painful medical procedures, separation from parents, and demands for learning new and difficult skills often present educational and emotional problems for children with serious physical impairments or diseases. (Merrell Wood/The Image Bank)

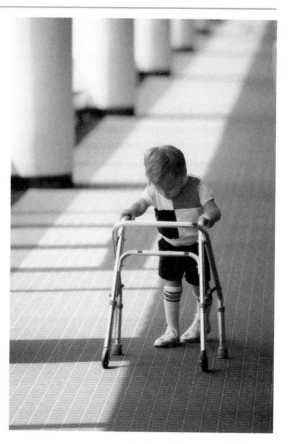

therapeutic management in the classroom, and encouraging independence and good work habits. Teachers should be particularly concerned about how to handle and position the child so that the risk of further physical disability is minimized and independent movement and manipulation of educational materials are most efficiently learned.

Specialists in prosthetics and orthotics design and build artificial limbs, braces, and other devices that help physically disabled individuals function more conventionally. By conferring with such specialists, the teacher will get a better grasp of the function and operation of a child's prosthesis or orthosis and understand what the child can and cannot be expected to do.

Social workers and psychologists are the professionals with whom most teachers are quite familiar. Cooperation with them may be particularly important in the case of a physically disabled child. Work with the child's family and community agencies is often necessary to prevent lapses in treatment. The child may also be particularly susceptible to psychological stress, so the school psychologist may need to be consulted to obtain an accurate assessment of intellectual potential.

Speech/language therapists are often called on to work with physically disabled children, especially those with cerebral palsy. The teacher will want advice from the speech/language therapist on how to maximize the learning of speech and language.

EARLY INTERVENTION

Two concerns of all who work with young physically disabled children are (1) early identification and intervention and (2) development of communication. Identifying signs of developmental delay so that intervention can begin as early as possible is important in preventing further disabilities that can result from lack of teaching and proper care. Early intervention is also important for maximizing the outcome of therapy. Communication skills are difficult for some physically disabled children to learn, and they are one of the critical objectives of any preschool program (see Chapter 6).

Probably the first and most pervasive concerns of teachers of young physically disabled children should be handling and positioning. *Handling* refers to how the child is picked up, carried, held, and assisted; *positioning* refers to providing support for the child's body and arranging instructional or play materials in certain ways. Proper handling makes the child more comfortable and receptive to education. Proper positioning maximizes physical efficiency and ability to manipulate materials. It also inhibits undesirable motor responses while promoting desired growth and motor patterns (Fraser & Hensinger, 1983).

What constitutes proper positioning for one child may not be appropriate for another. It is important that the teacher of physically disabled children be aware of some general principles of positioning and handling; in addition, he or she must work closely with physical therapists and physicians so that each child's particular needs are met.

The physical problems that most often require special handling and positioning involve muscle tone. Some children have **spastic** muscles—chronic increased muscle tone. As a result, their limbs are either flexed or extended all the time. If nothing is done to counteract the effects of the chronic imbalance of muscle tone, the child develops **contractures**—permanent shortening of muscles and connective tissues that results in deformity and further disability. Other children have athetosis or fluctuating muscle tone that results in almost constant uncontrolled movement.

If these movements are not somehow restrained, the child cannot accomplish many motor tasks successfully. Still other children have muscles that are **hypotonic.** These children appear floppy—their muscles are flaccid and weak. The hypotonia may prevent them from learning to hold up their heads, sit, or stand. All these muscle tone problems can occur together in the same child, they can occur with varying degrees of severity, and they can affect various parts of the body differently.

Another major problem that involves handling and positioning is the presence of abnormal reflexes. These are reflexes that most children exhibit during certain developmental periods but do not show after a given age. An example is the **asymmetrical tonic neck reflex (ATNR),** which babies normally show from birth to about four months but which is definitely abnormal or pathological if exhibited by a child who is a year old. The stimulus that elicits ATNR is turning the head to either side while lying on the back. The reflex is characterized by extension of the arm and leg on the side toward which the head is turned and flexion of the other arm and leg (see Figure 9.11). Utley, Holvoet, and Barnes (1977) have noted the problems caused by a pathological ATNR: First, rolling over is difficult or impossible; second, the child who is on all fours will collapse if the face is turned to either side; third, the child may not be able to get both hands to the midline for manual activities; fourth, self-feeding and walking are difficult.

Handling and positioning the physically disabled child demand attention to support of the child's body at various points and how various postures influence muscle tone and ability to move. There are several key points—neck and spine, shoulder

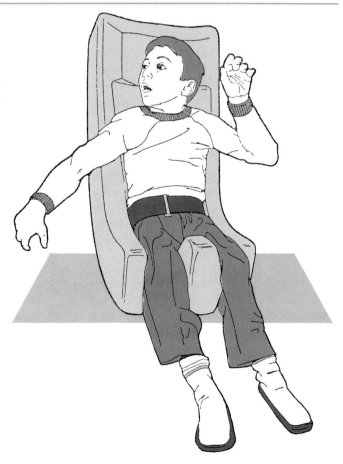

Figure 9.11 Asymmetrical tonic neck reflex. As shown in this illustration, the ATNR causes a student to assume a "fencing" position every time his head is turned.

SOURCE: B. A. Fraser and R. N. Hensinger, *Managing Physical Handicaps: A Practical Guide for Parents, Care Providers, and Educators* (Baltimore: Paul H. Brooks, 1983), p. 167. Copyright © 1983. Used with permission.

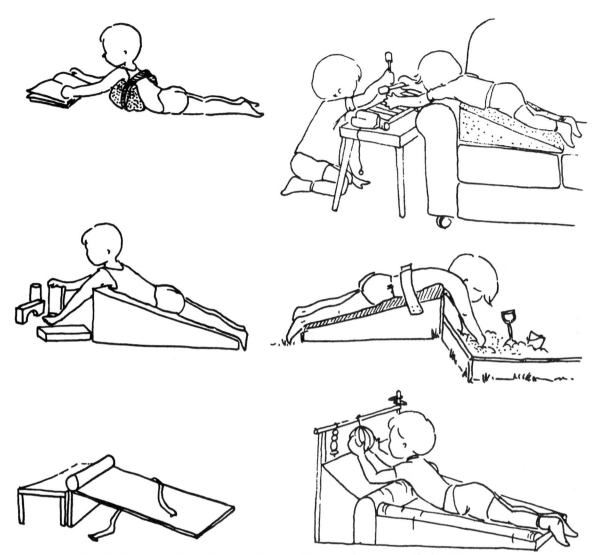

Figure 9.12 *Children positioned on wedges so they are free to use their arms and hands to reach and grasp. A wedge can be made of foam rubber, padded boards, or rolled blankets or towels to achieve proper support and positioning.*

SOURCE: N. R. Finnie, *Handling the Young Cerebral Palsied Child at Home,* 2nd ed. Copyright © 1974 by Nancie R. Finnie, F.C.S.P. Additions for U.S. edition copyright © 1975 by E. P. Dutton. Reprinted by permission of the publisher, E. P. Dutton and Wm. Heinemann Medical Books, London.

girdle, and pelvic area—where support should be given because pressure on these points controls muscle tone in the extremities and influences voluntary movement. Picking up, carrying, or handling children without attention to support at these key points may only make the child's voluntary movements more difficult (Hanson & Harris, 1986). Simple adaptive equipment is frequently required to keep the child positioned properly for movement and learning. Often such equipment can easily be made (DuBose & Deni, 1980; Fraser & Hensinger, 1983; Hanson & Harris, 1986; Verhaaren & Connor, 1981a, 1981b). Three examples of such positioning equipment are shown in Figures 9.12, 9.13, and 9.14. Some adaptive equipment for positioning can be purchased, but it often needs to be tailored to the needs of the individual child.

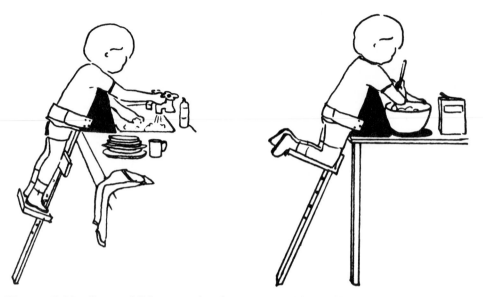

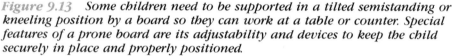

Figure 9.13 *Some children need to be supported in a tilted semistanding or kneeling position by a board so they can work at a table or counter. Special features of a prone board are its adjustability and devices to keep the child securely in place and properly positioned.*

SOURCE: N. R. Finnie, *Handling the Young Cerebral Palsied Child at Home* (New York: Dutton, 1975).

The teacher of young children with physical disabilities must know how to teach gross motor responses such as head control, rolling over, sitting, standing, and walking. Fine-motor skills such as pointing, reaching, grasping, and releasing are also critically important. These motor skills are best taught in the context of daily lessons that involve self-help and communication. That is, motor skills are not taught in isolation but as part of daily living and learning activities that will increase the child's communication, independence, creativity, motivation, and future

Figure 9.14 *Various adaptive equipment can be devised for maintaining a child in a side-lying position. Boards forming a right angle can be used, as shown here, but sandbags or even the right angle formed by a wall and the floor can be used.*

SOURCE: R. F. DuBose and K. Deni, "Easily Constructed Adaptive and Assistive Equipment," *Teaching Exceptional Children 12* (1980), 116–123. Copyright 1980 by The Council for Exceptional Children. Reprinted with permission.

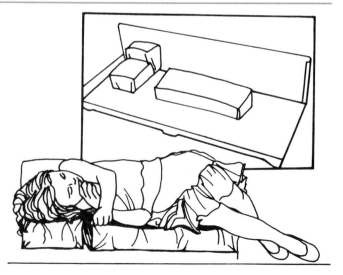

learning. Motor and communication skills necessary for daily living are not the only areas in which the teacher must provide instruction. Learning social responsiveness, appropriate social initiation, how to play with others, and problem solving, for example, are important goals for which the teacher must develop instructional strategies. Some children who are well beyond the typical preschooler's age may still be functioning at a very early developmental level. Consequently, the muscle tone, posture, and movement problems we discuss here, as well as the approach to teaching we just described, apply to some older students too.

TRANSITION

Transition involves a turning point, a change from one situation or environment to another. When special educators speak of transition, they typically refer to change from school to work or from adolescence to adulthood. For children with physical disabilities, however, transition is perhaps a more pervasive concern than for children with other disabilities. It may involve discharge from intensive care or transition from hospital to home at any age. Neisworth and Fewell (1989) have noted that "in an era of increasingly sophisticated medical technology, transition begins for some families at or shortly after the birth of a child" (p. xi). Nevertheless, we focus our attention here on the transition concerns of adolescents and young adults.

Two areas of concern for transition stand out clearly for physically disabled adolescents and young adults: careers and sociosexuality. Adolescents begin contemplating and experimenting with jobs, social relations, and sexuality in a direct and serious way. For the adolescent with a physical disability, these questions and trial behaviors are often especially perplexing, not just to themselves but to their families as well. "Can I get and hold a satisfying job?" "Can I become independent?" "Will I have close and lasting friendships?" "Will anyone find me physically attractive?" "How can I gratify my sexual needs?" Ordinary adolescents have a hard time coming to grips with these questions and the developmental tasks they imply; adolescents with physical disabilities often have an even harder time.

As we pointed out in our discussion of psychological characteristics, there is no formula for predicting the emotional or behavioral problems a person with a given physical disability will have. Much depends on the management and training the person has received. So it is particularly important to provide both career education and sociosexual education for physically disabled students.

Choice of Career

For the physically disabled adolescent or young adult, career considerations are extremely important (Fonosch, Arany, Lee, & Loving, 1982). In working out an occupational goal, it is vital to appraise realistically the individual's specific abilities and disabilities and to assess motivation carefully. Some disabilities clearly rule out certain occupational choices. With other disabilities, high motivation and full use of residual function may make it possible to achieve unusual professional status. For instance, Tom Dempsey, one of football's best field-goal kickers, had a congenitally deformed arm, hand, and foot.

One of the greatest problems in dealing with physically disabled adolescents is helping them attain a realistic employment outlook. Intelligence, emotional characteristics, motivation, and work habits must be assessed more carefully than physical limitations. Furthermore, the availability of jobs and the demands of certain occupations must be taken into account. The child who is moderately mentally retarded and has severe spastic quadriplegia is obviously not going to have a career as a lawyer, a laboratory technician, or a clerk-typist. But what of one who has severe spastic quadriplegia and a bright mind? Such a person may be able to overcome both the physical limitation and the associated social stigma and be successful in a wide variety of fields in which the work is more mental than physical.

There are no simple conclusions regarding the occupational outlook for students with physical disabilities. Those with mild or transitory handicapping conditions may not be affected at all in their occupational choices. Some with relatively mild physical disabilities may be unemployed, or even unemployable, because of inappropriate social and emotional behavior or poor work habits; they may need vocational rehabilitation training to function even in a vocation with limited demands. Some people with severe physical disabilities are able to use their intelligence, social skills, and residual physical abilities to the fullest and become competitive employees (or employers) in demanding occupations.

Sociosexuality

Until fairly recently, physical disabilities were assumed to cancel human sexuality. People who were not whole physically, especially if they had limited mobility, were thought of as having no sex appeal for anyone and as having little or no ability or right to function sexually. These ideas are reflected in the words of

Participation in social life and sociosexual activities are often special concerns of youths with physical disabilities. (© Bohdan Hrynewych/Southern Light)

William L. Rush (1977), a physically disabled young man whose romantic feelings were rejected by the first young woman he felt he loved: "Only two roads are open for the severely physically handicapped in dealing with their feelings of love: the road of expecting and accepting only platonic love or the road of fantasizing. Neither is very satisfactory" (p. 6).

Fortunately attitudes and experiences are changing. It is now recognized that handicapped people have a right to family life education, including sex education, and to a full range of human relationships, including appropriate sexual expression (Duncan & Canty-Lemke, 1986; Edmonson, 1980). Sociosexual education for physically disabled students, as such education for nonhandicapped children and youths, should begin early, continue through adulthood, and include information about the structure and functions of bodies, human relationships and responsibilities, and alternative modes of sexual gratification.

Physically disabled youths need to experience close friendships and warm physical contact that is not sexually intimate. But it is neither realistic nor fair to expect people with physical disabilities to keep all their relationships platonic or to limit themselves to fantasy. Most physical disability, even if severe, does not in itself kill sexual desire or prevent sexual gratification; nor does it preclude marriage and children. The purpose of special education and rehabilitation is to make exceptional individuals' lives as full and complete as possible. In the case of youths with physical disabilities, this may involve teaching or providing alternative means of sexual stimulation and accepting sexual practices and relationships that are different from the norm, as discussed by Lewandowski and Cruickshank (1980). With sensitive education and rehabilitation, satisfying sociosexual expression can be achieved by all but a small minority (DeLoach & Greer, 1981).

SUGGESTIONS FOR TEACHING STUDENTS WITH PHYSICAL DISABILITIES IN GENERAL EDUCATION CLASSROOMS

What to Look for in School

As you know from reading this chapter, children and adolescents attending school have a wide range of health and physical problems. This range is increasing as medical, educational, and technological advancements make possible the integration into the classroom of students with severe disabilities. Although many children with physical problems will be diagnosed before being mainstreamed, some may undergo changes in their conditions or in their reactions to medication during the school year, and other students may develop illnesses or be involved in accidents after entering school. The following questions may help you to identify potential problems (Dykes & Venn, 1983). Ask yourself if your student

- Seems as energetic as usual
- Initiates contact as usual
- Has normal skin tone
- Has any sores, rashes, cuts, and so on that you haven't seen before
- Is wearing clothing that seems to fit differently than usual
- Indicates verbally or nonverbally that he or she has discomfort or pain?

How to Gather Information

Although as a teacher you are not expected to be a medical diagnostician, you may have more opportunities than any other adult to observe your students. You therefore have an important responsibility to be aware of changes in your students' physical conditions and to notify the school nurse and parents or guardians of your observations so that they can arrange for medical examination and/or treatment.

For those students in your class with diagnosed physical and health impairments you will want to gather information that enables you to answer these questions (Lewis & Doorlag, 1987):

Medical Concerns:
1. Does the child take medication? How frequently? In what amounts? Is the school authorized to administer the medication during school hours?
2. What are the side effects of the medication?
3. What procedures should be followed in the event of a seizure, insulin shock diabetic coma, or other problem?
4. Should the child's activities be restricted in any way?

Travel:
1. How will the child be transported to school?
2. Will the child arrive and leave at the usual school times?
3. Will the child need special accommodations to travel within the school building or the classroom?

Communication:
1. Can the child write? Type? How?
2. Is an electronic communication aid used? If so, are there special instructions necessary for the child to use it or for the teacher to understand and maintain it?
3. Can the child make his or her needs known to the teacher? How?
4. Are there other aids or devices that I should know about?

Self-Care:
1. What types of self-care help, such as feeding and toileting, does the child need? Who is responsible for providing this care?
2. What equipment does the child need?

Positioning:
1. What positioning aids or devices (braces, pillows, wedges) does the child use?
2. What particular positions are most useful for specific academic activities and for resting?
3. Are there other aids or devices that I should know about?

Reading your students' individualized educational programs (IEPs) and consulting other school personnel who work with them (see p. 380) may provide answers to these questions. For additional medical information about specific diseases and disorders and practical suggestions for teachers, see *Physically Handicapped Children: A Medical Atlas for Teachers* (Bleck & Nagel, 1982) and the chapters concerning physical disabilities and emergency medical procedures in the *Handbook of Special Education* (Verhaaren & Connor, 1981).

Teaching Techniques to Try

The interventions required in school for students with physical disabilities vary greatly, depending on the type and severity of the students' conditions. Some students may require specialized assistance or training in such areas as mobility or communications. Others may need additional support to manage the sensory, learning, and behavioral disorders that can accompany some physical disabilities (see the appropriate chapters for these interventions). Still others may require no modifications or only minimal adjustments. For example, teachers may simply need to extend the deadline for students to complete assignments when they are absent or fatigued by their illnesses or the treatment of their illnesses. In fact, most physically and health-impaired students attend regular education classes for most of the school day and are expected to progress through the same curricular materials as nondisabled students (Reynolds & Birch, 1982). Many of these students, however, require some adaptation of instructional materials and activities in order to succeed in school and to maximize their independence.

Instructional Adaptations

One of the most common adaptations teachers make for physically disabled students is to modify the ways in which they respond to academic tasks.

WRITTEN RESPONSES. To complete class written activities some students need simple modifications and/or assistance in selecting the appropriate materials. These adaptations include the following (Hale, 1979, pp. 25–26):

- Writing on a pad of paper, rather than on loose sheets.
- Using tape, a clipboard, or a metal cookie sheet on which magnets are placed to secure loose papers
- Placing a rubber strip on the back of a ruler or using a magnetic ruler to prevent slipping when measuring or drawing lines
- Using pens (felt tip) and pencils (soft lead) that require less pressure
- Using pens and pencils that are easier to grasp. Twisting a rubber band around the shaft of the pen or pencil or slipping corrugated rubber or plastic tubing, a form curler, a golf practice ball, or a sponge rubber ball over the writing instrument makes it easier to hold.
- Using an electronic typewriter, word processor, or computer
- Using typing aids such as a pointer stick attached to a head or mouthpiece to strike the keys, a keyboard guard that prevents striking two keys at once, line spacers that hold written materials while typing, corrective typewriter ribbons that do not require the use of erasers.
- Writing or typing at a table that adjusts to appropriate heights for wheelchairs
- Using calculators to perform computations
- Audiotaping assignments, lectures, and other instructional activities that require extensive writing

For students who have more limited strength, muscular control, or mobility, selecting and designing instructional materials that require no letter and word formation may simplify responding to written tasks. For example, you may use worksheets and tests that direct students to put a line through the correct answer, providing enough space between the answer alternatives so that students can indicate their choice without marking another response accidentally (Bigge, 1982).

Still other adaptations do not require students to hold a pencil or pen. For example, you may arrange for students to move magnetic letters and numbers on a metal cookie sheet to indicate their responses or ask them to put a wooden block on top of their answer choice (Bigge, 1982).

Electronic devices also facilitate responding. Computers can be equipped with a variety of switches that allow students to operate them with a single movement. Selection of the type of switch will depend on the type of movement the student can best perform. Touch-sensitive screens, another computer adaptive device, enable students to respond to instructions and questions by touching a specific area of the screen.

ORAL RESPONSES. Speech synthesizers voice the responses nonverbal or severely speech-impaired students type on the computer and thereby enable them to participate in class discussions and to ask questions immediately. Less expensive communication boards, charts of pictures, symbols, numbers, or words, allow students to indicate their responses to specific items represented on the charts. To facilitate communication using these boards, Bigge (1982) recommends that listeners name the picture or say the letter or word quickly so that the conversation moves along more rapidly. Teachers have also found less comprehensive response adaptations useful during oral activities. For example, you can give students color-coded objects, such as blocks of wood that are easy to handle and do not slip, to indicate their responses to polar questions such as true/false, agree/disagree/don't know, or same/different.

READING TASKS. Devices that facilitate reading include book holders; reading stands that adjust to reclining, sitting, and standing positions; and page turners that range from pencil erasers to electric-powered devices that can be operated with minimal mobility (Hale, 1979). Talking books enable students who cannot hold books to tape lectures and to enjoy a wide variety of recorded novels, textbooks, and magazines. Specialized talking books, called compressed speech machines, play at faster than usual speeds and may be helpful to students who must learn large amounts of information (Dykes & Venn, 1983). This equipment is available at no cost from the Library of Congress.

In addition to these devices, instructional materials can be adapted for use during reading and thinking activities. For example, you can mount materials used in classifying and matching activities on cardboard, to help students handle them more easily, and supply containers with different category labels into which students can drop their answers, to eliminate papers falling from desks or wheelchair trays (Bigge, 1982). Teachers have also found it helpful to use photo albums that have sticky backings and plastic cover sheets and plastic photo cubes to hold instructional materials, such as pictures or word cards. This latter adaptation allows students to move the cubes to respond to a variety of tasks (Bigge, 1982).

Helpful Resources

School Personnel

Because students with health impairments and physical disabilities often require the expertise of a variety of professionals, several individuals may provide services to your student. Understanding the role of each is important in coordinating instructional and medical interventions. The following list describes the functions professionals typically fulfill in the treatment of physically disabled students (Dykes & Venn, 1983, pp. 261–263):

Physicians are licensed medical doctors who provide services that include diagnosing; prescribing medication; making referrals for physical therapy, occupational therapy, or orthopedic treatment; and recommending the extent and length of various activities and treatments. Specialized physicians include: orthopedists (specialists in diagnosing and treating joint, bones, and muscles impairments), neurologists (specialists in diagnosing and treating impairments to the nervous system such as cerebral palsy and muscular dystrophy), radiologists (specialists in using X rays and radioactive substances to diagnose and treat conditions such as cancer).

School nurses' responsibilities vary depending on the school system in which they are employed. Often they administer student medications at school, treat medical emergencies, provide medical information to students and staff, and help in identifying community health agencies for families.

Occupational therapists provide medically-prescribed assistance to help individuals manage their impairments. They may teach various self-help, daily-living, prevocational, leisure-time, and perceptual-motor skills and provide instruction in the use of adaptive devices including one-hand typewriters and hand splints.

Rehabilitation counselors provide a range of services related to vocational training and employment. For example, they may conduct vocational assessment and counseling and arrange for work training and experience. Typically they are employed by the state vocational rehabilitation agency, rather than by the school district.

Physical therapists provide services designed to restore or improve physical functioning and engage, in part, in such activities as exercising to increase coordination, range of motion, and movement. They also work to relieve pain.

Instructional Methods and Materials

Bigge, J. L. (1982). Teaching individuals with physical and multiple disabilities. Columbus, OH: Chas. E. Merrill.

Campbell, P. H. (1989). Students with physical disabilities. In R. Gaylord-Ross (Ed.), *Integration strategies for students with handicaps.* Baltimore: Brookes.

Eastman, M. K., & Safran, J. S. (1986). Activities to develop your students' motor skills. *Teaching Exceptional Children, 19,* 24–27.

Fithian, J. (Ed.). (1984). *Understanding the child with a chronic illness in the classroom.* Phoenix, AZ: Oryx Press.

Fraser, B. A., & Hensinger, R. N. (1983). *Managing physical handicaps.* Baltimore: Brookes.

Fredrick, J., & Fletcher, D. (1985). Facilitating children's adjustment to orthotic and prosthetic applicances. *Teaching Exceptional Children, 17,* 228–230.

Miller, S. E., & Schaumberg, K. (1988). Physical education activities for children with severe cerebral palsy. *Teaching Exceptional Children, 20,* 9–11.

Orelove, F. P., & Sobsey, D. (1987). *Educating children with multiple disabilities.* Baltimore: Brookes.

Self, P. C. (1984). *Physical disability: An annotated literature guide.* New York: Marcel Dekker.

Thornton, C. A., Tucker, B. F., Dossey, J. A., & Bazik, E. F. (1983). *Teaching mathematics to children with special needs.* Menlo Park, CA: Addison-Wesley.

Umbreit, J. (Ed.). (1983). *Physical disabilities and health impairments: An introduction.* Columbus, OH: Chas. E. Merrill.

Curricular Materials for and about Students with Physical Disabilities

*Brown, S., Hemphill, N. J., & Voeltz (1982). *The smallest minority: Adapted regular education social studies curricula for understanding and integrating severely disabled students. Lower elementary: Understanding self and others.* Honolulu: University of Hawaii/Manoa, Hawaii Intergration Project.

*Hemphill, N. J., Zukas, D., & Brown, S. (1982). *The smallest minority: Adapted regular education social studies curricula for understanding and integrating severely disabled students. The secondary grades: Understanding alienation.* Honolulu: University of Hawaii/Manoa, Hawaii Integration Project.

*Noonan, M. J., Hemphill, N. J., & Levy, G. (1983). *Social skills curricular strategy for students with severe disabilities.* Honolulu: University of Hawaii/Manoa, Hawaii Integration Project.

Office for the Education of Children with Handicapping Conditions (1982). *Motor impairment: Accepting individual differences.* Albany: New York State Education Department.

*Voeltz, L., Hemphill, N. J., Brown, S., Kishi, G., Klein, R., Fruehling, R., Levy, G., Collie, J., & Kube, C. (1983). The Special Friends program: A trainer's manual for integrated school settings. Honolulu: University of Hawaii/Manoa, Hawaii Integration Project.

* Available from Media Productions and Distributions, University of Hawaii, Castle Memorial Hall, 1776 University Avenue, Honolulu, HI 96822.

PHYSICAL DISABILITIES

Literature about Physically Disabled Individuals

ELEMENTARY: AGES 5–8 AND 9–12

Carlson, N. (1990). *Arnie and the new kid.* New York: Viking. (Ages 9–12)

Christian, M. B. (1985). *Growin' pains.* New York: Macmillan. (Ages 9–12)

Dana, M. (1988). *No time for secrets.* Mahwah, NJ: Troll Associates. (Ages 9–12)

Gorman, C. (1987). *Chelsey and the green-haired kid.* Boston: Houghton Mifflin. (Ages 9–12)

Gould, M. (1986). *The twelfth of June.* Philadelphia: Lippincott. (Ages 9–12, cerebral palsy)

Lasker, J. (1980). *Nick joins in.* Chicago: Albert Whitman. (Ages 5–8)

Rabe, B. (1981). *The balancing girl.* New York: Dutton. (Ages 5–8)

Roth, D. (1980). *The hermit of Fog Hollow.* Station, NY: Beaufort. (Ages 9–12)

Stern, C. (1981). *A different kind of gold.* New York: Harper & Row (ages 9–12)

Stover, M. F. (1989). *Midnight in the dollhouse.* Niles, IL: Albert Whitman. (Ages 9–12)

SECONDARY: AGES 13–18

Adler, C. S. (1981). *Down by the river.* New York: Coward, McCann, & Geoghegan. (Ages 13–18)

Blos, J. W. (1985). *Brothers of the heart: A story of the old northwest, 1837–1839.* New York: Scribner. (Ages 9–15).

Greenberg, J. (1983). *No dragons to slay.* New York: Farrar, Straus, & Giroux. (Ages 13–18, cancer)

Levy, M. (1982). *The girl in the plastic cage.* New York: Ballantine Books/Fawcett Juniper Books. (Ages 13–15, scoliosis)

Miklowitz, G. D. (1987). *Good-bye tomorrow.* New York: Delacorte Press. (Ages 13–18, AIDS)

Radley, G. (1984). *CF in his corner.* Soquel, CA: Four Winds Press (Ages 13–15, cystic fibrosis)

Ress, L. (1980). *Horse of air.* New York: Methuen (Ages 13–18)

Richmond, S. (1985). *Wheels for walking.* New York: Atlantic Monthly Press. (Ages 13–18, quadriplegia)

Slepian, J. (1980). *The Alfred summer.* New York: Macmillan (Ages 13–18, cerebral palsy.)

Software

(The following programs may be operated by an adaptive switch or touch-sensitive screens.)

Adventures of Jimmy-Jumper, Exceptional Children's Software, P.O. Box 487, Hays, KS 67601; (913) 625-9281 (prepositions; speech synthesizer required).

Counting Critters, MECC, 3490 Lexington Avenue, N., St. Paul, MN 55126; (612) 481-3500, (800) 228-3504.

Exploratory Plan, PEAL Software, 5000 North Parkway Calabasas, Ste. 105, Calabasas, CA 91302; (818) 883-7849 (communication).

First Verbs, Laureate Learning Systems, 110 East Spring Street, Winoski, VT 05404; (800) 655-4755 (speech synthesizer required).

First Words I and II, Laureate Learning Systems, 110 East Spring Street, Winoski, VT 05404; (800) 655-4755 (speech synthesizer required).

Interaction Games, Don Johnston Developmental Equipment, 1000 North Rand Road, Building 115, P.O. Box 639, Wauconda, IL 60084; (312) 526-2682 (row and column scanning).

Keyboarding for the Physically Handicapped, Gregg/McGraw-Hill, 1221 Avenue of the Americas, New York, NY 10020; (800) 262-4729.

Keyboarding with One Hand, Educational Electronic Technologies, LTD, 1088 Wantaugh Avenue, Wantaugh, NY 11793; (800) 4 EET USA.

Keytalk, PEAL Software, 5000 North Parkway Calabasas, Ste. 105, Calabasas, CA 91302; (818) 325-2001 (electronic communication aid).

Picture Programs, I, II, III, Parrol Software, P.O. Box 1139, State College, PA 16804; (812) 237-7282 (function, association, and rhyming words).

Rabbit Scanner, Exceptional Children's Software, P.O. Box 487, Hays, KS 67601; (913) 625-9281 (scanning trainer).

Representional Play, PEAL Software, 5000 North Parkway Calabasas, Ste. 105, Calabasas, CA 91302; (818) 883-7849 (communication).

Sunny Days, Don Johnston Developmental Equipment, 1000 North Rand Road, Building 115, P.O. Box 639, Wauconda, IL 60084; (312) 526-2682 (word recognition, spelling, and reading skills).

Switchmaster, Expert Systems Software, Ste. 316, Nashville, TN 37215; (615) 292-7667 (operation of switches).

Touch and Match, Exceptional Children's Software, P.O. Box 487, Hays, KS 67601; (913) 625-9281.

Organizations

AIDS

National AIDS Network, 2033 M Street, N.W., Suite 800, Washington, DC 20036; (202) 293-2437.

National Association of People with AIDS, 2025 I Street, N.W., Suite 415, Washington, DC 20006; (202) 429-2856.

Arthritis

Arthritis Foundation, 1314 Spring Street, N.W., Atlanta, GA 30309; (404) 872-7100.

Asthma

National Foundation for Asthma, P.O. Box 300069, Tucson, AZ 85751; (602) 323-6046.

Birth (Congenital) Defects

Association of Birth Defect Children, 3526 Emerywood Land, Orlando, FL 32812; (407) 859-2821.

March of Dimes Birth Defects Foundation, 1275 Mamaroneck Avenue, White Plains, NY 10605; (914) 428-7100.

Cancer

American Cancer Society, 1599 Clifton Road, Atlanta, GA 30329; (404) 320-3333.

Cancer Information Service, c/o National Cancer Institute, NIH Building 31, Room 10A24, Bethesda, MD 20892; (800) 4-CANCER.

Cerebral Palsy

United Cerebral Palsy Associations, 66 East Thirty-Fourth Street, New York, NY 10016; (212) 481-6300.

Child Abuse

American Association for Protecting Children, c/o American Humane Association, 9725 East Hampden Avenue, Denver, CO 80231; (303) 695-0811.

CHILDHELP U.S.A., Inc., 6463 Independence Avenue, Woodland Hills, CA 91370; (818) 347-7280.

National Child Abuse Hotline: (800) 4-A-CHILD.

Diabetes

American Diabetes Association, National Service Center, P.O. Box 25757, 1660 Duke Street, Alexandria, VA 22313; (703) 549-1500.

Epilepsy

Epilepsy Foundation of America, 4351 Garden City Drive, Landover, MD 20785; (301) 459-3700.

Muscular Dystrophy

Muscular Dystrophy Association, 810 Seventh Avenue, New York, NY 10019; (212) 586-0808.

Multiple Sclerosis

National Multiple Sclerosis Society, 205 East Forty-Second Street, New York, NY 10017; (212) 986-3240.

Bibliography for Teaching Suggestions

Bigge, J. L. (1982). *Teaching individuals with physical and multiple disabilities.* Columbus, OH: Chas. E. Merrill.

Bleck, E. E., & Nagel, D. A. (1982). *Physically handicapped children: A medical atlas for teachers* (2nd ed.). New York: Grune & Stratton.

Dykes, M. K., & Venn, J. (1983). Using health, physical, and medical data in the classroom. In J. Umbreit (Ed.), *Physical disabilities and health impairments: An introduction.* Columbus, OH: Chas. E. Merrill.

Hale, G. (1979). *The source book for the disabled.* Philadelphia: Saunders.

Lewis, R. B., & Doorlag, D. H. (1987). *Teaching special students in the mainstream.* Columbus, OH: Chas. E. Merrill.

Oettinger, L., & Coleman, J. (1981). Emergency medical procedures. In J. M. Kauffman & D. P. Hallahan (Eds.), *Handbook of special education.* Englewood Cliffs, NJ: Prentice-Hall.

Reynolds, M. C., & Birch, J. W. (1982). *Teaching exceptional children in all America's schools* (rev. ed.). Reston, VA: Council for Exceptional Children.

Verhaaren, P., & Connor, F. P. (1981). Physical disabilities. In J. M. Kauffman & D. P. Hallahan (Eds.), *Handbook of special education.* Englewood Cliffs, NJ: Prentice-Hall.

SUMMARY

Children with physical disabilities are those whose non-sensory physical limitations or health problems interfere with school attendance or learning to such an extent that special services, training, equipment, materials, or facilities are required. These children may have other disabilities such as mental retardation and emotional/ behavioral disorders. The medical nature of the problem highlights the need for interdisciplinary cooperation in special education.

Less than 0.5 percent of the child population receives special education and related services. Because of advances in medical technology, more children with severe disabilities are surviving, and many more are surviving disease or injury with mild impairments such as hyperactivity and learning disabilities. The needs of children and youths with physical disabilities and chronic illnesses far outstrip the public programs and services for them.

Children with neurological impairments have suffered damage to or deterioration of the central nervous system. Their behavioral symptoms include mental retardation, learning problems, perceptual-motor dysfunction, paralysis, seizures, and emotional/behavioral disorders. The causes of neurological impairments include infections, diseases, hypoxia, poisoning, congenital malformations, accidents, and child abuse.

Cerebral palsy (CP), a condition characterized by paralysis, weakness, uncoordination, and/or other motor dysfunction, accounts for about half of the children with physical impairments in the United States. It is nonprogressive brain damage that occurs before or during birth or in early childhood. Classification of CP is generally made according to the limbs involved and the type of motor disability. The educational problems associated with CP are varied because of the multiplicity of symptoms; a careful clinical appraisal must be made of each

individual to determine the type of special education needed.

Seizures are caused by an abnormal discharge of electrical energy in the brain. They may be generalized or partial. Recurrent seizures are referred to as epilepsy. Most people with seizure disorders are able to function normally, except when having a seizure. Intelligence is not directly affected by a seizure disorder, so educational procedures consist chiefly of attaining knowledge of the disorder and how to manage seizures, as well as a commitment to help dispel the ignorance and fear connected with seizures.

Spina bifida is a congenital midline defect resulting from failure of the bony spinal column to close completely during fetal development. The resulting damage to the nerves generally causes paralysis and/or lack of sensation below the site of the defect. The cause of spina bifida is not known. Educational implications of spina bifida are determined by the extent of the paralysis and medical complications, as well as the child's cognitive and behavioral characteristics. Intelligence and physical stamina are not directly affected by spina bifida, so most children with this condition attend regular classes.

An increasingly frequent cause of neurological impairment is traumatic head injury, frequently occurring as a result of vehicular accidents. The brain injury may range from mild to profound. Medical and educational personnel must work together as a team to provide transition from hospital or rehabilitation center to school. Frequent educational problems are focusing or sustaining attention, remembering, and learning new skills. Emotional, behavioral, and social problems may also be apparent.

A number of physical disabilities derive from musculoskeletal conditions, in which there are defects or diseases of the muscles or bones. Children with such disabilities have a range of difficulties in walking, standing, sitting, or using their hands. Muscular dystrophy is a degenerative disease causing a progressive weakening and wasting away of muscle tissues. Progressive physical immobility and the prospect of total disability or death make this condition especially difficult to manage. But intellectual capacity is not affected, and with proper motivation and educational procedures, most of these children can benefit from regular or special education programs. Arthritis is a disease that causes acute inflammation around the joints; its symptoms vary from mild to profound, and it affects children as well as adults. These and other musculoskeletal conditions do not cause lowered intelligence, so educational considerations include overcoming the child's limited mobility so that he or she can continue learning in as normal a way as possible.

Congenital malformations can involve any organ system, including the head and face, the heart and/or blood vessels, the hip or other joints, or the extremities (e.g., webbed or extra fingers or toes or other deformities of the hands or feet). Some malformations are genetic (caused by faulty chromosomes); others are caused by teratogens. Teratogens are deformity-producing factors, such as chemicals or infections, that interfere with normal fetal development. Alcohol is now the most common teratogen.

Accidents that bring about neurological impairment, disfigurement, or amputation are an important cause of physical disabilities among children and youths. AIDS, a fatal viral infection, is now forcing schools to make controversial decisions regarding sex education and inclusion of children and adults with the disease in the classroom. The number of infants and young children with AIDS is increasing dramatically because pregnant women with AIDS transmit the disease to their babies. The complications of the disease in its advanced stages include mental retardation, psychosis, seizures, and neurological impairment similar to cerebral palsy.

Adolescent pregnancy often results in children with physical disabilities. Teenage mothers are more likely than older women to give birth to premature babies or babies with disabilities and more likely also to abuse or neglect their children.

Besides alcohol, women may abuse other substances during pregnancy and thereby give birth to a child with disabilities. Use of cocaine and intravenous drugs by pregnant women is resulting in the birth of more babies with severe physiological, cognitive, and emotional problems.

Children dependent on ventilators are being returned home from hospitals in increasing numbers. Many of these children are returning to public schools. Careful consideration of the mainstreaming of these children is required.

Abused and neglected children represent an alarming and large number of those with physical disabilities. Many thousands of children each year are damaged—emotionally and physically—by adults who neglect, burn, beat, sexually molest, starve, and otherwise brutalize them. Children who already have disabilities are more likely than those without disabilities to be abused. Teachers must be especially alert to signs of possible child abuse and neglect.

As a group, children with physical disabilities represent the total range of impairment, and their behavioral and psychological characteristics thus vary greatly. The necessity for hospitalization, bed rest, prosthetic devices, and so on means that their academic achievement depends on individual circumstances, motivation, and the caliber of care received both at home and at school. The two major effects of a physical disability, especially if it is severe or prolonged, are that a child may be deprived of educationally relevant experiences and that he or she may not be able to learn to manipulate educational materials and respond to educational tasks the way most children do.

There does not appear to be a personality type associated with particular physical disabilities. The reactions of the public, family, peers, and educational personnel—as well as the child's own reactions to the disability—are all closely interwoven in the determination of any particular child's personality, motivation, and progress. Given ample opportunity to develop educationally, socially, and emotionally in as normal a fashion as possible, many children with physical disabilities are able to make a healthy adjustment to their impairments.

A prosthesis replaces a missing body part. An orthosis is a device that enhances the partial function of a body part. An adaptive device aids a person's daily activity. Important considerations in choosing prostheses, orthoses, and adaptive devices are simplicity, reliability, and the use of residual function.

Education for students with physical disabilities must focus on making the most of their assets. Behavior modification techniques have been valuable in helping children with physical disabilities achieve and perform at their maximum level. The student's individual characteristics (intellectual, sensory, physical, and emotional) must be considered when developing educational plans. Plans for young children must include service to the family. Increasingly, students with physical disabilities are being placed in regular classrooms. The problem of educating students with physical disabilities is often a problem of educating nonhandicapped students about the needs of people with disabilities. Along with scholastic education, the child may need special assistance in daily living, mobility, and occupational skills. Consequently, many other disciplines may be involved. The major considerations are to help each child become as independent and self-sufficient in daily activities as possible, to provide basic academic skills, and to prepare for advanced education.

Besides early identification and intervention to develop communication, handling and positioning are important considerations. Motor skills must be taught as part of daily lessons in self-help and communication.

Career choice and sociosexuality are two primary concerns of youths with physical disabilities. Career considerations must include careful evaluation of the young person's intellectual, emotional, and motivational characteristics as well as physical capabilities. Young people with physical disabilities have the right to the social relationships and modes of sexual expression afforded others in our society.

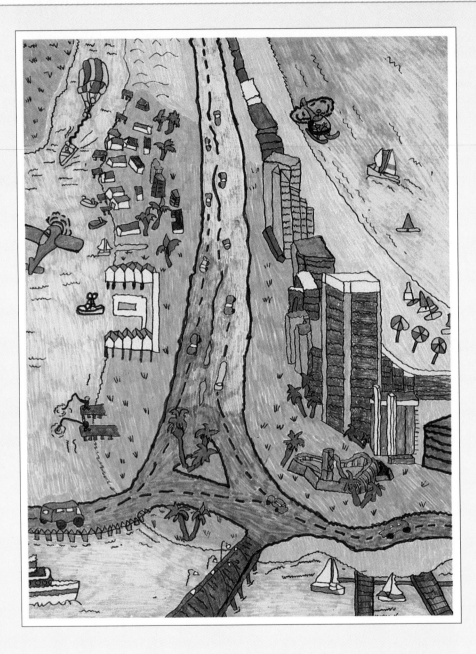

AERIAL VIEW
Udith A. Morton, Courtesy Very Special Arts

10

Giftedness

I think Jim Gillis was a much more remarkable person than his family and his intimates ever suspected. He had a bright and smart imagination and it was of the kind that turns out impromptu work and does it well, does it with easy facility and without previous preparation, just builds a story as it goes along, careless of whether it is proceeding, enjoying each fresh fancy as it flashes from the brain and caring not at all whether the story shall ever end brilliantly and satisfactorily or shan't end at all. Jim was born a humorist and a very competent one. When I remember how felicitous were his untrained efforts, I feel a conviction that he would have been a star performer if he had been discovered and had been subjected to a few years of training with a pen. A genius is not very likely to ever discover himself; neither is he very likely to be discovered by his intimates; they are so close to him that he is out of focus to them and they can't get at his proportions; they cannot perceive that there is any considerable difference between his bulk and their own. They can't get a perspective on him and it is only by a perspective that the difference between him and the rest of their limited circle can be perceived.

(*The Autobiography of Mark Twain*)

P eople who have special gifts, or at least have the potential for gifted performance, can go through life unrecognized. As Mark Twain pointed out (see page 397), they may seem unremarkable to their closest associates. Sometimes gifted children and youths are not discovered because their families and intimates simply place no particular value on their special abilities. Sometimes they are not recognized because they are not given the necessary opportunities or training. Especially in the case of those who are poor or members of minority groups, gifted children may be deprived of chances to demonstrate and develop their potential. How many more outstanding artists and scientists would we have if every talented child had the opportunity and the training necessary to develop his or her talents to the fullest possible extent? There is no way of knowing, but it is safe to say we would have more.

Unlike mental retardation and other handicapping conditions, giftedness is something to be fostered, not eliminated. Yet giftedness is not something a child can show without risk of stigma and rejection. Many people have a low level of tolerance for those who are intellectually superior or who eclipse the ordinary individual in some area of achievement. A child who achieves far beyond the level of his or her average peers may be subject to criticism or social isolation by other children or their parents. Had Jim Gillis been discovered, given a few years of training with a pen, and become a gifted writer, it is possible that some of his intimates would have found his giftedness hard to accept.

Some of the problems presented by giftedness parallel those presented by the handicapping conditions we have discussed in the other chapters of this book. For instance, the definition and identification of gifted children involve the same sort of difficulties that exist in the case of children with mental retardation or an emotional/behavioral disorder. But there is an underlying philosophical question regarding giftedness that makes us think differently about this exceptionality. Most of us feel a moral obligation to help those who are at some disadvantage compared to the average person, who have a deficiency that prevents them from achieving an ordinary level of competence unless they are given special help. In the case of gifted students, though, we may wonder about our moral obligation to help those who are already advantaged to become even better, to distinguish themselves further by fulfilling the highest promise of their extraordinary resources. It is on this issue— the desirability or necessity of helping our most capable children become even better—that special education for gifted students is likely to founder.

DEFINITION

Children with special gifts are in some way superior to a comparison group of other children of the same age. Beyond this almost meaningless statement, you will find little agreement about how giftedness should be defined (Gallagher, 1985; Maker, 1986). The disagreements are due primarily to differences of opinion regarding the following questions:

1. *In what way are gifted children superior?* Are they superior in general intelligence, insight, creativity, special talents, and achievements in academic subjects or in a valued line of work, moral judgment, or some combination of such factors? Perhaps nearly everyone is gifted in some way or other. What kind

We are indebted to Dr. Carolyn M. Callahan of the University of Virginia for her invaluable assistance in the preparation of this chapter.

MISCONCEPTIONS ABOUT PERSONS WITH GIFTEDNESS

Myth	Fact
Gifted people are physically weak, socially inept, narrow in interests, and prone to emotional instability and early decline.	Although there are wide individual variations, gifted individuals as a group tend to be exceptionally healthy, well adjusted, socially attractive, and morally responsible.
Gifted individuals are in a sense "superhuman."	Gifted people are not "superhuman"; rather, they are human beings with extraordinary gifts in particular areas.
Gifted children are usually bored with school and antagonistic toward those who are responsible for their education.	Gifted children usually like school and adjust well to their peers and teachers.
Gifted people tend to be mentally unstable.	Those who are gifted are likely to be well-adjusted, emotionally healthy people.
We know that 3 to 5 percent of the population is gifted.	The percentage of the population that is gifted depends on the definition of giftedness that one uses. Some definitions include only 1 or 2 percent of the population, others over 20 percent.
Giftedness is a stable trait, always consistently evident in all periods of a person's life.	Some gifted people's remarkable talents and productivity develop early and continue throughout life; in other cases, a person's gifts or talents are not noticed until adulthood, and occasionally a child who shows outstanding ability becomes a nondescript adult.
Gifted people do everything well.	Some people known as gifted have superior abilities of many kinds; others are clearly superior in only one area.
A person is gifted if he or she scores above a certain level on intelligence tests.	IQ is only one indication of giftedness. Creativity and high motivation are as important indications as general intelligence.
Gifted students will excel without special education. Students who are truly gifted need only the incentives and instruction that are appropriate for all students.	Some gifted children will perform at a remarkably high level without special education of any kind. Some will make outstanding contributions even in the face of great obstacles to their achievement. But most will not come close to achieving at a level commensurate with their potential unless their talents are deliberately fostered by incentives and instruction that are appropriate for their advanced abilities.

of giftedness is most important? What kind of giftedness should we try to encourage?

2. *How is superiority measured?* Is it measured by standardized tests of aptitude, teacher judgments, past performance in school or in everyday life, or by some other means? If it is measured in one particular way, some individuals will be overlooked. If past performance is the test, we are defining giftedness after the fact. What measurement techniques can we have confidence in?

What measurements will tell us which children have the potential to become gifted?

3. *To what degree must a child be superior to be considered gifted?* Must the child do better than 50 percent, 80 percent, 90 percent, or 99 percent of the comparison group? The number of gifted individuals will vary depending on the criterion (or criteria) for giftedness. What percentage of the population do we want to be gifted?

4. *Who should make up the comparison group?* Should it be every child of the same chronological age, the other children in the child's school, all children of the same ethnic or racial origin, or some other grouping? Almost everyone is the brightest or most capable in some group. What group should set the standard?

You may have concluded already that giftedness is whatever we choose to make it, just as mental retardation is whatever we choose to say it is. Someone can be considered gifted (or retarded) one day and not the next simply because we have changed an arbitrary definition. There is no inherent rightness or wrongness in the definitions professionals use. Some definitions may be more logical, more precise, or more useful than others, but we are still unable to say they are more "correct" in some absolute sense. We have to struggle with the concept of giftedness and the reasons for identifying gifted individuals before we can make any decisions about definition. Our definition of giftedness will be shaped to a large extent by what our culture believes is most useful or necessary for its survival. Giftedness is invented, not discovered (Sternberg & Davidson, 1986).

Even the terminology of giftedness can become rather confusing. Besides the word *gifted*, a variety of other terms have been used to describe individuals who are superior is some way: *talented, creative, insightful, genius,* and *precocious,* for example. **Precocity** refers to remarkable early development. Many highly gifted children show precocity in particular areas of development, such as language, music, or mathematical ability, and the rate of intellectual development of all gifted children exceeds the rate for nongifted children. **Insight** may be defined as separating relevant from irrelevant information, finding novel and useful ways of combining relevant bits of information, or relating new and old information in a novel and productive way. **Genius** has sometimes been used to indicate a particular aptitude or capacity in any area. More often, it has been used to indicate extremely rare intellectual powers (extremely high IQ or creativity). **Creativity** refers to the ability to express novel and useful ideas, to sense and elucidate novel and important relationships, and to ask previously unthought of, but crucial, questions. The word **talent** ordinarily has been used to indicate a special ability, aptitude, or accomplishment. **Giftedness,** as we use the term in this chapter, refers to cognitive (intellectual) superiority (not necessarily of genius caliber), creativity, and motivation in combination and of sufficient magnitude to set the child apart from the vast majority of age-mates and make it possible for him or her to contribute something of particular value to society (Renzulli, Reis, & Smith, 1981).

Changes in the Definition of Giftedness

The traditional definition of giftedness is based on general intelligence as measured by an individually administered intelligence test, usually the Stanford-Binet or the Wechsler Intelligence Scale for Children–Revised. That is, children have traditionally been considered gifted if they scored above a particular level on the Binet or the WISC–R. A definition of giftedness based solely on IQ was used in the classic

Insight: A Qualitative Difference in Thinking

The thinking of gifted children is qualitatively different from that of ordinary people. Many times I have, in classes of gifted children, written on the blackboard:

$$1 + 2 + 4 + 8 + \text{and so on} + 1024 = ?$$

and asked the children to find the sum. Very often, I have hardly stated the problem before someone shouts out "2047!" If I ask, "How did you get it so fast?," a typical answer might be "1 + 2 is 3, and 4 more is 7, and the sum is always one less than the next number."

When I teach the same topic to average college students, I must explain the concept of a geometrical progression, how to recognize this problem as such, how to derive a formula for the sum, and then show how to apply it to this special case. The gifted children have a capacity for insights which cannot be taught at any level. If this ability exists, it can be developed and stimulated.

SOURCE: P. C. Rosenbloom, "Programs for the Gifted in Mathematics," *Roeper Review*, 8 (1986), 243.

studies of gifted children by Lewis Terman and his associates (published under the general title *Genetic Studies of Genius*). This definition (high IQ) has been used in many other studies and programs for the gifted. In recent years, however, there has been great dissatisfaction with the use of IQ as the single (or even most important) criterion for defining giftedness.

Intelligence and giftedness are more complex than the relatively narrow band of performances required to score exceptionally high on an intelligence test.* Furthermore, giftedness seems to be characterized by qualitative differences in thinking and insightfulness, which may not be clearly reflected by performance on intelligence tests (see Reis, 1989; Sternberg & Davidson, 1983). The box above illustrates the type of insight that might be shown by a student who is gifted in mathematics. Because of the limitations of IQ tests, intelligence is being reconceptualized.

Reconceptualization of Intelligence

Whereas the usual tests of intelligence assess the ability to think deductively and arrive at a single answer that can be scored "right" or "wrong," tests of creativity, suggest many different potential answers. Recognition of the many facets of human intelligence led to dissatisfaction with previous conceptualizations of "general" intelligence or "primary mental abilities" (Maker, 1986). Nevertheless, some researchers continue searching for the cognitive characteristics that define *general* intelligence (Grinder, 1985). For example, Sternberg and Davidson (1983) describe *insight* skills, which they believe may be the primary characteristics that define intellectual giftedness. Although giftedness may be manifested by performance in specific domains (e.g., mathematics, writing, visual arts, interpersonal skills, music), the factor that makes such performance possible may be general intelligence (Horowitz & O'Brien, 1985).

---

* Recall that the limitations of IQ have become obvious also in the definition of mental retardation. An exceptionally low IQ by itself is no longer sufficient to define mental retardation but must be accompanied by deficits in adaptive behavior (see Chapter 3 and Zigler & Farber, 1985).

Giftedness and talent of many kinds are recognized. Stephen Hawking is recognized for his brilliance as an astrophysicist; Anne Tyler, author of Breathing Lessons, *for her creative writing; Steffie Graf for her athletic prowess; Connie Chung for her excellence as a television reporter; Bill Cosby for his greatness as a comedic writer and actor; Mikhail Baryshnikov for his genuis in dance.* (Stephen Allen/Globe Photos; Diana Walker; AP/Wide World Photos; R. Prigent/Sygma; Ralph Dominguez/Globe Photos; J. Donoso/Sygma)

Today researchers are finding evidence of multiple intelligences rather than a single general intelligence (Gardner & Hatch, 1989). Seven different kinds of intelligence, their end states (adult roles assumed by people high in that intelligence), and core components are shown in Table 10.1. Gardner and Hatch (1989) are convinced that these seven intelligences are highly independent and that nearly all children and adults show distinctive profiles of strength and weakness in the different kinds of intelligence. They suggest that these intelligences cannot all be measured through the usual types of testing but must be assessed in the natural contexts in which they can be exhibited. Consequently, Gardner and Hatch and other researchers are devising curriculum activities that allow children to develop and demonstrate their intelligences in common or typical contexts. For example, young children's intelligences may be assessed by using the kinds of materials and activities with which they have become familiar in their preschool.

Whether intelligence should be lumped into a general characteristic or split into distinctive parts is an ongoing debate with significant implications for defining giftedness (Reis, 1989). Regardless how the debate is ultimately resolved, it is clear that we have come a long way since the invention of the IQ in conceptualizing human intelligence.

Perhaps giftedness is not a fixed or absolute human characteristic. A person may be gifted if the conditions are right for gifted performance—if, besides possessing

TABLE 10.1 *The Seven Intelligences*		
Intelligence	End-States	Core Components
Logical-mathematical	Scientist Mathematician	Sensitivity to, and capacity to discern, logical or numerical patterns; ability to handle long chains of reasoning.
Linguistic	Poet Journalist	Sensitivity to the sounds, rhythms, and meanings of words; sensitivity to the different functions of language.
Muscial	Composer Violinist	Abilities to produce and appreciate rhythm, pitch, and timbre; appreciation of the forms of musical expressiveness.
Spatial	Navigator Sculptor	Capacities to perceive the visual-spatial world accurately and to perform transformations on one's initial perceptions.
Bodily-kinesthetic	Dancer Athlete	Abilities to control one's body movements and to handle objects skillfully.
Interpersonal	Therapist Salesman	Capacities to discern and respond appropriately to the moods, temperaments, motivations, and desires of other people.
Intrapersonal	Person with detailed, accurate self-knowledge	Access to one's own feelings and the ability to discriminate among them and draw upon them to guide behavior; knowledge of one's own strengths, weaknesses, desires, and intelligences.

SOURCE: H. Gardner & T. Hatch, Multiple intelligences go to school: Educational implications of the theory of multiple intelligences, *Educational Researcher, 18*(8) (1989), 6.

above-average ability and creativity, the person is given opportunities and incentives to perform at an extraordinarily high level. Perhaps we should speak of people who exhibit *gifted behavior* rather than of *gifted people* because people typically act gifted only under particular circumstances. These are relatively new ideas about giftedness that have been suggested by Keating (1980) and Renzulli, Reis, and Smith (1981).

More recently, Horowitz and O'Brien (1985) have conceptualized giftedness, retardation, and all levels of performance between these extremes in terms of a developmental model. Giftedness may be thought of as a superior to extraordinary developmental outcome resulting from the joint function of a relatively unimpaired and invulnerable organism and a facilitative environment. That is, a child can attain a gifted level of performance only when he or she is (1) relatively free of biological impairments, (2) mostly invulnerable to environmental stresses that tend to limit performance, and (3) reared in an environment that supports performance.

An important assumption of Horowitz and O'Brien's model is that children may function as gifted or nongifted in specific domains. For example, a child with cerebral palsy could not perform at a gifted level in a motor performance impaired by his or her brain injury. This child might, however, function at the gifted level with respect to cognitive development or in motor skills unimpaired by his or her brain injury. A child whose legs alone are seriously affected by cerebral palsy might become an eminent scientist or violinist, but this child could not become a gifted dancer. Furthermore, with the right technology, this child's motor performance could be improved.

Figure 10.1 **A developmental model for considering giftedness.**

SOURCE: F. D. Horowitz and M. O'Brien, "Epilogue: Perspectives on Research and Development," in F. D. Horowitz and M. O'Brien (Eds.), *The Gifted and Talented: Developmental Perspectives* (Washington, DC: American Psychological Association, 1985), p. 442. Copyright 1986 by the American Psychological Association. Reprinted by permission of the publisher and author.

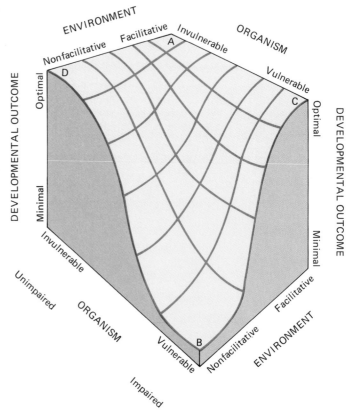

Gifted children have superior cognitive abilities that allow them to compete with older individuals of average intellect. (Timothy Eagan/Woodfin Camp & Associates)

The interactions among environment and organism hypothesized by Horowitz and O'Brien are depicted in Figure 10.1. The figure shows a cube shaped so that the curved surface represents the performance of children under various combinations of vulnerability, impairment, and environmental facilitation. The far upper corner (A) represents gifted performance, which would be produced by an unimpaired, invulnerable organism in a highly facilitative environment. The near lower corner (B) represents profound retardation or developmental failure, which would be the product of severe impairment and vulnerability in a nonfacilitative environment. The right upper corner (C) represents the optimal developmental outcome that can be expected in a facilitative environment, given an impaired and vulnerable organism. The left upper corner (D) represents the optimal outcome given an unimpaired and invulnerable child in a nonfacilitative environment. Note that the right and left corners represent the best outcomes that can be expected under the poorest circumstances—outcomes that, although optimal for the individual child, do not represent giftedness. Outcomes do not reach the gifted level at the left corner of the model because the child's environment does not facilitate performance; at the right corner, giftedness is not achieved because the organism is damaged.

In short, giftedness today is seen as a much more complex phenomenon than it was even a decade ago. The field is moving toward an appreciation of the neurophysiological factors involved in gifted performance and the ways in which intelligence is manifested in various domains of human endeavor.

A Suggested Definition

As mentioned earlier, an adequate definition of giftedness includes the requirement that a person show at least the *potential* for making a remarkable and valued contribution to the human condition. The problem, then, is one of predicting

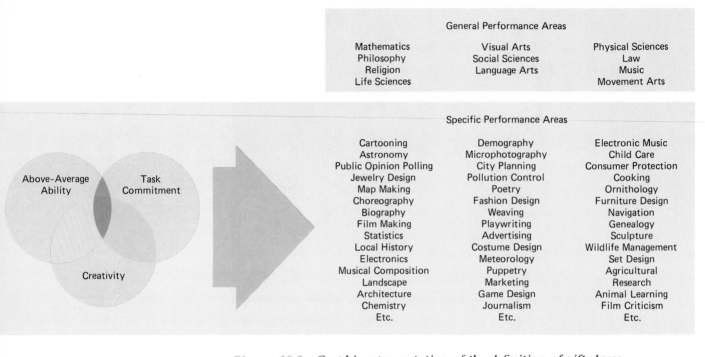

General Performance Areas

Mathematics	Visual Arts	Physical Sciences
Philosophy	Social Sciences	Law
Religion	Language Arts	Music
Life Sciences		Movement Arts

Specific Performance Areas

Cartooning	Demography	Electronic Music
Astronomy	Microphotography	Child Care
Public Opinion Polling	City Planning	Consumer Protection
Jewelry Design	Pollution Control	Cooking
Map Making	Poetry	Ornithology
Choreography	Fashion Design	Furniture Design
Biography	Weaving	Navigation
Film Making	Playwriting	Genealogy
Statistics	Advertising	Sculpture
Local History	Costume Design	Wildlife Management
Electronics	Meteorology	Set Design
Musical Composition	Puppetry	Agricultural
Landscape	Marketing	Research
Architecture	Game Design	Animal Learning
Chemistry	Journalism	Film Criticism
Etc.	Etc.	Etc.

Above-Average Ability · Task Commitment · Creativity

Figure 10.2 *Graphic representation of the definition of giftedness.*
SOURCE: J. S. Renzulli, S. M. Reis, and L. H. Smith, *The Revolving Door Identification Model* (Mansfield, CT: Creative Learning Press, 1981), p. 28. Reprinted with permission.

future performance. Given what is known about people whose achievements have been remarkable, we believe that gifted children should be defined (as suggested by Renzulli, Reis, & Smith, 1981) for purposes of education as those who have demonstrated or shown potential for

1. High ability (including high intelligence)
2. High creativity (the ability to formulate new ideas and apply them to the solution of problems)
3. High task commitment (a high level of motivation and the ability to see a project through to its conclusion)

The reason for using the multiple-criterion definition is that all three characteristics—high ability, high creativity, and high task commitment—seem to be necessary for truly gifted performance in any field.

Figure 10.2 illustrates the notion that giftedness is defined as a combination of these three characteristics (the shaded area shared by the three circles), but only when an individual applies them to performance in a specific endeavor. In an operational definition of giftedness, general ability is less important than specific performance; as Renzulli, Reis, and Smith (1981) state, "We do not offer courses or college majors in IQ, nor do people pursue careers or avocational activities in ideational fluency or semantic transformations . . . these are general abilities within the clusters that are *brought to bear* on specific areas of human expression" (p. 27).

PREVALENCE

It has been assumed in federal reports and legislation that 3 to 5 percent of the school population could be considered gifted or talented. Obviously the prevalence of giftedness is a function of the definition chosen. If giftedness is defined as the top x percent on a given criterion, the question of prevalence has been answered. Of course, if x percent refers to a percentage of a national sample, the prevalence of gifted pupils in a given school or cultural group may vary from the comparison group. When IQ is used as the sole or primary criterion for giftedness, more gifted children will come from homes of higher socioeconomic status, have fewer siblings, and have better-educated parents. Although giftedness by nearly any definition occurs in all socioeconomic strata, gifted children are not distributed equally across all social classes when IQ is the primary means of identification. This is one of the reasons for abandoning IQ as the sole criterion for defining giftedness.

Renzulli (1982) argues convincingly that the assumption that only 3 to 5 percent of the population is gifted is needlessly restrictive and may result in many potentially gifted students' contributions being overlooked. He suggests that 15 to 25 percent of all children may have sufficient ability, motivation, and creativity to exhibit gifted behavior at some time during their school career.

ORIGINS OF GIFTEDNESS

It is not really surprising that brilliant parents are more likely to have gifted children than are parents of average or retarded intelligence. We also know that an impoverished environment is less likely to produce children who will fulfill their potential for gifted behavior than one in which models of gifted performance, opportunities for learning, and appropriate rewards are richly provided. Of course, the giftedness of some children becomes evident even though their parents are intellectually dull and even though they experience environmental disadvantages. But the statistical probability of giftedness increases when the child's parents have higher than average intelligence and provide a better than average environment for the child. Some things that are not fully understood about the origins of giftedness and will take particularly well-designed research to discover, include the *relative* contribution of **genetic** and environmental factors to giftedness and the *precise nature* of the genetic and environmental factors that contribute to giftedness.

Genetic and Other Biological Factors

The proposition that intelligence and highly valued abilities are inherited is not a very popular one in our egalitarian society. It can be used as a springboard for arguments for selective reproduction of humans (with intelligence or other characteristics being the primary factors in selection of mates) and as a reason to downplay the importance of improving environmental conditions for citizens already born or conceived. Americans' distaste for the notion that intelligence is inherited is illustrated by the avalanche of outraged criticism that followed the publication of Arthur Jensen's 1969 article in which he argued that black children do not score as high as white children on intelligence tests because of genetic factors. Nevertheless, a considerable body of child development research supports the assertion that among white children living in America and Europe, 50 to 75 percent of the *variation* in intelligence is due to genetic factors (Bouchard & McGue, 1981).

New conceptions of intelligence and giftedness might at first thought seem to allow us to sidestep the issue of genetic factors in giftedness. That is, if IQ is abandoned as the criterion for defining giftedness in favor of a variety of practical intelligences (see Table 10.1), giftedness might be seen as something that is less affected by genetics. Research in behavioral genetics, however, suggests that every type of behavioral development is affected significantly by genes.

> The first message of behavioral genetic research is that genetic influence on individual differences in behavioral development is usually significant and often substantial. Genetic influence is so ubiquitous and pervasive in behavior that a shift in emphasis is warranted: Ask not what is heritable, ask what is not heritable. (Plomin, 1989, p. 108)

The fact that giftedness is partly inherited, regardless how it is defined, should not be misinterpreted as an indication that environmental factors are unimportant. Although genetic influences on the development of superior abilities cannot be denied, these biological influences are clearly no more important than the environments in which children are nurtured.

Biological factors that are not genetic may also contribute to the determination of intelligence. Nutritional and neurological factors, for example, may partially determine how intellectually competent a child becomes. In previous chapters we pointed out that severe malnutrition in infancy or childhood, as well as neurological damage at any age, can result in mental retardation. But it does not follow that superior nutrition and neurological status early in life contribute to superior intelligence.

Studies of individuals with high IQ, such as Terman's classic studies, typically have shown them to be physically superior to others of lesser intelligence in characteristics such as height, weight, attractiveness, and health in adulthood as well as in childhood. However, it is not clear whether these physical characteristics are a result of generally advantaged environments or of another factor that accounts for superior intellect.

More males than females are considered gifted and creative. By an overwhelming margin, men achieve outstanding status and recognition more frequently than women of the same age. However, there is little evidence that these performance differences are the result of biological differences. The available research points far more clearly to social and cultural expectations as an explanation for the disproportionate number of males who are recognized as gifted (Conroy, 1989; Eccles, 1985).

In summary, genetic factors clearly are involved in the determination of giftedness. Environmental influences alone cannot account for the fact that some individuals perform so far above the average. We emphasize, however, that an individual does not inherit an IQ or talent. What is inherited is a collection of genes that, along with experiences, determine the limits of intelligence and other abilities (Zigler & Farber, 1985).

Environmental Factors

Families, schools, and communities obviously have a profound influence on the development of children's abilities. Stimulation, opportunities, expectations, demands, and rewards for performance affect children's learning. For decades, researchers have found a correlation between socioeconomic level and IQ, undoubtedly in part because the performances measured by standard intelligence tests are based on what families, schools, and communities of the upper classes expect and teach. As definitions of intelligence and giftedness are broadened to include a wider range of skills and abilities that are not so specific to socioeconomic class, we will no doubt see changes in the way we view environmental effects on giftedness.

Plomin (1989) suggests that we must recognize the important influence of genetics in behavioral development, but this is not his only message:

> The second message [of behavioral genetic research] is just as important: These same data provide the best available evidence of the importance of environment. The data . . . suggest pandemic genetic influence, but they also indicate that nongenetic factors are responsible for more than half of the variance in most complex behaviors. . . . The phrase "behavioral genetics" is in a sense a misnomer because it is as much the study of nurture as nature. (p. 108)

We must ask, therefore, how families, schools, and the larger culture can nurture children's giftedness.

Research has shown that parents differ greatly in their attitudes toward and management of their gifted children. Some parents view having a gifted child as positive, some as negative; fathers appear to see their children as gifted less often than mothers (Cornell, 1983). A study of individuals who have been successful in a variety of fields has shown that the home and family, especially in the child's younger years, are extremely important (Bloom, 1982; Bloom & Sosniak, 1981). The following were found to occur in the families of highly successful persons:

- Someone in the family (usually one or both parents) had a personal interest in the child's talent and provided great support and encouragement for its development.
- Most of the parents were role models (at least at the start of their child's development of talent), especially in terms of life-style.
- There was specific parental encouragement of the child to explore, to participate in home activities related to the area of developing talent, and to join the family in related activities. Small signs of interest and capability by the child were rewarded.
- Parents took it for granted that their children would learn in the area of talent, just as they would learn language.
- Expected behaviors and values related to the talent were present in the family. Clear schedules and standards for performance appropriate for the child's stage of development were held.
- Teaching was informal and occurred in a variety of settings. Early learning was exploratory and much like play.
- The family interacted with a tutor/mentor and received information to guide the child's practice (interaction included specific tasks to be accomplished, information or specific points to be emphasized or problems to be solved, a set time by which the child could be expected to achieve specific goals and objectives, and the amount of time to be devoted to practice).
- Parents observed practice, insisted that the child put in the required amount of practice time, provided instruction where necessary, and rewarded the child whenever something was done especially well or when a standard was met.
- Parents sought special instruction and special teachers for the child.
- Parents encouraged participation in events (recitals, concerts, contests, etc.) in which the child's capabilities were displayed in public.

We may conclude that children who realize their potential for accomplishment most fully have families that are stimulating, directive, supportive, and rewarding

Environmental conditions that contribute to the development of giftedness include opportunities to learn advanced skills, guidance and support from parents or other adults, appropriate role models, encouragement to explore interests and talents, availability of special teachers, clear expectations for achievement, and recognition for performance. (left: Michal Heron/Woodfin Camp & Associates; right: Erika Stone)

of their abilities. Research does not, however, indicate much else about how families encourage gifted performance. Moreover, little is known regarding the appropriate and helpful involvement of parents in their gifted children's schooling (Colangelo & Dettmann, 1983; Page, 1983).

We have paid too little attention to how schools themselves may nurture children's giftedness. The ways in which schools identify giftedness, group children for instruction, design curricula, and reward performance have a profound effect on what the most able students achieve. When schools facilitate the performance of all students who are able to achieve at a superior level in specific areas, giftedness is found among children of all cultural and socioeconomic groups (Feldhusen, 1989; Frazier, 1989; Whitmore, 1987).

Several studies, including Terman's early work, have found that some cultural or ethnic groups (especially Jews) produce a higher than average number of gifted children even when differences in socioeconomic level are taken into account (Mistry & Rogoff, 1985). It may be that striving for upward social mobility and the high value attached to achievement in specific areas among certain cultural and ethnic groups contribute to giftedness. (Remember that motivation to achieve is an important feature of our definition.) However, in all studies of social and cultural factors related to giftedness it has been difficult or impossible to separate these factors from genetic influences.

Cultural factors work against the development and recognition of gifted females (Eccles, 1985). Females simply have not been provided with the motivation to enter into many academic disciplines or careers that have by tradition been dominated by males, such as chemistry, physics, medicine, and dentistry. When females do enter these fields, they are often rewarded inappropriately (according to irrelevant criteria or with affection rather than promotion) for their performance. English literature has tended to portray females as wives, mothers, or "weaker" sisters who are either dependent on males or sacrifice themselves for the sake of males who are dominant. These barriers to giftedness in females have only recently been brought forcefully to public attention, and it is too early to tell what benefits will result from their removal.

In summary, environmental influences have much to do with how a child's genetic endowment is expressed in performance. But neither environment nor genetics can be entirely responsible for the performance of gifted or retarded individuals. Genetic factors apparently determine the range within which a person will function, and environmental factors determine whether the individual will function in the lower or upper reaches of that range.

SCREENING AND IDENTIFICATION

Measurement of giftedness is a complicated matter. Some components cannot be assessed by traditional means. In addition, the particular definition of giftedness will determine how test scores are interpreted. But if it is indeed important to identify gifted children early so that they will be aided in the development of their special potential to make a unique and valuable contribution to society, it is important that good screening and measurement methods be used.

Effectiveness and Efficiency of Screening Techniques

According to Renzulli, Reis, and Smith (1981), a case study approach, in which aptitude and achievement test scores, teacher ratings, past academic performance, parent ratings, and self-ratings are taken into account, has advantages over the more traditional procedures based only on test scores. The advantages are greater efficiency and effectiveness and greater effectiveness in identifying minority group students. Sisk (1988) also recommends a case study approach using multiple sources of data. Note that part of the case study approach is obtaining aptitude (intelligence) and achievement test scores. This approach uses *additional* information; it does not substitute other sources of data for test scores.

Renzulli and Delcourt (1986) note that four criteria have been used in identifying gifted students: (1) test scores; (2) academic mastery in specific domains (e.g., mathematics); (3) creative productivity in specific domains or interdisciplinary areas, with products being assessed by teacher judgment and student interest and willingness to pursue advanced follow-up activities; and (4) long-range creative productivity (the ultimate criterion, which can be used to identify gifted persons only after the fact of their performance). Test scores have been the most widely used criteria, although selection on the basis of testing alone is now widely viewed as inappropriate:

> The test-score-as-criterion design has undoubtedly been popular because of its convenience and tidyness of arbitrarily equating giftedness with certain levels of IQ scores. But the performance-based designs help us to raise important issues about how one uses . . . intelligence *and other* potentials in situations that require the display and development of gifted behaviors. As one person put it, "I know IQ is important, but you just can't major in IQ." (p. 23)

Measuring Creativity

Nearly every definition of giftedness that is taken seriously today includes an explicit statement that the gifted person is highly creative (Callahan, in press; Torrance,

1986). But how can creativity be measured? As Petrosko (1978) notes, measuring creativity presents a challenging paradox—devising a standardized way of capturing a nonstandard behavioral product. Because of the convenience of test scores, to which Renzulli and Delcourt (1986) referred, researchers and publishers are often pressured to devise creativity tests. But as Treffinger (1986) has commented, "We must recognize that creativity is one of the most complex of human functions; it is unrealistic to expect that there ever will be (or that there should be) a single, easily administered, simply scored test booklet that educators can use to decide who is at least one standard deviation above other students in creativity" (p. 16).

Tests have been criticized as inadequate measures of creativity on much the same grounds that tests have been criticized as measures of intelligence. That is, scores on the tests are affected by many factors that have nothing to do with the actual ability one wishes to measure. Instead of defining creativity in terms of test scores, Wallach (1985) notes that "creativity may be best understood as what characterizes the work done at the cutting edge of a given field by those who have mastered it" (p. 117). Wallach suggests that research should focus on the identification of discipline-specific approaches to improving instruction and the study of creative people's accomplishments as they develop across their entire life spans.

What does creative performance entail? How can it be fostered? Answers to these questions demand analysis of the structure of the particular discipline. The box below is an example of a gifted mathematician's approach to fostering creativity in mathematics. Many of us find the notion of creativity in mathematics foreign, although we may readily understand what is involved in creativity in other disciplines.

PHYSICAL, PSYCHOLOGICAL, AND BEHAVIORAL CHARACTERISTICS

Although intellectual precocity has been recognized throughout recorded history there has been a persistent stereotype of the gifted individual as one who is physically weak, socially inept, narrow in interests, and prone to emotional instability and early decline. Terman's early studies, and many others, shattered the myth that giftedness carries with it a set of undesirable characteristics. In fact, it now appears that gifted children tend to be superior in every way—in intelligence, in physique, in social attractiveness, in achievement, in emotional stability, even in moral character. The danger now is a developing stereotype of the gifted child as "superhuman," as someone immune to ordinary frailties and defects.

Creative Work in Mathematics

Most school people have no conception of creative work in mathematics. When I teach gifted students, I start them on "baby research," at whatever level they are ready for. Since even in special classes for the gifted, there are usually wide variations in ability, I like to give problems where it is easy to get some interesting results, but where one can go as far as one's ability permits.

Thus with very young children (6–7 years old), I may tell about Lower Slobbovia,

themselves among their peers in adulthood. Occupationally, as educationally, they are winners (Gallagher, 1985; Terman, 1926; Terman & Oden, 1959).

But again, it is important to remember that this description does not hold true for *every* gifted person. It is not unusual for a gifted child to be unrecognized by school personnel or to become unpopular with teachers because of such characteristics as inquisitiveness, unusual knowledge and wit, or boredom with unchallenging school work. It is an unfortunate fact that much talent goes to waste because school personnel are oblivious of the needs of gifted children or refuse to alter the lockstep plan of education for the sake of superior students.

Social and Emotional Characteristics

Gifted children tend to be happy and well liked by their peers. Many are social leaders at school. Most are emotionally stable and self-sufficient and are less prone to neurotic and psychotic disorders than average children. They have wide and varied interests and perceive themselves in positive terms (Coleman & Fultz, 1985; Janos & Robinson, 1985).

When gifted students complain, what are their gripes? Galbraith (1985) studied the complaints of over 400 gifted students in six states. Approximately equal numbers of boys' and girls' responses to surveys and interviews were obtained. The students ranged in age from 7 to 18 years. The eight most frequent complaints are listed in the box on page 418. Notice that most of these gripes are not peculiar to students identified as gifted. However, Galbraith's findings do suggest that gifted students need more than intellectual challenge in order to feel good about themselves and use their special abilities to the fullest.

One common and persistent notion regarding gifted people, especially those who excel in the arts, is that they are prone to mental disease.* Freud theorized that artists turn away from the real world and toward creative endeavors because of unconscious conflicts. Such ideas have made it especially difficult to destroy the myth that creative excellence is linked to mental illness. Some great artists, musicians, and scientists have gone through periods of mental instability or psychosis, but their achievements were probably made in spite of, not because of, their emotional distress.

The misconception that gifted people tend to be social misfits and emotional cripples was abetted by a classic study by Leta Hollingworth (1942) of children who tested at 180 or higher IQ on the Stanford-Binet. She reported that these children were quite isolated from their peers and not very well adjusted as adults. But we should check into the representativeness of her sample of gifted children:

> In twenty-three years' seeking in New York City and the local metropolitan area, the densest center of population in this country and at the same time a great intellectual center attracting able persons, I have found only twelve children who test at or above 180 IQ (S-B). This number represents the winnowing from thousands of children tested, hundreds of them brought for the testing because of their mental gifts. (p. xiii)

To categorize gifted people as those with IQs of 180 or higher is roughly like categorizing retarded individuals as only those with IQs of 20 or less (Zigler &

---

* Lombroso (1905) wrote, "Just as giants pay a heavy ransom for their stature in sterility and relative muscular and mental weakness, so the giants of thought expiate their intellectual force in degeneration and psychoses. It is thus that the signs of degeneration are found more frequently in men of genius than even in the insane" (p. vi).

The Eight Great Gripes of Gifted Kids

1. No one explains what being gifted is all about—it's kept a big secret.
2. The stuff we do in school is too easy and it's boring.
3. Parents, teachers and friends expect us to be perfect, to "do our best" all the time.
4. Kids often tease us about being smart.
5. Friends who *really* understand us are few and far between.
6. We feel too different and wish people would accept us for what we are.
7. We feel overwhelmed by the number of things we can do in life.
8. We worry a lot about world problems and feel helpless to do anything about them.

SOURCE: J. Galbraith, "The Eight Great Gripes of Gifted Kids: Responding to Special Needs," *Roeper Review*, 7 (1985), 16.

Farber, 1985). Certainly it is reasonable to expect that children with such very high IQs might have more social problems and emotional difficulties than the more typical gifted child with an IQ in the 130 to 150 range, although follow-up research does not indicate that this is the case (White & Renzulli, 1987). Most societies have a great deal of trouble dealing with extreme deviance of any kind, and someone with an IQ of 180 is certainly unusual. However, to characterize all extremely gifted people as maladjusted and eccentric plainly contradicts the facts.

Again, it is well to consider *individual* children. The young genius may have unique problems in socialization, although the extraordinary resources that go with genius may equip such a child to handle unusual social situations. If the child is fortunate enough to have intelligent and caring parents in addition to superior mental powers, it is reasonable to expect that social adjustment will be quite good. Mike Grost, a child with an extremely high (over 180) IQ, was described by his mother as a happy and gregarious boy who could easily adapt to play with his peers or to social relationships with adults, as the situation demanded. His wit and charm helped him achieve acceptance among classmates at Michigan State University even at the tender age of ten. Here is one example of how things went in his college classes (Grost, 1970, p. 133):

"Now today our topic is 'Changing Sexual Mores' in the societies and cultures under study . . . let there be light! . . . nobody wants to open the discussion, eh? Maybe we should all go home and I'll take your reticence into consideration the next . . . well, our 10-year-old is going to volunteer some insightful remarks—go ahead. . . ."

"Well, not that I speak from experience, but. . . ."

Pandemonium.

"Quiet! Quiet! Class! Ahem! Perhaps, Mike, you had better qualify your position."

"Yes sir. I apologize for unwittingly disrupting the class. And may I say that I didn't mean to imply that anyone else in this class *could* speak from experience. . . ."

Chaos.

All this is not to say that gifted students are immune to social and emotional problems. They may be particularly susceptible to difficulties if they have extremely high IQs or if they are subject to social conditions, such as peer pressure toward mediocrity, that mitigate against mental health (Janos & Robinson, 1985). It should come as no surprise to find that gifted students become upset and maladjusted when they are discriminated against and prevented from realizing their full potential (see the box below). But that reaction is not peculiar to any group of children, exceptional or average along any dimension. Finally, it should be noted that as in the case of physical superiority, socioeconomic status may partially account for

Being Gifted: Some Unhappy Feelings

On Being Gifted, written by twenty gifted and talented high school students, contains a few brief comments by fourth-, fifth-, and sixth-graders from Norwich, Connecticut, that illustrate the negative self-perceptions and social stigma that gifted and talented students sometimes experience.

PEER PRESSURE

To many with exceptional talents a problem arises concerning their peers and contacts with other people. Of course the gifted student is proud of his powers but his peer group makes it very difficult for him.

People with special gifts get a great deal of attention from the society around them. For me it is not as great a problem as for others simply because I am in my own age group. However, prodding, teasing, and resentment do present themselves as foolish obstacles.

Students in my peer group are jealous about my ability. I do my best to share with them my knowledge and I try to help them whenever possible but all this is to no avail. (Jealousy stirs teasing—which gets to be a drag.)

CAUGHT IN THE MIDDLE

As I sit in a classroom of a smalltown high school, I am listening to the teacher begin a lecture for the day. He asks a question regarding the assigned homework, chapter 25 in our book. I raise my hand and respond correctly to his query. He continues to ask questions and I continue to answer them. After a couple of rounds I begin to look around sheepishly to see if anyone else has his hand raised. No one does so I answer again. I hear annoyed mutterings from my classmates. I just know they're thinking, "She thinks she knows everything." So in a futile effort to conform and satisfy them, I sink down in my seat just a little and let the rest of the questions slide by. The teacher becomes angry that no one has read the assignment and feels he must repeat the chapter. And another day is wasted.

So goes it, and unfortunately, too often. As a result, I do not feel challenged nor do I attempt to be when I find myself in such a class. One alternative, which in my school is extremely limited, is to sign up for those courses which are designed for people planning to major in that specific area. But alas, not enough teachers, nor enough money in the budget for books or supplies. So suffer, kid!

PRESSURES FROM TEACHERS

Often our peers get their cues when our teachers begin to reject us. This often happens when an instructor feels threatened by the exceptional student. In my school this takes the form of neglect. The teacher does not fill my needs because he will not devote extra time to me and often totally ignores my suggestions.

Often, instructors, though not actually threatened, feel that the gifted student has had enough recognition and therefore bypass him. Many times one of my teachers has preferred to work extremely hard with his favorite remedial workshop student than to talk to me. This sort of behavior has caused me to doubt my priorities concerning education.

WHO'S ON OUR SIDE?

Occasionally teachers seem to be foes rather than allies. Unfortunately, many times teachers are on an ego trip, preferring to help slower students so that they might appear to be all-powerful and all-knowing.

If a student happens to learn rapidly or already has a knowledge of the subject from prior exposure, the teacher develops a deep resentment for the child.

In my case, I had a teacher of algebra who developed this type of resentment. I understood the material because of previous contact with the subject. I seldom missed problems on tests, homework or on the board; when I did, I caught his wrath.

I don't know the psychological reasons; I only know this situation shouldn't exist.

SOURCE: *On Being Gifted* (New York: American Association for Gifted Children, 1978), pp. 21–29. © 1978 by the American Association for Gifted Children. Used by permission of Walker & Co.

the apparent social superiority of gifted children and youths. Higher socioeconomic status is a correlate of social acceptance and emotional health, and its relative influence compared to the influence of cognitive superiority is unknown.

Moral and Ethical Characteristics

There is a tendency among most of us to hope that those who are the brightest are also the best—that moral attributes such as fairness, honesty, compassion, and justice go along with intelligence. Gifted individuals should be able to do the right as they see it, and they should be able to see the right more quickly or more profoundly than the average person. However, the corruptibility of major figures in every profession in every society raises questions about the moral and ethical superiority of gifted persons. The atrocities of the Nazis in Germany, some of whom were able, creative, motivated individuals, testify to the fact that gifted and talented people *can* make criminal use of their potential. But are the moral and ethical shortcomings of these figures characteristic of gifted people as a group?

Here again, we must qualify the discussion by stating that there are individual differences among gifted people and that not every gifted person will be characterized by the description that fits the group. Most studies show gifted people to be superior to average individuals in concern for moral and ethical issues and in moral behavior (Gallagher, 1985). At an earlier age than most, gifted children tend to be concerned with abstract concepts of good and evil, right and wrong, justice and injustice (Galbraith, 1985; Hollingworth, 1942; Terman, 1926). They tend to be particularly concerned with social problems and the ways they can be resolved. The immoral, unethical gifted individual seems to be the exception rather than the rule. It may be that gifted people are the ones who have the greatest potential for helping individuals and societies resolve their moral and ethical dilemmas. It is worth remembering that almost any definition of giftedness will include people who are recognized as moral giants (Gruber, 1985).

ATTITUDES TOWARD GIFTED CHILDREN AND THEIR EDUCATION

It is relatively easy to find sympathy for handicapped children, but more than a little difficult to turn that sympathy into public support for effective educational programs. It is difficult to elicit sympathy for gifted children, and next to impossible to arrange sustained public support for education that meets their needs (Reis, 1989). When the Russians launched the world's first artificial satellite in the late 1950s, American pride and competitiveness and the obsession with "national security" aroused special interest in gifted children who could keep us in the space race. But when America pulled far ahead, society's attitudes toward the most capable of our children reverted to the traditional indifference or even resentment.

As many writers have pointed out, support for education of gifted and talented students runs in cycles. When national security is a major concern, programs for the gifted flourish because excellence is seen as a means of defense; when the nation feels secure from outside threats, programs are allowed to wither in favor of emphasis on educational equity. Gallagher (1986) notes that the relative emphasis on equity and excellence is an international as well as a national phenomenon.

We can state two rational arguments for providing special education for gifted children:

1. Every child is entitled to public education that meets his or her needs. Because of their exceptional abilities, gifted children need special education if they are to realize their potential for personal fulfillment and social contribution. To deny gifted children special education suited to their needs is to deny them equal opportunity, their birthright as American citizens.
2. Society will be best served if the talents of its most capable problem solvers are cultivated. Gifted children are the most precious natural resource for solving the future problems of society, and that resource can be ignored only at great peril. As Terman remarked, "It should go without saying that a nation's resources of intellectual talent are among the most precious it will ever have. The origin of genius, the natural laws of its development, and the environmental influences by which it may be affected for good or ill, are scientific problems of almost unequaled importance for human welfare" (1926, p. v).

These two arguments for providing special education for gifted students—do it for the sake of the children and do it for the sake of us all—are seldom enough to bring about either a wave of sentiment or a flurry of action on their behalf. In fact, the attitude we often encounter is that if gifted children are really so capable, they will find ways to help themselves.

In the mid-1980s, however, national interest in the education of gifted students increased, sparked by President Reagan's National Commission on Excellence in Education—the "A Nation at Risk" report published in 1983. Federal legislation supporting education of gifted children has been enacted, and many states have increased their budgets for educating their gifted children (Reis, 1989). Nevertheless, gifted children and youths remain the most underserved population in our nation's schools. Programs for gifted students are not yet safe from antagonistic attitudes and attacks on their evaluation.

Gallagher (1986) describes American society's attitude toward gifted and talented students as a love-hate relationship. Our society loves the good things that gifted people produce, but it hates to acknowledge superior intellectual performance. Opponents of special education for gifted students argue that it is inhumane and un-American to segregate gifted students for instruction, to allocate special resources for the education of those already advantaged, and that there is a danger of leaving some children out when only the ablest are selected for special programs. Yet segregation in special programs, allocation of additional resources, and stringent selectivity are practices enthusiastically endorsed by the American public when the talent being fostered is athletic. The opposition develops only when the talent is academic or artistic.

Let us take a closer look at the arguments against special education for gifted and talented students that have been advanced by Baer (1980), Myers and Ridl (1981), and Sapon-Shevin (1984). Note that the same arguments can be used against special education for handicapped children.

1. The children cannot be identified with great reliability (compare the difficulties in identifying students with E/BD, LD, and EMR).
2. More children are identified in some social classes or ethnic groups than in others.
3. Identified children receive special educational resources that others do not, although many nonidentified students could profit from those same resources.
4. Students may have special needs in one area but not in another, or at one time but not at another.
5. Identified students are set apart from their peers in a way that may stigmatize them.

In our opinion, one cannot argue against special education for gifted and talented students without arguing against special education in general, for all special education involves the recognition of individual differences and the accommodation of those differences in schooling.

The lack of research evidence supporting the effectiveness of educational programs for gifted students is also a factor underlying the fickle support of education for such children. There is simply not enough scientific research clearly indicating that gifted children become gifted adults who contribute to the social welfare or are personally fulfilled because of the influence of special education programs (Weiss & Gallagher, 1982). Although it can be argued on the basis of sound logic, common sense, and anecdotal reports that special education should be provided for gifted children, it is impossible to point to many controlled research studies showing the effects of such education. Callahan (1986) suggests that the wrong questions are often asked in evaluating programs. When the primary objective of a program is the provision of education that is appropriate for the capabilities of the students, the major evaluation questions should involve the appropriateness of the education provided, not the outcome of producing more productive citizens.

Legal arguments for education of gifted students are quite different from those for education of handicapped students. Much of the litigation for educating handicapped children was based on the fact that they were being excluded from school or from regular classes, leading to the argument that they were being denied equal protection of law. Gifted students are seldom denied an education or access to regular classes, so the legal basis for special provisions to meet their needs is less clear (Stronge, 1986).

NEGLECTED GROUPS OF GIFTED STUDENTS

There has been recent concern for neglected groups—gifted children and youths who are disadvantaged by economic needs, racial discrimination, handicaps, or sex bias—and it is not misplaced. We must face two facts: (1) Gifted children from higher socioeconomic levels already have many of the advantages, such as more appropriate education, opportunities to pursue their interests in depth, and intellectual stimulation, that special educators recommend for those who are gifted. (2) There are far too many disadvantaged and handicapped gifted individuals who have been overlooked and discriminated against, resulting in a tremendous waste of human potential (Whitmore, 1986).

The Problem of Underachievement

Students may fail to achieve at a level consistent with their abilities for a variety of reasons. Many females achieve far less than they might because of social or cultural barriers to their selection or of progress in certain careers. Students who are members of racial or ethnic minorities are often underachievers because of bias in identification or programming for their abilities. Students with obvious handicaps are frequently overlooked or denied opportunities to achieve. Still, underachievement cannot be explained simply by sex, race, or handicap discrimination; many males, nonminority, and nonhandicapped students also are underachievers. Underachievement of gifted and talented children can result from any of the factors that lead to underachievement in any group, such as emotional conflicts or a poor home environment. A very frequent cause is an inappropriate school program—school work that is unchallenging and boring because the gifted student has already mastered most of the material. And gifted underachievers often develop negative self-images and negative attitudes toward school (Delisle, 1982; Whitmore, 1980). When a student shows negative attitudes toward school and self, any special abilities he or she may have are likely to be overlooked.

Whitmore (1986) suggests that lack of motivation to excel is usually a result of a mismatch between the student's motivational characteristics and opportunities provided in the classroom. Students are typically highly motivated when (1) the social climate of the classroom is nurturant, (2) the curriculum content is relevant to the students' personal interests and is challenging, and (3) the instructional process is appropriate to the students' natural learning style. Whitmore suggests an approach to the problem of underachievement that is consistent with gifted students' advanced reasoning abilities. First, the teacher should study the problem systematically by observing the student's performance and behavior in various settings. Second, the teacher should share those observations with the student, indicating the hypothesized causes of the problem. Third, the teacher should attempt to develop a sense of partnership between the student and the parent or teacher(s) involved in the problem.

This sense of partnership is most likely to evolve when the teacher works with the student to define the problem precisely in terms of specific behavior and its probable consequences, generate alternative ways in which the student and adults could respond to the problem, select an alternative, and evaluate the outcome (or select another alternative if the prior attempt failed). This approach is consistent with the suggestion of Belcastro (1985) that behavior modification techniques may enhance certain desirable attributes of gifted students—their ability to analyze situations and devise means of coping with hostile or boring environments.

Underachievement must not be confused with nonproductivity (Delisle, 1981). A lapse in productivity does not necessarily indicate that the student is underachieving. Gifted students should not be expected to be constantly producing something remarkable. But this points up our difficulty in defining giftedness: How much time must elapse between episodes of creative productivity before we say that someone is no longer gifted or has become an underachiever? We noted earlier that giftedness is in the performance, not in the person. Yet we know that the unrelenting demand for gifted performance is unrealistic and can be inhumane.

Gifted Minority Students

Three characteristics may be used to define gifted students with unique needs because of their minority status: cultural diversity, socioeconomic deprivation, and geographic isolation (Baldwin, 1985). These characteristics may occur singly or in combination. They create unique needs for different reasons. Children from minority cultural groups may be viewed negatively, or the strengths and special abilities valued in their culture may conflict with those of the majority (see the box on p. 425). Children reared in poverty may not have toys, reading materials, opportunities for travel and exploration, good nutrition and medical care, and many other advantages typically provided by more affluent families. Lack of basic necessities and opportunities for learning may mask intelligence and creativity. Children living in remote areas may not have access to many of the educational resources that are typically found in more populated regions.

Adjustments must be made in identification procedures and programming to include minorities in education of gifted and talented students. Different cultural and ethnic groups place different values on academic achievement and areas of performance. Stereotypes can easily lead us to overlook intellectual giftedness or to over- or underrate children on any characteristic because they do not conform to our expectations based on their ethnic identity or socioeconomic status (Frazier, 1989).

Gifted Handicapped Students

The education of gifted handicapped students is a field that is just emerging (Whitmore & Maker, 1985). The major goals of the field today are identification of gifted students with specific disabilities, research and development, preparation of professionals to work with gifted handicapped children and youths, improvement of interdisciplinary cooperation for the benefit of such children and youths, and preparation of students for adult living.

A substantial percentage of eminent persons have been handicapped. Nevertheless, the special abilities of handicapped people are often overlooked. Whitmore and Maker (1985) note that our stereotypic expectations for disabled people frequently keep us from recognizing their abilities. For example, if a child lacks the ability to speak or to be physically active or presents the image associated with intellectual dullness (e.g., drooling, slumping, dull eyes staring), we tend to assume that the child is mentally retarded. The following is an example of how the gifted handicapped child is typically overlooked:

> Kim was classified at birth as "profoundly handicapped," owing to cerebral palsy of severe degree. Early treatment began with a physical therapist and a language develop-

A Minority Within a Minority: The Culturally Different Gifted and Talented

In 1975, a special conference was held to which twenty gifted and talented high school juniors and seniors were invited. One outcome of the conference was publication of a book, *On Being Gifted*, which was written entirely by the young participants. The reflections of these young people on their experiences and feelings and their recommendations for other gifted and talented youths make fascinating reading. One of the topics dealt with by several of the contributors is the problems of cultural minorities. A young native American wrote:

ARE YOU A MINORITY WITHIN OUR GIFTED AND TALENTED MINORITY?

Our Indian culture views gifted and talented youth in a type of religious manner. For our part, it takes quite a bit of intelligence to understand what goes on around us—such as the religious ceremonies. The elderly people believe you are nothing unless as an Indian you know you *are* an Indian and are fully aware of your culture.

But, in retrospect, we have the same interpretations of various aspects in life, whether it be of old legends or of religious beliefs.

Sometimes I am quite confused over certain things because of my two different cultures. I feel you have to adjust yourself to completely understand society *now*.

Educational opportunities for gifted and talented native Americans are a lot stronger now. There are more chances for higher education at more institutions, but we definitely need an even greater force to educate the rural gifted and talented native American.

Living in a rural area is undoubtedly different from living in an urbanized residence. I don't have much of an opportunity to increase my learning ability. Libraries and various other learning centers are situated in distant places requiring transportation and time for further studying. Yet, living in a rural area does have a basic learning value also, such as studying in secluded places where "city noise" is non-existent or sometimes just studying life itself. We have time and a place to do that without distraction.

Although I feel I have matured quite fast in the last several months since early admission to the local university, my life has not changed much because of my so-called "unique learning needs." Other than that, our school requires the usual classes to be taken in order to graduate with a certain amount of credit hours. This is where kids become bored. We all need a change of environment which goes along with selecting a wider variety of chosen fields. I myself became very depressed when higher educational opportunities were non-existent for students with unique learning needs. In addition, our community also fails to cooperate. *I mean, there are all these organizations helping the underachieving students, when I feel I need help, too!*

SOURCE: *On Being Gifted* (New York: American Association for Gifted Children, 1978). © 1978 by the American Association for Gifted Children. Used by permission of Walker & Co.

ment specialist, but at 7 years of age, Kim still had extremely limited motor control and no expressive language. Confined to a wheelchair, she slumped considerably and had difficulty holding her head erect. Her droopy posture, continual drooling, and lack of language skills led professionals to design educational experiences for her that were identical to those provided for mentally retarded children. She was placed in a public school for the profoundly and multiply handicapped, in which development of basic self-help skills comprised the principal educational goals.

Kim's parents, who were teachers, had observed through the years her increased effort to communicate with her eyes and began to believe there was more intellect within that severely limited body than they had assumed. They stimulated her with questions and problems to solve while providing her with a relatively simple means of indicating responses. When a group of students from the school for multiply handicapped were scheduled to be mainstreamed into an open-space elementary school, they insisted that Kim be included. After two months of stimulation in a normal classroom setting, the provision of an adapted communicator she could manage, and participation in a more normal instructional program, Kim evidenced remarkable development. She exhibited a capacity to learn quickly and to remember exceptionally well; superior problem-solving and reasoning skills; and a keen interest in learning. Within four months she was reading on grade level (second) despite missing two years of appropriate reading instruction in school. An adapted form of the Stanford-Binet was administered, and her performance qualified her as mentally gifted. (p. 16)

We do not want to foster the myth that giftedness is found as often among handicapped students as among those who are not handicapped. But clearly gifted handicapped students have been a neglected population. Whitmore and Maker (1985) estimate that at least 2 percent of handicapped children may be gifted (recall that 3 to 5 percent is the typical estimate for the general population).

EDUCATIONAL CONSIDERATIONS

Today, the consensus of leaders in the field is that special education for gifted and talented students should have three characteristics: (1) a curriculum designed to accommodate the students' advanced cognitive skills, (2) instructional strategies consistent with the learning styles of gifted students in the particular content areas of the curriculum, and (3) administrative arrangements facilitating appropriate grouping of students for instruction. States and localities have devised a wide variety of plans for educating gifted students (Callahan & Reis, in press). Generally, the plans can be described as providing **enrichment** (additional experiences provided to students without placing them in a higher grade) or **acceleration** (placing the students ahead of their age-peers). Seven plans for grouping students and modifying the curriculum for gifted and talented students are described by Weiss and Gallagher (1982) as follows:

1. *Enrichment in the classroom:* Provision of a differentiated program of study for gifted pupils by the classroom teacher within the regular classroom, without assistance from an outside resource or consultant teacher.
2. *Consultant teacher program:* Differentiated instruction provided within the regular classroom by the classroom teacher with the assistance of a specially trained consultant teacher.
3. *Resource room/pullout program:* Gifted students leave the classroom on a regular basis for differentiated instruction provided by a specially trained teacher.
4. *Community mentor program:* Gifted students interact on an individual basis with selected members of the community for an extended time period on a topic of special interest to the child.
5. *Independent study program:* Differentiated instruction consists of independent study projects supervised by a qualified adult.
6. *Special class:* Gifted students are grouped together and receive instruction from a specially trained teacher.

7. *Special school:* Gifted students receive differentiated instruction in a specialized school established for that purpose.

Not every community offers all the options listed here. In fact, there is great variation in the types of services offered within the school systems of a given state and from state to state (Renzulli, 1986). As one might expect, large metropolitan areas typically offer more program options than small towns or rural areas. New York City, for example, has a long history of special high schools for gifted and talented students.

The future holds particularly exciting possibilities for the education of gifted and talented students. Fox and Washington (1985) note that advances in telecommunications, the presence of microcomputers in the home and classroom, and the call for excellence in American education are three developments with implications for educating our most able students. Telecommunications, including instructional television, telephone conferencing, and electronic mail, are technological means of facilitating the interaction of gifted students and their teachers over wide geographical areas. These communication systems are important for extending appropriate education to gifted students in rural and remote areas. The possible uses of microcomputers for enhancing the education of gifted students are enormous. Using software tutorials, accessing data banks, playing or inventing computer games that are intellectually demanding, writing and editing in English and foreign languages, learning computer languages, and solving advanced problems in mathematics are only a few of the possibilities. The concern for excellence, especially in science and math education, spurred by the report of the National Commission on Excellence in Education in the early 1980s, is an important impetus for educating gifted students. If efforts to reform American education are continued and if they include attention to upgrading instruction for students at all levels of ability, special programs for gifted and talented students may become more common (Callahan & Reis, in press).

Acceleration

Acceleration has not been a very popular plan, except with extremely gifted students. Nevertheless, the evidence in favor of acceleration is quite positive. Feldhusen, Proctor, and Black (1986) summarize the research on advanced placement of precocious students as follows:

> Examination of the research literature reveals that acceleration contributes to academic achievement. No negative effects on social or emotional development have been identified. If adjustment problems occur, they tend to be minor and temporary in nature. Conversely, failure to advance a precocious child may result in poor study habits, apathy, lack of motivation, and maladjustment. (p. 27)

Opponents of acceleration fear that gifted children who are grouped with older students will suffer negative social and emotional consequences or that they will become contemptuous of their age-peers (see Southern, Jones, & Fiscus, 1989). Proponents of acceleration argue that appropriate curriculums and instructional methods are available only in special schools or in regular classes for students who are older than the gifted child. Furthermore, proponents argue that by being grouped with other students who are their intellectual peers in classes in which they are not always first or correct, gifted students acquire a more realistic self-concept and learn tolerance for others whose abilities are not so great as their

Collaboration: A Key to Success

INGRID WOERNER   DIANNE MAYBERRY-HATT

INGRID: I teach twenty-seven students in a self-contained classroom in a school that serves grades K–6. My training and experience as an early childhood educator (I taught for over ten years prior to taking my present position) have provided a good basis for me.

DIANNE: Having been in education for twenty-four years, I understand the frustrations of the job. If a teacher is concerned about a particular student, I'll often discuss the problem with him or her to arrive at a mutually acceptable solution. A personal approach is too often missing in schools, particularly in urban areas. Admittedly, this approach is time-consuming and sometimes nerve-wracking, but it works by creating the best setting for compromise.

INGRID: Understanding the community in which we work is important. Plainfield is an urban/suburban community with a diverse socioeconomic and racial population. The public school population—approximately 6,600—is approximately 94 percent African-American, 5 percent Hispanic, and 1 percent other. About 1,200 of the city's students attend private schools.

DIANNE: The structure of our gifted and talented (G/T) program is important, too. Three years ago the program evolved from a pull-out program to full-time special classes. Identified students in grades three to six are assigned to self-contained classes, often with the same teacher for two years. We have a multiphase identification procedure that includes evaluation of academic performance, standardized achievement test scores, teacher and peer nominations, interviews, and group discussions.

INGRID: Initially, Dianne and I worked together as fifth- and sixth-grade teachers. As the sixth-grade teacher, Dianne often taught my students. We shared lunch and playground duties. So we talked a lot. We discovered that we shared a keen interest in environmental issues, which led us to organize a three-day overnight excursion to an environmental center with our classes. Our first trip caused quite a sensation. Many of the children had never been away from home, much less to the wilderness of New York State! That was eight years ago, and now this trip is the highlight of hundreds of children's school years. In fact, the first thing former students who are now in college ask us about is that trip! This is perhaps our greatest success as a team, but if we had to pick an individual it would be Katie, an eleven-year-old who entered the G/T program as a sixth-grader showing a complete lack of self-confidence.

DIANNE: Most of the other students had been in the program for several years. This was Katie's first year, so we felt she was overwhelmed by what she thought was expected. She believed she was not measuring up when in fact she was performing above average in all her subjects and had an admirable academic record. Katie hid behind a mask of quietness; she rarely spoke or smiled. When given a choice, she most often opted to stand in the back of the line or sit in the last seat. When we asked a question she looked the other way so as not to be noticed or called on. Katie rarely volunteered answers or raised her hand for any reason. She usually cried when she earned a lower than average grade on a test. Fortunately, her grades were usually well above average. Katie seemed fearful of sharing anything that might leave her open to criticism. She'd cover up her difficulties with a particular assignment; she didn't want to ask for help and preferred to work through problems herself. Conferences with her mother offered little insight. As a rule, her projects and special assignments were always very carefully executed. Oral reports, however, were not. After a few words, she invariably lost her composure and could not complete the report. We organized a class meeting (without Katie) to discuss the problem. Because the other students were concerned, they decided that they should encourage Katie more and asked me to ask questions that

- Seeks involvement of others in discovery
- Develops flexible, individualized programs
- Provides feedback; stimulates higher mental processes
- Respects creativity and imagination

Renzulli (1980) has said that these traits are pure "American Pie" and one would hope that *all* teachers would show them. One is probably safe in assuming, however, that teachers must exceed most of their pupils in creativity, intelligence, energy, and task commitment. Consequently, a teacher of gifted students must be above the average for all teachers on many of these traits. Outstanding teachers of gifted students have been found to differ from average teachers in the following ways (Whitlock & DuCette, 1989):

- Having enthusiasm for own work with gifted students
- Having self-confidence in ability to be effective
- Being a facilitator of other people as resources and learners
- Being able to apply knowledge of theory to practice
- Having a strong achievement orientation
- Being commited to the role of educator of gifted students
- Building program support for gifted education programs.

EARLY INTERVENTION

Early identification of exceptional abilities is important. Tests have particular limitations in identifying young gifted children (Fatouros, 1986). Intelligence test scores of young children are not very stable; they tend to change a lot over a period of time, so that without other information they are not very good indicators of even potential giftedness. Robinson, Roedell, and Jackson (1979) believe that tests of academic achievement are useful in early identification if they are used as part of a carefully chosen and competently administered test battery. The battery must sample a wide range of abilities and must allow the child to demonstrate his or her *best* performance. Some tests designed for young children simply do not contain items difficult enough to tap skills at the top of the gifted child's ability. Furthermore, many young children are not easy to test. They are anxious or shy or so inquisitive about the testing materials that a particularly experienced and skillful examiner is required for accurate assessment of their abilities.

Robinson, Roedell, and Jackson (1979) note that young gifted children can be identified by the fact that they exhibit skills like those of ordinary children who are older. For example, an eighteen-month-old child may use language like that of most children who are thirty months; a three-year-old may do multiplication and division problems like those done by average third-graders; or a four-year-old may be able to read and draw maps as well as most adults (see examples of Chris and Jonathan in the box on p. 434). Robinson (1977) argues that gifted youngsters are not qualitatively different in cognitive characteristics, only quantitatively different. That is, their minds do not work in an essentially different way from the minds of most children; they only work faster and at a more advanced level. Gifted children, according to Robinson, are not cognitively different; they are developmentally advanced.*

---

* Recall that in Chapter 3 we discussed the theory that mentally retarded children are not cognitively different from most children, but rather show a developmental delay or lag in learning. These theories suggest that the cognitive characteristics of retarded individuals are the mirror image of those of gifted ones.

Any program for meeting the educational needs of young gifted children must take into account the fact that they can perform like older children in particular skill areas. The conclusion of some researchers (Robinson, 1977; Robinson, Roedell, & Jackson, 1979) is that since gifted children are only quantitatively different in their abilities, they do not need special programs. Instead, what young gifted children need is the freedom to make full and appropriate use of the school system as it now exists. They need the freedom to study with older children in specific areas where their abilities are challenged. Gifted children need to be able to get around the usual eligibility rules so they can go through the ordinary curriculum at an accelerated rate. Unfortunately, relatively few gifted preschoolers receive the kind of educational programming that is appropriate for their abilities. This is especially the case for young gifted children who are also handicapped, poor, or from minority families.

The Gifted Preschooler: Chris and Jonathan

Chris came running into the house, bubbling over with excitement, "Mommy, mommy. I did it! I put the bird back together. Its bones were scattered all around. Look. I have a skeleton of a bird! I guess I am a paleontologist for real! Let's go to the library and find out what species it is."

Chris, only 4, resembles Stephen Gould, world renowned paleontologist whose interest also began at an early age. A visit to the dinosaur exhibit at the American Museum of Natural History inspired both to the world of paleontological inquiry. Will Chris eventually become a paleontologist? Chris has both advanced knowledge and an all-consuming interest in paleontology.

From this scenario we can attest readily to his superior levels in vocabulary development and comprehension skills. Intense interest, in-depth knowledge, and accelerated development in language provide positive evidence of giftedness. But more important, these characteristics strongly imply that Chris has educational needs different from most 4-year-olds.

Will these special needs be met within the school setting? Unfortunately there are a limited number of educational programs adequately equipped to address the unique requirements of children like Chris. Chris' parents, like most parents of bright preschoolers, voice their concern since many of these youngsters are already reading, composing original stories, and computing simple addition and subtraction problems on their own.

One would only have to listen and watch children like Chris to confirm the need for such services. These children frequently demonstrate advanced vocabularies and often an early ability to read. In addition, they seem to learn easily and spontaneously. Logic appears early in some bright youngsters, often to the embarrassment of adults.

For instance, Jonathan, at 3, requested a grilled cheese sandwich at a restaurant. The waitress explained that grilled cheese was not on the menu. Jonathan, determined to have his way, queried, "Do you have cheese and bread?" The waitress nodded, "We do. . . ." "Then," Jon blurted, "do you have a pan?" Jon got his sandwich. When the sandwich arrived, the waitress took beverage orders. Jonathan ordered a milkshake, but this time the waitress was one step ahead. "Jonathan, we have milk and ice cream, but I'm sorry we don't have any syrup." To which Jon asked, "Do you have a car?"

Other youngsters may show advanced abilities in number concepts, maps, telling time, and block building. Their skills in such activities far exceed that of their agemates. Not only do these characteristics define gifted preschoolers but also provide a rationale and structure for intervention.

SOURCE: S. Baum, "The Gifted Preschooler: An Awesome Delight," *Gifted Child Today*, 9(4) (1986), 42–43.

Gifted preschool children demonstrate an ability to do things that older children of average ability do. (Daemmrich/Stock, Boston)

Gifted preschoolers may be intellectually superior and have above-average adaptive behavior and leadership skills as well. Their advanced abilities in many areas, however, do not mean that their development will be above average across the board. Emotionally, they may develop at an average pace for their chronological age. Sometimes their uneven development creates special problems of social isolation, and adults may have unrealistic expectations for their social and emotional skills because their cognitive and language skills are so advanced. They may require special guidance by sensitive adults who not only provide appropriate educational environments for them but also discipline them appropriately and teach them the skills required for social competence (Baum, 1986; Roedell, 1985). They may need help, for example, in acquiring self-understanding, independence, assertiveness, sensitivity to others, friend-making skills, and social problem-solving skills.

TRANSITION

For gifted students who are achieving near their potential and are given opportunities to take on adult roles, the transitions from childhood to adolescence to adulthood and from high school to higher education or employment are typically not very problematic. In many ways, transition for gifted youths tends to be a mirror image of the problems in transition faced by adolescents and young adults with disabilities. Consider the case of Raymond Kurzweil, inventor of the Kurzweil reading machine for blind persons (see Chapter 8).

A summer job, at age 12, involved statistical computer programming. Could a kid comprehend IBM's daunting Fortran manual? He very well could. Soon, in fact, IBM would be coming to young Kurzweil for programming advice.

By the time he was graduated from high school, the whiz kid had earned a national reputation, particularly for a unique computer program that could compose original music in the styles of Mozart and Beethoven, among others.

After carefully weighing all his options, Kurzweil decided to enroll in the Massachusetts Institute of Technology so that he could mingle with the gurus of the then-emerging science of artificial intelligence. Kurzweil was in his element. He was also rather quickly in the chips. (Neuhaus, 1988, p. 66)

Today, in his forties, Kurzweil is a highly successful entrepreneur who is chairman of three high-tech corporations he founded.

Not all adolescents and young adults who are gifted take transitions in stride, however. Many need personal and career counseling and a networking system that links students to school and community resources (Clifford, Runions, & Smyth, 1986). Some are well served by an eclectic approach that employs the best features of enrichment and acceleration (Feldhusen & Kolloff, 1986).

If there is a central issue in the education of gifted adolescents, it is that of acceleration versus enrichment. Proponents of enrichment feel that gifted students need continued social contact with their age-peers. They argue that gifted students should follow the curriculum of their age-mates and study topics in greater depth. Proponents of acceleration feel that the only way to provide challenging and appropriate education for those with special gifts and talents is to let them compete with older students. They argue that since the cognitive abilities of gifted students are advanced beyond their years, they should proceed through the curriculum at an accelerated pace (see the box on pp. 414–415 describing the program at Mary Baldwin College).

One of the most articulate proponents of acceleration is Julian Stanley, who directs a special program of accelerated study in mathematics at Johns Hopkins University in Baltimore. His project, the Study of Mathematically Precocious Youth (SMPY), is a longitudinal research program that began in 1971 (Benbow, 1986). Each year a mathematics talent search is conducted in the seventh, eighth, and ninth grades of the Baltimore metropolitan area. Students who have already scored in the top 5 percent on an achievement test are given two tests designed primarily for above-average eleventh- and twelfth-graders: the College Board's Scholastic Aptitude Test, mathematical part (SAT-M), and the Mathematics Achievement Test, Level I. Individual students are then given counseling about educational options.

Depending on how precocious they are in mathematics, their motivation to do advanced study, and personal considerations, the students may pursue a variety of acceleration programs such as skipping a grade, doing early part-time college study, earning college credit by examination or correspondence courses, entering college early, or attending special fast-paced classes. The students will be followed over a period of more than two decades to observe their achievements and personal adjustment.

The outcomes of the SMPY program are reported to be very positive and include increased zest for learning and for life, enhanced feelings of self-worth and accomplishment, and reduction of egotism and arrogance. Furthermore, these positive results have apparently been obtained also in the Minnesota Talented Youth Mathematics Program (Keating, 1979). Acceleration may be the better choice for students who are precocious in areas of study requiring reasoning that is not dependent on social experience. For students whose precocity is in areas requiring verbal skills and social reasoning, such as literature, it is more feasible to devise enrichment that is an adequate substitute for grade acceleration.

SUGGESTIONS FOR TEACHING THE GIFTED AND TALENTED STUDENT IN GENERAL EDUCATION CLASSROOMS

What to Look for in School

As you know from reading the chapter, students who demonstrate gifted behavior are superior in some way, and exhibit abilities and sensitivities that may allow them to: express themselves in special ways; learn quickly; be self-sufficient; or understand their own and others' feelings, motivations, and strengths and weaknesses. Although this combination of characteristics, coupled with exceptional eagerness and curiosity, may make gifted students easy to recognize in your class, formally identifying students for gifted and talented programs may be more difficult.

How to Gather Information

Because there is no federal definition of gifted and talented, each state has established its own criteria for identifying these students and then developed programs based on these criteria. Consequently, programs differ from state to state. If you think any of your students may be gifted, ask your principal for the state guidelines to determine if he or she might qualify for your district's specialized program. You may also contact the person in your building or in the central office who serves as coordinator for the gifted program and discuss the criteria your system has established. If you believe your student may meet these guidelines, collect samples of the student's work and record your observations of the student's productivity and creativity and show them to the gifted coordinator, who then may initiate a referral to the gifted and talented program.

Teaching Techniques to Try

Even in school systems that have comprehensive identification procedures and specialized resource programs, classroom teachers assume the responsibility during most of the school day for providing the educational experiences for gifted and talented students (Starko, 1986). One type of experience experts agree benefits academically-gifted students is self-directed learning, which helps students systematically move from teacher-determined and -directed instruction toward independent learning. Treffinger and Barton (1988, p. 28) summarize the goals of self-directed learning:

1. learning to function effectively in one's total environment,
2. learning to make choices and decisions based on self-knowledge of needs and interests,
3. learning to assume responsibility for choices and decisions by completing all activities at a satisfactory level of achievement and in an acceptable time frame,
4. learning to define problems and to determine a course of action for their solution, and
5. learning to evaluate one's own work.

These educators believe that the process of self-directed learning culminates in students being able to "initiate plans for their own learning, identify resources, gather data, and develop and evaluate their own products and projects" (p. 30). Teachers use a variety of techniques such as curriculum compacting, learning centers, independent study, and contracting to promote self-directed learning in regular education classes at all grade levels.

Educators emphasize that although self-directed learning options provide gifted students with advanced-level materials, they also can limit the students' interactions with other students and with the teacher without careful planning and direction by the teacher (Howley, Howley, & Pendarvis, 1986).

Curriculum Compacting

Curriculum compacting is a procedure in which the teacher modifies the regular curriculum to provide additional time for gifted students to pursue alternative learning activities. To make these modifications, you must first identify the academic strengths of your gifted students, using a variety of information sources such as school records, previous teacher recommendations, standarized and informal test results, and observation. Once you decide what curricular areas are most appropriate for compacting, consider the following questions:

1. What does the student already know?
2. What does the student need to learn?
3. What activities will meet the students' learning needs?

For example (Starko, 1986), one teacher determined that Michael, a gifted student, had already mastered all the skills presented in reading units 3 and 4, except outlining. Next she decided that he would complete only the assignments that focused on outlining skills; located these assignments in the reading book, using the Scope and Sequence charts; and recorded the work Michael would complete independently or with the class. Finally, she identified and outlined the activities that would meet Michael's needs based on his strengths and interests. Having made these assessment and instructional decisions, you next must decide how to provide appropriate alternative educational activities.

Learning Centers

Teachers often use learning centers to provide enrichment activities to their gifted students. To promote self-directed learning, however, these centers must offer in-structional opportunities in areas that are specifically designed and sequenced to encourage student independence.

Teachers in Richland County, Ohio found they could offer activities in regular education classes that developed the productivity and creativity of their gifted students by designing interest development centers (IDCs) (Burns, 1985). Unlike traditional learning centers, which help students master basic curriculum skills, IDCs facilitate students' independent exploration of a wide range of topics not included in the regular curriculum. The teachers stocked their centers with manipula-tive and media and print materials along with several suggestions for examining and experimenting in special interest areas. In keeping with the Renzulli model (see p. 430), they also included methodological resources that helped promote interest in long-term research. For example, one teacher developed a center about bicycling that contained materials on how to create a bike path and how to approach the city council for permission to build bike racks near businesses that students frequented.

To plan an IDC, the teachers first identified the interests of their students and then with other teachers brainstormed ideas that would invite and stimulate exploration. After they recorded these ideas and the materials they would include in the IDC, they began collecting materials in the following areas:

1. Narrative information contained in magazines, professional journals, video- and audiotapes, introductory textbooks, career brochures, and newspapers
2. Community resources such as the names, addresses, and telephone numbers of persons in the area who would let students visit their workplace or interview them
3. Display objects, including such items as slides, specimens, photographs, poetry, and art books

Once they had gathered these materials from other teachers, parents, students, and community organizations, clubs, or agencies, they arranged them in an attractive center in the classroom. When the center was completed, they introduced it to students in order to generate their interest and orient them to the topic and to available resources. Finally, they scheduled time each day for IDC exploration to give students the opportunity to become involved in the thinking and work inspired by the center. For additional information and specific independent learning center resources and ideas, see Burns (1985).

Independent Study

Sometimes students will develop and/or maintain great interest in a topic they have explored. When this occurs, you may decide to help students conduct an independent study on this topic. Independent study involves not only the exploration of a topic in depth but also the production of an original product that is disseminated to an appropriate audience. Because directing an independent study is time consuming and requires an understanding of the topic, teachers often solicit the help of the gifted program's resource teacher or another person who is knowledgeable about the subject and willing to participate in the project (Pendarvis, Howley, & Howley, 1990). The role of the teacher and resource person(s) is not to be director of the study; rather, they serve as assistants who help the students define and frame the problem, establish realistic goals and time lines, become aware of a variety of usable resources, identify both a product that the study will produce and an audience for the product, and evaluate their study. In addition, the adults involved in the project must reinforce the student's work throughout the study and provide methodological help when necessary. To learn more about the process of guiding gifted students through independent study see Reis and Cellerino (1983).

Contracts

You can also facilitate self-directed learning by providing individualized exploration and instruction in the form of student contracts. Like business contracts these documents are negotiated with the student and describe the area the student will study and the procedures and resources he or she will use in the investigation. When contracts are used to guide independent study, they also can specify the intended audience, the means of dissemination, deadlines for stages or steps in the study, and dates and purposes of periodic meetings with the teacher (Tuttle & Becker, 1983).

Helpful Resources

School Personnel

In the pursuit of ideas, information, and materials to use in self-directed learning activities, the school media specialist can be a valuable resource. He or she can orient students to the variety of materials that are available, including yearbooks; geographical, political, and economic atlases; career files; subject-related dictionaries; periodical indexes; bibliographic references and databases; and information available on microfilm and microfiche. Specialists also can help students learn how to evaluate resource material by assessing such factors as the purpose of the work and its intended audience; the author's (or editor's) credentials; completeness of index and reference citations; and accuracy and completeness of charts, statistics, graphs, time lines, and other illustrative materials (Flack, 1986, p. 175).

For students involved in independent studies, media specialists may be helpful resources in the creation of research products by instructing students in the use of such processes as videotaping, laminating, and making transparencies. They also may encourage and facilitate the dissemination of the products. For example, a second-grade student decided to write a children's talking book on Tchaikovsky that was intended for other elementary students and that would be housed permanently in his school's library (Reis & Cellerino, 1983).

Instructional Methods and Materials

Adams, D. M., & Hamm, M. E. (1989). *Media and literacy: Learning in an electronic age—Issues, ideas, and teaching strategies.* Springfield, IL; Chas. C Thomas.

Cook, C., & Carlisle, J. (1985). *Challenges for children: Creative activities for gifted and talented primary students.* West Nyack, NY: The Center for Applied Research in Education.

Cox, J., Daniel, N., & Boston, B. O. (1985). *Educating able learners: Programs and promising practices.* Austin: University of Texas Press.

Cushenbery, D. C. (1987). *Reading instruction for the gifted.* Springfield, IL: Chas. C Thomas.

Davis, G. A., & Rimm, S. B. (1989). *Education of the gifted and talented.* Englewood Cliffs, NJ: Prentice-Hall.

Dirkes, M. A. (1988). Self-directed thinking in the curriculum. *Roeper Review, 11,* 92–94.

Gallagher, J. J. (1986). *Teaching the gifted child* (3rd ed.). Newton, MA: Allyn & Bacon.

Kondziolka, G., & Normandeau, P. (1986). Investigation: An interdisciplinary unit. *Gifted Child Today, 9,* 52–54.

Lukasevich, A. (1983). Three dozen useful information sources on reading for the gifted. *Reading Teacher, 36,* 542–548.

Milgram, R. M. (1989). *Teaching gifted and talented learners in regular classrooms.* Springfield, IL: Chas. C Thomas.

Parker, B. N. (1989). *Gifted students in regular classrooms.* Boston: Allyn & Bacon.

Pendarvis, E. D., Howley, A. A., & Howley, C. B. (1990). *The abilities of gifted children.* Englewood Cliffs, NJ: Prentice-Hall.

Polette, N. (1984). *The research book for gifted programs.* O'Fallon, MO: Book Lures.

Ross, E. P., & Wright, J. (1987). Matching teaching strategies to the learning styles of gifted readers. *Reading Horizons, 28,* 49–56.

Schlichter, C. L. (1988). Thinking skills instruction for all classrooms. *Gifted Child Today, 11,* 24–28.

Schmitz, C. C., & Galbraith, J. (1985). Managing the social and emotional needs of the gifted. Minneapolis, MN: Free Spirit.

Sisk, D. (1987). *Creative teaching of the gifted.* New York: McGraw-Hill.

Curricular Models and Adaptations

Betts, G. T. (1985). *Autonomous learner model for the gifted and talented.* Greeley, CO: Autonomous Learning Publication and Specialists.

Bloom, B. S. (Ed.). (1974). *Taxonomy of Educational Objectives.* New York: McKay.

Feldhusen, J. F., & Kolloff, M. B. (1988). A three-stage model for gifted education. *Gifted Child Today, 11,* 14–18.

Guilford, J. P. (1967). *The nature of human intelligence.* New York: McGraw-Hill.

Hollingsworth, P. L. (1985). Enaction theory, simulation, and the gifted. *Roeper Review, 8,* 93–95.

Renzulli, J. (1977). *The enrichment triad model.* Mansfield, CT: Creative Learning Press.

Renzulli, J. S., Reise, S. M., & Smith, L. H. (1981). *The revolving door identification model.* Mansfield, CT: Creative Learning Press.

Robinson, A. (1986). Elementary language arts for the gifted: Assimilation and accommodation in the curriculum. *Gifted Child Quarterly, 30*, 178–181.

Taylor, C. W. (1978). How many types of giftedness can your program tolerate? *Journal of Creative Behavior, 12*, 39–51.

Treffinger, D. J. (1975). Teaching for self-directed learning: A priority for the gifted and talented. *Gifted Child Quarterly, 12*, 46–59.

Treffinger, D. J. (1978). Guidelines for encouraging independence and self-direction among gifted students. *Journal of Creative Behavior, 12*, 14–19.

Wallace, B. (1986). Curriculum enrichment then curriculum extension: Differentiated educational development in the context of equal opportunities for all children. *Gifted Education International, 4*, 4–9.

Williams, F. (1979). *Classroom ideas for encouraging thinking and feelings.* Buffalo, NY: D.O.K. Publishers.

Literature About Gifted and Talented Individuals

ELEMENTARY: AGES 5–8 AND 9–12

Calvert, P. (1980). *The snowbird.* New York: Scribner's.

Fitzgerald, J. D. (1967). *The great brain.* New York: Dial Press.

Greenwald, S. (1987). *Alvin Webster's surefire plan for success (and how it failed).* Boston: Little, Brown.

Hassler, J. (1981). *Jemmy.* New York: Atheneum.

Oneal, Z. (1980). *The language of goldfish.* New York: Viking Press.

Sobol, D. J. (1963). *Encyclopedia Brown: Boy detective.* New York: Thomas Nelson.

Wells, R. (1980). *When no one was looking.* New York: Dial Press.

MIDDLE AND HIGH SCHOOL: AGES 13–18

Evernden, M. (1985). *The dream keeper.* New York: Lothrop, Lee & Shepard Books.

Pfeffer, S. B. (1989). *Dear Dad, love Laurie.* New York: Scholastic.

Voigt, C. (1982). *Tell me if the lovers are losers.* New York: Atheneum.

Software

Adventure Master, CBS Software, 1 Fawcett Place, Greenwich, CT 06836.

Analogies, Hartley Courseware, Box 419, Dimondale, MI 48821; (800) 247-1380.

Animate, Broderbund, 17 Paul Drive, San Rafael, CA 94913; (800) 527-6263.

Appleworks, Claris, 440 Clyde Avenue, Mountain View, CA 94043; (415) 960-1500 (word processing).

Astronomy, The Voyager Company, 2139 Manning Avenue, Los Angeles, CA 90025.

Bank Street Music Writer, MIndscape, Inc., 344 Dundee Road, North Brook, IL 60062.

Bank Street School Filer Databases, Sunburst Communication, 39 Washington Avenue, Pleasantville, NY 10570; (800) 431-1934.

Command Series (D-Day/Battle of the Bulge), MicroProse Software, 120 Lake Front Drive, Hunt Valley, MD 21031.

Creativity Unlimited, Sunburst Communications, 39 Washington Avenue, Pleasantville, NY 10570; (800) 431-1934.

Dazzle Draw, Broderbund, 17 Paul Drive, San Rafael, CA 94903.

The Electronic Encyclopedia, Grolier Electronic Publishing, Inc., Sherman Turnpike, Danbury, CT 06816; (800) 858-8858.

The Fermi-Pico-Bagel Logo Game, Trillium Press, Box 921, Madison Square Station, New York, NY 10159; (212) 505-1440.

Gears, Sunburst Communications, 39 Washington Avenue, Pleasantville, NY 10570; (800) 431-1934.

The Incredible Laboratory, Sunburst Communications, 39 Washington Avenue, Pleasantville, NY 10570; (800) 431-1934.

In Search of the Amazing Thing, Spinnaker, 1 Kendall Square, Cambridge, MA 02139; (617) 494-1200.

Mathware, Trillum Software, Box 921, Madison Square Station, New York City, NY 10159.

Music Studies, Activision, Inc., 2350 Bayshore Frontage Road, Mountain View, CA 94043.

National Gallery of Art, The Voyager Company, 2139 Manning Avenue, Los Angeles, CA 90025; (213) 475-3524.

Newsroom, Springboard, 7807 Creekridge Creek, Minneapolis, MN 55435; (800) 6554-6301.

Operation Fog, Scholastic, Inc., P.O. Box 7503, 2931 East McCarty Jefferson City, MO 65102; (800) 654-6301.

Planetary Construction Set, Sunburst Communications, 39 Washington Avenue, Pleasantville, NY 10570; (800) 431-1934.

The Print Shop, Broderbund, 17 Paul Drive, San Rafael, CA 94913.

Science Tool Kit, Broderbund, 17 Paul Drive, San Rafael, CA 94913; (800) 527-6263.

Slide Show, Videodiscovery, P.O. Box 85878, Seattle, WA 98145; (206) 547-7981.

The Super Factory, Sunburst Communications, 39 Washington Avenue, Pleasantville, NY 10570; (800) 431-1934.

The Whatsit Corporation, Sunburst Communications, 39 Washington Avenue, Pleasantville, NY 10570; (800) 431-1934.

Organizations

Association for Gifted and Talented Students, Northwestern State University, Natchitoches, LA 71301; (318) 357-4572.

Association for the Gifted, the Council for Exceptional Children, 1920 Association Drive, Reston, VA 22091; (703) 620-3660.

Gifted Child Society, 190 Rock Road, Glen Rock, NJ 07452; (201) 444-6530.

National Association for Gifted Children, 4175 Lovell Road, Suite 140, Circle Pines, MN 55014; (612) 784-3475.

Bibliography for Teaching Suggestions

Burns, D. E. (1985). Land of opportunity. *Gifted Child Today*, issue 37, 41–45.

Flack, J. D. (1986). A new look at a valued partnership: The library media specialist and gifted students. *School Library Media Quarterly, 14*, 174–179.

Howley, A., Howley, C. B., & Pendarvis, E. D. (1986). *Teaching gifted children.* Boston: Little, Brown.

Pendarvis, E. D., Howley, A. A., & Howley, C. B. (1990). *The abilities of gifted children.* Englewood Cliffs, NJ: Prentice Hall.

Reis, S. M., & Cellerino, M. (1983). Guiding gifted students through independent study. *Teaching exceptional children.* 15, 136–139.

Starko, A. (1986). Meeting the needs of the gifted throughout the school day: Techniques for curriculum compacting. *Roeper Review, 9*, 27–33.

Treffinger, D. J., & Barton, B. L. (1988). Foster independent learning. *Gifted Child Today, 11*, 28–30.

Tuttle, F. B., & Becker, L. A. (1983). *Program design and development for gifted and talented students* (2nd ed.). Washington, DC: National Education Association.

SUMMARY

Disagreements about definitions of giftedness center around the questions of exactly how gifted children are superior; how this superiority is measured; the degree to which the individual must be superior to be considered gifted; and who should make up the comparison group. Even the terms used can be confusing: *Precocity* indicates remarkable early development; *insight* involves separating relevant from irrelevant information and combining information in novel and productive ways; *genius* refers to rare intellectual powers; *creativity* has to do with the ability to express novel and useful ideas, to see novel relationships, to ask original and crucial questions; *talent* indicates a special ability within a particular area.

The use of individually administered intelligence tests as the only basis for defining giftedness has met with increasing dissatisfaction for several reasons. First, traditional intelligence tests are limited in what they measure. Second, intelligence is being reconceptualized. The thinking of people with high intelligence appears to be qualitatively different from that of average people, perhaps along such dimensions as insightfulness. Leading researchers are searching for cognitive characteristics that define either *general* intelligence or *specific* intelligences. Whether intelligence should be lumped into a general characteristic or split into distinctive parts is an ongoing controversy. Third, new ideas about giftedness include the hypothesis that gifted performance is attainable only when a child is relatively free of biological impairments, mostly invulnerable to environmental stresses that limit performance, and reared in an environment that is supportive of high performance. However, children exhibit gifted performance in specific domains; it would be possible, for example, for a physically disabled child to attain giftedness in any area not impaired by that child's specific physical disability.

Giftedness may be defined as demonstration of high ability, high creativity, and high task commitment. Therefore, a given child may be gifted at one time, in one area of performance, or in one situation and not in another.

Giftedness is not an absolute, fixed human characteristic. Furthermore, it can be defined to include many or only very few people. Consequently the prevalence of giftedness cannot be precisely established. Perhaps 15 to 25 percent of the population has the potential for exhibiting gifted behavior at some time during their schooling in at least one area of performance.

Genetic factors are known to contribute significantly to behavioral development, including intelligence and gifted performance. Environmental factors—families, schools, and communities—are also known to influence the development of giftedness. Giftedness, then, is a result of combined biological and environmental influences—nature *and* nurture. Current research suggests that one's collection of genes sets limits of performance; the actual performance within those limits is determined by environmental factors.

The most effective and efficient means of screening for giftedness is a case study approach, which includes aptitude and achievement test scores, teacher ratings, records of past performance, parent ratings, and self-ratings. Test scores alone are now seen as an inadequate basis for the identification of gifted students. Creativity is an important aspect of giftedness, although measuring creativity is very difficult. Creativity is best understood as a characteristic of the behavior of people who have mastered a given field and are working at the cutting edge in their discipline.

The stereotype of brilliant people as physically weak, socially inept, and prone to emotional instability still exists. But considered as a group, gifted individuals tend to be superior not only in intelligence but also in physique, social attractiveness, achievement, emotional stability, and even moral character. They are not, however, "superhuman." Gifted people tend to excel in academic and occupational pursuits, although there are still many underachieving gifted children. Socially and emotionally, intellectually superior individuals tend, as a group, to be happy, well liked, stable, and less apt to have psychotic and neurotic disorders than average people. Despite historical and psychoanalytic theories to the contrary, genius and insanity are not linked. Like most of us, brilliant people can be corrupt and unscrupulous, but the majority appear to have a great concern for moral and ethical issues and behavior.

Current attitudes toward special education for gifted students leaves much to be desired. Those who argue against special education for gifted students may in reality be arguing against special education for any type of exceptional child. In recent years interest in education of gifted children has increased, but most gifted students in American public schools still receive no special services appropriate to their abilities.

Neglected groups of gifted students include underachievers—those who fail to achieve at a level consistent with their abilities, whatever the reason. Underachievement is often a problem of minority and handicapped students, whose special abilities tend to be overlooked because of biased expectations and/or the values of the majority.

Education of gifted and talented students should have three characteristics: curriculum designed to accommodate advanced cognitive skills, instructional strategies consistent with learning styles in particular curriculum areas, and administrative facilitation of grouping for instruction. Programs and practices in the education of gifted students are extremely varied and include special schools, acceleration, special classes, tutoring, and enrichment during the school year or summer. Administrative plans for modifying the curriculum include enrichment in the classroom, use of consultant teachers, resource rooms, community mentors, independent study, special classes, and special schools. Acceleration has not been a popular plan for educating gifted students, although considerable research supports it. Models of enrichment include a "revolving door" plan in which students continue to engage in enrichment activities for as long as they are able to go beyond the usual curriculum of their age-mates and a schoolwide enrichment model that is designed to improve the learning environment for all students.

Teachers of gifted students should exhibit characteristics that are desirable for all teachers. However, they probably must be particularly intelligent, creative, energetic, enthusiastic, and committed to excellence.

Early intervention entails early identification of special abilities, providing stimulation to preschool children to foster giftedness, and special provisions such as acceleration to make education appropriate for the young child's advanced skills. Gifted young children appear to have particular skills much like those of older nongifted children. We may need to take special care not to assume that a child's emotional and social development are advanced just because his or her language and cognitive skills are advanced.

Transitions to adolescence, adulthood, and higher education and employment are typically not the problems for high-achieving gifted children that they are for children with disabilities. Nevertheless, many do need personal and career counseling and help in making contacts with school and community resources. A major issue is acceleration versus enrichment. Programs of acceleration (especially in mathematics, in which students skip grades or complete college-level work early) have been evaluated very positively.

WHEN I WAS BORN
Camille Holvoet, Creative Growth Art Center

11

Parents and Families

Sun shone that day long ago in Corcloon. Yvonne was gone to school. Asleep in his blue bed Joseph looked the picture of pleasant childlike thimblework. Nora serenely simpered as she lifted him. Washed and powdered he sat on her lap. Fondly she slipped the geansai [jersey] over his blonde head. His head tilted boldly forward then suddenly it shot backwards. He faced his mother. He gazed his hurt gaze, lip protruding, eyes busy in conversation. He ordered her to look out the window at the sunshine. He looked hard at her ear ordering her to listen to the birds singing. Then jumping on her knees he again asked her to cock her ear and listen to the village children out at play in the school yard. Now he jeered himself. He showed her his arms, his legs, his useless body. Beckoning his tears he shook his head. Looking at his mother he blamed her, he damned her, he mouthed his cantankerous why, why, why me? Distracted by his youthful harshness of realization she tried to distract him. Lifting him in her arms she brought him outside into the farmyard. "Come on till I show you the calves," she coaxed. His lonely tears rushed even faster. He knew why she tried to divert his boyish questioning. He childishly determined not to look at the calves and shaking his head he gazed the other way. His mother tried again. "Look over at the lambs," she said, pointing at the sheep feeding at their trough in the field. He cried so loud he brought her to her senses. "Alright," she said, "we'll go back inside and talk." Placing him in his chair she then sat down and faced her erstwhile boy, yes, her golden-haired accuser. Meanwhile he cried continuously, conning himself that he had beaten her to silence. Looking through his tears he saw her as she bent low in order to look into his eyes. "I never prayed for you to be born crippled," she said. "I wanted you to be full of life, able to run and jump and talk just like Yvonne. But you are you, you are Joseph not Yvonne. Listen here Joseph, you can see, you can hear, you can think, you can understand everything you hear, you like your food, you like nice clothes, you are loved by me and Dad. We love you just as you are." Pussing still, snivelling still, he was listening to his mother's voice. She spoke sort of matter-of-factly but he blubbered moaning sounds. His mother said her say and that was that. She got on with her work while he got on with his crying.

The decision arrived at that day was burnt forever in his mind. He was only three years in age but he was now fanning the only spark he saw, his being alive and more immediate, his being wanted just as he was.

Source: Nolan, C. (1987). *Under the eye of the clock: The life story of Christopher Nolan*. New York: St. Martin's Press, pp. 37–38.

A fertile ground for conflict or harmony, the family, especially the family of the 1990s—and more especially the family of the 1990s with a disabled family member—is the perfect locale for the study of the interplay of human emotion and behavior. Think of your own family as you were growing up. Think of the dynamics of interaction among you and your sibling(s) and parent(s). These interactions were no doubt carried out within the full range of human emotions. Now, add to this mixture of human interaction a dose of disability. Consider how much more complex living in your family would have been if you had had a brother, like Joseph, with severe cerebral palsy (see p. 445).

In addition to underscoring the complexities of living with a family member with disabilities, the autobiographical account of Joseph and his mother also demonstrates how resilient some families can be in the face of extreme difficulties. A child with disabilities does not always threaten the well-being of a family. Reactions of family members to the individual with a disability can run the gamut from absolute rejection to absolute acceptance, from intense hate to intense love, from total neglect to total overprotection. In fact, some parents and siblings assert that having a family member with a disability has actually strengthened the family. As highlighted by the interaction between Joseph and his mother, however, coping with the stress of raising and living with a disabled child rarely comes easily.

In this chapter, we explore the dynamics of families with disabled children and discuss parental involvement in their treatment and education. Before proceeding further, however, it is instructive to consider the role of parents of exceptional children from a historical perspective.

PROFESSIONALS' CHANGING VIEWS OF PARENTS

Today, the knowledgeable professional who works with exceptional individuals is aware of the importance of the family. We now recognize that the family of the disabled individual, especially the parents, can help us in our educational efforts. To ignore the disabled student's family is shortsighted because it can lessen the effectiveness of teaching. Though today we recognize how crucial it is to consider the concerns of parents and families in treatment and educational programs for disabled individuals, this was not always the case.

Professionals' views of the role of parents have changed dramatically. In the not too distant past, some professionals looked to the parents primarily as a cause of some of the child's problems or as a place to lay blame when practitioners' interventions were ineffective. According to one set of authorities, negative views of parents were in some ways a holdover from the eugenics movement of the late nineteenth and early twentieth centuries (Turnbull & Turnbull, 1990). Professionals associated with the **eugenics movement** believed in the selective breeding of humans. They proposed sterilization of mentally retarded people because they erroneously believed that virtually all cases of mental retardation were caused by heredity.

Although the eugenics movement had largely died out by the 1930s and few professionals any longer blamed disabilities primarily on heredity, the climate was ripe for some of them to blame a variety of disabilities, especially emotional problems, on the child-rearing practices of parents. For example, until the 1970s and 1980s, when research demonstrated a biochemical basis for autism, it was quite popular to pin the blame for autism on the parents, especially mothers. The leading proponent of this viewpoint, Bruno Bettelheim, asserted that mothers who were cold and

MISCONCEPTIONS
ABOUT PARENTS AND FAMILIES OF DISABLED INDIVIDUALS

Myth	Fact
Parents must go through a series of emotional reactions—shock and disruption, denial, sadness, anxiety and fear, anger—before adapting to the birth of a child with disabilities.	Parents do not go through emotional reactions in a lockstep fashion. They may experience some, or all, of these emotions, but not necessarily in any particular order.
Parents are to blame for many of the problems of their disabled children.	Regardless of whether the child is disabled, the direction of cause and effect between parent and child is a two-way street. Parents can influence their children's behavior, but so, too, can children affect how their parents behave. In addition, research has demonstrated that some children with disabilities are born with more difficult temperaments, which can also have an effect on parental behavior.
Many parents of infants with disabilities go from physician to physician, "shopping" for an optimistic diagnosis.	Anecdotal accounts from parents indicate that just the opposite is often true. Parents frequently suspect that something is wrong with their baby but are told by physicians not to worry, that the child will "outgrow" the problem. They thus seek another opinion.
The "typical" family in the United States has two parents, is middle class, and only the father works outside the home.	Although this was once the case, demographics are changing rapidly. By the year 1995 almost two-thirds of preschoolers and three-quarters of school-age children will have a mother in the work force. In addition, one out of five families with a child under eighteen years is headed by a single parent, and about one in every five children lives in poverty.
Parents who elect not to be actively involved (e.g., attending and offering suggestions at IEP meetings or visiting the school frequently) in their disabled child's education and treatment are neglectful.	Although it is desirable for parents to be actively involved in their children's education, it is sometimes very difficult for them to do so because of their commitments to other family functions (e.g., work and child care). We should encourage parents to participate actively but not try to coerce them to do so or automatically assume that those who remain passive do not care about their children's welfare.
Professionals are always in the best position to provide help to families of individuals with a disability.	Research indicates that informal sources of support, such as extended family, friends, neighbors, church groups, and social clubs, are often more effective than formal sources of support, such as professionals and agencies, in helping families adapt to a family member with disabilities.

unresponsive toward their children—"refrigerator moms"—produced autism in their children (Bettelheim, 1950, 1967).

In the late 1970s and early 1980s professionals became less likely to blame parents automatically for the problems of their children. There were at least two reasons for this more positive view. First, Richard Bell forwarded the notion that the direction of causation between child and adult behavior is a two-way street (Bell & Harper, 1977). Sometimes the parent changes the behavior of the child or infant; sometimes the reverse is true. With specific regard to exceptional children, some researchers point out that disabled children, even as infants, sometimes possess difficult temperaments, which influence how parents respond to them (Brooks-Gunn & Lewis, 1984; Mahoney & Robenalt, 1986). Some disabled infants, for example, are relatively unresponsive to stimulation from their parents, making it more difficult to carry on interactions with them. With an understanding of the reciprocal nature of parent-child interaction we are thus more likely, for example, to sympathize with a mother's frustration in trying to cuddle a severely retarded infant or a father's anger in attempting to deal with his behavior-disordered teenager.

Second, professionals began to recognize the potentially positive influence of the family in the educational process. Although at first many of them tended to think that parents needed training to achieve a positive effect on their children, more and more have recognized that parents often have as much, and in some cases more, to offer than professionals regarding suggestions for the treatment of their children. The prevailing philosophy now dictates that whenever possible, professionals should seek out the special insights that parents can offer by virtue of living with their exceptional child.

For at least three reasons, professionals now have a more positive attitude toward the role of parents:

1. More and more special educators are supporting the idea that early intervention that takes place in the home and/or uses the home as a basis for curricular objectives has the best chance of success (McDonnell & Hardman, 1988). Early childhood special educators have noted that education should be focused on enabling preschool children to function in the home because a large portion of their time is spent in that setting.

2. Parents themselves have become more and more active in advocating services in an organized and effective way for their children. In the process, they have frequently argued that they themselves should be given a voice in how schools educate their children.

3. Because of the efforts of parental and professional organizations, Congress has passed federal laws (PL 94-142 and PL 99-457) stipulating that schools make a concerted effort to involve parents and families in the education of their disabled children. Among other things, for example, PL 94-142 specifies that schools attempt to include parents of handicapped children in the development of an individualized education plan (IEP) (see Chapter 1). In the case of children under three years of age, PL 99-457 dictates that schools must involve parents in the development of an **individualized family service plan (IFSP).** The focus of the IFSP is not only on the individual handicapped child but also on his or her family. It specifies services the family needs to enhance the child's development.

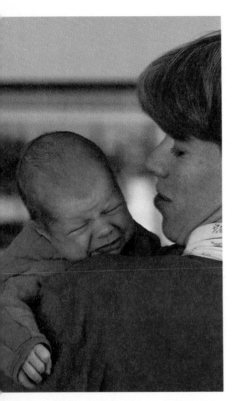

Parents' behaviors are shaped by the behaviors of their children and vice versa. (Erika Stone)

THE EFFECTS OF A DISABLED CHILD ON THE FAMILY

The birth of any child can have a significant effect on the dynamics of the family. Parents and other children in the family must undergo a variety of changes to adapt to the presence of a new member. The effects on the family of the birth of a disabled child can be even more profound. Disabled infants and children are frequently characterized by extremes of behavior, which in turn influence the interactions they have with parents and siblings. The extra care and special accommodations required by some exceptional children often alter how parents and siblings interact with the disabled child as well as with nondisabled family members.

Not only is the study of families of disabled individuals difficult because of the complexity of the interactions that take place, but it is also complicated by the fact that the area relies so much on subjective impressions. When talking about the impact an exceptional child has on a family, we are talking to a great extent about *feelings*—the feelings of parents toward the child and toward society's reactions to the child, the feelings of the child's siblings toward the child and society, and the feelings of the disabled child. When talking about feelings, of course, we are in the realm of subjectivity. Psychologists are notoriously good at describing people's emotions but poor at understanding them. The subjective and complex nature of the familial feelings aroused by disabled children make our job of comprehending their nature extremely difficult.

Parental Reactions

A Stage Theory Approach

Traditionally researchers and clinicians have suggested that parents go through a series of stages after learning they have a disabled child. Some of these stages parallel the proposed sequence of responses that accompany a person's reactions to the death of a loved one. A representative set of stages based on interviews of parents of infants with serious physical disabilities includes shock and disruption, denial, sadness, anxiety and fear, anger, and finally adaptation (Drotar, Baskiewicz, Irvin, Kennell, & Klaus, 1975).

Several authorities have questioned the wisdom of this stage approach in understanding parental reactions (Turnbull & Turnbull, 1990). It is clear that we should not think of parents as marching through a series of stages in lockstep fashion. It would be counterproductive, for example, to think, "This mother is now in the anxiety and fear stage; we need to encourage her now to go through the anger stage so she can finally adapt."

One argument against a strict stage model comes from the fact that many parents report that they do not engage in denial. In fact, they are often the first to suspect a problem. It is largely a myth that parents of disabled children go from physician to physician, shopping for a more favorable diagnosis. It is all too frequently the case that they have to convince the doctor that there is something wrong with their child (Akerley, 1985).

Although they may not go through these reactions in a rigid fashion, some parents do experience some or all of these emotions at one time or another. A common reaction, they report, is guilt.

The Role of Guilt

Parents of disabled children frequently wrestle with the terrifying feeling that they are in some way responsible for their child's condition. Even though in the vast majority of cases there is absolutely no basis for such thoughts, guilt is one of the most commonly reported feelings of parents of exceptional children. The high prevalence of guilt is probably due to the fact that the primary cause of so many disabilities is unknown. Uncertainty about the cause of the child's disability creates an atmosphere conducive for speculation by the parents that they themselves are to blame. Mothers are particularly vulnerable. As Featherstone (1980), the mother of a boy who is blind and has hydrocephaly, mental retardation, cerebral palsy, and seizures, relates:

> Our children are wondrous achievements. Their bodies grow inside ours. If their defects originated *in utero*, we blame our inadequate bodies or inadequate caution. If . . . we accept credit for our children's physical beauty (and most of us do, in our hearts), then inevitably we assume responsibility for their physical defects.
>
> The world makes much of the pregnant woman. People open doors for her, carry her heavy parcels, offer footstools and unsolicited advice. All this attention seems somehow posited on the idea that she is creating something miraculously fine. When the baby arrives imperfect, the mother feels she has failed not only herself and her husband, but the rest of the world as well.
>
> Soon this diffuse sense of inadequacy sharpens. Nearly every mother fastens on some aspect of her own behavior and blames the tragedy on that. (pp.73–74)

In addition to ambivalence concerning the cause of the child's disability, parents can also feel vulnerable to criticism from others about how they deal with their child's problems. Again, Featherstone (1980) relates,

> The exceptional family stands in a strange, and at times rather sad, relationship to outside opinion. Guilty, unsure, unprepared, and lonely, both parents and children long for understanding, reassurance, and approval. In the war against inner demons, they turn to others. I remember my struggles during Jody's earliest years. We had to decide whether to keep our difficult baby at home or to look around for a good residential school. Many things played into this momentous decision, but I remember, quite uncomfortably, that one factor was the opinion of other people. I was afraid that the world would judge me a rejecting, inadequate mother if I let Jody live somewhere else. If there was one person left in all the world who opposed placement, I did not want to do it. I paid no attention to a phalanx of friends and relatives advising institutional care. I figured I was doing more, not less than they advised.
>
> The whole situation recalled a problem that had troubled me as a child: the problem of the hero. Most of us, I reasoned, are neither heroes nor cowards, and no one judges us in these terms. We are ordinary people. Yet suppose I, an ordinary person, am walking alone beside an icy, isolated river, and see someone drowning. I have two options: I can jump in and try to save him (risking death myself), or I can agonize on the shore. In the first case I am a hero; in the second, a coward. There is no way I can remain what I was before—an ordinary person. As the mother of a profoundly retarded child, I felt I was in the same position: I had to look like a hero or a coward, even though actually I was still an ordinary person. (pp. 83–84)

The Role of the Father

Virtually all the research on parental reactions to disabled children has focused on the mother. Consequently, we know very little about fathers of disabled children, of how they influence and are influenced by their children. Authorities posit that most fathers of disabled children play an even more peripheral parental role than do fathers of nondisabled children. Although today's fathers are more involved with their children than were fathers of previous generations, the available evidence indicates that the father's part in influencing the development of his disabled child is more indirect than direct (Bristol & Gallagher, 1986; Kazak & Marvin, 1984). He can affect how the mother will interact with the child by his attitudes toward

More and more experts are recognizing the significant role fathers can play in the development of their children. (Erika Stone)

her and the family. His support, or lack of it, can have a significant effect on family harmony.

The reasons why fathers of disabled children should play a more peripheral parenting role than fathers of nondisabled children are not known. Because society still largely expects women to engage in caretaking, it may be that men find it easy to defer to their wives when a child requires extra care. However, some have speculated that the sharp differentiation of the two roles—the mother being the caretaker and the father being the supportive spouse—may be functional for some families (Kazak & Marvin, 1984). That is, they hypothesize that specialization of parental duties may be an efficient solution to the daily pressures of raising some exceptional children.

Parental Adjustment

There is abundant evidence that parents of disabled children undergo more than the average amount of stress (Breslau & Davis, 1986; Hanson, Ellis, & Deppe, 1989; Pahl & Quine, 1987; Singer & Irvin, 1989; Vietze & Coates, 1986). The stress is usually not the result of major catastrophic events, but rather the consequence of daily burdens related to child care. It may be that a single event, such as a family member coming down with a serious illness, will precipitate a family crisis, but its effects are even more devastating if the family was already under stress because of a multitude of "daily hassles."

There is no universal parental reaction to the added stress of raising a disabled child. Much depends on the parents' prior psychological makeup, the severity of the child's disability, and the amount of support the parents receive from friends, relatives, and professionals. Although there are exceptions, it is fair to say that parents who were well adjusted before the birth of the exceptional child have a better chance of coping with the situation than those who were already having psychological problems. It is also evident that parents of children with more severe disabilities usually have a more difficult time than parents of children with mild disabilities because the child-care burdens are greater. Again, however, there are exceptions. As Bronicki and Turnbull (1987) state,

> A more severe disability does not always produce greater stress. As one parent of a young adolescent commented:
>
> *Don has been labelled profoundly retarded. He is not able to do anything to take care of himself, cannot walk, and has no language. Sure, he creates strains and stresses. But I remind myself that I never have to chase him around the house, he never talks back or sasses, he doesn't have to enter the rat race of teen-age years like my other sons, and he does not try to hurt himself.* (p. 23)

It is important to keep in mind that the vast majority of parents of disabled children do not have major psychological problems. The types of problems some of them may be at risk to develop, for example, would be characterized as relatively mild forms of depression (Carr, 1988; Singer & Irvin, 1989).

Some parents report that the addition of a disabled child to the family actually has some unanticipated positive results. Some parents note, for example, that they have become more concerned about social issues and are more tolerant of differences in other people than they were before. Moreover, some parents claim that the birth of their disabled child has brought the family closer together.

Siblings' Reactions

Although there is a relatively large body of literature pertaining to parental reactions, there is much less information about siblings of exceptional individuals. What is available, however, indicates that siblings can, and frequently do, experience the same emotions—fear, anger, guilt, and so forth—that parents do. In fact, in some ways siblings may have an even more difficult time than their parents in coping with some of these feelings. First, being less mature, they may have trouble putting some of their negative sensations into proper perspective. Second, they may not have as broad a base of individuals with whom they can discuss their feelings (Featherstone, 1980). And third, they may be uncomfortable asking their parents the questions that bother them, for example, whether they will "catch" what their brother has, whether they were in some way responsible for their sister's disability, whether they will be called on to take care of their brother after their parents die.

Although some feelings about their sibling's disability may not appear for many years, a substantial number of accounts indicate that nondisabled siblings are aware at an amazingly early age that their brother or sister is different in some way. Jewell (1985), for example, recounts how her sister would make allowances for her cerebral palsy by playing a special version of "dolls" with her, a version in which all the dolls had disabilities. Though they may have a vague sense that their disabled sibling is different, the young nondisabled siblings may still have misconceptions about the nature of their sibling's condition, especially regarding its cause. Some parents have found children's literature useful in helping young children cope with their feelings about their disabled brother or sister. (See the box on p. 454 for an example of one of these books.)

As nondisabled siblings grow older, their concerns often become more focused on how society views them and their disabled siblings. Adolescence can be a particularly difficult period. As Featherstone (1980) notes, it is important for teenagers not to be considered different by their peers, but at the same time to be considered special, with all the attention that goes with being special, within the confines of their own family. Being the brother or sister of a child with a disability, however, often singles a person out as being different. At the same time, the nondisabled sibling can feel slighted because his or her exceptional brother or sister receives so much attention from their parents. The following account, by the sister of a brother with cerebral palsy and mental retardation, is an example of the reactions of some siblings:

> I cannot pinpoint exactly the time or the circumstance when I first became aware of Robin's handicaps. Several incidents come to mind, all of which occurred around the time I was eleven years old. One involved a trip to the shoe store where Robin was to be fitted for orthopedic shoes; another, a trip to the town near our country home for dinner at the YMCA. On both of these occasions, I can remember being acutely embarrassed by the ill-concealed stares our family received as we entered pushing Robin in his wheelchair. I was certain that everyone was looking at my brother with his obvious handicap and then wondering what was wrong with the rest of us. As a result of the feelings aroused in me by these occurrences, I began to refuse to go out to dinner or shopping with my family and took precautions to avoid being seen on the street or in the yard with Robin.
>
> These avoidance procedures on my part were not taken without an accompanying sense of guilt. I knew that it was wrong for me to be ashamed of my brother. I loved Robin dearly and realized that the opinions (real or imagined) of others should have no bearing on my relationship with him. . . .
>
> Following my period of avoidance, I entered a phase of false pretenses. I forced myself to appear in public with him—but only if I looked my very best (freshly washed hair, make-up, snazzy outfit, etc.). My specious reasoning was that if people were going to stare, they weren't going to find anything wrong with me. Also, though I am reluctant to admit such a selfish thought, I suppose I wanted to encourage people to think along the lines of "Oh, dear, look at that sweet young girl pushing her poor crippled brother around. What a wonderful child she must be." (The Helsel Family, 1985, pp. 94–95)

Siblings' Adjustment

Children, like parents, can adapt well or poorly to a disabled sibling. Research indicates that some siblings have trouble adjusting, some have no trouble adjusting, and some actually appear to benefit from the experience (Seligman & Darling, 1989; Senapati & Hayes, 1988). Like parents, however, siblings of exceptional children are at a greater risk than siblings of nondisabled children to have difficulties in adjustment.

Why some individuals respond negatively, whereas others do not, is not completely understood. Authorities, however, point to three situations that can make it particularly difficult for a child to develop positive attitudes toward their disabled sibling:

1. When the two siblings are close in age there is more chance of conflict (Simeonsson & Bailey, 1986). Apparently, the similarity in age makes the differences in ability between the two siblings more obvious.
2. Siblings of the same sex are more likely to experience conflict (Simeonsson & Bailey, 1986).

He's My Brother

There are now many children's books that deal with the subject of exceptional children. The following excerpts from Joe Lasker's *He's My Brother* deal specifically with the feelings a brother or sister of a handicapped child often has.

Jamie's my brother.
He doesn't have many friends.
Little kids play with him.
Sometimes a big kid plays when no one else is around.
Jamie gets teased.
He doesn't know how to answer back.
When he tries, he gets in trouble, and comes home.
Becka is our sister.
She likes Jamie.
She bakes brownies for him.
When kids on the block choose up teams, they choose Jamie last.
It took Jamie a long time to learn to tie his shoelaces.
He still has trouble hanging up his clothes.
I guess I have, too.
School is easy for me.
But hard for Jamie.
Jamie gets mixed up at school.
Especially when it gets noisy.

It took Jamie a long time

to learn to tie his shoelaces.

When it's time for a test, Jamie thinks he knows the answers.
Then everything goes wrong.
Sometimes the kids make fun of Jamie.
They take his cookies or spill his milk.
Sometimes I get mad at him because he is so slow.
Then I feel sorry and play a game of checkers with him.
But there are things Jamie likes a lot.
He loves babies.
He loves animals . . .
He never hurts them.
One day Jamie said, "Wouldn't it be nice if we could be friends with all the animals in the world?"
I wish I'd thought of that! . . .
Mom helps Jamie with his schoolwork.
Dad reads to Jamie.
I make up stories for Jamie.
Stories to tell him we love him.
He laughs.
He's my brother.

SOURCE: J. Lasker, *He's My Brother* (Chicago: Whitman, 1974). Reprinted with permission.

3. Nondisabled girls who are older than their disabled siblings are likely to have negative attitudes when they reach adolescence because they often shoulder child-care responsibilities (Stoneman, Brody, Davis, & Crapps, 1988).

FAMILY INVOLVEMENT IN TREATMENT AND EDUCATION

As noted earlier, today's professionals are more likely to recognize the positive influence parents can have on their exceptional children's development than was once the case. This more positive attitude toward parents is reflected in how parents are now involved in the treatment and education of their children. At one time, professionals primarily viewed parents as the passive recipients of their advice, whereas today they are much more likely to consider parents equal partners in the development of treatment and educational programming for their children (Turnbull & Turnbull, 1990). That is, professionals are beginning to realize that parents often have insights regarding the characteristics and needs of their children that can be helpful in devising the treatment and educational programs.

The effort to build professional-parent partnerships is consistent with the current thinking of child-development theorists who stress the importance of the social context within which child development occurs. Urie Bronfenbrenner (1979), a renowned child-development and family theorist, has been most influential in stressing that we cannot understand an individual's behavior without understanding the influence of the family on the behavior of the individual. Furthermore, we cannot understand the behavior of the family without considering the influence of other social systems, such as the extended family (e.g., grandparents), friends, and professionals, on the behavior of the family. The interaction between the family and the surrounding social system is critical to how the family functions. A supportive

Collaboration: A Key to Success

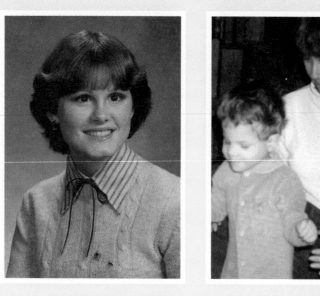

KATHY WYATT ANDREWS

SARAH ANN KLIER

KATHY: I have a personal interest in deafness because my sister and I have profound, unilateral, sensorineural hearing losses. Since 1985, I've been the parent infant advisor for a deaf education program. The children I serve vary greatly in ability levels and in the extent of their handicapping conditions. Several of my students have additional handicaps involving vision impairments, mental retardation, epilepsy, emotional disturbance, cerebral palsy, and poor health. The communication modes demonstrated by the children include pointing, gestures, unintelligible vocalizations, facial expressions, physical contact, and/or meaningful one- and two-word phrases using their voices or formal signs. Where I teach in Houston we have a mixture of black, white, and Hispanic families. I serve families with a variety of structures, including two-parent families, single mothers, and divorced parents. One of the families I work with is the Kliers, who have Daniel.

ANN: Daniel has been diagnosed as developmentally delayed, autistic, and mildly hearing impaired. His medical problems were overwhelming from birth. With his first cry, we knew he had many physical complications. He weighed 3 lbs. 14 oz., and he stopped breathing within two hours of delivery. The next month was a never-ending roller coaster ride of fear, guilt, and constant crises. When the day finally arrived for Daniel to come home, the decision to discharge him was made by the insurance company. Although he had not achieved the minimal requirements of adequate feeding ability, weight maintenance, and body temperature maintenance, the medical staff all but washed their hands of Daniel. It was a terrifying

experience, as the doctors gave us no guidance in how we should care for Daniel. The nature of his problems had not yet been diagnosed, nor could his potential be fully assessed. Our family stepped into the world of the unknown quite alone. After months of fear and frustration, medical experts finally agreed that Daniel was a gravely ill child, but they couldn't explain why. Eventually, Daniel was diagnosed as having a mild, mixed hearing loss. We were then referred to the deaf education cooperative, where we met Kathy.

KATHY: I met the Klier family when Daniel was two years and four months old. He had been recently diagnosed as having a mild, mixed hearing loss in the right ear and a moderate, primarily sensorineural hearing loss in the left ear. In addition, Daniel's hearing loss fluctuated because of chronic middle ear infections. Because of his weak condition, Daniel was sitting independently and crawling, but he was unable to support his weight in order to walk alone. His skills in the areas of socialization, self-help, motor ability, cognition, and language were all delayed by fourteen to twenty-two months. He was subsequently diagnosed as mentally retarded.

Daniel preferred to perform self-stimulation behaviors, such as rocking, flicking door handles and door stops, banging his head, and staring at lights and objects. He disliked physical contact and did not seek personal attention. He displayed an increasing number of autistic characteristics and was unable to sleep through the night. He would awaken screaming and crying and begin self-abusive behavior, including scratching, biting, and hitting.

ANN: Kathy began by evaluating Daniel at home in an environment that was familiar to him. She tested him with no preconceived opinions and gave him the opportunity to demonstrate his capabilities. Afterward, she presented us with an IEP outlining a program that would take Daniel through a series of steps toward achieving specific tasks. She scheduled weekly two-hour home visits. In introducing each new project, Kathy took the time to explain the significance of mastering the main goal and all the intermediate steps. She often adjusted the teaching procedures based on my feedback. She frequently brought articles, books, and audiovisual tapes that further explained Daniel's handicaps or offered techniques for teaching new skills. Kathy also accompanied me on doctor's visits as needed. She taught me how to prepare written questions to ask the physicians as well as how to get important information from them, including phone numbers, referrals, or another appointment as necessary. We were a *team*; we each played an important role in Daniel's education. When it was time for Daniel to be enrolled in a school-centered program at the age of three, Kathy explained the available preschool options and we visited each of the potential placements while the classes were in session.

KATHY: Our deaf education program uses a curriculum specifically designed to address the needs of hearing-impaired infants and their families. It's a home-based curriculum that permits the parent advisor to take advantage of the child's natural surroundings and familiar experiences. In implementing the program, I schedule weekly or biweekly home visits of an hour or two with each of the families. I act as a teacher and advisor to the families. The parents are expected to be their child's primary teachers and care givers. It's my responsibility to educate the parents in four major areas of hearing impairment: hearing aid usage, auditory training, communication skills, and oral and/or manual language skills. In addition, we monitor and address the child's progress in socialization, self-help skills, motor skills, and cognition. I have four major goals. First, I provide professional and emotional support during the early stages of identification, treatment, and placement, and throughout the delivery of the program. Second, I assess the needs of the parents and the child in conjunction with other professionals and plan the program based on the assessment. Third, I implement my services unobtrusively within the current structure of the family's culture and philosophy. Fourth, I teach the parents new skills through modeling, while providing the rationale and several suggestions for implementing the skills.

ANN: One of our real challenges was to present a variety of activities and materials that would maintain Daniel's focus and not encourage self-stimulation. Even though Daniel needed much repetition to learn a new skill, we had to teach the task in very short intervals over a long period of time. This was really frustrating! We had to remind ourselves constantly of our objectives so we didn't lose hope.

> *. . . a teacher should assist parents in acquiring the skills and confidence to raise a handicapped child . . .*

KATHY: Another challenge was to determine Daniel's specific medical problems, according to the behaviors he displayed. Once the behaviors were diagnosed, his parents and I sought solutions through the medical community. Medication and surgeries to remove his adenoids and place pressure-equalization tubes in his ears were really helpful. Naturally, communication is the essence of any teacher-parent relationship. Respect and honesty are the foundation for effective communication. We had to be open to each other's ideas and concerns. An honest relationship demanded that I say "I don't know" when I was uncertain of the next step or lacked the information they requested. It also required the parents to be honest about their implementation of the teaching plans and in reporting Daniel's success. The Kliers and I had to cooperate in our problem-solving. We didn't know what methods and materials would benefit Daniel. We had to develop teaching plans, implement the strategies, and finally revise those plans as needed. This effort meant that we sometimes had to accept frustration and defeat.

ANN: As we developed a common interest in Daniel and a close working relationship with Kathy, we felt comfortable in sharing personal feelings that assisted us in healing our anger, guilt, and heartache. As Kathy opened the door to our understanding Daniel's handicaps, my family became his teachers and advocates. I also learned that through active participation in Daniel's education, my family can best assist him in reaching his fullest potential. I've found that his teachers feel appreciated and respond positively to my presence. They realize that they don't have to shoulder the entire burden of Daniel's education. The results have been greater than we expected! Daniel is now able to walk independently, feed himself with minimal assistance, show affection toward others, interact appropriately with his environment, color, point to several objects, and gesture to express his wants, and he is beginning to verbalize.

KATHY: It has been exciting to see Ann and her husband develop self-confidence in their parenting skills. They are very capable of handling the new difficulties which will arise in the future. The Kliers have always had the potential to teach Daniel and to solve crises, but now they are aware of those abilities. Ultimately a teacher should assist parents in acquiring the skills and confidence to raise a handicapped child rather than make the parents dependent on educators' efforts. A child will have many teachers, but he will have the same parents all his life. Too often, teachers fail to realize all of the responsibilities and roles required of parents, which include spouse, employee, housekeeper, and parent to the child's other siblings. My greatest challenge is learning to accept the philosophies, priorities, and life-styles of individual families.

KATHY WYATT ANDREWS:
Parent infant advisor for families with hearing-impaired children from birth to age three, North Harris County Cooperative for the Education of the Deaf, Houston, Texas; B.S., Education of the Deaf and Elementary Education, Ball State University; M.Ed., Educational Administration and Supervision, Sam Houston State University; pursuing master's degree in special education

SARAH ANN KLIER:
Married mother of two children—Katie, eight, and Daniel, four

network of professionals, and especially friends, can be very beneficial to the family with a disabled child.

Current approaches to involving families in treatment and education of their exceptional children take into account how the family fits within the broader societal context. We now discuss two such approaches—the family systems approach of the Turnbulls (Turnbull & Turnbull, 1990) and the social support systems approach of Dunst and his colleagues (Dunst, Trivette, & Deal, 1988; Dunst, Trivette, Gordon, & Pletcher, 1989). These two approaches are very similar and overlap in many ways. They only differ with regard to emphasis. The family systems approach considers events that occur within the family as well as the broader social context. The social systems approach, although hardly ignoring the inner workings of the family unit, tends to focus more on the family's relationship with its social environment.

A Family Systems Approach

The philosophy behind a family systems approach is that all parts of the family are interrelated, so that events affecting any one family member also have an effect on the others. The more treatment and educational programs take into account the relationships and interactions among family members, the more likely they are to be successful. In other words, family systems theorists advocate that the family rather than the individual should be the focus of intervention efforts. The Turnbulls' model includes four interrelated components: *family characteristics, family interaction, family functions,* and *family life cycle* (Turnbull & Turnbull, 1990).

Family Characteristics

Family characteristics provide a description of basic information related to the family. They include characteristics of the exceptionality (e.g., the type of exceptionality and the severity of the disability), characteristics of the family (e.g., size, cultural background, socioeconomic status, and geographic location), personal characteristics of each family member (e.g., health and coping styles), and special conditions (e.g., child or spousal abuse and poverty). Family characteristics help determine how family members interact with themselves and with others outside the family. To begin to understand how a family functions, we need to have a good picture of its characteristics. It will probably make a difference, for example, whether the disabled child is retarded or hearing impaired, the disabled child is an only child or has five siblings, the family is upper middle class or lives in poverty, and so forth.

Recent changes in our society make it even more important for teachers and other professionals who work with families to take into account family characteristics. Demographic changes that have occurred over the past few decades make it imperative for professionals to be prepared to encounter a wide diversity of families. The middle-class nuclear family with two parents and only the father working outside the home is no longer the norm. For example, there has been a tremendous increase in the number of families in which both parents work outside the home. Demographers predict that by the year 1995 almost two-thirds of preschool-age children and over three-quarters of school-age children will have a mother in the work force (Hofferth & Phillips, 1987). Furthermore, the number of single-parent families has risen steadily to the point that about one out of five families with children under eighteen years of age is headed by a single parent (Norton & Glick, 1986). There has also been an increase in the number of families in poverty (Baumeister, Kupstas, & Klindworth, 1990). Approximately one in every five children lives below the poverty level in an environment of substandard housing, poor nutrition, and poor health care, and 54 percent of children of female-headed households live in poverty.

These dramatic demographic changes present a formidable challenge for professionals working with families. As the configuration of families changes, professionals will need to alter their approaches. For example, the same approaches that are very successful with middle-class, two-parent families may not be the ones required for single mothers.

Family Interaction

Family members can have a variety of functional and dysfunctional modes of interacting with one another. Turnbull and colleagues note that the amount of family cohesion and adaptability will determine how individuals within families interact. In general, families are healthier if they have moderate degrees of cohesion and adaptability.

COHESION. Cohesion refers to the degree to which an individual family member is free to act independent of other family members. An appropriate amount of family cohesion permits the individual to be his or her "own person" while at the same time allowing him or her to draw on other family members for support as needed. Families with low cohesion may not offer the exceptional child the necessary support, whereas the overly cohesive family may overprotect the disabled child and not allow him or her enough freedom.

It is frequently very difficult for otherwise healthy families to find the right balance of cohesion. They sometimes go overboard in wanting to help their children, and in so doing, limit their children's independence. A particularly stressful time can be adolescence, when the teenager strives to break some of the bonds that have tied him or her to the family. This need for independence is a normal behavior. What makes the situation so difficult for many families of disabled children is that the exceptional child, because of his or her disability, has often by necessity been more protected by parents. As one psychologist severely disabled by cerebral palsy has recounted,

> I remember the first time I wanted to travel alone, I had just turned sixteen. Some friends had invited me to stay with them in Baltimore. I sat down and discussed this with my parents. I said that I wanted to go by train, and that my friends would meet me in Baltimore at the train station. My parents were frightened and said so openly. They expressed their fears of my physical safety. . . . We talked and argued and cried for hours. The decision was that I was to go. . . . I'll never forget that day. My mother did not go to the train station with my father and me. She said she could give her permission for this to happen, but she couldn't watch it. My father settled me in a train seat and stood on the platform waving goodbye. I was trying not to cry and so was he. Blinking back tears, I waved goodbye to my father from the train window. He was vigorously waving goodbye with one hand—for his other was resting on the arm of my wheelchair. The train began pulling out of the station, and a panic gripped me. "My God! He still has my wheelchair. . . . Stop this train!" By this time we were a few blocks out of the station. What a ridiculous scene this must have appeared, this wriggly, little kid (I always looked young for my age) screaming at the top of my lungs to stop the train. . . . [The conductor] pulled the emergency cord and stopped the train. The words stuck in my throat as I looked up at this towering man. What a big question this little kid was about to ask, "Would you please back up the train so that I can get my wheelchair?" As the train backed up to the

platform, there was my poor father still standing there waving goodbye with one hand and holding my wheelchair with the other, unaware of anything but his departing daughter. He was shocked out of his numb pose only when the conductor jumped off the train and wrenched the chair from his hand. (Diamond, 1981, pp. 41–42)

At the same time as exceptional children ultimately need to gain as much independence from their family as possible, they also need to feel like a part of the family. They require a responsible role within the family such that other family members come to rely on them for what they contribute. Parents, for example, can consider giving household chores to the disabled child. Certain adaptations might be necessary, such as taping a dish towel to the hands of a cerebral palsied child so that it will not drop on the floor and allowing more time for him or her to complete the chore (Diamond, 1981), but the important thing is to provide the opportunity for the disabled child to be a contributing member of the family.

ADAPTABILITY. Adaptability refers to the degree to which families are able to change their modes of interaction when they encounter unusual or stressful situations. Some families are so chaotic that it is difficult to predict what any one member will do in a given situation. In such an unstable environment, the needs of the disabled family member may be overlooked or neglected. At the other end of the continuum are families characterized by extreme rigidity. Each family member has his or her prescribed role in the family. Such rigidity makes it difficult for them to adjust to the addition of a disabled family member. The addition of any child requires adjustment on the part of the family, but it is even more important if the child has special needs. For example, it may be that the mother's involvement in transporting the disabled child from one therapy session to another will necessitate that the father be more involved than previously in household chores and taking care of the other children.

Family Functions

Family functions refer to the numerous tasks and activities in which families engage to meet their many and diverse needs. According to Turnbull and Turnbull (1990) these needs fall into seven broad categories: economic, daily care, recreation, socialization, self-definition, affection, and educational/vocational.

An important point to consider is that education is only one of the several functions in which families are immersed. Several investigators have reported that many families of disabled students prefer a passive rather than an active degree of involvement in their children's education (Lynch & Stein, 1982; Vaughn, Bos, Harrell, & Lasky, 1988). Although some have been troubled by the fact that many parents are not more involved, others are less perplexed. They warn that we should not automatically assume, for example, that parents who do not contribute many suggestions at their child's IEP meeting are neglectful. Given the number of functions for which families are responsible and the configuration of some of the families noted earlier (e.g., single-parent families), some authorities do not find it surprising that

> . . . some families may make a decision to delegate educational responsibilities to teachers so that they will have additional time to invest in responding to their child's needs in other functional areas (for which there are no services) or to their own needs, as well as the needs of other family members. The fact that parents are not involved as advocates or intervenors with educational programs does not in any way

imply that they are not involved with their child in meeting needs in other functional areas (MacMillan & Turnbull, 1983); too frequently this is overlooked. (Benson & Turnbull, 1986, p. 145)

Professionals may not always appreciate the time and effort required from parents, especially those with a disabled child. As one parent of a severely and multiply disabled child has related,

> I remember the day when the occupational therapist at Jody's school called with some suggestions from a visiting nurse. Jody has a seizure problem which is controlled with the drug Dilantin. Dilantin can cause the gums to grow over the teeth—an effect that is especially likely if the gums are irritated by either poor hygiene or erupting teeth. The nurse had noted that nearly all the preschoolers at the school suffered from this overgrowth, and recommended, innocently enough, that the children's teeth be brushed four times a day, for five minutes, with an electric toothbrush. The school suggested that they could do this once on school days, and that I should try to do it the other three to four times a day. I trotted out a valid and convenient excuse: Jody's dentist had advised against an electric toothbrush.
>
> Although I tried to sound reasonable on the phone, this new demand appalled me. I rehearsed angry, self-justifying speeches in my head. Jody, I thought, is blind, cerebral palsied, and retarded. We do his physical therapy daily and work with him, change him, bathe him, dry him, put him in a body cast to sleep, launder his bed linens daily, and go through a variety of routines designed to minimize his miseries and enhance his joys and his development. (All this in addition to trying to care for and enjoy our other young children and making time for each other and our careers.) Now you tell me that I should spend fifteen minutes every day on something that Jody will hate, an activity that will not help him to walk or even defecate, but one that is directed at the health of his gums. This activity is not for a finite time but forever. It is not guaranteed to help, but "it can't hurt." And it won't make the overgrowth go away but may retard it. Well, it's too much. Where is that fifteen minutes going to come from? What am I supposed to give up? Taking the kids to the park? Reading a bedtime story to my eldest? Washing the breakfast dishes? Sorting the laundry? Grading students' papers? Sleeping? Because there is no time in my life that hasn't been spoken for, and for every fifteen minute activity that is added, one has to be taken away. (Featherstone, 1980, pp. 77–78)

Family Life Cycle

Several family theorists have noted that the impact of a disabled child on the family changes over time (Beckman & Pokorni, 1988; Fewell, 1986; Seligman & Darling, 1989; Turnbull & Turnbull, 1990). For this reason, some have pointed to the value of looking at families with disabled children from a life-cycle perspective. Turnbull and Turnbull (1990), for example, have presented four major life-cycle stages that are representative of other family theorists: birth and early childhood (zero to five years), childhood (six to twelve years), adolescence (twelve to twenty-one years), and adulthood (twenty-one years and up). Table 11–1 depicts some of the possible issues that parents and siblings of exceptional children encounter during each of these four stages.

Transition points between stages in the life cycle are particularly stressful for families, especially families with a disabled child. For example, as parents face moving their child from the relatively intimate confines of infant programs to the larger context of the public schools, they may have several fears. As one parent relates,

TABLE 11.1   Possible Issues Encountered at Life Cycle Stages

Life Cycle Stage	Parents	Siblings
Early Childhood, ages 0–5	• Obtaining an accurate diagnosis • Informing siblings and relatives • Locating services • Seeking to find meaning in the exceptionality • Clarifying a personal ideology to guide decisions • Addressing issues of stigma • Identifying positive contributions of exceptionality • Setting great expectations	• Less parental time and energy for sibling needs • Feelings of jealousy over less attention • Fears associated with misunderstandings of exceptionality

Life Cycle Stage	Parents	Siblings
School Age, ages 6–12	• Establishing routines to carry out family functions • Adjusting emotionally to educational implications • Clarifying issues of mainstreaming v. special class placement • Participating in IEP conferences • Locating community resources • Arranging for extracurricular activities	• Division of responsibility for any physical care needs • Oldest female sibling may be at risk • Limited family resources for recreation and leisure • Informing friends and teachers • Possible concern over surpassing younger sibling • Issues of "mainstreaming" into same school • Need for basic information on exceptionality

Life Cycle Stage	Parents	Siblings
Adolescence, ages 12–21	• Adjusting emotionally to possible chronicity of exceptionality • Identifying issues of emerging sexuality • Addressing possible peer isolation and rejection • Planning for career/vocational development • Arranging for leisure time activities • Dealing with physical and emotional change of puberty • Planning for postsecondary education	• Overidentification with sibling • Greater understanding of differences in people • Influence of exceptionality on career choice • Dealing with possible stigma and embarrassment • Participation in sibling training programs • Opportunity for sibling support groups

Life Cycle Stage	Parents	Siblings
Adult-hood, ages 21–	• Planning for possible need for guardianship • Addressing the need for appropriate adult residence • Adjusting emotionally to any adult implications of dependency • Addressing the need for socialization opportunities outside the family for individuals with exceptionality • Initiating career choice or vocational program	• Possible issues of responsibility for financial support • Addressing concerns regarding genetic implications • Introducing new in-laws to exceptionality • Need for information on career/living options • Clarify role of sibling advocacy • Possible issues of guardianship

Source: Turnbull, A. P. & Turnbull, H. R. (1990). *Families, professionals, and exceptionality: A special partnership.* (2nd ed.), Columbus OH: Charles E. Merrill.

As my daughter's third birthday approached, I lived in dread, not wishing to leave the familiar, comfortable environment of her infant program. The infant program had become home away from home for me. It was supportive and intimate. I had made some lifelong friendships, as well as having established a comfortable routine in our lives. I saw making the transition to a preschool program in the school district as an extremely traumatic experience, second only to learning of Amy's diagnosis.

What were my fears? First, I was concerned that my husband and I, along with professionals, would be deciding the future of our child. How could we play God? Would our decisions be the right ones? Second, I feared loss of control, as I would be surrendering my child to strangers—first to the school district's intake assessment team and then to the preschool teacher. The feeling of being at the mercy of professionals was overwhelming. In addition, I had more information to absorb and a new system with which to become familiar. Finally, I feared the "label" that would be attached to my child and feared that this label would lower the world's expectations of her. (Hanline & Knowlton, 1988, p. 116)

At the other end of the age spectrum, parents often encounter problems adjusting to the young disabled adult's transition from the home to a more independent work and living setting. Professionals now recognize that family attitudes are a key factor in the successful transition to work settings in the community (Carney & Orelove, 1988; Heal, Gonzalez, Rusch, Copher, & DeStefano, in press).

Transitions between stages are difficult because of the uncertainty that each new phase presents to the family. One of the reasons for the uncertainty pertains to replacements of the professionals who work with the disabled child. In particular, parents of a multiply disabled child, who requires services from multiple professionals, can be anxious about the switches in therapists and teachers that occur many times throughout the child's life, especially at transition points. (The box on pp. 464–465 describes one strategy for alleviating some of the problems resulting from changes in professionals.)

A Social Support Systems Approach

Like a family systems approach, a social support systems approach focuses education and treatment efforts on the broader social context rather than on individuals (Dunst, Trivette, & Deal, 1988). There are two important features of this approach. First, it focuses on informal rather than formal sources of support. More and more authorities are pointing to informal sources of support, such as extended family, friends, church groups, neighbors, and social clubs, as more effective than professionals and agencies in helping families cope with the stress of having a disabled child. Unfortunately, these informal supports, once so prevalent in our society, are fast disappearing (Zigler & Black, 1989). Largely because of the demographic changes noted earlier (e.g., increases in single-parent families and increases in poverty), families are less able today to rely on informal social networks for support.

Second, a social support systems approach focuses on helping families help themselves. Because many families do not have their own informal sources of support, a social systems approach helps to establish them. Its goal is to enhance the self-esteem of families by setting up a situation in which the help-seeker is less dependent on the help-giver than is the case in more traditional approaches. The model

. . . de-emphasizes help-seeker responsibility for causing problems and emphasizes help-seeker responsibility for acquisition of competencies necessary to solve problems, meet needs, realize personal projects, or otherwise attain desired goals. . . .

Getting to Know You

Parents of children with disabilities, especially those with multiple disabilities, must deal with a multitude and variety of professionals, some of whom may change from time to time. If the child is mainstreamed into general education, he or she may get a new teacher or set of teachers each year. A change from elementary to middle school or from middle to high school also brings additional changes in personnel. These many changes make it difficult for parents to keep all of the many professionals informed about their child's particular needs. The mother of a child with cerebral palsy, mental retardation, severe hearing impairment, and lack of speech has come up with a strategy for familiarizing professionals with her child. She recommends that the family develop a "My Story" booklet pertaining to the child, which can be updated periodically (Comegys, 1989). Following are excerpts from her daughter's booklet when she was in her early teens:

MY GOALS

1. I want to be as independent as I can possibly be.
2. I want to make friends with my nonhandicapped peers, at the high school, and participate in all school activities which interest me, including afterschool activities.
3. I want to be included in community functions such as recreational and park activities; church and social functions.
4. I plan on living and working in my home town after I graduate from high school.
5. I plan to work in the community (with support)—*not* in a sheltered workshop.
6. I want to learn to communicate with people better (eye contact, smile, and actions).
7. I want to learn to do things *for* people.
8. I want to learn to do more things for myself such as feed myself and participate more fully in dressing.
9. I want to develop my own sense of worth.
10. I want to be able to ride my bike by myself.
11. I am eager to operate the computer for my recreation now (*Fire Organ, Sticky Bears,* and *Musicomp* are some of the software used at home). Later I hope to apply these skills to a real job. I enjoy working a Xerox machine now.
12. I want to make choices for: partners in activities; when to stop or start an activity, etc.; my clothes, leisure, food.
13. I want to be asked to go out by a friend spontaneously—not always preplanned.

MY INTERESTS

I enjoy lights, windows, the computer, photographs and slides of familiar activities and people, and TV (nature, sports, comedy), and watching a fire in the fireplace.
I enjoy books, magazines, newspapers and catalogues, and maps. Geometric designs, too.
I like to swim, ride horseback, ride my bike around town.
I like to go places in a car. I like the school bus.
I like warmth much better than cold—it helps my muscles—spring and summer, sunbathing, warm baths, warm feet and hands are important to me.
I like to be at the piano with people who can play it.
I like to be read to.
I like to be hugged—if you know me well enough. I also like to be tickled.
I like birds and fish, very much! I have a parakeet: Pete!
I have long enjoyed many family slides on the Ectagraphic which I can fully operate alone with a special switch.

I am very interested in cookies and good things to drink (frappes, tonics, etc.)!

I like lots of daily physical exercise—walking two city blocks is prescribed—it helps me sleep and helps my digestion.

I MAY NOT SPEAK—BUT I DO COMMUNICATE

I use total communication (visual, audiological, physical cues). I communicate in many ways: here are three—

- **Line Drawings.** I use both single and multiple line drawings (called "Commenting Boards") which are black and white or lightly colored. They enable me to both give and receive cues. If you show me a line drawing for *car*, I will know we are going out for a drive and I will start to move toward the door. I tap some line drawings to let *you* know what I want. I use many line drawings. A few of them appear in this booklet. [not shown here]
- **Signs.** I understand some of your signs. I am learning to make some signs. Some are my own gestures and others are formal signs. Here is a list: [not shown here]
- **Body Language and Sounds.** Please *watch* me closely and you will see that I:

  1. point with my knuckles, or a finger, or a sweep of my arm.
  2. nod my head "yes."
  3. pull you when I want you to do something.
  4. push an object away (I may or may not want it).
  5. pull or push the bathroom door shut for privacy.
  6. tilt my head up and back which can mean I want to get up.
  7. rotate my head which can mean that it's time to get moving.

Please *listen* to my tone of voice. It changes constantly, and indicates pleasure, frustration, humming, questioning, loneliness, hunger. It helps when you pair these directions with a gesture, sign, or line drawing. For example, when it is time for me to get up from the chair and go somewhere, you might sign *stand* and show me the line drawing of *car*.

Please do not talk "around or through" me as though I am not in the room. It hurts my feelings. Include me by asking my opinion, questioning me, and showing me the appropriate line drawings and signs. It will make both of us much happier.

SOURCE: Comegys, A. (1989). Integration strategies for parents of students with handicaps. In R. Gaylord-Ross (Ed.), *Integration strategies for students with handicaps*. Baltimore, MD: Paul H. Brookes Publishing Co., pp. 345–346.

Help seekers are expected to play a major role in deciding what is important to them, what options they will choose to achieve intentions, and what actions they will take in carrying out plans. The help seeker is the essential agent of change; the help giver supports, encourages, and creates opportunities for the help seeker to become competent. The help giver does not mobilize resources on behalf of the help seeker, but rather creates opportunities for the help seeker to acquire competencies that permit him or her to mobilize sources of resources and support necessary to cope, adapt, and grow in response to life's many challenges. (Dunst, Trivette, and Deal, 1988, p. 44)

What many family theorists advocate is that rather than providing families with only direct services, professionals should also "enable families to help themselves and their children" (Zigler & Berman, 1983, p. 904). A major rationale for this emphasis is that it allows families to take more control over their own lives, thus

Parent support groups can be very helpful to many parents of children with disabilities.
(J. Pickerell/FPG)

avoiding the dependency sometimes associated with typical professional-family relationships. Situations in which the family looks to professionals for all of its help can result in the family members becoming dependent on professionals and losing their feelings of competence and self-esteem.

There are a variety of social supports that professionals can help parents establish. There are often a number of untapped resources that particular communities have to offer. (One creative alternative is depicted in the box below.)

Jay, Pat, and the Greeks: A Story about Transition

BY RUD AND ANN TURNBULL

"What do you do when you graduate? What do you do when you transition?"

Ask those questions of Jay Turnbull and he'll tell you, "I hang out at SAE with Pat, Chuck, and the guys."

He might also add, "I work at KU."

In these days when one of the buzzwords is "transition" and when Developmental Disabilities Planning Councils are rightly concerned about the unacceptable rate of employment and underemployment for people with developmental disabilities, Jay's answer may come as a surprise.

It's not surprising that he works at the University of Kansas, in supported employment. That is one of the goals he and his family had for many years. As Jay himself said, after a summer working on the production line of a factory in a sheltered-workshop enclave, "I want to wear a coat and tie to work." In his present job, he can if he wants to, and he would be appropriately dressed.

What may be surprising, however, is that he has been made an honorary member of the local chapter of Sigma Alpha Epsilon Fraternity. For Jay and for the members of the SAE chapter, transition means friendship. And that means growth in many dimensions for many people.

Jay spends all of the afternoons and most of the evenings every Tuesday and Thursday at the fraternity house. That means two meals a day, twice a week, and plenty of hanging out in the members' rooms. His photograph is in the exact center of the pledge class rows in the fraternity's 1988–89 composite photograph. He is the proud wearer of SAE sweatshirts and tee-shirts, given to him by the chapter. And when the chapter held its winter formal in one of Kansas City's best hotels, Jay and July Hardin, a KU junior from Evanston, Ill. who belongs to Delta Gamma sorority, tripped the light fantastic together, after Jay treated her and his best buddy, Pat Hughes and Pat's date, to dinner "in town."

How did all of this come about? It took only two people other than Jay to make it work. One of them is Pat, a KU junior who also is from Evanston and who spent a good part of last year working in a special education program in Evanston.

The other is Chuck Rhodes, the SAE resident educational advisor, a graduate student at KU working with the Beach Center on Families and Disability.

Pat met Jay one afternoon at the SAE house, when Chuck, who had been training Jay in weight lifting, brought him there to meet his roommate and other SAE members. As Chuck would say, "I wanted to enlarge Jay's circle of friends, for his benefit and theirs." As it happened, Pat and some of his fraternity brothers were listening to John Denver's music . . . and Jay knows all of that music. Quite naturally, Jay began to sing the words, and soon he was accompanied by several fraternity members. From that simple beginning—from an incident that occurred very naturally and that, as luck would have it, allowed Jay to show his competence and sociability—there evolved a friendship between Pat and Jay, complementing the one that Chuck and Jay had formed. And from Pat, there grew other friendships with SAE members, all with Chuck's careful and subtle monitoring.

A few weeks later, the SAE chapter admitted Jay as an honorary member; in their words, they "adopted" him.

What has it meant to everyone involved? Jay will say, by word and deed, that he has acquired new friends. When Tuesdays and Thursdays roll around, Jay has a special zip to his affect. His job coach, Sharon Donner, has observed it: "He works more to get to be with the guys than to finish his job." And his supervisor, Dorothy Johanning, has noted, "Jay loves to start work early. I think the fact that July Hardin comes in early has something to do with it." No doubt, relationships are affecting job performance.

For "the guys," as Jay calls them, it means human development in the intellectual, spiritual, and social dimensions. J. R. Rielly, the SAE chapter president, put it well when he said,

"When we first started working with Jay, I was somewhat skeptical. I had never been around someone with mental retardation, and I did not know what to expect or how to treat him. Now, after spending time with Jay, I realize that my ignorance was keeping me from becoming friends with a super person."

Troy Lewis, an SAE brother, added,

"During the short time that I have come to know Jay, I have learned a lot about myself and the world around me. I have come to the realization just how shallow people in general really are. If we all just opened our hearts a little and let someone like Jay into our lives, maybe we could put an end to all the hatred and discrimination there is in the world."

The SAE guys have become such a part of Jay's life that some have begun to "hang out" at his home. They are in demand as "big brothers" to Jay's sisters, Amy (14) and Kate (11).

Kate put it this way,

"It's so cool to say that my brother is hanging out with fraternity guys, because fraternities are really in. Also, having the SAE guys come to our house is like having a normal big brother."

And Amy commented,

"When Jay is with the SAE guys, I can really relax about his being accepted. I don't have to interpret for Jay or always be on guard to make sure he fits in. The SAE brothers are like big brothers to all of us, because they took Jay in as one of them. Pat, for example, is doing more than most big brothers of my friends—he's the disc jockey at my birthday party next week."

Pat sums it up when he says,

"JT's my buddy, my pal. And he's really part of our house. There is no problem with him eating there or sleeping over or partying. Jay's in the community, but, with us, he can participate in the same kind of life as the rest of us. There's no difference, really. All the differences are on the surface."

Chuck notes,

"It's amazing how much Jay has grown. His self-confidence is way up. His independence is, too, because we treat him like everyone else. And he thoroughly enjoys himself here. But that's true of the members, too. They have grown and they enjoy Jay. It's a win-win situation. Nothing beats it. Nothing can." Just this very month, SAE, which is headquartered in Evanston, has committed to a new national community service project. Care to guess what it is?

Yes, it's Project Friendship. Perhaps it will not be called that, not formally at least. But SAE national is so impressed with the Kansas University activity that it wants to replicate it nationally. To that end, the fraternity and the Beach Center are investigating how to get the money together so that Chuck, Pat, Jay, and "the guys" can take their "transition plan" and export it to many of SAE's 200-plus chapters.

So, ask again, "What do you do when you transition?" You "hang out" and create a new world. Is it in your IEP or ITP? Not likely. Is it in your power? Most certainly.

For more information and for any suggestions please contact Mr. Pat Hughes, 2440 Orrington, Evanston, IL 60201; (312) 869-9249.

Jay Turnbull is 21 years old and has been classified as having low-moderate mental retardation. His parents are Ann and Rud Turnbull, co-directors of the Beach Center on Families and Disability, a rehabilitation research and training center funded by National Institute on Disability and Rehabilitation Research. They are the authors of "Disability and the Family: A Guide to Decisions for Adulthood," published by Paul Brookes Publishing Co., Baltimore, MD. That book provides advice on how families can shape the future according to their choices and those of their member with a disability. They also are the authors of "Parent, Professionals, and Exceptionality: A Special Partnership," published by Charles E. Merrill Publishing Co., Columbus, Ohio. That book describes how parents and professionals can work as a team.

The Beach Center welcomes your comments about families. Write them at Beach Center, c/o Bureau of Child Research, 4138 Haworth Hall, The University of Kansas, Lawrence, Ks. 66045, and ask for their newsletter, if you are interested in families.

SOURCE: Turnbull, H. R., & Turnbull, A. P. (1989). Jay, Pat, and the Greeks: A story about transition. *Directions: Newsletter of the Illinois Planning Council on Developmental Disabilities.*

One of the most beneficial types of social support, especially for parents of recently diagnosed exceptional children, is that of parental support groups. These consist of parents of children with the same or similar disabilities. Such groups can be relatively unstructured, meeting infrequently with unspecified agendas, or they can be more structured. For example, some authorities have recommended that parents of older children be paired with those of younger children so that the latter can have the benefit of learning from the former (Turnbull & Turnbull, 1990). In any case, parental groups provide a number of benefits, "including (1) alleviating loneliness and isolation, (2) providing information, (3) providing role models, and (4) providing a basis for comparison" (Seligman & Darling, 1989, p. 44).

Communication Between Parents and Professionals

Virtually all family theorists agree that no matter which particular approach one uses to work with parents, the key to the success of the program is how well parents and professionals are able to work together. Even the most creative, well-conceived model is doomed to fail if professionals and parents are unable to communicate effectively. Unfortunately, special education does not have a long tradition of excellent working relationships between parents and teachers (Morgan, 1982). This is not too surprising if you consider the ingredients of the situation. On the one hand, you have the parents, who as discussed earlier may be trying to cope with the stresses of raising a disabled child in a complex and changing society. On the other hand, you have the professionals—teachers, speech therapists, physicians, psychologists, physical therapists, and so forth—who may be frustrated because they do not have all of the answers to the child's problems. As the parent of an autistic child has stated,

> We don't begin in anger. We start out the way all parents of all children do: with respect, reverence really, for the professional and his skills. The pediatrician, the teacher, the writer of books and articles on child development, they are the sources of wisdom from which we must draw in order to be good parents. We believe, we consult, we do as we are told, and all goes well unless . . . one of our kids has a handicap.
>
> We parents are almost always the first to notice that something is amiss, and one of our early consolations is often our pediatrician's assurance that "it's nothing—he'll

The traditional parent-teacher conference is an effective form of communication (Willie L. Hill, Jr./Stock, Boston)

outgrow it." That, of course, is exactly what we want to hear because it corresponds perfectly to the dwindling hope in our hearts, so we defer to the expert and our child loses another year. Finally, the time does come when not even the most conservative professional can deny the existence of a problem. The difficulty now is to define it and plan accordingly. With luck, our pediatrician refers us to an appropriate specialist and we are (or should be) on our way.

We transfer our trust to the new god and wait expectantly for the oracle to speak. Instead of the strong authoritative voice of wisdom, we more often hear an evasive stammer: "Can't give you a definite diagnosis . . . uh, mumble, mumble . . . virtually untestable . . . let's see him . . . cough, cough . . . again in a year." Ironically, when the oracle is loud and clear, it is often wrong: "Seriously emotionally disturbed; it's a severe withdrawal reaction to maternal ambivalence." The parents have just been treated to their first dose of professional puffery, and it is a very bitter medicine, all the more so for being almost totally ineffective.

Its one potentially redeeming feature may be realized if the parents react with sufficient anger to take charge, to assert their right to be their child's "case manager." Unfortunately, this is not likely to happen at such an early stage; it takes more than one false god to make us give up religion entirely. And when (or if) we do manage to assert ourselves, our behavior is viewed by professionals as the final stage in our own pathology; and any of us who may still be practicing religion are immediately excommunicated. (Akerley, 1985, pp. 23–24)

This parent's frustrating experiences and that of many others could be avoided if professionals were better prepared to communicate effectively with parents. Fortunately, more and more educators are developing better ways of facilitating teacher-parent communication. Teachers and parents can communicate in a variety of ways. To meet the individual needs of particular families, it is essential that teachers have an assortment of methods from which to choose. We briefly discuss two methods of communicating: the traditional parent-teacher conference, used by teachers with virtually all parents, and a strategy more specific to parents of exceptional children—a "traveling" notebook. (See Turnbull & Turnbull, 1990, for more strategies for teacher-parent communication.)

Parent-Teacher Conferences

Parent-teacher conferences can be an effective way for teachers to impart information to parents. Likewise, it is an opportunity for teachers to learn from parents more about the students from the parents' viewpoint. Turnbull and Turnbull (1990) assert that the key to holding a successful conference is planning, and the planning revolves around three stages: preconference, conference, and postconference.

The Turnbulls have recommended several questions that teachers can ask themselves in order to plan for conferences and/or to evaluate their performance before, during, and after conferences. See Table 11.2 for a list of some of these questions.

Traveling Notebooks

A major advantage to a well-planned parent-teacher conference is that the teacher and parent can cover a lot of topics in a relatively short period of time. There are, however, at least two disadvantages. First, the degree of preparation required and the difficulty fitting them into the busy schedules of teachers and parents limits how often parent-teacher conferences can be held. Second, parents can sometimes feel intimidated by their child's teacher in a relatively formal setting, especially if the meetings are infrequent.

An excellent way to keep more frequent and informal lines of communication

TABLE 11.2 *Questions for Teachers to Ask Themselves Regarding Parent-Teacher Conferences*

Preconference Preparation

Notifying Families
— Did I, or the school, provide parents with written notification of the conference?
— Did I provide a means of determining that the parents knew the date and time (e.g., by calling the parents or requesting them to return a signed form indicating that they were able to attend)?

Preparing for the Conference
— Did I review the student's cumulative records?
— Did I assess the student's progress and pinpoint areas of concern?
— Did I gather examples of the student's work to show parents?
— Did I prepare a written agenda that was the right length and that was flexible enough?
— Did I consult with other relevant professionals about the student's progress?
— Did I plan ahead about how to bring up any sensitive topics (e.g., suspected child abuse, change of child's placement)?
— Did I mentally rehearse and review what I was going to say at the conference?

Preparing the Physical Environment
— Did I consider the most appropriate location including the possibility of holding the conference in the parents' home?
— Did the setting provide enough privacy?
— Did the setting provide enough comfort?

Conference Activities

Developing Rapport
— Did I allow time for all participants to talk informally for a few minutes before starting the meeting?
— Did I introduce participants who were unfamiliar with each other?
— Did I express appreciation for the parents' coming to the meeting?

Obtaining Information From Parents
— Did I ask enough open-ended questions?
— Did my body language indicate interest in what parents were saying? (Did I maintain eye contact and look attentive?)
— Did I ask for clarification on points I didn't understand?

Providing Information to Parents
— Did I speak as positively as possible about the student?
— Did I use jargon-free language?
— Did I use specific examples to clarify my points?

Summarizing and Follow-Up
— Did I review the main points to determine next steps?
— Did I restate who was responsible for completing the next steps and by when?
— Did I end the meeting on a positive note?
— Did I thank the parents for their interest in attending the meeting?

Postconference Follow-Up

— Did I consider reviewing the meeting with the student?
— Did I share the results with the appropriate other professionals who work with the student?
— Did I make a record of the conference proceedings?

Source: Adapted from A. P. Turnbull, & H. R. Turnbull, *Families, Professionals, and Exceptionality: A Special Partnership*, 2nd ed. (Columbus, OH: Chas. E. Merrill, 1990).

open is through the use of a traveling notebook, a notebook that goes back and forth every day between school and home. The teacher and other professionals, such as the speech or physical therapist, can write brief messages to the parents and vice versa. In addition, a traveling notebook allows the different professionals to keep up with what each of them is doing with the student. (The box below provides examples of excerpts from a traveling notebook of a two-year-old child with cerebral palsy.)

The Traveling Notebook

The following short excerpts are taken at random from a notebook that accompanies two-year-old Lauren, who has cerebral palsy, back and forth to her special class for preschoolers. The notebook provides a convenient mode for an ongoing dialogue among her mother, Lyn; her teacher, Sara; her occupational therapist, Joan; and her speech therapist, Marti. As you can see from this representative sample, the communication is informal but very informative on a variety of items relating to Lauren.

Lyn,   9/7
    Lauren did _very_ well – We had several criers but – She played & worked very nicely. She responds so well to instruction – that's such a plus!
    She fed herself crackers & juice & did a good job. She was very vocal & enjoyed the other children too. She communicated c̄ me very well for the 1st day.
    Am pleased c̄ her first day.
                                Sara

Sara,   9/15
    Please note that towel, toothbrush/paste + clean clothes may be removed from bag today – WED. We witnessed an apparently significant moment in her

oral communication: She'll try to say "all done" after a meal. The execution is imperfect, to say the least, but she gets an "A" for effort. Could you please reinforce this after snack? Just ask her, "What do you say after you finish your snack?"

Thanks,

Lyn

9/28

Lauren had an esp. good day! She was jabbering a lot! Being very expressive ō her vocalness & jabbering. I know she said "yes" or an approximate thereof, several times when asked if she wanted something. She was so cute ō the animal sounds esp. pig & horse – she was really trying to make the sounds. It was the first time we had seen such a response. Still cruising a lot! She walked ō me around the room & in the gym. She used those consonant & vowel sounds: dadada, mama ma – her jabbering was just so different & definitely progressive. I am sending her work card ō stickers home tomorrow for good working.

Several notes:

① Susie (VI) came today & evaluated Lauren. She will compile a report & be in touch with you and me. She seemed very pleased c̄ Lauren's performance.

② Marti (speech) will see Lauren tomorrow at 11 AM for evaluation. She'll be in touch afterwards.

③ Susie informed me about the addition to the IEP meeting on Mon. Oct. 4 at 10 AM here at Woodbrook.

How is the tape + cards working at home? I know you both are pleased c̄ her jabbering. She seems so ready to say "something" – we are very, very pleased. See you tomorrow.

Sara

9/29

Lauren was a bit fussy during O.T. today – she stopped fussing during fine motor reaching activities (peg board, block building) but wasn't too pleased with being handled on the ball. She did a great job with the peg board + readily used her left hand.

I want to bring in some different spoons next week to see if she can become more independent in scooping with a large handle spoon or a spoon that is covered.

Joan

Joan —   10/1

Although Lauren would very much approve of your idea for making her more independant during feeding, we'd rather not initiate self-feeding with an adaptive spoon at this time. Here's why:

① When I feed Lauren or get her to grip a spoon and then guide her hand, I can slip the entire bowl of the spoon into her mouth and get her to close her lips on it. When Lauren uses a spoon without help, she turns it upside-down to lick it or inserts just the tip of it into her mouth and then sucks off the food...

② Lauren has always been encouraged to do things "normally". She never had a special cup or a "Tommy Tippee", for instance. Of course, it took a year of practice before she could drink well from a cup, and she still dribbles a little occasionally; but she's doing well now. We really prefer to give Lauren practice in using a regular spoon so that she doesn't get dependant on an adaptive utensil. I'd like to assure you that we appreciate your communication about sessions with Lauren and ideas for her therapy. Coordinating her school, home, and CRC programs is going to be a challenge, to say the least.

                                    Lyn

☺! Lauren walked all the way
from the room to Gym & back —
She also walked up & down the full
length of the gym!
   Several other teachers saw her and
were thrilled.
   She fell maybe twice!
But picked herself right up —
                              Sara

3/2
   Lauren had a great speech
session! We were playing
with some toys and she
said "I want help" as
plain as day. Later she
said "I want crackers"
and at the end of the
session, she imitated "Cindy,
let's go." Super!
                              Marti

IN CONCLUSION

Today's knowledgeable educator recognizes the tremendous impact a disabled child
can have on the dynamics of a family. They appreciate the negative, as well as the
positive, influence an exceptional child can exert. Today's knowledgeable educator
also realizes that the family of a disabled child can be a bountiful reservoir of
support for the child as well as an invaluable source of information for the teacher.
Although there have been tremendous advances, we are just beginning to tap the
potential families have for contributing to the development of their exceptional
children. We are just beginning to enable families to provide a supportive and en-
riching environment for their children. We are just beginning to harness the expertise of families so that we can provide the best possible programs for their children.

SUMMARY

At one time the prevailing attitude toward parents of disabled individuals was negative. Professionals viewed them as causes of their children's problems or as roadblocks to educational efforts. Two factors have contributed to a much more positive attitude toward parents. First, Bell introduced the theory that children, even young infants, can cause changes in adults' behavior. Thus, professionals began to look at adult-child interaction as a two-way street—sometimes adults affect children's behavior and sometimes the reverse is true. Second, professionals began to see parents as a potential source of information about how to educate their children. This second factor has come about because (1) professionals recognize that early intervention efforts that focus on the home are more effective, (2) parents have become effective advocates for their children, and (3) federal legislation dictates that parents be involved in the education of their handicapped children.

Many theorists and clinicians believe that parents go through a series of stages after learning that they have a disabled child. There are limitations to a stage approach, however, including the tendency to view *all* parents as progressing through *all* the stages in the same order. Nevertheless, many parents do have some emotional reactions, for example, feelings of guilt. Most research on parents of disabled children has focused on the mother. Research on fathers indicates that they have more of an indirect effect on the child; that is, their attitudes toward the mother and the family influence how the mother interacts with the child. Parents of exceptional children undergo a great deal of stress. How parents cope with the stress varies. Although very few of them experience major psychological disturbances, they are at risk for mild forms of depression.

Siblings of individuals with disabilities experience some of the same emotions that parents do. Because they are less mature, may not have a broad base of people to talk with, and may be hesitant to talk over sensitive issues with their parents, siblings may have a difficult time coping with their emotions. As they grow older, their feelings often become more centered on how society views them and their family. Like parents, most of them are able to adjust to a disabled sibling. However, adjustment is especially difficult when the two siblings are close in age and/or of the same sex. Also, older nondisabled girls may experience problems because they are often called on to take care of their disabled sibling.

Current family theorists stress the influence of the social context on child development. They note that the family as a whole affects individual family members and that society affects the family. Two educational approaches to families that consider the social context are the Turnbulls' family systems approach and Dunst and others' social support systems approach.

The Turnbulls' model includes four components: *family characteristics*, *family interaction*, *family functions*, and *family life cycle*. Family characteristics comprise the type and severity of the disability as well as such things as the size, cultural background, and socioeconomic background of the family. Family interaction refers to how cohesive and adaptable the family is. Family functions include economics, daily care, recreation, socialization, self-definition, affection, and educational/vocational. The family life cycle is made up of birth and early childhood, childhood, adolescence, and adulthood. The model suggests that the impact of a disabled child on the family as well as the impact of the family on the disabled child are determined by the complex interactions within and between the four components.

A social support systems approach like that of Dunst and his colleagues stresses the importance of the broader societal influence on family functioning. It emphasizes the value of informal sources of social support, such as the extended family, friends, neighbors, and church groups. A particularly effective social support is that of parent support groups, made up of parents who have children with similar disabilities. A social support systems philosophy is built on the assumption that it is better to enable families to help themselves than to provide only direct services to them.

Family theorists agree that the key to working and involving parents is communication. The parent-teacher conference is one of the most common avenues, and preparation is the key to a successful conference. Teachers need to consider *preconference*, *conference*, and *postconference* activities. Before the conference they need to notify the families, prepare for the conference, and prepare the physical environment. During the conference they need to develop rapport, obtain information from and provide information to parents, and summarize the conference and state a plan for follow-up. After the conference they should consider sharing the results with the student and other involved professionals. In addition to parent-teacher conferences, there are a variety of less formal means of communicating. The traveling notebook is a notebook that accompanies the child to and from school every day in which the parent, teacher, and other professionals can write messages to one another concerning the child's progress.

Glossary

Acceleration. Educating gifted students by placing them in grade levels ahead of their peers in one or more academic subjects.

Acquired aphasia. Loss or impairment of the ability to understand or formulate language because of accident or illness.

Acquired immune deficiency syndrome (AIDS). A fatal virus-caused illness resulting in a breakdown of the immune system. Currently, no known cure exists.

Adventitious deafness. Deafness occurring through illness or accident in an individual who was born with normal hearing.

Alcohol embryopathy. Fetal alcohol syndrome.

American Sign Language (Ameslan). A signing system for the hearing impaired that has its own grammatical rules and is considered by many to be a true language.

Amniocentesis. A medical procedure that allows examination of the amniotic fluid around the fetus; sometimes recommended to determine the presence of abnormality.

Analytic touch. Involves the touching of various parts of an object and then mentally constructing these separate parts.

Anoxia. Reduced supply of oxygen for a long enough time to cause brain injury.

Apert's syndrome. A condition characterized by a narrowing of the skull such that proper development of the brain is inhibited; results in mental retardation if not surgically corrected.

Aphasia (dysphasia). Loss or impairment of the ability to understand or formulate language; caused by neurological damage.

Applied behavior analysis. The application and evaluation of principles of learning theory applied to teaching situations; used with all types of disabled students, but particularly appropriate for severely and profoundly disabled persons. It consists of six steps: identifying overall goals, accumulating further information through baseline measurement, specifying learning objectives, implementing the intervention, monitoring student performance, and evaluating the intervention.

Apraxia. The inability to move the muscles involved in speech or other voluntary acts.

Aqueous humor. A watery substance between the cornea and the lens of the eye.

Arthritis. A disease involving inflammation of the joints.

Arthrogryposis. A congenital condition in which muscles of the limbs are missing or are smaller and weaker than normal, resulting in stiffness or deformity of the limbs and trunk.

Articulation. Refers to the movements the vocal tract makes during production of speech sounds; enunciation of words and vocal sounds.

Asthma. A chronic respiratory condition causing repeated episodes of difficulty in breathing (dyspnea).

Astigmatism. Blurred vision caused by an irregular cornea or lens.

Asymmetrical tonic neck reflex (ATNR). A normal reflex in babies up to about four months of age in which turning the head to one side results in extension of the arm and leg on the side toward which the head is turned and flexion of the opposite arm and leg. It is an abnormal reflex indicative of brain injury in infants older than about four months.

Ataxia. A condition characterized by awkwardness of fine and gross motor movements, especially those involved with balance, posture, and orientation in space; a type of *cerebral palsy*.

Athetosis. A condition in which there are sudden involuntary, jerky, writhing movements, especially of the fingers and wrists; a type of *cerebral palsy*.

Atresia. A condition in which the external auditory canal isn't formed completely.

Atrophy. Degeneration of tissue, such as muscles or nerves.

Attributions. Explanations given by people for their successes and failures. Attributions may be internal or external.

Audiogram. A graphic representation of the weakest sound a person can hear at several frequency levels.

Audiology. A science dealing with hearing impairments, their detection, and remediation.

Audiometric zero (zero decibel level). Lowest level at which normal people can hear.

Auditory training. The procedure of teaching deaf or hard-of-hearing children to make full use of their residual hearing ability.

Augmentative communication. Alternative forms of communication that do not use the oral sounds of speech.

Aura. A sensation, such as the perception of certain odors, sounds, images, etc., sometimes experienced just before a seizure.

Auricle. The visible part of the ear, composed of cartilage; collects the sounds and funnels them via the external auditory canal to the eardrum.

Autism. A childhood disorder characterized by extreme withdrawal, self-stimulation, cognitive deficits, language disorders, and onset before the age of thirty months.

Baseline. Used to assess the effects of an intervention. The therapist or teacher measures the client's or student's skill or behavior before instruction.

Battered child syndrome. Evidence of physical, psychological, and/

or sexual abuse or neglect of a child that is threatening to the child's health or life.

Behavioral assessment (direct daily measurement). A method of observing and recording particular behaviors continually over a specific length of time.

Blindisms. Repetitive, stereotyped movements such as rocking or eye rubbing; also characteristic of some severely retarded and disturbed children.

Braille. A system in which raised dots are used to allow blind people to "read" with their fingertips; consists of a quadrangular cell containing from one to six dots whose arrangement denotes different letters and symbols.

Brain dysfunction. A term applied to those in whom there is suspected malfunctioning of the brain; used instead of the term *brain damage* or *brain injury* because it does not specify tissue damage. Many professionals, especially educators, have avoided use of this term because of its ambiguity.

Cancer. Abnormal growth of cells in any of the body's organ systems.

Cataracts. A condition caused by a clouding of the lens of the eye; affects color vision and distance vision.

Catheterization. Insertion of a tube into the urethra to drain urine from the bladder.

Cerebral palsy. A condition characterized by paralysis, weakness, incoordination, and/or other motor dysfunction because of damage to the brain before it has matured.

Cerumen (earwax). A bitter substance in the ear; can repel insects and discourage their entry into deeper parts of the ear.

Chisanbop. A Korean method of using the fingers for math calculations; recommended by some for use with the visually impaired.

Chromosome. A rod-shaped entity in the nucleus of the cell; contains *genes*, which convey hereditary characteristics.

Chronological age. Refers to how old a person is; used in comparison with *mental age* to determine the IQ score of an individual:

$$IQ = \frac{MA}{CA} \times 100.$$

Cleft palate, cleft lip. Condition in which there is a rift or split in the upper part of the oral cavity or the upper lip.

Closed caption. Program captions visible only on TV sets equipped with a decoder.

Clubfoot. A congenital condition in which one or both feet are turned at the wrong angle at the ankle.

Cochlea. A snail-shaped organ that lies below the vestibular mechanism; its parts convert the sound coming from the middle ear into an electrical signal in the inner ear, which is transmitted to the brain.

Cognitive behavior modification. A training approach that emphasizes teaching individuals to control their own thought processes; often used with learning-disabled children who are in need of an educational approach that stresses self-initiative and learning strategies.

Cognitive mapping. A nonsequential way of conceptualizing the spatial environment that allows a visually impaired person to know where several points in the environment are simultaneously; allows for better mobility than does a strictly sequential conceptualization of the environment.

Cognitive training. Training procedures designed to change thoughts or thought patterns.

Coloboma. A degenerative disease in which the central and/or peripheral areas of the retina are incompletely formed, resulting in impairment of the visual field and/or central visual acuity.

Community residential facility (CRF). A place, usually a group home, in an urban or residential neighborhood where from about three to ten retarded adults live under supervision.

Comprehension monitoring. The ability to keep track of one's own comprehension of reading material and to make adjustments to comprehend better while one is reading; often deficient in learning-disabled students.

Congenital. Existing at birth.

Congenital anaphthalmos. Lack of development of the eye and parts of the brain; usually characterized by mental retardation.

Congenitally deaf. Deafness that is present at birth; can be caused by genetic factors, by injuries during fetal development, or by injury incurred at birth.

Contractures. Permanent shortening of muscles and connective tissues and consequent distortion of bones and/or posture because of neurological damage.

Convergent thinking. The tendency to think deductively and arrive at a single answer that could be scored "right" or "wrong."

Cornea. A transparent cover in front of the iris and pupil in the eye; responsible for most of the refraction of the light rays in focusing on an object.

Cranmer abacus. An adaptation of the Japanese abacus for the visually impaired; consists of beads that can be manipulated through touch for math computations.

Creativity. Ability to express novel and useful ideas, to sense and elucidate new and important relationships, and to ask previously unthought of but crucial questions.

Criterion-referenced test. A procedure used to determine a child's level of achievement; when this level is established, a criterion, or goal, is set to fix a level at which the child *should* be achieving.

Cultural-familial retardation. Mild retardation with no evidence of brain pathology in someone from an economically disadvantaged background.

Curriculum-based assessment. This approach to assessment is a formative evaluation method designed to evaluate performance in the particular curriculum to which students are exposed. It usually involves giving students a small sample of items from the curriculum in use in their schools. Proponents of this assessment technique argue that it is preferable to comparing students with national norms or using tests that do not reflect the curriculum content learned by students.

Cystic fibrosis. An inherited disease characterized by chronic respiratory and digestive problems.

Decibel. A unit of relative intensity of a sound; zero decibels designates the point at which people with normal hearing can just detect sound.

Defective syntax. Inability to put words together to express ideas in grammatically complete sentences.

Deviance. Behavior that is at variance with the socially accepted norm.

Diabetes. A hereditary or developmental problem of sugar metabolism caused by a failure of the pancreas to produce enough insulin; *diabetes mellitus* is the common type.

Diabetic retinopathy. A condition resulting from interference of the blood supply to the retina; the fastest-growing cause of blindness.

Diagnostic-perscriptive center. Facilities provided for exceptional children; usually such children are placed there for a short time so their needs can be assessed and a plan of action established for their education.

Dimensional classification. Classification of behavior disorders according to several types or dimensions comprised of behaviors that statistical analyses indicate tend to occur together.

Diplegia. A condition in which the legs are paralyzed to a greater extent than the arms.

Direct instruction. A method of teaching academics, especially reading and math, that is similar to behavior analysis. It emphasizes structure among solution strategies and the selection of examples.

Discourse. Conversation; skills used in conversation, such as turn-taking and staying on the topic.

Divergent thinking. The ability to think inductively and suggest many different potential answers.

Dizygotic. Refers to twins who are not genetically identical because they came from two separate eggs.

Doppler effect. Term used to describe the phenomenon of the pitch of a sound rising as the listener moves toward the source of that sound.

Double hemiplegia. A condition in which both halves of the body are paralyzed but, unlike in *quadriplegia*, the two sides are affected differently.

Down syndrome. A condition resulting from a chromosomal abnormality; characterized by mental retardation and such physical signs as slanted-appearing eyes, flattened features, shortness, tendency toward obesity. The three major types of Down syndrome are *trisomy 21*, *mosaicism*, and *translocation*.

Dysarthria. A condition in which brain damage causes impaired control of the muscles used in articulation.

Dyslexia. An impairment of the ability to read.

Dystrophy. Hereditary, progressive weakening and wasting away of muscle tissue in which there is no evidence of neurological disease.

Echolalia. The meaningless repetition (echoing) of what has been heard.

Ecological approach. A position that stresses the interaction between the individual and environment; proponents of this position believe that labeling a child's exceptionality is harmful.

Educable mentally retarded (EMR). The traditionally used educators' classification label for an individual whose IQ is between 50 and 75; considered to be capable of learning basic academic subjects; loosely corresponds to the AAMR category of *mild retardation*.

Electrodermal audiometry (EDA). Used in testing young and/or hard-to-test children; based on measurement of skin resistance in response to sounds.

Electroencephalogram (EEG). A graphic recording of the brain's electrical impulses.

Emotional lability. Frequent changes of mood.

Encephalitis. An inflammation of the brain; can affect the child's mental development adversely.

Endogenous. A term used to refer to mental retardation caused by social or genetic factors; infrequently used today.

Enrichment. Provision of additional learning experiences for gifted students while they remain in the grade level appropriate for their chronological age.

Epilepsy. Recurrent seizures.

Eugenics movement. A drive by some professionals to "better" the human race through selective breeding and sterilization of "unfit" parents such as people with mental retardation. This popular movement of the late nineteenth and early twentieth centuries resulted in laws restricting the marriage of mentally retarded individuals and sterilization of some mentally retarded people.

Eustachian tube. The tube connecting the middle ear and the throat.

Evoked-response audiometry. A technique involving electroencephalograph measurement of changes in brain-wave activity in response to sounds.

Executive control processes. Strategies an individual can use to do better on a variety of tasks involving concept learning, memory, attention, and language; an example would be rehearsal of to-be-learned items on a memory task; often deficient in learning-disabled and mentally retarded children.

Exogenous. A term used to refer to mental retardation caused by brain damage; infrequently used now.

Expressive language disabilities. Problems associated with the inability to express oneself verbally.

External locus of control. A personality characteristic in which individuals believe chance factors or people other than themselves are responsible for personal successes and failures; analogous to *outer-directedness*.

External otitis (swimmer's ear). An infection of the skin of the external auditory canal.

Fetal alcohol syndrome. Abnormalities associated with the mother's drinking alcohol during pregnancy. Defects range from mild to severe, including growth retardation, brain damage, mental retardation, hyperactivity, anomalies of the face, and heart failure.

Fingerspelling. Spelling the English alphabet by various finger positions on one hand.

Fluency. The flow with which oral language is produced.

Focal seizure. A partial seizure involving a discharge in a fairly circumscribed part of the brain, thus causing only a limited motor or sensory effect.

Formative evaluation methods. Measurement procedures used to monitor an individual student's progress. They are used to compare an individual to himself or herself, in contrast to standardized tests, e.g., which are primarily used to compare an individual to other students.

Functional. Nonorganic; without apparent structural or organic cause.

Functional academics. Practical skills rather than academic learning.

Galactosemia. A disease involving the body's inability to metabolize galactose; a metabolic genetic disorder that can result in mental retardation.

Gene. Responsible for hereditary characteristics; arranged at specific locations in the chromosomes within each cell.

Generalization. A principle of learning referring to a person's ability to learn something in one situation or setting and then demonstrate it in another situation or setting; difficult for many disabled students, especially those with learning disabilities or mental retardation.

Generalized seizure. A seizure involving a large part of the brain.

Genetics. The biological study of heredity.

Genius. A word sometimes used to indicate a particular aptitude or capacity in any area; rare intellectual powers.

German measles. See *rubella*.

Giftedness. Refers to cognitive (intellectual) superiority, creativity, and motivation of sufficient magnitude to set the child apart from the vast majority of age-mates and make it possible for him or her to contribute something of particular value to society.

Glaucoma. A condition of excessive pressure in the eyeball; the cause is unknown but if untreated, blindness results.

Group auditory trainers. Devices that amplify sound for a group of hearing-impaired individuals. Wireless FM systems allow freedom of movement for teacher and students.

Handicapism. A term used by activists who fault the unequal treatment of handicapped individuals. This term is parallel to the term *racism*, coined by those who fault unequal treatment based on race.

Hemiplegia. A condition in which one-half (right or left side) of the body is paralyzed.

Hemophilia. A rare, sex-linked disorder of the blood; occurs almost exclusively in males and is transmitted through a recessive gene carried by the mother.

Herpes simplex. A type of veneral disease that can cause cold sores or fever blisters; if it affects the genitals and is contracted by the mother-to-be in the later stages of fetal development, it can cause mental subnormality in the child.

Hertz (Hz) unit. A measurement of the frequency of sound; refers to highness or lowness of a sound.

Homophenes. Sounds identical in terms of revealing movements (visible articulatory patterns).

Hospital and homebound instruction. A service to provide for the educational needs of exceptional children who are unable to attend the regular school because of their disability.

Hydrocephalus. A condition characterized by enlargement of the head because of excessive pressure of the cerebrospinal fluid.

Hyperactivity. A higher degree of inappropriate motor activity than is considered typical for a particular age group.

Hyperopia. Farsightedness; usually results when the eyeball is too short.

Hypertonic. Muscle tone that is too high; muscles that are too tense.

Hypoglycemia. A condition characterized by abnormally low blood sugar.

Hyporesponsive. Slow to respond; opposite of *hyperactive* or distractible; characteristic of some learning-disabled children.

Hypotonic. Muscle tone that is too low; flabby muscles.

Hypoxia. Deficiency in the amount of oxygen reaching the tissues of the body.

Impulsivity. The tendency to respond quickly without carefully considering the alternatives; responding without adequate reflection.

Incus. Anvil-shaped bone in the ossicular chain of the middle ear.

Individualized education program (IEP). PL 94-142 requires an IEP to be drawn up by the educational team for each exceptional child; the IEP must include a statement of present educational performance, instructional goals, educational services to be provided, and criteria and procedures for determining that the instructional objectives are being met.

Individualized family service plan (IFSP). Planning required under PL 99-457 to ensure that services for infants and toddlers under age 3 are provided in the context of the family.

Individualized transition plan. Included as part of the IEP, this plan is developed during secondary school to plan for community adjustment and employment once the student has left school.

Informal reading inventory (IRI). A procedure used to appraise a child's level of reading competence in a particular area; consists of sequentially graded reading paragraphs.

Inner-directedness. A personality characteristic in which individuals rely on their own resources to solve problems; analogous to *internal locus of control.*

Insight. Ability to separate and/or combine various pieces of information in new, creative, or useful ways.

Internal locus of control. A personality characteristic in which individuals believe they are responsible for their own successes and failures; analogous to *inner-directedness.*

IQ (intelligence quotient). A measure of intellectual functioning; determined by dividing *mental age* (the age level at which the person is functioning) by *chronological age* and multiplying by 100.

IQ-achievement discrepancy. Academic performance markedly lower than what would be appropriate for a student's intellectual capability.

Iris. The colored portion of the eye; contracts or expands depending on the amount of light striking it.

ISO standard. The International Standard Organization's determination of the average hearing levels, in which slight hearing loss is considered to be from 27 to 40 dB loss; mild, 41 to 55 dB loss; marked, 56 to 70 dB loss; severe, 71 to 90 dB loss; and extreme, 91 dB or more loss.

Itinerant teacher. Goes from school to school on a regular schedule to perform special instructional services for exceptional children; also consults with regular teacher about special problems or techniques.

Kinesthesis. The sensation of bodily movements as perceived through the muscles, tendons, and joints; the feeling of movement.

Kurzweil Reading Machine. A computerized device that converts print into speech for the visually impaired. The user places the printed material over a scanner that then "reads" the material aloud by means of an electronic voice.

Language. An arbitrary code or system of symbols to communicate meaning.

Language disorder. A lag in the ability to understand and express ideas that puts linguistic skill behind an individual's development in other areas, such as motor, cognitive, or social development.

Larynx. The structure in the throat containing the vocal apparatus (vocal cords); *laryngitis* is a temporary loss of voice caused by inflammation of the larynx.

Laser cane. Operates on the principle that the individual can learn to locate objects by means of echoes; can be used by the visually impaired like a *long cane* or can be used as an electronic aid in mobility.

Learned helplessness. A motivational term referring to a condition wherein a person believes that no matter how hard he or she tries, failure will result.

Least restrictive environment (LRE). A legal term referring to the fact that exceptional children must be educated in as "normal" an environment as possible.

Legg-Calve-Perthes disease. A condition involving a flattening of the head of the femur or hip bone and including destruction of bone tissue, pain, muscular spasm, or limping. Usually occurs in children aged three to eleven.

Lens. A structure that refines and changes the focus of the light rays passing through the eye.

Locus of control. A motivational term referring to how people attribute their successes or failures; people with an *internal* locus of control believe that they themselves are the reason for success or failure, whereas people with an *external* locus of control believe outside forces (e.g., other people) influence how they perform.

Long cane. A mobility aid used by visually impaired individuals who sweep it in a wide arc in front of them; requires considerable training to be used properly. It is the mobility aid of choice for most blind travelers.

Low vision. A term used by educators to refer to individuals whose visual impairment is not so severe that they are uanble to read print of some kind. They may read large or regular print, and they may need some kind of magnification.

Maintenance. A principle of learning referring to a person's ability to demonstrate what he or she has learned a relatively long time (two or three months) after he or she first learned it; difficult for many disabled students, especially those with learning disabilities or mental retardation.

Malleus. Hammer-shaped bone in the ossicular chain of the middle ear.

Mediation. A strategy of attaching a verbal label to something so that it can be more easily remembered.

Meningitis. A bacterial or viral infection of the linings of the brain or spinal cord.

Meningocele. A tumorlike sac containing cerebrospinal fluid; a type of *spina bifida.*

Mental age. Refers to the IQ test score that specifies the age level at which an individual is functioning.

Mental retardation. Below-average intellectual functioning abilities. Both IQ and adaptive skills are considered today as measures of the level of retardation; those who are retarded were traditionally divided by IQ test scores as *educable, trainable,* and *custodial;* today the more commonly used AAMR division includes *mild, moderate, severe,* and *profound* categories.

Metacognitive skills. Those abilities that people use to know their own cognitive processes. Metacognition refers to one's understanding of what strategies are available for learning and what strategies are best used in which situations.

Metacognitive strategy instruction. Providing alternative thinking strategies to students to facilitate the learning process.

Microcephalus. A condition causing development of a small head with a sloping forehead; proper development of the brain is prevented, resulting in mental retardation.

Mild retardation. A classification used by the AAMR to specify an individual whose IQ test score is between 55 and 68 or 69; corresponds to educators' label of *educable retarded;* individual is capable of learning basic academic subjects.

Minimal brain dysfunction (MBD). A term used to describe a child who shows behavioral but not neurological signs of brain injury; the term is not as popular as it once was, primarily because of its lack of diagnostic utility—i.e., some children who learn normally show signs indicative of MBD.

Mixed cerebral palsy. A type of cerebral palsy in which two or more types, such as *athetosis* and *spasticity*, occur together.

Mixed dominance. A term describing a person whose preferred anatomical sides are mixed—e.g., right-eyed, left-footed, and right-handed. Occurs slightly more frequently in learning-disabled compared to normal children but not enough to be diagnostically useful; e.g., many individuals who learn normally have mixed dominance.

Mnemonic keyword method. A cognitive training strategy used to help children with memory problems remember curriculum content. The teacher transforms abstract information into a concrete picture, which depicts the material in a more meaningful way.

Modeling. Showing or demonstrating to others how to perform particular behaviors.

Moderate retardation. A classification used by the AAMR to specify an individual whose IQ test score is between 40 and 55; corresponds to educators' label of *trainable retarded*; individual can usually learn functional academics and vocational skills.

Monoplegia. A condition in which only one limb is paralyzed.

Monozygotic. Refers to twins who are genetically identical because they came from the same egg.

Morphology. The study within psycholinguistics of word formation; of how adding or deleting parts of words changes their meaning. Learning-disabled students often make morphological errors.

Mosaicism. A type of Down syndrome in which some of the cells, owing to faulty development, have an extra chromosome and some do not.

Multiple sclerosis. A chronic, slowly progressive disease of the central nervous system in which there is a hardening or scarring of the protective myelin sheath of certain nerves.

Muscular dystrophy. A hereditary disease characterized by progressive weakness caused by degeneration of muscle fibers.

Mutation. A change in one or more of the genes, the arrangement of genes, or the quantity of chromosomal material.

Myelomeningocele (meningomyelocele). A tumorlike sac containing part of the spinal cord itself; a type of *spina bifida*.

Myopathy. A weakening and wasting away of muscular tissue in which there is no evidence of neurological disease or impairment.

Myopia. Nearsightedness; usually results from a too-long eyeball.

Nephritis. A chronic disease of the kidneys characterized by swelling of the body tissues.

Nephrosis. A degenerative kidney disease.

Neurosis (psychoneurosis). A condition marked by anxiety, inability to cope with inner conflicts; doesn't interfere as seriously with everyday activity as does *psychosis*.

Noise. A term used to describe features of the environment or the speaker—poor acoustics in a room or poor syntax in a speaker—that contribute to a person's difficulty in hearing sounds.

Nonsheltered work environments. Work environments in which handicapped persons are engaged in competitive employment side by side with nonhandicapped co-workers.

Nonsupperative otitis. Inflammation of the middle ear that occurs without an infection; often preceded by infectious otitis media. (See *serous otitis media*.)

Normalization. A philosophical belief in special education that every individual, even the most handicapped, should have an educational and living environment as close to normal as possible.

Nystagmus. A condition in which there are rapid involuntary movements of the eyes; sometimes indicates a brain malfunction and/or inner ear problems.

Open caption. TV captions that can be seen on all sets; used with selected programs since the 1970s.

Ophthalmology. The science of dealing with eye diseases.

Optacon. A device used to enable the blind to "read"; consists of a camera that converts print into an image of letters, which are then produced via vibration onto the finger.

Organic. Inherent, inborn; involving known neurological or structural abnormality.

Orthosis. A device designed to restore, partially or completely, a lost function of the body (e.g., a brace or crutch).

Orthotics. A professional specialty concerned with restoration of lost function of body parts with braces, adaptive devices, etc.

Ossicles. Three tiny bones (*malleus, incus,* and *stapes*) that together make possible an efficient transfer of sound waves from the eardrum to the *oval window*, which connects the middle ear to the inner ear.

Osteogenesis imperfecta. A hereditary condition in which the bones are formed improperly and break very easily.

Osteomyelitis. A bacterial infection of the bone.

Otitis media. Inflammation of the middle ear.

Otology. The medical specialty dealing with the ear and its diseases.

Otosclerosis. A hereditary disease of the bone in which the *stapes* bone is abnormally attached to the *oval window* of the ear.

Outer-directedness. A personality characteristic in which individuals rely on people other than themselves for cues to solve problems; analogous to *external locus of control*.

Oval window. Connects the middle and inner ear.

Palate. The roof of the mouth.

Paraplegia. A condition in which both legs are paralyzed.

Partially sighted. According to the legal definition, those individuals whose visual acuity falls between 20/70 and 20/200 in the better eye with correction (e.g., eyeglasses); sometimes also referred to as partially blind.

Partial seizure. A seizure beginning in a localized area and involving only a small part of the brain.

Pathsounder. A device worn around a blind person's neck that emits a noise when an object is approached.

Peer tutoring. A method that can be used to integrate handicapped students in regular classrooms, based on the notion that students can effectively tutor one another. The role of learner or teacher may be assigned to either the handicapped or the nonhandicapped student.

Perception. An individual's ability to process stimuli meaningfully; the ability to organize and interpret sensory information.

Perkins Brailler. A system making it possible to write in *Braille*; has six keys, one for each of the six dots of the cell, which leave an embossed print on paper.

Perseveration. Persistent repetition of an activity or behavior.

Phenylketonuria (PKU). A metabolic genetic disorder caused by the inability of the body to convert phenylalanine to tyrosine; an accumulation of phenylalanine results in abnormal brain development.

Phocomelia. A deformity in which the limbs of the baby are very short or missing completely, the hands and feet attached directly to the torso-like flippers; many cases resulted from maternal use of the drug thalidomide during pregnancy.

Phonation. The process involved in control of the breath stream to produce speech sounds.

Phonology. The study of how individual sounds make up words.

Physically disabled. Not able to perform significant physical activities required in everyday living that most persons of the same age and sex are able to perform without special assistance.

Physically handicapped. Individuals whose nonsensory physical limitations or health problems interfere with school or learning to such an extent that they require special education.

Picture cues. Illustrations or photographs that provide a visual cue for completing a task; often used with workers who are mentally retarded to help them perform more independently on the job.

Pitch. The tonal frequency (high or low tone) of one's voice.

PL 94-142. The Education for All Handicapped Children Act, which contains a mandatory provision stating that to receive funds under the Act, every school system in the nation must make provision for a free, appropriate public education for every child between the ages of three and eighteen (now extended to ages three to twenty-one) regardless of how, or how seriously, he or she may be handicapped.

PL 99-457. Extended the requirements of PL 94-142 to children aged three to five.

Play audiometry. A method of testing hearing in which young children are taught to respond to an auditory signal during a game.

Poliomyelitis (polio, infantile paralysis). An infectious disease that attacks the nerve tissue in the spinal cord and/or brain.

Postlingual deafness. Deafness occurring after the development of speech and language.

Pragmatics. The study within psycholinguistics of how one uses language in social situations; emphasizes functional use of language rather than its mechanics. Learning-disabled students often have problems in the pragmatics of language.

Preacademic skills. Behaviors that are needed before formal academic instruction can begin (e.g., ability to identify letters, numbers, shapes, and colors).

Precocity. Remarkable early development.

Prelingual deafness. Deafness that occurs before the development of spoken language, usually at birth.

Process test. A procedure to determine the effectiveness of psychological (usually perceptual or linguistic) processes.

Profound retardation. A classification used by the AAMR to specify an individual whose IQ test score is below 25.

Prosody. The patterns of stress and rate given to spoken words; rhythm.

Prosthesis. A device designed to replace, partially or completely, a part of the body (e.g., artificial teeth or limbs).

Prosthetics. A professional specialty concerned with replacing missing body parts with artificial substitutes (*prostheses*).

Psychoanalysis. A system developed by Sigmund Freud to treat mental and emotional disorders; unconscious motivations are considered to be at the root of such problems.

Psychoneurosis (neurosis). A condition marked by anxiety, inability to cope with inner conflicts; doesn't interfere as seriously with everyday activity as does *psychosis*.

Psychosis. A major mental disorder exhibited in seriously disturbed behavior and lack of contact with reality; childhood *schizophrenia* and *autism* are forms of psychosis.

Pupil. The contractile opening in the middle of the iris of the eye.

Pure-tone audiometry. A system whereby tones of various intensities and frequencies are presented to determine a person's hearing loss.

Quadriplegia. A condition in which all four limbs are paralyzed.

Readiness skills. Skills deemed necessary before academics can be learned (e.g., attending skills, the ability to follow directions, knowledge of letter names).

Reauditorization. A defect in the ability to understand and recognize words so that they can be remembered and retrieved for later use.

Receptive language disabilities. Difficulties that derive from the inability to understand spoken language.

Reciprocal teaching. A teaching method in which students and teacher are involved in dialogue to facilitate reading comprehension.

Reflex audiometry. The testing of responses to sounds by observation of such reflex actions as the orienting response and the Moro reflex.

Regular education initiative (REI). A philosophy that maintains that general education, rather than special education, should be primarily responsible for the education of mildly (and some moderately) handicapped students.

Residential school. A facility in which the exceptional child receives total care, usually away from his or her home community.

Resonance. Refers to the quality of the sound imparted by the size, shape, and texture of the organs in the vocal tract.

Resource teacher. Typically provides services for exceptional children and their teachers within one school; assesses the particular needs of such children and sometimes teaches them individually or in small groups, using any special materials or methods that are needed; consults with regular teachers, advising on the instruction and management of the child in the classroom and demonstrating instructional techniques.

Retina. The back portion of the eye, containing nerve fibers connected to the optic nerve.

Retinitis pigmentosa. A hereditary condition resulting in degeneration of the retina; causes a narrowing of the field of vision.

Retinoblastoma. A hereditary disease characterized by a malignant tumor of the eye; associated with above-average intelligence.

Retinopathy of prematurity (ROF). Formerly referred to as retrolental fibroplasia, a condition resulting from administration of an excessive concentration of oxygen at birth; causes scar tissue to form behind the lens of the eye.

Reverse mainstreaming. The practice of placing nonhandicapped students in classes that are predominantly composed of handicapped students.

Rheumatic fever. A condition sometimes following a strep throat or scarlet fever; noted by painful swelling and inflammation of the joints.

Rheumatoid arthritis. A systemic disease with major symptoms involving the muscles and joints.

Rigidity cerebral palsy. A rare type of cerebral palsy that is characterized by diffuse, continuous muscle tension and consequent "lead-pipe" stiffness.

Rubella (German measles). A serious viral disease, which, if it occurs during the first trimester of pregnancy, is likely to cause a deformity in the fetus.

Schizophrenia. Psychotic behavior manifested by loss of contact with reality, bizarre thought processes, and inappropriate actions.

Scoliosis. Curvature of the spine, either congenital or acquired from poor posture, disease, or muscular weakness caused by certain conditions such as *cerebral palsy* or *muscular dystrophy*.

Seizure (convulsion). A sudden alteration of consciousness, usually accompanied by motor activity and/or sensory phenomena; caused by an abnormal discharge of electrical energy in the brain.

Self-instructional training. A type of *cognitive behavior modification* technique that requires individuals to talk aloud and then to themselves as they solve problems.

Self-monitoring. A type of *cognitive behavior modification* technique that requires individuals to keep track of their own behavior.

Semantic. Pertaining to meaning in language.

Serous otitis media. Inflammation of the middle ear that occurs without an infection; often preceded by infectious otitis media. (See *nonsupperative otitis media*.)

Severely and profoundly handicapped (SPH). A term applied to mentally retarded individuals whose IQs fall below 25; these are the most seriously impaired of the mentally retarded, often characterized by physical and sensory impairment as well as mental retardation.

Severe retardation. A classification used by the AAMR to specify an individual whose IQ test score is between 25 and 40; educational efforts usually concentrate on basic communication and self-help skills.

Sheltered workshop. A facility that provides a structured environment for handicapped persons in which they can learn skills; can be either a transitional placement or a permanent arrangement.

Sickle cell anemia. A severe, chronic blood disease that occurs only in those who inherit the abnormal sickle gene from both parents; the gene produces an abnormal form of hemoglobin; occurs almost exclusively among persons of African descent.

Signing English systems. Used simultaneously with oral methods in the total communication approach to teaching deaf students; different from American Sign Language because it maintains the same word order as spoken English.

Sign language. A manual system in which there is sometimes similarity between the configuration of each gesture and the meaning it represents.

Slate and stylus. A method of writing in *Braille* in which the paper is held in a slate while the stylus is pressed through openings to make indentations in the paper. With this method the Braille cells are written in reverse order, and thus it is more difficult to use than the *Perkins Brailler.*

Snellen chart. Used in determining visual competence; consists of rows of letters or *E*'s arranged in different positions; each row corresponds to the distance at which a normally sighted person can discriminate the letters; does not predict how accurately a child will be able to read print.

Sociopath. A person whose behavior is aggressively antisocial and who shows no remorse or guilt for misdeeds.

Sociopathic. Behavior characteristics of a *sociopath*; someone who exhibits behavior characteristic of a sociopath.

Sonic glasses. Developed by Kay in 1973; operates on the principle that humans, like bats, can learn to locate objects by means of echoes.

Spastic. Sudden, involuntary contraction of muscles that makes accurate, voluntary movement difficult; a type of *cerebral palsy.*

Spasticity. A condition in which there are sudden, involuntary contractions of the muscles, causing voluntary movements to be difficult and inaccurate; a type of *cerebral palsy.*

Spatial cognition. The ability to understand the spatial aspects of the environment in which one lives; especially difficult, but not impossible, for blind individuals.

Special day schools. Provide all-day, segregated education for exceptional children.

Special self-contained class. Enrolls exceptional children with a particular diagnostic label; usually children in such a class need full-time instruction in this placement and are only integrated with their normal classmates for a few activities, if any.

Speech. Forming and sequencing oral language sounds during communication.

Speech audiometry. A technique that tests a person's detection and understanding of speech rather than using pure tones to detect hearing loss.

Speech disorder. Oral communication that involves abnormal use of the vocal apparatus, is unintelligible, or so inferior that it draws attention to itself and causes anxiety, feelings of inadequacy, or inappropriate behavior in the speaker.

Speech flow. The sequence or rhythm with which speech sounds are produced.

Speech-Plus Talking Calculator. An electronic calculator designed especially for the visually impaired. The device "says" the numbers aloud as they are punched and "says" the answers aloud.

Speechreading. A method that involves teaching children to use visual information from a number of sources to understand what is being said to them; more than just lipreading, which uses only visual clues arising from the movement of the mouth in speaking.

Speech reception threshold (SRT). The decibel level at which a person can understand speech.

Spina bifida. A congenital midline defect resulting from failure of the bony spinal column to close completely during fetal development.

Standard deviation. A measure of the amount by which an individual test score differs from the mean (average) score; a statistical construct that divides normal distribution into areas, making it possible to predict the percentage that falls above or below a score.

Standardized achievement test. A procedure to determine a child's relative achievement level; administered to a large group of children so that any one child's score can be compared to the norm.

Stapes. Stirrup-shaped bone in the ossicular chain of the middle ear.

Stereotypic behaviors. Any of a variety of repetitive behaviors (e.g.,

eye rubbing) that are sometimes found in blind, retarded, or psychotic individuals. Sometimes referred to as stereotypies or blindisms.

Stereotypies. (See *stereotypic behaviors*).

Stimulus reduction. A concept largely forwarded by Cruickshank; an approach to teaching distractible and hyperactive children that emphasizes reducing extraneous (nonrelevant to learning) material.

Strabismus. A condition in which the eyes are directed inward (crossed eyes) or outward.

Structured program. A concept largely forwarded by Cruickshank; emphasizes a teacher-directed approach in which activities and environment are structured for distractible and hyperactive children.

Stuttering. Speech characterized by abnormal hesitations, prolongations, and repetitions; may be accompanied by grimaces, gestures, or other bodily movements indicative of a struggle to speak, anxiety, blocking of speech, or avoidance of speech.

Superphone. A device that enables a deaf person to communicate with someone who has a pushbutton phone; it changes the keyboard message typed by the deaf person into an electronic voice; the hearing person can then type a response on the phone keys that will appear on the deaf person's typewriter.

Sweep test. An audiometric test designed to screen people rapidly to determine whether or not they have hearing impairment.

Syntax. The way words are joined together to structure meaningful sentences.

Synthetic touch. Refers to a person's tactual exploration of objects that are small enough to be enveloped by one or both hands.

Syphilis. A venereal disease that can cause mental subnormality in a child, especially if it is contracted by the mother-to-be during the latter stages of fetal development.

Tactual vocoder. A device that transforms sound into vibrations.

Talent. A special ability, aptitude, or accomplishment.

Tay-Sachs disease. An inherited condition that can appear when both mother and father are carriers; results in brain damage and eventual death; it can be detected before birth through *amniocentesis.*

Teletext. System for presenting information on a standard television screen, which the viewer can see whenever he or she wishes; requires a decoder and keypad for retrieving information.

Teletypewriter (TTY). A device connected to a telephone by a special adapter; allows communication between the hearing and hearing impaired over the telephone.

Temperament. Inborn behavioral style, including general level of activity, regularity or predictability, approach or withdrawal, adaptability, intensity of reaction, responsiveness, mood, distractibility, and persistence. The temperament is present at birth but may be modified by parental management.

Teratogens. Deformity-producing factors that interfere with normal fetal development.

Total communication approach. An approach for teaching the hearing impaired that blends oral and manual techniques.

Trainable mentally retarded (TMR). The traditionally used educators' classification label for an individual whose IQ is between 25 and 50; corresponds to AAMR categorization of *moderate retardation*; the educational emphasis is on self-help and vocational skills.

Transition programming. A program to provide disabled individuals with educational support during the transition from school to workplace. The degree of support provided will vary according to the individual's handicapping condition.

Translocation. A type of Down syndrome in which the extra chromosome (the result of faulty development) in the twenty-first set breaks off and attaches itself to another of the chromosome pairs.

Tremor cerebral palsy. A rare type of cerebral palsy that is characterized by rhythmic, involuntary movement of certain muscles.

Triplegia. A condition in which three limbs are paralyzed; a type of cerebral palsy.

Trisomy 21. A type of Down syndrome in which the twenty-first chromosome is a triplet, making forty-seven, rather than the normal forty-six, chromosomes in all.

Tuberculosis. An infectious disease potentially causing tissue destruction in many organ systems, particularly the lungs.

Tuberous sclerosis. A rare type of brain disease; a biochemical disorder caused by an abnormal dominant gene; can result in mental retardation ranging from mild to severe.

Tympanic membrane (eardrum). The anatomical boundary between the outer and middle ear; the sound gathered in the outer ear vibrates here.

Velum. The soft palate.

Vestibular mechanism. Located in the upper portion of the inner ear; consists of three soft, semicircular canals filled with a fluid that is sensitive to head movement, acceleration, and other movements related to balance.

Vibrotactile pulser. A device used by Azrin, Jones, and Flye in 1968 to deliver a rhythmic pulse to the palm of the hand; a behavior modification technique aimed at helping children learn to read faster.

Visual efficiency. A term used to refer to how well one uses one's vision, including such things as control of eye movements, attention to visual detail, and discrimination of figure from background. It is believed by some to be more important than visual acuity alone in predicting a person's ability to function visually.

Vitreous humor. A transparent gelatinous substance that fills the eyeball between the retina and the lens of the eye.

Work-study program. Designed to introduce students to a variety of vocational opportunities while still in school. On-the-job training is provided, and the student's performance is evaluated.

References

Chapter 1

Anderson, B. (1989, March 13). Angel on the ascent. *Sports Illustrated*, *70*, 27.

Bateman, B. D., & Herr, C. M. (1981). Law and special education. In J. M. Kauffman & D. P. Hallahan (Eds.), *Handbook of special education*. Englewood Cliffs, NJ: Prentice Hall.

Baumeister, A. A., Kupstas, F. & Klindworth, L. M. (1990). New morbidity: Implications for prevention of children's disabilities. *Exceptionality*, *1*, 1–16.

Bricker, D. D. (1986). An analysis of early intervention programs: Attendant issues and future directions. In R. J. Morris & B. Blatt (Eds.), *Special education: Research and trends* (pp. 28–65). New York: Pergamon Press.

Clark, D. L., & Astuto, T. A. (1988). Education policy after Reagan—What next? Occasional paper No. 6, Policy Studies Center of the University Council for Educational Administration, University of Virginia, Charlottesville.

Cruickshank, W. M. (1977). Guest editorial. *Journal of Learning Disabilities*, *10*, 193–194.

Edgar, E., (1987). Secondary programs in special education: Are many of them justifiable? *Exceptional Children*, *53*, 555–561.

Hendrick, I. G., MacMillan, D. L., & Balow, I. H. (1989, April). *Early school leaving in America: A review of the literature*. Riverside: University of California, California Educational Research Cooperative.

Itard, J. M. G. (1962). *The wild boy of Aveyron*. (Trans. George & Muriel Humphrey). Englewood Cliffs, NJ: Prentice Hall.

Jenkins, J. R., Odom, S. L., & Speltz, M. L. (1989). Effects of social integration on preschool children with handicaps. *Exceptional Children*, *55*, 420–428.

Johnson, D. R., Bruininks, R. H., & Thurlow, M. L. (1987). Meeting the challenge of transition service planning through improved interagency cooperation. *Exceptional Children*, *53*, 522–530.

Kanner, L. (1964). *A history of the care and study of the mentally retarded*. Springfield, IL: Chas. C Thomas.

Martin, E. W. (1976). A national commitment to the rights of the individual—1776–1976. *Exceptional Children*, *43*, 132–135

Morse, W. C. (1984). Personal perspective. In B. Blatt & R. Morris (Eds.)., *Perspectives in special education: Personal orientations*. Glenview, IL: Scott, Foresman.

Neel, R. S., Meadows, N., Levine, P., & Edgar, E. B. (1988). What happens after special education: A statewide follow-up study of secondary students who have behavioral disorders. *Behavioral Disorders*, *13*, 209–216.

U.S. Department of Education. (1989). *Eleventh annual report to Congress on the implementation of The Education of the Handicapped Act*. Washington, DC: U.S. Government Printing Office.

Verstegen, D. A., & Clark, D. L. (1988). The diminution of federal expenditures for education during the Reagan administration. *Phi Delta Kappan*, *70*, 134–138.

Werner, E. E. (1986). The concept of risk from a developmental perspective. In B. K. Keogh (Ed.), *Advances in special education*, *Vol. 5: Developmental problems in infancy and the preschool years*. Greenwich, CT: JAI Press.

Winzer, M. A. (1986). Early developments in special education: Some aspects of Enlightenment thought. *Remedial and Special Education*, *7*(5), 422–49.

Wolman, C., Bruininks, R., & Thurlow, M. (1989). Dropouts and drop out programs: Implications for special education. *Remedial and Special Education*, *10*(5), 6–20, 50.

Yanok, J. (1986). Free appropriate public education for handicapped children: Congressional intent and judicial interpretation. *Remedial and Special Education*, *7*(2), 49–53.

Zelder, E. Y. (1953). Public opinion and public education for the exceptional child—court decisions 1873–1950. *Exceptional Children*, *19*, 187–198.

Zetlin, A. G., & Hosseini, A. (1989). Six postschool case studies of mildly learning handicapped young adults. *Exceptional Children*, *55*, 405–411.

Chapter 2

Balla, D. (1976). Relationship of institution size to quality of care: A review of literature. *American Journal of Mental Deficiency*, *81*, 117–124.

Banks, J. A. (1988). *Multiethnic education: Theory and practice* (2nd ed.). Boston: Allyn & Bacon.

Bauwens, J., Hourcade, J. J., & Friend, M. (1989). Cooperative teaching: A model for general and special education. *Remedial and Special Education*, *10*(2), 17–22.

Bender, W. N. (1988). The other side of placement decisions: Assessment of the mainstream learning environment. *Remedial and Special Education*, *9*(5), 28–33.

Bickel, W. E., & Bickel, D. D. (1986). Effective schools, classrooms, and instruction: Implications for special education. *Exceptional Children, 52,* 489–500.

Biklen, D. (1986, winter). Framed: Journalism's treatment of disability. *Social Policy,* pp. 45–51.

Blatt, B., & Kaplan, F. (1966). *Christmas in Purgatory: A photographic essay on mental retardation.* Boston: Allyn & Bacon.

Bogdan, R. (1986). The sociology of special education. In R. J. Morris & B. Blatt (Eds.), *Special education: Research and trends* (pp. 344–359). New York: Pergamon Press.

Bogdan, R., & Biklen, D. (1977). Handicapism. *Social Policy, 7*(5), 14–19.

Brantlinger, E. A., & Guskin, S. L. (1987). Ethnocultural and social-psychological effects on learning characteristics of handicapped children. In M. C. Wang, M. C. Reynolds, & H. J. Walberg (Eds.), *Handbook of special education: Research and practice. Vol. 1. Learner characteristics and adaptive education* (pp. 7–34). New York: Pergamon Press.

Brody, H. (1989). The great equalizer: PCs empower the disabled. *PC Computing, 2*(7), 82–93.

Butterfield, E. C. (1967). The role of environmental factors in the treatment of institutionalized mental retardates. In A. A. Baumeister (Ed.), *Mental retardation: Appraisal, education, and rehabilitation.* Chicago: Aldine.

Carnine, D., & Kameenui, E. J. (1990). The regular education initiative and children with special needs: A false dilemma in the face of true problems. *Journal of Learning Disabilities, 23*(3), 141–144.

Cavalier, A., & Mineo, B. A. (1986). The application of technology in the home, classroom, and work place: Unvoiced premises and ethical issues. In A. Gartner & T. Joe (Eds.), *Images of the disabled/disabling images.* New York: Praeger.

Chalfant, J. C. (1989). Learning disabilities: Policy issues and promising approaches. *American Psychologist, 44,* 392–398

Chalfant, J. C., Pysh, M. V., & Moultrie, R. (1979). Teacher assistance teams: A model for within-building problem solving. *Learning Disability Quarterly, 2,* 85–96.

Children's Museum of Boston, with WGBH Boston. (1978). *What if you couldn't? An elementary school program about handicaps.* Weston, MA: Burt Harrison & Co.

Chinn, P. C., & Hughes, S. (1987). Representation of minority students in special education classes. *Remedial and Special Education, 8*(4), 41–46.

Cohen, S. (1977). *Accepting individual differences.* Allen, TX: Developmental Learning Materials.

Conroy, J., Efthimiou, J., & Lemanowicz, J. (1982). A matched comparison of the developmental growth of institutionalized and deinstitutionalized mentally retarded clients. *American Journal of Mental Deficiency, 86,* 581–587.

Council for Children with Behavioral Disorders. (1989). White paper. Best assessment practices for students with behavioral disorders: Accommodation to cultural diversity and individual differences. *Behavioral Disorders, 14,* 263–278.

Crowley, E. P. (1986). Television and disability: A literature review. Unpublished manuscript, University of Virginia, Charlottesville.

Delpit, L. D. (1988). The silenced dialogue: Power and pedagogy in educating other people's children. *Harvard Educational Review, 58,* 280–298.

Deno, S. L. (1985). Curriculum-based measurement: The emerging alternative. *Exceptional Children, 52,* 219–232.

Duff, R. S., & Campbell, A. G. M. (1973). Moral and ethical dilemmas in the special care nursery. *New England Journal of Medicine, 289,* 890–894.

Duke, D. L. (1990). *Teaching: An introduction.* New York: McGraw-Hill.

Fiedler, C. R., & Simpson, R. L. (1987). Modifying the attitudes of nonhandicapped high school students toward handicapped peers. *Exceptional Children, 53,* 342–349.

Foster, G. G., Ysseldyke, J. E., & Reese, J. H. (1975). "I wouldn't have seen it if I hadn't believed it." *Exceptional Children, 41,* 469–473.

Friend, M. (1988). Putting consultation into context: Historical and contemporary perspectives. *Remedial and Special Education, 9*(6), 7–13.

Gallagher, J. J. (1972). The special education contract for mildly handicapped children. *Exceptional Children, 38,* 527–535.

Gartner, A., & Joe, T. (1986). Introduction. In A. Gartner & T. Joe (Eds.), *Images of the disabled/disabling images.* New York: Praeger.

Gartner, A., & Lipsky, D. K. (1989). *The yoke of special education: How to break it.* Rochester, NY: National Center on Education and the Economy.

Gerber, M. M., & Kauffman, J. M. (1981). Peer tutoring in academic settings. In P. S. Strain (Ed.), *The utilization of classroom peers as behavior change agents* (pp. 155–187). New York: Plenum.

Gerber, M. M., & Semmel, M. I. (1984). Teacher as imperfect test: Reconceptualizing the referral process. *Educational Psychologist, 19,* 137–148.

Gerber, M. M., & Semmel, M. I. (1985). Microeconomics of referral and reintegration: A paradigm for evaluation of special education. *Studies in Educational Evaluation, 11*(1), 13–29.

Gottlieb, J., & Leyser, Y. (1981). Facilitating the social mainstreaming of retarded children. *Exceptional Children, 1*(4), 57–69.

Greenspan, S., & Cerreto, M. (1989). Normalization, deinstitutionalization, and the limits of research: Comment on Landesman and Butterfield. *American Psychologist, 44,* 448–449.

Hallahan, D. P., Kauffman, J. M., Lloyd, J. W., & McKinney, J. D. (Eds.). (1988). The regular education initiative. *Journal of Learning Disabilities, 21*(1), special issue.

Hallahan, D. P., Keller, C. E., McKinney, J. D., Lloyd, J. W., & Bryan, T. (1988). Examining the research base of the regular education initiative: Efficacy studies and the Adaptive Learning Environments Model. *Journal of Learning Disabilities, 21,* 29–35.

Hentoff, N. (1985, January). The awful privacy of Baby Doe. *The Atlantic Monthly,* pp. 54–62.

Hilliard, A. G. (1989). Teachers and cultural styles in a pluralistic society. *NEA Today, 7*(6), 65–69.

Howell, K. W., & Morehead, M. K. (1987). *Curriculum-based evaluation for special and remedial education.* Columbus, OH: Chas. E. Merrill.

Idol, L. (1988). A rationale and guidelines for establishing special education consultation programs. *Remedial and Special Education, 9*(6), 48–58.

Jacob, E., & Jordan, C. (Eds.). (1987). Explaining the school performance of minority students. *Anthropology and Education Quarterly, 18*(4), special issue.

Jacobson, J. W., & Schwartz, A. A. (1983). The evaluation of community living alternatives for developmentally disabled persons. In J. L. Matson & J. A. Mulich (Eds.), *Handbook of mental retardation* (pp. 39–26). New York: Pergamon Press.

Jenkins, J. R., & Jenkins, L. M. (1987). Making peer tutoring work. *Educational Leadership, 44*(6), 64–68.

Johnson, D. W., & Johnson, R. (1986). Mainstreaming and cooperative learning strategies. *Exceptional Children, 52,* 553–561.

Johnson, L. J., Pugach, M. C., & Hammitte, D. J. (1988). Barriers to effective special education consultation. *Remedial and Special Education, 9*(6), 41–47.

Kent, D. (1986). Disabled women, portraits in fiction and drama. In A. Gartner & T. Joe (Eds.), *Images of the disabled/disabling images.* New York: Praeger.

Kidder, J. T. (1989). *Among schoolchildren.* Boston: Houghton Mifflin.

Kleinberg, J., & Galligan, B. (1983). Effects of deinstitutionalization on adaptive behavior of mentally retarded adults. *American Journal of Mental Deficiency, 88,* 21–27.

Klobas, L. (1985, January–February). TV's concept of people with disabilities: Here's lookin' at you. *The Disability Rag,* pp. 2–6.

Kopelman, L. M., Irons, T. G., & Kopelman, A. E. (1988). Neonatologists judge the "Baby Doe" regulations. *New England Journal of Medicine, 318,* 677–683.

Kriegel, L. (1986). The cripple in literature. In A. Gartner & T. Joe (Eds.), *Images of the disabled/disabling images.* New York: Praeger.

Landesman, S., & Butterfield, E. C. (1987). Normalization and deinstitutionalization of mentally retarded individuals: Controversy and facts. *American Psychologist, 42,* 809–816.

Larrivee, B. (1985). *Effective teaching for successful mainstreaming.* New York: Longman.

Lloyd, J. W., Crowley, E. P., Kohler, F. W., & Strain, P. S. (1988). Redefining the applied research agenda: Cooperative learning, prereferral, teacher consultation, and peer-mediated interventions. *Journal of Learning Disabilities, 21,* 43–52.

Lloyd, J. W., Keller, C. E., Kauffman, J. M., & Hallahan, D. P. (1988, January). *What will the regular education initiative require of general education teachers?* Washington, DC: U.S. Department of Education, Office of Special Education Programs.

Longmore, P. K. (1985). Screening stereotypes: Images of disabled people. *Social Policy, 16,* 31–37.

McCann, S. K., Semmel, M. I., & Nevin, A. (1985). Reverse mainstreaming: Nonhandicapped students in special education classrooms. *Remedial and Special Education, 6*(1), 13–19.

McMurray, G. L. (1986). Easing everyday living: Technology for the physically disabled. In A. Gartner & T. Joe (Eds.), *Images of the disabled/disabling images.* New York: Praeger.

Martin, D. S. (1987). Reducing ethnocentrism. *Teaching Exceptional Children, 20*(1), 5–8.

Mehta, V. (1989). *The stolen light.* New York: W. W. Norton & Co.

Minow, M. (1985). Learning to live with the dilemma of difference: Bilingual and special education. In K. T. Bartlett & J. W. Wegner (Eds.), *Children with special needs* (pp. 375–429). New Brunswick, NJ: Transaction Books.

Odom, S. L., Deklyen, M., & Jenkins, J. R. (1984). Integrating handicapped and nonhandicapped preschoolers: Developmental impact on nonhandicapped children. *Exceptional Children, 51,* 41–48.

Reschly, D. J. (1987). Learning characteristics of mildly handicapped students: Implications for classification, placement, and programming. In M. C. Wang, M. C. Reynolds, & H. J. Walberg (Eds.), *Handbook of special education: Research and practice, Vol. 1: Learner characteristics and adaptive education.* New York: Pergamon Press.

Reynolds, M. C., & Lakin, K. C. (1987). Noncategorical special education: Models for research and practice. In M. C. Wang, M. C. Reynolds, & H. J. Walberg (Eds.), *Handbook of special education: Research and practice, Vol. 1: Learner characteristics and adaptive education.* New York: Pergamon Press.

Rogoff, B., & Morelli, G. (1989). Culture and American children. *American Psychologist, 44,* 341–342.

Rosenshine, B. (1983). Teaching functions in instructional programs. *The Elementary School Journal, 83,* 335–354.

Rotegard, L. L., Hill, B. K., & Bruininks, R. H. (1983). Environmental characteristics of residential facilities for mentally retarded persons in the United States. *American Journal of Mental Deficiency, 88,* 49–56.

Schram, L., Semmel, M. I., Gerber, M. M., Bruce, M. M., Lopez-Reyna, N., & Allen, D. (1984). Problem solving teams in California. Unpublished manuscript, University of California at Santa Barbara.

Scruggs, T. E., & Richter, L. (1986). Tutoring learning disabled students: A critical review. *Learning Disability Quarterly, 9,* 2–14.

Slavin, R. E. (1988). Cooperative learning and student achievement. *Educational Leadership, 46*(2), 31–33.

Soeffing, M. Y. (1974). The way to know: Normalization of services for the mentally retarded—A conversation with Dr. Wolf Wolfensberger. *Education and Training of the Mentally Retarded, 9,* 202–208.

Stainback, W. C., & Stainback, S. B. (1984). A rationale for the merger of special and regular education. *Exceptional Children, 51,* 517–521.

Vergason, G. A., & Anderegg, M. L. (1989). Save the baby! A response to "Integrating the children of the second system." *Phi Delta Kappan, 71,* 61–63.

Walberg, H. J. (1984). Improving the productivity of America's schools. *Educational Leadership, 41*(8), 19–30.

Wang, M. C., Reynolds, M. C., & Walberg, H. J. (1986). Rethinking special education. *Educational Leadership, 44*(1), 26–31.

Wang, M. C., Reynolds, M. C., & Walberg, H. J. (1988). Integrating the children of the second system. *Phi Delta Kappan, 70,* 248–251.

Wang, M. C., Reynolds, M. C., & Walberg, H. J. (1989). Who benefits from segregation and murky water? *Phi Delta Kappan, 71,* 64–67.

Wesson, C., & Mandell, C. (1989). Simulations promote understanding of handicapping conditions. *Teaching Exceptional Children, 22*(1), 32–35.

Will, M. C. (1984). Let us pause and reflect—but not too long. *Exceptional Children, 51,* 11–16.

Will, M. C. (1986). Educating children with learning problems: A shared responsibility. *Exceptional Children, 52,* 411–415.

Wolf, B. (1974). *Don't feel sorry for Paul.* Philadelphia: Lippincott.

Wolfensberger, W. (1972). *The principle of normalization in human services.* Toronto: National Institute on Mental Retardation.

Ysseldyke, J. E., & Cristenson, S. L. (1987a). Evaluating students' instructional environments. *Remedial and Special Education, 8*(3), 17–24.

Ysseldyke, J. E., & Marston, D. (1988). Issues in the psychological evaluation of children. In V. B. Van Hasselt, P. S. Strain, & M. Hersen (Eds.), *Handbook of developmental and physical disabilities* (pp. 21–37). New York: Pergamon Press.

Zaner, R. M. (1986). Soundings from uncertain places: Difficult pregnancies and imperiled infants. In P. R. Dokecki & R. M. Zaner (Eds.), *Ethics of dealing with persons with severe handicaps: Toward a research agenda* (pp. 71–92). Baltimore: Paul H. Brookes.

Zigler, E. (1973). The retarded child as a whole person. In D. K. Routh (ed.), *The experimental psychology of mental retardation.* Chicago: Aldine.

Zigler, E. (1988, July). The social context of research design: From theory to practice in the care and education of retarded individuals. *Proceedings: Research in education of the handicapped project directors' meeting.* Washington, DC: U.S. Department of Education, Office of Special Education Programs.

Chapter 3

Allore, R., O'Hanlon, D., Price, R., Neilson, H., Willard, H. F., Cox, D. R., Marks, A., & Dunn, R. J. Gene encoding the β subunit of S100 protein is on chromosome 21: Implications for Down syndrome. (1988, March 11). *Science,* pp. 1311–1313.

Balla, D., & Zigler, E. (1979). Personality development in retarded persons. In N..R. Ellis (Ed.), *Handbook of mental deficiency: Psychological theory and research* (2nd ed.). Hillsdale, NJ: Erlbaum.

Bates, P., Renzaglia, A., & Wehman, P. (1981). Characteristics of an appropriate education for severely and profoundly handicapped students. *Education and Training of the Mentally Retarded, 16,* 142–149.

Batshaw, M. L., & Perret, Y. M. (1986). *Children with handicaps: A medical primer* (2nd ed.). Baltimore: Paul H. Brookes.

Baumeister, A. A., Kupstas, F., & Klindworth, L. M. (1990). New morbidity: Implications for prevention of children's disabilities. *Exceptionality, 1*(1), 1–16.

Berkell, D. (1988). Identifying programming goals for productive employment. In B. L. Ludlow, A. P. Turnbull, & R. Luckasson (Eds.), *Transitions to adult life for people with mental retardation: Principles and practices* (pp. 159–175). Baltimore: Paul H. Brookes.

Berrueta-Clement, J. R., Schweinhart, L. J., Barnett, W. S., Epstein, A. S., & Weikart, D. P. (1984). *Changed lives: The effects of the Perry Preschool Program on youths through age 19.* (Monograph of the High/Scope Educational Research Foundation No. 8.) Ypsilanti, MI: High/Scope Press.

Blackman, J. A. (1984a). Down syndrome. In J. A. Blackman (Ed.), *Medical aspects of developmental disabilities in children birth to three,* (Rev. 1st ed., pp. 92–95). Rockville, Md.: Aspen Systems Corp.

Blackman, J. A. (1984b). Low birth weight. In J. A. Blackman (Ed.), *Medical aspects of developmental disabilities in children birth to three* (Rev. 1st ed., pp. 143–146). Rockville, MD: Aspen Systems Corp.

Borkowski, J. G., and Cavanaugh, J. C. (1979). Maintenance and generalization of skills and strategies by the retarded. In N. R. Ellis (Ed.), *Handbook of mental deficiency: Psychological theory and research* (2nd ed.). Hillsdale, NJ: Lawrence Erlbaum.

Borkowski, J. G., Peck, V. A., & Damberg, P. R. (1983). Attention, memory, and cognition. In J. L. Matson & J. A. Mulich (Eds.), *Handbook of mental retardation* (pp. 479–497). New York: Pergamon Press.

Borkowski, J. G., & Wanschura, P. B. (1974). Mediational processes in the retarded. In N. R. Ellis (Ed.), *International review of research in mental retardation,* Vol. 7. New York: Academic Press.

Bray, N. W. (1979). Strategy production in the retarded. In N. R. Ellis (Ed.), *Handbook of mental deficiency: Psychological theory and research* (2nd ed.). Hillsdale, NJ: Lawrence Erlbaum.

Brooks, P. H., & McCauley, C. (1984). Cognitive research in mental retardation. *American Journal of Mental Deficiency, 88,* 479–486.

Brown, A. L. (1974). The role of strategic behavior in retardate memory. In N. R. Ellis (Ed.), *International review of research in mental retardation,* Vol. 7. New York: Academic Pres.

Brown, L., Shiraga, B., Ford, A., Nisbet, J., Van Deventer, P., Sweet, M., York, J., & Loomis, R. (1986). Teaching severely handicapped students to perform meaningful work in nonsheltered vocational environments. In R. J. Morris & B. Blatt (Eds.), *Special education: Research and trends* (pp. 131–189). New York: Pergamon Press.

Capron, C., & Duyme, M. (1989, August 17). Assessment of effects of socio-economic status on IQ in a full cross-fostering study. *Nature,* pp. 552–553.

Craik, F. I. M., & Lockhart, R. S. (1972). Levels of processing: A framework for memory research. *Journal of Verbal Learning and Verbal Behavior, 11,* 671–684.

Craik, F. I. M., & Tulving, E. (1975). Depth of processing and the retention of words in episodic memory. *Journal of Experimental Psychology: General, 104,* 268–294.

Cravioto, J., & DeLicardie, E. R. (1975). Environmental and nutritional deprivation in children with learning disabilities. In W. M. Cruickshank & D. P. Hallahan (Eds.), *Perceptual and learning disabilities in children.* Vol. 2: *Research and theory.* Syracuse, NY: Syracuse University Press.

Diamond, G. W., & Cohen, H. J. (1987, December). AIDS and developmental disabilities. *Prevention Update,* National Coalition on Prevention of Mental Retardation.

Doll, E. A. (1941). The essentials of an inclusive concept of mental deficiency. *American Journal of Mental Deficiency, 46,* 214–219.

Ellis, N. R. (1982). A behavioral research strategy in mental retardation: Defense and critique. In E. Zigler & D. Balla (Eds.), *Mental retardation: The developmental-difference controversy* (pp. 189–202). Hillsdale, NJ: Erlbaum.

Epstein, M. H., Polloway, E. A., Patton, J. R., & Foley, R. (1989). Mild retardation: Student characteristics and services. *Education and Training in Mental Retardation, 24*(1), 7–16.

Estes, W. K. (1970). *Learning theory and mental development.* New York: Academic Press.

Forness, S. R., & Kavale, K. A. (1984). Education of the mentally retarded: A note on policy. *Education and Training of the Mentally Retarded, 19,* 239–245.

Glidden, L. M. (1985). Semantic processing, semantic memory, and recall. In N. R. Ellis (Ed.), *International review of research in mental retardation,* Vol. 13. (pp. 247–278). New York: Academic Press.

Goodman, J. F. (1979). Is tissue the issue? A critique of SOMPA's models and tests. *The School Psychology Digest, 8,* 47–62.

Greenspan, S., & Shoultz, B. (1981). Why mentally retarded adults lose their jobs: Social competence as a factor in work adjustment. *Applied Research in Mental Retardation, 2*(1), 23–38.

Grossman, H. J. (Ed.). (1983). *Classification in mental retardation.* Washington, DC: American Association on Mental Deficiency.

Guthrie, R. (1984). Explorations in prevention. In B. Blatt & R. Morris (Eds.), *Perspectives in special education: Personal orientations* (pp. 157–172). Glenview, IL: Scott, Foresman.

Hallahan, D. P., & Cruickshank, W. M. (1973). *Psychoeducational foundations of learning disabilities.* Englewood Cliffs, NJ: Prentice-Hall.

Hansen, H. (1978). Decline of Down's Syndrome after abortion reform in New York State. *American Journal of Mental Deficiency, 83,* 185–188.

Hasazi, S. B., & Clark, G. M. (1988). Vocational preparation for high school students labeled mentally retarded: Employment as a graduation goal. *Mental Retardation, 26*(6), 343–349.

Hasazi, S. B., Collins, M., & Cobb, R. B. (1988). Implementing transition programs for productive employment. In B. L. Ludlow, A. P. Turnbull, & R. Luckasson (Eds.), *Transitions to adult life for people with mental retardation—Principles and practices* (pp. 177–195). Baltimore: Paul H. Brookes.

Hasazi, S. B., Gordon, L. R., Roe, C. A., Hull, M., Finck, K., & Salembier, G. (1985). A statewide follow-up on post-high school employment and residential status of students labeled "mentally retarded." *Education and Training of the Mentally Retarded, 20*(6), 222–234.

Heber, R. F. (1959). A manual on terminology and classification in mental retardation. *American Journal of Mental Deficiency Monograph.*

Hetherington, E. M., & Parke, R. D. (1986). *Child psychology: A contemporary viewpoint* (3rd ed.). New York: McGraw-Hill.

Justice, E. M. (1985). Metamemory: An aspect of metacognition in the mentally retarded. In N. R. Ellis (Ed.), *International review of research in mental retardation,* Vol. 13 (pp. 79–107). New York: Academic Press.

Kamphaus, R. W. & Reynolds, C. R. (1987). Clinical and research applications of the K-ABC. Circle Pines, MN: American Guidance.

Kaufman, A. S., & Kaufman, N. L. (1983). *The Kaufman Assessment Battery for Children.* Circle Pines, MN: American Guidance Service.

Lagomarcino, T. R., Hughes, C., & Rusch, F. R. (1989). Utilizing self-management to teach independence on the job. *Education and Training of the Mentally Retarded, 24*(2), 139–148.

Lambert, N., & Windmiller, M. (1981). *AAMD Adaptive Behavior Scale—School Edition.* Washington, DC: American Association of Mental Deficiency.

Lazar, I., & Darlington, R. (1982). Lasting effects of early education: A report from the Consortium for Longitudinal Studies. *Monographs of the Society for Research in Child Development, 47*(2–3, Serial No. 195).

Leahy, R., Balla, D., & Zigler, E. (1982). Role taking, self-image, and imitation in retarded and non-retarded individuals. *American Journal of Mental Deficiency, 86,* 372–379.

Luftig, R. L. (1988). Assessment of the perceived school loneliness and isolation of mentally retarded and nonretarded students. *American Journal of Mental Retardation, 92*(5), 472–475.

MacMillan, D. L. (1982). *Mental retardation in school and society* (2nd ed.). Boston: Little, Brown.

MacMillan, D. L. (1988). Issues in mild mental retardation. *Education and Training in Mental Retardation, 23*(4), 273–284.

MacMillan, D. L., & Borthwick, S. (1980). The new educable mentally retarded population: Can they be mainstreamed? *Mental Retardation, 18,* 155–158.

McCall, R. B. (1983). Environmental effects on intelligence: The forgotten realm of discontinuous nonshared within family factors. *Child Development, 54,* 408–415.

McCall, R. B., Appelbaum, M. I., & Hogarty, P. S. (1973). Developmental changes in mental performance. *Monographs of the Society for Research in Child Development, 38,* (Ser. No. 150).

Martin, J. E., Mithaug, D. E., & Burger, D. L. (1990). Effects of visual cues upon the vocational task performance of students with mental retardation. *Exceptionality, 1*(1), 41–59.

Martin, J. E., Rusch, F. R., Tines, J. J., Brulle, A. R., & White, D. M. (1985). *Mental Retardation, 23*(3), 142–147.

McGue, M. (1989, August 17). Nature-nurture and intelligence. *Nature,* pp. 507–508.

Mercer, J. R. (1973). *Labelling the mentally retarded.* Berkeley: University of California Press.

Mercer, J. R., & Lewis, J. F. (1977). *Adaptive behavior inventory for children, parent interview manual: System of multicultural pluralistic assessment.* New York: The Psychological Corporation.

Oakland, T. (1979). Research on the adaptive behavior inventory for children and the estimated learning potential. *The School Psychology Digest, 8,* 63–70.

Patterson, D. (1987). The causes of Down syndrome. *Scientific American, 257*(2), 52–57, 60.

Patton, J. R., & Spears, J. L. (1986). Adult and community issues. In J. R. Patton, J. S. Payne, & M. Beirne-Smith (Eds.), *Mental retardation* (2nd ed.) (pp. 445–486). Columbus, OH: Chas. E. Merrill.

Plomin, R. (1989). Environment and genes: Determinants of behavior. *American Psychologist, 44*(2), 105–111.

Polloway, E. A. (1985). Identification and placement in mild retardation programs: Recommendations for professional practice. *Education and Training of the Mentally Retarded, 20,* 218–221.

President's Committee on Mental Retardation. (1970). *The six-hour retarded child.* Washington, DC: U.S. Government Printing Office, 1970.

Ramey, C. T., & Campbell, F. A. (1984). Preventive education for high-risk children: Cognitive consequences of the Carolina Abecedarian Project. *American Journal of Mental Deficiency, 88,* 515–523.

Robinson, N. M., & Robinson, H. B. (1976). *The mentally retarded child: A psychological approach* (2nd ed.). New York: McGraw-Hill.

Rowe, D. C., & Plomin, R. (1981). The importance of nonshared (E.) environment influences in behavioral development. *Developmental Psychology, 17,* 517–531.

Rubinstein, A. (1989). Background, epidemiology, and impact of HIV infection in children. *Mental Retardation, 27*(4), 209–211.

Rusch, F. R., & Hughes, C. (1988). Supported employment: Promoting employee independence. *Mental Retardation, 26*(6), 351–355.

Rusch, F. R., Martin, J. E., & White, D. M. (1985). Competitive employment: Teaching mentally retarded employees to maintain their work behavior. *Education and Training of the Mentally Retarded, 20*(3), 182–189.

Sailor, W., Halvorsen, A., Anderson, J., Goetz, L., Gee, K., Doering, K., & Hunt, P. (1986). Community intensive instruction. In R. H. Horner, L. H. Meyer, & H. D. Fredericks (Eds.), *Education of learners with severe handicaps: Exemplary service strategies* (pp. 251–288). Baltimore: Paul H. Brookes.

Salend, S. J., & Giek, K. A. (1988). Independent living arrangements for individuals with mental retardation: The landlords' perspective. *Mental Retardation, 26*(2), 89–92.

Salzberg, C. L., Lignugaris/Kraft, B., & McCuller, G. L. (1988). Reasons for job loss: A review of employment termination studies of mentally retarded workers. *Research in Developmental Disabilities, 9,* 153–170.

Schalock, R. L., & Harper, R. S. (1978). Replacement from community-based mental retardation programs: How well do clients do? *American Journal of Mental Deficiency, 83,* 240–247.

Schalock, R. L., Harper, R. S., & Carver, G. (1981). Independent living placement: Five years later. *American Journal of Mental Deficiency, 86,* 170–177.

Schalock, R. L., & Lilley, M. A. (1986). Placement from community-based mental retardation programs: How well do clients do after 8 to 10 years? *American Journal of Mental Deficiency, 90*(6), 669–676.

Schalock, R. L., McGaughey, M. J., & Kiernan, W. E. (1989). Placement into nonsheltered employment: Findings from national employment surveys. *American Journal of Mental Retardation, 94*(1), 80–87.

Schultz, E. E., Jr. (1983). Depth of processing by mentally retarded and MA-matched nonretarded individuals. *American Journal of Mental Deficiency, 88,* 307–313.

Schultz, F. R. (1984). Fetal alcohol syndrome. In J. A. Blackman (Ed.), *Mental aspects of developmental disabilities in children birth to three* (rev. 1st ed., pp. 109–110). Rockville, MD: Aspen Systems Corp.

Sitkei, E. G. (1980). After group home living—what alternatives? Results of a two year mobility follow-up study. *Mental Retardation, 18,* 9–13.

Skeels, H. M. (1966). Adult status of children with contrasting early life experiences. *Monographs of the Society for Research in Child Development, 31* (Ser. No. 105).

Skeels, H. M., & Dye, H. B. (1939). A study of the effects of differential stimulation on mentally retarded children. *Convention Proceedings,* American Association on Mental Deficiency, 44, 114–136.

Snell, M. E. (1988). Curriculum and methodology for individuals with severe disabilities. *Education and Training in Mental Retardation, 23*(4), 302–314.

Sternberg, R. J., & Spear, L. C. (1985). A triarchic theory of mental retardation. In N. R. Ellis (Ed.), *International review of research in mental retardation,* Vol. 13 (pp. 301–326). New York: Academic Press.

Stodden, R. A., & Browder, P. M. (1986). Community-based competitive employment preparation of developmentally disabled persons: A program description and evaluation. *Education and Training of the Mentally Retarded, 21,* 43–53.

Streissguth, A. P., Barr, H. M., & Martin, D. C. (1983). Maternal alcohol use and neonatal habituation assessed with the Brazelton Scale. *Child Development, 54*(5), 1109–1118.

U.S. Department of Education (1989). *Eleventh Annual Report to Congress on The Implementation of the Education of the Handicapped Act.* Washington, DC: U.S. Government Printing Office.

Walker, H. M., McConnell, S., Holmes, D., Todis, B., Walker, J., & Golden, N. (1983). *The Accepts Program.* Austin, TX: Pro-Ed.

Wehman, P., Hill, M., Hill, J. W., Brooke, V., Pendleton, P., & Britt, C. (1985). Competitive employment for persons with mental retardation: A follow-up six years later. *Mental Retardation, 23*(6), 274–281.

Wehman, P., Moon, M. S., Everson, J. M., Wood, W., & Barcus, J. M. (1988). *Transition from school to work: New challenges for youth with severe disabilities.* Baltimore: Paul H. Brookes.

Wheeler, J. J., Bates, P., Marshall, K. J., & Miller, S. R. (1988). Teaching appropriate social behaviors to a young man with moderate mental retardation in a supported competitive employment setting. *Education and Training in Mental Retardation, 23*(2), 105–116.

Wolery, M., Bailey, D. B., & Sugai, G. M. (1988). *Effective teaching: Principles and procedures of applied behavior analysis with exceptional students.* Boston: Allyn & Bacon.

Zeaman, D., & House, B. J. (1963). The role of attention in retardate discrimination learning. In N. R. Ellis (Ed.), *Handbook of mental deficiency.* New York: McGraw-Hill.

Zetlin, A. G., & Murtaugh, M. (1988). Friendship patterns of mildly handicapped and nonhandicapped high school students. *American Journal of Mental Retardation, 92*(5), 447–454.

Zetlin, A. G., Turner, J., & Winik, L. (1987). Socialization effects on the community adaptation of adults who have mild retardation. In S. Landesman & P. Vietze (Eds.), *Living environments and mental retardation* (pp. 293–313). Washington, DC: American Association on Mental Retardation.

Zigler, E., & Balla, D. (1982). Introduction: The developmental approach to mental retardation. In E. Zigler & D. Balla (Eds.), *Mental retardation: The developmental difference controversy* (pp. 3–8). Hillsdale, NJ: Erlbaum.

Chapter 4

American Psychiatric Association. (1987). *Diagnostic and statistical manual of mental disorders (DSM-III-R)* (3rd ed. rev.). Washington, DC: American Psychiatric Association.

Baker, L. (1982). An evaluation of the role of metacognitive deficits in learning disabilities. *Topics in Learning and Learning Disabilities*, *2*(1), 27–35.

Bateman, B. D. (1968). *Interpretations of the 1961 Illinois Test of Psycholinguistic Abilities.* Seattle: Special Child Publications.

Belmont, L., & Birch, H. G. (1965). Lateral dominance, lateral awareness, and reading disability. *Child Development*, *34*, 57–71.

Billingsley, B. S., & Wildman, T. M. (1988). The effects of prereading activities on the comprehension monitoring of learning disabled adolescents. *Learning Disabilities Research*, *4*(1), 36–44.

Boder, E. (1973). Developmental dyslexia: A diagnostic approach based on three atypical reading-spelling patterns. *Developmental Medicine and Child Neurology*, *15*, 663–687.

Borkowski, J. G., Estrada, M. T., Milstead, M., & Hale, C. A. (1989). General problem-solving skills: Relations between metacognition and strategic processing. *Learning Disability Quarterly*, *12*(1), 57–70.

Brown, A. L., & Campione, J. C. (1984). Three faces of transfer: Implications for early competence, individual differences, and instruction. In M. E. Lamb, A. L. Brown, & B. Rogoff (Eds.), *Advances in developmental psychology*, (Vol. 3, pp. 143–192). Hillsdale, NJ: Lawrence Erlbaum.

Bryan, J. H., & Perlmutter, B. (1979). Immediate impressions of learning disabled children by female adults. *Learning Disability Quarterly*, *2*, 80–88.

Bryan, J. H., Sonnefeld, J., & Greenberg, F. (1981). Children's and parent's views about integration tactics. *Learning Disability Quarterly*, *4*, 170–179.

Bryan, T. H. (1974). Peer popularity of learning disabled children. *Journal of Learning Disabilities*, *7*, 621–625.

Bryan, T. H., & Bryan, J. H. (1986). *Understanding learning disabilities.* Palo Alto, CA: Mayfield Publishing Company.

Bryan, T. H., Donahue, M., & Pearl, R. (1981). Learning disabled children's peer interactions during a small group problem solving task. *Learning Disability Quarterly*, *4*, 13–22.

Bryan, T. H., Donahue, M., Pearl, R., & Sturm, C. (1981). Learning disabled children's conversational skills—The "TV Talk Show." *Learning Disability Quarterly*, *4*(3), 250–260.

Bryan, T. H., Sherman, R., & Fisher, A. (1980). Learning disabled boy's nonverbal behaviors with a dyadic interview. *Learning Disability Quarterly*, *3*, 65–72.

Bryan, T., Werner, M. A., & Pearl, R. (1982). Learning disabled students' conformity responses to prosocial and antisocial situations. *Learning Disability Quarterly*, *5*, 344–352.

Carpenter, D., & Miller, L. J. (1982). Spelling ability of reading disabled LD students and able readers. *Learning Disability Quarterly*, *5*, 65–70.

Chapman, J. W. (1988). Learning-disabled children's self-concepts. *Review of Educational Research*, *58*(3), 347–371.

Clements, S. D. (1966). *Minimal brain dysfunction in children: Terminology and identification.* NINDB Monograph No. 3. Washington, DC: U.S. Department of Health, Education and Welfare.

Cravioto, J., & DeLicardie, E. R. (1975). Environmental and nutritional deprivation in children with learning disabilities. In W. M. Cruickshank & D. P. Hallahan (Eds.), *Perceptual and learning disabilities in children. Vol. 2: Research and Theory.* Syracuse, NY: Syracuse University Press.

Cruickshank, W. M., Bentzen, F. A., Ratzeburg, F. H., & Tannhauser, M. T. (1961). *A teaching method for brain-injured and hyperactive children.* Syracuse, NY: Syracuse University Press.

Cullinan, D., Epstein, M. H., & Lloyd, J. (1981). School behavior problems of learning disabled and normal girls and boys. *Learning Disability Quarterly*, *4*, 163–169.

Deci, E. L., & Chandler, C. L. (1986). The importance of motivation for the future of the LD field. *Journal of Learning Disabilities*, *19*(10), 587–594.

Deno, S. L. (1985). Curriculum-based measurement: The emerging alternative. *Exceptional Children*, *52*(3), 219–232.

Deshler, D. D., & Schumaker, J. B. (1986). Learning strategies: An instructional alternative for low-achieving adolescents. *Exceptional Children*, *52*(6), 583–590.

Ellis, E. S., Deshler, D. D., & Schumaker, J. B. (1989). Teaching adolescents with learning disabilities to generate and use task-specific strategies. *Journal of Learning Disabilities*, *22*(2), 108–119, 130.

Englemann, S. E. (1977). Sequencing cognitive and academic tasks. In R. D. Kneedler & S. G. Tarver (Eds.), *Changing perspectives in special education.* Columbus, OH: Chas. E. Merrill.

Engelmann, S., Carnine, L., Johnson, G., & Meyers, L. (1988). *Corrective reading: Decoding.* Chicago: Science Research Associates.

Engelmann, S., Carnine, L., Johnson, G., & Meyers, L. (1989). *Corrective reading: Comprehension.* Chicago: Science Research Associates.

Englert, C. S., Raphael, T. E., Anderson, L. M., Anthony, H. M., Fear, K. L., & Gregg, S. L. (1988). A case for writing intervention: Strategies for writing informational text. *Learning Disabilities Focus*, *3*(2), 98–113.

Epstein, M. H., Cullinan, D., & Lloyd, J. W. (1986). Behavior-problem patterns among the learning disabled: III—Replication across age and sex. *Learning Disability Quarterly*, *9*(1), 43–54.

Federal Register (1977, December 29). Procedures for evaluating specific learning disabilities. Washington, DC: Department of Health, Education and Welfare.

Fernald, G. M. (1943). *Remedial techniques in basic school subjects.* New York: McGraw-Hill.

Finucci, J., and Childs, B. (1983). Dyslexia: Family studies. In C. Ludlow & G. Cooper (Eds.), *Genetic aspects of speech and language disorders.* New York: Academic Press.

Foorman, B. R., & Liberman, D. (1989). Visual and phonological processing of words: A comparison of good and poor readers. *Journal of Learning Disabilities*, *22*(6), 349–355.

Frostig, M., & Horne, D. (1964). *The Frostig program for the development of visual perception. Teacher's guide.* Chicago: Follett.

Frostig, M., Lefever, D. W., & Whittlesey, J. R. B. (1964). *The Marianne Frostig developmental test of visual perception.* Palo Alto, CA: Consulting Psychology Press.

Fuchs, L. S. (1986). Monitoring progress among mildly handicapped pupils: Review of current practice and research. *Remedial and Special Education*, *7*(5), 5–12.

Fuchs, L., Deno, S. L., & Mirkin, P. K. (1984). The effects of frequent curriculum-based measurement and evaluation of pedagogy, student achievement and student awareness of learning. *American Educational Research Journal*, *24*(2), 449–460.

Fuchs, L. S., & Fuchs, D. (1986). Effects of systematic formative evaluation: A meta-analysis. *Exceptional Children*, *53*(3), 199–208.

Fuchs, L. S., Fuchs, D., & Strecker, P. M. (1989). Effects of curriculum-based measurement on teachers' instructional planning. *Journal of Learning Disabilities*, *22*(1), 51–59.

Gadow, K. D., Torgesen, J. K., Greenstein, J., & Schell, R. (1986). Learning disabilities. In M. Hersen (Ed.), *Pharmacological and be-*

bavioral treatment: An integrative approach (pp. 149–177). New York: John Wiley.

Gajar, A. H. (1989). A computer analysis of written language variables and a comparison of compositions written by university students with and without learning disabilities. *Journal of Learning Disabilities, 22*(2), 125–130.

General Accounting Office. (1981). Disparities still exist in who gets special education. Report to the Chairman, Subcommittee on Select Education, Committee on Education and Labor, House of Representatives of the United States. Gaithersburg, Md.: GAO.

Gerber, M. M., & Hall, R. J. (1981). Development of spelling in learning disabled and normally-achieving children. Unpublished manuscript, University of Virginia Learning Disabilities Research Institute, Charlottesville.

Germann, G., & Tindal, G. (1985). An application of curriculum-based assessment: The use of direct and repeated measurement. *Exceptional Children, 52*(3), 244–265.

Getman, G. N., Kane, E. R., & McKee, G. W. (1968). *Developing learning readiness programs.* Manchester, MO: McGraw-Hill.

Gillingham, A., & Stillman, B. (1956). *Remedial training for children with special disability in reading, spelling, and penmanship.* Cambridge, MA: Educators Publishing Service.

Gottlieb, B. W., Gottlieb, J., Berkell, D., & Levy, L. (1986). Sociometric status and solitary play of LD boys and girls. *Journal of Learning Disabilities, 19*(10), 619–622.

Gresham, F. M., & Reschly, D. J. (1986). Social skill deficits and low peer acceptance of mainstreamed learning disabled children. *Learning Disability Quarterly, 9*(1), 23–32.

Griffey, Q. L., Zigmond, N., & Leinhardt, G. (1988). The effects of self-questioning and story structure training on the reading comprehension of poor readers. *Learning Disabilities Research, 4*(1), 45–51.

Hallahan, D. P. (1975). Comparative research studies on the psychological characteristics of learning disabled children. In W. M. Cruickshank & D. P. Hallahan (Eds.), *Perceptual and learning disabilities in children. Vol. 1: Psychoeducational practices.* Syracuse, NY: Syracuse University Press.

Hallahan, D. P., & Bryan, T. H. (1981). Learning disabilities. In J. M. Kauffman & D. P. Hallahan (Eds.), *Handbook of special education.* Englewood Cliffs, NJ: Prentice Hall.

Hallahan, D. P., & Cruickshank, W. M. (1973). *Psychoeducational foundations of learning disabilities.* Englewood Cliffs, NJ: Prentice Hall.

Hallahan, D. P., Gajar, A. H., Cohen, S. B., & Tarver, S. G. (1978). Selective attention and locus of control in learning disabled and normal children. *Journal of Learning Disabilities, 4*, 47–52.

Hallahan, D. P., & Kauffman, J. M. (1975). Research on the education of distractible and hyperactive children. In W. M. Cruickshank & D. P. Hallahan (Eds.), *Perceptual and learning disabilities in children. Vol. 2: Research and theory.* Syracuse, NY: Syracuse University Press.

Hallahan, D. P., & Kauffman, J. M. (1977). Labels, categories, behaviors: ED, LD, and EMR reconsidered. *The Journal of Special Education, 11*, 139–149.

Hallahan, D. P., Kauffman, J. M., & Ball, D. W. (1973). Selective attention and cognitive tempo of low achieving and high achieving sixth grade males. *Perceptual and Motor Skills, 36*, 579–583.

Hallahan, D. P., Kauffman, J. M., & Lloyd, J. W. (1985). *Introduction to learning disabilities.* Englewood Cliffs, NJ: Prentice Hall.

Hallahan, D. P., Kneedler, R. D., & Lloyd, J. W. (1983). Cognitive behavior modification techniques for learning disabled children: Self-instruction and self-monitoring. In J. D. McKinney & L. Feagans (Eds.), *Current topics in learning disabilities,* Vol 1. Norwood, NJ: Ablex.

Hallahan, D. P., Lloyd, J. W., Kauffman, J. M., & Loper, A. B. (1983). Academic problems. In R. J. Morris & T. R. Kratochwill (Eds.),

Practice of child therapy: A textbook of methods (pp. 113–141). New York: Pergamon Press.

Hallahan, D. P., Lloyd, J., Kosiewicz, M. M., Kauffman, J. M., & Graves, A. W. (1979). Self-monitoring of attention as a treatment for a learning disabled boy's off-task behavior. *Learning Disability Quarterly, 2*, 24–32.

Hallahan, D. P., Lloyd, J. W., & Stoller, L. (1982). *Improving attention with self-monitoring: A manual for teachers.* Charlottesville: University of Virginia Learning Disabilities Research Institute.

Hallahan, D. P., & Reeve, R. E. (1980). Selective attention and distractibility. In B. K. Keogh (Ed.), *Advances in special education. Vol. 1: Basic constructs and theoretical orientations.* Greenwich, CO: J.A.I. Press.

Hallgren, B. (1950). Specific dyslexia (congenital word blindness: A clinical and genetic study). *Acta Psychiatrica er Neurologica, 65,* 1–279.

Hammill, D. D. (1990). On defining learning disabilities: An emerging consensus. *Journal of Learning Disabilities.*

Hammill, D. D., & Larsen, S. (1974). The effectiveness of psycholinguistic training. *Exceptional Children, 41,* 5–15.

Hammill, D. D., Leigh, J. E., McNutt, G., & Larsen, S. C. (1981). A new definition of learning disabilities. *Learning Disability Quarterly, 4,* 336–342.

Heins, E. D., Hallahan, D. P., Tarver, S. G., & Kauffman, J. M. (1976). Relationship between cognitive tempo and selective attention in learning disabled children. *Perceptual and Motor Skills, 42,* 233–234.

Henker, B., & Whalen, C. K. (1980). The changing faces of hyperactivity: Retrospect and prospect. In C. K. Whalen & B. Henker (Eds.), *Hyperactive children: The social ecology of identification and treatment.* New York: Academic Press.

Henker, B., & Whalen, C. K. (1989). Hyperactivity and attention deficits. *American Psychologist, 44*(2), 216–223.

Hetherington, E. M., & Parke, R. D. (1986). *Child psychology: A contemporary viewpoint* (3rd ed). New York: McGraw-Hill.

Hewett, F. M., with Forness, S. R. (1974). *Education of exceptional learners.* Boston: Allyn & Bacon.

Horowitz, E. C. (1981). Popularity, decentering ability and role-taking skills in learning disabled and normal children. *Learning Disability Quarterly, 4,* 23–30.

Hynd, G. W., & Semrud-Clikeman, M. (1989). Dyslexia and neurodelopmental pathology: Relationships to cognition, intelligence, and reading acquisition. *Journal of Learning Disabilities, 22*(4), 204–216, 220.

Ingram, T. T. S. (1969). Developmental disorders of speech. In P. J. Vinken & G. W. Bruyn (Eds.), *Handbook of clinical neurology* (Vol. 4). Amsterdam: North Holland.

John, E. R., Prichep, L. S., Ahn, H., Kaye, H., Brown, D., Easton, P., Karmel, B. Z., Toro, A., & Thatcher, R. (1989). *Neurometric evaluation of brain function in normal and learning disabled children.* Ann Arbor: University of Michigan Press.

Johnson, D. J., & Myklebust, H. (1967). *Learning disabilities: Educational principles and practices.* Orlando, FL: Grune & Stratton.

Kauffman, J. M. (1975). Behavior modification. In W. M. Cruickshank & D. P. Hallahan (Eds.), *Perceptual and learning disabilities in children. Vol. 2: Research and theory.* Syracuse, NY: Syracuse University Press.

Kauffman, J. M., & Hallahan, D. P. (1979). Learning disability and hyperactivity (with comments on minimal brain dysfunction). In B. B. Lahey & A. E. Kazdin (Eds.), *Advances in clinical child psychology, Vol. 2.* New York: Plenum.

Kavale, K. A. (1988). The long-term consequences of learning disabilities. In M. C. Wang, M. C. Reynolds, & H. J. Walberg (Eds.), *Handbook of special education: Research and practice. Vol. 2: Mildly handicapped conditions.* New York: Pergamon Press.

Keilitz, I., & Dunivant, N. (1986). The relationship between learning disability and juvenile delinquency: Current state of knowledge. *Remedial and Special Education*, 7(3), 18–26.

Keogh, B. K., & Glover, A. T. (1980, November). Research needs in the study of early identification of children with learning disabilities. *Thalamus* (Newsletter of the International Academy for Research in Learning Disabilities).

Kephart, N. C. (1971, 1975). *The slow learner in the classroom* (2nd ed.) Columbus, OH: Chas. E. Merrill.

Kephart, N. C. (1975). The perceptual-motor match. In W. M. Cruickshank & D. P. Hallahan (Eds.), *Perceptual and learning disabilities in children. Vol. 1: Psychoeducational practices*. Syracuse, NY: Syracuse University Press.

Kinsbourne, M., & Warrington, E. K. (1963). Developmental factors in reading and writing backwardness. *British Journal of Psychology*, 54, 145–156.

Kirk, S. A., & Kirk, W. D. (1971). *Psycholinguistic learning disabilities: Diagnosis and remediation*. Urbana: University of Illinois Press.

Kirk, S. A., McCarthy, J. J., & Kirk, W. D. (1961, 1968). *Illinois test of Psycholinguistic abilities*. Urbana: University of Illinois Press.

Kneedler, R. D. (1980). The use of cognitive training to change social behaviors. *Exceptional Education Quarterly*, 1, 65–73.

Kneedler, R. D., & Hallahan, D. P. (1984). Self-monitoring as an attentional strategy for academic tasks with learning disabled children. In B. Gholson & T. Rosenthal (Eds.), *Applications of cognitive development theory*. New York: Academic Press.

Kosiewicz, M. M., Hallahan, D. P., Lloyd, J. W., & Graves, A. W. (1982). Effects of self-instruction and self-correction procedures on handwriting performance. *Learning Disability Quarterly*, 5, 71–78.

Liscio, M. (1986). *A guide to colleges for learning-disabled students*. Orland, FL: Academic Press.

Lloyd, J. W. (1988). Direct academic interventions in learning disabilities. In M. C. Wang, M. C. Reynolds, & H. J. Walberg (Eds.), *Handbook of special education: Research and practice. Vol. 2: Mildly handicapped conditions*. New York: Pergamon Press.

Lloyd, J., Hallahan, D. P., Kosiewicz, M. M., & Kneedler, R. D. (1980). *Self-assessment versus self-recording: Two comparisons of reactive effects on attention to task and academic productivity*. Charlottesville: University of Virginia Learning Disabilities Research Institute, Technical Report No. 29.

Lovejoy's four-year college guide for learning disabled students. (1985). New York: Simon & Schuster.

Lovitt, T. C. (1975a). Applied behavior analysis and learning disabilities—Part I: Characteristics of ABA, general recommendations, and methodological limitations. *Journal of Learning Disabilities*, 8, 432–443.

Lovitt, T. C. (1975b). Applied behavior analysis and learning disabilities—Part II: Specific research recommendations and suggestions for practitioners. *Journal of Learning Disabilities*, 8, 504–518.

Lovitt, T. C. (1977). *In spite of my resistance . . . I've learned from children*. Columbus, OH: Chas. E. Merrill.

Lynch, E. M., & Jones, S. D. (1989). Process and product: A review of the research on LD children's writing skills. *Learning Disability Quarterly*, 12(2), 74–86.

Mann, V. A., Cowin, E., & Schoenheimer, J. (1989). Phonological processing, language comprehension, and reading ability. *Journal of Learning Disabilities*, 22(2), 76–89.

Marston, D., & Magnusson, D. (1985). Implementing curriculum-based measurement in special and regular education settings. *Exceptional Children*, 52(3), 266–276.

Mastropieri, M. A., & Scruggs, T. E. (1988). Increasing content area learning of learning disabled students: Research implementation. *Learning Disabilities Research*, 4(1), 17–25.

Mastropieri, M. A., Scruggs, T. E., & Fulk, B. (in press). Teaching abstract and concrete vocabulary with the keyword method: Effects on recall and comprehension. *Journal of Learning Disabilities*.

Mathinos, D. A. (1988). Communicative competence of children with

learning disabilities. *Journal of Learning Disabilities*, 21(7), 437–443.

McConaughy, S. H., & Ritter, D. R. (1986). Social competence and behavioral problems of learning disabled boys. *Journal of Learning Disabilities*, 19(1), 39–45.

McGuire, J. M., & Shaw, S. F. (1987). A decision-making process for the college-bound student: Matching learner, institution, and support program. *Learning Disability Quarterly*, 10, 106–111.

McKinney, J. D. (1987a). Research on conceptually and empirically derived subtypes of specific learning disabilities. In M. C. Wang, M. C. Reynolds, & H. J. Walberg (Eds.), *Handbook of special education: Research and practice*. New York: Pergamon Press.

McKinney, J. D. (1987b). Research on the identification of LD children: Perspectives on changes in educational policy. In S. Vaughn & C. Bos, *Future directions and issues in research for the learning disabled*. San Diego, CA: College-Hill Press.

McKinney, J. D. (1989). Longitudinal research on the behavioral characteristics of children with learning disabilities. *Journal of Learning Disabilities*, 22(3), 141–150, 165.

McKinney, J. D., & Feagans, L. (1984). Academic and behavioral characteristics: Longitudinal studies of learning disabled children and average achievers. *Learning Disability Quarterly*, 7, 251–265.

McKinney, J. D., Short, E. J., & Feagans, L. (1985). Academic consequences of perceptual-linguistic subtypes of learning disabled children. *Learning Disabilities Research*, 1(1), 6–17.

McKinney, J. D., & Speece, D. L. (1986). Academic consequences and longitudinal stability of behavioral subtypes of learning disabled children. *Journal of Educational Psychology*, 78(5), 365–272.

McLeod, T. M., & Armstrong, S. W. (1982). Learning disabilities in mathematics—skill deficits and remedial approaches at the intermediate and secondary level. *Learning Disability Quarterly*, 5, 305–311.

Meichenbaum, D. H. (1975, June). Cognitive factors as determinants of learning disabilities: A cognitive-functional approach. Paper presented at the NATO Conference on The Neuropsychology of Learning Disorders: Theoretical Approaches, Korsor, Denmark.

Meichenbaum, D. H., & Goodman, J. (1971). Training impulsive children to talk to themselves: A means of developing self-control. *Journal of Abnormal Psychology*, 77, 115–126.

Mercer, C. D., Algozzine, B., & Trifiletti, J. (1979). Early identification—An analysis of the research. *Learning Disability Quarterly*, 2, 12–24.

Minskoff, E. H., Wiseman, D. E., & Minskoff, J. G. (1974). *The MWM Program for Developing Language Abilities*. Ridgefield, NJ: Educational Performance Associates.

Morris, N. T., & Crump, W. D. (1982). Syntactic and vocabulary development in the written language of learning disabled and non-learning disabled students at four age levels. *Learning Disability Quarterly*, 5, 163–172.

Murphy, D. M. (1986). The prevalence of handicapping conditions among juvenile delinquents. *Remedial and Special Education*, 7(3), 7–17.

Olson, R., Wise, B., Conners, F., Rack, J., & Fulker, D. (1989). Specific deficits in component reading and language skills: Genetic and environmental influences. *Journal of Learning Disabilities*, 22(6), 339–348.

Orton, S. (1937). *Reading, writing and speech problems in children*. New York: W. W. Norton & Co.

Owen, F. W., Adams, P. A., Forrest, T., Stolz, L. M., & Fisher, S. (1971). Learning disorders in children: Sibling studies. *Monographs of the Society for Research in Child Development*, 36 (4, Ser. No. 144).

Palincsar, A. S. (1986). Metacognitive strategy instruction. *Exceptional Children*, 53(2), 118–124.

Pearl, R., Bryan, T., & Donahue, M. (1980). Learning disabled children's attributions for success and failure. *Learning Disability Quarterly*, 3, 3–9.

Pearl, R., & Cosden, M. (1982). Sizing up a situation: LD children's understanding of social interactions. *Learning Disability Quarterly*, 4, 371–373.

Pelham, W. E. (1983). The effects of psychostimulants on academic achievement in hyperactive and learning-disabled children. *Thalamus* (Newsletter of the International Academy for Research in Learning Disabilities), 3(1), 2–48.

Pelham, W. E., & Murphy, H. A. (1986). Attention deficit and conduct disorders. In M. Hersen (Ed.), *Pharmacological and behavioral treatment: An integrative approach* (pp. 108–148). New York: John Wiley.

Peter, L. J. (1965). *Prescriptive teaching.* New York: McGraw-Hill.

Pressley, M., Symons, S., Snyder, B. L., & Cariglia-Bull, T. (1989). Strategy instruction comes of age. *Learning Disability Quarterly*, 12(1), 16–30.

Rivera, D., & Smith, D. D. (1988). Using a demonstration strategy to teach midschool students with learning disabilities how to compute long division. *Journal of Learning Disabilities*, 21(2), 77–81.

Robinson, F. P. (1946). *Effective study.* New York: Harper & Row.

Schumaker, J. B., Deshler, D. D., Alley, G. R., Warner, M. M., & Denton, P. H. (1982). Multipass: A learning strategy for improving reading comprehension. *Learning Disability Quarterly*, 5(3), 295–304.

Schunk, D. H. (1989). Self-efficacy and cognitive achievement: Implications for students with learning problems. *Journal of Learning Disabilities*, 22(1), 14–22.

Seligman, M. E. (1975). *Helplessness: On depression, developmental, and death.* San Francisco: W. H. Freeman.

Shaywitz, S. E., & Shaw, R. (1988). The admissions process: An approach to selecting learning disabled students at the most selective colleges. *Learning Disabilities Focus*, 3(2), 81–86.

Shaywitz, S. E., & Shaywitz, B. A. (1987). Attention deficit disorder: Current perspectives. Paper presented at National Conference on Learning Disabilities, Bethesda, MD: National Institutes of Child Health and Human Development (NIH).

Short, E. J., & Weissberg-Benchell, J. (1989). The triple alliance for learning: Cognition, metacognition, and motivation. In C. B. McCormick, G. E. Miller, & M. Pressley (Eds.), *Cognitive strategy research: From basic research to educational applications* (pp. 33–63). New York: Springer-Verlag.

Siperstein, G. N. (1988). Students with learning disabilities in college: The need for a programmatic approach to critical transitions. *Journal of Learning Disabilities*, 21(7), 431–436.

Speece, D. L., McKinney, J. D., & Appelbaum, M. I. (1985). Classification and validation of behavioral subtypes of learning-disabled children. *Journal of Educational Psychology*, 77(1), 67–77.

Sroufe, L. A. (1975). Drug treatment of children with behavior problems. In F. D. Horowitz (Ed.), *Review of child development research* (Vol. 4, pp. 347–407). Chicago: University of Chicago Press.

Strauss, A. A., & Kephart, N. C. (1955). *Psychopathology and education of the brain-injured child. Vol. II. Progress in theory and clinic.* New York: Grune & Stratton.

Strauss, A. A., & Lehtinen, L. E. (1947). *Psychopathology and education of the brain-injured child.* New York: Grune & Stratton.

Swanson, H. L. (Ed.). (1987). *Memory and learning disabilities: Advances in learning and behavioral disabilities.* Greenwich, CT: J.A.I. Press.

Swanson, H. L. (1989). Strategy instruction: Overview of principles and procedures for effective use. *Learning Disability Quarterly*, 12(1), 3–14.

Symons, S., Snyder, B. L., Cariglia-Bull, T., & Pressley, M. (1989). Why be optimistic about cognitive strategy instruction? In C. B. McCormick, G. E. Miller, & M. Pressley (Eds.), *Cognitive strategy research: From basic research to educational applications.* New York: Springer-Verlag.

Thomas, C. C., Englert, C. S., & Gregg, S. (1987). An analysis of errors and strategies in the expository writing of learning-disabled students. *Remedial and Special Education*, 8(1), 21–30, 46.

Torgesen, J. K. (1977). The role of nonspecific factors in the task performance of learning disabled children: A theoretical assessment. *Journal of Learning Disabilities*, 10, 27–34.

Torgesen, J. K. (1988). Studies of children with learning disabilities who perform poorly on memory span tasks. *Journal of Learning Disabilities*, 21(10), 605–612.

Torgesen, J. K., & Kail, R. V. (1980). Memory processes in exceptional children. In B. K. Keogh (Ed.), *Advances in special education. Vol. 1: Basic constructs and theoretical orientations.* Greenwich, CT: J.A.I. Press.

U.S. Department of Education (1989). *Eleventh annual report to Congress on the implementation of The Education of the Handicapped Act.* Washington, DC: U.S. Government Printing Office.

Vellutino, F. R. (1987). Dyslexia. *Scientific American. 256*(3), 34–41.

Vogel, S. A. (1977). Morphological ability in normal and dyslexic children. *Journal of Learning Disabilities*, 10, 41–49.

Vogel, S. (1987). Issues and concerns in LD college programming. In D. Johnson & J. Blalock (Eds.), *Adults with learning disabilities* (pp. 239–275). New York: Grune & Stratton.

Weiss, E. (1984). Learning disabled children's understanding of social interactions of peers. *Journal of Learning Disabilities*, 17, 612–615.

Werner, H., & Strauss, A. A. (1941). Pathology of figure-background relation in the child. *Journal of Abnormal and Social Psychology*, 36, 236–248.

Whalen, C. K., & Henker, B. (1980). The social ecology of psychostimulant treatment: A model for conceptual and empirical analysis. In C. K. Whalen & B. Henker (Eds.), *Hyperactive children: The social ecology of identification and treatment.* New York: Academic Press.

White, O., & Haring, N. (1980). *Exceptional teaching.* Columbus, OH: Chas. E. Merrill.

Wiig, E. H., Semel, E. M., & Abele, E. (1981). Perception of ambiguous sentences by learning disabled twelve-year-olds. *Learning Disability Quarterly*, 4, 3–12.

Wong, B. Y. L. (1979). Increasing retention of main ideas through questioning strategies. *Learning Disability Quarterly*, 2, 42–47.

Wong, B. Y. L., & Wong, R. (1980). Role-taking skills in normal achieving and learning disabled children. *Learning Disability Quarterly*, 3, 11–18.

Zigmond, N., & Sansone, J. (1986). Designing a program for the learning disabled adolescent. *Remedial and Special Education*, 7(5), 13–17.

Chapter 5

Achenbach, T. M. (1985). *Assessment and taxonomy of child and adolescent psychopathology.* Beverly Hills, CA: Sage Publications.

Bandura, A. (1973). *Aggression: A social learning analysis.* Englewood Cliffs, NJ: Prentice Hall.

Baumeister, A. A., Kupstas, F., & Klindworth, L. M. (1990). New morbidity: Implications for prevention of children's disabilities. *Exceptionality*, 1(1), 1–16.

Becker, W. C. (1964). Consequences of different kinds of parental discipline. In M. L. Hoffman & L. W. Hoffman (Eds.), *Review of child development research* (Vol. 1). New York: Russell Sage Foundation.

Bower, B. (1989). Remodeling the autistic child. *Science News, 136*, 312–313.

Bower, E. M. (1981). *Early identification of emotionally handicapped children in school* (3rd ed.). Springfield, IL: Chas. C Thomas.

Bower, E. M. (1982). Defining emotional disturbance: Public policy and research. *Psychology in the Schools*, 19, 55–60.

Chivian, E., Mack, J. E., Waletzky, J. P., Lazaroff, C., Doctor, R., & Goldenring, J. M. (1985). Soviet children and the threat of nuclear war: A preliminary study. *American Journal of Orthopsychiatry*, 55, 484–502.

Cline, D. (in press). Interpretations of emotional disturbance and social maladjustment as policy problems: A legal analysis of initiatives to exclude handicapped/disruptive students from special education. *Behavioral Disorders.*

Drabman, R. S., & Patterson, J. N. (1981). Disruptive behavior and the social standing of exceptional children. *Exceptional Education Quarterly, 1,* 45–55.

Durand, V. M., & Carr, E. G. (1988). Autism. In V. B. Van Hasselt, P. S. Strain, & M. Hersen (Eds.), *Handbook of developmental and physical disabilities.* New York: Pergamon Press.

Edelbrock, C. S., & Achenbach, T. M. (1984). The teacher version of the Child Behavior Profile: I. Boys aged 6–11. *Journal of Consulting and Clinical Psychology, 52,* 207–217.

Edgar, E. B. (1987). Secondary programs in special education: Are many of them justifiable? *Exceptional Children, 53,* 555–561.

Forness, S. R. (1988). School characteristics of children and adolescents with depression. In R. B. Rutherford, C. M. Nelson, & S. R. Forness (Eds.), *Bases of severe behavioral disorders of children and youth.* Boston: Little, Brown.

Fuchs, D., Fuchs, L. S., Fernstrom, P., & Hohn, M. (in press). Achieving responsible reintegration of behaviorally disordered students. *Behavioral Disorders.*

Garmezy, N. (1987). Stress, competence, and development: Continuities in the study of schizophrenic adults, children vulnerable to psychopathology, and the search for stress-resistant children. *American Journal of Orthopsychiatry, 57,* 159–174.

Goldstein, A. P. (1983). United States: Causes, controls, and alternatives to aggression. In A. P. Goldstein & M. H. Segall (Eds.), *Aggression in global perspective.* New York: Pergamon Press.

Grosenick, J. K. & Huntze, S. L. (1983). *More questions than answers: Review and analysis of programs for behaviorally disordered children and youth.* Columbia: Department of Special Education. University of Missouri.

Guetzloe, E. (1987). *Suicide and depression, the adolescent epidemic: Education's responsibility* (rev. ed.). Orlando, FL: Advantage Consultants.

Harris, K. R., Wong, B. Y. L., & Keogh, B. K. (Eds.). (1985). Cognitive-behavior modification with children: A critical review of the state-of-the-art. *Journal of Abnormal Child Psychology, 13,* special issue.

Hawton, K. (1986). *Suicide and attempted suicide among children and adolescents.* Newbury Park, CA: Sage Publications.

Henggeler, S. W. (1989). *Delinquency in adolescence.* Newbury Park, CA: Sage.

Hewett, F. M. (1968). *The emotionally disturbed child in the classroom.* Boston: Allyn & Bacon.

Hobbs, N. (1975). *The futures of children.* San Francisco: Jossey-Bass.

Huntze, S. (1985). A position paper of the Council for Children with Behavioral Disorders. *Behavioral Disorders, 10,* 167–174.

Institute of Medicine. (1989). *Research on children and adolescents with mental, behavioral, and developmental disorders.* Washington, DC: National Academy Press.

Kauffman, J. M. (1989). *Characteristics of children's behavior disorders* (4th ed.). Columbus, OH: Chas. E. Merrill.

Kazdin, A. E. (1987). *Conduct disorders in childhood and adolescence.* Beverly Hills, CA: Sage Publications.

Kazdin, A. E. (1989). Developmental psychopathology: Current research, issues, and directions. *American Psychologist, 44,* 180–187.

Kerr, M. M., & Nelson, C. M. (1989). *Strategies for managing behavior problems in the classroom* (2nd ed.). Columbus, OH: Ch. E. Merrill.

Kerr, M. M., Nelson, C. M., & Lambert, D. L. (1987). *Helping adolescents with learning and behavior problems.* Columbus, OH: Chas. E. Merrill.

Klein, R. G., & Last, C. G. (1989). *Anxiety disorders in children.* Newbury Park, CA: Sage Publications.

Knitzer, J. (1982). *Unclaimed children: The failure of public responsibility to children and adolescents in need of mental health services.* Washington, DC: Children's Defense Fund.

Koegel, R. L., Rincover, A., & Egel, A. L. (1982). *Educating and understanding autistic children.* San Diego: College Hill Press.

Kovacs, M. (1989). Affective disorders in children and adolescents. *American Psychologist, 44,* 209–215.

Leone, P. E., Price, T., & Vitolo, R. K. (1986). Appropriate education for all incarcerated youth: Meeting the spirit of P. L. 94–142 in youth detention facilities. *Remedial and Special Education, 7(4),* 9–14.

Lloyd, J. W., Kauffman, J. M., & Kupersmidt, J. B. (1990). Integration of students with behavior disorders in regular education environments. In K. Gadow (Ed.), *Advances in learning and behavioral disorders,* Vol. 6. Greenwich, CT: JAI Press.

Lovaas, O. I. (1987). Behavioral treatment and normal educational and intellectual functioning in young autistic children. *Journal of Consulting and Clinical Psychology, 55,* 3–9.

Lozoff, B. (1989). Nutrition and behavior. *American Psychologist, 44,* 231–236.

Lyman, R. D. (1984). The effect of private and public goal setting on classroom on-task behavior of emotionally disturbed children. *Behavior Therapy, 15,* 395–402.

Maslow, A. (1962). *Toward a psychology of being.* New York: D. Van Nostrand.

McDowell, R. L., Adamson, G. W., & Wood, F. H. (Eds.). (1982). *Teaching emotionally disturbed children.* Boston: Little, Brown.

Meichenbaum, D. (1977). *Cognitive-behavior modification: An integrative approach.* New York: Plenum.

Morse, W. C. (1985). *The education and treatment of socio-emotionally impaired children and youth.* Syracuse, NY: Syracuse University Press.

Murphy, D. M. (1986). The prevalence of handicapping conditions among juvenile delinquents. *Remedial and Special Education, 7(3),* 7–17.

National Mental Health Association. (1986). *Severely emotionally disturbed children: Improving services under the Education of the Handicapped Act (P.L. 94–142).* Washington, DC.

Neel, R. S., Meadows, N., Levine, P., & Edgar, E. B. (1988). What happens after special education: A statewide follow-up study of secondary students who have behavioral disorders. *Behavioral Disorders, 13,* 209–216.

Nelson, C. M., & Kauffman, J. M. (1977). Educational programming for secondary school age delinquent and maladjusted pupils. *Behavior Disorders, 2,* 102–113.

Nelson, C. M., & Rutherford, R. B. (in press). Troubled youth in the public schools: Emotionally disturbed or socially maladjusted? In P. Leone (Ed.), *Troubled and troubling youth: Multidisciplinary perspectives.* Newbury Park, CA: Sage Publications.

Nelson, C. M., Rutherford, R. B., & Wolford, B. I. (Eds.). (1987). *Special education in the criminal justice system.* Columbus, OH: Chas. E. Merrill.

Newcomb, M. D., & Bentler, P. M. (1989). Substance use and abuse among children and teenagers. *American Psychologist, 44,* 242–248.

Patterson, C. J., Kupersmidt, J. B., & Griesler, P. C. (1989). Self-concepts of children in regular education and in special education classes. Unpublished manuscript, Virginia Behavior Disorders Project, University of Virginia.

Patterson, G. R., DeBaryshe, B. D., & Ramsey, E. (1989). A developmental perspective on antisocial behavior. *American Psychologist, 44,* 329–335.

Petty, L. K., Ornitz, E. M., Michelman, J. D., & Zimmerman, E. G. (1984). Autistic children who become schizophrenic. *Archives of General Psychiatry, 41,* 129–135.

Plomin, R. (1989). Environment and genes: Determinants of behavior. *American Psychologist, 44,* 105–111.

Prior, M., & Werry, J. S. (1986). Autism, schizophrenia, and allied disorders. In H. C. Quay & J. S. Werry (Eds.), *Psychopathological disorders of childhood* (3rd ed.). New York: John Wiley.

Quay, H. C. (1981). Classification. In H. C. Quay & J. S. Werry (Eds.), *Psychopathological disorders of childhood (3rd ed.)*. New York: Wiley.

Quay, H. C., & Peterson, D. R. (1987). *Manual for the Revised Behavior Problem Checklist*. Coral Gables, FL.

Rogers, C. (1969). *Freedom to learn*. Columbus, OH: Chas. E. Merrill.

Rogoff, B., & Morelli, G. (1989). Perspectives on children's development from cultural psychology. *American Psychologist, 44*, 343–348.

Rutter, M. (1985). Family and school influences on behavioral development. *Journal of Child Psychology and Psychiatry, 26*, 349–368.

Rutter, M., & Schopler, E. (1987). Autism and pervasive developmental disorders: Concepts and diagnostic issues. *Journal of Autism and Developmental Disorders, 17*, 159–186.

Sameroff, A. J., Seifer, R., Zax, M. (1982). Early development of children at risk for emotional disorder. *Monographs of the Society for Research in Child Development, 47* (Ser. No. 199).

Sherburne, S., Utley, B., McConnell, S., & Gannon, J. (1988). Decreasing violent or aggressive theme play among preschool children with behavior disorders. *Exceptional Children, 55*, 166–172.

Sprafkin, J., Gadow, K. D., & Dussault, M. (1986). Reality perceptions of television: A preliminary comparison of emotionally disturbed and nonhandicapped children. *American Journal of Orthopsychiatry, 56*, 147–152.

Strain, P. S., & Fox, J. E. (1981). Peers as behavior change agents for withdrawn classmates. In A. E. Kazdin & B. B. Lahey (Eds.), *Advances in clinical child psychology* (Vol. 4, pp. 167–198). New York: Plenum.

Strain, P. S., Steele, P., Ellis, T., & Timm, M. (1982). Long-term effects of oppositional child treatment with mothers as therapists and therapist trainers. *Journal of Applied Behavior Analysis, 15*, 163–169.

Thomas, A., & Chess, S. (1984). Genesis and evolution of behavioral disorders: From infancy to early adult life. *American Journal of Psychiatry, 141*, 1–9.

Walker, H. M., Severson, H., Stiller, B., Williams, G., Haring, N., Shinn, M., & Todis, B. (1988). Systematic screening of pupils in the elementary age range at risk for behavior disorders: Development and trial testing of a multiple gating model. *Remedial and Special Education, 9*(3), 8–14.

Walker, H. M., Stieber, S., & O'Neill, R. E. (in press). Middle school behavioral profiles of antisocial behavior and at risk control boys: Descriptive and predictive outcomes. *Exceptionality*.

Wenar, C., Ruttenberg, B. A., Kalish-Weiss, B., & Wolf, E. G. (1986). The development of normal and autistic children: A comparative study. *Journal of Autism and Developmental Disorders, 16*, 317–333.

Wolf, M. M., Braukmann, C. J., & Ramp, K. A. (1987). Serious delinquent behavior as part of a significantly handicapping condition. *Journal of Applied Behavior Analysis, 20*, 347–359.

Chapter 6

American Speech-Language-Hearing Association. (1982). Definitions: Communicative disorders and variations. *ASHA, 24*, 949–950.

American Speech-Language-Hearing Association. (1983). Position of the American Speech-Language-Hearing Association on social dialects. *ASHA, 25*, 23–25.

Andrews, G., Craig, A., Feyer, A., Hoddinott, S., Howie, P., & Neilson, M. (1983). Stuttering: A review of research findings and theories circa 1982. *Journal of Speech and Hearing Disorders, 48*, 226–246.

Baca, L., & Amato, C. (1989). Bilingual special education: Training issues. *Exceptional Children, 56*, 168–173.

Baca, L., & Cervantes, H. (1989). *The bilingual special education interface* (2nd ed.). Columbus, OH: Chas. E. Merrill.

Bernstein, D. K., & Tiegerman, E. (1989). *Language and communica-tion disorders in children* (2nd ed.). Columbus, OH: Chas. E. Merrill.

Blank, M., & White, S. J. (1986). Questions: A powerful form of classroom exchange. *Topics in Language Disorders, 6*(2), 1–12.

Blosser, J. L., & DePompei, R. (1989). The head-injured student returns to school: Recognizing and treating deficits. *Topics in Language Disorders, 9*(2), 67–77.

Bull, G. L., Cochran, P. S., & Snell, M. E. (1988). Beyond CAI: Computers, language, and persons with mental retardation. *Topics in Language Disorders, 8*(4), 55–76.

Butler, K. G. (1986a). *Language disorders in children*. Austin, Tex.: Pro-Ed.

Butler, K. G. (1986b). Language research and practice: A major contribution to special education. In R. J. Morris & B. Blatt (Eds.), *Special education: Research and trends* (pp. 272–302). New York: Pergamon Press.

Campbell, S. L., Reich, A. R., Klockars, A. J., & McHenry, M. A. (1988). Factors associated with dysphonia in high school cheerleaders. *Journal of Speech and Hearing Disorders, 53*, 175–185.

Carrow-Woolfolk, E. (1988). *Theory, assessment and intervention in language disorders: An integrative approach*. Philadelphia: Grune & Stratton.

Casby, M. W. (1989). National data concerning communication disorders and special education. *Language, Speech, and Hearing Services in the Schools, 20*, 22–30.

Cheng, L. L. (1989). Service delivery to Asian/Pacific LEP children: A cross-cultural framework. *Topics in Language Disorders, 9*(3), 1–14.

Delpit, L. (1988). The silenced dialogue: Power and pedagogy in educating other people's children. *Harvard Educational Review, 58*, 280–298.

Devany, J. M., Rincover, A., & Lovaas, O. I. (1981). Teaching speech to nonverbal children. In J. M. Kauffman & D. P. Hallahan (Eds.), *Handbook of special education*. Englewood Cliffs, N.J.: Prentice Hall.

Ensher, G. L. (1989). The first three years: Special eduction perspectives on assessment and intervention. *Topics in Language Disorders, 10*(1), 80–90.

Fairweather, B. C., Haun, D. H., & Finkle, L. J. (1983). *Communication systems for severely handicapped persons*. Springfield: Ill.: Charles C. Thomas.

Falvey, M. A., McLean, D., & Rosenberg, R. L. (1988). Transition from school to adult life: Communication strategies. *Topics in Language Disorders, 9*(1), 82–86.

Fey, M. E. (1986). *Language intervention with young children*. San Diego: College-Hill Press.

Foster, H. L. (1986). *Ribin', jivin', and playin' the dozens* (2nd ed.). Cambridge, MA: Ballinger.

Fradd, S. H., Figueroa, R. A., & Correa, V. I. (1989). Meeting the multicultural needs of Hispanic students in special education. *Exceptional Children, 56*, 102–103.

Goldstein, H., & Strain, P. S. (1989). Peers as communication intervention agents: Some new strategies and research findings. *Topics in Language Disorders, 9*(1), 44–57.

Hallahan, D. P., Kauffman, J. M., & Lloyd, J. W. (1985). *Introduction to learning disabilities* (2nd ed.). Englewood Cliffs, N.J.: Prentice Hall.

Hoffnung, A. S. (1989). The nature of language. In P. J. Valletutti, M. McKnight-Taylor, & A. S. Hoffnung (Eds.), *Facilitating communication in young children with handicapping conditions: A guide for special educators*. Boston: Little, Brown.

Koegel, R. L., Koegel, L. K., Voy, V. K., & Ingham, J. C. (1988). Within-clinic versus outside-of-clinic selfmonitoring of articulation to promote generalization. *Journal of Speech and Hearing Disorders, 53*, 392–399.

Koegel, R. L., O'Dell, M. C., & Koegel, L. C. (1987). A natural language teaching paradigm for nonverbal autistic children. *Journal of Autism and Developmental Disabilities, 17*, 187–200.

Koegel, R. L., Rincover, A., & Egel, A. L. (1982). *Educating and understanding autistic children.* San Diego: College Hill Press.

Kuczaj, S. A. (1983). *Crib speech and language play.* New York: Springer-Verlag.

Lahey, M. (1988). *Language disorders and language development.* New York: Macmillan.

Lane, H. (1976). *The wild boy of Aveyron.* Cambridge, Mass.: Harvard University Press.

Langdon, H. W. (1989). Language disorder or difference? Assessing the language skills of hispanic students. *Exceptional Children, 56,* 160-167.

LaPointe, L. L. (1986). Neurogenic disorders of speech. In G. H. Shames & E. H. Wiig (Eds.), *Human communication disorders* (2nd ed.) (pp. 495–530). Columbus, Ohio: Chas. E. Merrill.

Larson, V. L., & McKinley, N. L. (1985). General intervention principles with language impaired adolescents. *Topics in Language Disorders,* 5(3), 70–77.

Leonard, L. (1986). Early language development and language disorders. In G. H. Shames & E. H. Wiig (Eds.), *Human communication disorders* (2nd ed.) (pp. 291–330). Columbus, Ohio: Chas. E. Merrill.

Lord, C. (1988). Enhancing communication in adolescents with autism. *Topics in Language Disorders,* 9(1), 72–81.

McCormick, L., & Schiefelbusch, R. L. (1984). *Early language intervention.* Columbus, Ohio: Chas. E. Merrill.

McKnight-Taylor, M. (1989). Stimulating speech and language development of infants and other young children. In P. J. Valletutti, M. McKnight-Taylor, & A. S. Hoffnung (Eds.), *Facilitating communication in young children with handicapping conditions: A guide for special educators.* Boston: Little, Brown.

McMorrow, M. J., Foxx, R. M., Faw, G. D., & Bittle, R. G. (1986). *Looking for the words: Teaching functional language strategies.* Champaign, Ill.: Research Press.

McReynolds, L. V. (1986). Functional articulation disorders. In G. H. Shames & E. H. Wiig (Eds.), *Human communication disorders* (2nd ed.) (pp. 139–182). Columbus, Ohio: Chas. E. Merrill.

McWilliams, B. J. (1986). Cleft palate, In G. H. Shames & E. H. Wiig (Eds.), *Human communication disorders* (2nd ed.) (pp. 445–482). Columbus, Ohio: Chas. E. Merrill.

Meyers, S. (1986). Qualitative and quantitative differences and patterns of variability in disfluencies emitted by preschool stutterers. *Journal of fluency Disorders, 11,* 293–306.

Mirenda, P., & Schuler, A. L. (1988). Augmenting communication for persons with autism: Issues and strategies. *Topics in Language Disorders,* 9(1), 24–43.

Moore, P. (1986). Voice disorders. In G. H. Shames & E. H. Wiig (Eds.), *Human communication disorders* (2nd ed.) (pp. 183–229). Columbus, Ohio: Chas. E. Merrill.

Mysak, E. D. (1986). Cerebral palsy. In G. H. Shames & E. M. Wiig (Eds.), *Human communication disorders* (2nd ed.). Columbus, OH: Chas. E. Merrill.

Naremore, R. C. (1980). Language disorders in children. In T. J. Hixon, L. D. Shriberg, & J. H. Saxman (Eds.), *Introduction to communication disorders.* Englewood Cliffs, N.J.: Prentice Hall.

Newman, P. W., Creaghead, N. A., & Secord, W. (1985). *Assessment and remediation of articulatory and phonological disorders.* Columbus, OH: Chas. E. Merrill.

Owens, R. E. (1986). Communication, language, and speech. In G. H. Shames & E. H. Wiig (Eds.), *Human communication disorders* (2nd ed.) (pp. 27–79). Columbus, Ohio: Chas. E. Merrill.

Owens, R. E., & House, L. I. (1984). Decision-making processes in augmentative communication. *Journal of Speech and Hearing Disorders, 49,* 18–25.

Roberts, J. E., Babinowitch, S., Bryant, D. M., Burchinal, M. R., Koch, M. A., & Ramey, C. T. (1989). Language skills of children with different preschool experiences. *Journal of Speech and Hearing Research, 32,* 773–786.

Schiefelbusch, R. L., & McCormick, L. P. (1981). Language and speech disorders. In J. M. Kauffman & D. P. Hallahan (Eds.), *Handbook of special education.* Englewood Cliffs, N.J.: Prentice Hall.

Shames, G., & Rubin, H. (Eds.). (1986). *Stuttering: Then and now.* Columbus, Ohio: Merrill.

Shprintzen, R. J. (1988). Cleft palate and craniofacial disorders: Where we have been, where we need to go. In S. E. Gerber & G. T. Mencher (Eds.), *International perspectives on communication disorders.* Washington, DC: Gallaudet University Press.

Spradlin, J. E., & Siegel, G. M. (1982). Language training in natural and clinical environments. *Journal of Speech and Hearing Disorders, 47,* 2–6.

Starkweather, C. W. (1983). *Speech and language: Principles and processes of behavior change.* Englewood Cliffs, N.J.: Prentice Hall.

Stephens, M. I. (Ed.) (1985). Language impaired youth: The years between 10 and 18. *Topics in Language Disorders,* 5(3), special issue.

U. S. Department of Education. (1989). *Eleventh annual report to Congress on implementation of P.L. 94–142.* Washington, DC: U. S. Government Printing Office.

Vanderheiden, G. C. (1984). High and low technology approaches in the development of communication systems for severely physically handicapped persons. *Exceptional Education Quarterly, 4(4),* 40–56.

Wallach, G. P., & Miller, L. (1988). *Language intervention and academic success.* Boston: Little, Brown.

Wiig, E. H. (1986). Language disabilities in school-age children and youth. In G. H. Shames & E. H. Wiig (Eds.), *Human communication disorders* (2nd ed.) (pp. 331–383). Columbus, Ohio: Chas. E. Merrill.

Yairi, E. (1983). The onset of stuttering in two- and three-year-old children: A preliminary report. *Journal of Speech and Hearing Disorders, 48,* 171–178.

Ylvisaker, M., & Szekeres, S. F. (1989). Metacognitive and executive impairments in head-injured children and adults. *Topics in Language Disorders,* 9(2), 34–49.

Chapter 7

Baker, C., & Battison, R. (1980): *Sign Language and the deaf community: Essays in honor of William C. Stokoe.* Silver Spring, MD: National Association of the Deaf.

Boatner, E., Stuckless, E., & Moores, D. F. (1964) *Occupational status of the young deaf adults of New England and their need and demand for a regional technical vocational training center.* West Hartford, CI: American School for the Deaf.

Boothroyd, A. (1987). Technology and science in the management of deafness. *American Annals of the Deaf, 132,* 326–329.

Bornstein, H., Hamilton, L., & Saulnier, K. (1983). *The comprehensive Signed English dictionary.* Washington, DC: Gallaudet University Press.

Brill, R. G., MacNeil, B., & Newman, L. R. (1986). Framework for appropriate programs for deaf children. *American Annals of the Deaf, 131(2),* 65–77.

Carney, E., & Verlinde, R. (1987). Caption decoders: Expanding options for hearing impaired children and adults. *American Annals of the Deaf, 132(2),* 73–77.

Castiglia, P. T., Aquilina, S. S., & Kemsley, M. (1983). Focus: Nonsuppurative otitis media. *Pediatric Nursing, 9,* 427–431.

Davis, H. (1978a). Abnormal hearing and deafness. In H. Davis & S. R. Silverman (Eds.), *Hearing and deafness* (4th ed.). New York: Holt, Rinehart & Winston.

Davis, H. (1978b). Audiometry: Other auditory tests. In H. Davis & S. R. Silverman (Eds.), *Hearing and deafness* (4th ed.). New York: Holt, Rinehart & Winston.

Fant, L. J. (1971). *Say it with hands.* Silver Spring, Md.: National Association for the Deaf.

Flexer, C., Wray, D., & Black, T. (1986). Support group for moderately hearing-impaired college students: An exanding awareness. *The Volta Review, 88*(4), 223–229.

Fry, D. B. (1966). The development of a phonological system in the normal and the deaf child. In F. Smith & G. A. Miller (Eds.), *The genesis of language: A psycholinguistic approach.* Cambridge, MA: M.I.T. Press.

Geoffrion, L. D. (1982). The Ability of hearing-impaired students to communicate using a teletype system. *The Volta Review, 84,* 96–108.

Goppold, L. (1988). Early intervention for preschool deaf children: The longitudinal academic effects relative to program methodology. *American Annals of the Deaf, 133,* 285–288.

Gustason, G., Pfetzing, D., & Zawolkow, E. (1972). *Signing Exact English.* Silver Spring, MD: National Association of the Deaf.

Hanshaw, J. B. (1982). On deafness, cytomegalovirus, and neonatal screening. *American Journal of Diseases of Children, 136,* 886–887.

Hoemann, H. W., & Briga, J. S. (1981). Hearing impairments. In J. M. Kauffman & D. P. Hallahan (Eds.), *Handbook of special education.* Englewood Cliffs, NJ: Prentice Hall.

Jacobs, M. A. (1982). Visual Communication (speechreading) for severely and profoundly hearing-impaired youth and adults. In D. G. Sims, G. G. Walter, & R. L. Whitehead (Eds.), *Deafness and communication: Assessment and training* (pp. 271–295). Baltimore: Williams & Wilkins.

Jordan, I. K., & Karchmer, M. A. (1986). Patterns of sign use among hearing impaired students. In A. N. Schildroth & M. A. Karchmer (Eds.), *Deaf children in America* (pp. 125–138). San Diego: College-Hill Press.

Kampfe, C. M., & Turecheck, A. G. (1987). Reading achievement of prelingually deaf students and its relationship to parental method of communication: A review of the literature. *American Annals of the Deaf, 132*(1), 11–15.

Karchmer, M. A., Milone, M. N. & Wolk, S. (1979). Educational significance of hearing loss at three levels of serverity. *American Annals of the Deaf, 124,* 97–109.

Klima, E. S., Bellugi, U. (1979). *The signs of language.* Cambridge, MA: Harvard University Press.

Lane, H. (1984). *When the mind hears: A history of the deaf.* New York: Random House.

Lane, H. (1987, July 17). Listen to the needs of deaf children. *New York Times.*

Liben, L. S. (1978). Developmental perspectives on the experiential deficiencies of deaf children. In L. S. Liben (Ed.), *Deaf children: Developmental perspectives,* New York: Academic Press.

Ling, D., & Ling, A. (1978). *Aural habilitation.* Washington, DC: Alexander Graham Bell Association for the Deaf.

Loeb, R., & Sarigiani, P. (1986). The impact of hearing impairment on self-perceptions of children. *The Volta Review, 88*(2), 89–100.

Martin, F. N. (1986). *Introduction to audiology* (3rd ed.). Englewood Cliffs, NJ: Prentice Hall.

Meadow, K. P. (1975). Development of deaf children. In E. M. Hetherington (Ed.), *Review of child development research* (Vol. 5). Chicago: University of Chicago Press.

Meadow, K. P. (1980). *Deafness and child development.* Berkeley: University of California Press.

Meadow, K. P. (1984). Social adjustment of preschool children: Deaf and hearing, with and without other handicaps. *Topics in Early Childhood and Special Education, 3,* 27–40.

Meadow-Orlans, K. P. (1987). An analysis of the effectiveness of early intervention programs for hearing-impaired children. In M. J. Guralnick & F. C. Bennett (Eds.), *The effectiveness of early intervention for at-risk and handicapped children* (pp. 325–362). New York: Academic Press.

Menchel, R. S. (1988). Personal experience with speechreading. *The Volta Review, 90*(5), 3–15.

Moog, J., & Geers, A. (1985). EPIC: A program to accelerate academic progress in profoundly hearing-impaired children. *The Volta Review, 87*(6), 259–277.

Moores, D. F. (1969). The vocational status of young deaf adults in New England. *Journal of Rehabilitation of the Deaf, 2,* 29–41.

Moores, D. F. (1982). *Educating the deaf: Psychology, principles, and practices.* (2nd ed.). Boston: Houghton-Mifflin.

Moores, D. F. (1987). *Educating the deaf: Psychology, principles, and practices.* 3rd ed. Boston: Houghton-Mifflin.

Moores, D. F. (1990). Research in educational aspects of deafness. In D. F. Moores & K. Meadow-Orlans (Eds.), *Educational and developmental aspects of deafness.* Washington, DC: Gallaudet University Press.

Moores, D. F., & Maestas y Moores, J. (1981). Special adaptations necessiated by hearing impairments. In J. M. Kauffman & D. P. Hallahan (Eds.), *Handbook of special education.* Englewood Cliffs, NJ: Prentice Hall.

Neisser, A. (1983). *The other side of silence.* New York: Knopf.

Newby, H. A. (1971). Clinical audiology. In L. E. Travis (Ed.), *Handbook of speech pathology and audiology.* Englewood Cliffs, NJ: Prentice Hall.

Niemoeller, A. E. (1978). Hearing aids. In H. Davis & S. R. Silverman (Eds.), *Hearing and deafness* (4th ed.). New York: Holt, Rinehart & Winston.

Padden, C., & Humphries, T. (1988). *Deaf in America: Voices from a culture.* Cambridge, MA: Harvard University Press.

Pelton, S., & Whitley, P. (1983). Otitis media: Current concepts in diagnosis and management. *Pediatric Annals, 12,* 207–218.

Prinz, P. M., & Nelson, K. E. (1985). A child-computer-teacher interactive method for teaching reading to young deaf children. In D. Martin (Ed.), *Cognition, education, and deafness: Directions for research and instruction* (pp. 124–127). Washington, DC: Gallaudet University Press.

Prinz, P. M., Pemberton, E., & Nelson, K. (1985). The ALPHA Interactive Microcomputer System for teaching reading, writing, and communication skills to hearing-impaired children. *American Annals of the Deaf, 130*(4), 441–461.

Quigley, S., Jenne, W., & Phillips, S. (1968). *Deaf students in colleges and universities.* Washington, DC: Alexander Graham Bell Association for the Deaf.

Rawlings, B. W., Karchmer, M. A., DeCaro, J., & Egelston-Dodd, J. (Eds.). (1986). *College and career programs for the deaf* (6th ed.). Washington, DC: Gallaudet University.

Rawlings, B. W., Trybus, R. J., & Biser, J. (1978, December). *A guide to college/career programs for deaf students.* Washington, DC: Office of Demographic Studies, Gallaudet University.

Sacks, O. (1989). *Seeing voices: A journey into the world of the deaf.* Berkeley: University of California Press.

Sanders, D. A. (1982). *Aural rehabilitation* (2nd ed.). Englewood Cliffs, NJ: Prentice Hall.

Saur, R., Coggiola, D., Long, G., & Simonson, J. (1986). Educational mainstreaming and the career development of hearing-impaired students: A longitudinal analysis. *The Volta Review, 88*(2), 79–88.

Schein, J. D., & Delk, M. T. (1974). *The deaf population of the United States.* Silver Spring, MD: National Association of the Deaf.

Schiff-Myers, N. B. (1982). Sign and oral language development of preschool hearing children of deaf parents in comparison with their mothers' communication system. *American Annals of the Deaf, 127,* 322–330.

Schildroth, A. N. (1986). Residential schools for deaf students: A decade in review. In A. N. Schildroth & M. A. Karchmer (Eds.), *Deaf children in America* (pp. 83–104). San Diego: College-Hill Press.

Schildroth, A. N., Rawlings, B. W., & Allen, T. E. (1989). Hearing-impaired children under age 6: A demographic analysis. *American Annals of the Deaf, 134*(2), 63–69.

Schow, R., & Nerbonne, M. (Eds.). (1980). *Introduction to aural rehabilitation.* Baltimore: University Park Press.

Slike, S. B., Chiavacci, J. P., & Hobbis, D. H. (1989). The efficiency and effectiveness of an interactive videodisc system to teach sign language vocabulary. *American Annals of the Deaf, 134,* 288–290.

Spradley, T. S., & Spradley, J. P. (1978). *Deaf like me.* Washington, DC: Gallaudet University Press.

Stedt, J., & Moores, D. F. (1990). Manual codes on English and American Sign Language: Historical perspectives and current realities. In H. Bornstein (Ed.), *Manual communication: Implications for education.* Washington, DC: Gallaudet University Press.

Stoel-Gammon, C., & Otomo, K. (1986). Babbling development of hearing-impaired and normally hearing subjects. *Journal of Speech and Hearing Disorders, 51,* 33–41.

Stoker, R. G. (1982). Telecommunications technology and the hearing impaired: Recent research trends and a look into the future. *The Volta Review, 84,* 147–155.

Stokoe, W. C. (1960). *Sign language structure.* Silver Spring, MD: Linstok Press.

Stokoe, W. C., Casterline, D. C., & Croneberg, C. G. (1976). *A dictionary of American Sign Language on linguistic principles* (2nd ed.). Silver Spring, MD: Linstok Press.

Sullivan, P. M. (1982). Administration modifications on the WISC-R Performance Scale with different categories of deaf children. *American Annals of the Deaf, 127,* 780–788.

Trybus, R. J., & Karchmer, M. A. (1977). School achievement scores of hearing impaired children. National data on achievement status and growth patterns. *American Annals of the Deaf, 122,* 62–69.

U.S. Department of Education (1989). *Eleventh annual report to Congress on the implementation of The Education of the Handicapped Act.* Washington, DC: U.S. Government Printing Office.

Vygotsky, L. S. (1962). *Thought and language.* New York: Wiley.

Walker, L. A. (1986). *A loss for words: The story of deafness in a family.* New York: Harper & Row.

Wilbur, R. B. (1979). *American Sign Language and sign systems.* Baltimore: University Park Press.

Wolk, S., & Schildroth, A. N. (1986). Deaf children and speech intelligibility: A national study. In A. N. Schildroth & M. A. Karchmer (Eds.), *Deaf children in America* (pp. 139–159). San Diego: College-Hill Press.

Chapter 8

Aitken, S., & Bower, T. G. R. (1982). The use of the Sonicguide in infancy. *Journal of Visual Impairment and Blindness, 76,* 91–100.

American Printing House for the Blind. (1985). *Distribution of January, 1985, quota registrations by school, grades, and reading media.* Louisville, KY: American Printing House for the Blind.

Andersen, E. S., Dunlea, A., & Kekelis, L. S. (1984). Blind children's language: Resolving some differences. *Journal of Child Language, 2,* 645–664.

Barraga, N. C. (1983). *Visual handicaps and learning* (rev. ed.). Austin, TX: Exceptional Resources.

Barraga, N. C., & Collins, M. E. (1979). Development of efficiency in visual functioning: Rationale for a comprehensive program. *Journal of Visual Impairment and Blindness, 73,* 121–126.

Bateman, B. D. (1963). Reading and psycholinguistic processes of partially seeing children. *Council for Exceptional Children Research Monograph,* Council for Exceptional Children (5).

Berkson, J. (1981). Animal studies of treatment of impaired young by parents and the social group. Paper presented at the Conference on the Blind Child in Social Interaction. *Journal of Visual Impairment and Blindness, 75,* 210–214.

Berlá, E. P. (1981). Tactile scanning and memory for a spatial display by blind students. *Journal of Special Education, 15,* 341–350.

Bischoff, R. W. (1979). Listening: A teachable skill for visually impaired persons. *Journal of Visual Impairment and Blindness, 73,* 59–67.

Bosbach, S. R. (1988). Precane mobility devices. *Journal of Visual Impairment and Blindness, 82,* 338–339.

Bower, T. J. R. (1977). Blind babies see with their ears. *New Scientist, 73,* 255–257.

Brody, H. (1989, July). The great equalizer: PCs empower the disabled. *PC Computing,* pp. 82–93.

Carter, K. (1983). Comprehensive preliminary assessments of low vision. In R. T. Jose (Ed.), *Understanding low vision.* New York: American Foundation for the Blind.

Collins, M. E., & Barraga, N. C. (1980). Development of efficiency in visual functioning: An evaluation process. *Journal of Visual Impairment and Blindness, 74,* 93–96.

Conant, S., & Budoff, M. (1982). The development of sighted people's understanding of blindness. *Journal of Visual Impairment and Blindness, 76,* 86–90.

Cutsforth, T. D. (1951). *The blind in school and society: A psychological study.* New York: American Foundation for the Blind.

Davidson, P. W. (1972). The role of exploratory activity in haptic perception: Some issues, data, and hypotheses. *Research Bulletin: American Foundation for the Blind* (24), 21–27.

Davidson, P. W., Dunn, G., Wiles-Kettenmann, M., & Appelle, S. (1981). Haptic conservation of amount in blind and sighted children: Exploratory movement effects. *Journal of Pediatric Psychology, 6,* 191–200.

Dodds, A. G., Howarth, C. I., & Carter, D. C. (1982). The mental maps of the blind: The role of previous visual experience. *Journal of Visual Impairment and Blindness, 76,* 5–12.

Dubose, R. F. (1976). Developmental needs in blind infants. *New Outlook for the Blind, 70,* 49–52.

Farkas, G. M., Sherick, R. B., Matson, J. L., & Loebig, M. (1981). Social skills training of a blind child through differential reinforcement. *The Behavior Therapist, 4,* 24–26.

Farmer, L. W. (1975). Travel in adverse weather using electronic mobility guidance devices. *New Outlook for the Blind, 69,* 433–451.

Farmer, L. W. (1980). Mobility devices. In R. L. Welsh & B. B. Blasch (Eds.), *Foundations of orientation and mobility.* New York: American Foundation for the Blind.

Ferrell, K. A. (1980). Can infants use the Sonicguide? Two years' experience of Project VIEW! *Journal of Visual Impairment and Blindness, 74,* 209–220.

Fletcher, J. F. (1981). Spatial representation in blind children. 3: Effects of individual differences. *Journal of Visual Impairment and Blindness, 75,* 46–49.

Fraiberg, S. (1975). The development of human attachments in infants blind from birth. *Merrill-Palmer Quarterly, 21,* 315–334.

Fraiberg, S. (1977). *Insights from the blind.* New York: Basic Books.

Fraiberg, S., Smith, M., & Adelson, E. (1969). An educational program for blind infants. *Journal of Special Education, 3,* 121–139.

Gaylord-Ross, C., Forte, J., Gaylord-Ross, R. (1986). The community classroom: Technological vocational training for students with serious handicaps. *Career Development for Exceptional Individuals, 9*(1), 24–33.

Genensky, S. M., Petersen, H. E., Clewett, R. W., & Yoshimura, R. J. (1978). A second-generation interactive classroom television system for the partially sighted. *Journal of Visual Impairment and Blindness, 72,* 41–45.

Gottesman, M. (1976). Stage development of blind children: A Piagetian view. *New Outlook for the Blind, 70,* 94–100.

Graves, W. H., & Lyon, S. (1985). Career development: Linking education and careers of blind and visually impaired ninth graders. *Journal of Visual Impairment and Blindness, 79,* 444–449.

Griffin, H. C., & Gerber, P. J. (1982). Tactual development and its implications for the education of blind children. *Education of the Visually Handicapped, 13,* 116–123.

Hanninen, K. A. (1975). *Teaching the visually handicapped.* Columbus, OH: Chas. E. Merrill.

Harris, L., Humphrey, G. K., Muir, D. M., Dodwell, P. C. (1985). Use of the Canterbury Child's Aid in infancy and early childhood: A case study. *Journal of Visual Impairment and Blindness, 79,* 4–11.

Hayes, S. P. (1942). Alternative scales for the mental measurement of the visually handicapped. *Outlook for the Blind and the Teachers Forum, 36,* 225–230.

Hayes, S. P. (1950). Measuring the intelligence of the blind. In P. A. Zahl (Ed.), *Blindness.* Princeton, NJ: Princeton University Press.

Herman, J. F., Chatman, S. P., & Roth, S. F. (1983). Cognitive mapping in blind people: Acquisition of spatial relationships in a large-scale environment. *Journal of Visual Impairment and Blindness, 77,* 161–166.

Hetherington, E. M., & Parke, R. D. (1986). *Child psychology: A contemporary viewpoint* (3rd ed.). New York: McGraw-Hill.

Hollyfield, R. L., & Foulke, E. (1983). The spatial cognition of blind pedestrians. *Journal of Visual Impairment and Blindness, 77,* 204–210.

Jackson, R. M., Peck, A. F., & Bentzen, B. L. (1983). Visually handicapped travelers in the rapid rail transit environment. *Journal of Visual Impairment and Blindness, 77,* 469–475.

Kay, L. (1973). Sonic glasses for the blind: A progress report. *Research Bulletin: American Foundation for the Blind* (25), 25–58.

Knight, J. J. (1972). Mannerisms in the congenitally blind child. *New Outlook for the Blind, 66,* 297–302.

Lowenfeld, B. (1971). Psychological problems of children with impaired vision. In W. M. Cruickshank (Ed.), *Psychology of exceptional children and youth* (3rd ed.). Englewood Cliffs, NJ: Prentice Hall.

Lowenfeld, B. (1973a). History of the education of visually handicapped children. In B. Lowenfeld (Ed.), *The visually handicapped child in school.* New York: John Day.

Lowenfeld, B. (1973b). Psychological considerations. In B. Lowenfeld (Ed.), *The visually handicapped child in school.* New York: John Day.

McGinnis, A. R. (1981). Functional linguistic strategies of blind children. *Journal of Visual Impairment and Blindness, 75,* 210–214.

McIntire, J. C. (1985). The future role of residential schools for visually impaired students. *Journal of Visual Impairment and Blindness, 79,* 161–164.

McLinden, D. J. (1988). Spatial task performance: A metaanalysis. *Journal of Visual Impairment and Blindness, 82,* 231–236.

Maloney, P. L. (1981). *Practical guidance for parents of the visually handicapped preschooler.* Springfield, IL: Chas. C Thomas.

Matsuda, M. M. (1984). Comparative analysis of blind and sighted children's communication skills. *Journal of Visual Impairment and Blindness, 78,* 1–5.

Mehta, V. (1982). *Vedi.* New York: W. W. Norton & Company.

Mehta, V. (1984). *The ledge between the streams.* New York: W. W. Norton & Co.

Mehta, W. (1985). *Sound-shadows of the new world.* New York: W. W. Norton & Co.

Mehta, V. (1989). *The stolen light: Continents of exile.* New York: W. W. Norton & Co.

Melrose, S., & Goodrich, G. L. (1984). Evaluation of voice-output calculators for visually handicapped users. *Journal of Visual Impairment and Blindness, 78,* 17–19.

National Society for the Prevention of Blindness (1964). Pub. V-7.

National Society for the Prevention of Blindness (1972). *Teaching about vision.*

Newland, T. E. (1979). The Blind Learning Aptitude Test. *Journal of Visual Impairment and Blindness. 73,* 134–139.

Palazesi, M. A. (1986). The need for motor development programs for visually impaired preschoolers. *Journal of Visual Impairment and Blindness, 80,* 573–576.

Pfouts, J. J., & Nixon, D. G. (1982). The reality of the dream: Present status of a sample of 98 totally blind adults. *Journal of Visual Impairment and Blindness, 76,* 41–48.

Pitman, D. J. (1965). The musical ability of blind children. *Research Bulletin: American Foundation for the Blind* (11), 63–79.

Rathgeber, A. J. (1981). Manitoba vision screening study. *Journal of Visual Impairment and Blindness, 75,* 239–243.

Rickelman, B. L., & Blaylock, J. N. (1983). Behaviors of sighted individuals perceived by blind persons as hindrances to self-reliance in blind persons. *Journal of Visual Impairment and Blindness, 77,* 8–11.

Rieser, J. J., Guth, D. A., & Hill, E. W. (1982). Mental processes mediating independent travel: Implications for orientation and mobility. *Journal of Visual Impairment and Blindness, 76,* 213–218.

Sampaio, E. (1989). Is there a critical age for using the Sonicguide with blind infants? *Journal of Visual Impairment and Blindness, 83,* 105–108.

Scott, E. P. (1982). *Your visually impaired student: A guide for teachers.* Baltimore, MD: University Park Press.

Scott, R. A. (1969). *The making of blind men.* New York: Russell Sage Foundation.

Smith, M. A., Chethik, M., & Adelson, E. (1969). Differential assessments of "blindisms." *American Journal of Orthopsychiatry, 39,* 807–817.

Stephens, B., & Grube, C. (1982). Development of Piagetian reasoning in congenitally blind children. *Journal of Visual Impairment and Blindness, 76,* 133–143.

Stewart, I. A., Van Hasselt, V. B., Simon, J., & Thompson, W. B. (1985). The Community Adjustment Program (CAP) for visually impaired adolescents. *Journal of Visual Impairment and Blindness, 79,* 49–54.

Storey, K., Sacks, S. Z., & Olmstead, J. (1985). Community-referenced instruction in a technological work setting: A vocational education option for visually handicapped students. *Journal of Visual Impairment and Blindness, 79,* 481–486.

Strelow, E. R. (1983). Use of the Binaural Sensory Aid by young children. *Journal of Visual Impairment and Blindness, 77,* 429–438.

Strelow, E. R., & Boys, J. T. (1979). The Canterbury Child's Aid: A binaural spatial sensor for research with blind children. *Journal of Visual Impairment and Blindness, 73,* 179–184.

Struve, N. L., Cheney, K. M., & Rudd, C. (1980). Chisanbop for blind math students. *Education of the Visually Handicapped, 11,* 108–112.

Suppes, P. (1974). A survey of cognition in handicapped children. *Review of Educational Research, 44,* 145–175.

Swallow, R. M., & Conner, A. (1982). Aural reading. In S. S. Mangold (Ed.), *A teachers' guide to the special educational needs of blind and visually handicapped children.* New York: American Foundation for the Blind.

Thomas, C. L. (Ed.). (1985). *Taber's cyclopedic medical dictionary* (15th ed.). Philadelphia: F. A. Davis Co.

Thurrell, R. J., & Rice, D. G. (1970). Eye rubbing in blind children: Application of a sensory deprivation model. *Exceptional Children, 36,* 325–330.

Tobin, M. J., & Hill, E. W. (1988). Visually impaired teenagers: Ambitions, attitudes, and interests. *Journal of Visual Impairment and Blindness, 82,* 414–416.

Tuttle, D. (1974). A comparison of three reading media for the blind: Braille, normal recording, and compressed speech. *Research Bulletin: American Foundation for the Blind,* No. 27, 217–230.

U. S. Department of Educations (1989). *Eleventh annual report to Congress on the implementation of The Education of the Handicapped Act.* Washington, DC: U.S. Government Printing Office.

Van Hasselt, V. B. (1983). Social adaptation in the blind. *Clinical Psychology Review,* 87–102.

Warren, D. H. (1981). Visual impairments. In J. M. Kauffman & D. P.

Hallahan (Eds.), *Handbook of special education*, Englewood Cliffs, NJ: Prentice-Hall.

Warren, D. H. (1984). *Blindness and early childhood development* (2nd ed.). New York: American Foundation for the Blind.

Warren, D. H., Anooshian, L. J., & Bollinger, J. G. (1973). Early vs. late blindness: The role of early vision in spatial behavior. *Research Bulletin: American Foundation for the Blind* (26), 151–170.

Warren, D. H., & Kocon, J. A. (1974). Factors in the successful mobility of the blind: A review. *Research Bulletin: American Foundation for the Blind* (28), 191–218.

Wellbourne, A., Lifschitz, S., Selvin, H., & Green, R. (1983). A comparison of the sexual learning experiences of visually impaired and sighted women. *Journal of Visual Impairment and Blindness*, 77, 256–259.

Willis, D. H. (1976). *A study of the relationship between visual acuity, reading mode, and school systems for blind students—1976.* Louisville, KY: American Printing House for the Blind.

Winkley, W. M. (1985). World without workshops. *Journal of Visual Impairment and Blindness*, 79, 462–465.

Chapter 9

Anastasiow, N. J. (1983). Adolescent pregnancy and special education. *Exceptional Children*, 49, 396–401.

Banker, B. Q., & Bruce-Gregorios, J. (1983). Neuropathology. In G. H. Thompson, I. L. Rubin, & R. M. Bilenker (Eds.), *Comprehensive management of cerebral palsy.* New York: Grune & Stratton.

Batshaw, M. L., & Perret, Y. M. (1986). *Children with handicaps: A medical primer.* Baltimore: Paul H. Brookes.

Baumeister, A. A., Kupstas, F., & Klindworth, L. M. (1990). New morbidity: Implications for prevention of children's disabilities. *Exceptionality*, 1, 1–16.

Blackman, J. A. (Ed.). (1984). *Medical aspects of developmental disabilities in children birth to three* (rev. 1st ed.). Rockville, MD: Aspen.

Bryan, D. P., & Herjanic, B. (1980). Depression and suicide among adolescents and young adults with selective handicapping conditions. *Exceptional Education Quarterly*, 1(2), 57–66.

Campbell, P. H., Green, K. M., & Carlson, L. M. (1977). Approximating the norm through environmental and child-centered prosthetics and adaptive equipment. In E. Sontag, J. Smith, & N. Certo (Eds.), *Educational programming for the severely and profoundly handicapped.* Reston, VA: Council for Exceptional Children.

Cavazzuti, G. B., Ferrari, P., & Lalla, M. (1984). Follow-up study of 482 cases with convulsive disorders in the first year. *Developmental Medicine and Child Neurology*, 26, 425–437.

Chadwick, D. (1989). Protecting abused kids. *NEA Today*, 8(5), 23.

Church, J. A., Allen, J. R. & Stiehm, E. R. (1986). New scarlet letter(s), pediatric AIDS. *Pediatrics*, 77, 423–427.

Crocker, A. C. (Ed.) (1989). Developmental disabilities and HIV infection: A symposium on issues and public policy. *Mental Retardation*, 27(4), special issue.

Cruickshank, W. M. (Ed.). (1976). *Cerebral palsy: A developmental disability* (3rd rev. ed.). Syracuse, NY: Syracuse University Press.

Delatte, J. G., Orgeron, K., & Preis, J. (1985). Project SCAN: Counseling teen-age parents in a school setting. *Journal of School Health*, 55(1), 24–26.

DeLoach, C., & Greer, B. G. (1981). *Adjustment to severe physical disability: A metamorphosis.* New York: McGraw-Hill.

DuBose, R. F., & Deni, K. (1980). Easily constructed adaptive and assistive equipment. *Teaching Exceptional Children*, 12, 116–123.

Duncan, D., & Canty-Lemke, J. (1986). Learning appropriate social and sexual behavior: The role of society. *The Exceptional Parent*, 16(5), 24–26.

Dyar, S. E. (1988). A step in the right direction. *Helex: The University of Virginia Health Sciences Quarterly*, 6(3), 5–11.

Edmonson, B. (1980). Sociosexual education for the handicapped. *Exceptional Education Quarterly*, 1(2). 67–76.

Eiben, R. M., & Crocker, A. C. (1983). Cerebral palsy within the spectrum of developmental disabilities. In G. H. Thompson, I. L. Rubin, & R. M. Bilenker (Eds.), *Comprehensive management of cerebral palsy.* New York: Grune & Stratton.

Finnie, N. R. (1975). *Handling the young cerebral palsied child at home.* New York: Dutton.

Fonosch, G. G., Arany, J., Lee. A., & Loving, S. (1982). Providing career planning and placement services for college students with disabilities. *Exceptional Education Quarterly*, 3(3), 67–74.

Fraser, B. A., & Hensinger, R. N. (1983). *Managing physical handicaps: A practical guide for parents, care providers, and educators.* Baltimore: Paul H. Brooks.

Freeman, J. M., Jacobs, H., Vining, E., & Rabin, C. E. (1984). Epilepsy and the inner city schools: A school-based program that makes a difference. *Epilepsia*, 25, 438–442.

Hanson, M. J., & Harris, S. R. (1986). *Teaching the young child with motor delays.* Austin TX: Pro-Ed.

Harmon, C., Furrow, D., Gruendel, J., & Zigler, E. (1980, Spring). Childhood accidents: An overview of the problem and a call for action. *Newsletter of the Society for Research in Child Development.*

Hauser, W. A., & Kurland, L. T. (1975). The epidemiology of epilepsy in Rochester, Minnesota, 1935 through 1967. *Epilepsia*, 16, 1–66.

Hoare, P. (1984). The development of psychiatric disorder among schoolchildren with epilepsy. *Developmental Medicine and Child Neurology*, 26, 3–13.

Hobbs, N., Perrin, J. M., & Ireys, H. T. (1984). *Chronically ill children and their families.* San Francisco: Jossey-Bass.

Hobbs, N., Perrin, J. M., Ireys, H. T., Moynahan, L. C., & Shayne, M. W. (1984). Chronically ill children in America. *Rehabilitation Literature*, 45, 206–213.

Hopkins, T. W., Bice, H. V., & Colton, K. C. (1954). *Evaluation and education of the cerebral palsied child.* Arlington, VA: Council for Exceptional Children.

Jacobs, I. B. (1983). Epilepsy. In G. H. Thompson, I. L. Rubin, & R. M. Bilenker (Eds.), *Comprehensive management of cerebral palsy.* New York: Grune & Stratton.

Klein, M., & Stern, L. (1971). Low birth weight and the battered child syndrome. *American Journal of Diseases of Children*, 122, 15–18.

Korabek, C. A., & Cuvo, A. J. (1986). Children with spina bifida: Educational implications of their medical characteristics. *Education and Treatment of Children*, 9, 142–152.

Lewandowski, L. J., & Cruickshank, W. M. (1980). Psychological development of crippled children and youth. In W. M. Cruickshank (Ed.), *Psychology of exceptional children and youth* (4th ed.). Englewood Cliffs, NJ: Prentice Hall.

Lyon, J. (1985). *Playing god in the nursery.* New York: W. W. Norton & Co.

Merina, A. (1989). Is your school ready for AIDS? *NEA Today*, 8(5), 10–11.

Miczio, P. M. (1983). *Parenting children with disabilities: A professional source for physicians and guide for parents.* New York: Marcel Dekker.

Migra, T. (1987). Impairment due to infectious disease ruled a handicap. *Education Week*, 6(24), 1, 21.

Moore, J. (1985). Technology is not magic. *The Exceptional Parent*, 15(7), 41–42.

National Head Injury Foundation (1988). *An educator's manual: What educators need to know about students with traumatic brain injury.* Southborogh, MA.

Neisworth, J. T., & Fewell, R. R. (Eds.). (1989). Transition. *Topics in Early Childhood Special Education*, 9(4).

Reed, S. (1988). Children with AIDS: How schools are handling the crisis. Kappan special report. *Phi Delta Kappan*, 69, K1–K12.

Robinson, N. M., & Robinson, H. B. (1976). *Mentally retarded child: A psychological approach* (2nd ed.). New York: McGraw-Hill.

Rush, W. L. (1977). Feelings of love. *The Exceptional Parent*, 7(6), 2–6.

Rutledge, D. N., & Dick, G. (1983). Spinal cord injury in adolescence. *Rehabilitation Nursing*, 8(6), 18–21.

Satz, J. (1986). Another first: The National Park Service opens summer work programs to students with disabilities. *The Exceptional Parent*, 16(2), 19–22.

Savage, R. C. (1988). Introduction to educational issues for students who have suffered traumatic brain injury. *An educator's manual: What educators need to know about students with traumatic brain injury.* Southborogh, MA.

Schonberger, L. B., Sullivan-Bolyai, J. Z., & Bryan, J. A. (1978). Poliomyelitis in the United States. *Advances in Neurology*, 19, 217–227.

Scott, D. (1973). *About epilepsy* (rev. ed.). New York: International Universities Press.

Shannon, K. M., & Ammann, A. J. (1985). Acquired immune deficiency syndrome in childhood. *Journal of Pediatrics*, 106, 332–342.

Snell, M. E., & Browder, D. M. (1986). Community-referenced instruction: Research and issues. *Journal of the Association for Severely Handicapped*, 11, 1–11.

Stores, G. (1978). School-children with epilepsy at risk for learning and behavior problems. *Developmental Medicine and Child Neurology*, 20, 502–508.

Torres, F. (1969). Convulsive disorders: A working classification and guidelines for diagnosis and treatment. *Medical Times*, 97, 152–156.

U.S. Department of Education. (1984). *Sixth annual report to Congress on the implementation of Public Law 94–142, The Education for All Handicapped Children Act.* Washington, DC: U.S. Government Printing Office.

U.S. Department of Education. (1989). *Eleventh annual report to Congress on the implementation of Education of the Handicapped Act.* Washington, DC.

Utley, B. L., Holvoet, J. F., & Barnes, K. (1977). Handling, positioning, and feeding the physically handicapped. In E. Sontag, J. Smith, & N. Certo (Eds.), *Educational programming for the severely and profoundly handicapped.* Reston, VA: Council for Exeptional Children.

Verhaaren, P., & Connor, F. (1981a). Physical disabilities. In J. M. Kauffman & D. P. Hallahan (Eds.), *Handbook of special education.* Englewood Cliffs, NJ: Prentice Hall.

Verhaaren, P., & Connor, F. (1981b). Special adaptations necessitated by physical disabilities. In J. M. Kauffman & D. P. Hallahan (Eds.), *Handbook of special education.* Englewood Cliffs, NJ: Prentice Hall.

Vinger, P. F., & Hoerner, E. F. (Eds.). (1986). *Sports injuries: The unthwarted epidemic* (2nd ed.). Littleton, MA: PSG Publishing Company.

Wilsnack, S. C., Klassen, A. D., & Wilsnack, R. W. (1984). Drinking and reproductive dysfunction among women in a 1981 national survey. *Alcoholism: Clinical and Experimental Research*, 8, 451–458.

Wolraich, M. L. (1984). Seizure disorders. In J. A. Blackman (Ed.), *Medical aspects of developmental disabilities in children birth to three* (rev. 1st ed., pp. 215–221). Rockville, MD: Aspen.

Zadig, J. M. (1983). The education of the child with cerebral palsy. In G. H. Thompson, I. L. Rubin, & R. M. Bilenker (Eds.), *Comprehensive management of cerebral palsy.* New York: Grune & Stratton.

Zirpoli, T. J. (1986). Child abuse and children with handicaps. *Remedial and Special Education*, 7(2), 39–48.

Ziter, F. A., & Allsop, K. G. (1976). The diagnosis and management of childhood muscular dystrophy. "Clinicians must provide the the best care and support possible." *Clinical Pediatrics*, 15, 540–548.

Chapter 10

Baer, N. A. (1980). Programs for the gifted: A present or paradox? *Phi Delta Kappan*, 61, 621–623.

Baldwin, A. Y. (1985). Programs for the gifted and talented: Issues concerning minority populations. In F. D. Horowitz & M. O'Brien (Eds.), *The gifted and talented: Developmental perspectives* (pp. 251–295). Washington, DC: American Psychological Association.

Baum, S. (1986). The gifted preschooler: An awesome delight. *Gifted Child Today*, 9(4), 42–45.

Belcastro, F. P. (1985). Gifted students and behavior modification. *Behavior Modification*, 9, 155–164.

Benbow, C. P. (1986). SMPY's model for teaching mathematically precocious students. In J. S. Renzulli (Ed.), *Systems and models for developing programs for the gifted and talented.* Mansfield, CT: Creative Learning Press.

Bloom, B. S. (1982). The role of gifts and markers in the development of talent. *Exceptional Children*, 48, 510–522.

Bloom, B. S., & Sosniak, L. A. (1981). Talent development vs. schooling. *Educational Leadership*, 39, 86–94.

Bouchard, T. J., & McGue, M. (1981). Familial studies of intelligence: A review. *Science*, 212, 1055–1059.

Callahan, C. M. (1983). Issues in evaluating programs for the gifted. *Gifted Child Quarterly*, 27(1), 3–7.

Callahan, C. M. (1986). Asking the right questions: The central issue in evaluating programs for the giftd and talented. *Gifted Child Quarterly*, 30, 38–42.

Callahan, C. M. (in press). The assessment of creativity. In N. Colangelo & G. Davis (Eds.), *Handbook of gifted education.* Boston: Allyn & Bacon.

Callahan, C. M., & Reis, S. M. (in press). The education of the gifted and talented student. In C. C. Yeakey (Ed.), *Schools as conduits: Educational policy making during the Reagan years.* New York: Preager.

Clark, B. (1979). *Growing up gifted.* Columbus, OH: Chas. E. Merrill.

Clifford, J. A., Runions, T., & Smyth, E. (1986). The Learning Enrichment Service (LES): A participatory model for gifted adolescents. In J. S. Renzulli (Ed.), *Systems and models for developing programs for the gifted and talented.* Mansfield, CT: Creative Learning Press.

Colangelo, N., & Dettmann, D. F. (1983). A review of research on parents and families of gifted children. *Exceptional Children*, 50, 20–27.

Coleman, J. M., & Fultz, B. A. (1985). Special class placement, level of intelligence, and the self-concepts of gifted children: A social comparison perspective. *Remedial and Special Education*, 6(1), 7–12.

Conroy, M. (1989). Where have all the smart girls gone? *Psychology Today*, 23(2), 20.

Cornell, D. G. (1983). Gifted children: The impact of positive labeling on the family system. *American Journal of Orthopsychiatry*, 53, 322–335.

Delisle, J. (1981). The non-productive gifted child: A contradiction of terms? *Roeper Review*, 3, 20–22.

Delisle, J. (1982). The gifted underachiever: Learning to underachieve. *Roeper Review*, 4, 16–18.

Delisle, J. R., & Renzulli, J. S. (1982). The revolving door identification and programming model: Correlates of creative production. *Gifted Children Quarterly*, 26(2), 89–95.

Dettmer, P. (1982). Preventing burnout in teachers of the gifted. *Gifted/Creative/Talented*, January-February, pp. 37–41.

Eccles, J. S. (1985). Why doesn't Jane run? Sex differences in educational and occupational patterns. In F. D. Horowitz & M. O'Brien (Eds.), *The gifted and talented: Developmental perspectives* (pp. 251–295). Washington, DC: American Psychological Association.

Fatouros, C. (1986). Early identification of gifted children is crucial . . . but how should we go about it? *Gifted Education Internatinal*, 4, 24–28.

Feldhusen, J. F. (1989). Synthesis of research on gifted youth. *Educational Leadership, 46*(6), 6–11.

Feldhusen, J., & Kolloff, P. B. (1986). The Purdue secondary model for gifted and talented youth. In J. S. Renzulli (Ed.), *Systems and models for developing programs for the gifted and talented.* Mansfield, CT: Creative Learning Press.

Feldhusen, J. F., Proctor, T. B., & Black, K. N. (1986). Guidelines for grade advancement of precocious children. *Roeper Review, 9,* 25–27.

Frazier, M. M. (1989). Poor and minority students can be gifted too! *Educational Leadership, 46*(6), 16–18.

Fox, L. H., Brady, L., & Tobin, D. (Eds.). (1983). *Learning-disabled/gifted children.* Baltimore: University Park Press.

Fox, L. H., & Washington, J. (1985). Programs for the gifted and talented: Past, present, and future. In F. D. Horowitz & M. O'Brien (Eds.), *The gifted and talented: Developmental perspectives* (pp. 197–221). Washington, DC: American Psychological Association.

Galbraith, J. (1985). The eight great gripes of gifted kids: Responding to special needs. *Roeper Review, 7,* 15–18.

Gallagher, J. J. (1985). *Teaching the gifted child* (3rd ed.). Boston: Allyn & Bacon.

Gallagher, J. J. (1986). Our love-hate affair with gifted children. *Gifted Child Today, 9*(3), 47–49.

Gallagher, J. J., & Weiss, P. (1979). *The education of gifted and talented students: A history and prospectus.* Washington, DC: Council for Basic Education.

Gardner, H., & Hatch, T. (1989). Multiple intelligences go to school: Educational implications of the theory of multiple intelligences. *Educational Researcher, 18*(8), 4–9.

George, W. C. (1979). The talent search concept: An identification strategy for the intellectually gifted. *Journal of Special Education, 13,* 221–237.

Grinder, R. E. (1985). The gifted in our midst: By their divine deeds, neuroses, and mental test scores we have known them. In F. D. Horowitz & M. O'Brien (Eds.), *The gifted and talented: Developmental perspectives* (pp. 5–35). Washington, DC: American Psychological Association.

Grost, A. (1970). *Genius in residence.* Englewood Cliffs, NJ: Prentice Hall.

Gruber, H. E. (1985). Giftedness and moral responsibility: Creative thinking and human survival. In F. D. Horowitz & M. O'Brien (Eds.), *The gifted and talented: Developmental perspectives* (pp. 301–330). Washington, DC: American Psychological Association.

Hollingworth, L. S. (1942). *Children above 180 IQ, Stanford-Binet: Origin and development.* Yonkers-on-Hudson, NY: World Book Company.

Horowitz, F. D., & O'Brien, M. (1985). Epilogue: Perspectives on research and development. In F. D. Horowitz & M. O'Brien (Eds.), *The gifted and talented: Developmental perspectives* (pp. 437–454). Washington, DC: American Psychological Association.

Humphreys, L. G. (1985). A conceptualization of intellectual giftedness. In F. D. Horowitz & M. O'Brien (Eds.), *The gifted and talented: Developmental perspectives* (pp. 331–360). Washington, DC: American Psychological Association.

Janos, P. M., & Robinson, N. M. (1985). Psychosocial development in intellectually gifted children. In F. D. Horowitz & M. O'Brien (Eds.), *The gifted and talented: Developmental perspectives* (pp. 149–195). Washington, DC: American Psychological Association.

Jensen, A. (1969). How much can we boost IQ and scholastic achievement? *Harvard Educational Review, 39,* 1–123.

Karnes, F. A., & Collins, E. C. (1980). *Handbook of instructional resources and references for teaching the gifted.* Boston: Allyn & Bacon.

Kauffman, J. M. (1981). Historical trends and contemporary issues in special education in the United States. In J. M. Kauffman & D. P. Hallahan (Eds.), *Handbook of special education.* Englewood Cliffs, NJ: Prentice Hall.

Keating, D. P. (1979). Secondary school programs. In A. H. Passow (Ed.), *The 78th yearbook of the National Society for the Study of Education, Part I. The gifted and talented.* Chicago: University of Chicago Press.

Keating, D. P. (1980). Four faces of creativity: The continuing plight of the intellectually underserved. *Gifted Child Quarterly, 24*(2), 56–61.

Lindsey, M. (1980). *Training teachers of the gifted and talented.* New York: Teachers College Press.

Lombroso, C. (1905). *The man of genius* (2nd ed.). New York: Walter Scott.

Maker, C. J. (1977). *Providing programs for the gifted handicapped.* Reston, VA: Council for Exceptional Children.

Maker, C. J. (1986). Education of the gifted: Significant trends. In R. J. Morris & B. Blatt (Eds.), *Special education: Research and trends* (pp. 190–221). New York: Pergammon Press.

Marland, S. P. (Submittor). (1972). *Education of the gifted and talented: Report to the Congress of the United States by the U.S. Commissioner of Education.* Washington, DC: U.S. Government Printing Office.

Mistry, J., & Rogoff, B. (1985). A cultural perspective on the development of talent. In F. D. Horowitz & M. O'Brien (Eds.), *The gifted and talented: Developmental perspectives* (pp. 125–144). Washington, DC: American Psychological Association.

Mitchell, P., & Erickson, D. K. (1978). The education of gifted and talented children: A status report. *Exceptional Children, 45,* 12–16.

Myers, D. G., & Ridl, J. (1981). Aren't all children gifted? *Today's Education, 70,* 15–20.

Neuhaus, C. (1988). Genius at work. *US Air, 10*(2), 64–68.

Nichols, R. C. (1965). *The inheritance of general and specific ability.* Research Report No. 1. Evanston, IL: National Merit Scholarship Corporation.

Olenchak, F. R., & Renzulli, J. S. (1989). The effectiveness of the schoolwide enrichment model on selected aspects of elementary school change. *Gifted Child Quarterly, 33*(1), 36–46.

Page, B. A. (1983). A parent's guide to understanding the behavior of gifted children. *Roeper Review, 5*(4), 39–42.

Parke, B. N. (1989). Educating the gifted and talented: An agenda for the future. *Educational Leadership, 46*(6), 4–5.

Perry, S. M. (1986). I'm gifted . . . and I'm not supposed to know it. *Gifted Child Today, 9*(3), 52–54.

Petrosko, J. M. (1978). Measuring creativity in elementary school: The current state of the art. *Journal of Creative Behavior, 12*(2), 109–119.

Plomin, R. (1989). Environment and genes: Determinants of behavior. *American Psychologist, 44,* 105–111.

Reis, S. M. (1989). Reflections on policy affecting the education of gifted and talented students: Past and future perspectives. *American Psychologist, 44,* 399–408.

Renzulli, J. S. (1977). *The enrichment triad model: A guide for developing defensible programs for the gifted and talented.* Wethersfield. CT: Creative Learning Press.

Renzulli, J. S. (1978). What makes giftedness? Re-examining a definition. *Phi Delta Kappan, 60*(3), 180–184, 261.

Renzulli, J. S. (1980). Will the gifted child movement be alive and well in 1990? *Gifted Child Quarterly, 24*(3), 3–9.

Renzulli, J. S. (1982). Dear Mr. and Mrs. Copernicus: We regret to inform you. . . . *Gifted Child Quarterly, 26*(1), 11–14.

Renzulli, J. S. (1983). Guiding the gifted in the pursuit of real problems: The transformed role of the teacher. *Journal of Creative Behavior, 17*(1), 49–59.

Renzulli, J. S. (Ed.). (1986). *Systems and models for developing programs for the gifted and talented.* Mansfield Center, CT: Creative Learning Press.

Renzulli, J. S., & Delcourt, M. A. B. (1986). The legacy and logic of research on identification of gifted persons. *Gifted Child Quarterly,* *30,* 20–23.

Renzulli, J. S., Hartman, R. K., & Callahan, C. M. (1975). Scale for rating the behavioral characteristics of superior students. In W. B. Barbe & J. S. Renzulli (Eds.), *Psychology and education of the gifted* (2nd ed.). New York: Irvington.

Renzulli, J. S., & Owen, S. V. (1983): The revolving door identification model: If it ain't busted don't fix it: If you don't understand it don't nix it. *Roeper Review,* 6(91), 39–41

Renzulli, J. S., & Reis, S. M. (1985). *The schoolwide enrichment model: A comprehensive plan for educational excellence.* Mansfield Center, CT: Creative Learning Press.

Renzulli, J. S., Reis, S. M., & Smith, L. H. (1981). *The revolving door identification model.* Mansfield Center, CT: Creative Learning Press.

Renzulli, J. S., & Smith, L. H. (1977). Two approaches to identification of gifted students. *Exceptional Children, 43,* 512–518.

Robinson, H. B. (1977). Current myths concerning gifted children. In *Gifts, talents, and the very young.* Ventura, CA: National/State Leadership Training Institute on the Gifted and Talented.

Robinson, H. B., Roedell, W. C., & Jackson, N. E. (1979). Early identification and intervention. In A. H. Passow (Ed.), *The 78th yearbook of the National Society for the Study of Education, Part I. The gifted and talented.* Chicago: University of Chicago Press.

Roedell, W. C. (1985). Developing social competence in gifted preschool children. *Remedial and Special Education,* 64(4), in press.

Rosenbloom, P. C. (1986). Programs for the gifted in mathematics. *Roeper Review, 8,* 243–246.

Sapon-Shevin, M. (1984). The tug-of-war nobody wins. Allocation of educational resources for handicapped, gifted, and "typical" students. *Curriculum Inquiry, 14,* 57–81.

Sisk, D. A. (1988). Children at risk: The identification of the gifted among the minority. *Gifted Education International, 5,* 138–141.

Southern, W. T., Jones, E. D., & Fiscus, E. D. (1989). Practitioner objections to the academic acceleration of gifted children. *Gifted Child Quarterly,* 33(1), 29–35.

Starko, A. J. (1986). *It's about time: Inservice strategies for curriculum compacting.* Mansfield Center, CT: Creative Learning Press.

Sternberg, R. J., & Davidson, J. E. (1983). Insight in the gifted. *Educational Psychologist, 18,* 51–57.

Sternberg, R. J., & Davidson, J. E. (1985). Cognitive development in the gifted and talented. In F. D. Horowitz & M. O'Brien (Eds.), *The gifted and talented: Developmental perspectives* (pp. 37–74). Washington, DC: American Psychological Association.

Sternberg, R. J., & Davidson, J. E. (Eds.) (1986). *Conceptions of giftedness.* New York: Cambridge University Press.

Stronge, J. H. (1986). Gifted education: Right or privilege? *Gifted Child Today,* 9(3), 52–54.

Terman, L. M. (1926). *Genetic studies of genius, Vol. I: Mental and physical traits of a thousand gifted children* (2nd ed.). Palo Alto, CA: Stanford University Press.

Terman, L. M., & Oden, M. H. (1959). *Genetic studies of genius, Vol. V: The gifted group at midlife.* Palo Alto, CA: Stanford University Press.

Torrance, E. P. (1986). Glimpses of the "Promised Land." *Roeper Review, 8,* 246–251.

Treffinger, D. J. (1986). Research on creativity. *Gifted Child Quarterly, 30,* 15–19.

Treffinger, D. J., Renzulli, J. S., & Feldhausen, J. F. (1975). Problems in the assessment of creative thinking. In W. B. Barbe & J. S. Renzulli (Eds.) *Psychology and education of the gifted* (2nd ed.). New York: Irvington.

Van Tassel-Baska, J. (1989). Appropriate curriculum for gifted learners. *Educational Leadership,* 4(6), 13–15.

Wallach, M. A. (1985). Creativity testing and giftedness. In F. D. Horowitz & M. O'Brien (Eds.). *The gifted and talented: Developmental perspectives* (pp. 99–123). Washington, DC: American Psychological Association.

Weiss, P., & Gallagher, J. J. (1982). *Report on education of gifted* (Vol II). Chapel Hill, NC: Frank Porter Graham Child Development Center.

White, W. L., & Renzulli, J. S. (1987). A forty year follow-up of students who attended Leta Hollingworth's school for gifted students. *Roeper Review, 10,* 89–94.

Whitlock, M S., & DuCette, J. P. (1989). Outstanding and average teachers of the gifted: A comparative study. *Gifted Child Quarterly, 33,* 15–21.

Whitmore, J. R. (1980). *Giftedness, conflict, and underachievement.* Boston: Allyn & Bacon.

Whitmore, J. R. (1986). Understanding a lack of motivation to excel. *Gifted Child Quarterly, 30,* 66–69.

Whitmore, J. R., & Maker, C. J. (1985). *Intellectual giftedness in disabled persons.* Rockville, MD: Aspen.

Whitmore, J. (1987). Conceptualizing the issue of underserved populations of gifted students. *Journal for the Education of the Gifted, 10,* 141–153.

Zigler, E., & Farber, E. A. (1985). Commonalities between the intellectual extremes: Giftedness and mental retardation. In F. D. Horowitz & M. O'Brien (Eds.), *The gifted and talented: Developmental perspectives* (pp. 378–408). Washington, DC: American Psychological Association.

Chapter 11

Akerley, M. S. (1985). False gods and angry prophets. In H. R. Turnbull & A. P. Turnbull (Eds.), *Parents speak out: Then and now* (2nd ed., pp. 23–31). Columbus, OH: Chas. E. Merrill.

Baumeister, A., Kupstas, F., & Klindworth, L. M. (1990). New morbidity: Implications for prevention of children's disabilities. *Exceptionality,* 1(1), 1–16.

Beckman, P. J., & Pokorni, J. L. (1988). A longitudinal study of families of preterm infants: Changes in stress and support over the first two years. *Journal of Special Education,* 22(1), 55–65.

Bell, R. Q., & Harper, L. V. (1977). *Child effects on adults.* Hillsdale, NJ: Lawrence Erlbaum.

Benson, H. A., & Turnbull, A. P. (1986). Approaching families from an individualized perspective. In R. H. Horner, L. H. Meyer, & H. D. B. Fredericks (Eds.), *Education of learners with severe handicaps: Exemplary service strategies* (pp. 127–157), Baltimore: Paul H. Brookes.

Bettelheim, B. (1950). *Love is not enough.* New York: Macmillan.

Bettelheim, B. (1967). *The empty fortress.* New York: Free Press.

Breslau, N., & Davis, G. C. (1986). Chronic stress and major depression. *Archives of General Psychiatry, 43,* 309–314.

Bristol, M. M., & Gallagher, J. J. (1986). In J. J. Gallagher & P. M. Vietze (Eds.), *Families of handicapped persons: Research, programs, and policy issues* (pp. 81–100). Baltimore: Paul H. Brookes.

Bronfenbrenner, U. (1979). *The ecology of human development: Experiments by nature and design.* Cambridge, MA: Harvard University Press.

Bronicki, G. J., & Turnbull, A. P. (1987). Family-professional interactions. In M. E. Snell (Ed.), *Systematic instruction of persons with severe handicaps* (pp. 9–35). Columbus, OH: Chas. E. Merrill.

Brooks-Gunn, J., & Lewis, M. (1984). Maternal responsivity in interactions with handicapped infants. *Child Development,* 55(3), 858–868.

Carney, I. H., & Orelove, F. P. (1988). Implementing transition programs for community participation. In B. L. Ludlow, A. P. Turnbull, & R. Luckasson (Eds.), *Transitions to adult life for people with mental retardation—Principles and practices* (pp. 137–157). Baltimore: Paul H. Brookes.

Carr, J. (1988). Six weeks to twenty-one years old: A longitudinal study of children with Down's syndrome and their families. *Journal of Child Psychology and Psychiatry,* 29(4), 407–431.

Comegys, A. (1989). Integration strategies for parents of students with handicaps. In R. Gaylord-Rodd (Ed.), *Integration strategies for students with handicaps* (pp. 339–350). Baltimore: Paul H. Brookes.

Diamond, S. (1981). Growing up with parents of a handicapped child: A handicapped person's perspective. In J. L. Paul (Ed.), *Understanding and working with parents of children with special needs.* New York: Holt, Rinehart & Winston.

Drotar, D., Baskiewicz, A., Irvin, N., Kennell, J., & Klaus, M. (1975). The adaptation of parents to the birth of an infant with a congenital malformation: A hypothetical model. *Pediatrics, 56,* 710–717.

Dunst, C. J., Trivette, C. M., & Deal, A. (1988). *Enabling and empowering families.* Cambridge, MA: Brookline Books.

Dunst, C. J., Trivette, C. M., Gordon, N. J., & Pletcher, L. L. (1989). Building and mobilizing informal family support networks. In G. H. S. Singer & L. K. Irvin (Eds.), *Support for caregiving families: Enabling positive adaptation to disability* (pp. 121–141). Baltimore: Paul H. Brookes.

Featherstone, H. (1980). *A difference in the family: Life with a disabled child.* New York: Basic Books.

Fewell, R. R. (1986). A handicapped child in the family. In R. R. Fewell & P. F. Vadasy (Eds.), *Families of handicapped children: Needs and supports across the life span* (pp. 3–34). Austin, TX: Pro-Ed.

Hanline, M. F., & Knowlton, A. (1988). A collaborative model for providing support to parents during their child's transition from infant intervention to preschool special education public school programs. *Journal of the Division for Early Childhood, 12*(2), 116–125.

Hanson, M. J., Ellis, L., & Deppe, J. (1989). Support for families during infancy. In G. H. S. Singer & L. K. Irvin (Eds.), *Support for caregiving families: Enabling positive adaptation to disability* (pp. 207–219). Baltimore: Paul H. Brookes.

Heal, L. W., Gonzalez, P., Rusch, F., Copher, J. I., & DeStefano, L. (in press). A comparison of successful and unsuccessful placements of youths with mental handicaps into competitive employment. *Exceptionality.*

The Helsel Family. (1985). The Helsels' story of Robin. In H. R. Turnbull & A. P. Turnbull (Eds.), *Parents speak out: Then and now* (2nd ed., pp. 81–89). Columbus, OH: Chas. E. Merrill.

Hofferth, S. L., & Phillips, D. A. (1987). Child care in the United States, 1970 to 1995. *Journal of Marriage and the Family, 49,* 559–571.

Jewell, G. (1985). *Geri.* New York: Ballantine Books.

Kazak, A. E., & Marvin, R. S. (1984). Differences, difficulties, and adaptation: Stress and social networks in families with a handicapped child. *Family Relations, 33,* 67–77.

Lynch, E. W., & Stein, R. (1982). Perspectives on parent participation in special education. *Exceptional Education Quarterly, 3*(2), 56–63.

McDonnell, A., & Hardman, M. (1988). A synthesis of "best practice"

guidelines for early childhood services. *Journal of the Division for Early Childhood, 12*(2), 328–341.

MacMillan, D. L., & Turnbull, A. P. (1983). Parent involvement with special education: Respecting individual preferences. *Education and Training of the Mentally Retarded, 18*(1), 5–9.

Mahoney, G., & Robenalt, K. (1986). A comparison of conversational patterns between mothers and their Down syndrome and normal infants. *Journal of the Division for Early Childhood, 10,* 172–180.

Morgan, D. P. (1982). Parent participation in the IEP process: Does it enhance appropriate education? *Exceptional Education Quarterly, 3*(1), 33–40.

Nolan, C. (1987). *Under the eye of the clock: The life story of Christopher Nolan.* New York: St. Martin's Press.

Norton, A. J., & Glick, P. C. (1986). One parent families: A social and economic profile. *Family Relations, 35*(1), 9–17.

Pahl, J., & Quine, L. (1987). Families with mentally handicapped children. In J. Orford (Ed.), *Treating the disorder, treating the family.* Baltimore: Johns Hopkins University Press.

Seligman, M., & Darling, R. B. (1989). *Ordinary families, special children: A systems approach to childhood disability.* New York: Guilford Press.

Senapati, R., & Hayes, A. (1988). Sibling relationships of handicapped children: A review of conceptual and methodological issues. *International Journal of Behavioral Development, 11*(1), 89–115.

Simeonsson, R. J., & Bailey, D. B. (1986). Siblings of handicapped children. In J. J. Gallagher & P. M. Vietze (Eds.), *Families of handicapped persons: Research, programs, and policy issues* (pp. 67–77). Baltimore: Paul H. Brookes.

Singer, G. H. S., & Irvin, L. K. (1989). Family caregiving, stress, and support. In G. H. S. Singer & L. K. Irvin (Eds.), *Support for caregiving families: Enabling positive adaptation to disability* (pp. 3–25). Baltimore: Paul H. Brookes.

Stoneman, Z., Brody, G. H., Davis, C. H., & Crapps, J. M. (1988). Childcare responsibilities, peer relations, and sibling conflict: Older siblings of mentally retarded children. *American Journal of Mental Retardation, 93*(2), 174–183.

Turnbull, A. P., & Turnbull, H. R. (1990). *Families, professionals, and exceptionality: A special partnership* (2nd ed.). Columbus, OH: Chas. E. Merrill.

Vaughn, S., Bos, C., Harrell, J., & Lasky, B. (1988). Parent participation in the initial placement/IEP conference 10 years after mandated involvement. *Journal of Learning Disabilities, 21*(2), 82–89.

Vietze, P. M., & Coates, D. L. (1986). Research with families of handicapped persons: Lessons from the past, plans for the future. In J. J. Gallagher & P. M. Vietze (Eds.), *Families of handicapped persons: Research, programs, and policy issues* (pp. 291–301). Baltimore: Paul H. Brookes.

Zigler, E., & Berman, W. (1983). Discerning the future of early childhood intervention. *American Psychologist, 38*(8), 894–906.

Zigler, E., & Black, K. B. (1989). America's family support movement: Strengths and limitations. *American Journal of Orthopsychiatry, 59*(1), 6–19.

Author Index

M

Subject Index